Inside Consumption

What do we know about consumer motives, goals, and desires?

Why do we choose to buy and consume certain products and services from the many available in the marketplace?

Following the pioneering and successful volume *The Why of Consumption* (2000), the same editors have brought together an all-new cast of leading scholars to address modern-day issues in consumer motivation. Representing diverse viewpoints and drawing on relevant theories and frameworks grounded in fields such as cognitive, clinical, and social psychology, behavioral decision theory, sociology, semiotics, cultural anthropology, and culture studies, the chapters in this volume address a variety of topics related to research on consumer motives, goals and desires.

Topics include:

- the interplay between the heart and the mind in what consumers desire
- hedonic, utilitarian, and variety-seeking motives
- implications of a promotion versus prevention focus in consumer decision-making
- motives for engaging in socially undesirable consumer behaviors
- how individual consumers, communities, and cultures come to value brands, fashion goods, and objects of art
- intergenerational as well as information age influences on the motives underlying consumers' identities, both present and future.

This provocative and important book provides insights for students, scholars, and practitioners who seek to understand the vital relationship between motivation and consumption.

S. Ratneshwar holds the Bailey K. Howard World Book Chair of Marketing and is also the Chair of the Marketing Department at the College of Business, University of Missouri (Columbia).

David Glen Mick is the Robert Hill Carter Professor of Marketing at the McIntire School of Commerce, University of Virginia.

Inside Consumption

Consumer motives, goals, and desires

Edited by

S. Ratneshwar and David Glen Mick

 Routledge
Taylor & Francis Group

LONDON AND NEW YORK

First published 2005
by Routledge
2 Park Square, Milton Park, Abingdon, Oxon OX14 4RN

Simultaneously published in the USA and Canada
by Routledge
270 Madison Ave, New York, NY 10016

Routledge is an imprint of the Taylor & Francis Group

Typeset in 10/12 Baskerville by RefineCatch Ltd, Bungay, Suffolk
Printed and bound in Great Britain by MPG Books Ltd, Bodmin

British Library Cataloguing in Publication Data
A catalogue record for this book is available from the British Library

Library of Congress Cataloging in Publication Data
Inside consumption/S. Ratneshwar and David Glen Mick
    [editors].—1st ed.
        p. cm
    Includes bibliographical references and index.
1. Consumer behavior. 2. Consumers—Research. I. Ratneshwar, S.
II. Mick, David Glen.
    HF5415.32.I57   2005
    339.4'7—dc22
                                                    2004028913

ISBN 0–415–34193–0 (hbk)
ISBN 0–415–34194–9 (pbk)

**For our children,
Priya, Sumitra, Owen, and Neal**

Contents

List of illustrations	xi
Notes on contributors	xiii
Acknowledgments	xxii

1 Inside consumption: new insights on what we buy and consume   **1**
S. RATNESHWAR AND DAVID GLEN MICK

2 Promotion and prevention in consumer decision-making: the state of the art and theoretical propositions   **8**
MICHEL TUAN PHAM AND E. TORY HIGGINS

3 Why and how consumers hope: motivated reasoning and the marketplace   **44**
GUSTAVO E. DE MELLO AND DEBORAH J. MACINNIS

4 Death, where is thy sting? Mortality and consumer motivation in the writings of Zygmunt Bauman   **67**
DARACH TURLEY

5 Making consumption decisions by following personal rules   **86**
ON AMIR, ORLY LOBEL, AND DAN ARIELY

6 Variety for the sake of variety? Diversification motives in consumer choice   **102**
BARBARA E. KAHN AND REBECCA K. RATNER

7 Consuming fashion as flexibility: metaphor, cultural mood, and materiality   **122**
SUSAN B. KAISER AND KARYL KETCHUM

 8 **A behavioral decision theory perspective on hedonic
    and utilitarian choice**   144
    UZMA KHAN, RAVI DHAR, AND KLAUS WERTENBROCH

 9 **Interplay of the heart and the mind in decision-making**   166
    BABA SHIV, ALEXANDER FEDORIKHIN, AND STEPHEN M. NOWLIS

10 **Social marketing messages that may motivate
    irresponsible consumption behavior**   185
    CORNELIA PECHMANN AND MICHAEL D. SLATER

11 **We are who we were: intergenerational influences in
    consumer behavior**   208
    ELIZABETH S. MOORE AND WILLIAM L. WILKIE

12 **Consumer identity motives in the information age**   233
    JOHN DEIGHTON

13 **Communal consumption and the brand**   252
    THOMAS C. O'GUINN AND ALBERT M. MUÑIZ, JR

14 **How societies desire brands: using cultural theory to
    explain brand symbolism**   273
    DOUGLAS B. HOLT

15 **Transformations in consumer settings: landscapes and
    beyond**   292
    GEORGE RITZER, MICHAEL RYAN, AND JEFFREY STEPNISKY

16 **Star gazing: the mythology and commodification of
    Vincent van Gogh**   309
    GARY J. BAMOSSY

17 **Conscious and unconscious processing in consumer
    motives, goals, and desires**   330
    W. FRED VAN RAAIJ AND GEWEI YE

18 **What consumers desire: goals and motives in the
    consumption environment**   340
    MARSHA L. RICHINS

    Author index   348
    Subject index   352

Illustrations

Figures

2.1	A stylized model of consumer decision-making	14
2.2	Regulatory focus and problem recognition	15
2.3	Regulatory focus and information search	17
2.4	Regulatory focus and consideration set formation	21
2.5	Regulatory focus and evaluation of alternatives	23
2.6	Regulatory focus and choice	29
2.7	Regulatory focus and post-choice processes	35
3.1	The three faces of consumer hope	47
3.2	Definitions for the three faces of consumer hope	47
3.3	Having hope and its relation to motivated reasoning	51
7.1	Fashioning flexibility: the intersections among metaphor, cultural mood, and materiality	123
7.2	Fashion as metaphor	129
7.3	Fashion as cultural mood	132
7.4	Fashion as materiality	138
8.1	Conceptual distinctions in the types of preferences studied by prior researchers	145
8.2	A self-attribution model of hedonic choice	159
9.1	Affective-cognitive framework	167
10.1	Counterinformative messages: adverse effects that are easiest to avoid	190
10.2	Theory of offsetting behavior	201
11.1	Marketplace manifestations of intergenerational (IG) influences	215
11.2	Sources with potential to disrupt intergenerational (IG) influences	220
11.3	Sustaining forces for intergenerational (IG) influences	222
12.1	Degrees of buyer identity	238
12.2	How identity programs engage the motive to share self-related information	243
17.1	Levels of processing model	331

Tables

10.1	Types of adverse effects that may be caused by messages	187
10.2	Studies documenting that social marketing messages caused adverse effects relative to a nonexposed control group	188
12.1	Buyer identity and implications for exchange relations	245

Contributors

On Amir (PhD, Massachusetts Institute of Technology) is Assistant Professor of Marketing in the Yale School of Management. His research focuses on understanding the various mechanisms underlying decision-making, the psychology of using money, and on the psychological implications of price promotions.

Dan Ariely (PhD in Cognitive Psychology, UNC–Chapel Hill; PhD in Business Administration, Duke University) is the Luis Alvarez Renta Professor at the Sloan School of Management and the Media Laboratory, both at MIT. His research examines consumer decision-making and behavioral economics with a focus on the nature of utility, especially issues such as the value of money, hedonic utility, utility from labor, and honesty. His articles have been published in the *Journal of Consumer Research, Journal of Consumer Psychology, Marketing Science, Journal of Interactive Marketing, Marketing Letters, Management Science, Psychological Science, Journal of Experimental Psychology, Journal of Behavioral Decision-Making, Journal of Organizational Behavior and Human Decision Processes, Quarterly Journal of Economics, RAND Journal of Economics, Journal of Economic Behavior and Organization*, and miscellaneous other journals. He currently serves on the editorial boards of the *Journal of Consumer Research, Journal of Marketing Research* and the *Journal of Interactive Marketing*.

Gary Bamossy (PhD, University of Utah) is Professor of Marketing and Director of the Global Business Program at the David Eccles School of Business, University of Utah. He was previously Professor of Marketing at the Vrije Universiteit in Amsterdam, and continues to have a part-time appointment there. His research focuses on the globalization of consumer culture and cross-cultural research methods. He is co-author with Michael Solomon and Søren Askegaard of *Consumer Behavior: A European Perspective*, and co-editor with Janeen Costa of *Marketing in a Multicultural World*. His research has been published in *International Journal of Research in Marketing, Journal of Business Research, Journal of Cultural Economics*, and other journals. He serves on the editorial review board of *Journal of Public Policy and Marketing* and *Journal of Macromarketing*. Since 1999 he has been invited by the Bank of Sweden to nominate a candidate for the Nobel Prize in Economics.

John Deighton is the Harold M. Brierley Professor of Business Administration at the Harvard Business School. His research deals with interactive marketing and is published in the *Journal of Consumer Research*, *Journal of Marketing Research*, *Journal of Marketing*, *Harvard Business Review*, *Sloan Management Review*, and other journals. He is an associate editor of the *Journal of Consumer Research* and on the editorial board of the *Journal of Marketing*, where he received an Alpha Kappa Psi "best article" award. He won the Robert B. Clarke Outstanding Educator Award of the Direct Marketing Education Foundation and the Hillel J. Einhorn Excellence in Teaching Award, University of Chicago Graduate School of Business. He was at the University of Tokyo as the Hakuhodo Visiting Professor of Marketing, and Duke University as a visiting scholar at the Teradata Center for Customer Relationship Management. His PhD is from the Wharton School, University of Pennsylvania.

Gustavo E. de Mello was a doctoral candidate at the Marshall School of Business, University of Southern California. His main area of research centered on the cognitive biases arising from affective factors and the pursuit of goals, particularly in the choice and evaluation of products. His research has appeared in the *Journal of Marketing*, *Journal of Consumer Research*, and the *International Journal of Internet Marketing and Advertising*, as well as in the proceedings of the Association for Consumer Research and the Society for Consumer Psychology conferences. His dissertation, which analyzes the role of motivated reasoning in consumers' evaluations of products, received the 2003 SCP-Sheth Dissertation Proposal Award.

Ravi Dhar is Professor of Marketing and Co-director of the Center for Customer Insights at the Yale School of Management. He also has a joint appointment as Professor of Psychology in the Department of Psychology, Yale University. His research awards include the AMA Doctoral Dissertation Award (Honorable Mention), Finalist for the Paul Green Award, and Finalist for the O'Dell award. He is an expert in consumer behavior and branding, marketing management and marketing strategy. His research involves using psychological and economic principles to identify successful consumer and competitive strategies in the offline and online marketplace. He has been a visiting professor at HEC Graduate School of Management in Paris, at Erasmus University in the Netherlands, and at the Graduate School of Business, Stanford University. He has written more than 25 articles and serves on the editorial boards of leading marketing journals, such as *Journal of Consumer Research*, *Journal of Marketing Research*, and *Marketing Science*.

Alexander Fedorikhin (PhD, University of Iowa) is Assistant Professor of Marketing, University of Southern California. His research concentrates on the interplay of affective and cognitive influences in consumer decision-making. He studies the influence of affect elicited by stimuli, ambient affect (or mood), and specific emotions on consumer decisions. His research has appeared in *Journal of Consumer Research*, *Organizational Behavior and Human Decision Processes*, and the *Journal of Consumer Psychology*.

E. Tory Higgins (PhD, Columbia) is the Stanley Schachter Professor of Psychology, Professor of Business, and Director of the Motivation Science Center at Columbia University. He works at the intersection of motivation and cognition, and is an expert on motivational models of performance, judgment, and decision-making. His most recent research addresses the general question, "Where does value come from?" and the more specific question, "What makes a decision good?" He received the Donald T. Campbell Award in Social Psychology in 1996, and the Thomas M. Ostrom Award in Social Cognition in 1999. In 2000, he was the recipient of both the William James Fellow Award from the American Psychological Society and the Distinguished Scientist Award from the American Psychological Association. He was Associate Editor of *Social Cognition* for 20 years. In 2004, he was the recipient of Columbia's Presidential Award for Outstanding Teaching. In 2005, he received the Society of Experimental Social Psychology's Distinguished Scientist Award.

Douglas B. Holt (PhD, Northwestern University) is the L'Oréal Professor of Marketing at the Said Business School, University of Oxford. He applies a socio-cultural lens to address central questions in branding (iconic brands, global brands), advertising (organizational processes), and consumer culture (social class, masculinity, race, consumerism). His research has appeared frequently in the *Journal of Consumer Research* and the *Harvard Business Review*. He is editor of *The Consumer Society Reader* (with Juliet Schor; The New Press, 2000) and author of *How Brands Become Icons: The Principles of Cultural Branding* (Harvard Business School Press, 2004). He currently serves as an Associate Editor for the *Journal of Consumer Research*.

Barbara E. Kahn (PhD, Columbia University) is the Dorothy Silberberg Professor of Marketing at the Wharton School, University of Pennsylvania. Her research focuses on customer decision-making, specifically variety-seeking, variety or assortment issues and medical decision-making in high consequence/stressful environments. Her research has appeared in the *Journal of Consumer Research, Journal of Marketing Research, Marketing Science, Journal of Consumer Psychology*, and *Journal of Retailing* among other outlets. She is co-author of *Grocery Revolution: New Focus on the Consumer*. Professor Kahn is currently on or has been on the editorial boards of *Journal of Marketing Research, Journal of Marketing, Marketing Science, Journal of Consumer Research*, and *Marketing Letters*, and is President of the policy board of *Journal of Consumer Research*. She is a past Area Editor of *Marketing Science* and a current Associate Editor of *Journal of Consumer Research*. She is an academic trustee of the Marketing Science Institute.

Susan B. Kaiser (PhD, Texas Woman's University) is a Professor and Chair of Textiles and Clothing, as well as a Professor of Women and Gender Studies, at the University of California, Davis. Her current research focuses on fashion theory, the production-consumption interface in global textile/apparel systems, and (re)constructions of masculinity through style and fashion. She is the author of *The Social Psychology of Clothing: Symbolic Appearances in Context* (2nd edition, revised, Fairchild Publications, 1997) and articles in *Clothing and Textiles Research Journal, Cultural Studies, Symbolic Interaction, Sociological Inquiry*, and *Journal of Consumer Culture*. She is a Fellow and past President of the International Textile and Apparel Association and serves on the Editorial Board of *Fashion Theory*. Other honors include: Outstanding Faculty Mentor Award (UC Davis), Green Honors Visiting Professorship (Texas Christian University), and Outstanding Alumna Award, University of Texas at Austin.

Karyl Ketchum is a visual artist and advanced doctoral student in the Cultural Studies Department at the University of California, Davis. Her current areas of research include the role of fashion and aesthetics in constructing cultural memory, vision and Internet technologies, and the role of the pixel in globalizing photographic sign systems. Her dissertation explores the role of technologies of vision, and visions of technology, in reifying cultural understandings of gender, race, and whiteness.

Uzma Khan is a doctoral candidate at Yale School of Management. Her research interests include sequential decision-making, consumer goals, self-control, and inter-temporal choice. Her dissertation research, which examines how choices made in isolation are different from choices made in connection with similar future choices, received the 2004 Sheth Dissertation Award (honorable mention) from the Society of Consumer Psychologists and the Whitebox Advisors Fellowship from the International Center for Finance, Yale University.

Orly Lobel (SJD Harvard Law School, expected 2005) is the Sydney Knafel Fellow at the Weatherhead Center for International Affairs, Harvard University. She is also a Visiting Lecturer at Yale Law School, teaching in the area of employment law. Her research focuses on new models of regulation and governance in the context of the new economy, the labor market, privatization, and new public management techniques. Her publications include a book on Israeli labor and employment law and articles in the *Michigan Law Review, Minnesota Law Review*, and *University of Pennsylvania Employment and Labor Law Journal*. She has clerked on the Israel Supreme Court and served as a Fellow at the Kennedy School of Government.

Deborah J. MacInnis (PhD, University of Pittsburgh) is Professor of Marketing at the University of Southern California. She has published papers in the *Journal of Consumer Research, Journal of Marketing Research, Journal of Marketing, Journal of Consumer Psychology, Journal of Personality and Social Psychology Journal of the Academy of Marketing Science, Journal of Advertising, Psychology and Marketing*, and *Journal of Business Research* in the areas of marketing communications, information processing, imagery, emotions, and brand images. She has served as an Associate Editor for the *Journal of Consumer Research* and has served on the editorial review boards of the *Journal of Marketing Research, Journal of Consumer Research, Journal of Marketing, Journal of the Academy of Marketing Science*, and several other journals. She is a past President of the Association for Consumer

Research, and has served as Vice-President of Conferences and Research for the Academic Council of the AMA.

David Glen Mick (PhD, Indiana University) is the Robert Hill Carter Professor of Marketing at the McIntire School of Commerce, University of Virginia. His research has primarily centered on the nature and role of meaning in consumer behavior, particularly in the domains of advertising processing, self-gifts, technological products, customer satisfaction, and quality of life. His research has appeared in the *Journal of Consumer Research, Journal of Marketing, Harvard Business Review, International Journal of Research in Marketing, Journal of Retailing, Journal of Business Ethics,* and *Semiotica,* among other outlets. He currently serves on the editorial review boards of the *Journal of Consumer Research, Journal of Consumer Psychology,* and the *Journal of Marketing,* and he has served previously as Associate Editor and then Editor of the *Journal of Consumer Research.* He is a Fellow in the Society for Consumer Psychology and recently President (2005) of the Association for Consumer Research.

Elizabeth S. Moore (PhD, University of Florida) is Associate Professor of Marketing at the University of Notre Dame. Her research interests are in marketing and society, consumer behavior of households, and marketing to children. Her research has appeared in the *Journal of Marketing, Journal of Consumer Research, Journal of Public Policy & Marketing, Journal of the Academy of Marketing Science,* and *Journal of Macromarketing.* She currently serves on the editorial board of the *Journal of Public Policy & Marketing.* She has received several awards for her research, including the Best Article Award (2002) and the Robert Ferber Award (Honorable Mention), both from the *Journal of Consumer Research.* Prior to joining Notre Dame, she served on the faculty at the University of Illinois where she received the Outstanding Undergraduate Teacher Award in the College of Commerce. At Notre Dame, she was recently awarded the BP Amoco Outstanding Teacher Award.

Albert M. Muñiz, Jr (PhD, University of Illinois, Urbana-Champaign) is Assistant Professor of Marketing at DePaul University. His research interests are in the sociological aspects of consumer behavior and branding, and his teaching interests include consumer behavior, consumer culture, and Internet marketing. He has published in the *Journal of Consumer Research* and the *Journal of Interactive Marketing.*

Stephen M. Nowlis (PhD, University of California at Berkeley) is the AT&T Distinguished Research Professor of Marketing in the W. P. Carey School of Business at Arizona State University. His research interests include consumer decision-making and choice; brand management; and consumption enjoyment. His articles have been published in the *Journal of Consumer Research, Journal of Marketing Research, Marketing Science, Journal of Consumer Psychology, Marketing Letters,* and *Annual Review of Psychology.* He is an Associate Editor at the *Journal of Consumer Research* and serves on the editorial boards of the *Journal of Marketing Research* and *Marketing Letters.* He is the winner of the 2001 William F.

O'Dell Award and a finalist for the 2002 Award, and the winner of the 2001 Early Career Contribution Award from the Society for Consumer Psychology – Sheth Foundation.

Thomas C. O'Guinn (PhD, Communications, University of Texas at Austin) is Professor of Advertising and Sociology, University of Illinois at Urbana-Champaign. His research focuses on the sociology of consumption, particularly with respect to media, advertising, and brands. His most recent work extends into social history. He is also known for his work on compulsive consumption. He has published widely, served on many editorial boards, and is a multiple time winner of the Best Article Award of the *Journal of Consumer Research*. He is also an award-winning teacher.

Cornelia (Connie) Pechmann (PhD, Vanderbilt University) is Professor of Marketing at the Graduate School of Management, University of California, Irvine. She primarily conducts controlled experiments to examine the effects of controversial forms of advertising on consumers, including comparative advertising and tobacco advertising. She has received $1 million in grants to study the effects of pro- and anti-smoking media messages on adolescents. Dr Pechmann has published over 50 refereed articles, chapters, and proceedings in outlets such as the *Journal of Consumer Research, Journal of Marketing, Journal of Marketing Research*, and *American Journal of Public Health*, and her work has been cited in *The Wall Street Journal* and other major newspapers. She serves on the editorial review boards of the *Journal of Consumer Research, Journal of Marketing*, and *Journal of Public Policy and Marketing*. She has served as a consultant to the US Office of National Drug Control Policy's youth anti-drug media campaign.

Michel Tuan Pham (PhD, University of Florida) is Professor of Business at the Graduate School of Business of Columbia University, New York. His research concentrates on three overlapping sets of issues: the role of affect in consumer judgment and decision-making, the motivational analysis of consumer judgment and decision-making, and the importance of constructive processes in marketing communications and persuasion. His articles have been published in the *Journal of Consumer Research, Journal of Marketing Research, Journal of Consumer Psychology, Organizational Behavior and Human Decision Processes, Journal of Economic Psychology, Marketing Letters, Recherche et Applications en Marketing*, and other journals. He serves on the editorial boards of the *Journal of Consumer Research, Journal of Marketing Research, Journal of Consumer Psychology*, and *Recherche et Applications en Marketing*.

Rebecca K. Ratner (PhD, Princeton University) is Associate Professor of Marketing at the Kenan-Flagler Business School, University of North Carolina. Her research focuses on reasons why people deviate from optimal decisions when making choices over time, including the role of perceived social norms, prediction, and memory errors in guiding such behavior. Her research has appeared in the *Journal of Consumer Research, Marketing Letters, Journal of Personality and Social Psychology, Organizational Behavior and Human Decision Processes*, and

Journal of Personal and Social Relationships, among other outlets. She currently serves on the editorial review board of the *Journal of Economic Psychology*.

S. Ratneshwar (PhD, Vanderbilt University) holds the Bailey K. Howard World Book Chair of Marketing and is also Chair of the Marketing Department at the College of Business, University of Missouri (Columbia). His research interests include consumer goals and motivation; consumer memory, judgment and decision-making; timestyle and time consumption; brand positioning and advertising; and marketing strategy. His articles have been published in the *Journal of Consumer Research*, *Journal of Marketing Research*, *Journal of Marketing*, *International Journal of Research in Marketing*, *Journal of Consumer Psychology*, *Journal of the Academy of Marketing Science*, *Journal of Business Research*, *Marketing Letters*, *Journal of Strategic Marketing*, *Journal of Leisure Research*, and miscellaneous other journals. He currently serves on the editorial boards of the *Journal of Consumer Research*, *Journal of the Academy of Marketing Science*, and *Journal of Interactive Marketing*.

Marsha L. Richins (PhD, University of Texas) is the Myron Watkins Distinguished Professor in the Department of Marketing, University of Missouri (Columbia). Her research has dealt with materialism, consumption values, and the role those values play in choice and consumption decisions. Her research has been published in the *Journal of Consumer Research*, *Journal of Marketing*, *Journal of Consumer Psychology*, *Journal of Economic Psychology*, *American Behavioral Scientist*, and elsewhere. She is a past President of the Association for Consumer Research, has served as Associate Editor for the *Journal of Consumer Research*, and was co-chair and organizer of an international conference on materialism.

George Ritzer is Distinguished University Professor at the University of Maryland where he has also been a Distinguished Scholar-Teacher and won a Teaching Excellence Award. He was awarded the 2000 Distinguished Contributions to Teaching Award by the American Sociological Association. He has served as Chair of two different Sections of the American Sociological Association. In addition to *The McDonaldization of Society* (1993, 1996, 2000, 2004; translated into a dozen languages), his other efforts to apply social theory to the everyday realms of the economy and consumption include *Expressing America: A Critique of the Global Credit Card Society* (1995), *The McDonaldization Thesis: Explorations and Extensions* (1998), *Enchanting a Disenchanted World: Revolutionizing the Means of Consumption* (1999; 2005), *McDonaldization: The Reader* (2002), and *The Globalization of Nothing* (2004). He is co-founding editor (with Don Slater) of the *Journal of Consumer Culture*. In addition to the above, he has authored and edited many works in social theory and other areas of sociology.

Michael Ryan is a PhD student at the University of Maryland, College Park. His research interests include social theory, consumption, globalization, sexuality, and social psychology. He has published in *The Hedgehog Review*, *Social Thought & Research*, and the *Encyclopedia of Social Theory*. He is currently Senior Managing Editor of the forthcoming *Encyclopedia of Sociology* and Managing Editor of the *Journal of Consumer Culture*.

Baba Shiv (PhD, Duke University) is Associate Professor at the Graduate School of Business, Stanford University. The broad thrust of his research is on "mindless" (i.e., very low-involvement) decision-making. His current work focuses on the role of affect in decision-making, the neuro-physiological bases of emotions, and non-conscious mental processes. He has published articles in *Marketing Letters, Organizational Behavior and Human Decision Processes, Journal of Consumer Psychology*, and the *Journal of Consumer Research*. He serves on the editorial boards of the *Journal of Marketing Research, Journal of Consumer Psychology*, and the *Journal of Consumer Research*. He was invited to the first ever Marketing Science Institute Young Scholar program in 2001. Prior to Stanford, he taught at the Tippie College of Business, University of Iowa, where he was named "Outstanding Faculty" in the *Business Week Guide to the Best Business Schools, 6th Edition* (McGraw-Hill).

Michael D. Slater (PhD, Stanford) is Professor of Journalism and Technical Communication, Colorado State University. His research interests include communication and public health, media effects on attitudes and behavior, persuasion processes, effects of narrative, and research methods. Recent publications have appeared in *Communication Research, Journal of Communication, Health Communication, Journalism and Mass Communication Quarterly, American Journal of Public Health*, and *Public Policy and Marketing*. He is the Chair of the Coalition for Health Communication.

Jeffrey Stepnisky is a doctoral student in sociology at the University of Maryland, and holds a Masters Degree in theoretical psychology from the University of Alberta, Canada. His area of specialization is social theory with particular interest in theories of the self, biomedicalization, and consumption. His dissertation, *The Psychotropic Self*, will explore the relationship between self-understanding and psychiatric medications. In recent years, he has served as the Managing Editor for *The Encyclopedia of Social Theory* (2004), the *Journal of Consumer Culture*, and the *Encyclopedia of Sociology* (forthcoming, Blackwell). He is also the co-author of an essay in *Challenges to Theoretical Psychology* (1999), and several entries on consumption that are to appear in the *Encyclopedia of Economic Sociology*.

Darach Turley (PhD, Dublin City University) is Senior Lecturer in Consumer Behavior and Associate Dean at the Business School, Dublin City University. His research interests have focused on consumption and the older consumer and the relationship between death, bereavement, and consumption. He has written a number of book chapters on these areas and has also published in *Industrial Marketing Management* and the *Journal of Business and Industrial Marketing*. He is currently Associate Editor of the *Irish Marketing Review*.

W. Fred van Raaij (PhD, Tilburg University) is Professor of Economic Psychology at the Department of Social Sciences, Tilburg University, The Netherlands. His research interests include financial behavior of consumers and investors, consumer and investor confidence, money illusion, effects of marketing communication, new media, consumer pro-environmental behavior, heuristics and biases, and economic decision-making. He was the founding Editor of the *Journal of Economic Psychology*. His work has appeared in the *Journal of Consumer Research, International Journal of Research in Marketing, Psychology & Marketing, Journal of Economic Psychology, Journal of Marketing Communications, Journal of Business Research, Kyklos, Marketing and Public Policy, Annals of Tourism Research*, and many other (Dutch, German) journals. He served/serves on the editorial boards of the *Journal of Economic Psychology, Journal of Consumer Research, Journal of Consumer Psychology, Marketing Theory, Journal of Marketing Communications*, and *Zeitschrift für Marketing*. He is the former President of the GVR, the Dutch Association for Marketing Communication.

Klaus Wertenbroch is an Associate Professor of Marketing at INSEAD, Singapore. Before joining INSEAD, he was a member of the faculties of Duke University and Yale University. He holds a PhD and an MBA from the University of Chicago and an MSc (Diplom) in Psychology from Darmstadt University of Technology in his native Germany. Dr Wertenbroch studies consumer decision-making and its strategic marketing implications (such as pricing implications of consumption self-control and of impulsive and hedonic choice). His research won the 1995 American Marketing Association Annual Award for the Best Dissertation in Marketing. His work has appeared in leading academic journals such as the *Journal of Consumer Research, Journal of Marketing Research, Marketing Science*, and *Psychological Science*. He serves on the editorial boards of the *Journal of Marketing Research* and the *Journal of Consumer Research* and was guest editor of a special issue of *Marketing Letters*.

William L. Wilkie is the Aloysius and Eleanor Nathe Professor of Marketing at the University of Notre Dame. His research centers on marketing and society, consumer behavior, and advertising. Professor Wilkie has been recognized with the American Marketing Association's highest honor, the Distinguished Marketing Educator Award, and with the President's Award and BP/Amoco Outstanding Teacher Award at Notre Dame. He has served as President of the Association for Consumer Research, and on the editorial boards of the *Journal of Consumer Research, Journal of Marketing Research, Journal of Marketing*, and *Journal of Public Policy & Marketing*. One of his articles has been named a "Citation Classic in the Social Sciences" by the Institute for Scientific Information. Prior to Notre Dame, he served on the faculties at Purdue, Harvard, and Florida, as in-house consultant at the FTC (Consumer Protection), and as Research Professor at MSI. Professor Wilkie's undergraduate degree is from Notre Dame and he holds graduate degrees from Stanford University.

Gewei Ye (PhD, Tilburg University) has studied psychology and computer science. He is Assistant Professor of Marketing and e-Business at Towson University. His research interests include consumer choice, brand-switching, unconscious affect, investment behavior, research methodology, e-business, and Internet technology. He published in the *Journal of Marketing Communications*.

Acknowledgments

It is our pleasure to gratefully recognize the many individuals whose enthusiastic efforts and unstinting help made it possible for us to bring this project to fruition. We thank Francesca Heslop, our commissioning editor, for her strong encouragement throughout this endeavor. We are also indebted to Emma Joyes and the other staff at Routledge for their ready assistance at every stage. We are deeply appreciative of the following chapter reviewers who offered timely, insightful, and highly constructive comments: Jennifer Aaker, Rashmi Adaval, Rohini Ahluwalia, Craig Andrews, Eric Arnould, Russ Belk, Lauren Block, Chris Breward, Susan Broniarczyk, Les Carlson, Ziv Carmon, Terry Childers, Suraj Commuri, June Cotte, Diana Crane, Mary Lynn Damhorst, Aimee Drolet, Sasha Fedorikhin, Gary Alan Fine, Jim Gentry, Güliz Ger, Patrick Hetzel, Margaret Hogg, Shailendra Jain, Jamy Joy, Frank Kardes, Ran Kivetz, Susan Kleine, Rob Kozinets, Angela Lee, Jonathan Levav, Charlotte Mason, Rick Netemeyer, Nathan Novemsky, Steve Nowlis, Ray Oldenberg, Ginger Pennington, Raj Raghunathan, Suresh Ramanathan, Hope Schau, Bernd Schmitt, John Schouten, Jonathan Schroeder, Baba Shiv, Itamar Simonson, Mike Solomon, Susan Spiggle, Michal Strahilevitz, Jim Twitchell, and Luk Warlop. We thank Tilo Chowdhury, Mandy Earley, Scott Radford, and Jane Olorenshaw for their help in editing the manuscript. We are grateful to Swales & Willis for their work in producing this book. Finally, we are truly indebted to the many fine scholars who contributed their ideas, efforts, and time to write the chapters in this volume.

S. R.
D. G. M.

1 Inside consumption

New insights on what we buy and consume

S. Ratneshwar and David Glen Mick

> What a life means is what that life purposes . . . The disposition to live purposefully is built into the most fundamental architecture of zoological organisms, and the disposition to seek meaning stems straightforwardly from the evolution of purposiveness together with human intellect.
>
> (Klinger 1998: 28, 30)

It seems incontrovertible, whether one champions or castigates this state of affairs, that consumption in our era has become the defining phenomenon of human life and society. Moreover, since consumer behavior – from eating and drinking to leisure and cultural pursuits – is always a goal-consumption sequence (Klinger 1998), the way to understand consumer behavior, to get "inside" in the most perceptive manner, is through the door of consumer motivations, goals, and desires.

On such a philosophical and theoretical foundation rests the volume you hold in your hand, the second we have edited on this theme. Five years ago we worked with our colleague Cynthia Huffman and put together the first edited book of leading scholars addressing the complex and multifaceted nature of consumer motives, goals, and desires, in *The Why of Consumption* (Ratneshwar *et al.* 2000). We were fortunate and delighted that it exceeded our expectations in its impact on subsequent scholarship on this topic. Our series editors and publisher were also buoyed by that book's reception and use, to the extent that they encouraged us to develop a subsequent volume of all-new research on the same theme and with a similarly pluralistic approach. The result is what we hope is the second in a continuing series of scholarly merit for consumer researchers worldwide.

Just as we did before, we have sought out several of the most creative and renowned academic minds that have studied different aspects of motivation and purpose in consumer behavior. We challenged them to choose a topic of their expertise and to summarize the current state of knowledge, and in this process to afford provocative perspectives and forward-looking theoretical frameworks that would contain strong heuristic value for stimulating further research. And as we did in the first volume, we deliberately pursued very diverse scholars who collectively represent the many different research paradigms that are needed to comprehensively understand consumer motives, goals, and desires. We were gratified that nearly all of the individuals we approached agreed to contribute to the book. As a result, our second volume includes not only well-known consumer scholars from North American and Europe, but also contributors such as Tory Higgins, Susan Kaiser, and George Ritzer who work outside of the academic discipline of marketing where consumer behavior has been most predominantly studied in recent decades.

In the introduction to our first book, we outlined an integrative framework of "5 W's and an H" (Who, What, When, Where, Why, and How) for analyzing consumption behavior (see Ratneshwar *et al.* 2000). Correspondingly, a central and unifying premise across all of the chapters in this second volume is the same, namely, in order to understand *what* people buy and consume, we have to inquire intensively into *why* – their motives, goals, and desires. To effectively answer the questions of what and why, researchers must dig into the question of *how*, particularly regarding the cognitive and affective processes implicated in consumption decisions. Further, it is necessary to delve into the question of *who*, namely, the systemic tendencies and variations across individuals, families, communities, and cultures. Finally, since Lewin (1936), it has been widely recognized that human behaviors and their underlying purposes and meanings are situated in both physical and psychological time and space, and thereby the vital context questions of *when* and *where* must be also be addressed to fully comprehend consumer behavior.

This overarching framework for consumption behavior is variously invoked across the fifteen chapters and two commentaries in this new book. The authors blend this framework with their own theories, frameworks, and conceptual tools from assorted fields such as economics, psychology, behavioral decision theory, sociology, semiotics, anthropology, and cultural studies. The substantive topics are equally varied and fascinating, including consumer hope and consumer motives surrounding mortality; the hedonic, utilitarian, and variety-seeking motives of consumer behavior, including fashion as one particular case; the implications of a promotion versus prevention focus in consumer decision-making; the interplay between the heart and the mind in what consumers desire; the motives for engaging in socially undesirable consumer behaviors; the valuation of brands in consumer communities and developed societies; the purposes behind the consuming of art and retail landscapes; and the intergenerational and digital influences on motives for consumers' identities, both present and future.

Book organization and a preview of the chapters

Consumer approach and avoidance behaviors

Chapters 2, 3 and 4 of the book emphasize the theme of consumer approach and avoidance behaviors. In Chapter 2, Pham and Higgins address this topic from the perspective of how consumers self-regulate their behaviors in the service of attaining desirable goals. Building on Higgins's regulatory focus theory (1998), they discuss in detail the implications of having a *promotion* focus (e.g., eager, risk-approaching means of accomplishing a goal) versus a *prevention* focus (e.g., vigilant, risk-avoiding ways of reaching the same goal). Drawing on prior empirical research as well as offering new theorizing, they develop many interesting propositions for various stages of the consumer decision-making process.

In Chapter 3, de Mello and MacInnis examine approach behaviors by focusing on the nature of consumer *hope*. Consumers are motivated by all kinds of hopes. In affluent societies, these range from hoping to lose weight or drive gorgeous cars, to hoping to cure cancer. In less affluent societies, there are more primordial hopes, including the hope to provide sufficient food, clothing, and shelter for one's family. De Mello and MacInnis first distinguish among three "faces" of hope (i.e., to hope, to have hope, and to be hopeful) in terms of appraisal theory, and they point out that having hope is ultimately critical for a "meta-goal" of sustaining hope. They then discuss at length how the act of having hope links to the processes by which consumers engage in motivated or biased reasoning in the marketplace.

In Chapter 4, Turley reflects on the writings of the sociologist Zygmunt Bauman (1992) regarding how consumption behaviors are indispensable for people to dodge and avoid mortality notions. As Turley argues, it is "precisely in and through consumption that any culturally mediated bid for immortality must be sought." He discusses how culture and culturally sanctioned consumption function to avoid and repress the terror of death. We "approach" immortality initially by deconstructing the concept of death into manageable and impersonal thought fragments, and by engaging in a myriad of death-denying consumption actions. But as cultures evolve from a modern to a postmodern ethos, things go further. We deconstruct immortality itself by shrugging off its previous meanings of permanence and the here-after, preferring instead to slice and dice here-and-now consumer life into fleeting moments of heavenly bliss.

Rules, variety, and flexibility in consumer choice

Chapters 5, 6, and 7 deal with how individuals go about choosing what products and services to buy and consume. Some may rigidly follow personal rules, while others may deliberately pursue variety, and still others may cherish flexibility. In Chapter 5, Amir, Lobel, and Ariely discuss how consumption decisions are often based on implicit *rules*, in the form of "shoulds" and "should nots," many of which are derived from abstract or higher-order socio-cultural norms and principles. Tracing the parallels between decision-making rules and legal system rules, they distinguish their concept of rules from decision heuristics and examine the role of rules in daily consumer decisions. Amir *et al.* further discuss how rules get activated and used, and when and how decision rules are overridden by the principle of pleasure maximization.

In Chapter 6, Kahn and Ratner focus on the quest for *variety* in choosing what to consume. Proceeding from a utility-maximization perspective, they review the beneficial as well as detrimental value of variety-seeking motives and behaviors. In the latter half of their chapter, Kahn and Ratner take a closer look at the notion of "too much variety," the intriguing idea that consumers may often buy less-preferred products because they simply overestimate or otherwise misjudge the value of variety in choice. The authors then suggest several interesting directions for future research, including questions such as when high-variety-seekers might be judged favorably by others, and how consumers might be cured ("de-biased") from seeking too much variety.

In Chapter 7, Kaiser and Ketchum inquire into the consumption of fashion and the performance of fashionability, when it comes to consumer choices regarding body and appearance styles. The authors point to the central role of flexibility in both communicating, as well as steering through, the ambiguity inherent in the world of fashion. In Kaiser and Ketchum's terms, flexibility in fashion and fashionability is constructed at the intersection of metaphor, cultural mood, and materiality: metaphor, because consumers have the opportunity, within a culturally shared system of meanings, to "broadcast" something about who they are by how they dress; cultural mood, because fashion can serve as a "mood board," a way of capturing and portraying collective as well as individual feelings, hopes, tensions, and anxieties; materiality, because branded physical objects (e.g., a pair of Calvin Klein jeans), and their relationships with the human body (e.g., the extent to which the jeans are tight or baggy on a person), afford the ambiguous makings for mood- imbued, cultural statements.

Sense and sensibility in consumption decisions

Chapters 8, 9, and 10 address in diverse ways the theme of "sensible" consumption decisions (i.e., those based on rational or instrumental reasons) versus decisions based on one's sensibilities (i.e., those that are guided by emotions, impulses, or pure pleasure). In Chapter 8, Khan, Dhar, and Wertenbroch examine this problem from a behavioral decision theory perspective. They focus on the concept of experiential preferences and review the research done on how consumers trade off between hedonic and utilitarian goals, and how they weigh immediate gratification against long-term consumption benefits. Khan *et al.* further discuss consumers' strategies for self-control in the face of temptation and then propose a self-attribution model of hedonic choice. They suggest, for example, that the choices made between products that variously represent vice and virtue can initiate, consciously or unconsciously, inferences in consumers' minds about their own self-identities, which in turn can affect, in a feedback loop, the nature of these very choices on future occasions.

In Chapter 9, Shiv, Fedorikhin, and Nowlis take an in-depth look at the interplay between emotions and cognitions in consumption decisions. Integrating neurological as well as psychological perspectives, they trace the paths that lead from automatic processing of stimuli to lower-order emotions and contrast such emotions to higher-order ones that are produced by more deliberative cognitive processes. Shiv *et al.* then propose how the affective-cognitive system overall, as well as the interactions among the individual components of this system, influence the motives that underlie consumption decisions. In the final section of their chapter, the authors lay out a number of conceptual and methodological issues that remain to be addressed in this fast burgeoning area of research.

In Chapter 10, Pechmann and Slater examine whether, when, and how social marketing messages can inadvertently fuel the types of irresponsible ("senseless") consumption behaviors (e.g., alcohol and drug abuse) these messages are actually meant to curb. The authors review a large body of literature on such boomerang effects, and they distinguish between messages that are counterinformative, messages that elicit backlash because of psychological reactance or fear-control responses, and messages that are inherently problematic. Pechmann and Slater then go on to discuss how messages can be specifically tailored to avoid such adverse consequences and they outline additional areas for research.

Consumer identity: history and virtuality

Chapters 11 and 12 connect consumer motivation to identity issues. In Chapter 11, Moore and Wilkie address the topic of intergenerational (IG) influences on consumption preferences in terms of how information, resources, and beliefs are transferred from one generation to the next within families. The authors first provide a broad overview of prior research done in this area, with an emphasis on socialization theory. Next, they discuss the nature and extent of IG influences on product and brand preferences as well as buying styles. Moore and Wilkie then inquire into the "why" of IG influences in motivational terms, identifying factors such as simplifying choice heuristics and emotional bonds between parents and their adult sons and daughters. Finally, the authors discuss the extent to which IG influences might be permanent, and they identify several different areas for future research.

In Chapter 12, Deighton examines the issue of consumer identity in the context of interactive marketing. In the age of information, buyers can take on digital identities, which include aspects of their unique characteristics that can be electronically coded by sellers. Moreover, this information can be manipulated in various ways by those sellers at later points in time (e.g., in selecting which previous customers from a database to target for a new offering). Digital identities thus enable sellers to know their customers at an individual level, a concept Deighton calls *customer branding*. Deighton discusses how the "motive to be identified and to identify, to evade identification and to police it," is beginning to occupy a central place in consumer behavior as well as marketing thinking. He distinguishes between four different levels of intensity with which customers can be branded, based on the complexity and richness of the identity elements involved in buyer-seller exchanges. Deighton then relates the intensity of the identity program to consumer motives for sharing information with marketers. He also discusses the buyer side as well as the seller side of the privacy debate that has been engendered by the phenomenon of digital identities.

Community and culture in valuing brands

Chapters 13 and 14 move the story from the individual consumer to community and culture, and does so in regard to their respective roles in bestowing *brands* with desirable and valuable meanings. In Chapter 13, O'Guinn and Muñiz make a strong case that brands need to be understood in their social context. They focus on the concept of brand communities and describe its three defining character- istics as: (1) consciousness of kind, i.e., a sense of belonging to an in-group, thanks to a brand that is patronized by all of the group members; (2) rituals and tradi- tions that surround the brand; and (3) moral obligations that are often, but not always, shared by members of the group (e.g., in regard to product repairs and service). O'Guinn and Muñiz go on to discuss several facets of brand com- munities such as their opposition to out-group members (those loyal to competing brands), brand and group membership legitimacy issues, how rumors and com- munity narratives function to transform brands into legends, and the role of the community in politicizing brand meanings.

In Chapter 14, Holt moves up the level of analysis from communities to cultures, and he explains how major brands are increasingly built out of cultural symbolism. He first critiques conventional psychological accounts of strong brands and brand equity, which center on the individual consumer and emphasize con- cepts such as cognitive representations and abstract associations of brands. Holt then describes a case study of how Corona became an iconic brand in the US market. He traces the history of the brand and its advertising messages, and he describes how the brand successfully parlayed the cultural symbolism of stories involving people relaxing at Mexican beaches so as to create a mythic identity for Corona. He argues that cultural mythmaking is ultimately a cause, not a consequence, of favorable brand associations. He then outlines some of the key principles of "cultural branding" and relates the appeal of iconic brands to societal desires for smoothing over anxieties and contradictions in everyday life.

Consuming authenticity versus triviality

Chapters 15 and 16 offer two ruminations on the nature of modern consumption. The authors of the two chapters come at it from different perspectives and address different domains of consumption, but they converge in their concerns about how the marketplace has the power to trivialize the authentic. Using the terms coined by Ritzer (2004), it is possible to take a *something* that is intrinsically rich in substantive content and turn it into a *nothing*, a consumption object that is mostly devoid of real content. In Chapter 15, Ritzer, Ryan, and Stepnisky consider consumption landscapes, which are collections of proximally situated business that work synergistically to encourage people to consume, and often in very extravagant ways (e.g., the Las Vegas Strip). Proceeding from a theory of sociology of space, the authors argue that consumption landscapes, as created by large-scale economic interests, serve not only as marketplaces, but also as tangible manifestations of popular cultural ideals and images. Ritzer *et al.* consider the case of Easton Town Center in Columbus, Ohio. The authors observe that Easton is a shopping mall designed to simulate a small town community of 1950s America. They point out, however, that Easton has many inherent contradictions and its highly orchestrated rationality undermines any real possibility of building an organic community. In the authors' analysis, notwithstanding the efforts of its creators to give Easton the qualities of a something, it turns out to be a nothing, indeed even a "non-place."

In Chapter 16, Bamossy examines how popular mythology has inflated Vincent van Gogh and his work into larger-than-life creations and, importantly, how certain myths motivate and sustain many acts of consumption related to van Gogh and his paintings. Bamossy outlines the roles of the many dramatis personae involved in the van Gogh mythmaking, including art critics, literary scholars, biographers, film makers, physicians, and pilgrims. In conjunction with the van Gogh myths, exhibitions of his work have spawned a huge commercial enterprise of mass-produced, "low art" goods and images that serve to create and propagate still more myths, even as they become kitschy staples of modern culture. Bamossy points out that, in the final analysis and despite becoming the objects of commodification, van Gogh the man and his art will likely endure as contemporary myths of substance.

Summing up

Finally, van Raaij and Ye (Chapter 17) and Richins (Chapter 18) provide discerning commentaries on the previous chapters and also offer their own insights on current and undiscovered areas of research on consumer motives, goals, and desires.

Overall, we hope this second volume will offer new and invigorating insights for scholars, practitioners, and public policy-makers who wish to more fully grasp the essential relationships among human purposes, meanings, and consumption behaviors.

References

Bauman, Z. (1992) *Mortality, Immortality, and Other Life Strategies*, Cambridge: Polity Press.

Higgins, E. T. (1998) "Promotion and prevention: Regulatory focus as a motivational principle," in *Advances in Experimental Social Psychology* 30: 1–46.

Klinger, E. (1998) "The search for meaning in evolutionary perspective and its clinical implications," in P. T. P. Wong and P. S. Fry (eds) *The Human Quest for Meaning: A Handbook of Psychological Research and Clinical Applications*, Mahwah, NJ: Erlbaum: 27–50.

Lewin, K. (1936) *Principles of Topological Psychology*, New York: McGraw-Hill.

Ratneshwar, S., Mick, D. G., and Huffman, C. (2000), "Introduction: The 'why' of consumption," in S. Ratneshwar, D. G. Mick, and C. Huffman (eds) *The Why of Consumption: Contemporary Perspectives on Consumer Motives, Goals, and Desires*, London and New York: Routledge: 1–8.

Ritzer, G. (2004) *The Globalization of Nothing*, Thousand Oaks, CA: Pine Forge Press.

2 Promotion and prevention in consumer decision-making

The state of the art and theoretical propositions

Michel Tuan Pham and E. Tory Higgins

Our understanding of consumer decision-making has historically been dominated by information-processing theory and, more recently, by behavioral decision research. These two perspectives have undeniably offered important insights about the cognitive processes underlying consumers' decisions. However, there is more to consumer decision-making than computer-like mental processes, judgment heuristics, and preference construction. Clearly missing from these perspectives is the motivational dimension of consumer decision-making. Consumers' decisions – which brand to purchase, where to go on vacation, or how to decorate the house – do not take place in a motivational vacuum. These decisions take place in the context of goals that consumers are pursuing, needs that they seek to fulfill, and drives that color their thoughts.

The purpose of this chapter is to discuss how regulatory focus theory (Higgins 1997, 1998, 2002) – a theory of motivation and self-regulation that has been rapidly gaining prominence in consumer research (e.g., Aaker and Lee 2001; Briley and Wyer 2002; Pham and Avnet 2004; Zhou and Pham 2004) – can be drawn upon to explain a variety of consumer decision-making phenomena. We briefly review the major tenets of the theory, which proposes a fundamental distinction between two modes of self-regulation called promotion and prevention. Drawing on existing empirical evidence and new conceptual analyses, we then develop a series of theoretical propositions about the effects of promotion and prevention on consumer decision-making. These propositions are organized along the traditional stages of the decision-making process postulated by standard consumer behavior theory (i.e., problem recognition, information search, consideration set formation, etc.). Some of these propositions have already received empirical support, but most await formal empirical testing in consumer research. This propositional inventory can thus be viewed as a research agenda for studying the role of regulatory focus in consumer decision-making. We hope that this agenda will help revive consumer and marketing scholars' interest in the motivational analysis of consumer decision-making.

An overview of regulatory focus theory

Because regulatory focus theory has been covered extensively elsewhere (e.g., Higgins 1997, 1998), we will discuss here only three aspects of the theory: (1) its major tenets and how it relates to other perspectives on approach and avoidance motivation; (2) examples of empirical findings that support the theory's basic tenets; and (3) the major antecedents of regulatory focus.

Regulatory anticipation, reference, and focus in approach-avoidance

Motivation is generally conceived of as being driven by the approach of pleasure and by the avoidance of pain – a basic idea known as the hedonic principle. The approach of pleasure and the avoidance of pain has been studied from three different perspectives, each associated with its own principle: (1) the principle of regulatory anticipation, (2) the principle of regulatory reference, and (3) the principle of regulatory focus. According to the principle of regulatory anticipation, motivation arises from people's *expectations* or *anticipations* about the *consequences* or *outcomes* of their actions. These anticipated consequences can be either positive ("pleasure") or negative ("pain"). It is in terms of these anticipated consequences that approach and avoidance is conceptualized in regulatory anticipation. People are believed to approach anticipated pleasures and avoid anticipated pains. When Freud (1920/1950) described motivation as "hedonism of the future," he was referring to the principle of regulatory anticipation. Notions such as "reward" and "punishment" (e.g., Lewin 1935) are characteristic of regulatory anticipation. Mowrer (1960), for instance, viewed regulatory anticipation as the fundamental principle underlying motivated learning. He saw the motivation to learn as driven primarily by "hope" and "fear." de Mello and MacInnis's discussion (this volume) of the notion of hope is written from a regulatory anticipation perspective. The standard economic theory of choice, which models choice as a function of expected utility, is also formulated from the perspective of regulatory anticipation.

Whereas regulatory anticipation focuses on the person's expectations of pleasant versus painful consequences, the principle of regulatory reference focuses on the *point of reference* that the person uses in self-regulation. Holding outcome expectations constant, self-regulation can operate either in reference to a desired end-state or in reference to an undesired end-state. For example, two students could be equally hopeful when taking an exam, but one may be hopeful that she will be successful in obtaining an "A," whereas the other may be hopeful that she will be successful in avoiding a "C." Similarly, two consumers could be equally apprehensive while choosing a gift, but one may be fearful that she might not able to get "the perfect gift" (a failure to attain a desired end-state), whereas the other may be fearful that she might end-up selecting "a totally inappropriate gift" (a failure to avoid an undesired end-state). In regulatory reference, approach and avoidance is therefore conceptualized in terms of *movement* toward desired end-states (approach) or away from undesired end-states (avoidance). Like the principle of regulatory anticipation, the principle of regulatory reference has a long history in psychology. Most animal-learning and biological models of motivation make a fundamental distinction between approaching desired end-states and avoiding undesired end-states (e.g., Hull 1952; Lang 1995). This distinction also appears in cybernetic and control process models of self-regulation in the form of positive and negative reference values (e.g., Carver and Scheier 1981; Miller *et al.* 1960). However, even if many models make a distinction between self-regulation toward desired end-states, and self-regulation away from undesired end-states, the major focus in the psychological literature has been on self-regulation toward desired end-states (see, e.g., Carver and Scheier 1981; Kardes and Cronley 2000; Miller *et al.* 1960).

In regulatory focus theory (Higgins 1997, 1998), approach and avoidance is not conceptualized in terms of anticipated outcomes (i.e., anticipated pleasure or pain) or in terms of reference end-states (desired or undesired). Instead, it is conceptualized in terms of *strategic means for self-regulation*. Self-regulation toward desired end-states – that is, *holding regulatory reference constant* – can be pursued either with means that are approach-oriented or with means that are avoidance-oriented. For example, a person whose desired end-state or goal is to become a college-level tennis player may select strategies that are approach-oriented such as practicing drills two-hours per day and enrolling in a tennis academy, or strategies that are avoidance-oriented such as refraining from smoking and keeping away from junk-food. Self-regulation dominated by strategic means that are approach-oriented is called *promotion*-focused, and self-regulation dominated by strategic means that are avoidance-oriented is called *prevention*-focused. According to regulatory focus theory, promotion-focused self-regulation is more likely in the pursuit of goals that are related to advancement and accomplishment. Prevention-focused self-regulation is more likely in the pursuit of goals that are related to security and protection. Promotion-focused self-regulation is characterized by greater *eagerness*. In signal-detection terms, promotion-oriented individuals are primarily concerned with insuring "hits" and minimizing "errors of omission" (i.e., missed opportunities or lack of accomplishment). In contrast, prevention-focused self-regulation is characterized by greater *vigilance*. In signal-detection terms, prevention-oriented individuals are primarily concerned with insuring "correct rejections" and minimizing "errors of commission" (i.e., making "mistakes"; see Crowe and Higgins 1997).

Consider, for instance, two students with the same goal of receiving an "A" in a course (i.e., the same reference end-state). Assume further that they have similar expectations with respect to success versus failure (comparable anticipations of pleasant versus painful outcomes). They may still differ in whether they represent the goal as a matter of accomplishment or as a matter of security. The former would trigger promotion; the latter would trigger prevention. The difference between promotion and prevention would not reside in the students' desired end-state or in their expectations, but in their strategic preferences for *how* to attain the desired end-state. The promotion-focused student would be inclined to use eager approach strategies for attaining the desired goal (e.g., reading non-required materials to gain extra credit), whereas the prevention-focused student would be inclined to use vigilant avoidance strategies for attaining the desired goal (e.g., being careful to finish all requirements on time).

It should be noted that promotion and prevention differ not only in how desired end-states are approached, but also in how undesired end-states are avoided (see Higgins *et al.* 1994). When avoiding undesired end-states, individuals with a promotion focus would use eager means to move away from the undesired end-state, which involves *approaching mismatches* to the undesired end-estate. In contrast, individuals with a prevention focus would use vigilant means to avoid the undesired end-state, which involves *avoiding matches* to the undesired end-state. Consider a person whose goal is to avoid conflict with a roommate (an undesired end-state). If the person is promotion-oriented, he or she might attempt to avoid conflict by organizing a meeting with the roommate to work out a schedule for cleaning the shared apartment (approaching a mismatch to conflict as the undesired end-state). If the person is prevention-oriented, he or she may instead leave the apartment whenever the roommate starts to argue (avoiding a match to conflict as the undesired end-state).

Support for regulatory focus theory

The major tenets of regulatory focus theory are supported by a considerable amount of empirical evidence (for reviews, see Higgins 1997, 1998). As examples, we describe two particular studies. The first study is a study by Förster *et al.* (1998), which provides a clear demonstration of the difference between promotion and prevention in approaching the same desired end-state. The study focused on the classic "goal looms larger" effect, which refers to the fact that the intensity of motivation typically increases as people move closer to completing their goals (see Lewin 1935). Several months prior to the actual study, participants' chronic regulatory focus was assessed through the accessibility of their ideals (a measure of promotion orientation) and the accessibility of their "oughts" (a measure of prevention orientation). In the actual study, all participants were given the same desirable goal to be approached – to identify as many solutions as possible to a series of anagrams. As participants were solving the anagrams, their strategic eagerness versus vigilance was assessed by recording their arm-pressure during arm-flexion (a behavioral signal of eager approach) and during arm-extension (a behavioral signal of vigilant avoidance). Among promotion focus participants, arm-flexion pressure increased as they moved closer to the last anagram, signaling increased eagerness as participants approached goal completion. Among prevention focus participants, it was arm-extension pressure that increased, signaling increased vigilance as participants approached goal completion. Thus, both promotion and prevention participants became more motivated as they approached the desired end-state, but they differed in the strategic orientation of their motivation (eagerness versus vigilance).

In another study, Crowe and Higgins (1997) used a recognition memory paradigm to show that promotion is characterized by greater eagerness and prevention is characterized by greater vigilance. Participants were first shown a list of target items. After a delay, they were given test items that included both "old" (target) items from the original list and "new" (distractor) items not from the original list. Participants were to respond "yes" if they believed that the test item was an old target item and "no" if they believed that the test item was a new distractor item. There were four possible outcomes:

(a) "Hit" (saying "yes" to a target item);
(b) "Miss" (saying "no" to a target item);
(c) "False Alarm" (saying "yes" to a distractor item); and
(d) "Correct Rejection" (saying "no" to a distractor item).

Because eagerness entails an inclination toward hits and against misses, it was predicted that promotion would produce a propensity to say "yes," resulting in a risky bias. In contrast, because vigilance entails an inclination toward correct rejections and against false alarms, it was predicted that prevention would produce a propensity to say "no," resulting in a conservative bias. These predictions were supported (see also Friedman and Förster 2001).

Although space limitations prevent us from reviewing additional studies, numerous other studies indicate that regulatory focus differences in strategic emphasis influence other basic decision processes (for a review, see Higgins and Spiegel, in press), including categorization (e.g., Molden and Higgins 2004), expectancy-valuation (e.g., Shah and Higgins 1997), affective responses to decision-making (e.g., Higgins *et al.* 1997; Idson *et al.* 2004), and willingness to consider new options and multiple options (e.g., Liberman *et al.* 1999, 2001).

Sources of regulatory focus

Promotion and prevention focus are *motivational states*; they are states of an individual during goal pursuit. A major source of these states lies in the individual's socialization. According to *self-discrepancy theory* (Higgins 1987), certain modes of caretaker-child interactions foster children's acquisition of either goals representing their own or significant others' hopes, wishes, and aspirations for them – goals called *ideals* – or goals representing their own or significant others' beliefs about their duties, obligations, and responsibilities – goals called *oughts*. Promotion arises from caretaker-child interactions in which pleasure is experienced as a "presence of positive" and pain is experienced as an "absence of positive." An example of "presence of positive" pleasure would be when the caretaker hugs and kisses or praises the child for his or her accomplishments. An example of "absence of positive" pain would be when the caretaker acts disappointed when the child fails to fulfill the caretaker's hopes. By emphasizing advancement, aspirations, and accomplishments, this kind of socialization creates a promotion focus that will subsequently be reflected in a chronic accessibility of the person's ideals (Higgins and Silberman 1998). In contrast, prevention arises from caretaker-child interactions where pleasure is experienced as an "absence of negative" and pain is experienced as a "presence of negative." An example of "absence of negative" pleasure would be when the caretaker reassures the child by removing something the child find threatening. An example of "presence of negative" pain would be when the caretaker scolds or punishes the child when the child misbehaves or acts irresponsibly. By emphasizing protection, safety, and responsibility, this kind of socialization creates a prevention focus that will subsequently be reflected in a chronic accessibility of the person's oughts (ibid.).

Note that people's chronic promotion and prevention orientations are theoretically independent. Hence, individuals can be high in promotion focus only, high in prevention focus only, high in both, or low in both. It has also been found that individuals from individualist cultures (e.g., North Americans, Western Europeans) tend to be chronically more promotion-focused, whereas individuals from collectivist cultures (e.g., Middle Easterners, East Asians) tend to be chronically more prevention-focused (see Lee *et al.* 2000; Pham and Avnet 2004, Study 4).

States of promotion and prevention focus can also be determined by situational factors. For example, task instructions framed in terms of "gains" versus "nongains" tend to activate a promotion focus, whereas task instructions framed in terms of "losses" versus "non-losses" tend to activate a prevention focus (e.g., Shah and Higgins 1997; see also Lee and Aaker 2004; Zhou and Pham 2004). In addition, activation or priming of individuals' ideals or oughts can temporarily increase their accessibility, thereby creating momentary states of promotion or prevention focus, respectively (e.g., Higgins *et al.* 1994; Liberman *et al.* 2001; Pham and Avnet 2004). We now turn to how differences in regulatory focus may affect consumer decision-making.

Promotion, prevention, and consumer decision-making

Standard consumer theory depicts consumer decision-making as a series of stages progressing through

(1) problem recognition,
(2) information search,
(3) formation of a consideration set,
(4) evaluation of alternatives,
(5) choice/purchase, and
(6) post-choice/post-purchase processes (e.g., Hoyer and MacInnis 2003).

This stylized stage-model, illustrated in Figure 2.1, provides a convenient way of organizing our theoretical propositions.

Problem recognition (or need arousal)

Consumer decision-making is assumed to be triggered by the recognition of a problem or the arousal of a need. Problem recognition is typically conceptualized

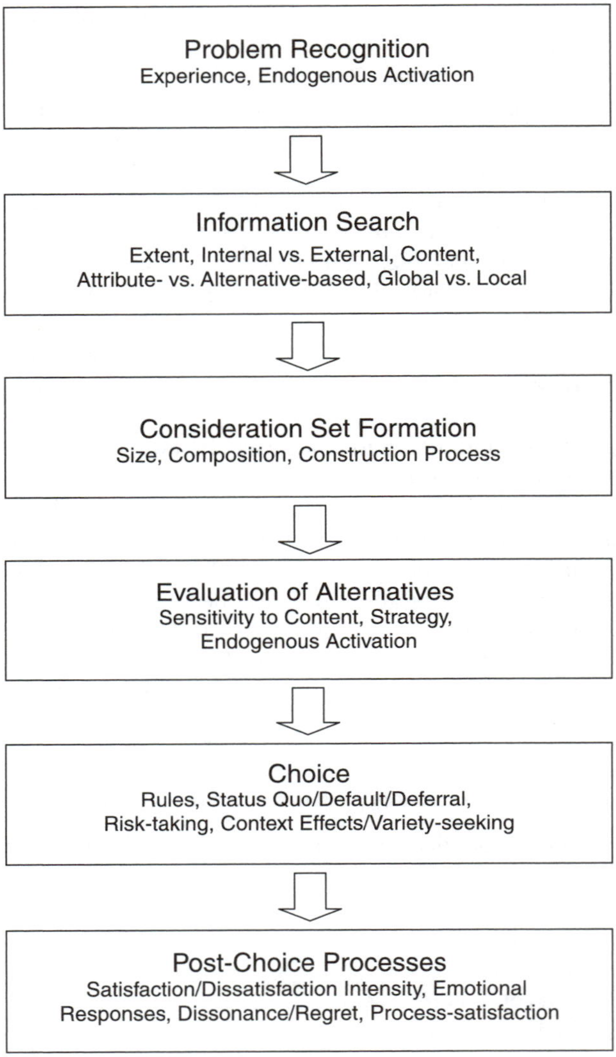

```
┌─────────────────────────────────────────────┐
│           Problem Recognition                 │
│      Experience, Endogenous Activation        │
└─────────────────────────────────────────────┘
                      ⇩
┌─────────────────────────────────────────────┐
│           Information Search                  │
│    Extent, Internal vs. External, Content,    │
│  Attribute- vs. Alternative-based, Global vs. Local │
└─────────────────────────────────────────────┘
                      ⇩
┌─────────────────────────────────────────────┐
│         Consideration Set Formation           │
│    Size, Composition, Construction Process    │
└─────────────────────────────────────────────┘
                      ⇩
┌─────────────────────────────────────────────┐
│         Evaluation of Alternatives            │
│      Sensitivity to Content, Strategy,        │
│            Endogenous Activation              │
└─────────────────────────────────────────────┘
                      ⇩
┌─────────────────────────────────────────────┐
│                  Choice                       │
│     Rules, Status Quo/Default/Deferral,       │
│   Risk-taking, Context Effects/Variety-seeking │
└─────────────────────────────────────────────┘
                      ⇩
┌─────────────────────────────────────────────┐
│           Post-Choice Processes               │
│ Satisfaction/Dissatisfaction Intensity, Emotional │
│ Responses, Dissonance/Regret, Process-satisfaction │
└─────────────────────────────────────────────┘
```

Figure 2.1 A stylized model of consumer decision-making.

as the detection by the consumer of a discrepancy between an actual state (e.g., the fridge is empty) and a desired state (e.g., the children should eat dinner by 7 p.m.). This discrepancy may arise in two distinct manners (Brunner and Pomazal 1988). First, a desired state may move away from a current state that is stationary. For instance, a consumer who, until now, has been satisfied with owning a single car (the current state) may now experience a new need or want for a second car (a change in desired state). Changes in desired states may occur as a result of new personal circumstances (e.g., a new job out of town), marketing pressures (e.g., advertising, price promotions), or social comparisons (e.g., witnessing other consumers enjoy having a second car). A second type of discrepancy between actual and desired states arises when a current state moves away from a desired state that is stationary. For instance, a temporary illness in a normally healthy consumer creates a discrepancy between the new current state of sickness and the unchanged desire to be healthy. Our theoretical propositions with respect to problem recognition in consumer decision-making are summarized in Figure 2.2 (in each table the predictions that remain to be tested empirically are marked with an asterisk).

Experience of problem recognition

We propose that pre-existing states of promotion versus prevention will induce different perceptions of discrepancy between actual and desired states and result in different experiences of problem recognition (Proposition 1.1). Individuals in a promotion state are concerned with advancement and pursue advancement by adding "hits." Thus, under promotion, consumers will pay relatively more attention to the desired state (perceived as advancement) compared to the actual state. In contrast, individuals in a prevention state seek to prevent problems and want to reject mistakes. Thus, under prevention, consumers will pay relatively more attention to the actual state (perceived as a problem) compared to the desired state. For example, we predict that a promotion-oriented consumer who needs a second car because of a new out-of-town job will tend to focus on the desirability of the second car, whereas a prevention-oriented consumer in the same situation will

Proposition 1.1*	Under promotion, consumers will pay relatively more attention to the desired state than to the actual state, and experience problem recognition as a need to be met. Under prevention, consumers will pay relatively more attention to the actual state than to the desired state, and experience problem recognition as a problem to be resolved.
Proposition 1.2	Discrepancies between actual states and desired ideals will trigger a promotion focus in decision-making, whereas discrepancies between actual states and desired oughts will trigger a prevention focus.
Proposition 1.3*	Holding the desired end-state constant, problem recognition that arises from a change in the desired state will trigger promotion, whereas problem recognition that arises from a change in the current state will trigger prevention.

Note: Propositions that are yet to be tested empirically are denoted with an asterisk, both in this figure and in Figures 2.3–2.7.

Figure 2.2 Regulatory focus and problem recognition.

tend to focus on the problem of *not* having a second car. In this example, both consumers would be motivated to move from their current state to the desired end-state; however, they would likely attend to different aspects of the situation. In general, promotion-oriented consumers will tend to experience the situation as a "need to be met," whereas prevention-oriented consumers will tend to experience the same situation as a "problem to be fixed."

Activation of promotion versus prevention

Not only can states of promotion and prevention influence the experience of problem recognition, they can also be differentially activated by different types of problem recognition. Different types of discrepancies between actual and desired states may result in different activations of promotion and prevention and, therefore, in different patterns of decision-making. As mentioned previously, there is a fundamental distinction between two types of desirable end-states (Higgins 1987): (a) ideals, which refer to consumers' aspirations, hopes, and wishes (e.g., wanting a beautiful house, dreaming of an exotic vacation); and (b) oughts, which refer to consumers' obligations, duties, and responsibilities (e.g., having to provide for a child's education, having to repay one's debts). According to regulatory focus theory (Higgins 1997, 1998), discrepancies between consumers' actual states and desired ideals will trigger states of promotion, whereas discrepancies between consumers' actual states and their desired oughts will trigger states of prevention (Proposition 1.2). Although this prediction has not been directly tested in a consumer decision-making context, it has received ample support in other contexts (e.g., Higgins *et al.* 1994; Pham and Avnet 2004). Higgins *et al.* (1994) have found, for instance, that respondents whose ideals were primed or chronically accessible tended to favor approach strategies in self-regulation (e.g., being emotionally supportive of friends), whereas respondents whose oughts were primed or chronically accessible tended to favor avoidance strategies instead (e.g., keeping secrets about friends).

We additionally hypothesize that, holding the type of desired state constant (e.g., the need for a new car), discrepancies that arise from a change in the desired state (e.g., a new job requires an additional car) will tend to activate states of promotion, whereas discrepancies that arise from a change in the actual state (e.g., the current car broke down) will tend to activate states of prevention (Proposition 1.3). In both cases, there should be a motivation to move from the current state toward the desired state (e.g., a desire for a new car). However, if the motivation arises from a change in the desired state (e.g., a new car for a new job), the movement should be experienced as advancement, activating a promotion focus. In contrast, if the desire arises from a change in the actual state (e.g., a new car to replace a broken-down car), the movement should be experienced as correcting a problem, activating a prevention focus. The implications of this distinction are currently being investigated. Propositions 2 and 3 highlight an important recent development of regulatory focus theory: In addition to exerting *exogenous* influences on consumer decision-making, regulatory focus can also be *endogenously* determined by various aspects of this decision-making process (see Zhou and Pham 2004).

Information search

Once a problem has been recognized, a search for information is assumed to follow. Consumers' information search can be characterized along several dimensions (e.g., Bettman 1979; Hoyer and MacInnis 2003):

(a) the extensiveness of the search;
(b) the direction of the search, internal or external;
(c) the type of information searched; and
(d) the structure of the search, which can be alternative-based or attribute-based, and global or local.

Our propositions with respect to these four dimensions of information search are summarized in Figure 2.3.

Proposition 2.1*	Promotion- and prevention-oriented individuals should devote comparable amounts of effort to information search and will search for comparable amounts of information.
Proposition 2.2	The number of alternatives or options searched will be greater under promotion than under prevention.
Proposition 2.3*	Under promotion, information search will be relatively more internal, whereas under prevention, information search will be relatively more external.
Proposition 2.4	Under promotion, information search will tend to focus on positive signals about the available options, whereas under prevention, information search will tend to focus on negative signals.
Proposition 2.5	Promotion will foster a preferential search for attribute information related to advancement and accomplishments, whereas prevention will foster a preferential search for attribute information related to security and protection.
Proposition 2.6*	Under promotion, information search will concentrate on seeking information about additional alternatives while holding the number of attributes constant; under prevention, information search will concentrate on seeking information about additional attributes while holding the number of alternatives constant.
Proposition 2.7*	Under promotion, information will be searched in a more global and "top-down" manner; under prevention information will be searched in a more local and "bottom-level," serial manner.

Figure 2.3 Regulatory focus and information search.

Extensiveness of search

The effects of regulatory focus on the extensiveness of search should depend on how this extensiveness is operationalized. If the extensiveness of search is defined in terms of sheer amount of information searched or amount of effort devoted to searching, there should be no systematic difference between promotion and prevention. Amount of information searched and search effort depend primarily on the consumer's level of involvement (motivation intensity) with the decision and their level of knowledge about the product category involved (e.g., Beatty and Smith 1987; Brucks 1985). To the extent that regulatory focus is theoretically independent of motivation intensity and expertise, promotion- and prevention-oriented individuals should devote comparable amounts of effort to search and search for comparable amounts of information (Proposition 2.1). Although this proposition remains to be tested, indirect support for this prediction comes from the finding that, in persuasion settings, activation of promotion and prevention produces similar depths of processing (Avnet and Pham 2004; Pham and Avnet 2004).

However, if extensiveness of search is defined in terms of how many alternatives or options are considered, search should be more extensive under promotion than under prevention (Proposition 2.1). Individuals with a promotion focus should not want to overlook options or "miss hits." In contrast, individuals with a prevention focus should want to consider only as many options as are necessary for the task at hand, since adding unnecessary options increases the chance of making mistakes. Previous studies have shown that more alternatives are indeed generated and considered when people have a promotion focus than when they have a prevention focus (e.g., Crowe and Higgins 1997; Friedman and Förster 2001; Liberman *et al.* 2001).

Internal versus external search

Search for information can be internal and based on the consumer's knowledge and memory, or external and directed to the environment. Pham and Avnet (2004) recently hypothesized that promotion-focused consumers will engage in relatively more internal search than prevention-focused consumers, whereas prevention-focused consumers will engage in relatively more external search than promotion-focused consumers (Proposition 2.3). This hypothesis was based on the finding that promotion triggers a more eager form of exploration, whereas prevention triggers a more vigilant form of exploration (e.g., Crowe and Higgins 1997). Eagerness should theoretically encourage the reliance on heuristic modes of judgment (see Förster *et al.* 2003), which include the reliance on internal knowledge structures (Pham and Avnet 2004). In contrast, vigilance should encourage scrutiny of the environment and thus the reliance on external information (e.g., Bless *et al.* 1996; Förster *et al.* 2000).

Content of information searched

Because promotion is characterized by a strategy of approaching matches to the desired end-state, it should foster a preferential search for positive (rather than negative) signals about the available options. In contrast, because prevention is characterized by a strategy of avoiding mismatches to the desired end-state, it should foster a search for negative (rather than positive) signals about the options (Proposition 2.4). Consistent with this prediction, Pham and Avnet (2004) recently found that, in persuasion, promotion-focused consumers were more influenced by positive affective cues (an attractive ad execution) than by negative affective cues (an unattractive ad execution). In contrast, prevention-focused consumers were more influenced by negative substantive information (weak product claims) than by positive substantive information (strong product claims).

Promotion should also foster a preferential search for attribute information related to advancements and accomplishments, whereas prevention should foster a preferential search for attribute information related to security and protection (Proposition 2.5). The results of a study by Safer (1998; see Higgins 2002) are consistent with this prediction. Participants instructed to imagine that they wanted to purchase a computer were provided a list of 24 questions they could ask about the computer: 8 about innovative features (e.g., how creative or advanced it was), 8 about reliability features (e.g., its ability to prevent system crashes or other problems), and 8 about neutral features (e.g., total weight of the unit). Participants were asked to select those 10 questions whose answers would be most helpful in making their purchase decision. As predicted, participants with a stronger promotion focus were more likely to seek information concerning innovation than reliability, whereas the reverse was true for participants with a stronger prevention focus.

Alternative- versus attribute-based search

A major tenet of decision research is that information search may be structured either in terms of alternatives (e.g., different brands) or in terms of attributes of the alternatives (see Payne *et al.* 1993; Bettman *et al.* 1998). We propose that, under promotion, information search will concentrate on seeking information about additional alternatives while holding the number of attributes constant; under prevention, information search will concentrate on seeking information about additional attributes while holding the number of alternatives constant (Proposition 2.6). This prediction is based on the thesis that promotion is mostly geared toward identifying and capturing opportunities, whereas prevention is mostly geared toward avoiding mistakes (see Crowe and Higgins 1997). One's ability to identify opportunities obviously increases when more alternatives are considered. However, one's ability to avoid mistakes is more likely to increase when more information about each alternative is considered.

Global versus local search

Information can be searched in a global, "big picture" manner or in a more local, detail-oriented manner. A global search tends to proceed in a "top-down" fashion, whereas a local search tends to proceed in a "bottom-level," serial fashion. We propose that under promotion information search will be more global and proceed in a top-down manner, whereas under prevention information search will be more local and proceed in a bottom-level, serial manner (Proposition 2.7). For example, we predict that promotion-focused patrons in a restaurant would tend to examine the food menu by first scanning the menu's main categories (appetizers versus entrees), then searching for possible subcategories within each main category (e.g., meat versus fish within entrees), and then look for specific dishes within the selected subcategory (e.g., sole meuniere within fish). Prevention-focused patrons would instead tend to proceed by scanning the menu serially at the specific dish level (e.g., first dish under appetizers, second dish under appetizer, etc.). Although this proposition remains to be tested, indirect support for this prediction was recently obtained in a study by Förster and Higgins (2004). Participants were presented with composite stimuli consisting of large letters made up of small letters. They were asked to respond as quickly as possible to a target letter (e.g., H) that appeared either at the global level (e.g., a large H made of small Ts) or at the local level (e.g., a large T made of small Hs). Individuals with a promotion focus were found to respond more quickly at the global level than at the local level, whereas the reverse was true for individuals with a prevention focus.

Consideration set formation

Based on an initial gathering of information, consumers are assumed to narrow down the available set of options to a subset called the consideration set, that is, the set of alternatives that "the consumer considers seriously when making a purchase and/or consumption decision" (Hauser and Wernerfelt 1990: 393). Alternatives enter the consideration set based on two factors: (a) their goal-satisfying properties, and (b) their salience or accessibility at the time of the decision (Shocker *et al.* 1991). Consideration sets can be characterized by their size, by their composition, and by the process by which they are generated. Our propositions about the effects of regulatory focus on consideration set formation are summarized in Figure 2.4.

Set size

Consideration sets have been found to contain typically between three and seven alternatives across a broad range of product categories (see Hauser and Wernerfelt 1990). Consistent with Propositions 2.2 and 2.6, we hypothesize that the consideration sets of promotion-oriented consumers will generally be larger than those of prevention-oriented consumers (Proposition 3.1). Again, this is because promotion activates goals of maximizing hits and minimizing misses

Proposition 3.1*	The consideration set of promotion-oriented consumers will generally be larger than the one of prevention-oriented consumers.
Proposition 3.2	Holding the size of the set constant, the consideration set of promotion-oriented consumers will be more heterogeneous than the one of prevention-oriented consumers.
Proposition 3.3*	Under promotion, consideration sets will tend to be formed through the gradual inclusion of alternatives, whereas under prevention, consideration sets will tend to be formed through the gradual exclusion of alternatives.
Proposition 3.4*	Under promotion, the screening of alternatives for further consideration is more likely to be based on a disjunctive rule; under prevention, this screening is more likely to be based on a conjunctive rule.

Figure 2.4 Regulatory focus and consideration set formation.

(errors of omission), which favors the consideration of a larger set of alternatives. In contrast, prevention emphasizes necessity and activates goals of maximizing correct rejection and minimizing false alarms (errors of commission), which favors the consideration of a smaller set of alternatives, mostly those perceived to be necessary.

Set composition

We also propose that the composition of the consideration set will differ under promotion versus prevention. Holding the size of the set constant, the consideration sets of promotion-oriented consumers will be more heterogeneous (exhibit greater variety) than those of prevention-oriented consumers (Proposition 3.2). The concern for maximizing opportunities that characterizes promotion has been found to trigger a more explorative mode of processing (e.g., Friedman and Förster 2001). This explorative mode of processing should favor the consideration of a more diverse set of options, which increases the chance of positive discovery. In contrast, a concern for minimizing mistakes should favor the consideration of a more homogeneous set of options, which reduces uncertainty. Consistent with this proposition, it has been found that, in problem solving, promotion-oriented individuals exhibit greater creativity than prevention-oriented individuals (ibid.). More direct support for this proposition comes from a recent study by Chowdhury (2004) who showed that, in gift-giving, consumers with a promotion focus have more heterogeneous consideration sets than consumers with a prevention focus.

Set construction process

We propose that regulatory focus will also influence the process by which consideration sets are formed. Whereas promotion-oriented consumers are expected to form consideration sets through the gradual inclusion of alternatives, prevention-oriented consumers are expected to form consideration sets through the gradual exclusion of alternatives (Proposition 3.3). This proposition follows directly from the approach versus avoidance strategies associated with promotion and prevention. Although the proposition still awaits formal empirical testing, it is consistent with recent findings from Shah *et al.* (2004) who observed that promotion-focused individuals exhibit a positive in-group bias (i.e., greater inclusion of in-group members), whereas prevention-focused individuals exhibit a negative out-group bias (i.e., greater exclusion of out-group members).

Promotion- and prevention-focused consumers would also be expected to follow different rules to include or exclude alternatives from the consideration set. Two choice rules are often mentioned with respect to how consumers narrow down the number of alternatives to a more manageable set (see Bettman 1979). The conjunctive rule consists in setting minimum cutoff values for all attributes and eliminating every alternative that fails to pass any of these cutoffs. This rule is conservative and weighs negative information more heavily. The disjunctive rule consists in setting more ambitious cutoffs for all attributes and accepting every alternative that exceeds any of these cutoffs. This rule is more aggressive and weighs positive information more heavily. We propose that under promotion, the screening of alternative for further consideration is more likely to be based on a disjunctive rule, whereas under prevention, this screening is more likely to be based on a conjunctive rule (Proposition 3.4). Although this prediction has not been tested directly, Brockner *et al.* (2002) found that individuals who are successful in promotion self-regulation – as evidenced by a congruence between their ideal and actual selves – are more accurate in estimating the probabilities of disjunctive events, whereas individuals who are successful in prevention self-regulation – as evidenced by a congruence between their ought and actual selves – are more accurate in estimating the probabilities of conjunctive events.

Evaluation of alternatives

Once a consideration set has been generated, a formal evaluation of the considered alternatives is expected to follow. During this evaluation stage, consumers are assumed to examine information about the attributes of the alternatives and integrate this information into summary evaluations of the alternatives. Of the six stages of the classic consumer decision-making process, it is the evaluation stage that has received the most attention from consumer researchers interested in regulatory focus theory (although most of this work has been on persuasion as opposed to true decision-making). We propose that regulatory focus influences both the type of evaluative *content* that consumers are sensitive to and the type of evaluation *strategy* that they follow. We also propose that promotion and prevention may also be activated *endogenously* by the alternative being evaluated (Zhou and Pham 2004). Our propositions are summarized in Figure 2.5.

Sensitivity to evaluative content

A variety of findings indicate the existence of a basic *matching principle* in how target objects are evaluated under different regulatory foci. Attribute information seems to carry a greater weight on how the option is evaluated when the content of this information is compatible with the person's regulatory focus than when it is incompatible. As a result, objects that are attractive (unattractive) on attribute

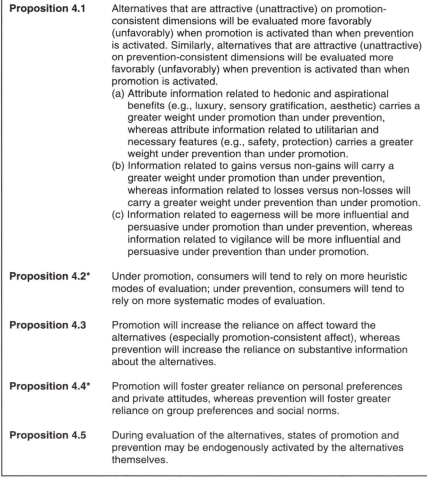

Proposition 4.1	Alternatives that are attractive (unattractive) on promotion-consistent dimensions will be evaluated more favorably (unfavorably) when promotion is activated than when prevention is activated. Similarly, alternatives that are attractive (unattractive) on prevention-consistent dimensions will be evaluated more favorably (unfavorably) when prevention is activated than when promotion is activated.
	(a) Attribute information related to hedonic and aspirational benefits (e.g., luxury, sensory gratification, aesthetic) carries a greater weight under promotion than under prevention, whereas attribute information related to utilitarian and necessary features (e.g., safety, protection) carries a greater weight under prevention than under promotion.
	(b) Information related to gains versus non-gains will carry a greater weight under promotion than under prevention, whereas information related to losses versus non-losses will carry a greater weight under prevention than under promotion.
	(c) Information related to eagerness will be more influential and persuasive under promotion than under prevention, whereas information related to vigilance will be more influential and persuasive under prevention than under promotion.
Proposition 4.2*	Under promotion, consumers will tend to rely on more heuristic modes of evaluation; under prevention, consumers will tend to rely on more systematic modes of evaluation.
Proposition 4.3	Promotion will increase the reliance on affect toward the alternatives (especially promotion-consistent affect), whereas prevention will increase the reliance on substantive information about the alternatives.
Proposition 4.4*	Promotion will foster greater reliance on personal preferences and private attitudes, whereas prevention will foster greater reliance on group preferences and social norms.
Proposition 4.5	During evaluation of the alternatives, states of promotion and prevention may be endogenously activated by the alternatives themselves.

Figure 2.5 Regulatory focus and evaluation of alternatives.

dimensions that are consistent with promotion are evaluated more positively (negatively) when promotion is activated than when prevention is activated. Similarly, objects that are attractive (unattractive) on attribute dimensions that are consistent with prevention are evaluated more positively (negatively) when prevention is activated than when promotion is activated (Proposition 4.1). This well-documented phenomenon has been observed for various kinds of compatibility between type of information and regulatory focus. For example, attribute information related to hedonic and aspirational benefits (e.g., luxury, sensory gratification, aesthetic) carries a greater weight under promotion than under prevention, whereas attribute information related to utilitarian and necessary features (e.g., safety, protection) carries a greater weight under prevention than under promotion (Proposition 4.1.a).[1] Consistent with this proposition, Safer (1998; cited in Higgins 2002) found that in choices between (a) products that score high on luxury dimensions but average on protection dimensions (e.g., a car with plush leather seats and regular brakes) and (b) products that score high on protection dimensions but average on luxury dimensions (e.g., a car with anti-locking brakes and regular fabric seats), promotion-focused individuals tended to choose the former, whereas prevention-focused individuals tended to choose the latter. Similarly, Aaker and Lee (2001) found that a fruit juice advertised in terms of energy benefits was evaluated more favorably by individuals with independent selves (who are more promotion-focused) than by individuals with interdependent selves (who are more prevention-focused); on the other hand, a fruit juice advertised in terms of cancer prevention benefits was evaluated more favorably by individuals with interdependent selves than by individuals with independent selves. Wang and Lee (2004) have obtained similar results when promotion and prevention are primed directly as opposed to indirectly through respondents' self-views.

Regulatory focus theory (Higgins 1997, 1998) also predicts that information related to gains and non-gains should carry a greater weight under promotion than under prevention, whereas information related to losses and nonlosses should carry a greater weight under prevention than under promotion (Proposition 4.1.b). Shah *et al.* (1998) found, for instance, that promotion-oriented individuals were more motivated by incentives framed in terms of gains and nongains, whereas promotion-oriented individuals were more motivated by incentives framed in terms of losses and nonlosses. Zhou and Pham (2004) recently found that financial products associated with promotion (e.g., individual stocks in brokerage accounts) are evaluated with higher sensitivity to potential gains and lower sensitivity to potential losses, whereas financial products associated with prevention (e.g., mutual funds in retirement accounts) are evaluated with higher sensitivity to potential losses and lower sensitivity to potential gains. Similarly, Lee and Aaker (2004) recently found that advertising taglines framed in terms of gains ("Get Energized!") resulted in more favorable attitudes when the rest of the ad was written in promotion terms (stressing the energy benefits of drinking grape juice) than when the rest of the ad was written in prevention terms (stressing the cancer reduction benefits of drinking grape juice). Taglines framed in loss terms ("Don't Miss Out on Getting Energized!") resulted in more favorable attitudes when the rest of the ad was written in prevention terms than when the rest of the ad was written in promotion terms.

Regulatory focus theory would also predict that, under promotion, information related to eagerness should be more influential and persuasive than information related to vigilance, whereas, under prevention, information related to vigilance should be more influential and persuasive than information related to eagerness (Proposition 4.1.c). Consistent with this prediction, Cesario *et al.* (2004) found that a persuasion message advocating a new public education policy was more effective when promotion-oriented participants received an eagerness-framed message than a vigilance-framed message, whereas the opposite was true for prevention-oriented participants. Similarly, Spiegel *et al.* (2004) found that promotion-focused individuals were more likely to complete a task when given means framed in terms of eagerness than when given means framed in terms of vigilance. In contrast, prevention-focused individuals were more likely to complete the task when given means framed in terms of vigilance than when given means framed in terms of eagerness.

Two types of mechanisms have been proposed to account for the regulatory "compatibility" phenomenon described in Proposition 4.1 (and Propositions 4.1.a, 4.1.b, and 4.1.c). First, it could be that a state of promotion or prevention raises attention to information that is compatible with this state and increases the weight that this information receives during judgment integration. If the weight of regulatory-focus-compatible information increases in judgment, options that are attractive on compatible dimensions will naturally be evaluated more favorably. Consistent with this explanation, Aaker and Lee (2001) found that, following exposure to a promotional message, respondents had better memory for information that was consistent with their state of regulatory focus than for information that was inconsistent with this state. Wang and Lee (2004) similarly found that promotion- or prevention-focused individuals spent more time processing information that was compatible with their state than information that was not compatible. Finally, Pham and Avnet (2004) found that information compatible with the regulatory state was perceived to be more diagnostic than information that was not compatible.

An alternative explanation is that a match between the information and the person's regulatory state – a situation called *regulatory fit* – creates a subjective experience of "feeling right" that is then used as information to make evaluations (Higgins 2000, 2002). Cesario *et al.* (2004) recently tested this explanation in a persuasion context. They hypothesized that, for a promotion-focused person, a message framed in eager terms would feel more "right" than a message framed in vigilant terms. Conversely, for a prevention-focused person, a message framed in vigilant terms would feel more "right" than a message framed in eager terms. These feelings of rightness would then be interpreted as meaning that the message is persuasive or that the person agrees with the message's position. Consistent with this hypothesis, Cesario *et al.* (2004) found that regulatory fit indeed increased the perceived persuasiveness of messages compared to situations of non-fit. They additionally found that this effect disappeared when the actual source of the feelings was made salient before message exposure. This latter finding supports the idea that the phenomenon is driven by a misattribution of the feelings of rightness to the object being evaluated (see Schwarz and Clore 1983). Lee and Aaker (2004) recently obtained similar results with different operationalizations of regulatory fit. We shall return to this notion of regulatory fit in our discussion of post-decisional processes.

Evaluation strategy

We also predict that regulatory focus will influence the strategy that consumers use to evaluate options. Specifically, we propose that under promotion, consumers will tend to rely on more heuristic modes of evaluation; whereas, under prevention, consumers will tend to rely on more systematic modes of evaluation (Proposition 4.2). Consistent with this proposition, Förster *et al.* (2003) found that promotion-oriented individuals tended to perform tasks with greater speed and lower accuracy, whereas prevention-oriented individuals tended to perform the same task with lower speed but greater accuracy. This is presumably because promotion induces eagerness in task performance, whereas prevention induces vigilance.

A major heuristic of evaluation is to rely on one's feelings, as in the "How-do-I-feel-about-it?" heuristic (Schwarz and Clore 1983, 1996; Pham 1998, 2004). Pham and Avnet (2004) recently hypothesized that promotion would increase the reliance on affective feelings toward the alternatives (especially promotion-consistent feelings), whereas prevention would increase the reliance on substantive information about the alternatives (Proposition 4.3). This is because promotion and eagerness encourage reliance on heuristic modes of judgment (Proposition 4.4) and internal information (see Proposition 2.3); in contrast, prevention and vigilance encourage the use of systematic modes of judgment and external information. Consistent with this hypothesis, Pham and Avnet (2004) found that, in an advertising setting, the priming of ideals increases the influence of the ad's aesthetic on brand attitudes, whereas the priming of oughts increases the influence of the ad's claim strength. In subsequent studies, they additionally found that the same phenomenon occurs in impression formation and in decision-making, even when the feelings toward the target are manipulated incidentally through a mood induction. It appears that the activation of promotion makes people believe – correctly or incorrectly – that their feelings are diagnostic. It should be noted, however, that in the Pham and Avnet studies, affective feelings were mostly of the promotion kind (e.g., attractiveness of an ad, charisma of a person, etc.) An interesting avenue for future research would be to investigate how regulatory focus moderates reliance on affective feelings of a prevention kind (e.g., feelings of anxiety versus relief). According to regulatory focus theory, affective feelings of a prevention kind should be weighted more heavily under prevention than under promotion, which would represent an important boundary condition of the Pham and Avnet findings. It has been found, for instance, that a promotion focus produces quicker evaluations of how happy or sad an object makes people feel, whereas a prevention focus produces quicker evaluations of how relaxed or nervous an object makes people feel (Shah and Higgins 2001).

We also predict that promotion will foster greater reliance on personal preferences and private attitudes, whereas prevention will foster greater reliance on group preferences and social norms (Proposition 4.4). Although this prediction has yet to be tested explicitly, it is consistent with the finding that promotion tends to be associated with independent self-representations, whereas prevention tends to be associated with interdependent self-representations (Lee *et al.* 2000). It is also consistent with the finding that the priming of avoidance motivation increases the endorsement of proverbs stressing the importance of balance and equity in social relations (Briley and Wyer 2002). Furthermore, ideals (which tend to trigger promotion) involve aspirations that are often personal, whereas oughts (which tend to trigger prevention) involve duties, obligations, and responsibilities that generally are interpersonal.

Endogenous activation of promotion and prevention

As formalized in Propositions 4.1–4.4, states of promotion versus preventions are expected to exert *exogenous* influences on consumers' preferences for differential content of attribute information about the alternatives. Zhou and Pham (2004) recently proposed that, during evaluation, states of promotion and prevention may also be *endogenously* activated by the alternatives themselves (Proposition 4.5). As mentioned previously, they found that in investment decisions certain financial products such as individual stocks in trading accounts were evaluated with greater sensitivity to gains and lower sensitivity to losses (a pattern of evaluation consistent with a promotion focus), whereas other financial products such as mutual funds in a retirement account were evaluated with greater sensitivity to losses and lower sensitivity to gains (a pattern of evaluation consistent with a prevention focus). In another experiment, they found that the mere act of evaluating financial products labeled either as "individual stocks in a trading account" or as "mutual funds in a retirement account" was sufficient to trigger distinct promotion or prevention tendencies that carried over to subsequent decisions in totally unrelated domains. These findings suggest that the types of financial products may actually dictate the criteria and goals that investors use to make their decisions. According to standard finance theory, however, it should be the investor's goals and criteria that dictate how they evaluate investment alternatives, not the reverse. Zhou and Pham (2004) observe that their findings imply a "means-dictate-the-ends" phenomenon that has important implications, not just for investment decisions, but for decision research in general.

Choice

The evaluation of the alternatives is assumed to culminate in the choice of one alternative. This choice process can be characterized by

(a) the rules that are used to arrive at the chosen alternative;
(b) the decision-maker's preference for the status quo, default option, or choice-deferral;
(c) the decision-maker's attitude toward risk; and
(d) the decision-maker's sensitivity to the context of choice and preference for variety.

Our propositions about the effects of regulatory focus on choice are summarized in Figure 2.6.

Choice rules

As mentioned previously, in consideration set formation promotion should encourage a process of inclusion, whereas prevention should encourage a process of exclusion (see Proposition 3.3). In addition, promotion should encourage the reliance on a disjunctive rule, whereas prevention should encourage the reliance on a conjunctive rule (see Proposition 3.4). The same motivational forces that underlie these predictions with regard to consideration set formation should exert similar influences once the consideration set is formed and shape the choice process *within* the consideration set. We therefore propose that, within the consideration set, choice will tend to be guided by a process of selection or acceptance under promotion and by a process of elimination or rejection under prevention (Proposition 5.1). We also propose that, within the consideration set, promotion will encourage the reliance on a disjunctive rule and prevention will encourage the reliance on a conjunctive rule (Proposition 5.2).

The conjunctive and disjunctive rules assume no ordering of the attributes in terms of their importance. However, attributes often have different importance for the consumer. Two well-known choice rules capitalize on the different importance attached to different attributes (see Bettman 1979). Under the lexicographic rule, the consumer first compares the options on the most important attribute and chooses the option with the highest score on this attribute. In case of a tie, the process is then repeated with the second most important attribute, and so on until only one option remains. Under an elimination-by-aspect-type rule (see Tversky 1972), the alternatives are also assessed based on the most important attribute, but are eliminated if they fail to meet a certain cutoff. If multiple alternatives clear the first screening, they are then assessed based on the second most important attribute, and so on until one alternative remains.[2] We propose that promotion will encourage the reliance on a lexicographic rule, whereas prevention will encourage the reliance on an elimination-by-aspect-type rule (Proposition 5.3). Again, this is because promotion is oriented toward the fulfillment of aspirations and maximal goals, whereas prevention is oriented toward the avoidance of mistakes and fulfillment of minimal goals.

Proposition 5.1*	Under promotion, choice within the consideration set will be guided by a process of selection or acceptance, whereas under prevention, choice within the consideration set will be guided by a process of elimination or rejection.
Proposition 5.2*	Within the consideration set, promotion will encourage the reliance on a disjunctive rule, whereas prevention will encourage the reliance on a conjunctive rule.
Proposition 5.3*	Promotion will encourage the reliance on a lexicographic rule of choice, whereas prevention will encourage the reliance on an elimination-by-aspect-type rule.
Proposition 5.4	In choices between the status quo and a new option, promotion will increase preference for the new option, whereas prevention will increase preference for the status quo.
Proposition 5.5*	In choices involving a default option, prevention-oriented consumers will be more likely to choose the default than promotion-oriented consumers.
Proposition 5.6*	Prevention-oriented consumers are more likely to defer choice or prefer no-choice options than promotion-oriented consumers.
Proposition 5.7.1	Promotion will generally trigger greater risk-taking in choice, whereas prevention will generally trigger greater risk-aversion.
Proposition 5.7.2	In choices between a modest but certain gain and a greater but uncertain gain, promotion-oriented consumers will tend to favor the former and exhibit relative risk-aversion.
Proposition 5.7.3	In choices between a modest but certain loss and a greater but uncertain loss, prevention-oriented consumers will tend to favor the latter and exhibit relative risk-seeking.
Proposition 5.7.4	If the current state is highly undesirable, prevention-focused individuals will be more likely to pursue "riskier" options that could remove the undesirable state than promotion-focused individuals.
Proposition 5.8*	The "attraction" effect will be stronger among promotion-focused consumers than among prevention-focused consumers.
Proposition 5.9	The "compromise" effect will be stronger among prevention-focused consumers than among promotion-focused consumers.
Proposition 5.10*	Variety-seeking will be more pronounced among promotion-oriented consumers than among prevention-oriented consumers.

Figure 2.6 Regulatory focus and choice.

Status quo, default, and choice deferral

Consumer decision-making often involves a choice between the status quo and a new option. Regulatory focus theory predicts that, given such choices, promotion-oriented consumers will tend to favor the new option, whereas prevention-oriented consumers will tend to favor the status quo (Proposition 5.4). This is because a promotion focus is generally associated with an openness to change, whereas a prevention focus is generally associated with a preference toward stability. Liberman *et al.* (1999) tested this prediction using an endowment-effect paradigm. In this paradigm, participants are typically given one object, the "endowed" option, and offered an opportunity to exchange it against another object of comparable monetary value. It is generally found that, whichever object people are initially endowed with, they are reluctant to exchange it for another object of comparable value. Liberman *et al.* (1999) found that the priming of prevention magnified the endowment effect (making participants even more reluctant to exchange the product they were endowed with), whereas the priming of promotion removed the endowment effect (making participants indifferent between the product they were endowed with and the other product).

Closely related to the notion of status quo is the notion of "default," that is, an option that is selected unless the decision-maker actively rejects it. A large body of evidence shows that, in choices where there is a default option, the default generally receives a disproportionate share of the choices (e.g., Johnson and Goldstein 2003). Multiple explanations have been offered for this phenomenon. Acceptance of the default may reflect sheer inertia, as opting out of a default requires extra effort (e.g., Madrian and Shea 2001). The phenomenon may also reflect greater anticipated regret from rejecting the default due to counterfactual thinking (e.g., Kahneman and Miller 1986). The setting of the default may additionally be seen as having information value (e.g., "It must be the option most people prefer."). We propose that, in choices involving a default option, prevention-oriented consumers will be more likely to choose the default than promotion-oriented consumers (Proposition 5.5). Again, this is because promotion is generally characterized by a greater openness to change and greater willingness to take risks, whereas prevention is generally characterized by a preference for stability and lower willingness to take risks. Moreover, the default option may be interpreted as reflecting some social norm (e.g., "This is what I am expected to choose."), which should increase its appeal to prevention-focused individuals (see Propositions 1.2 and 4.4).

Also related to the notion of status quo is the notion of choice-deferral. Sometimes, consumers simply elect to postpone choice, which some have called a preference for the no-choice option (e.g., Dhar 1997). We predict that compared to promotion-oriented consumers, prevention-oriented consumers will be more likely to defer choice and elect non-choice options (Proposition 5.6). Again, this is because promotion-oriented consumers should be more open to capturing opportunities and taking chances, whereas prevention-oriented consumers should be more concerned about avoiding mistakes.

Risk-taking

We propose that, in choice, promotion will generally – but not always (as discussed further below) – trigger greater risk taking, whereas prevention will generally – but not always – trigger greater risk aversion (Proposition 5.7.1). As discussed by Zhou and Pham (2004), two sets of mechanisms contribute to this phenomenon. First, as already mentioned, promotion is characterized by eagerness, which usually translates into greater openness to risk, whereas prevention is characterized by vigilance, which usually translates into lesser openness to risk (Higgins 1997, 1998). This tendency was apparent in the previously mentioned finding that in signal detection tasks promotion-focused participants exhibit a risky bias, whereas prevention-focused participants exhibit a conservative bias (Crowe and Higgins 1997). This tendency also transpired in the finding that promotion-oriented individuals tend to perform tasks with greater speed and lower accuracy, whereas prevention-oriented individuals tend to perform the same tasks with lower speed but greater accuracy (Förster *et al.* 2003).

According to Zhou and Pham (2004), a second mechanism lies in promotion and prevention's differential attention to gains and losses. In many domains, options (e.g., surgery) with greater potential upsides (e.g., complete riddance of medical condition) also present greater potential downsides (e.g., life-threatening complications), whereas options (e.g., continuous medication) with smaller potential downsides (e.g., few side-effects) are also those with smaller potential upsides (e.g., symptoms relief without complete cure). In a choice between (a) a risky alternative with greater upsides and greater downsides and (b) a conservative alternative with smaller downsides and smaller upsides, promotion focusing on positive outcomes would favor the risky option, whereas prevention focusing on negative outcomes would favor the conservative option.

In a recent test of Proposition 5.7.1, Zhou and Pham (2004) asked participants to assess their willingness to invest a sum of money in a risky business venture. In one condition, the money was to be withdrawn from a financial account associated with promotion (a brokerage account). In the other condition, the money was to be withdrawn from a financial account associated with prevention (a retirement account). As predicted, participants were more willing to invest (i.e., risk their money) if the money came from the promotion-oriented brokerage account than if the money came from the prevention-oriented retirement account. In another study, Zhou and Pham (2004) primed participants into promotion versus prevention by having them proofread a text and solve anagrams under either eager approach instructions or vigilant avoidance instructions. Participants were then asked to allocate a sum of money between shares of an individual stock (a more risky option) and shares of a mutual fund (a less risky option). As predicted, participants who were primed in terms of promotion allocated relatively more money to the individual stock than participants who were primed in terms of prevention. (Other results indicate that these effects cannot be accounted for by standard economic and finance principles.) Similarly, Raghunathan *et al.* (2004) recently observed that, when given a choice between (a) going out with a good friend the evening before an exam (a higher-risk/higher-reward option) and (b) staying at home to study (a lower-risk/lower-reward option), participants whose ideals were primed leaned toward the evening with the friend, whereas participants whose oughts were primed leaned toward the evening studying.

Although promotion *generally* entails greater risk-seeking and prevention *generally* entails greater-risk aversion (Proposition 5.7.1), this relationship ceases to hold in certain situations recently identified by Zhou (2002; cited in Zhou and Pham 2004). Specifically, in a choice between a modest but certain gain and a greater but uncertain gain, promotion-oriented individuals will tend to favor the former and thus exhibit relative risk-aversion (Proposition 5.7.2). In a choice between a modest but certain loss and a greater but uncertain loss, prevention-oriented individuals will tend to favor the latter and thus exhibit relative risk-seeking (Proposition 5.7.3). In one experiment (ibid.), respondents who had been primed with promotion or prevention were asked to imagine that they had achieved some moderate "paper" (unrealized) gains on the stock market. They were then presented with two options: (a) selling their shares now to realize their capital gains, or (b) holding on to their shares for a chance of even greater gains but at the risk of the stock returning to its original price (i.e., to miss out on a gain). Note that, in this scenario, the riskier option (b) is no longer a clear "achieving gains-seizing opportunities" option. In fact, the less risky option (a) could be construed as being more consistent with the achievement of gains and the seizing of opportunities. Thus, failure to choose (a) could be construed as an error of omission. As expected, in this scenario, respondents who were primed with promotion were more likely to choose the less risky option (a) (i.e., were more risk-averse) than respondents who were primed with prevention. In another experiment (ibid.), respondents who had also been primed with promotion or prevention were asked to imagine that they had incurred some moderate paper losses on the stock market. They had two options: (a) sell their shares and realize their capital loss, or (b) hold on to their shares for a chance of breaking even but at the risk of incurring even greater losses. Again, in this scenario, the less risky option (a) is no longer a clear "prevent losses" option. In fact, the more risky option (b), with its chance of breaking even, could be construed as being more consistent with the avoidance of losses. In this case, choosing (a) and realizing one's losses could be construed as an error of commission. As expected, in this scenario, respondents who were primed with prevention were more likely to choose the more risky option (b) (i.e., were more risk-seeking) than respondents who were primed with promotion.

Therefore, under certain conditions, promotion and prevention can be meaningfully dissociated from risk-seeking and risk-aversion. Reversal of the typical pattern of risk-seeking under promotion and risk-aversion under prevention is most likely in loss domains. Specifically, we propose that if the current state is highly undesirable, prevention-focused individuals will be more likely to pursue riskier options that could remove (or "subtract") the undesirable state – thereby exhibiting in effect greater risk-seeking behavior – than promotion-focused individuals (Proposition 5.7.4). This is because prevention-focused individuals would consider it a mistake to remain in the current state, and feel it necessary to choose the riskier option. Note that such seemingly risk-seeking choices under prevention would arise not because prevention-focused individuals really want to take risks, but rather because they see it as a *necessity* to "correctly reject" the option that would prolong the negative state with greater certainty.

Context effects and variety-seeking

A growing body of evidence indicates that consumer choice is determined not only by the attributes of the options but also by the context in which the options are presented. Two particular aspects of the choice context have received a great deal of attention. The asymmetric-dominance or "attraction" effect refers to the tendency of an option A that dominates another option B to benefit disproportionately from the introduction of B in the choice set relative to other options that do not dominate B (Huber *et al.* 1982).[3] Although various accounts have been offered for this phenomenon (see, e.g., ibid.; Ratneshwar *et al.* 1987), a major explanation seems to be that the presence of a dominance relationship can be quite seductive as a choice heuristic (e.g., Simonson 1989). We propose that, compared to the activation of prevention, the activation of promotion will magnify the asymmetric dominance effect (Proposition 5.8). This is because a dominance relation in a choice set can be seen as an opportunity to be seized and not to be missed, which should be especially attractive to eager consumers. In contrast, vigilant consumers may be more wary of using a mere dominance relation as a basis of choice.

Another well-known context effect is the compromise effect. This effect refers to the tendency of an option to gain a disproportionate share of the market when presented as a middle-of-the-road, compromise option relative to other options in the choice set (Simonson 1989). According to Simonson (1989), compromise alternatives tend to be appealing because they are easy to justify as a choice. Simonson and Tversky (1992) suggest that compromise options are also appealing because they present fewer disadvantages compared to more extreme options (i.e., options that are excellent on some dimensions but poor on other dimensions). We propose that, compared to the activation of promotion, the activation of prevention will magnify the compromise effect (Proposition 5.9). As suggested by Simonson and Tversky (1992), the attractiveness of compromise options lies in part in the fact that they *avoid* the *disadvantages* of the more extreme options. Choosing the compromise option can thus be seen as a form of vigilance, which should be magnified by the activation of prevention. Extreme options (i.e., options that excel on some dimensions but are poor on others), on the other hand, should be relatively more appealing to eager individuals who tend to weigh positive attributes more strongly than negative attributes. Moreover, compromises are more consistent with collectivist norms of decision-making (Briley *et al.* 2000), norms that have stronger association with prevention than with promotion (see Lee *et al.* 2000). Consistent with Proposition 5.9, Briley *et al.* (2000) found that the compromise effect is indeed more pronounced in collectivist cultures (which tend to be more prevention-oriented) than in individualist cultures (which tend to be more promotion-oriented). Briley and Wyer (2002) also found that the priming of avoidance motivation increases preference for compromise options. The relation between regulatory focus theory and the attraction and compromise effects is currently being investigated in related work by Kivetz and Leavav.

When the choice involves the simultaneous selection of multiple items (e.g., ordering multiple articles of clothing from a catalog) or occurs on a repeated basis (e.g., buying groceries every Saturday), *other items* selected may become part of the choice context. A substantial amount of evidence suggests that consumer choice often reflects a search for variety. That is, consumers often seem motivated to diversify their choices (for a review, see Kahn and Ratner, this volume). We propose that, in choice, variety-seeking will be more pronounced under promotion than under prevention (Proposition 5.10; see also Proposition 3.2). This is because, as mentioned previously, promotion-oriented individuals are generally more open to change (see Proposition 5.4) and more willing to take risks (see Proposition 5.7.1). For promotion-oriented individuals, variety offers a way of capturing additional opportunities. Failure to do so would be an error of omission. In contrast, prevention-oriented individuals are more likely to see variety as a potential mistake and possible error of commission. (The safer option would be to consistently choose the most preferred alternative). Although this prediction remains to be tested explicitly, it is consistent with the previously mentioned finding that in gift giving, more diverse alternatives are considered under promotion than under prevention (Chowdhury 2004).

Post-choice processes

According to standard consumer theory, the final stage of the consumer decision-making process is a post-choice assessment of the decision. As summarized in Figure 2.7, we propose that differences in regulatory focus will influence

(a) the intensity of consumers' satisfaction/dissatisfaction with desirable/undesirable outcomes,
(b) the type of emotion experienced in response to desirable or undesirable outcomes,
(c) the nature of any post-decisional dissonance, and
(d) the satisfaction with the decision-making process *independent* of its outcome.

Satisfaction/dissatisfaction intensity

Decisions that produce desirable outcomes (successes) will obviously result in greater satisfaction and lesser dissatisfaction than decisions that produce undesirable outcomes (failures). Holding the desirability of the outcome constant, the intensity of the satisfaction or dissatisfaction may differ, depending on the consumer's regulatory focus. This difference arises from the types of goals that are associated with promotion and with prevention. Again, promotion is usually

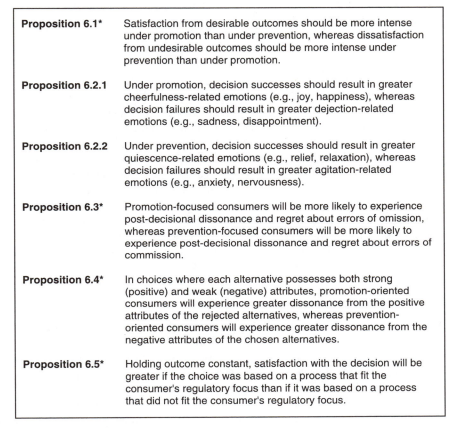

Proposition 6.1*	Satisfaction from desirable outcomes should be more intense under promotion than under prevention, whereas dissatisfaction from undesirable outcomes should be more intense under prevention than under promotion.
Proposition 6.2.1	Under promotion, decision successes should result in greater cheerfulness-related emotions (e.g., joy, happiness), whereas decision failures should result in greater dejection-related emotions (e.g., sadness, disappointment).
Proposition 6.2.2	Under prevention, decision successes should result in greater quiescence-related emotions (e.g., relief, relaxation), whereas decision failures should result in greater agitation-related emotions (e.g., anxiety, nervousness).
Proposition 6.3*	Promotion-focused consumers will be more likely to experience post-decisional dissonance and regret about errors of omission, whereas prevention-focused consumers will be more likely to experience post-decisional dissonance and regret about errors of commission.
Proposition 6.4*	In choices where each alternative possesses both strong (positive) and weak (negative) attributes, promotion-oriented consumers will experience greater dissonance from the positive attributes of the rejected alternatives, whereas prevention-oriented consumers will experience greater dissonance from the negative attributes of the chosen alternatives.
Proposition 6.5*	Holding outcome constant, satisfaction with the decision will be greater if the choice was based on a process that fit the consumer's regulatory focus than if it was based on a process that did not fit the consumer's regulatory focus.

Figure 2.7 Regulatory focus and post-choice processes.

associated with ideals (hopes, wishes, and aspirations), whereas prevention is usually associated with oughts (duties, responsibilities, and obligations). Because ideals are standards that the person *hopes* to attain, they tend to function like *maximal* goals. In contrast, because oughts are standards that the person *has to* meet, they tend to function like *minimal* goals (Brendl and Higgins 1996). Success in attaining a maximal goal should provide more intense pleasure than success in attaining a minimal goal, but failure to attain a minimal goal should provide more intense pain than failure to attain a maximal goal (Idson *et al.* 2000). Therefore, satisfaction from desirable outcomes should be more intense under promotion than under prevention, whereas dissatisfaction from undesirable outcomes should be more intense under prevention than under promotion (Proposition 6.1). Consistent with this prediction, Idson *et al.* (2000) found that pleasure from a positive outcome was more intense if the outcome was framed as a gain (a promotion success) than if it was framed as a non-loss (a prevention success). Pain from a negative outcome was more intense if the outcome was framed as a loss (a prevention failure) than if it was framed as a non-gain (a promotion failure).

Emotional responses to decision outcomes

Decision outcomes trigger not only summary judgments of satisfaction or dissatisfaction but also a variety of emotional responses (e.g., Westbrook and Oliver 1991). Consumers' emotional responses to decision successes and failures should be qualitatively different under promotion than under prevention. Under promotion, decision successes should result in greater elation-related emotions (e.g., joy, cheerfulness, happiness), whereas decision failures should result in greater dejection-related emotions (e.g., sadness, disappointment, discouragement) (Proposition 6.2.1). Under prevention, decision successes should result in greater quiescence-related emotions (e.g., relief, calm, relaxation), whereas decision failures should result in greater agitation-related emotions (e.g., anxiety, tension, nervousness) (Proposition 6.2.2). These propositions emanate directly from self-discrepancy theory (Higgins 1987) and have been documented in numerous studies (e.g., Higgins *et al.* 1997; Idson *et al.* 2000).

Post-decisional dissonance and regret

After a consumer has made a decision, the possibility that it could be the wrong decision can be source of emotional discomfort for the consumer. This discomfort may range from mild dissonance on account of the uncertainty as to whether the chosen alternative was in fact the right choice (e.g., when the outcome is still unknown), to acute regret from the conviction that the selected option was indeed the wrong choice (e.g., when the outcome is known).[4] The arousal of dissonance or regret is likely to be different under promotion versus prevention. As mentioned previously, eager, promotion-focused individuals tend to be more concerned with errors of omission, whereas vigilant, prevention-focused individuals tend to be more concerned with errors of commission (e.g., Crowe and Higgins 1997). We therefore propose that promotion-focused consumers will be more likely to experience post-decisional dissonance and regret in relation to errors of omission (e.g., failing to buy a product while it was on sale), whereas prevention-focused consumers will be more likely to experience post-decisional dissonance and regret in relation to errors of commission (e.g., buying a product that was not really needed; see Proposition 6.3). Consistent with this prediction, Roese *et al.* (1999) found that failures of promotion (e.g., failing to fulfill a romantic interest) tend to trigger *additive* counterfactuals that mutate inactions (e.g., "I should have asked her out"), whereas failures of prevention (e.g., inadvertently causing some food poisoning), tend to trigger *subtractive* counterfactuals that mutate actions (e.g., "I should not have given her that sandwich"). Similarly, Camacho *et al.* (2003) found that chronically promotion-oriented individuals experience stronger guilt following sins of omission (e.g., not offering help to a person in need) than following sins of commission (e.g., taking advantage of a friend), whereas the reverse was true for chronically prevention-oriented individuals.

The rationale behind Proposition 6.3 yields another related prediction. In many choice situations, each alternative possesses both strong (positive) and weak (negative) attributes. We propose that, after making such choices, promotion-oriented consumers will experience greater dissonance from the positive attributes of the rejected alternatives (which would be perceived as non-gains or forsaken "hits"). In contrast, prevention-oriented consumers will experience greater dissonance from the negative attributes of the chosen alternative (which would be perceived as losses or failures to correctly reject) (Proposition 6.4).

Process-based satisfaction

In a recent extension of regulatory focus theory, Higgins (2000, 2002) proposed the *value-from-fit hypothesis*. This hypothesis holds that people derive value (or "utility") not only from the outcomes of the choices they make, but also from the *process* by which those choices are made. Specifically, the hypothesis states that the value that a person will derive from a choice – holding the outcome of the choice constant – will be greater if the choice is made in a manner that is consistent with the person's regulatory orientation (a situation called *regulatory fit*) than if the choice is made in a manner that is inconsistent with this person's regulatory orientation (a situation called regulatory non-fit). To test this hypothesis, Higgins *et al.* (2003) recently asked chronically promotion-focused participants and chronically prevention-focused participants to make a choice between an inexpensive disposable pen and a university-branded coffee mug. The products were chosen such that virtually all participants would choose the much more desirable coffee mug (i.e., such that decision outcome would be constant). Half of the participants were asked to make the choice by considering what they would *gain* by choosing one product or the other (an eager strategy). The other half were asked to make the choice by considering what they would *lose* by choosing one product or the other (a vigilant strategy). As predicted, participants assigned a substantially greater monetary value to the mug when their choice strategy matched their chronic regulatory focus (when promotion-focused participants used an eager strategy and when prevention-focused participants used a vigilant strategy) than when their choice strategy did not match their chronic regulatory focus (when promotion-focused participants used a vigilant strategy and prevention-focused participants used an eager strategy). Additional studies indicate that the phenomenon arises because a regulatory fit produces a phenomenal experience of "feeling right" that is misattributed to the chosen alternative (Camacho *et al.* 2003; Cesario *et al.* 2004; Higgins *et al.* 2003). The process appears to be similar to the one posited by the affect-as-information model (Schwarz and Clore 1983, 1996; Pham 1998, 2004), except that the misattributed feelings are not typical emotional feelings of pleasantness, but metacognitive feelings of "being right" (see Cesario *et al.* 2004). We therefore propose that, holding the outcome of the decision constant, satisfaction with the decision will be greater if the choice was based on a process that fit the consumer's regulatory focus than if it was based on a process that did not fit the consumer's regulatory focus (Proposition 6.5).[5]

Concluding remarks

For much of the past 30 years, consumer researchers have focused primarily on a cognitive analysis of consumer decision-making (see Bettman *et al.* 1998 for a review). This work has generated numerous insights on how various cognitive factors – factors such as accessibility, diagnosticity, availability, congruency, commensurability, representativeness, and so on – influence consumers' decisions. Yet, however interesting and rigorous this body of work may be, one must not forget that consumer decision-making – and human cognition in general – do not operate in a motivational vacuum. Recent work has shown that consumer decision-making is influenced by a variety of motivational factors besides purely cognitive processes. For instance, decision processes have been shown to depend on the instrumental versus experiential nature of consumers' motives (e.g., Pham 1998), their need to justify the choice (e.g., Simonson 1989), their need to respect personal rules (Amir *et al.*, this volume), their desire to diversify their consumption (Kahn and Ratner, this volume), and their desire to shape their self-image (Khan *et al.*, this volume).

Studying consumer decision-making from a motivational perspective does raise a major challenge, however. Assuming that the field is past describing motivation simply in terms of its intensity (see, e.g., the vast amount of research on "involvement"), the range of decision-relevant motives or goals – that is, the range of outcomes that the consumer seeks to achieve through the decision – is almost unlimited. Regulatory focus theory presents a significant advantage in this respect. Unlike most other theories of motivation, the theory is not cast in terms of *desired outcomes* – desired outcomes that can be almost infinitely diverse (e.g., choice accuracy, impression management, ego-defense, terror management, dissonance reduction, achievement motivation, etc.) – but in terms of *strategic inclinations* for attaining these outcomes, which are classified into two basic categories, promotion- and prevention-focused. Studying consumer decision-making along these two types of strategic inclinations offers the epistemological advantage of parsimony.

We would like to offer two final suggestions. First, our organization of the predictions along well-defined stages of the decision-making process is mostly a matter of convenience. One should not forget that in reality consumer decision-making is inherently dynamic, and not purely linear. For example, as we have noted, not only can regulatory focus exert exogenous influences on decision-making, it can also be determined endogenously by the decision-making process itself (see Zhou and Pham, 2004). Therefore, analyzing the *dynamics* of promotion and prevention *throughout* the decision-making process would be an important extension of the ideas presented in this chapter. Second, although most of our predictions were cast as basic ("main") effects of promotion and prevention, many of these effects are likely to be qualified by meaningful contingencies (see, e.g., Propositions 5.7.1, 5.7.2, 5.7.3). Identifying these contingencies via further research would be important as well. Nevertheless, as indicated by the number of theoretical propositions advanced in this chapter, we believe that the basic distinction between promotion-eagerness and prevention-vigilance offers great potential for the study of motivated consumer decision-making. Whether the propositions we offer in this chapter will withstand future empirical verification, only the future can tell. On our part, we have guarded optimism that they will.

Acknowledgments

Preparation of this chapter was supported in part by a research grant to the first author from the Graduate School of Business of Columbia University. The authors thank Jennifer L. Aaker, Angela Y. Lee, and Ginger L. Pennington for their helpful comments on an earlier draft. Correspondence regarding this chapter may be addressed to either Michel Tuan Pham (tdp4@columbia.edu) or Tory Higgins (tory@paradox.psych.columbia.edu).

Notes

1 See Khan *et al.* (this volume) for a review of research on hedonic versus utilitarian consumption.
2 In Tversky's (1972) original formulation of the elimination-by-aspect heuristic, the order in which the attributes are examined is probabilistic (with the probability of examination proportional to the relative weight of each attribute) rather than being strictly determined by the weight of each attribute. We describe a deterministic version of the heuristic for clarity of exposition.
3 An option A is said to "dominate" another option B if A is superior to B on every choice-relevant dimension.
4 Like disappointment, regret is an unpleasant emotion that arises from counterfactual comparisons between "what is" and "what could have been." In disappointment what is being compared is the undesirable (disappointing) actual outcome with what this outcome could have been (the aspiration or standard). In regret what is being compared is the chosen course of action (or inaction) with what this course could have been (see Zeelenberg *et al.* 1998).
5 Note that the value-from-fit hypothesis is not restricted to fit to promotion versus prevention. Regulatory fit produces similar effects with other types of regulatory orientations (see, e.g., Avnet and Higgins 2003).

References

Aaker, J. L. and Lee, A. Y. (2001) " 'I' seek pleasures and 'we' avoid pains: The role of self-regulatory goals in information processing and persuasion," *Journal of Consumer Research* 28(1): 33–49.
Avnet, T. and Higgins, E. T. (2003) "Locomotion, assessment, and regulatory fit: Value transfer from 'how' to 'what,' " *Journal of Experimental Social Psychology* 39(5): 525–530.
Avnet, T. and Pham, M. T. (2004) "Comparing the attitude strength of promotion- and prevention-based evaluations," Unpublished manuscript, Columbia University.
Beatty, S. E. and Smith, S. M. (1987) "External search effort – An investigation across several product categories," *Journal of Consumer Research* 14(1): 83–95.

Bettman, J. R. (1979) *An Information Processing Theory of Consumer Choice*, Reading, MA: Addison-Wesley.

Bettman, J. R., Luce, M. F., and Payne, J. W. (1998) "Constructive consumer choice processes," *Journal of Consumer Research* 25(3): 187–217.

Bless, H., Schwarz, N., Clore, G. L., Golisano, V., and Rabe, C. (1996) "Mood and the use of scripts: Does a happy mood really lead to mindlessness?" *Journal of Personality and Social Psychology* 71(4): 665–679.

Brendl, C. M. and Higgins, E. T. (1996) "Principles of judging valence: What makes events positive or negative?" in *Advances in Experimental Social Psychology*, Vol. 28: 95–160.

Briley, D. A., Morris, M. W., and Simonson, I. (2000) "Reasons as carriers of culture: Dynamic versus dispositional models of cultural influence on decision-making," *Journal of Consumer Research* 27(2): 157–178.

Briley, D. A. and Wyer, R. S. (2002) "The effect of group membership salience on the avoidance of negative outcomes: Implications for social and consumer decisions," *Journal of Consumer Research* 29(3): 400–415.

Brockner, J., Paruchuri, S., Idson, L. C., and Higgins, E. T. (2002) "Regulatory focus and the probability estimates of conjunctive and disjunctive events," *Organizational Behavior and Human Decision Processes* 87: 5–24.

Brucks, M. (1985) "The effects of product class knowledge on information search behavior," *Journal of Consumer Research* 12(1): 1–16.

Brunner, G. C. and Pomazal, R. J. (1988) "Problem recognition: The crucial first stage of the consumer decision process," *Journal of Consumer Marketing* 5: 53–63.

Camacho, C. J., Higgins, E. T., and Luger, L. (2003) "Moral value transfer from regulatory fit: What feels right is right and what feels wrong is wrong," *Journal of Personality and Social Psychology* 84(3): 498–510.

Carver, C. S. and Scheier, M. F. (1981) *Attention and Self-Regulation: A Control-Theory Approach to Human Behavior*, New York: Springer-Verlag.

Cesario, J., Grant, H., and Higgins, E. T. (2004) "Regulatory fit and persuasion: Transfer from 'feeling right,'" *Journal of Personality and Social Psychology* 86(3): 388–404.

Chowdhury, T. G. (2004) "The role of variety-seeking trait in purchases made for others," Unpublished dissertation, University of Connecticut.

Crowe, E. and Higgins, E. T. (1997) "Regulatory focus and strategic inclinations: Promotion and prevention in decision-making," *Organizational Behavior and Human Decision Processes* 69(2): 117–132.

Dhar, R. (1997) "Consumer preference for a no-choice option," *Journal of Consumer Research* 24(2): 215–231.

Förster, J. and Higgins, E. T. (2004) "Regulatory focus and global versus local perception: Implications for performance and value," Unpublished manuscript, International University Bremen.

Förster, J., Higgins, E. T., and Bianco, A. T. (2003) "Speed/accuracy decisions in task performance: Built-in trade-off or separate strategic concerns?" *Organizational Behavior and Human Decision Processes* 90(1): 148–164.

Förster, J., Higgins, E. T., and Idson, L. C. (1998) "Approach and avoidance strength during goal attainment: Regulatory focus and the 'goal looms larger' effect," *Journal of Personality and Social Psychology* 75(5): 1115–1131.

Förster, J., Higgins, E. T., and Strack, F. (2000) "When stereotype disconfirmation is a personal threat: How prejudice and prevention focus moderate incongruency effects," *Social Cognition* 18(2): 178–197.

Freud, S. (1950) *Beyond the Pleasure Principle* (Original work published 1920), New York: Liveright.

Friedman, R. S. and Förster, J. (2001) "The effects of promotion and prevention cues on creativity," *Journal of Personality and Social Psychology* 81: 1001–1013.

Hauser, J. R. and Wernerfelt, B. (1990) "An evaluation cost model of consideration sets," *Journal of Consumer Research* 16(4): 393–408.

Higgins, E. T. (1987) "Self-discrepancy: A theory relating self and affect," *Psychological Review* 94(3): 319–340.

Higgins, E. T. (1997) "Beyond pleasure and pain," *American Psychologist* 52(12): 1280–1300.

Higgins, E. T. (1998) "Promotion and prevention: Regulatory focus as a motivational principle," in *Advances in Experimental Social Psychology*, Vol. 30: 1–46.

Higgins, E. T. (2000) "Making a good decision: Value from fit," *American Psychologist* 55(11): 1217–1230.

Higgins, E. T. (2002) "How self-regulation creates distinct values: The case of promotion and prevention decision-making," *Journal of Consumer Psychology* 12(3): 177–191.

Higgins, E. T., Idson, L. C., Freitas, A. L., Spiegel, S., and Molden, D. C. (2003) "Transfer of value from fit," *Journal of Personality and Social Psychology* 84(6): 1140–1153.

Higgins, E. T., Roney, C. J. R., Crowe, E., and Hymes, C. (1994) "Ideal versus ought predilections for approach and avoidance-distinct self-regulatory systems," *Journal of Personality and Social Psychology* 66(2): 276–286.

Higgins, E. T., Shah, J., and Friedman, R. (1997) "Emotional responses to goal attainment: Strength of regulatory focus as moderator," *Journal of Personality and Social Psychology* 72: 515–525.

Higgins, E. T. and Silberman, I. (1998) "Development of regulatory focus: Promotion and prevention as ways of living," in J. Heckhausen and C. S. Dweck (eds), *Motivation and Self-Regulation Across the Life Span*, New York: Cambridge University Press: 78–113.

Higgins, E. T. and Spiegel, S. (in press) "Promotion and prevention strategies for self-regulation: A motivated cognition perspective," in R. Baumeister and K. Vohs (eds), *Handbook of Self-Regulation*, New York: Guilford Press.

Hoyer, W. D. and MacInnis, D. J. (2003) *Consumer Behavior* (3rd ed.), Boston, MA: Houghton Mifflin.

Huber, J., Payne, J. W., and Puto, C. (1982) "Adding asymmetrically dominated alternatives: Violations of regularity and the similarity hypothesis," *Journal of Consumer Research* 9(1): 90–98.

Hull, C. L. (1952) *A Behavior System: An Introduction to Behavior Theory Concerning the Individual Organism* New Haven, CT: Yale University Press.

Idson, L. C., Liberman, N., and Higgins, E. T. (2000) "Distinguishing gains from nonlosses and losses from nongains: A regulatory focus perspective on hedonic intensity," *Journal of Experimental Social Psychology* 36(3): 252–274.

Idson, L. C., Liberman, N., and Higgins, E. T. (2004) "Imagining how you'd feel: The role of motivational experiences from regulatory fit," *Personality and Social Psychology Bulletin* 30(7): 926–937.

Johnson, E. J. and Goldstein, D. (2003) "Medicine – do defaults save lives?" *Science* 302(5649): 1338–1339.

Kahneman, D. and Miller, D. T. (1986) "Norm theory: Comparing reality to its alternatives," *Psychological Review* 93(2): 136–153.

Kardes, F. R. and Cronley, M. L. (2000) "The role of approach/avoidance asymmetries in motivated belief formation and change," in S. Ratneshwar, D. G. Mick, and C. Huffman (eds), *The Why of Consumption: Contemporary Perspectives on Consumer Motives, Goals, and Desires*, New York: Routledge: 81–97.

Lang, P. J. (1995) "The emotion probe – studies of motivation and attention," *American Psychologist* 50(5): 372–385.

Lee, A. Y. and Aaker, J. L. (2004) "Bringing the frame into focus: The influence of regulatory fit on processing fluency and persuasion," *Journal of Personality and Social Psychology* 86(2): 205–218.

Lee, A. Y., Aaker, J. L., and Gardner, W. L. (2000) "The pleasures and pains of distinct self-construals: The role of interdependence in regulatory focus," *Journal of Personality and Social Psychology* 78(6): 1122–1134.

Lewin, K. (1935). *A Dynamic Theory of Personality*. New York: McGraw-Hill.

Liberman, N., Idson, L. C., Camacho, C. J., and Higgins, E. T. (1999) "Promotion and prevention choices between stability and change," *Journal of Personality and Social Psychology* 77(6): 1135–1145.

Liberman, N., Molden, D. C., Idson, L. C., and Higgins, E. T. (2001) "Promotion and prevention focus on alternative hypotheses: Implications for attributional functions," *Journal of Personality and Social Psychology* 80: 5–18.

Madrian, B. C. and Shea, D. F. (2001) "The power of suggestion: Inertia in 401(k) participation and savings behavior," *Quarterly Journal of Economics* 116(4): 1149–1187.

Miller, G. A., Galanter, E., and Pribram, K. H. (1960) *Plans and the Structure of Behavior*, New York: Holt, Rinehart, and Winston.

Molden, D. C. and Higgins, E. T. (2004) "Categorization under uncertainty: Resolving vagueness and ambiguity with eager versus vigilant strategies," *Social Cognition* 22(2): 248–277.

Mowrer, O. H. (1960) *Learning Theory and Behavior*, New York: John Wiley.

Payne, J. W., Bettman, J. R., and Johnson, E. J. (1993) *The Adaptive Decision-Maker*, New York: Cambridge University Press.

Pham, M. T. (1998) "Representativeness, relevance, and the use of feelings in decision-making," *Journal of Consumer Research* 25(2): 144–159.

Pham, M. T. (2004) "The logic of feeling," *Journal of Consumer Psychology* 14(4): 360–369.

Pham, M. T. and Avnet, T. (2004) "Ideals and oughts and the reliance on affect versus substance in persuasion," *Journal of Consumer Research* 30(4): 503–518.

Raghunathan, R., Pham, M. T., and Corfman, K. (2004) "Anxiety, sadness, and consumer decision-making: Disentangling the effects of feelings and regulatory focus," Unpublished manuscript, University of Texas, Austin.

Ratneshwar, S., Shocker, A. D., and Stewart, D. W. (1987) "Toward understanding the attraction effect – the implications of product stimulus meaningfulness and familiarity," *Journal of Consumer Research* 13(4): 520–533.

Roese, N. J., Hur, T., and Pennington, G. L. (1999) "Counterfactual thinking and regulatory focus: Implications for action versus inaction and sufficiency versus necessity," *Journal of Personality and Social Psychology* 77: 1109–1120.

Safer, D. A. (1998) "Preference for luxurious or reliable products: Promotion and prevention focus as moderators," Unpublished dissertation, Columbia University, New York.

Schwarz, N. and Clore, G. L. (1983) "Mood, misattribution, and judgments of well-being – informative and directive functions of affective states," *Journal of Personality and Social Psychology* 45(3): 513–523.

Schwarz, N. and Clore, G. L. (1996) "Feelings and phenomenal experiences," in E. T. Higgins and A. W. Kruglanski (eds), *Social Psychology: Handbook of Basic Principles*, New York: Guilford Press: 433–465.

Shah, J. Y., Brazy, P. C., and Higgins, E. T. (2004) "Promoting us or preventing them: Regulatory focus and manifestations of intergroup bias," *Personality and Social Psychology Bulletin* 30: 433–446.

Shah, J. and Higgins, E. T. (1997) "Expectancy x value effects: Regulatory focus as determinant of magnitude and direction," *Journal of Personality and Social Psychology* 73(3): 447–458.

Shah, J. and Higgins, E. T. (2001) "Regulatory concerns and appraisal efficiency: Promotion and prevention as general concerns producing general efficiencies," *Journal of Personality and Social Psychology* 80: 693–705.

Shah, J., Higgins, E. T., and Friedman, R. S. (1998) "Performance incentives and means: How regulatory focus influences goal attainment," *Journal of Personality and Social Psychology* 74(2): 285–293.

Shocker, A. D., Ben-Akiva, M., Boccara, B., and Nedungadi, P. (1991) "Consideration set influences on consumer decision-making and choice: Issues, models, and suggestions," *Marketing Letters* 2(3): 181–197.

Simonson, I. (1989) "Choice based on reasons – the case of attraction and compromise effects," *Journal of Consumer Research* 16(2): 158–174.

Simonson, I. and Tversky, A. (1992) "Choice in context – trade-off contrast and extremeness aversion," *Journal of Marketing Research* 29(3): 281–295.

Spiegel, S., Grant-Pillow, H., and Higgins, E. T. (2004) "How regulatory fit enhances motivational strength during goal pursuit," *European Journal of Social Psychology* 3: 439–54.

Tversky, A. (1972) "Elimination by aspects: A theory of choice," *Psychological Review* 79 (July): 281–299.

Wang, J. and Lee, A. Y. (2004) "The role of regulatory fit on information search and persuasion," Unpublished manuscript, Northwestern University.

Westbrook, R. A. and Oliver, R. L. (1991) "The dimensionality of consumption emotion patterns and consumer satisfaction," *Journal of Consumer Research* 18(1): 84–91.

Zeelenberg, M., van Dijk, W. W., van der Pligt, J., Manstead, A. S. R., van Empelen, P., and Reinderman, D. (1998) "Emotional reactions to the outcomes of decisions: The role of counterfactual thought in the experience of regret and disappointment," *Organizational Behavior and Human Decision Processes* 75(2): 117–141.

Zhou, R. (2002) "Individual investors decision-making: The ubiquitous influence of promotion and prevention self-regulation," Unpublished dissertation, Columbia University, New York.

Zhou, R. and Pham, M. T. (2004) "Promotion and prevention across mental accounts: how financial products dictate consumers' investment goals," *Journal of Consumer Research* 31(2): 125–135.

3 Why and how consumers hope

Motivated reasoning and the marketplace

Gustavo E. de Mello and
Deborah J. MacInnis

Aspirations to achieve desired states drive, directly or indirectly, all of human behavior. This most basic and fundamental of principles is at the core of our quest to understand the why of consumer behavior and what processes and purposes lie inside the external manifestations of consumption. Tightly intertwined with these aspirations is the concept of hope: consumers hope to lose weight and to look younger; they hope to have beautiful houses and fashionable as well as flexible wardrobes (Kaiser and Ketchum, this volume); they hope to find enlightenment, and they even hope to avoid death (Turley, this volume). The possibility of achieving such goals drives consumption as consumers buy products or services regarded as means to achieve these ends. Indeed, the shopping experience itself engenders hope that a new and better self is in the offing (Kaiser and Ketchum, this volume).

As would be expected of a notion so intimately linked to human aspirations, hope is a common word in everyday language. Research by Shimanoff (1984) finds that in everyday conversations, hope is one of the most frequently named emotions. Religions and spiritual philosophies across cultures advocate the importance of hope for the health of the mind, body, and soul. Paradoxically, despite its prevalence in language and consumer culture, and its relevance to consumer goals, the study of hope in the literature in marketing and psychology is limited. Indeed, over forty years ago, Cohen (1958) observed, "Although life without hope is unthinkable, psychology without hope is not, judging by the conspicuous absence of any study of hope from the literature" (10). The status of the study of hope has changed little in the interim; as Lazarus (1999a: 653) expounds, "With a modest number of exceptions ... there has been a great reluctance on the part of psychologists to address the concept of hope." We surmise that the dearth of research on the topic is due to two factors: (1) historical conceptualizations of emotions that omit hope, and (2) lack of clarity in the definition of hope.

In the present chapter, we define the concept of hope using an appraisal theory perspective. This theory is particularly appropriate to the study of goals as it reflects consumers' assessments of the impact of the environment on goal achievement. Underlying the evocation of hope are appraisals that a future outcome is goal-congruent and possible. Complementing the use of appraisal theory, we also argue that the concept of hope can be studied in terms of its three "faces," specifically, (1) to hope, (2) to have hope, and (3) to be hopeful. *To hope* is to yearn for a goal-congruent outcome seen as possible; *to have hope* is to enjoy a positive feeling that such outcome is possible; finally, *to be hopeful* is to assign an expectation level to the possibility of the outcome. We elaborate on these distinctions later in the chapter as they relate to the depiction in Figure 3.1. Each "face" relates to the definition of hope, but focuses on a different aspect of the appraisal process. This chapter focuses on the second of these treatments of hope – *to have hope*. Consideration of the other two faces of hope are described elsewhere (e.g., MacInnis and de Mello 2005 focus on *to hope*; MacInnis *et al.* 2004 focus on *being hopeful*).

In the next sections, we expand on the topic of having hope, how this facet of the hope triptych is woven into consumption, and how having hope is linked to motivated information processing. We begin by defining *having hope* as it relates to the other two faces of *hoping* and *being hopeful*, encasing this definition in the framework of appraisal theory. We then define motivated reasoning and explain the mechanisms whereby it operates. Next, we link having hope with motivated reasoning, analyzing how the consumption of hope (as a marketable entity) is tightly coupled with cognitive biases. Here, we pay special attention to both adaptive and maladaptive consumer consequences of hope-motivated reasoning. Finally, we suggest directions for further study of this phenomenon.

An appraisal theory perspective on hope

According to appraisal theory, *emotions are caused by appraisals or perceptions of a given situation* (Ellsworth and Smith 1988; Frijda *et al.* 1989; Oatley and Johnson-Laird 1987; Roseman 1991). Appraisal theorists have identified a number of dimensions that individuals use to assess their environment, among them assessments of goal congruency, agency, certainty, normative/moral compatibility, and importance (Johnson and Stewart 2004; Roseman 1991).

In the appraisal theory framework, and as elaborated below, hope is defined as *a positive emotion evoked in response to a goal-congruent outcome appraised as possible* (MacInnis and de Mello 2005). As an emotion evoked in response to an appraisal, hope is characterized as a "high-road emotion," that is, one evoked in response to higher-order cognitions or appraisals (Shiv *et al.*, this volume).

Positive valence. A number of researchers have hypothesized or confirmed empirically that hope is a positive emotion (e.g., Shaver *et al.* 1987). Hope is a pleasurable state that helps those in distress cope with fear and anxiety over an uncertain future (Lazarus 1999a). Myers (2000) links hope to happiness, and Belk (1996) has aptly described it as a state of exciting, yet illusory, anticipatory desire that has the power to sustain and nourish us.

Goal-congruence. Research on human goals is predicated on a basic assumption: individuals have goals, or *desired outcomes* that they aspire to achieve, and they strive toward these ends until the experienced current state satisfactorily approximates the desired state (Gollwitzer and Moskowitz 1996). Hope is felt in response to outcomes appraised as favorable or goal-congruent (Lazarus 1991; Roseman 1991). Goal-congruence reflects the extent to which the environment is appraised as consistent with one's goals. In a benign environment, "goal-congruent" means that one makes an appraisal that a good, favorable, desired, or positive outcome (e.g., having a trim physique) could occur. In an aversive or threatening environment, "goal-congruent" means that a negative outcome could be avoided or solved (e.g., slow down aging). Hope thus applies equally to consumers with a promotion or a prevention focus (Pham and Higgins, this volume). In the case of a promotion focus, hope means that a good outcome can be realized, whereas in the case of a prevention focus, hope implies that a bad outcome that can be avoided.

Importantly, while hope relates to goals, it complements this literature in three ways: (1) it focuses on the outcomes presumed to result from goal achievement; (2) it adds an affective element to the study of goals by focusing on an emotion that arises from goal formulation and pursuit (Bagozzi *et al.* 2000); and (3) it indicates that consumers sometimes have a goal of having hope, as possession of this emotion is pleasurable and congruent with higher-order goals of seeking positive reinforcement.

Possibility. A critical factor for the elicitation of hope is that goal attainment is appraised as possible. This last factor pertains to the *certainty* dimension of appraisal theory. As a future-oriented emotion, hope refers to states that have not yet been attained and as such, are uncertain. However, it is necessary that along the certainty continuum (i.e., from certain to occur to certain not to occur) the outcome is deemed possible (Lazarus 1991; Roseman 1991). Indeed, the possibility factor is a characteristic that differentiates hope from mere desire. As Lazarus (1999a: 653) writes, "Although desire is an essential feature, hope is much more than desire," because hope also requires "the possibility of an uncertain outcome." Averill *et al.* (1990) found that the most common factor initiating hope was changes in perceptions of possibility, such as an increase in the probability of a previously unlikely event. When the attainment of a desired end-state is appraised as impossible (e.g., "I cannot get rid of my wrinkles"), the resulting emotions are linked to frustration, anger, disappointment, or despair (e.g., Higgins 1987). Indeed, hopelessness or despair is experienced when a desired goal is seen as impossible, inducing a state of depression (Seligman 1975).

The three facets of hope

While appraisal theorists seem to agree that hope is an emotion evoked in response to an outcome appraised as goal-congruent and possible, definitions of hope in the psychology literature suggest at least three facets of hope, all of which incorporate appraisal dimensions of goal congruency and possibility. They are: (1) to hope; (2) to be hopeful; and (3) to have hope. While similar in the core appraisal dimensions, they differ in emphasis. Importantly, these three facets of hope correspond with and help clarify definitional inconsistencies in hope as defined by a

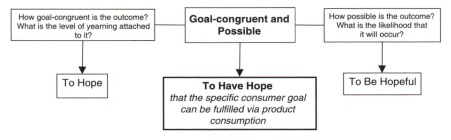

Figure 3.1 The three facets of consumer hope.

To Hope

Definition: A positive emotion that varies as a function of the degree of yearning for a *possible*, *goal-congruent*, future outcome.
- Pieper (1994): an emotion that occurs when what one is expecting is good signifying all that one longs for.
- Rycroft (1979): a feeling or emotion about it that includes two features: we desire something we do not have; and we desire something we believe we could or may gain.

To Have Hope

Definition: A positive emotion that arises when a *goal-congruent* future outcome is judged to be *possible*.
- Gelwick (1979): a belief that what is desirable and good is also possible.[3]
- Haase *et al.* (1992): an energized mental state involving feelings of uneasiness or uncertainty and characterized by a cognitive, action-oriented expectation that a positive future goal or outcome is possible.

To Be Hopeful

Definition: A positive emotion that rises as a function of expectations regarding the likelihood of a *possible future goal-congruent* outcome.
- Stotland (1969): a necessary condition for action to achieve a goal that is a function of the perceived probability of attaining the goal and the perceived importance of the goal.
- Staats (1987): the expectation of desirable future events.

Figure 3.2 Definitions for the three facets of consumer hope.

variety of researchers in psychology, medicine, and other disciplines. Figure 3.1 indicates various ways in which the "hope" construct has been defined. As shown, various definitions correspond with each of the three facets. Figure 3.1 depicts the relationship between the three facets of hope.

To *have hope* is to enjoy a positive feeling that a goal-congruent outcome is possible. The feeling of hope derives, then, from the consumer's assessment of goal possibility. This implies that such an affective state is acquirable, and may thus be a goal in itself, as discussed in the next section. As an emotion evoked in response to an appraisal, hope is characterized as a "high-road emotion", that is, one evoked in response to higher-order cognitions or appraisals (Shiv *et al.*, this volume). One either has hope or does not have hope; and the hope one has can be false or true. One has hope when one does not assess a goal-congruent outcome as impossible, but rather sees potential for its possibility.

Consider the consumer who wants to have hope that he will lose weight in the next few months, and suppose this consumer needs to assess this goal-congruent outcome (i.e., losing weight) as possible. One way to facilitate such positive assessment is to afford oneself of means to goal attainment, such as products that present themselves as goal-enablers – in the present example, an herbal supplement that boosts metabolism, for instance. When this consumer purchases such a product, the benefit he is acquiring is not only the potential effects of the supplement on his body weight, but also the feeling of hope that his goal is possible. As illustrated in this example, the focus we place on *having hope* is particularly relevant to this book since (a) consumers have hope that products and services will yield outcomes that are consistent (or congruent) with their goals, and (b) the pleasurable experience of having hope may itself be a goal.

To *hope* is to yearn for a goal-congruent outcome regarded as possible. Notice that the appraisal of possibility distinguishes *to hope* from simply *to yearn* – in fact, the latter is independent from possibility assessments, while for the former the notion of possibility is critical. This facet of hope incorporates the appraisal dimension of yearning or importance, and suggests not a binary state, but rather a continuous emotion that varies as a function of the extent to which the outcome is yearned (i.e., desired, important, entails deficiency in the self). While two individuals may both have hope for losing weight, the two may differ in the *extent* to which they hope to lose weight, with one consumer yearning more for this outcome than another. One might say that the degree of hope relates to the goal-congruency dimension, as the individual appraises not the *existence* of a possible goal-congruent outcome, but rather *how much yearning is associated with the goal-congruent outcome* (i.e., how goal-congruent is it; see Figure 3.2).

To *be hopeful* is to assign an expectation level or perceived likelihood to the possibility of a goal-congruent outcome. *To be hopeful* is not synonymous with *to have expectations*; while the former is outcome-dependent, the latter is independent of the goal-congruence of the outcome (for example, one can expect a downturn in the economy, but one certainly is not hopeful that it will occur). This facet of hope operates on the uncertainty dimension of appraisal theory, with degrees of hopefulness varying as a function of the perceived likelihood of the goal-congruent outcome. Two consumers could *have hope* for surviving cancer, and both could *hope* (yearn) for this outcome, however one may be more *hopeful* about overcoming the disease, assigning a relatively high likelihood to this outcome, while another sees the probability of this outcome as low. Though they may "hold out hope" that the disease will be overcome, they do not expect that it will. Being hopeful is related to the concept of optimism; however, optimism (when conceptualized as a state versus a trait variable) is a belief that incorporates the *confidence* assigned to the expectation level.

Having hope as a goal

Having hope has been seen, both by laypeople and scholars, as driver or means to goal achievement; for example, Stotland (1969) observed that hope is linked to goal-setting and pursuit. We should not overlook, however, the role of having hope as a goal in itself. As a pleasurable, uplifting emotion, having hope is a state we strive to attain. The quest for having hope, and the desire to sustain it, are powerful drivers of behavior. In light of Shiv *et al.*'s discussion (this volume) of the neurological effects of emotions, it is interesting that having hope has been associated with the release of neurotransmitters (endorphins and enkephalins) in the brain that are involved in the reduction of pain (Groopman 2004). As such, there may be a very primitive and biological basis for why individuals may put "having hope" as a goal in and of itself.

It is easy to understand why consumers would set "having hope" as a goal. As a positive emotion, hope uplifts and energizes. The evocation of hope engenders positive feelings that can induce a positive mood (Ellsworth and Smith 1988). The induction of a positive mood through hope relates to the concepts of mood repair and maintenance described in the mood literature (e.g., Isen 1987, 2001). The mood-enhancing qualities of having hope pertain both to consumers who focus on the achievement of positive outcomes, but also to those who focus on the avoidance of negative ones.[1]

The marketplace as a source of hope

If we are to have or possess hope, there must be some source from which the possession of hope is derived. One such source is the marketplace. Indeed, the marketplace affords consumers a myriad of ways to buy and have hope, which illustrates how hope is one of the powerful drivers inside consumption. In other words – and borrowing from Charles Revson's famous quote – factories make products, which in the stores are sold as hope. The consumption of hope from the marketplace is relevant to goals in multiple life domains and is derived from the availability of products and services that are viewed as making it possible for these goal-congruent outcomes to be realized.

Consumers assess the possibility of attaining their goals by evaluating the affordances available to them in themselves and their surrounding environment. Products are means that provide such affordances. Thus, by acquiring a hair-loss remedy that promises to stop hair loss, the consumer is buying a justification for his/her assessment of goal possibility, and in turn acquiring hope. If the product is effective at delivering the promised benefit, the consumer will have achieved two goals: the short-term goal of having hope, and the long-term goal of having a full head of hair.

Interestingly, the consumption of hope may outweigh a product's or service's ability to deliver on these hopes. From "ab machines" to fitness waters with negligible traces of vitamins and antioxidants, to magnetic bracelets that cure arthritis and "get rich overnight" pyramid schemes, the marketplace is rife with products and services that the dispassionate consumer would term, at best, as of dubious effectiveness. Nevertheless, many of these products enjoy a strong – and growing – share of consumer spending; to wit, the "alternative medicine" industry has been estimated at \$18 billion a year. The individuals spending these billions are neither ignorant nor uneducated: to the contrary, most are affluent and knowledgeable (Francese 2003). The acts of buying such products becomes less puzzling when we realize that consumers are not buying weight loss or improved health, but rather hope for achieving such outcomes.

Notice that when we consider the intermediate goal of "having hope" as an end in itself, the actual efficacy of the product becomes secondary. This simple implication helps explain many instances of consumer choice in which the consumer may seem to behave in unjustified or sub-optimal ways, as in the examples above. While the outside observer may be puzzled by a consumer who purchases a very unorthodox lotion to eliminate wrinkles, and may be tempted to tout such consumer as "irrational" or "uneducated," things take on a different perspective when we include "hope as a goal" in the equation; now, this consumer's behavior might be termed completely rational, as her actions map perfectly into her goal of having hope.

We propose below that while hope can be had through consumption of goods and services offered in the marketplace, the acquisition and sustenance of hope is linked to a series of biased cognitive processes known as motivated reasoning. We explore these issues below and use Figure 3.3 as our guide.

Motivated reasoning as a means to having hope

Motivated reasoning is defined as a tendency to think about and evaluate information in a way that supports a particular directional conclusion (Kunda 1990). Motivated reasoning can be contrasted with "objective reasoning," as when consumers process information so as to arrive at an accurate conclusion (truth). Such reasoning is evidenced in situations when consumers deeply process message arguments so as to assess their true merits, as would be the case with the Elaboration Likelihood Model's (ELM) "central route processing" (Petty and Cacioppo 1986). While both motivated and objective reasoning involve "motivation" and hence entail considerable processing of a message, the former involves a motivation to arrive at a *desired* conclusion while the latter involves a motivation to arrive at an *accurate* conclusion (see Kruglanski *et al.* 1993 for a detailed distinction between accuracy motivations and motivations for a specific closure).

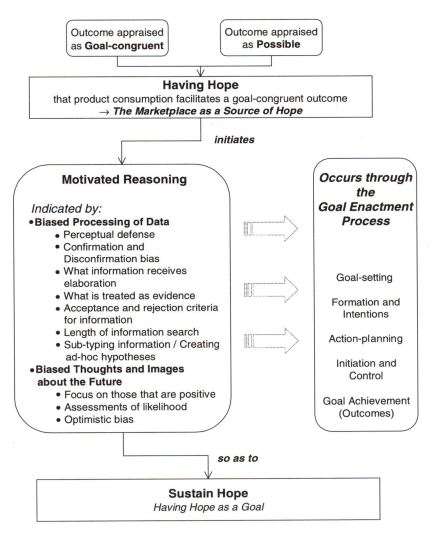

Figure 3.3 Having hope and its relation to motivated reasoning.

What affects motivated reasoning?

Extant research shows that several factors stimulate the propensity for motivated reasoning. One such factor is exposure to information that challenges a prior attitude or preference toward a position or an object, such as a product or brand (e.g., Lord *et al.* 1979; Russo *et al.* 1998; Meloy 2000). For example, Jain and Maheswaran (2000) found that when consumers were confronted with a message that either supported or did not support their perceptions of a previously preferred brand, they processed preference-inconsistent information more critically than they did preference-consistent information.

A second factor is the receipt of information that counters a desired self-concept. For example, Alloy *et al.* (1997) found that individuals were more likely to pay attention to and process positive self-relevant information and less likely to pay attention to and process less favorable information about themselves.

We argue here that a third factor affecting biased processing is hope. Sustaining hope sometimes may be possible only when consumers engage in motivated reasoning, as the directional nature of this type of biased cognitive processing may be necessary for continued assessments of the possibility of the goal-congruent outcome. Because the elicitation of hope is a function of goal-possibility assessments, we suggest that *having hope* that a goal-congruent outcome is possible affects the nature of judgment and decision-making via motivated reasoning. Motivated reasoning, we argue, is not only a response to having hope; it allows the individual to have and sustain hope, and thus fulfill a meta-goal of feeling good.[2]

The potential impact of having hope on motivated reasoning is supported by past writings describing the seductive power of hope in judgment processes. Averill *et al.* (1990) identified eight categories that reflect the ways in which people think about and experience hope. Of the eight, one stands out as irrefutably negative: *hope is deception.* In the same vein, Belk (1996) links hope with the "suspension of cynicism and disbelief." These observations fit squarely within our conceptualization of hope framed in appraisal theories of emotion: Since *having hope* is contingent on appraisals of the possibility of a goal-congruent outcome, consumers should be motivated to hold onto the idea that this outcome is possible, rather than giving in to the assessment that the outcome is impossible or that the possible outcome may be goal-incongruent. While the latter appraisal would result in emotions like hopelessness and despair, the former appraisal results in having hope. Accordingly, consumers should be motivated to process information in a selective way so as to reach this conclusion.

Hope-driven motivated reasoning

Motivated reasoning is revealed by a set of biases and illusions that pertain to (a) the manner in which we process data from the external world and (b) the types of thoughts and images that occur in our internal world (see Figure 3.3). We argue below that having hope evokes motivated reasoning, which in turn allows individuals to sustain hope. Figure 3.3 incorporates the twin ideas about having hope: (a) consumers have hope to achieve a goal-congruent outcome, and (b) sustaining hope is itself a goal as the feeling associated with hope is pleasurable and positive.

Biased processing of data

We propose that hope induces motivated reasoning of information encountered in the external world and that the impact of hope on motivated reasoning is revealed by a number of potential biases. We begin a brief review of some of these biases analyzing how *perceptual defense* may play a role in the pursuit of hope.

Perceptual defense (see Figure 3.3) is a bias in which the valence of available information affects the likelihood that such information is encoded and the speed with which it is processed. Research has shown that conscious recognition thresholds are higher for "taboo" concepts, negative emotional stimuli, etc., than for positive or neutral stimuli (Trope *et al.* 1997: 109). When consumers hope that arthritis can be relieved with magnetic therapy, they likely encode information supporting the effectiveness of a magnetic bracelet more readily and ignore or block information that suggests its ineffectiveness.

Two other biases are the *confirmation* and *disconfirmation bias*. Research reviewed by Johnson and Sherman (1990), Kunda (1990) and others indicates that individuals tend to focus on instances that confirm a favored hypothesis, labeled a *confirmation bias*. Sanbonmatsu *et al.* (1998) have extensively reviewed these types of biases that fall under the umbrella of "selective hypothesis testing." Individuals who have hope have a "favored hypothesis" – that is, that a goal-related product is effective, and thus the goal-congruent outcome is possible. In contrast, individuals tend to ignore or counterargue information that runs contrary to the conclusion they would like to reach: a bias called the *disconfirmation bias*. Having hope that cellulite can be eliminated should also affect the likelihood of a disconfirmation bias since evidence that a given product is not an effective treatment for this condition runs contrary to the conclusion consumers wish to reach, and would elicit emotions like disappointment and frustration as opposed to hope.

The confirmation and disconfirmation biases also suggest an interaction between having hope and the congruity of information on the nature of cognitive elaboration. If confronted with information that supports the possibility of the goal-congruent outcome, consumers may likely elaborate on this information and generate support arguments that confirm it. In contrast, information that runs counter to a favored conclusion (e.g., outcome is not possible or is goal-incongruent) is more likely to be scrutinized and counterargued. Thus, a consumer who has hope that he can become more productive by redesigning his office with feng-shui principles will more likely counterargue information showing that this technique is ineffective, arguing that feng-shui detractors lack an understanding of this philosophy.

In addition to its effects on attentional focus and the generation of support and counterarguments, having hope may also affect what information is treated as evidence and how strongly the evidence is regarded. Wyer and Frey (1983) found that subjects who received "failure" feedback in an intelligence test were more likely to judge such tests as less valid than those who had received "success" feedback. It makes sense to anticipate that consumers who wish to sustain hope for the possibility of a goal-congruent outcome may have more lenient acceptance criteria for information that supports its possibility and more rigorous acceptance criteria for information that points to its impossibility.

Rejecting a favored hypothesis means missing an opportunity to reach a goal-congruent outcome. For example, for a consumer who has hope about the possibility of quitting smoking, rejecting the hypothesis that "individuals who use product *A* are more likely to quit smoking than those who don't" implies facing the fact that the goal of quitting might be too difficult to achieve. Having hope may also cause consumers to evaluate product-favorable claims as stronger than consumers who do not have hope for a given outcome. In the same vein, information that runs counter to the possibility of a goal-congruent outcome may be judged as weak. Consistent with this hypothesis, Edwards and Smith (1996) found that when individuals were confronted with information that went against a favored conclusion, they tended to judge it as weaker than information compatible with a favored conclusion (18). For example, compared to consumers for whom weight loss is not goal-relevant, those who have hope that weight loss is possible may be more likely to discount an exposé of a diet system they are using, judging the presented information as weak. Those who have hope may, for example, argue that the research described in the exposé was conducted by a private party, and not by a well-respected body such as the American Medical Association.

Having hope may also interact with the valence of information to affect the length of information search (see Figure 3.3). Edwards and Smith (1996) argue that people should terminate search earlier (i.e., be content with fewer pieces of information) when the information supports a desired conclusion (e.g., when it suggests that a goal-congruent outcome is possible) than when it does not. When information supports the notion that the goal-congruent outcome can be achieved, individuals should be less motivated to search further as additional search runs the risk of identifying information that does not support it. In contrast, when information does not support the occurrence of the goal-congruent outcome or supports the occurrence of a goal-incongruent outcome, individuals might search longer, probably due to their motivated "skepticism" of goal-incongruent information, or perhaps to find information that will support it.

Finally, past research has found that consumers may *subtype information* that does not support a desired conclusion, treating it as an unusual or exceptional case, or creating *ad hoc* hypotheses that explain it away. For example, research by Kunda and Oleson (1995) in social groups and stereotyping showed that subjects tended to use irrelevant information or neutral attributes to subtype stereotype-disconfirming exemplars, and thus "protect" their stereotype. It appears, then, that individuals want to hold on to their beliefs, but feel they need a reason or justification to do so – however irrelevant it may be. We surmise that hope should also lead to subtyping of information that does not support the possibility of the goal-congruent outcome.

Biased thoughts and images about the future

Having hope for a goal-congruent outcome can also bias internally generated thoughts and images of possible uncertain futures (see Figure 3.3). Considerable research supports the notion that the content of future-oriented thoughts and images is biased in favor of outcomes that are positive, such as those that are goal-congruent. Fiske and Taylor (1991: 215) indicate that "over a wide variety of tasks, subjects' predictions of what will occur in the future correspond closely to what they would like to see happen or what is socially desirable, rather than what is objectively likely." This tendency to regard one's future as positive has been labeled an *optimistic bias*. A number of studies have shown that when thinking about the future individuals estimate the likelihood that they will experience a wide variety of pleasant (goal-congruent) events more so than will their peers. We have a tendency to believe, for example, that we are much more likely than our peers to get a good first job, get a good salary, or have a gifted child (Weinstein 1980). Conversely, when asked about the chances of experiencing a wide variety of negative (goal-incongruent) events including getting a disease (Menon *et al.* 2002), being victim of a crime (Perloff and Fetzer 1986), or being depressed (Kuiper *et al.* 1983) most people believe that they are less likely than their peers to experience such outcomes. Since hope involves a positive goal-congruent outcome, it is likely that the pursuit of having hope induces biases in the direction of positive versus negative states. Thus, use of the optimistic bias should allow consumers to sustain hope.

Hope may not only bias the content of future-oriented thoughts, but also the perceived likelihood that the possible goal-congruent outcome will actually occur. Thus, it can alter assessments of *possibility* into one of *likelihood* or *probability*, inducing the state of *being hopeful*. Research has found that imagining positive futures enhances the perceived likelihood that these experiences will actually occur. Markus and Nurius (1986) found that when asked about what the future holds, four times more positive than negative outcomes were anticipated by subjects. Matlin and Stang (1978) review evidence suggesting that people judge pleasant events (such as those we have hope for) as more likely than unpleasant ones even when the actual probabilities of the events are the same. Combined, the above research suggests that the goal congruency and possibility components of hope stimulate thoughts about a positive (goal-congruent) future and the expectations of its likelihood. Such an expectation should lead to having and sustaining hope.

One potential reason why we may be biased in our expectations of goal-congruent outcomes is a processing bias involved in mental simulation referred to as *focalism* (Wilson *et al.* 2000). Focalism is a tendency to focus future-oriented thoughts and images too much on a specific outcome and not enough on other possible outcomes that might occur. The assessment of possibility of a future outcome is thus constrained to the occurrence of the focal (goal-congruent) outcome and not others. Because consumers want to have and sustain hope that a goal-congruent outcome is possible, they will likely focus internal thoughts and images on scenarios and arguments that affirm the outcome's possibility (i.e., this product will work), not those that suggest its impossibility or the possibility of a goal-incongruent outcome (i.e., this product may fail or it may have side effects). One important implication of these biases is that the pursuit of hope may lead consumers to risky behaviors, as we will discuss later.

Having hope and the goal enactment process

Because hope is a goal-related emotion, the analysis of its dynamics must follow that of goal pursuit, particularly as it pertains to the appraisal of goal relevance and possibility. The assessment of goal possibility takes place at several stages along the goal pursuit process (see Figure 3.3). The cognitive processes involved in constructing and modifying goals are referred to as *goal determination* (Huffman *et al.* 2000). Goals that are of high personal relevance and are rooted in higher-order needs and motives usually require that consumers engage in processes of goal determination that involve several goal levels in a means-end chain type of progression. For example, a consumer who desires to be admired by his peers may wish to become more physically attractive. In order to attain this intermediate goal, he may set a goal to lose weight, which could be achieved by exercising more, which in turn could be done if he had more energy and stamina. This process that links goals from higher levels (e.g., life themes and values) to lower levels (e.g., current concerns, benefits sought, and consumption intentions) is referred to as *incorporation* (see Huffman *et al.* 2000, for a discussion).

During this process, the consumer must assess the possibility of each sub-goal along the chain, starting with the lower, most immediate sub-goal. In the example above, the consumer may need to determine whether there is a means (e.g., a product) that will provide him with the added energy and stamina that he needs in order to exercise more, which will lead to weight loss, to improved physical appearance, and finally to the admiration of his peers. After the initial overall evaluation of goal attainment, two basic anticipated emotional outcomes are possible: if attainment is seen as possible, our consumer will have hope; if not, he will experience anxiety and despair. Moreover, once evoked, having hope may affect the nature of information-processing across multiple stages of the goal-enactment process described by Bagozzi and Dholakhia (1999) as shown in Figure 3.3 and described below.

Having hope at the goal formation, intention, and choice stages

Bagozzi (1992) argues that the decision of which goals to pursue is a function of (among other things) the perceived likelihood that the pursuit of the goal will result in achievement. The biases reviewed above suggest that having hope can affect expectations or perceptions of outcome likelihood and hence impact consumer decision-making. Having hope, for example, may induce elaboration that suggests to consumers that the goal-congruent outcome is not only possible, but likely for them. The research on focalism and the optimistic bias mentioned earlier indicate that consumers are likely to imagine that things for which they have hope are more likely to happen to them than they are to happen to other people. The confirmation bias suggests that hope may make one susceptible, among other things, to the use of incomplete and unrepresentative data in forming expectations. For example, a consumer who has hope that there is a cure for cancer may be convinced that cancer eradication can be achieved through positive imagery because he has read about someone "who whipped the Big C after practicing mental imagery" (Gilovich 1991: 29). Hence, the biases just reviewed would lead us to expect that hope plays a key role in the formation of intentions as it increases consumers' perceptions that the goal-congruent outcome will occur. At this stage, consumers develop attitudes and beliefs congruent with their state of "having hope." For example, consumers may have hope that products can be found in the marketplace that will slow down or eliminate their signs of aging. The action tendencies generated from having hope carry the consumer to the next step in the goal pursuit process.

Having hope at the action-planning and initiation stages

At the action-planning stage, consumers derive a plan regarding how goals can be achieved and which behaviors should be initiated to foster goal achievement (Bagozzi and Dholakia 1999). Having hope for the achievement of the goal-congruent outcome may encourage motivated reasoning processes that suggest that actions designed to initiate the outcome are indeed likely to culminate in its occurrence. Thus, while elderly consumers who do not have hope (i.e., are hopeless) will most likely give up and resign themselves to the idea that "reversing aging" is not possible, and thus not invest any effort in searching for products related to this goal, those who have hope will likely start searching for products that are advertised as means to "looking and staying younger."

Having hope at the product evaluation stage

Because having hope fosters motivated reasoning, it will likely stimulate a number of biases and illusions when consumers initially evaluate products during their search for goal-related goods and services in the marketplace. Biased hypothesis testing and perceptual defense stimulated by hope may lead consumers to over-look disconfirming evidence and instead search for more elusive corroborating evidence that suggests that a product can indeed facilitate the outcome for which the consumer has hope. The confirmation bias may lead consumers to interpret ambiguous or irrelevant information stated in marketing communications as supportive of the product's quality. Having hope for the possibility of a goal-congruent outcome may lead consumers to adopt less rigorous acceptance criteria and stronger rejection criteria in evaluating evidence favoring a product's ability to achieve a goal-congruent outcome, making consumers more vulnerable to waffle words, incomplete comparisons, pragmatic implications, implied superiority, and puffery in advertising. By virtue of this optimism bias, consumers who have hope that a given outcome is possible may be more likely to count themselves outside the group of people for whom some products (e.g., drugs, beauty aids, and weight loss supplements) have side effects.

Having hope at the goal achievement stage

Finally, having hope may affect motivated reasoning in judgments of goal achievement. Particularly in cases where consumers do not have (or are not aware of) alternative means (i.e., products) for goal achievement, it becomes critical for them to perceive that goal achievement has occurred, or that progress towards it has been made. In other words, if the product in question is one of a very scarce list of alternatives to goal attainment, its effectiveness becomes critical, since failure entails the assessment that goal achievement may not be possible, thus terminating hope. This means that consumers have a motivation to believe that the product has indeed helped them to get closer to their goals, particularly when there are not many other products on the market that they could use if this one failed. By virtue of the confirmation bias, consumers may interpret as "supportive of product effectiveness" data gathered about the product post-consumption that they would normally catalog as unsupportive. Based on biased self-testing, consumers who have hope about a goal-congruent outcome may interpret ambiguous product experiences as evidence for its success. The confirmation and disconfirmation biases may cause consumers to selectively focus on information and other consumers that suggest that the product is good and to ignore information or consumer feedback that runs counter to it, as suggested by cognitive dissonance theory. Consumers may also use weaker acceptance criteria to judge product satisfaction. Even though product performance may be ambiguous or even slightly negative, consumers may preserve the initial affect attached toward the product. This is particularly likely to occur with credence products for which an objective measure of performance may not be available. For example, consumers cannot readily determine whether the antioxidants present in the supplements they are taking are actually slowing down the aging process, or whether a certain technique has "harmonized their metabolism." Past research supports the notion that motivated reasoning can impact evaluations of outcome performance. This phenomenon has been labeled the "illusion of success" (Taylor *et al.* 2000).

Clearly, a rational consumer would not continue purchasing a product that has proved to be ineffective. At some point, even the motivation to have and sustain hope must yield to objective reality. What we are arguing, however, is that giving up hope is an emotionally costly choice. When hope does not depend on just one product (i.e., when there are many alternative means to goal attainment), the "hope cost" of rejecting a product as ineffective is minimal, since the consumer can immediately try an alternative, and continue sustaining hope. On the other hand, when alternatives have become too scarce, consumers are likely to be more willing to give the "failing" product the benefit of the doubt and try it again, with the hope that this time it will yield the desired results.

The role of "perception of objectivity" in motivated reasoning

Though our arguments thus far suggest that consumers engage in motivated reasoning to imply that the goal-congruent outcome is possible, one might ask, why must a consumer engage in such an effortful cognitive process? Why not just believe that the goal is attainable? We believe the answer is twofold. First, we must understand the difference between faith and hope: while the former is a belief that is unquestioned and need not be founded in reason (e.g., religious faith), hope does have cognitive roots and demands a reason to believe that the future desired outcome may be possible. Second, individuals wish to perceive themselves as rational and objective. Indeed, Asch (1952) proposed that we tend to believe that we are "bias-free" – a basic principle of human experience that he labeled "naïve realism." Consumers who want to have hope must, then, find reasons to justify their entitlement to enjoying this cognitively laden emotion, and at the same time maintain their self-perception of being rational and objective. Thus, another important factor involved in motivated reasoning is the individual's need to not violate this self-perception, and to cater to the cognitive demands of hope.

Individuals have indeed been shown to exhibit a tendency that has been labeled the *illusion of objectivity* by Trope *et al.* (1997). The need for justifications (however irrelevant or neutral they may be) to form or retain an attitude has been shown in social psychology, and in the work by Kunda and Oleson (1995) cited earlier. Previous research in consumer behavior has shown that consumers do use irrelevant information in product choice decisions (e.g., Brown and Carpenter 2000). If the illusion of objectivity is a natural concomitant of motivated reasoning, and if the pursuit of hope induces motivated reasoning, consumers who have hope about a possible goal-congruent outcome might show evidence of trying to maintain this illusion. We have seen instances of this type of phenomenon in the discussion of motivated reasoning mechanisms in the previous section. The selective gathering of product information and the assessment of this information in terms of strength and diagnosticity are in fact efforts to imbue the processing effects of having hope with an aura of reason. Consider a consumer who has hope about the efficacy of a magnetic bracelet to relieve her arthritis: this consumer may treat information in an ad that describes the bracelet as "featuring magnetized copper and zinc spheres" as relevant to the product's effectiveness claims, regardless of the factual relevance of such attributes.

Consumer consequences of having hope

We will see that acquiring the hope that goals can be achieved through the marketplace is associated with both positive and negative outcomes; among the former are coping and goal achievement, while the latter include inaccurate assessments of risk and self-deception.

It has been proposed that emotions serve functional purposes (Izard and Ackerman 2000; Lazarus 1991). An evolutionary-psychological view of emotions presents affective reactions as functionally specialized for solving different adaptive problems, as if they triggered micro-programs (i.e., fight, flight, seek, avoid, etc.) that engage individuals in actions conducive to safeguarding their best interests. It has been observed, however, that the action tendencies triggered by emotions may have conflicting and maladaptive consequences (Cosmides and Tooby 2000). Having and sustaining hope can, too, have both adaptive and maladaptive possible consequences as described below.

Adaptive consequences

Coping and well-being

Considerable research shows that when individuals are faced with aversive outcomes (e.g., cancer), having hope acts as a coping mechanism, raising moods and protecting individuals from feelings of despair (Affleck *et al.* 2001; Lazarus 1999a). Having hope is often linked with coping and positive adaptation (Lazarus 1991; 1999b) perhaps because when situations appear bleak, all people have to hold onto are hopes that the goal-congruent outcome will occur. As Averill *et al.* (1990) note, hope is said to be the best medicine. It "nourishes, guides, uplifts, and supports a person in times of difficulty" (100). Perhaps the fact that "hope springs eternal" arises from its use as a coping mechanism to help survival in the bleakest of times.

Having hope has been shown to have positive psychological benefits in coping with medical illnesses, such as viewing aversive situations as having a silver lining and protecting individuals from negative moods. It has also been linked with coping with aversive physical conditions. Individuals who have hope for overcoming illness show greater pain endurance, more proactive and more positive self-care practices, delayed illness timing, and afflictions that are less severe of shorter duration (see Taylor *et al.* 2000, for reviews).

Having hope may motivate and sustain consumers in other difficult consumption contexts where coping resources are needed. Such consumer contexts would include loss of valued possessions through divorce, natural disasters, and institutionalization. Given its effects on coping, having hope and its effects on motivated reasoning may also positively influence consumer well-being.

Goal achievement

Having hope may also be adaptive because it affects goal achievement. The positive outlook inherent in hope can be easily associated with goal formation, intention, and action-planning. Indeed, feelings of hope are associated with action tendencies and drive toward goal pursuit (see Stotland 1969), to the extent that hope stimulates goal-setting, intention formation, and action-planning. Additionally, having hope should motivate action and control (i.e., commitment to the goal). Averill *et al.* (1990) suggest that having hope helps people remain loyal and committed to action even when logically they should, perhaps, be skeptical. Given the impact of having hope on stages of the goal enactment process (see Figure 3.3), it is not surprising that having hope is linked with actual goal achievement (Snyder *et al.* 1997).

Maladaptive consequences

Consumer risk

Having hope and its effects on motivated reasoning may also lead individuals to engage in risky consumption practices. In their eagerness to sustain hope, consumers may overlook or ignore the dangers involved in certain treatments or over-the-counter drugs (e.g., ephedra, St. John's wort). In the pursuit of goal-congruent outcomes, particularly as they vie to attain an ideal state, consumers may be led by an *approach* motive (Higgins 1998). Research has shown that this motive is accompanied by a *promotion* focus, which in terms of product information search and evaluation processes leads consumers to focus on the benefits rather than on the costs of such products (see Kardes and Cronley 2000, for a detailed discussion). The role of the pursuit of hope on consumer behavior complements the predictions of regulatory focus theory for promotion focus (Higgins 2002). We posit, however, that when consumption goals are framed in terms of having hope (i.e., acquiring this feeling as the result of consumption), cases normally seen as having an avoidance motivation (and a prevention focus) such as avoiding a disease, may actually elicit a promotion focus. For example, while the goal "avoiding arthritis" is clearly an avoidance goal, that of "having hope that arthritis will be avoided" is framed as an approach goal. Depending on the framing, thus, the consumer would be led by either a prevention or a promotion focus. This distinction has important implications that must be analyzed by future research.

A critical corollary of the above discussion is that it is not just that the pursuit of hope may raise the risk tolerance level for consumers (i.e., make them conscientiously more accepting of risk), but rather that it may prevent them from making an appropriate risk assessment on which to base their decisions. When this is the case, the consequences of pursuing hope through motivated reasoning are clearly maladaptive.

Self-deception

Snyder and Higgins (1988) coined the term "reality negotiation" to describe a process whereby individuals interpret outcomes in a self-serving manner in order to avoid revising their current beliefs in the face of challenging or discrepant information. It is thought to encompass "any strategy that serves to maintain positive beliefs about the self under conditions threatening to the self" (Elliott *et al.* 1991: 608), including the optimistic bias.

As part of reality negotiation, consumers may develop a false feeling of hope (i.e., having hope when they should not) about the possibility of a goal-congruent outcome (Snyder 1989). Polivy and Herman (2002: 678) studied false hopes in individuals and observed that, despite continuing failure, people persist in their self-change attempts, convincing themselves that "with a few adjustments, success will be within their grasp," in a cycle that is "liable to continue indefinitely." These individuals may set unrealistic goals to become slimmer, quit smoking, or create an improved new self. The importance of consumers learning to distinguish between feasible and impossible goals becomes clear: overconfidence and false hopes may lead to maladaptive consumer behavior so as to result in failure, distress, and unhappiness.

Conclusion

This chapter has advanced a theoretical framework that describes the concept of having hope, and proposed that arousal of this positive emotional state encourages motivated reasoning so as to sustain hope. We posit that having hope is a powerful affective state that individuals strive to attain and nourish. In order to do so, they search for and purchase products that are seen as means to achieve the individual's desired end-state. Throughout the process of goal pursuit – including product search, choice, and post-use evaluation – having hope is linked to motivated reasoning, and it informs consumers' cognitive processes: In assessing whether the product in question indeed affords having hope about the achievement of the desired end-state, consumers engage in motivated reasoning, whereby their search and evaluation of product information is biased toward a favorable appraisal of the target product.

An in-depth exploration of hope-related biased information-processing is called for, in view of its potential wide-reaching effects on consumer well-being: effects that range from positive adaptive coping during times of adversity, to minor nuisances (disappointment, small sums of misspent money) from realized self-delusion, to tragic outcomes (improper medication, injury, and death) from failure to encode and process potentially negative outcomes. The next step, thus, entails the development of models that allow us to maximize the benefits, and minimize the downsides, of our perennial pursuit of hope.

Acknowledgments

The authors wish to thank the invaluable input provided by the editors in the process of writing this chapter. Special thanks are due to Rashmi Adaval, Rohini Ahluwalia, Lauren Block, Shailendra Jain, and Frank Kardes for their many insightful comments and suggestions.

Notes

1   Importantly, while hope may *evoke* a positive mood the construct of hope is distinct from mood. First, the literature on mood links cognitive processes with more flexibility (e.g., consideration of alternatives), innovativeness/creativity, thoroughness (under certain circumstances, e.g., if the task is enjoyable), and efficiency (because of flexibility

and innovativeness mentioned above). The effects of hope are narrower, and, as we suggest below, are guided by *a motivation for specific closure* (i.e., "this goal-congruent outcome is possible"). The motivation for specific closure explains the outcomes we discuss here much better than "positive mood" would. Moreover, a person who is pursuing hope (but hasn't yet achieved it) is not necessarily in a positive mood yet.

2   Although future research on this topic is warranted, we surmise that the three facets of hope in Figure 3.1 are all related to motivated reasoning, though in different ways. While having hope may stimulate motivated reasoning, the *degree* to which consumers engage in motivated reasoning may be a function of the degree to which they hope for that outcome (i.e., yearn for it; see MacInnis and de Mello 2005). Hopefulness may be an *outcome* of motivated reasoning induced by hope as motivated reasoning may not only keep hope alive but may also alter the perceived likelihood that the goal-congruent outcome will occur.

3   The term "desirable" means "goal-congruent", and should not be confused with the degree of desirability or the amount of yearning one has for the goal-congruent outcome

References

Affleck, G., Tennen, H., and Apter, A. (2001) "Optimism, pessimism, and daily life with chronic illness," in E. C. Chang (ed.) *Optimism and Pessimism: Implications for Theory, Research, and Practice*, Washington, DC: American Psychological Association: 147–168.

Alloy, L. B., Abramson, L. Y., Murray, L. A., Whitehouse, W. G., and Hogan, M. E. (1997) "Self-referent information-processing in individuals at high and low cognitive risk for depression," *Cognition and Emotion Special Issue: The Cognitive Psychology of Depression* 11: 539–568.

Asch, S. E. (1952) *Social Psychology*, Oxford: Prentice-Hall.

Averill, J. R., Catlin, G., and Chon, K. K. (1990) *Rules of Hope*, New York: Springer-Verlag.

Bagozzi, R. P. (1992) "The self-regulation of attitudes, intentions, and behaviour," *Social Psychology Quarterly* 55: 178–204.

Bagozzi, R. P., Baumgartner, H., Pieters, R., and Zeelenberg, M. (2000) "The role of emotions in goal-directed behavior," in S. Ratneshwar, D. G. Mick, and C. Huffman (eds) *The Why of Consumption: Contemporary Perspectives on Consumer Motives, Goals, and Desires*, New York: Routledge: 36–58.

Bagozzi, R. P. and Dholakia, U. (1999) "Goal setting and goal striving in consumer behavior," *Journal of Marketing* 63: 19–32.

Belk, R. W. (1996) "On aura, illusion, escape, and hope in apocalyptic consumption," in S. Brown, J. Bell, and D. Carson (eds) *Marketing Apocalypse: Eschatology, Escapology and the Illusion of the End*, London: Routledge: 87–107.

Brown, C. L. and Carpenter, G. S. (2000) "Why is the trivial important? A reasons-based account for the effects of trivial attributes on choice," *Journal of Consumer Research* 26: 372–385.

Cohen, J. (1958) *Humanistic Psychology*, London: Allen and Unwin.

Cosmides, L. and Tooby, J. (2000) "Evolutionary psychology and the emotions," in M. Lewis and J. M. Haviland-Jones (eds) *Handbook of Emotions*, New York: Guilford Press: 91–115.

Edwards, K. and Smith, E. E. (1996) "A disconfirmation bias in the evaluation of arguments," *Journal of Personality and Social Psychology* 71: 5–24.

Elliott, T. R., Witty, T. E., Herrick, S., and Hoffman, J. T. (1991) "Negotiating reality after physical loss – hope, depression, and disability," *Journal of Personality and Social Psychology* 61: 608–613.

Ellsworth, P. C. and Smith, C. A. (1988) "Shades of joy: Patterns of appraisal differentiating pleasant emotions," *Cognition and Emotion* 2: 301–331.

Fiske, S. T. and Taylor, S. E. (1991) *Social Cognition* (2nd edn), New York: Mcgraw-Hill Book Company.

Francese, P. (2003) "Consumers today," *American Demographics* 25: 28–29.

Frijda, N. H., Kuipers, P., and Schure, E. T. (1989) "Relations among emotion, appraisal, and emotional action readiness," *Journal of Personality and Social Psychology* 57: 212–228.

Gelwick, R. (1979) "Post-critical belief," in R. Fitzgerald (ed.) *The Sources of Hope*, Rushcutters Bay, Australia: Pergamon Press (Australia): 124–143.

Gilovich, T. (1991) *How We Know What Isn't So: The Fallibility of Human Reason in Everyday Life*, New York: The Free Press.

Gollwitzer, P. M. and Moskowitz, G. B. (1996) "Goal effects on action and cognition," in E. T. Higgins and A. W. Kruglanski (eds) *Social Psychology: Handbook of Basic Principles*, New York: Guilford Press: 361–399.

Groopman, J. (2004) *The Anatomy of Hope: How People Prevail in the Face of Illness*, New York: Random House.

Haase, J. E., Britt, T., Coward, D., Leidy, N., and Penn, P. (1992) "Simultaneous concept analysis of spiritual perspective, hope, acceptance, and self-transcendence," *Journal of Nursing Scholarship* 24: 141–147.

Higgins, E. T. (1987) "Self-discrepancy: A theory relating self and affect," *Psychological Review* 94: 319–340.

Higgins, E. T. (1998) "Promotion and prevention: Regulatory focus as a motivational principle," in M. P. Zanna (ed.) *Advances in Experimental Social Psychology*, Vol. 30, New York: Academic Press: 1–46.

Higgins, E. T. (2002) "How self-regulation creates distinct values: The case of promotion and prevention decision-making," *Journal of Consumer Psychology* 12: 177–191.

Huffman, C., Ratneshwar, S., and Mick, D. G. (2000) "Consumer goal structures and goal-determination processes," in S. Ratneshwar, D. G. Mick, and C. Huffman (eds) *The Why of Consumption: Contemporary Perspectives on Consumer Motives, Goals, and Desires*, New York: Routledge: 9–35.

Isen, A. M. (1987) "Positive affect, cognitive processes and social behavior," in L. Berkowitz (ed.) *Advances in Experimental Social Psychology*, Vol. 20, New York: Academic Press: 203–253.

Isen, A. M. (2001) "An influence of positive affect on decision-making in complex situations: Theoretical issues with practical implications," *Journal of Consumer Psychology* 11: 75–85.

Izard, C. E. and Ackerman, B. P. (2000) "Motivational, organizational, and regulatory functions of discrete emotions," in M. Lewis and J. M. Haviland-Jones (eds) *Handbook of Emotions*, New York: Guilford Press: 253–264.

Jain, S. P. and Maheswaran, D. (2000) "Motivated reasoning: A depth-of processing perspective," *Journal of Consumer Research* 26: 358–371.

Johnson, A. R. and Stewart, D. W. (2004) "A re-appraisal of the role of emotion in consumer behavior: Traditional and contemporary approaches," *Review of Marketing Research* 1.

Johnson, M. K. and Sherman, S. J. (1990) "Constructing and reconstructing the past and the future in the present," in E. T. Higgins and R. M. Sorrentino (eds) *Handbook of Motivation and Cognition*, Vol. 2, New York: Guilford Press: 482–526.

Kardes, F. R. and Cronley, M. L. (2000) "The role of approach/avoidance asymmetries in motivated belief formation and change," in S. Ratneshwar, D. G. Mick, and C. Huffman (ed) *The Why of Consumption: Contemporary Perspectives on Consumer Motives, Goals, and Desires*, New York: Routledge: 81–97.

Kruglanski, A. W., Webster, D. M., and Klem, A. (1993) "Motivated resistance and openness to persuasion in the presence or absence of prior information," *Journal of Personality and Social Psychology* 65: 861–876.

Kuiper, N. A., MacDonald, M. R., and Derry, P. A. (1983) "Parameters of a depressive self-schema," in J. Suls and A. G. Greenwald (eds) *Psychological Perspectives on the Self,* Vol. 2, Hillsdale, NJ: Erlbaum: 191–217.

Kunda, Z. (1990) "The case for motivated reasoning," *Psychological Bulletin* 108: 480–498.

Kunda, Z. and Oleson, K. C. (1995) "Maintaining stereotypes in the face of disconfirmation – constructing grounds for subtyping deviants," *Journal of Personality and Social Psychology* 68: 565–579.

Lazarus, R. S. (1991) *Emotion and Adaptation,* New York: Oxford University Press.

Lazarus, R. S. (1999a) "Hope: An emotion and a vital coping resource against despair," *Social Research* 66: 653–660.

Lazarus, R. S. (1999b) *Stress and Emotion: A New Synthesis,* New York: Springer.

Lord, C. G., Ross, L., and Lepper, M. R. (1979) "Biased assimilation and attitude polarization: The effects of prior theories on subsequently considered evidence," *Journal of Personality and Social Psychology* 37: 2098–2109.

MacInnis, D. J. and de Mello, G. E. (2005) "The concept of hope and its relevance to product evaluation and choice," *Journal of Marketing* 69(1): 1–14.

MacInnis, D. J., de Mello, G. E., and Patrick, V. M. (2004) "Consumer hopefulness: construct, relevance to internet marketing, antecedents and consequences," *International Journal of Internet Marketing and Advertising* 1: 174–195.

Markus, H. and Nurius, P. (1986) "Possible selves," *American Psychologist* 41: 954–969.

Matlin, M. and Stang, D. (1978) *The Pollyanna Principle,* Cambridge, MA: Schenkman.

Meloy, M. G. (2000) "Mood-driven distortion of product information," *Journal of Consumer Research* 27: 345–359.

Menon, G., Block, L. G., and Ramanathan, S. (2002) "We're at as much risk as we're led to believe: Effects of message cues on judgments of health risk," *Journal of Consumer Research* 28: 533–549.

Myers, D. G. (2000) "Hope and happiness," in J. E. Gillham (ed.) *The Science of Optimism and Hope: Research Essays in Honor of Martin E. P. Seligman,* Philadelphia, PA: Templeton Foundation Press: 323–336.

Oatley, K. and Johnson-Laird, P. N. (1987) "Towards a cognitive theory of emotions," *Cognition and Emotion* 1: 29–50.

Perloff, L. S. and Fetzer, B. K. (1986) "Self-other judgments and perceived vulnerability to victimization," *Journal of Personality and Social Psychology* 50: 502–510.

Petty, R. E. and Cacioppo, J. T. (1986) *Communication and Persuasion: Central and Peripheral Routes to Attitude Change,* New York: Springer.

Pieper, J. (1994) *Hope and History: Five Salzburg Lectures,* San Francisco: Ignatius.

Polivy, J. and Herman, C. P. (2002) "If at first you don't succeed: False hopes of self-change," *Amercian Psychologist* 57(9): 677–689.

Roseman, I. J. (1991) "Appraisal determinants of discrete emotions," *Cognition and Emotion* 5: 161–200.

Russo, J. E., Meloy, M. G., and Medvec, V. H. (1998) "Predecision distortion of product information," *Journal of Marketing Research* 35: 438–452.

Rycroft, C. (1979) "Steps to an ecology of hope," in R. Fitzgerald (ed.) *The Sources of Hope,* Rushcutters Bay, Australia: Pergamon Press (Australia): 3–23.

Sanbonmatsu, D. M., Posavac, S. S., Kardes, F. R., and Mantel, S. P. (1998) "Selective hypothesis testing," *Psychonomic Bulletin and Review* 5: 197–220.

Seligman, M. E. P. (1975) *Helplessness: On Depression, Development, and Death*, San Francisco, CA: Freeman.

Shaver, P., Schwartz, J., Kirson, D., and O'Connor, C. (1987) "Emotion knowledge: Further exploration of a prototype approach," *Journal of Personality and Social Psychology* 52: 1061–1086.

Shimanoff, S. B. (1984) "Commonly named emotions in everyday conversations," *Perceptual and Motor Skills* 58: 514.

Snyder, C. R. (1989) "Reality negotiation – from excuses to hope and beyond," *Journal of Social and Clinical Psychology* 8: 130–157.

Snyder, C. R., Cheavens, J., and Sympson, S. C. (1997) "Hope: An individual motive for social commerce," *Group Dynamics: Theory, Research and Practice* 1: 107–118.

Snyder, C. R. and Higgins, R. L. (1988) "From making to being the excuse – an analysis of deception and verbal nonverbal issues," *Journal of Nonverbal Behavior* 12: 237–252.

Staats, S. (1987) "Hope: Expected positive affect in an adult sample," *Journal of Genetic Psychology* 148: 357–364.

Stotland, E. (1969) *The Psychology of Hope*, San Francisco, CA: Josey Bass.

Taylor, S. E., Kemeny, M., Reed, G. M., Bower, J. E., and Gruenwald, T. L. (2000) "Psychological resources, positive illusions and health," *American Psychologist* 55: 99–109.

Trope, Y., Gervey, B., and Liberman, N. (1997) "Wishful thinking from a pragmatic hypothesis-testing perspective," in M. S. Myslobodsky (ed.) *The Mythomanias: The Nature of Deception and Self-deception*, Mahwah, NJ: Lawrence Erlbaum Associates: 105–131.

Weinstein, N. D. (1980) "Unrealistic optimism about future life events," *Journal of Personality and Social Psychology* 39: 806–820.

Wilson, T. D., Wheatley, T., Meyers, J. M., Gilbert, D. T., and Axsom, D. (2000) "Focalism: A source of durability bias in affective forecasting," *Journal of Personality and Social Psychology* 78: 821–836.

Wyer, R. S. and Frey, D. (1983) "The effects of feedback about self and others on the recall and judgments of feedback-relevant information," *Journal of Experimental Social Psychology* 19: 540–559.

4 Death, where is thy sting?

Mortality and consumer motivation in the writings of Zygmunt Bauman

Darach Turley

Mortality and consumer motivation seem to sit uncomfortably alongside each other. At one level this is understandable; death seen either as annihilation or transformation marks the termination of all human needs and desires. However, if death is taken to mean awareness of mortality, a different picture emerges. In the work of Polish sociologist Zygmunt Bauman, awareness of personal death, besides being the hallmark of being human, is also the "mother of all motives," the wellspring of all cultural activity. The sweep of his argument cannot be overstated. Knowledge of individual mortality, the passage from "is" to "is not," engenders such vertiginous terror that we turn to culture to furnish a worldview, a "survival policy," that will both suppress this haunting realization and proffer some strategy for immortality to counter it. Herein lies death's deadliest sting.

Bauman is not the only twentieth-century social thinker to foreground the centrality of awareness of personal death in human affairs (Heidegger 1962; Berger 1967). Indeed, in many respects the pivotal role he accords the awareness of death parallels that of Ernest Becker (1973). For both, this awareness is a universal phenomenon; cultures not only serve to repress it but also proffer a means of transcending death and achieving immortality. In this light, history can best be read as a series of immortality ideologies. Becker is credited with being one of the psychoanalytic progenitors of Terror Management Theory (TMT; Pyszczynski *et al.* 1997), a theory that is beginning to feature in consumer behavior research (Arndt *et al.* 2004). This theory, as its name suggests, claims that the terror attendant upon awareness of death can be managed through cultural worldviews and values that assure immortality to those who subscribe to them. In addition, this terror can be further assuaged through the sense of self-esteem that flows from being a compliant and valued member of such worldviews.

TMT proponents have drawn on Becker's fundamental tenet to develop a body of experimental research where subjects' mortality salience is typically manipulated to assess its impact on a range of dependent variables, variables that increasingly involve consumer behavior constructs. Thus, priming mortality salience has been found to heighten materialism and the "urge to splurge," both of which are core values of contemporary worldviews (Kasser and Sheldon 2000: Arndt *et al.* 2004); to bolster perceptions of domestic products that embody "home values" (Maheswaran and Agrawal 2004); to increase interest in purchasing high-status luxury brands that confirm the consumer's sense of being valued (Mandel and Heine 1999); and to depress consumption of high-calorie fattening foods that impact negatively on both body and self-image (Shiv *et al.* 2004).

This chapter's overview of Bauman's thinking on the fear of death should hopefully serve both as complement and counterpoint to the contribution of TMT researchers. At one level, his views on the relationship between awareness of mortality and contemporary marketplace behavior are arguably more sweeping and holistic. He sees contemporary society above all else as a consumer society – the defining activity of individuals in present-day society *is* consuming (1995). Consumption is not some extra-mural activity to which people resort when weary of weightier matters. As a result, it is precisely in and through consumption that any culturally mediated bid for immortality must be sought. The marketplace is where immortality stakes are decided, where they are ultimately won or lost.

This chapter is an attempt, with the aid of marketplace examples, to show how the writings of Bauman reveal mortality as a wellspring of much contemporary consumer behavior. The first half begins by introducing two central features of death in Bauman's thinking: its impermeability to reason – the fact that we simply cannot think through or make sense of death, and its personal private character – "my death" as opposed to say, death in general or death of some third party. Following this, a section on "Death and Culture" illustrates how he sees all cultural activity energized by the need to suppress this conception of death. The second half of the chapter presents Bauman's portrayal and critique of the two most prominent survival strategies being played out in contemporary Western societies, with particular reference to the integral role of consumer behavior and marketing in each of those strategies.

Over its relatively short and colorful lifespan, consumer research has portrayed the consumer in a variety of guises: need-satisfier, decision-maker, problem-solver, meaning-seeker, identity-creator, addict, bricoleur, and rebel. At a time when an anti-foundationalist ethos prevails, it may be worth calling to mind that, however much they may vary, however fragmented they become in profile or consumption, and however impressive the ministrations of medics, 100 percent of consumers continue to die. Put another way, all consumers are on death row. They may not be aware of it; they may hope to cheat death by behaving as though they are simply doing life. Others may be seeking or may have been granted temporary reprieves and stays of execution. Yet others may be dreaming up subterfuges, escape plans, tunnels. One thing is certain though – nobody gets his or her sentence commuted to life. Seen in this light, all consumers are incarcerated and all their experiences are pretty near-death experiences.

In general, consumer behavior as a discipline has deftly side-stepped this dimension of the human predicament, possibly out of deference to consumers' sensibilities. At the risk of forcing the custodial metaphor, those few authors who have ventured into this dark domain have typically drawn attention to one of four aspects of the condemned consumer's predicament. The first concerns those who have had brushes with death on foot of encounters with or remissions from serious illness (Pavia and Mason 2004). Findings indicate that consumption plays a critical and reflexive role in negotiating both the trauma of initial diagnosis and the ensuing sense of uncertainty regarding future undertakings. The second group of authors has considered the prisoner's plight as execution looms imminently. Foci here include voluntary and involuntary disposition of possessions and the distillation of personal inventory as role decrements increase and life runs out (Young and Wallendorf 1989; Pavia 1993; Stevenson and Kates 1999; Price *et al.* 2000; Kates 2001). Typically this subset of consumers has, on foot of senescence or sickness, consciously acknowledged the impending final curtain. The third aspect concerns less the occupant on death row than those who have to live with and perhaps even witness the approaching departure. A small cadre of consumer researchers have begun to explore the functioning of friends, family, and spouses in the lead up to and passage through this peri-mortal penumbra (Gentry *et al.* 1995; Gabel *et al.* 1996; Bonsu and Belk 2003). The fourth aspect also concerns those left behind, but focuses on how they comport themselves once the immediate post-mortem period has passed. Their liminal status has to be relegated so that incorporation can be realistically attempted. Research here has charted the post-mortem journey of bereaved consumers as they embark on a sense-making, memory-maintenance enterprise in the hope that if they cannot get over their loss, they may at least get used to it (Gentry *et al.* 1994; Gentry and Goodwin 1995).

With this overview, all angles would appear to have been covered; all that is, except for the point at which it began – the inmate nestling in his penitential necrospace on death row. Here, death may feature minimally. The mindless routine of the prison regime may help muffle any inner misgivings. If death does loom large, it does so primarily for the occupant in the condemned cell itself at the dead end of the prison corridor. This particular scenario – death as non-imminent, generalized mortality – may represent a fifth dimension in the consumer behavior canon and provides the central focus of both this chapter and the nascent corpus of terror management research mentioned earlier. Its emergence is a promising one. Too earnest a focus on posthumous happenings may well hamper insight into any possible invigorating role death may dance in the pre-humous life of seemingly untroubled consumers. By equating death with dying, this focus may have inadvertently occluded how the designation "death" in "death row" affects those who linger there.

Twentieth-century thanatologists have positioned contemporary attitudes towards death along a denial-acceptance axis (Ariès 1974; Giddens 1991; Walter 1994; Berridge 2001). But denial, defiance, acceptance, dismissal, rejection, and resignation are all collectively reactions *to* human mortality and, as such, presuppose some awareness of this mortality in the first place. Returning to the earlier designation of the consumer as the condemned occupant of death row, the issue here is the manner and extent to which awareness of being personally and ineluctably condemned to this fate informs individual behaviour. The operative term here is "personal" mortality and should serve to distinguish it from the generalized and more palatable realization that this fate awaits all fellow inmates.

Death as unreasonable

Much of Bauman's understanding of the current social order parallels that of Giddens (1990, 1991), an order marked by pervasive reflexivity, radical doubt, and the privatization of meaning. The privatization of meaning burdens humans with the onus of constructing individual meanings of death. Communal framings of mortality have been debunked, unreflexive custom is insufficient and, at the end of the day, it is reason, the hallmark of emancipation from the pre-modern, that is charged with the lonesome and fragile task of making sense of death. This is the core of Bauman's thesis. His cryptic and provocative prose in *Mortality, Immortality, and Other Life Strategies* (1992a) evokes this predicament of human reason writhing and wrestling like a trapped animal, hemmed in on all sides, desperately essaying to break out of the smothering, suffocating effect of the thought of death. Thought cannot think its own not being there; in this sense, death is unthinkable. Thought is defeated in the very act of trying to think its death; in this sense it is offensive.

Coined in these sober terms, death is "the scandal of modernity" (1995: 168), a realization that may explain why it has been both privatized and socially sequestered. The thought of death as rational impasse, as "contradiction in terms" (1992a: 13) marks its most distinctive aspect. Death is now "out of control." Furthermore, with the demise of communal prescriptions and tradition, one of reason's more noble roles was to be that of "guide to good choice" (1992b: 1) in the onerous problem of forging self-identity. Yet again it falls short; it fails to deliver and does so because, besides not being a "problem," death emphatically is not a matter of choice.

Death as my death

For Bauman, death today is utterly private. "Private" in the sense of being individualized, "private" too in the related sense of lacking any communally shared framework or ritual. This results in a "trained incapacity" (1992a: 135) to know both how to behave towards and how to speak of death. And even if the necessary courage could be mustered, language could not accommodate us. Death is literally unspeakable. Human language is a "language of survival . . . an instrumental language that deals with causes and events with a vocabulary geared to [death's] collective and public denial" (1992b: 8). His theoretical argument concerning the incapacity of language to cope with death translates into the everyday aversion of ordinary folk to speaking to and about the dying, the palpable relief on extricating oneself from a house of the dying or the recently dead, gauche gestures and mutterings towards the bereaved, consumers lost for words when penning sympathy cards.

Throughout his writings, Bauman is at pains to emphasize that the death to which he alludes is the individual's own death, not death in general or death of any other individuals. He draws on Freud's (2001 [1915]) observation:

It is indeed impossible to imagine our own death; and whenever we attempt to do so we can perceive that we are in fact still present as spectators. Hence the psycho-analytic school could venture on the assertion that at bottom no one believes in his own death (289).

When asked to ponder death, most people assume the role of onlooker at their own deathbed or attendee at their own funeral. This is precisely why death is imponderable, why we are so mistaken. Death is the end of being able to spectate at anything. Imagined presence at our own funeral is not death but more a variation of premature burial syndrome, the staple of numerous Hammer horror movies. Faced with this impasse, death is typically imagined as death of others.

Truth to tell, the death of others encountered most often is not the harrowing death of a beloved other but the media-mediated death of distant strangers. The thousands of murders, assaults, hangings, stabbings, and executions we view usually occur somewhere else, to young males we do not know, and involve some form of violence (Fulton and Owen 1994). Courtesy of the camera's zoom lens, we can now see death close up, at a distance, as never before, safely cushioned at either end by ads and weather forecasts. "Death 'as seen on TV' is a drama played in *virtual reality*" (Bauman 1998: 65). "So banalised, death is made too familiar to be noted and much too familiar to arouse high emotions . . . its horror is exorcised through its omnipresence" (1997: 159).

Death and culture

Bauman contends that, while death has always has been traumatic, today, on foot of reason's humiliation, it takes on a uniquely parlous character. It is not so much death's macabre overlay of contamination, decay, and putrefaction that haunts us but its insidious inducement of ontological terror and the ensuing need to repress this terror, a need that energizes *all* cultural activity. This is the primary function of all cultures.

> Culture is after that permanence and durability which life, by itself, so sorely misses. . . . [Death] makes permanence into a task, into an urgent task, into a paramount task – a fount and a measure of all tasks – and so it makes culture, that huge and never stopping factory of permanence.
>
> (Bauman 1992a: 4)

So, humans surrender themselves to culturally sanctioned projects that are inherently open-ended and transcending: the creation of offspring, lineages, and pedigrees; building up commercial empires; amassing artifacts; acquiring money, possessions, and collections; and generating a colossus of learning, knowing all the while that this work will never be complete. Yet, much of the allure of these undertakings is their very open-endedness. Culture makes it our mission to cultivate permanence, to prevent these achievements from slipping down into the grave with us. It also promises to act as guarantor of this permanence and durability. The precise nature of the possessions and collectibles designated worthy of permanence is of lesser importance than that they embody the cultural consensus that confers mortality-defeating permanence in the first place. In the consumer behavior field some authors have already begun to explore this theme; both Belk (1988, 1995) and Hirschman (1990) have studied consumers striving to secure such secular immortality by amassing collections and endowing philanthropic ventures respectively.

To really appreciate what death can accomplish, all one need do is look at the myriad cultural forms throughout history, both occidental and oriental, to see how they have succeeded in enabling humans to live as though there were no death. Culture is the cover-up *par excellence*. Death's highest achievements are the very strategies to which it gives rise to stifle its own intimations. Its power is most evident where it seems to have been expunged, forgotten, or conquered. Death in Bauman's writings is suffused with dissimulation and concealment; it has to be.

> Culture is an elaborate counter-mnemotechnic device to forget what they [humans] are aware of. Culture would be useless if not for the devouring need of forgetting ... Thus, the constant risk of death – the risk always *knowable* even if flushed down into the murky depths of the subconscious – is, arguably, the very foundation of culture.
>
> (Bauman 1992a: 31)

Death dissembles and nowhere does this dissemblance succeed more deftly than where death and dying are relegated to consideration of the "last things." The self-sequestration of death is more radical and pervasive than the truncation of funeral cortèges, the consignment of the elderly to "geriatric ghettos" (1997: 159), and the relegation of the departed to vital statistics might indicate.

To illustrate how knowledge of mortality functions as the wellspring of cultural structuration, Bauman (1992a, 1992b, 1997, 1998) furnishes an exposé of the more notable, if inevitably doomed, expedients or strategies that have featured in recorded history. The Judeo-Christian afterlife, Buddist reincarnation, and survival in some de-individualized collectivity are among the more notable. Their precise number and localizations are less crucial than their common purpose – to stifle knowledge of death by proposing an immortality policy, if not for all, then for a select few. What culture deems durable – religious devotion, commitment to society, heroic deeds, wealth, social pedigree – lasts. Durability is the currency of immortality and, critically, its antithesis, "transience," cannot last.

There seems to be a specific form of cultural hegemony operative in the allocation of immortality to objects. Those most likely to own durables are likely to be the arbiters of what counts as durable and, in turn, what counts as durable is more than likely to be owned by them. Fortunately, the immortality aspirant can, courtesy of the "market game" (1992a: 56) purchase it second-hand. The highest value of possessions is their immortality value. Western culture has historically endorsed the tastes and discretions of the aristocracy as more durable than those of lower orders and has done so by privileging consumption of the ephemeral over mundane sensual enjoyment. This latter inferior consumption typically results in the consumed object being destroyed. Bauman thus adds a certain immortal veneer to social distinction as proposed by Bourdieu (1979). Whatever its historical modulations, the notion of "durable" in Bauman always retains one essential property. Possessions and objects assume this property by dint of their ability to confer immortality and in turn consumer desire for the durable is always at one with the desire to defeat mortality.

The modern survival strategy: mortality deconstructed

While Bauman portrays all social forms as manifestations of one or more survival strategies to cope with our knowledge of death, he reserves his most detailed, incisive and often corrosive commentary for the strategies evident in contemporary society. He is not overly exercised in demarcating time boundaries between the modern and postmodern and considers that strategies peculiar to each moment are apparent in current mindsets and marketplace behavior. He characterizes the modern survival strategy as one where mortality has been deconstructed. As was seen earlier, reason, the standard-bearer of modernity, is powerless, speechless and frozen, when confronted with the thought of its own not being there. However, if death could be diluted, deconstructed into a series of deaths, or more properly, types of death with their respective diseases, then reason could get to work. Problems, causes, and solutions are the stock in trade of reason and if death can, in this sense, be problematized, then the final solution may well be within our grasp. The consoling thing about individual deaths is that they have a cause: cancer, heart attack, kidney failure, AIDS, brain hemorrhage. So, while there is absolutely nothing that can be done about death itself, there is much we can do about:

> Death sliced and fragmented into innumerable small and smaller-still threats to survival . . . And fighting them back is an activity so time- and energy-consuming, that no time or energy is left for musing on the ultimate vanity of it all.
>
> (Bauman 1998: 65)

This fragmentation of death impacts at a number of levels. In an immediate sense it is evidenced in the growing professionalization and sanitization of the funeral process itself (Metcalf and Huntington 1991; Mitford 1998; Berridge 2001). The professionalization of medical care is both one of its symptoms and its contributory causes. Moller (1996) has observed the growth of specialisms in contemporary hospitals and institutions, each one charged with combating a specific death-threatening disease, the suffix "ologist" after each specialism denoting death dissected.

Death deconstructed is a death bereft of any unitary symbol. Grim reapers, scythes, nooses, skull and cross-bones have all had their day. Stripped of its coterie of contributory ailments, death itself is now no more than a skeleton, but not a shared symbolic one. Sequestration has taken care of that. This parallel symbolic fragmentation has percolated through to the array of distinctive floral and other emblems adopted by charitable bodies in campaigns to raise funds and public awareness of their particular disease or disability. A "Death Day" sounds like a non-starter.

Death decomposed and deconstructed fuels an array of preventive consumer behaviours. The thought of death means paralysis, the thought of an individual cause of death is a catalyst for action. For Bauman, death spells *angst*, disease spells *anxiety*, and it is anxiety that drives the cascade of contemporary health-enhancing, death-defying consumption. Anxiety is death's terror deconstructed into manageable intimations encountered on the

> innumerable traps and ambushes of daily life. One tends to hear it knocking now and again, daily, in fatty fast foods, in listeria-infected eggs, in cholesterol-rich temptations, in sex without condoms, in cigarette smoke, in asthma-inducing carpet mites, in "the dirt you see and the germs you do not," in lead-loaded petrol and the lead-free.
>
> (Bauman 1998: 65)

Much of consumption is thus a crusade against one or more lethal eventualities and our weekly amble through the shopping aisles could, if we were minded to listen, sound more like a stroll down mortality lane. You can buy your way out of deconstructed death.

If the marketplace is thus replete with a host of specific remedies and preventive possibilities and I fail to take steps, to purchase what is on offer, then I have nobody to blame save myself. Failure to listen to the inner rumblings of this marketplace redounds on the happy-go-lucky carefree consumer. What I will die of is an illness about which I could have done something or at least something more. In this sense, death in modernity is a matter of personal responsibility, ineluctably mine and therefore a thoroughly private affair. Bauman is at pains to stress that this modern strategy is not a variation on the *carpe diem* policy associated with Epicureanism where death is defiantly ignored so that life and all its pleasures can be savored to the full. Far from being a distant end point, death today is woven into the fabric of domestic and retail landscapes, its overtures vaguely audible, beckoning us to join battle armed with an arsenal of diets, workouts, supplements, spas, treatments, therapies, techniques, lotions, and potions; "consumer goods have *memento mori* written all over them, even if with an invisible ink" (1998: 28). Death is no more than an amalgam of curable diseases where something can be done about each. Bauman's contention that "Certainty of death incapacitates, uncertainty of outcome boosts energy and spurs into action" (1992a: 130) might well serve both as motto for modern consumption and as window on the breadth of death's motivational sway.

Deconstruction brings death within the ambit of causation, event, and solution. The modern craving for causes had been tellingly presaged by Freud (2001 [1915]):

> when [death] does happen ... Our habit is to lay stress on the fortuitous

causation of the death – accident, disease, infection . . . in this way we betray an effort to reduce death from a necessity to a chance event (290).

In a world where death is exhausted completely by the battery of diseases that bring it about, the expression "died from natural causes" sounds oxymoronic – in media reports, downright suspicious – and the term "died from old age" singularly unsatisfactory. Nobody is old enough to die of old age. Causes have become celebrities. Most deaths on television are caused (Fulton and Owen 1994) and, because they are caused, are potentially avoidable. Admittedly the cause of death is increasingly being sought within the victim. Crime fiction has had a fresh lease of life with a generation of female forensic pathologists, the "new femmes fatales" (Berridge 2001: 259), dissecting viscera, foraging for microscopic clues in the inner recesses of human cadavers. The real coup occurs when the cause is located; rounding up the culprit is routine, more and more part of the epilogue. A different, though related, phenomenon is apparent in news coverage of aircraft disasters. The drive to find the cause translates into a feverish scurry to locate and retrieve the black box that harbors it, a search that can overshadow coverage of the casualties of the disaster that was caused. So, if "who-done-its?" are permitted to embrace "what-done-its?," if either the butler or the bacterium can be guilty, then a sizeable portion of the media diet of modern consumers serves to reflect and reinforce the death deconstruction agenda.

The postmodern survival strategy: immortality deconstructed

Bauman is averse to delimiting survival strategies to time boundaries, but it is clear that he sees widespread evidence of a characteristically postmodern survival policy in contemporary Western societies. His understanding of the aptly named postmodern moment seems to focus mainly on its depiction in the writings of Baudrillard, Foucault, and Lyotard. With the linear developmental meta-narrative of modernity brought into disrepute, and with reason in retreat, there is no longer any need to justify the present by reference to some more perfect future. Stripped of its subservient role, the present can be liberated from "connexivity" with both past and future. Personal and social histories can shrug off any inhibiting *telos*, the better to savor the present moment into which the future has collapsed. Any distant immortality vested in that future can, as a result, be deconstructed into a myriad of heavenly moments, a merry-go-round of blissful "nows." Where modernity proposed a policy of deconstructing mortality, postmodernism has forged its counterpart, the deconstruction of immortality. Immortality no longer carries hues of permanence or cumulative identity-building. It has been dissolved into a miasmic procession of microscopic morsels. In such a world:

> Every present counts as much, or as little, as any other, and each one is – potentially – the gate opening into eternity. Thus the distinction between the

mundane and the eternal, transient and durable, mortal and immortal, is all but effaced. If in the pre-modern era *death* was "tamed" – now . . . it is *immortality* that has been "tamed."

(Bauman 1992a: 168)

Since Socratic times reason had been charged with the onerous task of distinguishing between opinion and true knowledge, between the epidermal realm of appearances and inner reality, between flux and what endures. In the postmodern moment there is parity of esteem for both reality and representation. There is "no division between things that mean and things that are meant" (183) and in such a semiotic hall of mirrors the most apt metaphor for living is a thespian one. Life is to be lived as a theatrical *mis en scène*. No two shows need be identical, however, each evanescent performance has a final curtain in which death is re-presented and, in the process, divested of its power to haunt and terrorize. Each theatrical rehearsal can serve as an inoculation against death in such a way that "if taken in daily, in partly detoxicated and thus non-deadly doses, the awesome poison seems to lose its venom" (188). Disappearance does not entail dissolution, however. What was formerly discarded or disdained can re-emerge, recoverable, as highly desired.

Immortality and desire for innovation

De-differentiation flows inevitably from the radical reversibility in postmodernity and the de-differentiation *par excellence*, the one that carries the postmodern day, is in Bauman's eyes that between mortality and immortality, between transience and durability. The contemporary marketplace is a kaleidoscopic fusion of durability and transience. Here consumers can have their cake and then have another later. What marketing terms "innovation" is, in his view, no more than a variation, albeit a pivotal one, on a broader theme being played out on the wider social landscape. Individuals' occupational, residential, and relational lives are increasingly marked by fluidity and transience (2003). So, too, with the world of goods: durations may vary, but disappearance is inevitable and necessary. The marketplace is the *locus classicus* where this ephemerality is played out to perfection. The endless parade of product and service innovations, the plethora of new, improved, "never-to-be-repeated" re-runs, upgrades, and product re-launches form the canvas on which this life strategy is writ largest. Ever-shortening life cycles for products and their subsequent reappearance as "new" models, the hegemony of the disposable, collectively serve as a vicarious reassurance that death is more a suspension than a cessation.

Bauman lends a delightful twist to postmodern consumers' lust for innovations. It is not because they desire the new, the improved, in itself, not because the new and improved offering resonates with the modern developmental meta-narrative (Hirschman 1980), not because the current version is faulty or deficient, but because we "do not wish it to be immortal" (Bauman 1992a: 188). They have to know that each consumption episode has an ending, but an ending followed by a fresh beginning. Durables are not permitted to endure. Indeed, marketing's own meta-narrative of the need to replace and renew may be less a matter of idolizing innovations, and more a matter of denigrating what is currently possessed. Postmodern consumers cannot afford to let products live out their natural lives. If they gave the matter sufficient thought, they would see chronic hiring rather than purchasing as the better offer. "Whoever chains themselves to an unseaworthy vessel risks going down with it at the next tide. By comparison, surfing seems a safer option" (2001a: 22). Strictly speaking, obsolescence is not inbuilt in products; it is a human requirement, a core element of this latter-day survival strategy. Old products never die, they are never allowed to do so. In mock biblical style, he excoriates those unable to partake in this spectacular cycle. "Woe to those who, because of a dearth of assets, are doomed to go on using goods that no longer hold a promise of new and untried sensations" (2003: 50).

Given his sociological orientation, Bauman's analysis of the postmodern motivational process may lack some of the terminological precision consumer researchers might wish for. Knowledge of death is the "mother of all threats, the threat that daily begets all threats and never lets them toddle out of reach" (1995: 106). Postmodern culture, as with all cultures, is charged with furnishing an all-in package that will both stifle this threat and provide a strategy for action comprising goals and desires for the purposes of securing immortality. In a postmodern context the pre-eminent goal, and duty, is the creation of personal identity, an immortal identity, and doing so autonomously, unfettered by normative underpinnings (Bauman 1998). Immortal identity is available in and through immortal moments of consumption or more precisely through the "thrilling, ravishing, enrapturing, ecstatic sensations" (1995: 116) they afford properly disposed consumers. In such a scenario the notion of a finite list of consumer needs is utterly redundant.

> The *spiritus movens* of consumer activity is not a set of articulated, let alone fixed, needs but *desire* – a much more volatile and ephemeral evasive and capricious, and essentially non-referential phenomenon; a self-begotten and self-perpetuating motive that calls for no justification or apology either in terms of an objective or a cause . . . it has itself for its paramount object, and for that reason is bound to stay insatiable.
>
> (Bauman 2001a: 13)

With this quotation Bauman's understanding of desire seems to resemble closely those of Campbell (1987) and Belk *et al.* (2000; Belk 2003), that the desired object is of lesser moment than that desire itself keep desiring: that the construction of identity "is a never ending and forever incomplete process, and must remain such to deliver on its promise" (2001b: 64).

The term "desire" clearly marks an advance on "need" in the consumer motivational register for Bauman, signaling as it does the liberation of choice from any regulatory framework. However, at times he seems to prefer the term "wish" rather than "desire" to denote the motivational state peculiar to the postmodern consumer (1992a, 2001a). He feels that desire harbors overtones of comparison, mimesis, and envy and thus fails to do justice to the fey, wisp-like whimsicality of the wish, its sense of abandon, volatility, and obliviousness of consequences.

He likens the self-perpetuating character of the self-creation project to that of a participant in the London Marathon. However, this is a marathon with a difference. Runners must keep running, opting out is not an option, and "the finishing line always moves faster than the fastest runner" (2000: 73). The race is its own justification. The inability to quit the race translates into the compulsion to consume. "The archetype of that particular race in which every member of a consumer society is running . . . is the activity of shopping" (ibid.). By "shopping" Bauman means not just its retail variety, but the broader urge to acquire skills, competencies, image, sex-appeal, and identity. This point is central to his thinking. Shopping *is* the race. Postmodern society is above all else a society of shoppers, and if it is to propose any credible survival policy, any plausible strategy for immortality, it must do so by locating transcendence within fragmented and fleeting shopped-for moments. Wish lists are ultimately shopping lists.

Desire for peak experiences and fitness

In former times, if moments of immortal otherworldly ecstasy were granted to a select mystical few as a reward for asceticism and disdain for earthly attachment, they have now been firmly grafted onto the postmodern marketplace. Goods have come full circle – from being an impediment to ecstasy to being the site where it may be savored exhaustively. Bauman labels consumer experiences delivering particular intensity, "peak experiences." Unlike their religious predecessors, present-day peak experiences are both a product of and a testament to human prowess and potential. He highlights a certain paradox here. All experiential moments are ostensibly equal, but some peak experiences are more equal than others. The difference is predicated more on intensity and quantity rather than quality. However, quantity does not mean accumulation: "this life favors lightness and speed. It is the turnover, not the volume of purchases that measures success in the life of *homo consumens*" (2003: 49).

The transcending immortal character of the peak experience derives from its consumption-carrying capacity, its ability to deliver an ever-increasing amount and intensity of sensation in an episodic cycle of enjoyment. Peak experiences are now inevitably consumer experiences; the converse does not hold, though it could. Bauman is less than forthcoming on what precise sensations he has in mind here; however, they would appear to include "transcendent heightened experiences" such as those described by Celsi *et al.* (1993) in their study of US skydivers.

Peak experiences create a bind of sorts for marketing and advertising professionals. On the one hand they are obligated to pledge more ample and varied peak experiences – they can even go the full nine yards and promote their products as *the* ultimate – on the other hand, such pledges must never be taken literally.

The promise of new, overwhelming, mind-boggling or spine-chilling, but always exhilarating experience, is the selling point of food, drinks, cars, cosmetics, spectacles or holiday packages. Each dangles the prospect of "living through" sensations never experienced before, and more intense than any tested before.

(Bauman 1998: 71)

In this context it is interesting to note that a European car manufacturer is currently promoting new models under the generic slogan: "The Ultimate Driving Experience." Bauman would probably like to believe that those at whom it is directed will read it with a liberal pinch of postmodern salt.

While access to transcendence and immortality through consumption is available to all – in theory there are no non-peakers – some adept consumers, by dint of training, marketplace nous, and practice, have turned consumption into an art. These cultivated individuals have honed their prowess in absorbing what the marketplace has to offer and have become what might colloquially be termed "A-list" peakers. Having purged themselves of any inner inhibitions or hang-ups, they stand poised to exact the maximum dividend their expanded consumption-carrying capacity can deliver. "Fitness," as opposed to health, is what these consumers are required to cultivate. Indeed, staying "fit" plays a central role in the postmodern motivational repertoire. It consists in maintaining the requisite poise, vigilance, heightened receptivity, and consumer literacy to savor the full payload of marketplace experiences, coupled with "a flexible, absorptive and adjustable body, ready to live through sensations not yet tried and impossible to specify in advance"(2000: 76).

However, the notion of fitness harbors an inherent ambiguity, one that can impact on consumer behavior in its own right. Bauman cites the example of the eager consumer willingly poised to savor the breadth of culinary pleasures on offer in the myriad cookbooks that bedeck contemporary bookstores. Yet this very willingness, if followed through too enthusiastically, may adversely affect the very bodily fitness on which it depends and, in turn, feed a retailing reaction where the same bookstore has to sport an equally broad assortment of dieting manuals. This paradox occasionally erupts into what he terms "body panics" (1995: 121), a siege mentality where consumers become overly exercised with ingredients, additives, workout regimes, carcinogens, diet plans, modified foodstuffs, brands, any one of which may impair fitness terminally.

Desire for freedom and expertise

In a marketplace overflowing with an excruciating assortment of immortality-laden produce, the postmodern consumer is condemned to choose. And while personal identity is no longer a project but a collage of disconnected fluid selves, each still has to be chosen, and chosen in the knowledge that it will be reflexively revisited at some future point (Giddens 1991). While unconstrained freedom is our sentence, its practice in the absence of any solid yardstick is absurd. Seen in this light, freedom and choice are truly tyrannical (Schwartz 2000); tyrannical, too, because immortal identity is at stake. If choice is unbounded it is also crucially important. In such an anomic vacuum there may not be "wrong" choices but there are "inept," "inappropriate," and "inadequate" versions; "inadequacy has replaced deviation as the most feared penalty for individual failure" (Bauman 1995: 113). So the flip side of this heady freedom is the lust for certainty, for the assurance that our experiences carry that immortality-bearing sparkle. Bauman sees the postmodern urge to expunge uncertainty as a key driver of contemporary consumer behavior.

Fortunately, the market is not found wanting in this regard; in fact, it offers the best "Two for the price of one" deal imaginable – total freedom and complete certainty at the same time. Certainty comes courtesy of an expertise system comprised of people "who know better" and "the authority of numbers" (2001b: 63). Expertise has a broad denotation and can be supplied in a number of guises: percentage of cat owners, proportion of dentists, celebrity endorsements, Oscar-winning make-up artists, personal trainers to the stars, star ratings for hotels, "must-see" movies, mentions in restaurant guides, write-ups in consumer reports. Consumers do not appear to be overly disconcerted by the fact that certainty is both plural and provisional, once it is available.

Bauman alludes to de Certeau's (1984) notion of "habitat" to illustrate the subtle interplay between expert servicescape and the manner in which individuals negotiate their passage through it. Expert systems are "self-propelling and self-reinforcing" and usually arrive uninvited into the lives of "consumers of expertise" (Bauman 1990: 200). That said, our dependence on them is addictive. He paints a delightful vignette of how this postmodern expert system orchestrates dependency by describing a typical newspaper weekend color supplement. The index sports sections on clothing, gardening, horoscopes, food, wine, travel, health, interior décor, dining in, dining out, agony aunts and uncles and relationships – how to get into them and how to get out of them (2003: 35), a maze of enticing expertise through which uncertain consumers wander.

One particular subspecies of expert are advertisers, "immortality brokers" (1992a: 172) who assure us that we have succeeded or at least tell us how to succeed. We need to *know* that choices are not inept, that our sensations carry the hallmark of immortality. Advertisers can truly be considered "masters of the moment." Their remit is to generate trust in consumers that they can manufacture and manipulate notoriety and muster a critical mass of non-critical applauders to sustain it in the forefront of public attention. The emergence and disappearance of fads and fashions in the contemporary marketplace is staged "transient durability" (185). The product that is "in," the song at the top of the charts, the "must-have" item of apparel, by virtue of being famous and fashionable, carry the luster of transcendence, and can be the stuff of peak experience. This quality stems in no way from the products in question; it is cultivated by and predicated on the fact that it is talked about and seen. Despite this, transience can be true, it can afford certainty especially when backed up by audience ratings, panel data and media cuttings. "Fame producers" (86) can even invest the apparent fall from fame with spectacular new life: tabloid coverage of pop virtuosos jostled outside courthouses, sporting greats denying doping charges, extra-marital misdemeanors, "back on the bottle" headlines, all in bold type.

In spite of this rather grim account of what marketing and advertising experts allegedly do, Bauman protests that they are not the prime movers in this process, although his exculpations are often less than wholesome. He does not subscribe to the view that these professions have within their power the ability to act as originators of consumer desire. Repeatedly, he characterizes consumers as "immortality bidders" (86). Advertising experts, as immortality brokers, are no more than unwitting accomplices in putting on offer an "all-in" survival policy where immortality is made available in momentary packages. The world of advertising with its stream of referential, repetitious, and disconnected messages resonates with and fosters the postmodern immortal moment in a particularly privileged fashion.

Epilogue

Awareness of mortality is the hallmark of humanity. It is a knowledge that automatically fuels the drive to escape and transcend itself, to secure immortality. The exigency for immortality, in turn, is what being human is about. According to Bauman, this exigency is death's sting, *vigor mortis*, and energizes all cultural activity. What any culture proposes to consumers by way of desired possessions, lifestyles, needs, goals, and values are collectively termed survival strategies or policies. The overriding exigency for immortality was seen to fuel a variety of goals and desires in the postmodern strategy: to create and re-create personal identity; to do so by dint of unregulated choice; to maintain and cultivate marketplace acuity; to ensure "body fitness;" to weather "body panics;" to aim for and extract an optimal sensory dividend from consumer choice; and to eschew inept and inadequate experiences and its corollary, the lust for certainty. Given the nature of the postmodern moment, it comes as no surprise that most of these have less to do with the precise objects of consumer desire than with the manner in which they should be chosen. Consumers are of course at liberty to invoke one or more policies and can be expected to stay with them as long as their immortality credentials remain believable, as long as their forgetfulness-inducing allure remains intact.

It might be queried whether, in Bauman's eyes, hope features in this portrayal of the contemporary consumer. The interplay between desire and hope has been promisingly explored by Belk *et al.* (2000, 2003) who adopted a definition similar to that outlined by de Mello and MacInnis (this volume) where hope is "a positive emotion evoked in response to a goal congruent outcome appraised as possible." On these terms, a modicum of hope does seem to imbue consumer choice in both strategies outlined here: in the mortality deconstruction strategy that a specific ailment or cause can be countered, and in the immortality deconstruction variety that consumer choice will yield an exhilarating if less than perfect quality of experience. However, if the super-ordinate human goal is that culture should suppress awareness of death, it seems reasonable that a concomitant objective is that its members be spared the trauma of appraising how their culture is faring in this regard. The prospect of a negative appraisal may be too dreadful to contemplate. In Bauman's eyes the situation of adherents of both strategies may, in this sense, be beyond hope.

Bauman's equation of culture and survival strategy results in an inevitable dissemblance. Culture is a "macro-conspiracy" (Dollimore 1999: 124). The theoretical sweep of his argument is such that death typically does not "appear under its own name" (1992a: 7). Death's sting is painful, powerful, and persuasive but always deceptively so. His characterizations of contemporary cultural strategies and their relative success often carry a barbed subversive rider that exposes their inherent fragility and futility and a lingering suspicion that perhaps they, more so than any predecessor, are incapable of supporting and legitimating a sustainable sense of immortality – a point that may elude some of his critics. For example, Warde (1994a, 1994b) advocates a more nuanced appreciation of the polyvalence of shopping, suggesting that in Bauman's work the melodrama of the shopping moment – that it is an anxiety-ridden exercise in free choice – is overplayed at the expense of what, for many consumers, is its predictable vapidity and tedium. One wonders, however, whether Bauman's point has less to do with championing a particular vision of shopping than pursuing the logic of an immortality strategy predicated on and purveyed exclusively through under-socialized consumer choice to its ultimate conclusion, a form of *reductio ad absurdum*.

While all strategies are, in theory, equal and equally flawed, the strategies discussed in this chapter seem to "fit" (Bauman 1992b: 21) the contemporary habitat more effectively. Observers and proponents of the postmodern survival policy will find in his writings a challenging, if sometimes withering, commentary on its workings and weaknesses. At heart, his reservations about this policy are twofold: that its protestations of parity and access for all to the shopping parousia are hollow, spurious, and unfulfilled, and that its equation of human freedom with consumer choice is overly reductive (1992c: 225).

What Bauman has to say should serve to underscore that the former deference shown by researchers towards death and its impact on consumer behavior on the basis that it was "none of their business" was misplaced. Death *is* their business. In much of contemporary Western culture consumption serves as both a means by which bids for immortality are worked out and a lens through which they can be studied. In this sense his contribution to marketing is perhaps best characterized as basic rather than applied; indeed manipulating consumers' death anxiety to maximize market share sounds like an ethical non-starter. That said, Bauman's depiction of the role of advertising affords a novel perspective for future research. The world of advertisements is one where the pain of anxiety attendant upon daunting and unlimited consumer choice can be mollified and assuaged. In this sense, advertising functions more as pandemic sedative than hideous persuader.

On a final note, his work may serve to prompt greater clarity on what is meant by "death" and its effect on consumer behavior. Clarion-like, he repeatedly emphasizes the distinctive impact of awareness of personal mortality as opposed to any other incarnations such as death of a loved one or generalized cataclysm. His insights into the contemporary marketplace may furnish a prism through which the consumer researcher who walks "the road less traveled" (Holbrook 1995: 149) can study the pervasive, if ultimately illusory, promise of culture to put paid to consumers' knowledge of death, once for all.

Acknowledgments

The author would like to gratefully acknowledge the support and helpful comments of Russell Belk, Jim Gentry, and Margaret Hogg in writing this chapter.

References

Ariès, P. (1974) *Western Attitudes towards Death: From the Middle Ages to the Present*, Baltimore, MD: Johns Hopkins University Press.
Arndt, J., Solomon, S., Kasser, T., and Sheldon, K. M. (2004) "The urge to splurge: A terror management account of materialism and consumer behavior," *Journal of Consumer Psychology* 14(3): 198–212.
Bauman, Z. (1990) *Thinking Sociologically*, Oxford: Basil Blackwell.
Bauman, Z. (1992a) *Mortality, Immortality, and Other Life Strategies*, Cambridge: Polity Press.
Bauman, Z. (1992b) "Survival as a social construct," *Theory, Culture and Society* 9: 1–36.
Bauman, Z. (1992c) *Intimations of Postmodernity*, London: Routledge.
Bauman, Z. (1995) *Life in Fragments: Essays in Postmodern Morality*, Oxford: Blackwell.
Bauman, Z. (1997) *Postmodernity and its Discontents*, Cambridge: Polity Press.
Bauman, Z. (1998) "Postmodern religion?" in P. Heelas (ed.) with D. Martin and P. Morris, *Religion, Modernity, and Postmodernity*, Oxford: Blackwell: 55–78.
Bauman, Z. (2000) *Liquid Modernity*, Cambridge: Polity Press.
Bauman, Z. (2001a) "Consuming life," *Journal of Consumer Culture* 1(1): 9–29.
Bauman, Z. (2001b) *Community: Seeking Safety in an Insecure World*, Cambridge: Polity Press.
Bauman, Z. (2003) *Liquid Love*, Cambridge: Polity Press.
Becker, E. (1973) *The Denial of Death*, New York: The Free Press.
Belk, R. (1988) "Possessions and the extended self," *Journal of Consumer Research* 15 (September): 139–168.
Belk, R. (1995) *Collecting in a Consumer Society*, London: Routledge.
Belk, R. (2003) "The fire of desire: A multisited inquiry into consumer passion," *Journal of Consumer Research* 30 (December): 326–351.
Belk, R., Ger, G., and Askegaard, S. (2000) "The missing streetcar named desire," in S. Ratneshwar, D. G. Mick, and C. Huffman (eds) *The Why of Consumption: Contemporary Perspectives on Consumer Motives, Goals, and Desires*, London: Routledge: 98–119.
Berger, P. L. (1967) *The Sacred Canopy: Elements of a Sociological Theory of Religion*, New York: Doubleday.
Berridge, K. (2001) *Vigor Mortis*, London: Profile Books.
Bonsu, S. K. and Belk, R. W. (2003) "Do not go cheaply into that good night: Death-ritual consumption in Asante, Ghana," *Journal of Consumer Research* 30 (June): 41–55.
Bourdieu, P. (1979) *Distinction: A Social Critique of the Judgment of Taste* (trans. Richard Nice), London: Routledge.
Campbell, C. (1987) *The Romantic Ethic and the Spirit of Modern Consumerism*, London: Blackwell.
Celsi, R. L., Rose, R. L., and Leigh, T. W. (1993) "An exploration of high-risk leisure consumption through skydiving," *Journal of Consumer Research* 20 (June): 1–23.

Certeau, M. de (1984) *The Practice of Everyday Life* (trans. S. Rem), Berkeley: University of California Press.

Dollimore, J. (1999) *Death, Desire, and Loss in Western Culture*, London: Penguin Books.

Freud, S. (2001 [1915]) *Thoughts for the Times on War and Death*, in The Standard Edition of the Complete Psychological Works of Sigmund Freud (Vol. XIV), (trans. J. Strachey), London: Vintage: 273–302.

Fulton, R. and Owen, G. (1994) "Death in contemporary American society," in R. Fulton and R. Bendiksen (eds) *Death and Identity* (3rd edn), Philadelphia, PA: Charles Press: 12–27.

Gabel, T. G., Mansfield, P., and Westbrook, K. (1996) "The disposal of consumers: An exploratory analysis of death-related consumption," in K. P. Corfman and J. G. Lynch (eds) *Advances in Consumer Research*, Vol. 23, Provo, UT: Association for Consumer Research: 361–367.

Gentry, J. W. and Goodwin, C. (1995) "Social support for decision-making during grief due to death," *American Behavioral Scientist* 38(4): 553–563.

Gentry, J. W., Kennedy, P. F., Paul, C., and Hill, R. P. (1994) "The vulnerability of those grieving the death of a loved one: Implications for public policy," *Journal of Public Policy and Marketing* 13(2): 128–142.

Gentry, J. W., Kennedy, P. F., Paul, C., and Hill, R. P. (1995) "Family transitions during grief: Discontinuities in household consumption patterns," *Journal of Business Research* 34: 67–79.

Giddens, A. (1990) *The Consequences of Modernity*, Cambridge: Polity Press.

Giddens, A. (1991) *Modernity and Self-Identity: Self and Society in the Late Modern Age*, Cambridge: Polity Press.

Heidegger, M. (1962 [1927]) *Being and Time* (trans. J. Macquarrie and E. S. Robinson), New York: Harper and Row.

Hirschman, E. (1980) "Consumer modernity, cognitive complexity, creativity and innovativeness," in R. P. Bagozzi (ed.) *Marketing in the 80's: Changes and Challenges*, Chicago, IL: American Marketing Association: 152–161.

Hirschman, E. (1990) "Secular immortality and the American ideology of affluence," *Journal of Consumer Research* 17 (June): 31–42.

Holbrook, M. (1995) *Consumer Research: Introspective Essays on the Study of Consumption*, Thousand Oaks, CA: Sage Publications.

Kasser, T. and Sheldon, K. M. (2000) "Of wealth and death: Materialism, mortality salience, and consumption behavior," *Psychological Science* 11(4): 348–351.

Kates, S. M. (2001) "Disposition of possessions among families of people living with AIDS," *Psychology and Marketing* 18(4): 365–387.

Maheswaran, D., and Agrawal, N. (2004) "Motivational and cultural variations in mortality salience effects: Contemplations on terror management theory and consumer behavior," *Journal of Consumer Psychology* 14(3): 213–218.

Mandel, N., and Heine, S. J. (1999) "Terror management and marketing: He who dies with the most toys wins," in E. J. Arnould and L. M. Scott (eds) *Advances in Consumer Research*, Vol. 26, Provo, UT: Association for Consumer Research: 527–532.

Metcalf, P. and Huntington, R. (1991) *Celebrations of Death: The Anthropology of Mortuary Ritual* (2nd edn), Cambridge: Cambridge University Press.

Mitford, J. (1998) *The American Way of Death Revisited*, London: Virago Press.

Moller, D. W. (1996) *Confronting Death: Values, Institutions and Human Mortality*, New York: Oxford University Press.

Pavia, T. (1993) "Disposition and perceptions of self in late stage HIV infection," in L. McAlister and M. L. Rotschild (eds) *Advances in Consumer Research*, Vol. 20, Provo, UT: Association for Consumer Research: 425–428.

Pavia, T. M. and Mason, M. J. (2004) "The reflexive relationship between consumer behavior and adaptive coping," *Journal of Consumer Research* 31(2): 441–454.

Price, L. L., Arnould, E. J., and Folkman, C. (2000) "Older consumers' disposition of special possessions," *Journal of Consumer Research* 27 (September): 179–201.

Pyszczynski, T., Greenberg, J., and Solomon, S. (1997) "Why do we need what we need? A terror management perspective on the roots of human social motivation," *Psychological Inquiry* 8(1): 1–20.

Schwartz, B. (2000) "Self-determination: The tyranny of freedom," *American Psychologist* 55(1): 79–88.

Shiv, B., Ferraro, R., and Bettman, J. R. (2004) "Let us eat and drink; for tomorrow we shall die: Mortality salience and hedonic choice," in B. E. Kahn and M. F. Luce (eds) *Advances in Consumer Research*, Vol. 31, Valdosta, GA: Association for Consumer Research: 118–119.

Stevenson, G. J. and Kates, S. M. (1999) "The last gift: The meaning of gift-giving in the context of dying of AIDS," in E. J. Arnould and L. M. Scott (eds) *Advances in Consumer Research*, Vol. 26, Valdosta, GA: Association for Consumer Research: 113–118.

Walter, T. (1994) *The Revival of Death*, New York: Routledge.

Warde, A. (1994a) "Consumption, identity-formation, and uncertainty," *Sociology* 28(4): 877–898.

Warde, A. (1994b) "Consumers, identity and belonging," in R. Keat, N. Whitely and N. Abercrombie (eds) *The Authority of the Consumer*, London: Routledge: 58–74.

Young, M. M. and Wallendorf, M. (1989) "Ashes to ashes, dust to dust: Conceptualizing consumer disposition of possessions," in T. L. Childers *et al.* (eds) *American Marketing Association Winter Educators' Conference*, Chicago: American Marketing Association: 33–39.

5 Making consumption decisions by following personal rules

On Amir, Orly Lobel, and Dan Ariely

In a vocal uproar, consumers protested against Amazon.com's strategy to price discriminate by charging their loyal customers higher prices, thereby extracting greater profits (Rosencrance 2000). Prior to this, the giant online retailer realized, as many others, that some consumers (e.g., its loyal customer base) were willing to pay a higher premium than other consumers. Following a simple economic logic, Amazon.com charged these consumers higher prices. Alas, when consumers found out about this strategy they became enraged: "no company *should* charge different consumers different prices" was a common cry. Two interesting and important facts stand out in this story. The first is that Amazon.com's strategy is on many counts equivalent to other price discrimination approaches commonly used, including the very popular targeted coupon campaigns employed by most retailers on and off line. The second, and central to this work, is the use of the term "should" in the consumer outcry above.

Another example relating to perceived violation of fairness is the Coca-Cola Company's attempt to price discriminate based on the momentary value of the drink to the individual. It was obvious to the company that consumers derive greater pleasure from drinking a cold can of Coke on a warm day than on a cold one. Simple economic logic dictates that consumers would therefore be willing to pay more for Coke on a warm day than they would on a cold day. To take advantage of this insight, Coke conducted a test in which temperature gauges were installed in vending machines to enable the machines to react to local weather conditions and change the price accordingly. Needless to say, the mere rumors about this made consumers furious. It wasn't that they didn't enjoy a cold Coke more on a warm day, but they simply felt they should not be charged more money for the same can of Coke; the company should not take advantage of them (King and Narayandas 2000).

The central argument in the current chapter is that our consumption reality is full of "shoulds" and "should nots," some of which are derived from higher principles, e.g. fairness, as in the example above, some others from social and cultural norms, and some from personally relevant experiences. In this chapter we present a mechanism consumers employ when making decisions – following rules. Following rules is a decision approach that is different from the attempt to optimally solve a decision problem or use close-enough shortcuts (i.e., heuristics) that are common in the traditional decision analytical framework. Instead, the rules we propose as a decision-making mechanism are much more similar to legal rules used in the justice system. In what follows, we describe what we mean by the term *rules*, why we chose this term, its various sources, and important characteristics that differentiate rules from other decision-making mechanisms. We also discuss implications and future direction of inquiry.

Why "rules"?

Imagine Tom, a middle-aged writer, who has to decide whether to go see the new *Lord of the Rings* movie at the premiere, or wait a couple of weeks, read the reviews, and then decide whether or not to go. There are several paths Tom may take in order to make his choice. He may toss a coin, and go to the movie if it lands on heads; he may sit and write down the balance of reasons for and against going; he may decide to shortcut this process by only thinking of the first reason that comes to mind; or he may realize that he is generally against postponing positive experiences, and simply go. By taking the last route, Tom is essentially excluding the balance of reasons, and acting upon a pre-existing rule. It is exactly this process of an exclusionary nature that we define here as following rules (Raz 1975).

We are not the first to import the notion of rules into decision-making. Following a substantial treatment in philosophy, Prelec (1991; see also Ainslie 1992; Baron 1994; March 1994) suggested a decision-making style that is independent from tastes or preferences, but is akin to the use of legal rules in matters of self-control and identity maintenance. In the context of Tom's decision above, such a rule may come into play if he asks himself whether he is the type of person who would rush to a premiere without hearing what the critics have to say, or whether he is the type of person who values movie premieres.

The rules discussed here are derived from higher-order principles that are acquired via moral or social context; but such principles, unlike rules, typically do not provide in and of themselves direct action prescriptions for what actions to take and what to avoid.[1] The "decisions by rules" perspective presented here is related to two other theories of individual decision-making: reason-based choice and heuristics. In this section, we discuss the relationship of the rules mechanism to these two theories.

According to the reason-based choice view (Shafir *et al.* 1993; Simonson 1989), people rely on reasons to justify choices, especially in the face of conflict, and sometimes even search for them when the reasons are not obvious – "people search for a compelling rationale for choosing one alternative over another." While reasons and rules can be considered close relatives, there are some important differences. Perhaps the most prominent is the following hierarchical asymmetry: rules can provide reasons and function as reasons, but reasons seldom become rules (but see Raz 1975 for an in-depth discussion on a hierarchy of reasons, some of which may be used as rules as defined in the current context). A more central difference lies in the hypothesized process: we propose that rules are used on the fly and usually at a low level of thoughtfulness, while most analyses of reason-based choice envision an elaborate process of weighing and comparing reasons for and against each available choice alternative (sometimes even after the choice has been made).

When we compare "heuristics" and "decisions by rules," it is clear that although these two mechanisms share some commonalities, there are some important differences. The first difference concerns the goal of using heuristics versus rules. Decision-makers use heuristic procedures to limit the amount of information processed or the complexity of the ways in which information inputs are combined (Frederick 2002). As such, heuristics are useful for simplifying computations under uncertainty, when cognitive resources are scarce, or when full computation is infeasible. Heuristics such as elimination by aspect (Tversky 1972) and representativeness (Kahneman and Tversky 1982) are examples of such mechanisms. In contrast, the rules we discuss here are different because they do not describe a computational or evaluative approach. These rules provide "do and don't do" action plans that are not meant to simplify decisions but rather to enforce certain conventions.

The second difference between heuristics and rules relates to preferences. Many heuristics are said to "work" at the service of preferences – aimed at maximizing the latter under a certain set of constraints (cost of thinking, time, effort, etc.). There are multiple examples of such heuristic-based trade-offs, perhaps the most notable one being the accuracy-effort trade-off framework (Payne *et al.* 1993). Rules, however, are not related to a sacrifice of utility for the purpose of local effort-benefits considerations. For example, consider a choice between an option that is a "better deal" (e.g., two products cost the same, but one had a higher original price) and one that provides higher personal utility (e.g., the product that is liked more). Under such conditions, Hsee (1999) has demonstrated that people are more likely to chose the "better deal" option, thereby implying that they follow the "value-seeking" rule rather than their own preferences (for a detailed treatment of this rule, see Hsee 1999; Hsee *et al.* 2003).

By their nature, rules are used for guiding decision-making even when the complexity of the task is trivial, and when there are no repercussions for *not* doing so (i.e., rules are often followed even in situations in which one does not stand to lose or suffer if the rule is not obeyed). Moreover, unlike people's preferences, these rules are assumed to be general, overarching guidelines for behavior and as such are applied broadly in a law-like manner – "do or do not do."[2] To define more precisely what a rule means, Raz (1975: 497) proposes a test of whether a behavioral guideline is a rule by identifying its overarching nature and seldom questioned validity:

> [By following a rule] What I am not doing is assessing the merits of the case taking all the relevant facts into consideration. I am not doing this for I have decided on a rule, that is, I have accepted an exclusionary reason to guide my behavior in such cases. I may occasionally, of course, examine the justification of the rule itself. If I re-examine the rule on every occasion to which it

applies, however, then it is not a rule which I have adopted. I may on the other hand examine the rule occasionally even when not confronted with a case to which it applies. This is the test by which to determine whether a person follows a rule.

The legal system and rules

One can obtain a different perspective on the "decision by rules" approach by tracing its evolutionary development. From this perspective, it is perhaps not a coincidence that the "decisions by rules" decision-making style has evolved, for it relies on principles similar to those that have guided the social evolution of legal systems. In other words, while the decision analytical perspective has developed outside of the natural ways in which social institutions have evolved, decisions by rules more closely resemble the natural development of human thought regarding decisions over the ages. Even a superficial analysis of the development of the legal system suggests that the current approach has improved and developed over the centuries. Primitive legal systems, such as the early Roman and English systems, evolved through ritual stages, in which blood feuds between clans were superseded as dispute resolution mechanisms by the judgments of monarch kings and patrician priests, who formalized rituals, invoking memorized rules to reduce violent episodes (Maine 1861; Gray 1997). Although rituals included processes that today seem unfair and arbitrary, by the move to a ritualized customary decision institution, the conception of law as a body of rules was born. Initially, trials by ordeal efficiently determined guilt or innocence by simple tests such as whether the accused would float when thrown into the local river. Later, the transition to the common law stage was characterized by the replacement of arbitrary local decision-making and divine intervention with written law, applied universally by a professional judiciary.

A further development, and perhaps the greatest evolution for this institution, was the use of analogical reasoning and precedents, allowing broader application of legal principles to particular contexts (Gray 1997). This development brings us to the present-day system where the institution of a judicial equity system allows the override of mechanical or strict adherence to certain results. If we take the current characteristics of the legal system as an advanced evolutionary state and try to apply these characteristics to the domain of individuals using rules for decision-making, two main principles emerge: memory and consciousness. Memory creates a dependency on past judgments and a set of easily prescribed paths for decisions in a variety of different cases. This is where precedents get their force and where early repeated behavior gets imprinted on future behaviors. Notwithstanding, consciousness allows us in some cases to override the prescribed path of behavior when the situation calls for a different set of decisions, albeit at the cost of extra consideration and deliberation. We return to these two important characteristics, invocation and override, when we describe empirical tests for the decisions-by-rules mechanism itself.

The possible downside of following rules

One consequence of the broad application of rules to different activities is that there are circumstances for which the rules are not suited and yet they are applied (as with many legal systems), resulting in actions that can at times be disassociated from preferences. For example, consider stopping and waiting at a red traffic light in an abandoned street in the middle of the night, with no apparent other traffic. According to some, it is by the very definition of rules that they exclude a set of considerations that may, at times, prove to be the right set of inputs to apply to the decision at hand (Raz 1975). As another example, suppose a person immensely enjoys smelling the fresh air in the park on his or her way to work, and even mentions this to co-workers every day. And suppose that a young entrepreneur overhears this information, and convinces city hall to start charging one cent for passage through the park when the flowers are in bloom. It is very likely that the protagonist will refuse to pay merely because this person does not believe that one should have to pay for a breath of fresh air, even though it is worth much more than one cent to him or her in terms of the happiness it brings to that individual's life. In this example, the protagonist's belief in the invalidity of the payment request functions as a rule in the person's decision. Nevertheless, using the rule can rob that person of valuable happiness. Note that we are not claiming that this individual is unable to comprehend the value of this experience – only that he or she is unwilling to directly pay for it. Indeed, if the same payment was to be framed differently, for example as a donation to the city park services, the same person might be willing to provide much more to ensure continued enjoyment from the fresh flowers.

It is important to understand that we emphasize the negative aspects of using rules only as a method to identify the mechanism. If the predictions of rule-use and preference maximization would have been identical, we would not have been able to tell the two apart. The mechanism of following rules has many personal and social advantages, and one should not mistake this chapter for saying otherwise!

In summary, theoretical views in psychology, philosophy, and decision-making (e.g., Prelec 1991; Ainslie 1992; Baron 1994; March 1994; Habermas 1996) suggest an additional mechanism for decisions and another reason for the inconsistency often observed between preferences and actions (e.g., Tversky and Simonson 1993; Fischoff 1991; Frederick 2002) – the use of decision rules.[3]

Rules in daily decisions

Decision rules can be based on personal, social, cultural, or moral conventions. Growing up in different cultures, or subcultures, is likely to teach individuals different "causal schemata" of the stimulus-response relations in their environment (Nisbett and Wilson 1977; Schwartz 1977; Gilbert 1995; see also Raz 1975). Some rules can be learned from personal experience (e.g., don't tell one's spouse dinner is not good; set a personal deadline one day before the actual deadline;

hide an extra key in the garden), while others can be based on social, cultural, and moral conventions one does not need to experience in order to learn (e.g., one should not steal; paying for sex is not a decent relationship; some offers are unfair). Thus, because these rules are learned and may be socially constructed they are also unlikely to be universal, and the specific rules that are applied by different individuals in different circumstances would almost certainly depend on individual, social, and cultural factors.

One outcome of the social construction of rules as decision mechanisms is that individuals may "drift" into following rules gradually over a period of time without ever consciously deciding to do so, and without being aware that they started adopting the use of a rule. In the terms of Kahneman and Frederick (2003), "system-2" processes are automated to become "system-1":

> A person may, however, come to follow a rule without having decided to do so. He may have been brought up from early childhood to believe in the validity of the rule and to respect it. He may have drifted into following the rule as an adult gradually over a period of time without ever really making up his mind to do so.
>
> (Raz 1975: 497)

As an example of such rules and also of the arbitrariness of their boundaries consider the distinction among the four meta-schemas of social order suggested by Fiske's theory of human sociability (1992). In this theory, the four forms of sociality (communal sharing, authority-ranking, equality-matching, and market-pricing relations) define four distinct sets of courses of action that are admissible and inadmissible behaviors and trade-offs. As an example of an unacceptable rule of conduct within a specific social order, consider the likelihood that after a fabulous meal at your mother in-law's you would take out your checkbook and ask how much you owe her for this dinner (for the ingredients and for her time). While this exchange would be unacceptable for most people, other exchanges would be appropriate in this case (e.g., painting your mother in-law's garage, fixing her deck, giving her a gift, etc.). This example illustrates not only the rules and how they can apply differently for the same person in their different social schemas, but also the arbitrariness of the exchange relationships that are acceptable and unacceptable within the different social schemas.

Another aspect of rules in everyday life relates to personal rules regarding desirable and undesirable behavior as a source of self-control. Based on views of eighteenth-century thinkers and focusing on issues of self-control, Ainslie (1992) argues that as a child develops, she consciously or unconsciously learns a general precept, such as "maintain health" or "be good," effectively uniting actions under a common rule towards a desired end. Such grouping of choices serves as the building blocks of one's willpower. This learned aspect of rules differentiates them from preference-based mechanisms (preferences can be either learned or endowed), and deserves further emphasis. Several other theorists have also argued that personal rules are the predominant mechanism for pre-commitment against follies of self-control (Raz 1975; Prelec 1991; Ainslie 1992). In these cases, rules may be conscious and self-generated in order to dictate future behavior and avoid future conflicts. For example, an ex-smoker may create a rule that prevents him or her from even an occasional, seemingly harmless, taste of a friend's cigarette for fear of increasing his or her own urge to smoke.

Theoretical summary

In summary, the rules that are the focus of the current chapter are analogues to legal or moral rules in that they are not binding constraints on behavior, but instead form guiding principles that are not always explicitly considered. We further propose that because these rules only form virtual constraints on decisions, they will be followed most frequently when they are strongly invoked, when decisions are made mindlessly (Langer 1989), when there is little experience in the domain, or when the rules are acquired via non-personal (social) experience (Reagan and Fazio 1977). Moreover, because rules are general in nature, behaviors that are guided by them will not always match optimizations according to preferences, and following rules could come at the expense of local personal utility.

Therefore, while there is no question that internal states (i.e., attitudes and preferences) are commonly used as inputs for consumers' decisions, the two main general claims of this chapter are that in cases where there is a feeling of "the right thing to do":

(1) When a rule is invoked, unless it is overridden, individuals will follow the rule in a "moral-like" fashion instead of basing their decisions on their preferences.
(2) The rules individuals follow can sometimes be invoked in situations that undermine preference maximization, leading to choices that provide lower consumption utility.

In the following sections, we will describe evidence supporting the rules-based mechanism by examining these specific claims. The first claim involves three components: invocation (activation), override (ignoring the rule), and the distinctiveness of rule-based decision-making from preference-based decision-making. The second claim involves examining disassociations between preferences and decisions. Note, however, that investigation of the second claim is more complex: it requires searching for instances where rule-based choice negates preference maximization. Because of this requirement we will focus the entire discussion of support for the rules-based mechanism on cases where maximizing preferences implies choosing one outcome, yet following a rule dictates making a different choice. But we note that there are most likely many cases in which rules would lead to the same choice outcomes as preferences, but these are obviously situations where it is hard to distinguish one decision mechanism from another.

Rule activation

The activation of personal rules is likely to be defined not only by social and cultural context, but also by the local context of the task (March 1994). For example, Fiske and Tetlock (1997) suggest that one can overcome one such type of rules, emerging from taboo trade offs, by obfuscating the trade off (i.e., hiding the invoking cue), and reframing the decision task in more comparable terms. When tasks are reframed, binding norms or decision rules are not invoked, making their violation easier (see also Ratner and Miller 2001, Experiment 4). For example, although it is not considered appropriate to pay with cash for a dinner one is invited to, it is acceptable (and even recommended) to "pay" back the hosts with a gift such as wine or flowers. The key here is attention to the appropriateness and applicability of the rules (Ainslie 1992). When attention is directed at a rule, it will be followed. On the other hand, in cases where attention is not directed at a rule, it will not be invoked and thus not followed. For example, Amir and Ariely (2004) find that consumers are likely to prefer a slightly delayed concert over an immediate one, because of the added benefit of savoring, and are also willing to exert more effort (driving time to get a ticket) to gain access to the delayed concert than to the immediate one. However, in contrast to this behavior, they find that consumers are willing to pay more for the immediate concert, because they have a rule opposing payment for delay. Amir and Ariely (2004) discuss this pattern of behavior in the context of a rule consumers follow whereby it is not acceptable to pay more for a delayed positive event. One of the interesting aspects of this example is that when the cost (payment) is framed in units of effort, this does not invoke the rule, but when the cost (payment) is framed in monetary terms the rule is invoked.

This sensitivity of behavior to the invoking cue (money in the case above) demonstrates the sensitivity of rules to the exact set of circumstances under which the judgment is made. Indeed, it has been suggested that the effect framing has on the activation of social norms may lie in focus of attention (Cialdini *et al.* 1991). When attention is focused on a particular norm as a standard for behavior, rules are likely to influence behavior, whereas when attention is not directed at a rule, following one's preference is likely to take precedence over following rules. The framing and attentional aspects of the activation of rules also implies that their activation is in many cases implicit, which renders their invocation exogenous. The exogenous activation means that manipulations such as differential framing of the same situation will determine whether the rule is invoked or not, which in turn will determine the reliance on the rule as a guiding principle for behavior. For example, Amir and Ariely (2004) find that whether or not consumers prefer to go to a high-end store and pay a premium for the service depends greatly on whether the premium is presented as a general price increase or whether this increase is associated directly with the service in the store. Specifically, when the service is bundled with the price of the product itself (e.g., a TV is more expensive in a good-service store compared to the same TV at an average-service store) consumers are much more likely to pay the service premium. On the other hand when the same price premium was defined as being an explicit payment for service, the pattern reversed and most consumers found this store to be less desirable. In other words, much like the cases with obfuscating taboo trade offs, consumers were not willing to pay directly for service but were willing to pay for it when it was a part of a bundle.

The rule invocation process that starts with the recognition of the exogenous situation may also be influenced by the decision-maker's internal goals such as preserving a current identity or striving towards a desired one (March 1994). For example, a consumer might wonder what other consumers would do in similar situations or what someone they admire would do if in a similar situation.

Using rules

Certain aspects of using rules as a decision-making mechanism are distinct from plausible alternatives and therefore enable us to differentiate and identify the actual mechanism used in the decision-making process. In this section, we will describe evidence supporting this conceptualization. We will first describe a case in which consumers' choices are disassociated from their preferences, and then provide evidence supporting a rule-based mechanism as opposed to alternative ones (e.g., preference maximization, the use of simplifying heuristics, or choosing based on the balance of reasons).

There are many cases in which consumers do not choose the most beneficial outcome: they could be making a mistake, their judgment could be biased, and so forth. In this section we would like to suggest that another mechanism responsible for such mistakes in choices (i.e., predicted happiness–decision inconsistencies) is rule-following. For example, consumers often follow a "value-seeking" rule, which implies attaching a greater importance to some larger but not-consumable gain in value relative to a smaller but consumable value. In everyday consumption settings, this translates, for example, to choosing a music CD that is liked less simply because its original (non-discounted) price was higher over a preferred CD whose original price was lower (Hsee *et al.* 1999). In this example, consumers are behaving as if they are in fact consuming the discount size rather than the CD!

Another example comes from the realm of negotiations, as depicted by the behavior of individuals playing ultimatum games. In this game there are two stages: in the first, one side makes a pie-dividing offer, and in the second, the other side decides whether to accept the offer or to reject it. If the offer is accepted, both sides receive their respective parts of the pie, and if not, both sides receive nothing. The theoretical best (equilibrium) strategy is for the first side to offer the minimal possible amount, and for the other side to accept any offer, as it has nothing to lose. The reality, however, is very different from theory; people hardly ever make low offers, and even when these offers are made, they are rarely accepted. In fact, pie distributions tend to be very close to the fair half-and-half divisions (see Roth 1995 for a review; Frederick 2002). Much like the Coke price discrimination example earlier, people refuse to accept a beneficial offer when it seems that this offer *should* not have been made.

Our third example has to do with intertemporal choice. As mentioned above, there are many experiences that we are better off having sooner rather than later (e.g., receiving the newest PDA), but there are some that are better a little later. The latter experiences usually are characterized by a strong component of savoring of their overall appeal, e.g., a concert by your favorite band, or receiving a kiss from your favorite movie star (Loewenstein 1987). The question that arises, then, is whether individuals are able to realize the exception to this generic case and, given this recognition, whether they would be willing to pay more for the more enjoyable, albeit delayed, experience. Based on the observation that there is only a small and exceptional set of experiences where delay of a positive experience is desirable, the strict rule-based perspective suggests that the rule that will be applied to these experiences will be the same as the rule applied to the large category of intertemporal choices, i.e., that it is not good to delay positive experiences. Thus, if individuals will not immediately recognize the value in delay, they will be willing to pay less for the delayed experience. The studies by Amir and Ariely (2004) show that when asked about which experience would provide them with more enjoyment (or which one they would drive further in order to secure) individuals are able to recognize without problems that the delayed experience is going to be associated with a higher level of enjoyment. Yet, when asked about payment, these same individuals indicated that they would pay less for these more pleasurable (delayed) experiences. Further, this payment pattern did not result from asymmetric market beliefs regarding which tickets should cost more and which should cost less. This example demonstrates that while individuals are able to recognize the value in delay, they are unwilling to pay more for these superior experiences. (As an intuitive example, consider whether you would be willing to pay Amazon to delay a shipment for a good you will enjoy anticipating).

The three examples presented here (deal-seeking, altruism, and preference for delays) demonstrate cases in which there is a preference – action inconsistency. Yet, thus far we have not presented evidence that rule following indeed generated this inconsistency between preferences and choices. We will now describe additional findings that differentiate rules from other mechanisms.

The first piece of evidence comes from one of the preference for delay experiments presented earlier, namely, showing that while individuals refused to pay more money for the delayed and more enjoyable experience, they were willing to invest more effort in order to do so. The fact that there was a disassociation between behavior and preferences, and that this disassociation appeared only when the payment form was monetary but not experiential, suggests that a rule is the decision mechanism that is involved, and that this rule is invoked by eliciting conventions regarding the use of money.

Another piece of evidence supporting the use of a rule-based mechanism pertains to individual differences. Because of the ways different rules come to be, various individuals may hold different rules, and even those who have the same rules may adhere to those rules to different degrees. Consequently, if some individuals are more likely to follow rules because of their personal propensity to do so, we should expect those same people to display greater discrepancies with their preferences in the situations mentioned above in which rules and preferences point in different directions. This pattern is precisely what Amir and Ariely (2004) found: individuals who were higher on personality traits that relate to adherence to rules showed a larger discrepancy between their preferences and their behaviors. These personality differences provide further, and perhaps the most direct, support for the distinction between rules on one hand and heuristics and normative, preference-based explanations on the other.

Rule override

A final aspect of the rules-based decision mechanism is the ability to override the rules. Rules are by definition overarching, such that if one examines the appropriateness of a rule on every occasion, then it is not a rule (Raz 1975). But our conceptualization leaves open the possibility of examining the adequacy of a rule from time to time and overriding it. This aspect of our theorizing also fits the legal metaphor since even judges examine the appropriateness and validity of rules every once in a while. When consumers wrongly apply a rule and reduce their overall happiness, as in the afore-mentioned cases, they could have been better off taking a moment to carefully consider whether applying the rule was the appropriate thing to do. For example, if consumers face a choice of payment for a delayed concert, instead of applying the rule against payment for delay they would be better off realizing that in this case there is value in postponement, i.e., the joy of savoring. Such consideration could arise from increasing the amount of time and attention individuals invest in making the decision, or from making the pleasure dimension more salient. Amir and Ariely (2004) tested these premises within the context of unwillingness to pay more for a delayed positive experience: participants were asked to either choose a concert date for which they would be willing to pay more or a concert date which would generate the greatest overall pleasure from two alternative dates (tonight or two weeks from tonight). Participants were either asked to respond to these questions with the first answer that comes to mind or to think carefully about their answer before responding. The findings indicate that, consistent with the rule-based decision-making approach, when delivering an immediate response, participants were more likely to favor the delayed concert when considering their overall pleasure, and the immediate concert when considering their willingness to pay. However, when carefully considering their response, participants were more likely to prefer the delayed concert in both types of questions (pleasure and money). These results suggest that where monetary responses are concerned, the application of rules is the immediate and primary reaction and that only with greater consideration can this first reaction be overridden such that decisions coincide more with preferences. This primacy of the rule is most likely based on automaticity and extensive experience with applying such rules to many situations over one's lifetime.

A conceptual replication using a very different manipulation revealed the same basic findings. In this case, the pleasure dimension was made more salient through the use of cognitive priming. Participants were first asked to describe pleasurable events, such as eating their favorite ice cream or having a full body massage, and then responded to the concert date choice question for overall happiness or willingness to pay. Consistent with the rule-based mechanism, its activation, and override, when the pleasure dimension was primed (and thus made more accessible), study participants were more likely to override the rule and choose the delayed concert even when asked about payment.

Again, manipulations of additional thinking or emotional priming should have little impact on preference – behavior inconsistency, according to the preference-based view of decisions (normative or heuristic). In contrast, the rules-based account of decisions proposed here assumes the ability to override rules as well as sensitivity to environmental conditions. Rule-based decisions therefore should be sensitive to these two manipulations and the results support the present viewpoint on human decision-making.

General discussion

Consumers make numerous decisions on a daily basis. Understanding the underlying mechanisms that drive the particular choices consumers make is invaluable. Our goal in this chapter was to argue and demonstrate that individuals sometimes make decisions according to preset rules and not their preferences, and that such a decision-making mechanism may lead them to make decisions that don't always maximize their consumption experience (utility). The general perspective on rules presented here is that these rules are overarching guidelines for behavior, that they are learned either from experience or from social exchange, and that they are followed almost blindly when invoked. The experimental evidence surveyed provides support for the decision by rules mechanism by showing that (1) when a rule is invoked and not overridden, instead of basing their decisions on preferences, consumers follow the rule; (2) rule-following consequently can lead to situations in which consumers make decisions that are suboptimal in that they do not maximize consumption utility, and consumers do so even in cases where it is obvious which choice alternative is likely to be associated with higher overall pleasure; and (3) that such rules are invoked when consumers deal with tasks framed in monetary terms. In other words, mentioning money is often sufficient to invoke such rules.

We believe that this mechanism is of high importance because it suggests that consumers do not always engage in cost-benefit trade-offs and in some cases prefer to not pay for things that are clearly preferred (which also means that market research based on preferences can be misleading in these cases). More broadly, understanding the set of rules consumers employ may allow us to identify the missing link between cultural and social norms and actual decision behavior. By aligning consumer behavior with a systematic network of rules, we may be able to disentangle individual, social, and situational determinants of the consumer choice-making process. The rules-based mechanism has a particular appeal for marketers since the environment and the conditions under which individuals make decisions can be artificially changed to influence the application of rules, and the likelihood that they will be overridden. This aspect has obvious consequences since the market can shape rules and obfuscate the conditions that evoke and override the rules in ways that can either fit or undermine preferences.

In summary, the common view held by both marketers and decisions scientists is that individuals make decisions according to a set of preferences by searching for an optimum, a local optimum, or a close-enough estimate when exact algorithms are too costly. In contrast, in the current work we suggest that this view does not always hold and that decision-makers sometimes do not try to consider the best alternative according to their preferences, but rather act upon pre-imposed decision rules that are based on moral or social norms and on behavioral guidelines (see also Prelec 1991; Ainslie 1992; Baron 1994; March 1994; Hsee *et al.* 2003).

Future research

As this stream of research is relatively young, there is still much to learn. There is a set of questions one may ask about rules in general as decision-making mechanisms: What is the exact process by which rules emerge, and what are the individual and cultural determinants by which consumers come to rely on specific rules in choice-making (see also Fiske 1992; Fiske and Tetlock 1997)? Another general question concerns the ways in which individuals can overcome the rules, and instead use their preferences as a guide for their decisions. Regarding this question, it is possible that being mindful (see Langer 1989) of the different rules might allow consumers to ignore them at the time of action or to pre-commit to ignoring them *ex ante*. A third general question concerns the categorization of different rules. There is one category of rules that are used to enforce behavior on oneself (Ainslie 1992; Prelec 2003). Yet not all rules seem to fit this category. What other categories of rules exist? A fourth question concerns the effects of rule violation. In discussing rules for self-control, Ainslie (1992) has argued that violating a rule can be a slippery slope to its demise, while Prelec (2003) believes that such violations can be highly informative to the decision-maker about his or her own persona. In domains not related to self-control, rule violation might have yet other consequences.

A different approach to better understand rules-based decisions is to examine the workings of particular rules. For example, one can ask, how does a rule such as the one against paying for delay actually emerge? It is possible that this rule stems from a generalized desire for immediate gratification; from a developmental perspective, the human ability to anticipate develops at a later stage than the need for immediate gratification. Also, can people be trained to never activate a rule or perhaps to more quickly override it?

Finally, the results discussed here shed some light on the possible negative aspects of using money as an exchange medium. Although money is generally viewed as a fabulous invention because it allows for better market exchanges, specialization etc., the results presented here also show that when it comes to monetary decisions, there is an increased propensity to activate rules, which might ultimately undermine preferences (see also Amir *et al.* 2004 regarding the psychology of monetary judgments). If this pattern holds across many domains, a higher reliance on barters and direct trade offs (or at least considering these explicitly when thinking about monetary exchanges) might lead to higher consumer welfare. The research surveyed in this chapter is only an initial step in understanding the interesting and important mechanism of decisions by rules. The generality of this mechanism and the applications for consumer decisions and welfare could be far reaching.

Notes

1 Social norms stand for many behavioral guidance mechanisms. Many of them are principles that require additional instructions to guide specific behavior (e.g., be nice). However, some social norms are actually specific rules (e.g., display a flag on Independence Day).
2 Hence the term "rules," as defining: x should [not] do y in situation S (Raz 1975).
3 A great deal of discourse in moral and legal philosophy is devoted to the overlap, hierarchy, and boundaries of a myriad of terms describing behavioral guidelines, such as rules, principles, norms, rationales, morals, and so forth. The locus of distinctions between such terms lies in the [superhuman] ability to identify the source, relevance, and distinct implications of each one, contrast, compare, and finally choose the correct manner of thought and action that follow from that choice (See, for example, Dworkin's "Judge Hercules" in Habermas 1996). In this work, the use of the term "rules" refers to a general underlying mechanism whereby people choose according to what they think they ought to do, and these "oughts" arise when a situational cue invokes them.

References

Ainslie, G. (1992) *Picoeconomics: The Strategic Interaction of Successive Motivational States Within the Person*, Cambridge: Cambridge University Press.

Amir, O. and Ariely, D. (2004) "Decisions by rules: Dissociation between preferences and willingness to act," Yale University, Working Paper.

Amir, O., Ariely, D., and Carmon, Z. (2004) "The locus and appropriateness of monetary evaluations: Why monetary assessments do not reflect predicted utility," Yale University, Working Paper.

Baron, J. (1994) "Nonconsequentialist decisions," *Behavioral and Brain Sciences* 17(1): 1–10.

Cialdini, R. B., Kallgren, C. A., and Reno, R. R. (1991) "A focus theory of normative conduct: A theoretical refinement and reevaluation of the role of norms in human behavior," in M. P. Zanna (ed.) *Advances in Experimental Social Psychology*, Vol. 24, New York: Academic Press: 201–234.

Fischoff, B. (1991) "Value elicitation: Is there anything in there?" *American Psychologist* 46: 835–847.

Fiske, A. P. (1992) "The four elementary forms of sociality: Framework for a unified theory of social relations," *Psychological Review* 99: 689–723.

Fiske, A. P. and Tetlock, P. E. (1997) "Taboo trade-offs: Reactions to transactions that transgress the spheres of justice," *Political Psychology* 18: 255–297.

Frederick, S. (2002) "Automated heuristics," in T. Gilovich, D. Griffing, and D. Kahneman (eds) *Heuristics and Biases: The Psychology of Intuitive Judgment*, Cambridge: Cambridge University Press.

Gilbert, D. T. (1995) "Attribution and interpersonal perception," in A. Tesser (ed.) *Constructing Social Psychology*, New York: McGraw-Hill.

Gray, P. N. (1997) *Artificial Legal Intelligence*, Brookfield, VT: Dartmouth Publishing Co.

Habermas, J. (1996) *Between Facts and Norms*, Cambridge, MA: MIT Press.

Hsee, C. K. (1999) "Value seeking and prediction–decision inconsistency: Why don't people take what they predict they'll like the most?" *Psychonomic Bulletin and Review* 6(4): 555–561.

Hsee, C. K., Zhang, J., Yu, F., and Xi, Y. (2003) "Lay rationalism and inconsistency between predicted experience and decision," *Journal of Behavioral Decision-Making* 16: 257–272.

Kahneman, D. and Frederick, S. (2003) "Representativeness revisited: Attribute substitution in intuitive judgment," in T. Gilovich, D. Griffing, and D. Kahneman (eds) *Heuristics and Biases: The Psychology of Intuitive Judgment*, Cambridge: Cambridge University Press.

Kahneman, D. and Tversky, A. (1982) "Subjective probability: A judgment of representativeness," in D. Kahneman, P. Slovic, and A. Tversky (eds) *Judgment Under Uncertainty: Heuristics and Biases*, New York: Cambridge University Press.

King, C. and Narayandas, D. (2000) "Coca-Cola's new vending machine (a): Pricing to capture value, or not?" *Harvard Business School Case* # 9-500-068.

Langer, E. J. (1989) "Minding matters: The consequences of mindlessness–mindfulness," in L. Berkowitz (ed.) *Advances in Experimental Social Psychology*, Vol. 22, San Diego, CA: Academic Press: 137–174.

Loewenstein, G. (1987) "Anticipation and the valuation of delayed consumption," *The Economic Journal* 97: 666–684.

Maine, H. S. (1861 and republished 1986) *Ancient Law*, New York: Dorset Press.

March, J. G. (1994) *A Primer on Decision-Making: How Decisions Happen*, New York: The Free Press: 57–102.

Nisbett, R. E. and Wilson, T. D. (1977) "Telling more than we can know: Verbal reports on mental processes," *Psychological Review* 84: 231–259.

Payne, J. W., Bettman, J. R., and Johnson, E. J. (1993) *The Adaptive Decision-Maker*, New York: Cambridge University Press.

Prelec, D. (1991) "Values and principles: Some limitations on traditional economic analysis," in A. Etzioni and P. R. Lawrence (eds) *Socio-Economics: Toward A New Synthesis*, Armonk, NY, M. E. Sharpe: 131–145.

Prelec, D. (2003) "Rules (are meant to be broken)," MIT Working Paper.

Ratner, R. K. and Miller, D. T. (2001) "The norm of self-interest and its effects on social action," *Journal of Personality and Social Psychology* 81(1): 5–16.

Raz, J. (1975) "Reasons for action, decisions, and norms," *Mind* 84(336) (October): 481–499.

Reagan, D. T. and Fazio, R. (1977) "On the consistency between attitudes and behavior: Look to the method of attitude formation," *Journal of Experimental Social Psychology* 13: 28–45.

Rosencrance, L. (2000) "Customers Balk at Variable DVD Pricing on Amazon.com," *CNN.com.technology>computing*, Online article, Sep. 13th.

Roth, A. E. (1995) "Bargaining experiments," in J. H. Kagel and A. E. Roth (eds) *Handbook of Experimental Economics*, Princeton, NJ: Princeton University Press.

Shafir, E., Simonson, I. and Tversky, A. (1993) "Reason-based choice," *Cognition* 49: 11–36.

Simonson, I. (1989) "Choice based on reasons: The case of attraction and compromise effects," *Journal of Consumer Research* 16(2): 158–174.

Schwartz, S. H. (1977) "Normative influences on altruism," in L. Berkowitz (ed.) *Advances in Experimental Social Psychology*, Vol. 10, New York: Academic Press: 221–279.

Tversky, A. (1972) "Elimination by aspects: A theory of choice," *Psychological Review* 79: 281–299.

Tversky, A. and Simonson, I. (1993) "Context-dependent preferences," *Management Science* 10: 1179–1189.

6 Variety for the sake of variety?

Diversification motives in consumer choice

Barbara E. Kahn and Rebecca K. Ratner

Suppose that you are planning the itinerary for your upcoming Hawaiian vacation. Imagine that you have been to Hawaii before and know that you enjoy relaxing on the beach more than other available activities such as deep-sea fishing, shopping, and mingling with strangers at the hotel-sponsored luau. How much time would you allow yourself to spend relaxing on the beach? Will you choose beach relaxation until you are ready for a change, or will you switch away from the beach experience to your less-favored experiences to incorporate diversity into your vacation? Casual observation of tourist's vacation habits suggests that you are likely to diversify your activities. Even in making more prosaic choices such as choosing among a selection of appetizers at a party or potentially more important choices, such as making donations to charity, people will sometimes incorporate less-liked items or experiences in order to obtain variety.

In this chapter we focus on the quest for variety, in and of itself, as a motivation for consumption. We begin with an examination of the need for variety in a normative sense – where the variety actually increases the overall utility of the consumption set. We then consider the situations in which consumers may choose too much variety – a bias which has been labeled the *diversification bias* (Read and Loewenstein 1995). We define "too much variety" as a set of choices in which consumers include items that they like less than other items they could have chosen. However, we discuss possible motivations and moderators for this kind of decision-making and note a range of goals that individuals may be trying to satisfy by straying from the highest-rated options. We conclude with a discussion of avenues for future research that will address several key under-researched questions pertaining to variety-seeking behavior.

The normative value of variety-seeking behavior

One could argue that from an evolutionary perspective, the pursuit of variety is necessary for growth and adaptation to a changing environment (Foxall 1993). Certainly, in many literatures (e.g., psychology, economics, nutrition) the consumer's desire for variety has been considered a natural and utility-maximizing motivation for behavior. In this section, we describe three key motivations for variety-seeking behavior that conceive of variety-seeking as a beneficial and adaptive choice strategy.

Basic drive for stimulation

Psychologists have focused on an individual's need for stimulation (Berlyne 1960) as a basic drive that can be satisfied through exploratory or varied behavior or through the consumption of novel stimuli (Faison 1977; Venkatesan 1973). This drive or need for stimulation has often been described as a single-peaked preference choice function (Coombs and Avrunin 1977) in which low levels of stimulus intensity provoke a desire for arousal that individuals attempt to satisfy by seeking variety; however, if the stimulus intensity gets too high, then individuals attempt to decrease the arousal by diminishing their variety-seeking behavior. Consistent with our opening example, Coombs and Avrunin describe this single-peaked choice function in the context of taking a vacation (1977: 218–219):

> Suppose an individual is considering taking a trip for a vacation and must decide how long a time to be gone. On the one hand, there are good consequences of traveling, the stimulation of novelty and new experiences for example, and the longer one travels, the more these experiences accumulate. The interest and satisfaction from new input is most rapid at first and then falls off – as traveling continues, the stimulation from it satiates. . . .

Psychologists have found that this drive for stimulation or for variety differs by individual (Steenkamp and Baumgartner 1992). There is heterogeneity with regard to how much stimulation an individual may feel is optimal; some people have greater needs for stimulation and are more likely to engage in exploratory or variety-seeking behavior – or to innovate and try new things – and others have lower needs for stimulation and thus are less likely to pursue these types of activities (Raju 1980). This difference in individuals' physical desires, need for stimulation, or variety has also been supported in the observation of the behavior of laboratory rats. In the laboratory, some rats had a greater propensity toward exploratory behavior than others (Dellu *et al.* 1996). The HR (high responders) rats were more likely to visit the novel arm (as opposed to the familiar arm) in a Y-shaped maze and were more likely to explore a higher number of arms in a complex maze than the LR (low responders) rats. The HR rats seek not only novelty, but variety and change. The researchers suggested that there was a difference in the activity in their hypothalamo-pituitary-adrenal (HPA) axis between the two groups of rats and that could explain the underlying biological difference between HR and LR rats. In other words, there is a link between the biological brain structure they have investigated (e.g., the HPA axis) and the types of novelty-seeking and variety-seeking behavior observed in the HR rats. If analogous effects occur in humans, this would support the idea that there is a biological reason for the drive for variety that some people exhibit.

Consistent with the notion that variety-seeking behavior can be driven by a desire to maintain an optimal stimulation level, research suggests that when the drive for variety on one dimension is satisfied, the desire for variety on other dimensions diminishes. For example, if consumers select choice environments that are more stimulating, they may try to simplify their purchase behavior and choose less variety because their desire for stimulation is satisfied through the more complex environment (Menon and Kahn 2002). Similarly, if the drive for stimulation is satisfied in one product category through increased variety-seeking, variety-seeking in a subsequent or parallel product category is diminished (Menon and Kahn 1995). The implication of these results is that in some regards, the stimulation derived from seeking variety across different dimensions is similar (or at least substitutable).

Desire to overcome satiation

Distinct from the notion that people like variety because they have a basic drive for stimulation is the idea that people like variety because they become satiated with the attribute levels of a given product and need or desire other products or experiences that offer a range of other attribute levels (e.g., McAlister 1982). Similar to the single-peak preference function stipulated by Coombs and Avrunin, some economists have suggested that consumers are likely to switch among different products because of the decreasing marginal value of the original item (Silberberg 1978) or the decreasing marginal utility of a specific attribute of the item (Lancaster 1971).

This satiation with existing choices can be affected by conditions in the choice environment. For example, in an experiment where positive mood was induced (through the unexpected gift of a bag of colorful candies), participants exhibited increased variety-seeking in selections among various consumer product choices as compared to the selections participants made in a control condition (Kahn and Isen 1993). The positive mood induction encouraged participants to elaborate and process the attributes of the offered alternatives more than in the control condition. In addition, the respondents in the positive-affect conditions were more optimistic in anticipation of consumption of the alternatives. These two factors encouraged those in the positive-affect conditions to become more satiated with repeated choices over time and thus to seek more variety than those in the control condition.

In another series of experiments (Mitchell *et al.* 1995), scents pumped into the environment that were either congruent or incongruent with the choice set stimuli affected variety-seeking tendencies. Stimuli-congruent scents increased satiation with repeated choice patterns and encouraged variety-seeking behavior. For example, participants choosing among chocolate candies chose more variety when the environment was scented with a chocolate fragrance than when the environment was scented with a flowery fragrance. In this case, the researchers found that variety-seeking increased in the congruent condition because the respondents exhibited increased cognitive flexibility: they processed information about the choice set items more holistically than those who were in the incongruent conditions. This attention to the trade-offs among attributes increased the perception of additional potential benefits that each of the different alternatives could yield.

Nutritionists have always noted a strong preference for variety in the consumption of food. Most dietary recommendations encourage people to sample widely to make sure to consume foods that offer a wide selection of nutritional requirements. Research has shown that even if these nutritional recommendations were not widely accepted, consumers would likely seek variety in their nutritional selections because they experience satiation when they repeatedly consume foods that are similar in sensory properties such as texture, flavor, or food type. For example, refugees who were forced to eat the same foods repeatedly for long periods of time experienced significantly reduced liking for those foods and a decreased willingness to eat those foods again (Rolls and de Waal 1985). If consumers switch among different types of food, e.g., moving from salty foods to sweet foods, the pleasantness of each of the items of food consumed increases (Rolls *et al.* 1981a). When consumers are exposed to novel tastes, they report increased liking for the foods and increased willingness to consume those foods (Birch and Marlin 1982). Therefore, repeated exposure to familiar foods produces monotony (more so for savory than sweet foods), but repeated exposure to novel foods increases acceptance (Hetherington *et al.* 2000) and learning about favorable features of the previously unfamiliar items.

The sensory satiety that occurs when consumers repeatedly eat the same foods suggests that if consumers are exposed to more actual variety or diversification in the offered choice sets, they may consume more. In fact, studies on consumption have found that although physiological factors such as hunger can account for some differences in consumption quantities, environmental contextual cues can also influence consumption (e.g., Herman and Mack 1975). For example, if consumers are offered an assortment with three different flavors of yogurt, they are likely to consume an average of 23 percent more yogurt than if they are offered an assortment featuring only one flavor (Rolls *et al.* 1981b). Thus it has been acknowledged that the availability of a variety of different foods is an important factor in the etiology of obesity (Rolls *et al.* 1983). It has also been shown that if actual variety is held constant, but the perceived variety of a consumption set increases because of the manner in which the choice options are displayed, consumption quantities can increase (Kahn and Wansink 2004).

In summary, the research described in these first two sections indicates that variety-seeking can emerge when the change itself produces desirable levels of stimulation or when switching allows people to recover from attribute satiation and obtain a combination of attributes across the choice set that no single option can provide.

Resolution of difficult decisions

People also choose variety for a number of reasons that reflect their belief that variety-seeking will help them resolve a decision that is otherwise difficult. For example, when choosing among unfamiliar items, consumers may choose a set of varied options to acquire information about the items in the set (Brickman and D'Amato 1975; McAlister 1982). Similarly, in choice occasions where there is a desire to find the perfect option (e.g., the classic secretary problem, Chow *et al.* 1964), individuals will likely sample a variety of options until they are willing to accept one as potentially optimal.

A related advantage to variety-seeking behavior is that it provides a mechanism for hedging one's bets. By choosing a portfolio of options a consumer can hedge against future uncertainty (Pessemier 1978). The uncertainty can be due to the inherent riskiness of the alternatives, the uncertainty in consumers' anticipated preference for the alternatives (Kahneman and Snell 1992), or changes in needs or personal goals (Simonson 1990). Simonson (1990) and Kahn and Lehmann (1991) suggest that people seek variety because they are risk-averse and uncertain about their future preferences. An implication of this approach is that variety-seeking should decline if the uncertainty or risk is reduced (Read and Loewenstein 1995).

Further, consumers may use variety-seeking as a choice heuristic to resolve conflict in difficult choice situations. Simonson (1990) suggests that sometimes consumers have difficulty choosing among familiar alternatives and are uncertain about their relative preferences for the different items. This kind of decision-making can incur discomfort, conflict, and even pain (Abelson and Levi 1985). One way to resolve that conflict without requiring too much cognitive effort would be to choose a variety of options. Thus this explanation for variety-seeking suggests that consumers use it as a conscious cognitive mechanism to avoid having to make more difficult trade-offs. An interesting implication for future research is that decisions that are subjectively perceived to be more difficult – even when the decision itself is unchanged (perhaps through manipulating the fluency with which the decision is processed, such as with a difficult-to-read font) – could produce greater variety-seeking.

Summary

The research we have reviewed thus far focuses on a number of sensible reasons why consumers may seek variety. They desire the stimulation that comes with experimentation, they seek a set of options that collectively provide needed attributes to overcome satiating on the attributes of any one option, and they seek variety when it is it is difficult to forecast future needs or when it is difficult to make decisions between items in the choice set. However, other research suggests that sometimes consumers go too far in their quest for variety and that this desire can manifest itself in ways that are arbitrary or even suboptimal. We describe this research in the section that follows.

Can variety-seeking behavior lead people astray?

Whereas the preceding perspectives focus on why variety-seeking behavior is beneficial, other approaches suggest that not all variety-seeking behavior is adaptive. In fact, it has been postulated that no explanation is needed for variety-seeking *per se*, but rather that there is a random character to the timing for the desire for variety (Bass *et al.* 1972). In this account, variety-seeking behavior occurs because although the probability of choosing the most-preferred brand is greatest, there is a stochastic component of choice such that consumers do not always choose their most-preferred brand.

Other research suggests that in many cases variety-seeking behavior emerges systematically rather than randomly, but in ways that reflect arbitrary decisions about the attribute or dimension on which the individual should seek variety. In some cases, variety-seeking actually leads individuals to abandon the choices that would provide the greatest utility. We discuss evidence for each of these approaches next.

Arbitrary dimensions of variety

One large class of arbitrary dimensions that impacts the overall variety chosen could be called framing or partitioning effects. For example, Read and Loewenstein (1995) find that the way a choice set is bracketed can systematically affect the final choice of items. Consumers tend to treat choices that are bracketed or framed together differently from those that are framed apart: items that are framed or linked together are considered as a type of portfolio choice, whereas items that are not linked as such are considered in isolation. Consumers are likely to choose a more varied sequence of items when considering the items as a portfolio of choices than when considering each of the offerings in isolation.

Other research indicates that partitioning a choice set affects the final choice such that consumers tend to engage in a rule such as "1/n" to justify their behavior (Fox *et al.* 2004). Individuals thus appear to apply a decision-making rule (Amir *et al.*, this volume) that they should not restrict their choices to their favorites. Participants tend to choose one item from each group into which the choice alternatives are clustered; so for example, Fox *et al.* find that participants are more likely to choose one wine from each region when items on a wine list are grouped by region than by grape, and they are more likely to choose one wine of each grape type when they are grouped by grape than by region. These effects are more pronounced for novices than experts, and are less pronounced when people indicate a lot of variance in their ratings (i.e., when they have strong favorites).

The arbitrary ways in which individuals obtain variety can have important implications. In one study (Fox *et al.* 2004), respondents were asked how to allocate financial aid among a variety of income ranges of college applicants. In one condition, respondents saw income ranges in which the low-income ranges were unpacked (e.g., the range of annual incomes were divided into five ranges of equal magnitude) and in the other condition, the high-income ranges were unpacked. Instructions indicated that the categories were arbitrary. Results showed a general trend of giving more money to less wealthy applicants but the amount given was affected by which income range was unpacked. When lower incomes were unpacked, 96 percent of the financial aid went to the lower income groups, but when higher incomes were unpacked, only 48 percent went to those same applicants. Thus the desire to spread one's choices across the range of salient options can lead to decisions that overrule one's own preferences.

Another set of arbitrary dimensions that affect how much variety consumers include in their choice sets could be termed "context effects." In these types of examples, changing the context in which the choice set is presented can affect the amount of variety chosen. For example, Menon and Kahn (1995) found that if consumers chose variety in one category, they then chose less variety in a subsequent category. Regardless of which category was used to provide the needed variety, if consumers encountered more variety in one category they chose less variety in the next.

Recent research (Drolet 2002) has suggested that consumers may not only crave variety among items within a choice set, but they may also crave variety in the decision processes that they use to choose these items. Similar to the arbitrariness of the variety incorporated in the choice of items, there seems to be a somewhat similar arbitrariness in individuals' choice of decision rules. In laboratory studies, consumers seemed to indicate a preference merely for a variety of choice rules rather than indicating any preference for the specific rules in and of themselves. For example, if a consumer first uses a "compromise option" choice rule, they were less likely to use that choice rule in a subsequent choice set and instead chose one of the extreme options. Further, change in the use of these choice rules over time was more likely to be seen in individuals with a higher dispositional need to demonstrate their uniqueness (see also Kim and Drolet 2003).

The research described here suggests that the dimensions on which individuals seek variety are often arbitrary. If individuals seek variety across randomly determined dimensions, the drive for variety will sometimes preclude individuals from choosing their favorite items in a choice set. Does variety-seeking behavior, then, sometimes reflect a sub-optimal decision strategy?

Choosing less-pleasing items

There is accumulating evidence that there are contexts in which individuals' choice of variety leads them to deviate from the items that would give them the greatest pleasure during consumption. In a seminal paper, Simonson (1990) cleverly showed that individuals' desire for variety depended on the timing of the choice decision rather than the utility of the items consumed. In a series of experiments, he asked participants to forecast in advance what snack foods they would want in future weeks. When consumers were asked to choose multiple items in a category for future consumption (simultaneous condition) they were more likely to seek variety than those who sequentially chose what they wanted to consume on each consumption occasion (sequential condition). Further, those respondents who chose sequentially were more likely to choose their most-preferred item each time than those who chose simultaneously.

Read and Loewenstein (1995) replicated these experiments and determined that people often felt that they had made a mistake when choosing variety in the simultaneous condition. Many of the participants indicated later that they wanted to trade in their originally chosen options to get less variety but more-preferred products. Read and Loewenstein called this choice anomaly a *diversification bias* and defined it as a pattern of choices where people chose more variety for future consumption relative to making separate choices immediately preceding consumption.

Another set of studies found that respondents chose to deviate from most-liked items even if they were not predicting choices for future consumption but rather making choices on each occasion about which item to experience next (Kahn *et al.* 1997; Ratner *et al.* 1999). In these studies, participants were asked to choose songs and then report their real-time utilities as they listened to their chosen songs. Participants tended to stray from favorite items during their self-constructed concerts, although they often ended their sequence with the choice of their favorite item. Their ratings during the concert indicated that consumers were choosing songs that they enjoyed less than they would have enjoyed repeating the already-listened-to songs that they preferred.

Why people include "too much" variety

Why might people decide to include so much variety that they end up not maximizing their real-time enjoyment during consumption? We suggest four explanations next, indicating that people

(1) attempt to maximize utility globally across the set of experiences rather than locally,
(2) mispredict how much enjoyment they will derive from the choices they make,
(3) seek to maximize their memory of the experience rather than their real-time enjoyment, and
(4) choose variety to signal something about themselves to others.

Global utility versus local utility

Research suggests that consumers make different decisions if they are thinking about them as isolated choices than if they are thinking about them as items within a sequence. Read and Loewenstein (1995) suggested that the diversification bias is attributable in part to *choice bracketing* effects, as described earlier: the tendency to treat choices that are bracketed or framed together differently from those that are framed apart. Using a formal condition of independence, the value of the sequence of choices should equal the sum of the value of its component parts. If the utilities of the items are held constant, consumers should choose the same items if they are choosing within a sequence as if they are choosing the items in isolation. However, consumers frequently do not behave that way (Loewenstein and Prelec 1993) but instead respond to the "gestalt" properties of the sequence. There are aspects of the sequence that become salient when people are thinking in terms of the sequence that disappear when consumers are just thinking in terms of the individual items. Thus, consumers do not seem to evaluate sequences of choices as merely the concatenation of those choices.

One way to think about the difference between the sequence of items and the sum of the individual items is to think about the differences between the global utility of the sequence and the local utility of each individual item (Kahn *et al.* 1997). If a consumer were choosing to maximize the local utilities, then consumers would choose to optimize their pleasure on each choice occasion, thereby failing to consider how their current choices would affect their later enjoyment. When faced with choices that provide differing rates of reinforcement, individuals could try to consume the alternatives that would yield the higher rates on any given trial (i.e., melioration, Herrnstein 1990a, b). Thus, if people are generally meliorating, they should tend to consume their favorites whenever they believed that those items would be even marginally more pleasing than the alternatives.

On the other hand, global maximization suggests that consumers consider the overall choice sequence and choose items across the sequence that would maximize their overall enjoyment. There is a stream of literature that suggests people indeed attempt to maximize utility globally rather than locally if the sequence is identified. However, many of the research findings indicate that when consumers think in terms of a sequence, they tend to include less-pleasing options and therefore choose too much variety to maximize pleasure across the sequence. Indeed, research that incorporates real-time ratings of enjoyment across the complete choice sequence suggests that individuals making a series of choices often fail to maximize either locally or globally because they include so many less-pleasing items (Kahn *et al.* 1997; Ratner *et al.* 1999).

There are several reasons postulated as to why the identification of a "sequence" changes the items chosen and increases the overall variety such that the consumption sequence ends up including less-pleasing choices. First, people prefer to spread out pleasurable things (Loewenstein and Prelec 1993). Thus, when offered the opportunity to choose something less good or even bad in between good things, people might seize the opportunity so that the pleasures are spread out. Second, people tend to prefer improving sequences and this can dictate the desire to add in less-liked items in the early parts of a sequence. For example, participants in one series of experiments overwhelmingly preferred the sequences that ended with a gain rather than with a loss (Ross and Simonson 1991). This has been found in other contexts as well: for example, people typically prefer increasing wage profiles to ones that are declining or flat (Loewenstein and Sicherman 1991). One possible reason for consumers' preference for improving sequences is that this format allows them to savor their reward for longer, whereas consuming an unavoidable, unpleasant item early eliminates feelings of dread (Loewenstein 1987).

Misprediction of future preferences

Another body of research suggests that the reason people choose varied sequences that include less-liked items is that consumption by definition must occur after choice, and people are bad forecasters of their own preferences (Kahneman and Snell 1992). As a result, they sometimes choose to deviate from their favorite(s), mistakenly believing that they will derive more utility from another option. For example, in a laboratory study, consumers who were asked to predict their enjoyment for yogurt, ice cream, and music over time did not predict their actual tastes very well. Participants generally assumed that their tastes across consumption occasions for a repeated item would decline more than they actually did. In contrast to the respondents' assumptions, their tastes for these products remained more stable across usage occasions than they predicted, and for many people, their evaluations of the products became more favorable over time. Other research confirms that consumers overestimate how quickly they will satiate on favored items (Read and Loewenstein 1995). Read and Loewenstein suggested that in addition to the choice-bracketing phenomenon discussed earlier, the diversification bias is largely attributable to *time contraction* – the tendency of individuals to treat long intervals as if they were much shorter and consequently to overestimate how quickly they will satiate on attributes of a particular product.

Another miscalibration that consumers are prone to is the prediction of how their evaluation of one object will affect their evaluation of another that is consumed close in time. This emerges specifically in predicting how contrast effects (Tversky and Griffin 1991) will affect utilities. The general consumer theory is that if there is a degree of relatedness between the items, the consumption of a more-pleasing item may benefit by being preceded by something less pleasing because the utility of the more-pleasing item will be enhanced by the contrast with the worse item. Thus the contrast hypothesis suggests that consumers may choose to consume items they do not like in order to make the items that they do like appear better. It is reminiscent of the adage of why people bang their heads against the wall ("because it feels so good to stop") or why some people prefer four seasons ("because it strengthens the appreciation of the milder ones"). Patterns of variety-seeking that include these less-liked items hence may be a strategy to increase preferences by purposefully including distasteful alternatives. The irony of this strategy is that it implies a consumer might choose to include less-pleasing items in the choice set even though research suggests that this type of intuitive belief about the nature of contrast effects is sometimes mistaken (Novemsky and Ratner 2003). In laboratory experiments, participants thought that they would enjoy an experience more if it had been preceded by something less pleasant when, in fact, real-time ratings indicated no contrast effects. More generally, people have inaccurate beliefs about how to space things over time to maximize (global) utility. Both of these overestimation effects could explain why people deviate from liked items to include other, less-liked ones.

Maximizing the retrospective experience

Yet another explanation for why consumers choose so much variety rests on the idea that consumers may be trying to maximize the retrospective experience, or their memory of the choice experience, as opposed to real-time experience. In a series of studies, participants rated the retrospective memory of the enjoyment of a highly varied musical sequence higher than they did for a less-varied sequence, even if the actual real-time enjoyment of the highly varied sequence was lower than that of the less-varied sequence (Ratner *et al.* 1999). These results suggest that sometimes consumers select a more varied sequence of items that includes less-pleasing goods, not because that sequence will lead to the greatest enjoyment in real time, but because it will lead to a better memory of the sequence. An interesting avenue for future research will be to examine situations in which people tend to seek present pleasure versus retrospective pleasure; for example, it may be that people who are forward-looking and good at delaying gratification tend to think about which experiences they expect to look back on favorably.

This strategy of maximizing future memories rather than real-time enjoyment may contribute to the variety-seeking behavior in our opening example. We suspect that it is common for vacationers to schedule many different types of activities, even if their preferred activity is relaxing at the beach. Since a vacation that consists only of sitting on the sand provides a less interesting memory than one that incorporates museum-visiting and deep-sea fishing, the tourist might choose activities that do not provide the most enjoyable experiences at the time but will create the best overall retrospective photo album.

Research in progress (Varghese *et al.*, in process) extends these findings of preference for variety in memory to the study of the effectiveness of persuasion appeals. Specifically, Varghese *et al.* have found that consumer products that have varied appeals (e.g., a mixture of emotional and objective appeals) are more preferred in memory than they are in real-time evaluation. Preliminary evidence suggests that these varied appeals are easier to retrieve in memory, and that these easier retrievals are associated with more positive affect and therefore higher preference.

Consumers may also deviate from favorite items in an effort to protect their past memories of favorite consumption experiences (Zauberman and Ratner, in process). The idea here is that people choose not to repeat experiences that were special in the past because they do not want to risk overwriting memories from the special experiences. For example, respondents report that they are reluctant to return to a vacation spot where they had a honeymoon with anyone other than their spouse, and they are less interested in returning to a restaurant where they had a very special evening than to a restaurant where they had a pleasant – but not particularly special – evening. Although such behaviors may be optimal if individuals derive considerable utility from memories, and they are able to protect their memories by engaging in variety-seeking behavior, such a strategy may fail to maximize utility during the moments of consumption. Interesting questions then arise as to whether the optimal strategy is to maximize memories rather than real-time pleasure.

Social motivations

Consumers sometimes choose more variety than their personal preferences warrant in an effort to manage observers' reactions to their choices. Ratner and Kahn (2002) find that people expect others to want more variety than they themselves prefer, and they anticipate that restricting their own choices to consumption of their favorite item(s) might make a negative impression on others; for example, others might conclude that they are dull, boring, or narrow-minded. Sampling a variety of items, on the other hand, allows consumers to express to others that they are creative and interesting people who enjoy many different things. As a result of this belief, laboratory experiments indicate that consumers are more likely to indulge in variety-seeking when consumption is public than when it is private. Further, this effect of public scrutiny on variety-seeking is attenuated when a social cue legitimates the decision to stick to one's favorites. Evidence for another type of interpersonal influence on variety-seeking behavior comes from a recent series of studies in which consumers ordering from a menu in a group context chose something other than their favorite item if another group member has already selected that item (Ariely and Levav 2000). In that situation, choosing something different from what another person had chosen allows consumers to get information about additional options as well as to assert their uniqueness. Similar results emerge in a cross-cultural context, in which members of individualistic cultures and those primed to be individualistic exhibit variety-seeking among decision rules in order to assert their uniqueness (Kim and Drolet 2003).

Implications and future research directions

The desire for variety is a strong motivation in consumer decision-making. Sometimes this desire for variety is normative – the items that the varied sequences contain are actually the most-liked items. At other times, the desire for variety is so strong that less-liked items are included in the consumption experience and the overall pleasure derived from consumption is lower than it could be. Whereas previous work has focused on whether variety-seeking behavior exists and the antecedents of variety-seeking behavior, we focus here on both the antecedents and consequences of variety-seeking. Specifically, we suggest that variety-seeking behavior often fails to maximize the utility summed across the moments of consumption although it may allow people to obtain other types of outcomes (e.g., to fulfill a desire for uniqueness or to create better retrospective memories).

It will be useful for researchers to develop theories that measure the impact of variety-seeking behavior across a range of outcomes. For example, some of the variables we have suggested here include self-image or self-presentational benefits of variety-seeking, the utility from memory of the consumption episode, and the more common measure of consumption utility. Investigating a broad array of goals and benefits that could be served by variety-seeking behavior is important because it is likely that different people incorporate variety for different reasons or to different degrees. For example, perhaps those with a promotions focus seek variety to explore new options, whereas those with a prevention focus seek variety because they think this is what others believe they ought to do; or perhaps those with a prevention orientation seek less variety than those with a promotion focus simply because they are risk-averse (Pham and Higgins, this volume).

In the sections that follow, we discuss a number of additional questions that could be explored in future research:

(1) When are those who seek variety in fact evaluated favorably by others and when might they be evaluated *less* favorably by others if they choose variety?
(2) What leads people to offer so much variety to others and how can this amount be reduced so that people are not overwhelmed by the amount of variety with which they are presented?
(3) How can one navigate high-variety choice offerings without choosing too much variety for oneself?
(4) What are the implications of variety-seeking for highly important, high-involvement domains?

We believe that each of these questions represents a currently under-researched area that would benefit from more empirical investigation.

When are variety-seekers evaluated favorably?

There is some evidence (Ratner and Kahn 2002) that people are in fact perceived more favorably when they select variety. However, it will be important to explore conditions under which observers perceive variety-seeking to reflect negative traits (such as disloyalty or indecisiveness) rather than open-mindedness or uniqueness. At what point do people perceive that another person has chosen too much variety? If the observers know that the decision-maker has knowingly selected less-liked items, will they consider that behavior to be irrational or will they consider it evidence of flexibility?

More generally, under what conditions does the set of options chosen reflect too much variety? To obtain some insight into this question, we conducted an exploratory, open-ended study in which we asked people to provide examples in which someone else would be choosing "too much variety." The most-frequently listed response indicated that having multiple romantic partners simultaneously was too much variety, clearly expressing preference for individuals who are willing to commit. Analogously, this may suggest that in certain marketing contexts if an initial commitment has been made to a brand (e.g., by signing up for a frequency program), then deviating from that product to other brands could be viewed by observers as choosing too much variety.

If the costs of seeking variety become too high (e.g., a high dollar amount or considerable effort), then it is likely that people will conclude that the variety-seeking behavior is unreasonable. In our exploratory study, one respondent listed "buying tank tops, T-shirts, long sleeve Ts, and sweaters at one time (when they're full price)" as examples of too much variety, and another listed "buying three colors of the same overpriced shoes." Another responded having "different video-game systems," suggesting that the costs of maintaining two different systems would be excessive for the marginal benefit of variety. Similarly, it may be that multiple romantic relationships are considered excessive, not because of a moral preference for commitment, but because of the high costs associated with maintaining the various relationships.

These examples suggest the need for the development of an overall framework that predicts when change is perceived to be optimal versus when consistency is desirable. There is a well-established literature in psychology on cognitive consistency that shows that individuals prefer that their many beliefs about the world (including other people) fit together (Festinger 1957), and that when there is a need to adjust one's own behaviors based on another's actions, it is helpful for the other person's behaviors to be predictable (Thibaut and Kelley 1959). For example, subordinates rate their superiors negatively to the extent that these supervisors engage in variable behavior (Aldag and Brief 1977). A high level of variety-seeking in jobs (identified as "job changes" by one of our respondents) also is not evaluated as favorably. But in other domains, observers expect people to exhibit more variety-seeking (less consistency). For example, seeking high amounts of variety in cuisine is often described as a good thing (in our exploratory study, many gave food examples such as "someone who always eats the same thing without trying new things" or "refuses to buy anything but two specific vegetables" as choosing too little variety). It may be that even in situations where consistency is at first preferable, such as in career development or romantic relationships, if a meaningful connection between the events could be established (for example, that a series of seemingly unrelated jobs enabled the person to develop their skills in managing new technologies), the variety might be lauded.

How to reduce the amount of variety presented to others?

Related to the issue of how much variety people expect others to seek is the issue of how much variety people provide when constructing choice sets for others. Observation in the marketplace shows that there has been a trend towards bigger and bigger assortments (Kahn and McAlister 1997). Large assortment strategies can backfire, however, if the complexity causes information overload such that a customer feels overwhelmed and dissatisfied, or chooses not to make a choice at all (Broniarczyk *et al.* 1998; Huffman and Kahn 1998; Iyengar and Lepper 2000). Clearly, one reason these assortments have grown so large is that retailers feel that customization or catering to everyone's unique tastes will result in market advantages. Notwithstanding, the growth in retail assortments may have to do with retailers' desires to cater to the variety required within each individual as well. In this latter case, retailers need to estimate how much variety each consumer will want. Some research has shown (Ratner and Kahn 2002), that there is an overestimation bias in these types of situations, such that people tend to choose a larger variety of items when choosing for others rather than for themselves. In particular, Ratner and Kahn found in one study that participants indicated that they would choose a greater number of different appetizer types for their peers than for themselves.

Further inquiry may help us determine why people tend to overestimate others' preferred amount of variety and help identify the natural boundary conditions for this effect as well. For example, the tendency to offer a wider assortment of items should diminish if it is known that the recipient has very strong favorites within the set. It will be useful to explore what mechanisms lead people to mispredict how much variety others want, and as a result better understand what types of feedback will help people determine the optimal amount of variety to offer. Perhaps people think that others' optimum stimulation levels are higher than they actually are, or perhaps the rate of others' satiation of favorites is miscalibrated.

It may be that even if people correctly assess how much variety others want, they may want to portray their own open-mindedness and creativity by presenting others with a varied set. For example, if a Hawaiian tour guide knows that a vacationer likes beach time the most, will the vacationer respond to the tour guide more favorably if he or she prints out only a list of "the island's best beaches" or, if in addition to the island's best beaches, the tour guide also prints a list of other non-beach activities? We suspect that the vacationer may provide positive feedback to the tour guide who offers more options, even if the individual is unlikely to take advantage of those options (Shin and Ariely 2004). Thus, it is likely that the desire to offer large choice sets is reinforced by the reactions of customers who say that they appreciate the large set. Perhaps if the tour guide receives feedback that vacationers become overwhelmed by too many choices, the guide will offer a more narrow range of options to customers in the future.

How to reduce the amount of variety chosen for oneself?

The finding that people are often overwhelmed by high-variety choice sets has generated considerable interest in better understanding conditions in which consumers will be able to manage such decisions. For example, it has been shown that people are better able to navigate a high-variety choice set when they know what they are looking for or have an ideal product in mind (Chernev 2003). Other research (Morales *et al.*, forthcoming) has shown that consumers' perceptions of variety and satisfaction with an assortment are dependent upon how a product category is organized, both internally by the consumer (mental schemas or shopping goals) and externally by the retailer (display organization or filtering mechanisms).

Future research should examine repeated-choice contexts (in which individuals can select more than one item from the set) as well as the more commonly studied single-choice contexts. It certainly would be in the interest of managers of a currently favored brand to communicate to consumers that they should not seek variety (e.g., to convey that variety-seeking away from their brand is a negative behavior that conveys inconsistency rather than the positive traits that consumers often associate with variety-seeking behavior). Future research could examine what types of manipulations will encourage individuals to stick with their favorites when making repeated choices over time. For example, will individuals learn to choose less variety in a supermarket after reading about the Simonson results about people's tendency to choose too much variety? If so, it will be important also to assess the impact of reduced variety-seeking on well-being: Are people happier in real-time because they are consuming more of their favorite items, or do they regret having forgone the varied set of items, which might have left them with less-liked flavors but feeling that they were more exciting people? The extent to which people derive utility from variety-seeking, like other consumption behaviors, may be influenced by the attributions people make about their own traits based on their behaviors (see Khan *et al.*, this volume). More generally, it will be interesting to explore the roles of affect and cognition in variety-seeking behavior: Do people feel that they would be happier if they chose less variety, but in fact end up choosing less-pleasing items based on beliefs about other consequences of their choices (e.g., the belief that experiencing less pleasure now will enable them to maximize enjoyment in the future)? If so, then factors that increase one's focus on affect (Shiv and Fedorikhin 1999; Shiv *et al.*, this volume) should decrease levels of variety-seeking.

What are the implications of variety-seeking behavior for high-involvement categories?

In most of the research that we have presented, the desire for variety has been explored in hedonic or low-involvement product categories. We believe that the desire for variety extends to utilitarian and high-involvement domains as well, and future research should explore these other contexts. Presumably if the quest for variety encourages people to include sub-optimal selections, there may be costs both at the individual level and the societal level.

Preliminary evidence suggests that a desire to seek variety, even across arbitrary dimensions, can lead people to make decisions that undermine other important goals. This is consistent with the results described earlier regarding people's tendency to distribute financial aid fairly evenly across whatever income groups had been presented (Fox *et al.* 2004); those making the financial allocation decisions seemed willing to overrule their beliefs that financial aid should be given primarily to lower-income students when presented with arbitrary partitions of the higher-income groups. Similarly, most universities and corporations believe that a diverse student body or employee base is preferable to one that involves people that are all similar to each other. In these cases, there is a belief that there is an inherent value to diversification. It will be useful to investigate the extent to which variety-seeking behavior in these high-involvement or utilitarian domains leads to optimal or sub-optimal decision-making. For example, although diversity along many dimensions may greatly enrich life on a college campus, there may be specific dimensions where variety is less valuable. The desire for a diverse population on a salient but unimportant dimension (e.g., a desire not to admit more than two people from any particular high school), could lead members of a selection committee to pass over candidates who actually are more diverse on more meaningful dimensions (e.g., life challenges experienced). Preliminary laboratory experiments (Avramov and Kahn, in process) that studied the college admissions process have found evidence of a variety-seeking bias caused by arbitrary bracketing based on geographic origin; research participants focused on maximizing high school diversity rather than attending to other meaningful attributes of each candidate. Indeed, college admissions policies that seek diversity across high schools as a way to obtain racial diversity – such as a policy in Texas to admit to public universities any high school student in the state who graduates in the top 10 percent of his or her high school – can become lightning rods for controversy, as critics perceive that the high-school diversity policy precludes admissions committees from considering other important student characteristics (Glater 2004).

These results suggest that variety-seeking behavior is not necessarily reduced for high-involvement decisions. We suspect that decision-makers making important allocation decisions (e.g., managers choosing how much money to allocate to projects; governments deciding how much aid to allocate to needy countries) may show the same desire to seek variety that has been demonstrated in the studies reviewed here.

Conclusions

We suggest in this chapter that the consequences of variety-seeking behavior are as complex as its antecedents. Our focus has been on ways in which variety-seeking behavior often fails to maximize the pleasure reported during the consumption episode or how such behavior leads people to select lower-ranked items. However, if the relevant outcomes are broadened to include other elements such as self-image, self-presentation, and memories of the experience, we may find that variety-seeking behavior accomplishes many different goals. Circumstances under which including variety does or does not achieve these many objectives will be an important area for further study.

Acknowledgments

We would like to thank Aimee Drolet, Nathan Novemsky, Itamar Simonson, and the editors for their helpful comments on this manuscript. We also gratefully acknowledge support from a Wharton-SMU Research Center grant from Singapore Management University to Barbara E. Kahn and the Cato Center for Applied Business Research Fund to Rebecca K. Ratner.

References

Abelson, R. P. and Levi, A. (1985) "Decision-making and decision theory," in G. Lindzey and E. Aronson (eds) *The Handbook of Social Psychology*, Vol. 1, New York: Random House: 231–309.
Aldag, R. J. and Brief, A. P. (1977) "Relationships between leader behavior variability indices and subordinate responses," *Personnel Psychology* 30 (Fall): 419–426.
Ariely, D. and Levav, J. (2000) "Sequential choice in group settings: Taking the road less traveled and less enjoyed," *Journal of Consumer Research* 27 (December): 279–290.

Bass, F. M., Pessemier, E. A., and Lehmann, D. R. (1972) "An experimental study of relationships between attitudes, brand preference and choice," *Behavorial Science* 17 (November): 532–541.

Berlyne, D. E. (1960) *Conflict, Arousal and Curiosity*, New York: McGraw Hill.

Birch, L. L. and Marlin, D. W. (1982) "I don't like it; I never tried it: Effects of exposure on two-year old children's food preferences," *Appetite* 3 (December): 353–360.

Brickman, P. and D'Amato, B. (1975) "Exposure effects in a free-choice situation," *Journal of Personality and Social Psychology* 32 (September): 415–420.

Broniarczyk, S. M., Hoyer, W. D., and McAlister, L. (1998) "Consumers' perceptions of the assortment offered in a grocery category: The impact of item reduction," *Journal of Marketing Research* 35 (May): 166–176.

Chernev, A. (2003) "When more is less and less is more: The role of ideal point availability and assortment in choice," *Journal of Consumer Research* 30 (September): 170–183.

Chow, Y. S., Moriguti S., Robbins, H., and Samuels, S. M. (1964) "Optimal selection based on relative rank (the 'secretary problem')," *Israel Journal of Mathematics* 2: 81–90.

Coombs, C. and Avrunin, G. S. (1977) "Single-peaked functions and the theory of preference," *Psychological Review* 84 (March): 216–230.

Dellu, F., Piazza, P. V., Mayo, W., Le Moal, M. *et al.* (1996) "Novelty-seeking in rats: Biobehavioral characteristics and possible relationship with the sensation-seeking trait in man," *Neuropsychobiology* 34(3): 136–145.

Drolet, A. (2002) "Inherent rule variability in consumer choice: Changing rules for change's sake," *Journal of Consumer Research* 29 (December): 293–305.

Faison, E. W. J. (1977) "The neglected variety drive," *Journal of Consumer Research* 4 (December): 172–175.

Festinger, L. (1957) *A Theory of Cognitive Dissonance*, Stanford, CA: Stanford University Press.

Fox, C. R., Ratner, R. K., and Lieb, D. (2004) "How subjective grouping of options influences choice and allocation: Diversification bias and the phenomenon of partition dependence," Unpublished manuscript, the Anderson School at UCLA.

Foxall, G. R. (1993) "Consumer behavior as an evolutionary process," *European Journal of Marketing* 27(8): 46–58.

Glater, J. D. (2004) "Diversity plan shaped in Texas is under attack," *New York Times* (June 13): 1.

Herman, C. P. and Mack, D. (1975) "Restrained and unrestrained eating," *Journal of Personality* 43 (December): 647–660.

Herrnstein, R. J. (1990a) "Behavior, reinforcement, and utility," *Psychological Science* 1 (July): 217–223.

Herrnstein, R. J. (1990b) "Rational choice theory: Necessary but not sufficient," *American Psychologist* 45 (March): 356–367.

Hetherington, M. M., Bell, A., and Rolls, B. J. (2000) "Effects of repeat consumption on pleasantness, preference, and intake," *British Food Journal* 102(7): 507–521.

Huffman, C. and Kahn, B. E. (1998) "Variety for sale: Mass customization or mass confusion?" *Journal of Retailing* 74 (Winter): 491–513.

Iyengar, S. S. and Lepper, M.R. (2000) "When choice is demotivating," *Journal of Personality and Social Psychology* 6: 995–1006.

Kahn, B. E. and Isen, A. M. (1993) "The influence of positive affect on variety-seeking among safe, enjoyable products," *Journal of Consumer Research* 20 (September): 257–270.

Kahn, B. E., and Lehmann, D. R. (1991) "Modeling choice among assortment," *Journal of Retailing* 67 (Fall): 274–299.

Kahn, B. E. and McAlister, L. (1997) *Grocery Revolution: The New Focus on the Consumer*, Reading, MA: Addison Wesley, Longman.

Kahn, B. E., Ratner, R. K., and Kahneman, D. (1997) "Patterns of hedonic consumption over time," *Marketing Letters* 8(1): 85–96.

Kahn, B. E. and Wansink, B. (2004) "The influence of assortment structure on perceived variety and consumption quantities," *Journal of Consumer Research* 30 (March).

Kahneman, D. and Snell, J. S. (1992) "Predicting a changing taste: Do people know what they will like?" *Journal of Behavioral Decision-Making* 5(3): 187–200.

Kim, H. and Drolet, A. (2003), "Choices and self-expression: A cultural analysis of variety-seeking," *Journal of Personality and Social Psychology* 85 (August): 373–382.

Lancaster, K. (1971) *Consumer Demand: A New Approach*, New York: Columbia University Press.

Loewenstein, G. F. (1987) "Anticipation and the valuation of delaying consumption," *Economic Journal* 97: 666–684.

Loewenstein, G. F. and Prelec, D. (1993) "Preferences for sequences of outcomes," *Psychological Review* 100(1): 91–108.

Loewenstein, G. F. and Sicherman, N. (1991) "Do workers prefer increasing wage profiles?" *Journal of Labor Economics* 9(1): 67–84.

McAlister, L. (1982) "A dynamic attribute satiation model of variety-seeking behavior," *Journal of Consumer Research* 9 (September): 141–150.

Menon, S. and Kahn, B. E. (1995) "The impact of context on variety-seeking in product choices," *Journal of Consumer Research* 22 (December): 285–295.

Menon, S. and Kahn, B. E. (2002) "Cross-category effects of induced arousal and pleasure on the internet hopping experience," *Journal of Retailing* 78 (Spring): 31–40.

Mitchell, D. J., Kahn, B. E., and Knasko, S. C. (1995) "There's something in the air: Effects of congruent or incongruent ambient odor on consumer decision-making," *Journal of Consumer Research* 22 (September): 229–238.

Morales, A., Kahn, B. E., McAlister, L. and Broniarczyk, S. M. (forthcoming) "Perceptions of assortment variety: The effects of congruency between consumers' internal and retailers' external organization," *Journal of Retailing*.

Novemsky, N. and Ratner, R. K. (2003) "The time course and impact of consumers' erroneous beliefs about hedonic contrast effects," *Journal of Consumer Research* 29: 507–516.

Pessemier, E. (1978) "Stochastic properties of changing preferences," *American Economic Review* 68(2): 380–385.

Raju, P. S (1980) "Optimum stimulation level: Its relationship to personality demographics and exploratory behavior," *Journal of Consumer Research* (December): 272–282.

Ratner, R. K. and Kahn, B. E. (2002) "The impact of private versus public consumption on variety-seeking behavior," *Journal of Consumer Research* (September): 246–258.

Ratner, R. K., Kahn, B. E., and Kahneman, D. (1999) "Choosing less-preferred experiences for the sake of variety," *Journal of Consumer Research* (June): 1–15.

Read, D. and Loewenstein, G. (1995) "Diversification bias: Explaining the discrepancy in variety-seeking between combined and separated choices," *Journal of Experimental Psychology: Applied* (March): 34–49.

Rolls, E. T. and de Waal, W. L. (1985) "Long term sensory-specific satiety: Evidence from an Ethiopian refugee camp," *Physiology and Behavior* (June): 1017–1020.

Rolls, B. J., Rolls, E. T., Rowe, E. A., and Sweeney, K. (1981a) "Sensory specific satiety in man," *Physiology and Behavior* (July): 137–142.

Rolls, B. J., Rowe, E. A., Rolls, E. T., Kindston, B., Megson, A., and Gunary, R. (1981b) "Variety in a meal enhances food intake in man," *Physiology and Behavior* (February): 215–221.

Rolls, B. J., Van Dujvenvoorde, P. M., and Rowe, E. A. (1983) "Variety in the diet enhances intake in a meal and contributes to the development of obesity in the rat," *Physiology and Behavior* 31(July): 21–27.

Ross, W. and Simonson, I. (1991) "Evaluation of pairs of experience: A preference for happy endings," *Journal of Behavioral Decision-Making* 4: 273–282.

Shin, J. and Ariely, D. (2004) "Keeping doors open: The effect of unavailability on incentives to keep options viable," *Management Science* 50(5): 575–586.

Shiv, B. and Fedorikhin, A. (1999) "Heart and mind in conflict: Interplay of affect and cognition in consumer decision-making," *Journal of Consumer Research* 26 (December): 278–282.

Silberberg, E. (1978) *The Structure of Economics*, New York: McGraw-Hill.

Simonson, I. (1990) "The effect of purchase quantity and timing on variety-seeking behavior," *Journal of Marketing Research* 27 (May): 150–162.

Steenkamp, J. B. and Baumgartner, H. (1992) "The role of optimum stimulation level in exploratory consumer behavior," *Journal of Consumer Research* 19 (December): 434–448.

Thibaut, J. W. and Kelley, H. H. (1959) *The Social Psychology of Groups*, New Brunswick, NJ: Transaction Publishers.

Tversky, A. and Griffin, D. (1991) "Endowment and contrast in judgments of well-being," in R. J. Zeckhauser (ed.) *Strategy and Choice*, Cambridge, MA: MIT Press: 297–318.

Venkatesan, M. (1973) "Cognitive consistency and novelty seeking," in S. Ward and T. S. Robertson (eds) *Consumer Behavior: Theoretical Sources*, Englewood Cliffs, NJ: Prentice-Hall: 355–384.

7 Consuming fashion as flexibility

Metaphor, cultural mood, and materiality

Susan B. Kaiser and Karyl Ketchum

To consume fashion and to perform fashionability is to access a complex and highly flexible system with which to negotiate meaning and navigate ambiguity. In this chapter, we are interested in the "why" of fashion consumption, with "fashion" referring to the collective process through which consumers participate in creating and altering "strong norms" (Crane 2000) about how to look and dress at a given point of time, within a given population (Kaiser *et al.* 1991). Fashion is a concept that applies to a wide range of consumer goods (e.g., clothes, food cars, various industrial products) and activities, as well as to science, media, and ideas in general (see Blumer 1969; Davis 1992). Here, however, we focus on the processes and strategies associated with consumers' ongoing modifications of their bodies and appearance styles.

Our goal is to suggest a model (see Figure 7.1) that provides a meta-theoretical framing for understanding the "why" issues associated with fashion consumption. This model highlights what we see as some of the key assumptions and concepts underlying fashion-theorizing, consumer discourses on fashion, and industrial discourse. Although we hope that the model will be useful in a wide range of contexts, especially in a global economy, we recognize that the producing, distributing, and consuming "playing field" is not level – aesthetically, culturally, economically, geographically, nationally, physically, or socially. Indeed, our intention is to offer this model as a vehicle to think through the complex ways in which inequalities coincide uneasily with identities, meanings, and pleasures.

Because fashion is a highly visual event, we have also created what we think of as a series of visual mappings designed to reflect on the movement of fashion through the three frames of metaphor, cultural mood, and materiality as they are developed within this chapter. As depicted in Figure 7.1 and throughout our images (Figures 7.2–7.4; for more details and versions in color, see http://textiles. ucdavis.edu/flexibility/), we argue that *flexibility* is central to an understanding of fashion consumption; indeed, it is probably what makes the fashion system – and our ability to theorize it – work at all.

We begin and end this chapter with discussions of flexibility as a meta-theory as well as a metaphor for fashion. Although flexibility has rarely been highlighted in theoretical discourse on fashion directly, we argue that it is an underlying assumption that becomes apparent if, as Guy *et al.* (2001) might put it, we "unpick the

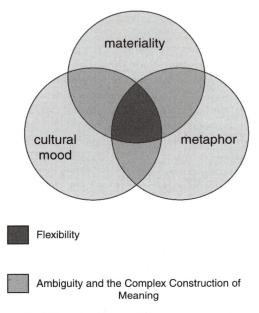

Figure 7.1 Fashioning flexibility: the intersections among metaphor, cultural mood, and materiality.

seams" of fashion theory. Further, we argue that flexibility represents a key intersection – a crosscutting theme – in pursuing understandings of fashion consumption. Notably, it becomes a relatively emphatic part of fashion's overlapping systems of production, distribution, and consumption.

Flexibility can be seen as related to *ambiguity* – a central concept in fashion theory (Wilson 1985; Enninger 1985; Davis 1985, 1992; Kaiser *et al.* 1991; Kaiser 1997). Contributing to flexibility as an intersectional force, we suggest, is its relationship to ambiguity. That is, flexibility becomes a "centering" strategy that enables navigating ambiguity. In many ways, flexibility places a positive and strategic spin on fashion's rampant ambiguity so as to make it more palatable, if not productive, in everyday life.

As shown in Figure 7.1, we argue that fashion makes and re-makes meaning in and through the ambiguous interplay among *metaphor* (abstract meanings and systems of signification), *cultural mood* (collective emotions), and *materiality* (the body, political economy, and the transformation of natural and synthetic materials into consumer products for the body). In the following sections, we discuss each of these concepts in turn, and then close by indicating how and why (and the limits to which) flexibility is a useful, meta-theoretical concept that helps to interpret the "why" underlying much of the academic, industrial, and popular discourse on fashion.

In proposing the model shown in Figure 7.1, we do not mean to reify abstractions to the point of nullifying diverse living, producing, and consuming bodies – bodies that are gendered, classed, raced, sexualized, and otherwise marked (and unmarked) in many ways. Nor is it our intent to pursue an in-depth analysis of individual consumers' psychological motives for consuming fashion, although neither do we want to exclude them as important contributors to the model. As O'Guinn and Muñiz (in this volume) and Holt (in this volume) reveal, there is a critical tension – within the consumer behavior and marketing fields – between psychological and socio-cultural frameworks; they argue for more attention to the latter – and, implicitly, for more connection between the two. We agree; fashion needs to be understood as a complex and profound interplay among micro and macro (and meso) frameworks (see Kaiser *et al.* 1995).

Following and extending the arguments by Polhemus (2000) and Muggleton (2000), we argue that "style surfing" goes beyond the realm of subcultural style and pertains more broadly to the "pick and mix" aesthetic in which many contemporary consumers find themselves engaging on a day-to-day basis, to the extent that resources or interests support such an aesthetic. This aesthetic process would not be possible without a sense of flexibility – a strategy that consumers use to navigate ambiguity – to negotiate the complex intersections depicted in Figure 7.1. In part, it is exactly because of the primacy of these intersectional meanings to fashion that we turn to the construction of images (and everyday looks or appearance styles) as a strategy. While the signifieds within an image can be slippery, within them we sense the complex multidimensional relationships between parts and wholes and the inflection and even volatility of identity, time, space, and the body. In a way similar to fashion, an image's "inner articulations" (Simmel 1904) define it, become what "it" *is*. The creation of these meanings is necessarily embodied, contingent, and political.

Flexibility

The term flexibility is complex and multidimensional. It refers to the capability to be bent, especially repeatedly; it also connotes the ability to adapt to new, diverse, and changing requirements, including external influences. At the same time, it can mean moving or tensing by means of contraction, as in the case of muscles that yield to the influence of exertion (*Oxford English Dictionary* 2004). Clothed bodies doing yoga come to mind as contemporary (and currently fashionable) visual and embodied metaphors of adapting, bending, and strengthening simultaneously. And on a more abstract level, we might even think of the flexibility of a form, texture or color as it moves through the contemporary moment, manifesting itself in, on, and through an increasing multitude of objects and materials – and gaining cultural capital – through *intertextuality*. The flexibility that enables intertextuality contributes importantly to fashion's feeling of an aesthetic "language of the moment" (note the intertextuality of form within the images of metaphor and cultural mood in Figures 7.2 and 7.3, respectively).

In-depth discussions of flexibility *per se* are scant in fashion theory, but the implication or assumption of flexibility surfaces repeatedly. Among the specific references are Wilson's (1985: 14–15) remark, in *Adorned in Dreams*, that fashion is "one of the most accessible and one of the most flexible means" available to consumers to express the ambiguities of everyday life: ambiguities surrounding capitalism ("with its great wealth and squalor"), identity ("of the relation of self to body and self to the world"), and art ("its purpose and meaning").

Studies of consumer discourse tend to be replete with references to the "contextual flexibility" of favorite articles of clothing (Kaiser *et al.* 1993; Kaiser 1997). These are the kinds of clothes that "travel" fluidly from one look to another or from one situation to the next. In a study of women's negotiations of business dress, Patricia Kimle and Mary Lynn Damhorst (1997: 63) developed a model to acknowledge the complex and "multiple meaning components [required to] facilitate the creative exploration of self-expression within flexible and vague boundaries."

Flexibility can be seen as a way of both articulating and navigating ambiguity – not only for consumers, but also for producers and retailers who need to adapt to changing demand and relevance. Focusing more specifically on the production end of the equation in *The Conquest of Cool*, Frank (1997) includes a chapter entitled "Fashion and Flexibility." His larger argument is that both menswear and advertising suffered from the doldrums in the 1950s and then experienced " 'revolutions' in their own right during the 1960s, with vast changes in corporate practice, in productive flexibility, and especially in that intangible phenomenon known as 'creativity' – and in both cases well before the counterculture appeared on the mass media scene" (Frank 1997: 27). Accordingly, he argues that in 1967 and 1968, advertising and menswear executives were well poised to capitalize upon the counterculture. At the same time, men's fashions could not have changed without a shift in the consciousness of adult men who could actually afford to buy the clothes associated with what the media termed as the "peacock revolution" of the late 1960s and early 1970s. Frank focuses primarily in his "Fashion and Flexibility" chapter on the awareness of retailers and manufacturers of the need "to make their production and buying techniques more flexible to accommodate the vagaries of fashion" (ibid.: 191). Those retailers and manufacturers who were most adaptive to change were "capable of great flexibility and uninhibited by Theory X corporate strictures" (ibid.: 198).

More generally, Harvey (1989) describes flexibility as the *modus operandi* of late capitalism. He distinguishes the contemporary, global model of flexibility (e.g., flexible accumulation, flexible manufacturing and contracting, flexible labor) from the earlier modern capitalist systems in which a Fordist, assembly line model operated. Whereas the Fordist system assumed that workers would buy the goods they produced, no such assumption underlies the late capitalist model – a model prone to a "disconnect" between production and consumption. Rather, the latter system's "flexible" workforce (one that is part-time or seasonal, or is hired and fired by sub-contractors) contributes to profitability as well as to global competitiveness.

Ong (1999) makes the case that it is important to understand the extent to which the new, transnational "human practices and cultural logics" of capitalism "induce subjects to respond fluidly and opportunistically to changing political-economic conditions." Somewhat similarly, Slater (1997: 189) argues that "flexibilization" extends well beyond the production line, influencing the "rapid and interconnected flows of information from points of sale through material suppliers (as in the idea of 'Benetton capitalism')." The business strategies of global fashion producers/retailers H&M, Zara, and GAP represent such models of flexibilization. This flexibility, afforded at least in part by new technologies, can foster customized products sold to highly segmented markets.

Also part of the agility of companies to compete is the concept of just-in-time production. According to Adair-Heeley (1991), just-in-time production means beating the competition by creating a culture of ongoing improvement – that is, by anticipating, and being adaptive to, the need for change, before it is too late. Reducing lead times and increasing flexibly, he argues, makes forecasting easier and hence more accurate.

So, in large part, advanced capitalist production has the objective of "flexibility and market responsiveness," so as to adapt quickly and strategically to consumer demand (Lowson *et al.* 1999). Also contributing to the market's flexibility is what Agins (1999) has identified as a breakdown of the traditional system of fashion into one of component parts – parts that are often branded. Flexibility can be seen as an interlocking theme between the production of branded separates (e.g., jeans, jackets, running shoes) and the ongoing accumulation of separates that require mixing and matching of new identities by consumers. Although the term "flexible accumulation" is used widely in global capitalist circles to encompass the creative and strategic opportunities involved in the gathering and managing of corporate capital, it can also be seen as applying to the ongoing consumer process of wardrobe replenishment, to the extent that personal resources and inclination allow. To consume fashion is to produce "looks" or appearance styles, enabling consumers to create, mix, and match (or not). This mixing and matching, not surprisingly, contributes to the ambiguity of personal fashion statements.

Ambiguity

Ambiguity prevails as an explanatory concept in fashion theory (Stone 1962; Wilson 1985; Enninger 1985; Davis 1985, 1992; Kaiser *et al.* 1991; Kaiser 1997). As a mode of communication, appearance style is non-linear and Gestalt-like – a visual broadcast signal whose range of meaning is extremely variable. Stone (1962) has described how the richest meanings are negotiated through appearances that are ambiguous – that require mindful interpretations rather than shortcut perceptions (e.g., stereotypes).

Davis (1992: 5) described clothing's code as

> incipient . . . although it must necessarily draw on the conventional visual and tactile symbols of a culture, [it] does so allusively, ambiguously, and inchoately, so that the meanings evoked by the combinations and permutations of the code's key terms (fabric, texture, color, pattern, volume, silhouette, and occasion) are forever shifting or "in process."

As consumers mix and match separates, within and across brands, identities, and social groups and situations, the potential for ambiguity is likely to intensify.

Meaning seldom emerges without some degree of ambiguity. This is the "refreshing paradox" (Stone 1977) that enables individuals to direct their attention toward appearance style, to engage in interpretive processes, and to participate in the social construction of meaning. According to Stone's (1962) analysis of appearance, ambiguity lies somewhere in between non-sense (where no meaning is shared; it is a "fly by") and boredom (where the meanings are so taken for granted or prescribed that little new happens in terms of interpretation). Ambiguity, it seems, can lead to the richest constructions of meaning, because it requires negotiation; it takes effort that is more mindful, creative, and constructive (Kaiser *et al.* 1991). Ambiguity contributes to "instructive confusions" (Levine 1985: 73).

Some consumers may appreciate the open possibilities – for personal style creation and interpretation alike – that ambiguity affords. For example, Hodkinson (2002) describes how goth style can be characterized as portraying a kind of (somewhat feminized) sexual ambiguity, with males and female alike wearing considerable amounts of makeup and jewelry, as well as clothing styles such as fishnet tights, frilly shirts, velvet jackets, and mesh tops (48–49). But consumer style ambiguity can be more subtle; in a study of professional women, Kimle and Damhorst (1997) found that they use style choices strategically to mediate between attractiveness and professionalism, carefully avoiding "danger zones" (e.g., extreme sexiness, cold conservatism) as they create hybrid constructions of identity that express preferred ways of being and succeeding. Similarly, Kunkel (1999) studied women's negotiations of the contradictions between femininity and feminism through style. And, Kaiser *et al.* (2001) found that academic women use style as a kind of strategic ambiguity. One professor shared the following thoughts:

> I can actually in my appearance play out all of the contradictions and complexities of my identity . . . How do you signify a combination of intellectual authority – a kind of sense of confidence of knowing what you're doing – with playfulness, you know, with questioning, with openness?
>
> (Kaiser *et al.* 2001: 133)

On the other hand, not all consumers revel in the sense of open-endedness, polysemy, or vagueness that ambiguity can generate in the minds of wearers and perceivers alike. Solomon (2003) notes that too many choices can lead to a paradox within consumer space; some consumers, at least, would appreciate a little less chaos and a little more guidance or direction. Nevertheless, in contemporary consumer space, consumers tend to make their own connections and to participate actively in the creation of their own "buzz" (e.g., through online communities), rather than passively receiving meanings from corporate hype.

As depicted in Figure 7.1, we are suggesting that ambiguity emerges from the complex overlap among the spheres of metaphor, cultural mood, and materiality. That is, these three realms of experience do not coincide easily or readily. Rather, it is through their ambiguous confluence that producers and consumers alike use flexibility as a strategic, if not a creative, device. Whereas ambiguity can be variously seen as open-ended, vague, multi-faceted, or frustrating, depending on one's point of view, flexibility can become a concept of maneuverability, adaptability, even hope. (See de Mello and MacInnis, in this volume, for a helpful discussion of hope and consumption.) This is not to say that ambiguity is necessarily negative and flexibility is necessarily positive, but rather to indicate that the latter is more likely to be *perceived* as a useful strategy for the articulation and negotiation of meaning, or even for doing everyday life.

Together, ambiguity and flexibility enable connecting and joining elements that would otherwise be disparate. At the same time, fashion has the capability to express that which culture cannot otherwise communicate clearly in words (see McCracken 1988). In Slack's (1996) discussion of articulation as a theory and method in cultural studies, she notes the importance of connecting, joining, and expressing that which otherwise might be disparate elements in order to illuminate what is going on in society. The articulation of emergent identities and meanings is accomplished, and limited, through metaphoric systems of meaning, through the collective moods or emotions that render a sense of cultural resonance, and through (last but certainly not least) the actual materiality of bodies and commodities. The following sections take up each of these three themes, pointing in the process to their complex intersections.

Metaphor

Making sense of ambiguity is an ongoing project – the root of much of the "why" of fashion consumption. Whereas language often locks us into binary constructions (i.e., mind versus body, production versus consumption, masculine versus feminine), the flexible accumulation of fashionable commodities allows consumers to articulate meanings and feelings metaphorically. Fashion offers a unique opportunity for an emphatic, albeit ambiguous, insistence of identity and community.

Inasmuch as fashion – and the performance of fashionability – accesses a complex and highly flexible metaphoric system, it enables the social construction of meaning, on an ongoing basis. Issues of time, cultural space, and identity/community all intervene in this construction, and from a consumer point of view, fashion is one of the key arenas that allow us – provisionally, of course – to represent ourselves and who we are becoming (and, somewhat ambiguously, who we hope we are *not* becoming; see Freitas *et al.* 1997) on an everyday basis. This system enables the articulation of self in relation to others at given points of time, within given cultural spaces. All of this is accomplished with the materials of consumption – materials that semiotically encode colors, textures, shapes, and combinations in ways that may come to *mean* something that often cannot quite be articulated adequately in words (see Figure 7.2).

To the extent that culture entrusts clothing and fashion with messages that it cannot otherwise articulate (McCracken 1988), the challenge is left to consumers to construct their messages visually on an everyday basis. And yet consumers may

Figure 7.2 Fashion as metaphor. Visual metaphors create connections that enable new meanings to flourish, or wither, through the self-conscious and unlikely mapping of conceptual domains. These metaphors depend on a certain stability within the systems of meaning through which they emerge, while at the same time they intend to disturb those same systems . . . productively.

well find it difficult to express verbally just what it is that they are trying to say about themselves and their identities (Freitas *et al.* 1997; Kaiser 1997). Part of the *why* of the consumption of fashion revolves around the actual process of styling meaning – giving it form and texture, while always remaining within its prescribed terms. The visual and tactile, nonlinear, "broadcast"-like quality of meaning construction through the use of materials is not easy to achieve. Further complicating such meaning construction is the ongoing change that is negotiated simultaneously at multiple levels of interaction and that coincides with the process of doing everyday life in and through consumption (i.e., purchase, use, and ultimate disposal).

There are some distinctive elements of signification that pertain to fashion as a form of communication that is at once material and metaphoric. Fashion seems to establish connections and contradictions at one and the same time; in the process, the consumption of fashion may seem frenetic and illogical on some levels. But it also enables a sense of cultural order, of collective selection in order to feel current. All of this is highly "in the moment" – connecting the dots of style in order to express a sense of timeliness. It can be productive to take note of the ways in which this communication is both similar to, and yet different, from linguistic models.

Fashion and fashionability rely on history and "etymologization" (Jakobson 1990: 424) for intelligibility. Jakobson writes of this process in the context of linguistics and, following Gabelentz, notes how with the acquisition of a mother tongue, intuition and feeling *etymologize* without regard for historical linguistics. That is, native speakers of a language do not need to look up a word in the dictionary – turn to a historical linguistic record of the word – in order to understand the various inflections it has taken on by way of the history of its usage.

In resorting to a neologism, "etymologize," Jakobson draws our attention to the recalcitrant nature of language when asked to reflect upon its own processes. In addition, by mobilizing a noun – "etymology" ("the tracing of a word or other form back as far as possible in its own language and to its source," *Webster's New World College Dictionary* 2003: 467) – and transforming it into a verb, the primacy of time and movement (of *process*) is highlighted. Thus this etymologizing process is not simply one of noting provenance, but also one that requires its user to understand (although not necessarily consciously) the historically specific inflections taken on by a word/sign as it has evolved through time. In other words, the native speaker harnesses inflection intuitively. Interrogating such a process is no easy matter.

Like language, the successful performance of fashion/fashionability requires an intimate awareness of this same etymologizing process. Textures, forms, and colors etymologize in relation both to space (culture, community, ethnicity, subculture) and time (history). Yet, and unlike conventional uses of language, fashion goes the additional step of requiring that this movement manifests itself in a relation of newness, "tapping" the cultural present with just the right measure of subtlety and conviction. Success or failure is, of course, registered within cycles of desire, consumption, and spectacle – in other words, through consumer capitalism. As Debord asserts, "everything that appears is good; whatever that is good will appear" (1994: 15). Fashion moves in metaphoric relation with the cultural present; it shifts sign currents – trends – through its formulaic, constructing them as equal to the contemporary moment. It is a kind of hypertext formation that extends itself deeply into the semiotics of the cultural present through a genealogy of form, color, and texture.

We can also look to Jakobson's linguistic model for other clues that might offer productive ways to analyze communication and the "why" of consumption and fashion. According to Jakobson, in the linguistic model communication takes place within the register of *feeling*, outside and beyond the literal word or image and with a diligent eye directed back at the past. This "outside and beyond" is also the realm of metaphor. It is a register where meanings are dynamically forged outside of their presence and literalness. By way of the "outside and beyond" realm of metaphor, historical semiotic systems are accessed and, in the case of fashion/fashionability, the ability to insist upon the self through the consummate operations of these codes is made possible. In the course of communication, perhaps the success and the quality of these metaphoric operations constitute the premiere motivation for consumer participation in the semiotic, and the economic, cycles of fashion/fashionability. As Cameron (1999) reminds us, there is a powerful effect of shared intimacy that develops through the successful exchange of a metaphor (126). She directs us to the concept of "paraphraseability," as it was raised by Aristotle. This concept refers to "the degree of ease with which the meaning of a metaphor can be explained in literal language" (Cameron 1999: 126); the more complex the metaphor, the more it relies on an exclusivity of shared systems of meaning (histories, both recent and not), and the less "paraphraseable" it is. The less paraphraseable, the more profound and affirming – in terms of intimacy – is the communication.

Fashion/fashionability offers perhaps the quintessential medium through which to forge such bonds of intimacy and community, as its requirements are so highly complex. A successful interlocutor must not only recognize and decode the familiar, but also have enough of a sense of the entire system to recognize novel relationships among signs that somehow might "speak" of the cultural present – indeed, speak *fashionability* itself. To quote Barthes (1990: 26), "a system of signs is not founded on the relation of a signifier to a signified . . . but on the relation among the signifiers themselves." In signifying fashion, this relationship, or more importantly the lack of this relationship to the larger system – the novelty and cultural resonance of the signifier – becomes over-determined. The successful performance of fashion requires a degree of difference within the plane of the signifier, which triggers, in the mind of the interlocutor, recourse to the register of metaphor and, in turn, excites a trope that resonates structurally and uniquely within the contemporary cultural moment. This is complex, and its successful execution invigorating, as within this moment the "I" is recognized as present, even despite systems of signification that seem otherwise determined to erase it. The fashion/fashionability cycle is perhaps unique in offering such an opportunity. Consumption, in dialogue with fashionability, allows us to connect to each other and to the cultural present outside of linguistics. However, this is an ironic kind of backhanded movement that both reifies systems of hegemonic capitalism, consumption and spectacle, while also offering them a peculiar kind of redemption – even in the face of the brute nature of their materiality (e.g., flexible hiring and firing of garment workers, sweatshops, credit card debt, discrimination based on the materiality of the body, as in the case of racism).

Thus far we have discussed the role of metaphor within the processes of fashion in terms of two distinct roles: as a form: fashion = cultural present, and as a formulaic, whose successful execution promises an, albeit problematic, affirmation of self and community through intersubjectivity. We propose one additional figuration of metaphor in relation to fashion and consumption: fashion as mixed metaphor. This figuration enables a deeper understanding of the hybrid identities or inner articulations – the idea of working the "in-between" spaces, the vague boundaries, and the overlapping nature of gender, ethnicity, sexuality, class, along with various lifestyle choices – that become represented in and through appearance style (see, for example, Kimle and Damhorst 1997; Freitas *et al.* 1997; Muggleton 2000; Kaiser *et al.* 2001; Hodkinson 2002).

A metaphor maps one semiotic structure onto another, creating an opportunity for new articulations between them. When we mix metaphors this mapping becomes hyperbolic, and even volatile. In particular, it is the ability of fashion to join disparate metaphors (to *mix* metaphors) in a given clothing or appearance style that allows for complex, visual articulations and for creative negotiations of meaning. The consumption of fashion becomes a process of visual simultaneity, enabling the joint communication of previously disparate identities and temporal and spatial contexts. Through appearance style, fashion consumers become subjects who design and negotiate a sense of who, when, and where they *are* and *are becoming* – a process conditioned by a complex relationship with capital (both cultural and economic) and inflected by cultural mood.

Cultural mood

Fashion speaks openly of time, and under its breath, it requests a certain kind of collective subjectivity. As an emotive discourse, fashion enables the visual articulation of shifting, collective feelings and emotions (see Figure 7.3). Much of this articulation is "outside and beyond" literal meaning, as in the context of metaphoric meaning. So, there is a complex overlap or interplay between metaphor and cultural mood. But there is also a need for some analytical distinction. For example, Davis (1992) points to the need to delineate, as well as to study the overlap between, ambiguity (related to mixed metaphors) and ambivalence (related to

Figure 7.3 Fashion as cultural mood. The self is never present within the field of vision. Is it the certainty of this removal, or absence, that preconditions fashion as a medium through which we can "see" (metaphorically, literally) the present and yet remain somehow securely removed from it? Could this be some of fashion's anxious spirit?

cultural mood). Whereas the former refers to multiple messages relayed through processes of signification, the latter refers to mixed emotions or feelings. Figure 7.1 points to the delineation as well as the overlap between the two concepts, as does Figure 7.2 (in a more visual and abstract fashion).

More fundamentally, metaphor uses pre-existing (historical) sets of meanings and maps them onto each other in new ways that (when successful) encourage new understandings. On its own, metaphor has no interest in the direction this movement takes. It is unmotivated; it is only interested in relishing its ability to shift domains of knowledge. On the other hand, cultural mood is a highly motivated conceptual category. Its object is the present, and its focus is quite singular. So, within the shifting and amorphous realm of fashion, metaphor provides the ability to make the conceptual shifts among sign systems, while cultural mood provides the direction those shifts will take. They are separate, and yet imbricated, as depicted in the Venn diagram (Figure 7.1) and as suggested variously in Figures 7.2, and even 7.3 and 7.4.

Inasmuch as mood itself is "a prevailing but temporary state of mind or feeling," it has a temporal element, with an awareness that it will change. Mood also refers to a "pervading atmosphere or tone . . . that quality of a work of art or literature [or fashion] which evokes . . . a certain emotion or state of mind." In general, connotations associated with mood include time, change, and feelings that cannot easily be put into words. We use the concept of cultural mood to refer to the idea of experiences, feelings, and sentiments that resonate culturally and that get expressed through the visual arts, popular culture, media, films, and music, as well as fashion (and indeed, fashion is present within each of the other listed kinds of cultural representations). We are not referring here to the specific or shifting emotions of a given consumer, although there may well be an important relationship between psychological and social/cultural moods. That is to say, consumers – or at least subsets of consumers – are likely to experience some "similar yearnings, tensions, concerns, or discontents, which, regardless of how we apprehend them, seek some form of expression" (Davis 1992: 17).

There is a certain ambiguity in fashion's ability to evoke or to emote: to represent collective subjectivity – not in the sense of representing an existing reality, but rather in the sense of constituting or constructing the experience of reality. That is, through fashion one can conjure feelings or construct interpretations about what is "going on" in society. This process of representation is, in part, an articulation of collective mood(s). It is a somewhat vague and polysemous discourse – an ongoing visual conversation that derives and evokes its feelings from textures, colors, and forms that are disseminated so as to form a palpable feeling of the times. This discourse preconditions fashion's existence, and it is both an individual and a collective affair – a mechanism for identification as well as differentiation. It expresses the interplay between these dimensions through a sense of being in the moment, of having a sense of momentum: moving forward toward an uncertain future.

To the extent that fashion can be loosely equated with the *Zeitgeist*, or "spirit of the times," it can be described as a fluid spirit – a questioning spirit – indeed, an anxious spirit. There is an "unquietness" to fashion. Anxiety, according to Kierkegaard (1980: 197), is the "ambiguity of subjectivity." In the case of fashion, cultural anxiety can be described as the ambiguity of *collective* subjectivity, or even *inter*subjectivity. Cultural anxiety involves uncertain and uneasy dispositions, which are put into discourse, visually and ambiguously, through fashion. There is no resolution to this discourse. Rather, the logic of anxiety, according to Kierkegaard, lies in the need to articulate subjectivity, which itself lacks content. This is a subjectivity with a future orientation, as anxiety entails an impatient anticipation of a future whose signifiers are still floating freely. It is an experience or emotion of ambiguous transition, of looking toward the future with a feeling "in one's bones that a storm is approaching" (ibid.: 115).

For example, Arnold (2001) argues that high fashion designers of the 1990s articulated a "disquieting feeling of anxiety" alongside an obsession with nostalgia (i.e., references to the past) and excess (i.e., extravagance and luxurious escape):

> McQueen's statuesque models may have been dressed in couture luxury but they were often adorned with animal skulls or layered with torn leathers that spoke of death and threat. Photographers also brought notes of brutality to fashion magazines, both in Juergen Teller's and Corinne Day's realist depiction of models as fragile mortals rather than invincible superhumans and Sean Ellis's gothic images of dark fetishes.
>
> (Arnold 2001: xiii)

In some ways, then, fashion offers some ambiguous content to subjectivity as it plays with cultural anxieties. It makes anxieties material; it embodies them through an interplay of diverse ideas and possible moods. Yet from a consumptive perspective, there is even more to this story. Fashion and appearance style also provide visual materials and methods with which to frame or shape a discourse and its issues. For example, the appearance styles of tween or teen consumers may articulate cultural anxieties regarding sexuality or violence (Hethorn and Kaiser 1998; Kaiser 2003). That is, tween or teen consumers create looks that both represent and stimulate the anxiety of adults and other youth. Inasmuch as tweens or teens themselves represent the future, their appearance styles participate in a discourse of anxiety.

Part of the ambiguity surrounding fashion is its complex way of dealing with time. At the same time it anticipates the future anxiously, using signifiers that float within and among media images and consumers' bodies, it also grabs images from the past to anchor a sense of reference. Following Walter Benjamin, Lehmann (2000) describes how fashion relies upon a "tiger's leap into the past" to develop its visual vocabulary. At the time of this writing, for example, a fresh and slightly "hot" pink has been very fashionable for the last couple of years, as has camouflage in various colors and textures. As with some of the 1950s-influenced swingy skirts and somewhat kitsch-like use of trim (e.g., rickrack, braid, ribbon) on sweaters or shirts, a semiotic leap enables a kind of freshness and represents an ambivalent cultural mood (somewhat nostalgic, but fresh and hopeful at the same time).

Fashion is also all about capturing the moment: of being *in* the emerging moment, as well as in the cultural mood. And, fashion as intersubjectivity participates in a process of momentum and visual negotiation that ambiguously awaits, and prepares for, the future. Anxiety as a concept is not just about fear or dread; it can also involve a sense of anticipation or even hope. As de Mello and MacInnis note (in this volume), consumers may have a goal of having hope; there is pleasure in having this goal – in and of itself. Shopping itself is a future-oriented activity, as well as one that may offer the thrill of being in the moment, of trying something new to anticipate how it might fit into one's future.

Herein lies some of the complex mixture of feelings associated with fashion. The same fashion process that may afford consumer pleasure, creative identity construction, temporal flexibility, and anticipation or even hope, also generates consumer debt, status differentiation, and questions about who benefits and suffers in the context of global capitalism. In large part, it is the commercial nature of fashion that makes consumers so ambivalent about it. As Wilson (1985) suggests, there is a modern Western cultural tendency to both love and hate fashion. In this case, fashion and capitalism are the objects of emotion. However, ambivalence and other mixed emotions (i.e., anxiety) are also the *subjects* of fashion; they serve to constitute consumers' collective subjectivity or mood.

Whereas anxiety is oriented toward the future, ambivalence seems to be an emotion that fashion creates and evokes in the moment, capturing a sense of the present. Both anxiety and ambivalence can be characterized as highly ambiguous or mixed in character and mood. However, the signifiers of anxiety are multiple and freely floating, while those of ambivalence are more likely to be binary: a juxtaposition of knowable opposites:

> Ambivalence confuses, devours, and tortures. But it also defines and orders, transforming the unknown into a knowable opposite. It constructively metaphors the world . . . A structural feature of every image and fantasy, the ambivalent fusion of opposites devours the soul. Mediated by recognition and acceptance, it is therapeutic, imaginative, originating, and joining.
>
> (Garrison 1982: 229)

Wilson (1985: 246–247) describes fashion as fundamentally ambivalent, because the process of dressing inscribes "upon our bodies the often obscure relationship of art, personal psychology, and the social order." In the context of designers' or consumers' creations of clothing and appearance styles, ambivalence can seem to offer an emotional moment of arbitrary closure, based on the social order that we know and yet resist on some level (for example, the melding of masculinity and femininity, feminism and femininity, coolness and professionalism). These are the moments of articulation that create hybrid appearances reliant on the contradictions between one identity variable and its opposite, or between one theme and its opposite.

Given that modern Western thought often frames its logic around binary categories – that is, it encourages thinking in twos, in polarizing opposites – it is not surprising that ambivalence represents the "aha!" moments of creative closure or synthesis. Yet in the longer view of modern Western fashion history, ambivalence can be seen as an ongoing discourse – one that incorporates the pushes and pulls of identities framed as dichotomies. Davis (1992) argued that ambivalences surrounding identity fuel fashion change:

> Among the more prominent ambivalences underlying such fashion-susceptible instabilities are the subjective tensions of youth versus age, masculinity versus femininity, androgyny versus singularity, inclusiveness versus exclusiveness, work versus play, domesticity versus worldliness . . . Fashion's code modifications seem constantly to move within and among symbols by which clothing encodes these tensions, now highlighting this, muting that, juxtaposing what was previously disparate, inverting major to minor and vice versa.
>
> (Davis 1992: 18)

Davis's analysis suggests that in the context of fashion, ambivalence becomes a visual context for melding and muting. In this context, "knowable" (in the context of language or "logical" thought) opposites may be juxtaposed, but a new articulation simultaneously emerges that complicates the idea of the binary categories themselves. In the terms of Figure 7.1, we are reminded of the need to think critically and creatively about the interface (the ambiguity) among materiality, cultural mood, and metaphor. For as the above quote by Davis suggests, there are moments and moods in which language fails us. When language's metaphors are too firmly rooted within formalism and convention (the old), they seem to lock us inextricably into reductive and essentializing binarisms (i.e., masculinity versus femininity, youth versus age, work versus play).

In contrast, fashion/fashionability is defined through its penchant to break convention and to deploy the new. It uses and translates binary (and other) systems as a resource or grab bag from which to create in the spirit of bricolage or collage, thereby evoking feelings that articulate a moment or a mood that is otherwise limited by binary categories. An analogy can be drawn with the metaphor of the "mood boards" used in fashion design and in marketing and advertising circles. This idea refers to "a collage of images intended to evoke or project a particular style or image." As described by a designer in the home section of the March 24, 1985 issue of the *Chicago Tribune*, "I work in my head, then do thumbnail sketches . . . Then I do a 'mood board.' I'll use fabric swatches, pull pictures . . . out of publications, etc." (*Oxford English Dictionary* 2004). A mood board can be used to create a new concept, a new logo, or a new way of thinking about contradictions.

Fashion designer Narciso Rodriguez pillages photography books, raids library and museum archives, and "obsessively takes snapshots during his travels," combining these seemingly disparate elements with a toy plastic swordfish and a Nike swoosh: "There is so much new culture, so much that is inspiring in everyday life. Nothing is too silly or humble to find a place," indicates Rodriguez. Designer

Anna Sui's board includes fabric swatches, and Zac Posen describes mood boards as "more metaphorical than literal" (La Ferla 2004: 5–6).

To the extent that consumers mix and match the appearance-related commodities they buy, in part, to articulate cultural ambivalences (Kaiser *et al.* 1991, 1995), they can be seen as becoming mobile "mood boards" – as creating collages of their own. In the process, the visual politics of fashion cannot be undermined, because appearance style articulates contradictions and ambiguities that language cannot. What language might frame as "this versus that" or "identity versus identity *not*" (see Freitas *et al.* 1997) can be articulated in greater depth and breadth through appearance style, evoking moods that simultaneously (and perhaps nostalgically) grab visual ideas from the past, express the ambivalent closure of the present, and anxiously anticipate an uncertain future. In this way, fashion bridges time as it represents the process of temporal change itself. Yet it does so with an attitude, with a complex array of moods that are continually in the making. These constructions rely upon materiality: the processes associated with technology, production, and the very fabrics of society that help to shape consumers' fashionings of their (also material) bodies in their everyday lives.

Materiality

In an essay entitled "Advertising: The Magic System," cultural studies scholar Williams (1993) argued that the problem is not so much that modern society is too materialistic. Rather, the problem is that it is *"not materialist enough"* (422, emphasis added). By this he referred in part to the need to use a materialist perspective (within Marxist discourse) to analyze the economic and historical realities experienced by those who actually make and use the materials of industrial capitalism. But Williams also pointed in this essay to the gap between the qualities of the actual materials (e.g., clothes and other materials of appearance style) and the "magical" images constructed to sell them to consumers. Such an interpretation, coupled with a more traditional Marxist analysis, calls for the need to understand the power relations involved in material life, including the political economy of not only production, but also distribution and consumption (see Figure 7.4). We have touched on such a materialist analysis in the "flexibility" section of this paper, in terms of the "flexible" process by which two-dimensional materials are converted into three-dimensional cultural objects that are made available in the marketplace (e.g., the political economy, the labor, the distribution, the branding, the affordability).

Here, we want to focus our attention more directly on the physical aspects of materiality: "the state or quality of being material" (*Webster's New World College Dictionary* 2003: 834). We are primarily interested here in the materiality of clothes and the body – and the interplay between the two. In this context, materiality pertains to the actual fabrics or garments (or other goods) and their tactile and other physical properties. It also includes the body itself as a physical entity – including issues of race and other constructions of scientific discourse that characterize ways of being and appearing in the world.

Figure 7.4 Fashion as materiality. Global capitalism's disconnect between consumption and production is continually under threat by materiality itself. After all, consumers have to know at some level that commodities are produced; these *things* came from . . . somewhere. Yet, it is increasingly difficult to know *where* in the context of global outsourcing. Further, in the commodity's requisite crossing of the divide – its movement from nature to culture – bodies (only *certain* bodies) are haunted by the possibility of their own denial; in certain spaces this is not merely symbolic.

Historically, the consumption of an article of clothing was an important investment with a long life cycle, durability permitting (Crane 2000). It is the very materiality of clothing that leads to contemporary debates in the field of fashion history. As Breward (1998) notes, this field's art historical focus in British academe after the Second World War was on

> the careful dating of surviving clothing and its representation in paintings . . . as a useful tool in processes of authentication and general connoisseurship. The emphasis on the creation of linear chronologies and stylistic progressions that art historical directions dictated at the time has to some extent influenced the nature of much fashion history writing since.
>
> (Breward 1998: 301)

Yet in the late 1970s, a number of debates began to challenge the assumptions that "had underpinned the serious study of fashion in the first place" (ibid.: 302). The newer paradigm drew on Marxism, feminism, psychoanalysis, and semiotics, bringing to the forefront a number of debates centered around the body, gender, race and ethnicity, and other issues related to identity and representation.

This newer paradigm of fashion, we argue, relies upon an assumption of flexibility. This assumption becomes material in the case, for example, of the global production, distribution, and consumption of jeans. Jeans embody contextual flexibility: They can be dressed up or down or in between, they can be worn for work as well as play, and they range from inexpensive to expensive. Their contextual flexibility relies on the other clothes and accessories worn with them. But aside from the social ramifications of their flexibility, there is the issue of the actual materials and their "goodness of fit" with the body – that is, how jeans and the body leave mutual marks on one another. In an article entitled, "The Fingerprint of the Second Skin," Hauser (2005) describes how the creases and wear patterns of worn denim are used in forensics to reveal something about the wearer's identity: how the jeans are washed or ironed, what s/he carries in the pockets, how s/he walks. But Hauser points out that to some extent the manufacturing process predetermines a certain kind of wear pattern (e.g., fading propensity, seam tension). She argues that while consumers impart their own shape on jeans through everyday wear patterns, the garments have their own materiality that is shaped by the actions and habits of invisible garment workers.

Conversely, the materiality of jeans leaves its very imprint on the materiality of the body. Kastrinakis (2004) describes the recent contextual flexibility of jeans – especially branded jeans – in terms of their relationship with the body, as a kind of "new corset." Interviewees (female college students on both coasts of the United States) in her study made pointed remarks about the degree to which jeans may not only disable flexible bodily movements, but also leave their mark on the body:

> I generally do not wear jeans that I cannot move or sit in.
> I prefer stretch so you don't feel like you cannot breathe in them, especially after you eat.
> If I can breathe normal and don't have to suck in constantly, that's comfort.
> I ask myself, "Will they be comfortable when I sit down?"
> I prefer jeans not too tight so as to cut off my circulation or leave indent marks on my waist.

Ultimately, the process of producing consumer identity in everyday life relies heavily on the materiality of the body, as well as the clothes and other commodities one has the resources or inclination to buy and use. As Butler (1993) famously puts it, "bodies matter." In the context of fashion, bodies materialize – in close contact with material goods – and point to the complex intersections among gender, sexuality, race, ethnicity, age, and other physical dimensions of identity. A recent *Time* website ("The Role of Race in Fashion," 2003) focuses on the black "model of the moment, Liya Kebede in a Marc Jacobs satin dress." Yet it goes on to raise a question that points to the material limits of flexibility (race is not as flexible as a change of clothes):

Everyone knows that a successful model boasts an enviable weight, height and bone structure, but must she also have the right color skin? It's a question the fashion industry has not entirely resolved.

Moving (flexibly?) through ambiguity

The Venn diagram depicted in Figure 7.1 gives us a semiotic mapping, or geography, calling attention to interrelationships and to the central role of flexibility as a method of adaptation and – perhaps paradoxically – assertion. Flexibility is a resource or strategy that enables us to "manage" the ambivalences and anxieties of fashion's material inevitability: working it through, so to speak. In the process, we come to adapt to and belong within its contemporary cacophony of contradiction and anxiety (e.g., labor, gross economic inequities, stereotypes of gender and race). Then, in what may seem to be a reverse move, we turn again to flexibility as a method of harnessing and re-articulating the signifying logics of appearance style and fashion, using them to speak of a differentiated self and to request recognition of this singularity. In this way, flexibility comes to be both a strategy of "fitting to" the cultural present, and a strategy of not "fitting to" it.

However, it is the nature of sign systems to be limited by their own lexicon and syntax, and fashion is no exception. The interplay among metaphor, cultural mood, and materials that comprises the fashion system is both contained and sustained by capitalism. And, this fact enables and denies a rhythm that, within the contemporary moment, seems to be functioning at a fevered pitch. While within this chapter, we have attempted to theorize the way in which flexibility has come to signify the cultural moment from materiality to abstraction, and from the individual to the collectivity, it is alternately of critical importance that we also theorize the limitations of flexibility.

For this is also a critical part of the *why* of fashion. When defining fashion as flexibility, we come toe to toe with the Hegelian "problem of identity," and this is productive (1969). Hegel's philosophical logic tells us that, in order to be equated, two terms must also lie outside of each other to some degree. The very equation, in this case fashion = flexibility, necessarily admits their singularity, while simultaneously acknowledging in some way that there is a remainder that does not fit into the second term. Thus, fashion itself must also be understood as having moments of rigidity and brittleness; it needs constant maintenance in order to ensure its status. It lies in opposition to flexibility, at the same moment that it constitutes flexibility (and relies desperately upon it). Therefore, ironically, we might begin to conceptualize fashion as "$_{(in)}$flexibility." That is, fashion relies equally on flexibility and *in*flexibility as a strategy. This formulation, "$_{(in)}$flexibility," helps to pinpoint the double (if not multiple) meanings of flexibility, and draws attention both to its ambivalent promise and its material limitations. It also points to fashion's *in*flexibility as a qualifying subtext constantly relegated to the back stage, or even to the invisible back room: where workers toil, where the "magic images" of advertising are constructed, and where racism, classism, sexism, and violence persist. At the same time, it is the very process of being *in* –

part of – flexibility that allows the system to work, despite the rampant ambiguity that cross-cuts the metaphors, cultural moods, and materiality of fashion.

The formulation "$_{(in)}$flexible," along with the Venn diagram, reminds us of the need to ground ambiguity in the actual concreteness of workers' and consumers' lives and material circumstances, the qualities of the materials themselves, and the visual and tactile responses to the materials that are themselves embodied. That is, the material limits of flexibility can be seen in paychecks and layoffs, credit card bills, trade regulations, and wardrobe malfunctions. Together with a capitalist economic system, ambivalence thrives on contradictions. And, it is the link between capitalism and ambivalence that makes fashion so compelling as an opportunity to articulate change and negotiate identity and meaning on an ongoing basis (Kaiser *et al.* 1991, 1995). Paradoxically, flexibility butts up against its limits as it simultaneously enables a complex global system of fashion to function. And this is how and where the "why" of fashion consumption becomes so compelling in everyday life. For fashion fosters a sense of going somewhere or moving forward flexibly, despite (and perhaps even more convincingly, *because of*) forces that work against such flexibility.

Acknowledgments

We are indebted to the reviewers of an earlier draft of this manuscript – Christopher Breward, Diana Crane, Mary Lynn Damhorst, and Michael Solomon – for their very thoughtful and helpful comments that helped, in diverse and stimulating ways, to shape our thinking for this final version. We are fortunate to have such critical and creative colleagues to review our work.

References

Adair-Heeley, C. B. (1991) *The Human Side of Just in Time: How to Make the Techniques Really Work*, New York: AMACOM.

Agins, T. (1999) *The End of Fashion: The Mass Marketing of the Clothing Business*, New York: William Morrow and Company.

Arnold, R. (2001) *Fashion, Desire and Anxiety: Image and Morality in the 20th Century*, New Brunswick, NJ: Rutgers University Press.

Barthes, R. (1990) *The Fashion System* (trans. M. Ward and R. Howard), Los Angeles: University of California Press.

Blumer, H. (1969) "Fashion: From class differentiation to collective selection," *Sociological Quarterly* 10: 275–292.

Breward, C. (1998) "Cultures, identities, histories: Fashioning a cultural approach to dress," *Fashion Theory* 2(4): 301–314.

Butler, J. (1993) *Bodies That Matter*, New York/London: Routledge.

Cameron, L. (1999) "Operationalising 'metaphor' for applied linguistic research," in L. Cameron and G. Low (eds) *Researching and Applying Metaphor*, New York: Cambridge University Press: 3–28.

Crane, D. (2000) *Fashion and Its Social Agendas: Class, Gender, and Identity in Clothing*, Chicago, IL: University of Chicago Press.

Davis, F. (1985) "Clothing and fashion as communication," in M. R. Solomon (ed.) *The Psychology of Fashion*, Lexington, MA: Lexington Books: 15–27.

Davis, F. (1992) *Fashion, Culture, and Identity*, Chicago, IL: University of Chicago Press.

Debord, G. (1994) *The Society of the Spectacle*, New York: MIT Press.

Enninger, W. (1985) "The design features of clothing codes: The functions of clothing displays in interaction," *Kodikas/Code* 8: 81–110.

Frank, T. (1997) *The Conquest of Cool: Business Culture, Counterculture, and the Rise of Hip Consumerism*, Chicago, IL: University of Chicago Press.

Freitas, A. J., Kaiser, S. B., Chandler, J. L., Hall, C., Kim, J. W., and Hammidi, T. (1997) "Appearance management as border construction: Least favorite clothing, group distancing, and identity . . . *not!*" *Sociological Inquiry* 67: 323–335.

Garrison, M. (1982) "The poetics of ambivalence," in J. Hillman (ed.) *Spring: An Annual of Archetypical Psychology and Jungian Thought*, Dallas, TX: Spring Publications.

Guy, A., Green, E., and Banim, M. (2001) *Through the Wardrobe: Women's Relationships with Their Clothes*, Oxford/New York: Berg.

Harvey, D. (1989) *The Condition of Postmodernity*, Oxford: Basil Blackwell.

Hauser, K. (2005) "The fingerprint of the second skin," in C. Breward and C. Evans (eds) *Fashion and Modernity*, Oxford: Berg.

Hegel, G. W. F. (1969) *Science of Logic* (trans. A. V. Miller), London: George Allen & Unwin, Ltd.

Hethorn, J. and Kaiser, S. (1998) "Youth style: Articulating cultural anxiety," *Visual Sociology* 14: 109–125.

Hodkinson, P. (2002) *Goth: Identity, Style, and Subculture*, Oxford/New York: Berg.

Jakobson, R. (1990) *On Language* (reprinted from 1896 edition, ed. and trans. L. R. Waugh and M. Monville-Burston), Cambridge, MA: Harvard University Press.

Kaiser, S. B. (1997) *The Social Psychology of Clothing: Symbolic Appearances in Context* (2nd edn, revised), New York: Fairchild Publications.

Kaiser, S. B. (2003) "Fashion, media, and cultural anxiety," in L. Fortunati, J. E. Katz, and R. Riccini (eds) *Mediating the Human Body: Technology, Communication, and Fashion*, Mahwah, NJ: Lawrence Erlbaum Associates: 155–161.

Kaiser, S., Chandler, J., and Hammidi, T. (2001) "Minding appearances in female academic culture," in A. Guy, E. Green, and M. Banim (eds) *Through the Wardrobe: Women's Relationships with their Clothes*, Oxford/New York: Berg.

Kaiser, S. B., Freeman, C. M., and Chandler, J. L. (1993) "Favorite clothes and gendered subjectivities: Multiple readings," in N. K. Denzin (ed.) *Studies in Symbolic Interaction*, Greenwich, CN: JAI Press, Vol. 15: 27–50.

Kaiser, S. B., Nagasawa, R. H., and Hutton, S. S. (1991) "Fashion, postmodernity, and personal appearance: A symbolic interactionist formulation," *Symbolic Interaction* 14: 165–185.

Kaiser, S. B., Nagasawa, R. H., and Hutton, S. S. (1995). "Construction of an SI theory of fashion: Part 1. Ambivalence and change," *Clothing and Textiles Research Journal* 13: 172–183.

Kastrinakis, D. (2004) "Jeans: Brand, Comfort and Value," MS Thesis, University of California, Davis.

Kierkegaard, S. (1980) *The Concept of Anxiety* (ed. and trans. R. Thomte and A. A. Anderson), Princeton, NJ: Princeton University Press.

Kimle, P. A. and Damhorst, M. L. (1997) "A grounded theory model of the ideal business image for women," *Symbolic Interaction* 20: 45–68.

Kunkel, C. A. (1999) "A visual analysis of feminist dress," in M. L. Damhorst, K. A. Miller, and S. O. Michelman (eds) *The Meanings of Dress*, New York: Fairchild: 183–188.

LaFerla, R. (2004) "Bless this mess: Fashion designers take inspiration and tack it to the wall," *New York Times*, February 8: ST1, 6.

Lehmann, U. (2000) *Tigersprung: Fashion in Modernity*, Cambridge, MA: MIT Press.

Levine, D. N. (1985) *The Flight from Ambiguity*, Chicago, IL: University of Chicago Press.

Lowson, R., King, R. E., and Hunter, N. A. (1999) *Quick Response: Managing the Supply Chain to Meet Consumer Demand*, Chichester, UK: John Wiley & Sons.

McCracken, G. D. (1988) *Culture and Consumption: New Approaches to the Symbolic Character of Consumer Goods and Activities*, Bloomington: Indiana University Press.

Muggleton, D. (2000) *Inside Subculture: The Postmodern Meaning of Style*, Oxford/New York: Berg.

Ong, A. (1999) *Flexible Citizenship: The Cultural Logics of Transnationality*, Durham, NC: Duke University Press.

Oxford English Dictionary (2004) <http://dictionary.oed.com/cgi/entry> Access date: November 17, 2004.

Polhemus, T. (2000) *Style Surfing: What to Wear in the 3rd Millennium*, London: Thames and Hudson.

Simmel, G. (1904) "Fashion," *International Quarterly*. Reprinted in *American Journal of Sociology* 62 (May 1957): 541–558.

Slack, J. D. (1996) "The theory and method of articulation in cultural studies," in D. Morley and K.-H. Chen (eds) *Stuart Hall: Critical Dialogues in Cultural Studies*, London: Routledge.

Slater, D. (1997) *Consumer Culture and Modernity*, Cambridge: Polity Press.

Solomon, M. R. (2003) *Conquering Consumerspace: Marketing Strategies for a Branded World*, New York: Amacom.

Stone, G. P. (1962) "Appearance and the self," in A. Rose (ed.) *Human Behavior and Social Processes*, Boston, MA: Houghton-Mifflin Company.

Stone, G. P. (1977) "Personal acts," *Symbolic Interaction* 1: 2–19.

"The Role of Race in Fashion" (2003) <http://www.time.com/time/fashion/20030908/race> Access date: November 17, 2004.

Webster's New World College Dictionary (2003) Springfield, MA: Merriam-Webster.

Williams, R. (1993) "Advertising: The magic system," in S. During (ed.) *The Cultural Studies Reader* (2nd edn), London: Routledge: 410–423.

Wilson, E. (1985) *Adorned in Dreams: Fashion and Modernity*, London: Virago Press.

8 A behavioral decision theory perspective on hedonic and utilitarian choice

Uzma Khan, Ravi Dhar, and
Klaus Wertenbroch

How do consumers choose whether to have a rich, creamy Häagen-Dazs ice cream for dessert or a healthy but perhaps less tasty bowl of fresh fruit? Whether to go on a beach vacation for a week or spend the time making progress on an important long-term project at work? Whether to choose an expensive apartment with a nice view far from work or a cheaper apartment without a view but close to the office?

Consumers are often faced with these types of choices between hedonic and utilitarian alternatives that are at least partly driven by emotional desires rather than cold cognitive deliberations. Hence, these choices represent an important domain of consumer decision-making. Yet much of the pioneering work in behavioral decision theory has largely focused on the cognitive aspects of decision-making without exploring its emotional dimensions (Kahneman 1991). This research program was initially juxtaposed against standard economic theory, according to which consumers maximize utility in a rational and cognitively driven manner. Research in behavioral decision-making therefore followed a paradigm of contrasting actual choices to predictions derived from these rational models. Parallel research on consumer information-processing took a similar approach and viewed consumers as rationally bounded yet emotionally dispassionate decision-makers who logically evaluate alternatives in terms of trade-offs among product attributes. This research, with its roots in problem-solving, has emphasized effort-accuracy trade-offs in decision-making and similarly neglected the emotional dimensions of choice (Payne *et al.* 1988). Neither approach has focused on systematically explaining consumer behavior with regards to goods or attributes whose selection and use is guided by emotional wants rather than functional needs (e.g., gourmet food, performing arts, paintings, movies, concerts, and fashion).

Nonetheless, emotional desires can often dominate functional motives in the choice of products (Maslow 1968). For example, when buying a house an emotional feature such as the view from the bedroom window can be more influential in the final decision than a more utilitarian concern with distance from work. One can, of course, incorporate such attributes into a traditional framework, treating them simply as additional considerations in choice. However, to fully understand the pattern of choice, it is important that any explanation of consumer behavior is accompanied by a complete understanding of the interplay between a consumer's functional goals and experiential preferences within the decision context. Consumer researchers have increasingly begun to investigate consumer choice based on distinctions that involve the purchase and consumption of goods for pleasure versus for more utilitarian and instrumental purposes. Two different theoretical perspectives broadly capture these distinctions. The first perspective is explicitly concerned with context effects on the trade-offs involved in choosing between alternatives that induce pleasure and alternatives that are instrumental to achieving some other goal, such as getting a kiss from one's favorite movie star or receiving $50 (e.g., Dhar and Wertenbroch 2000; Rottenstreich and Hsee 2001; O'Curry and Strahilevitz 2001). The second perspective that helps elucidate conflicts between functional goals and experiential preferences characterizes goods according to their capacity to induce temptation and impulsive choice at the expense of delayed benefits (e.g., tasty but fatty and salty potato chips). Research in this second category typically falls into the realm of time-inconsistent preferences (e.g., Hoch and Loewenstein 1991; Loewenstein *et al.* 2003; Wertenbroch 1998).

So far, the distinctions within and across both perspectives have coexisted loosely without much integration because they arose from different theoretical paradigms within consumer research and decision-making. In the next section of this chapter we attempt to take stock of, and organize, the two conceptualizations; we also review the empirical findings that are rooted in the different paradigms. The conceptualizations that stem from each perspective are shown in Figure 8.1. We discuss points of divergence between the different conceptualizations. We also examine commonalities and propose a self-attribution model of hedonic choice, which explains consumer choice of the types of goods characterized by these distinctions and integrates the two theoretical perspectives. Finally, we present a number of propositions for future research based on the model and our integrative viewpoint.

Preferences in the context of trade-offs with functional goals	Preferences in the context of time inconsistency

• Luxuries vs. necessities
  • Kivetz and Simonson (2002a, b)
	• Shoulds vs. wants
	  • Bazerman *et al.* (1998)

• Hedonic vs. utilitarian goods
  • Hirschman and Holbrook (1982)
  • Strahilevitz and Myers (1998)
  • Dhar and Wertenbroch (2000)
	• Affective vs. cognitive preferences
	  • Shiv and Fedorikhin (1999)

• Affect-rich vs. affect-poor goods
  • Rottenstreich and Hsee (2001)
  • Hsee and Rottenstreich (2004)
	• Vices vs. virtues
	  • Wertenbroch (1998)
	  • Read *et al.* (1999)

Figure 8.1 Conceptual distinctions in the types of preferences studied by prior researchers.

Experiential preferences and functional goals: conceptualizations and findings

As proposed above, two different research programs exist in the consumer choice literature that view experiential preferences either in the context of trade-offs with functional goals or in the context of time-inconsistent preferences. We now examine the various conceptualizations within these research perspectives along with their respective empirical findings.

Preferences in the context of trade-offs with functional goals

Several streams of literature have examined trade-offs between goods that are chosen and consumed to induce pleasure and make consumers feel good versus those that achieve an instrumental purpose. These streams have distinguished between luxuries and necessities, hedonic and utilitarian goods, and affect-rich and affect-poor products.

Luxuries versus necessities

A basic distinction between different types of goods is that between necessary and luxury items. Necessary items are essentials, items that are indispensable for the preservation of a minimum standard of living. Food, clothing, and medical care, for example, are basic requirements of life that cannot be avoided or denied. The word luxury is derived from Latin *luxus*, meaning excess. Luxuries are therefore objects of desire that provide a condition of abundance, pleasure, ease, and comfort. Necessities, on the other hand, are objects that relieve an unpleasant state of discomfort (Berry 1994). Psychologists have discussed the extent to which luxuries are less important than necessities in terms of a hierarchy of needs (Maslow 1968). This is consistent with how economists define luxuries as goods whose income elasticity of demand is positive, while necessities are goods whose income elasticity of demand is negative (Deaton and Muellbauer 1980).

Hedonic versus utilitarian goods

Some researchers have used the terms luxury and necessity more broadly, in a less technical sense, to imply that luxuries are consumed primarily for hedonic pleasure while necessities are required to meet more utilitarian goals (Dubois *et al.* 2004; Kivetz and Simonson 2002a, b; Strahilevitz and Myers 1998). Hedonic goods are multisensory and provide for experiential consumption, fun, pleasure, and excitement. Flowers, designer clothes, music, sports cars, luxury watches, and chocolate fall in this category. Utilitarian goods, on the other hand, are primarily instrumental, and their purchases are motivated by functional product aspects. Examples of utilitarian goods are microwaves, detergents, minivans, home security systems, or personal computers (Dhar and Wertenbroch 2000; Hirschman and Holbrook 1982; Strahilevitz and Myers 1998). Notice that both utilitarian and hedonic consumption are discretionary and the difference between the two is a matter of degree or perception. That is, in comparison to utilitarian consumption, hedonic consumption may be perceived as relatively more discretionary (Okada 2005).

Different products can be high or low in both hedonic and utilitarian attributes at the same time. In fact, most evaluations in our consumption profile are based on the degree to which various alternatives satisfy utilitarian and hedonic goals (Batra and Ahtola 1990). A person evaluating a pair of sneakers may care for both functional features (e.g., durability) as well as hedonic features (e.g., design). Usage and consumption motives are central in determining whether an item is perceived as primarily hedonic or utilitarian (e.g., Pham 1998). For example, purchasing a cell phone to access help in times of trouble makes a cell phone a utilitarian product. Buying the same phone to chat with friends makes it hedonic.

Affect-rich versus affect-poor goods

A related distinction in the literature has been drawn between affect-rich and affect-poor products. Affect-rich products elicit associative imagery while affect-poor goods evoke little or no such imagery. For example, a $100 coupon redeemable for payment towards a phone bill evokes little affective imagery compared to a coupon of similar monetary value redeemable towards a dinner for two at a fine restaurant (Rottenstreich and Hsee 2001). Affect-rich items are those whose choice is likely to be made intuitively. These products may be spontaneously evaluated on the basis of the liking or disliking that they evoke (e.g., Kahneman and Frederick 2002; Schwarz and Clore 1983). Unlike intuitive emotions, the choice of affect-poor goods is likely to be based on analytical rules and assessments. Moreover, Pham (1998) has shown that feelings are weighed more heavily under experiential motives than under instrumental motives, echoing the distinction between hedonic and utilitarian consumption goals. Goods that are consumed for hedonic purposes tend to be more affect-rich than those that are consumed for utilitarian purposes (although not all utilitarian products need to be affect-poor).

Of what relevance are these distinctions to consumer choice? Because experiential and functional considerations map onto independent product attributes, these distinctions have important implications for how consumers make trade-offs between these attributes depending upon the choice task or context. In the following section we discuss several findings in the literature that have been attributed to these distinctions in product attributes.

Response mode effects

Although hedonic versus utilitarian and affect-rich versus affect-poor distinctions are not between good and bad, consumer choice between the two seems to be driven by whether a preference for a hedonic item can be justified. Response modes that increase (decrease) the need for justification favor utilitarian (hedonic) options. For example, preferences are reported to reverse between hedonic and utilitarian items in separate versus joint evaluation tasks. In a field study, Okada

(2005) showed that, although restaurant clients preferred a relatively more hedonic dessert when only one dessert was offered, a relatively more utilitarian dessert was preferred when both desserts were offered together. The difficulty in justifying a hedonic option in comparison with a utilitarian option seems responsible for these effects. In a direct comparison, where choosing one option implies explicitly rejecting the other, the relatively more discretionary nature of the hedonic item may be highlighted and hence increase the guilt associated with its choice. The difficulty of choosing a hedonic alternative over a utilitarian option also seems to make hedonic options appear to be more popular as prizes than as purchases, whereas utilitarian options appear to be more popular as purchases than as prizes (O'Curry and Strahilevitz 2001). Passively receiving a reward does not require as much justification as does actively purchasing the same reward.

Several marketer-induced tactics can also provide guilt-reducing justifications that increase the attractiveness of hedonic products. For example, Kivetz and Simonson (2002a) demonstrated that higher requirements of effort in frequency programs shifted people's preferences towards receiving luxury as compared to necessity rewards. Exerting increased effort presumably makes people feel that their hard work has entitled them to the luxury reward. Strahilevitz and Myers (1998) showed that preferences for a hedonic option are enhanced when the purchase is tied to charity donations. Bundling products with promised charity donations was more successful in promoting frivolous luxuries than practical necessities. In the same vein, Khan and Dhar (2005) showed that, as compared to a control condition, preference for a hedonic option vis-à-vis a utilitarian option increased after a charitable act. Their explanation is based on the idea that a charitable act produces positive attributions that reduce the negative self-attributions associated with hedonic consumption. They further show that no preference for the hedonic option is observed if the charitable act (and hence the positive self-attributions) can be discredited by attributing it to a driving violation. Thus, perceived diagnosticity of positive self-attributions is an important driver of whether or not a prior act influences the subsequent action.

Range effects

Research has shown that people demonstrate more range insensitivity when evaluating affect-rich than affect-poor alternatives (e.g., Frederick and Fischhoff 1998; Kahneman *et al.* 2000). For example, when college students were asked how many hours they would be willing to work to earn $30 or $60 in cash versus in terms of a music book valued at $30 or $60, they demonstrated more sensitivity to the monetary difference when the reward was cash (affect-poor) than when it was an affect-rich music book (Hsee and Rottenstreich 2004). Affect-rich alternatives evoke valuation by feeling while affect-poor alternatives lead to valuation by calculation. When relying on feelings, people are sensitive to the presence or absence of a stimulus but are less sensitive to variations in range. In contrast, when people rely on calculation, they are generally sensitive to changes in range. Consistent with these findings, Wakefield and Inman (2003) suggest that consumers are generally less price-sensitive when buying products and services that have hedonic characteristics rather than when buying products that are primarily of a functional nature. Because hedonic products are consumed for fun and fantasy, saving may not be a big concern when one has finally decided to buy something hedonic. Also, people may be willing to spend more on hedonic items because of the relatively infrequent consumption of such items. Similarly, Strahilevitz (1999) demonstrated that consumers are less sensitive to the magnitude of the donation with hedonic products as compared with frivolous products. This too suggests that people may be less sensitive to range effects in frivolous purchases than in more functional, utilitarian purchases.

Role of uncertainty

Consistent with the above is also the finding that an affect-poor prize is preferred under certainty but an affect-rich prize is preferred under lack of certainty (Bazerman *et al.* 1998; Rottenstreich and Hsee 2001). For instance, it has been shown that people are willing to pay more in terms of time than money for hedonic items (Okada 2005). To the extent that monetary value of time is more ambiguous than that of hard currency, it is reasonable that people feel more ready to pay for hedonic items with time rather than money. Support for this also comes from O'Curry and Strahilevitz (2001) who show that individuals are more likely to choose a hedonic alternative over a utilitarian one when the probability of receiving the selected item was low than when the probability of receiving the selected item was high.

Reference dependence

Another effect that is credited to the difference in (affect-rich) hedonic and (affect-poor) utilitarian product types is that people are more loss-averse for hedonic attributes (Dhar and Wertenbroch 2000). For example, an apartment with a better view (relatively hedonic feature) is preferred over an apartment with a shorter commute to work (relatively utilitarian feature) when the decision-maker's current apartment has both a nice view and a short commute than when the current apartment has neither of the two features. In other words, when people are making a forfeiture decision they are more likely to give up the utilitarian option than the hedonic one. However, when choosing to acquire, people are more likely to prefer the utilitarian option to a hedonic alternative. This result suggests that, similar to its effect on range sensitivity (Hsee and Rottenstreich 2004) and perceptions of uncertainty (Rottenstreich and Hsee 2001), affect may also influence loss aversion.

It is important to note again that the hedonic versus utilitarian and affect-rich versus affect-poor distinctions are not between good and bad options. That is, hedonic (affect-rich) and utilitarian (affect-poor) alternatives could both be good but on different dimensions (e.g., one shampoo cleans better whereas another makes the user feel sexy). Now consider a very different kind of choice. Imagine a person who is thinking about whether to study for an upcoming exam or go to a party. She may *want* to go to the party but feel that she *should* work towards her exam instead. This person is faced with a classic *heart* versus *mind* conflict. Although working for the exam has long-term benefits, it has little immediate appeal. On the other hand, going to the party is immediately attractive but may compromise future academic success. Next, we discuss the conceptualizations used in the literature on impulsive consumption and self-control that seem to capture this related dimension of consuming for pleasure versus instrumental reasons within an intertemporal framework.

Preferences in the context of time-inconsistency

Research that falls into the domain of time-inconsistency contrasts the characteristics of consumption for immediate pleasure with the characteristics of consumption for longer-term benefits. Past literature has used several conceptually similar terms to capture these dimensions of consumption.

Shoulds versus wants

In Homer's *Odyssey*, Ulysses binds himself to the mast knowing that he would *want* to steer his ship toward the Sirens upon hearing their enchanting songs but that he *should* not do so because he would wreck it on the Sirens' shores. We all face such intrapersonal conflicts when what we want is not what we believe we should do (Bazerman *et al.* 1998). We may *want* to go to a movie with our friends but know that we *should* work towards an approaching deadline. Consumers may buy products that they feel they *should* buy (healthy or less expensive) instead of the ones they really *want* (less healthy but more tasty or expensive).

Affective versus cognitive preferences

The *should* versus *want* distinction is compatible with Hoch and Loewenstein's (1991) conflict between *desire* and *willpower*, or Shiv and Fedorikhin's (1999) discord between the *heart* and the *mind* (Shiv *et al.*, this volume). The unifying theme in this research is that it perceives people as choosing the immediately gratifying option on impulse. This crude impulsivity is overcome only if cognitive resources allow a careful and sophisticated consideration of the long-term consequences of alternatives. For example, Shiv and Fedorikhin (1999) found that when processing resources are limited, spontaneously evoked affective reactions rather than cognitions tend to have a greater impact on choice. In contrast, when the availability of processing resources is high, cognitions related to consequences of choice tend to have greater influence (see Millar and Tesser 1986).

Vices versus virtues

Casting the above conflict in terms of different types of consumption goods, Wertenbroch (1998) showed that intrapersonal dilemmas arise when people face choices between *vices* and *virtues*. A relative vice (virtue) is something that is preferred to a relative virtue (vice) when considering only the immediate (delayed) consequences of consumption and holding delayed (immediate) consequences fixed. Generally, a vice can be conceptualized as an affective want that is motivated by impulses, while a virtue can be seen as a more reasoned and cognitively preferred choice option. As compared to a virtuous option, choosing a vice entails small but immediate hedonic gratification with larger but delayed, less positive (or even negative) consequences (Read *et al.* 1999; Wertenbroch 1998).

The critical aspect in the above distinctions is that they relate to temporally inconsistent preferences – what is gratifying now is not what is preferred for the future. Intertemporal preference reversals arise from a disposition to give disproportionate weight to short-term benefits and costs, which is usually referred to as hyperbolic time discounting (Ainslie 1975). As a consequence, when consumption is still far away we might plan to have something that maximizes our long-run utility, but when consumption is imminent we might choose something that is bad for us in the long run but has more immediate appeal. For example, Read and Van Leeuwen (1998) reported that about half of their subjects chose a virtuous piece of fruit over junk food one week before they were to consume it, but immediately before consumption most of them changed their mind and ended up choosing chocolate bars or potato chips. This type of inconsistency has important implications for decision theory and has been used to explain several consumption phenomena, which we discuss next.

Response mode effects

Bazerman *et al.* (1998) showed that preferences for vice or *want* options are stronger when these option are evaluated separately as compared to when they are evaluated jointly with virtuous or *should* options, a result that is echoed by Okada's (2005) analogous findings for hedonic and utilitarian items. Similarly, Read *et al.* (1999) found that consumers choose more virtues in simultaneous choices of multiple items at the same time for consumption over several periods than in sequential choices of one item at a time just before each consumption occasion. Specifically, in a choice between highbrow movies (that offer less immediate fun but are educationally or culturally enriching, e.g., *Schindler's List*) and lowbrow movies (that generally provide little educational benefit but are good for entertainment and instant pleasure, e.g., *Speed*) people preferred more highbrow movies in simultaneous choice than in sequential choice. An undercurrent in this research is that when people act on their intrinsic preferences they are spontaneously tempted by, and attracted to, relative vices. It is only when cognitive factors kick in, either due to direct comparisons in joint evaluation or to the availability of processing resources as in Shiv and Fedorikhin (1999) that the long-term consequences of alternatives are taken into account.

Self-control

In general, when the short-term outcomes of an activity are in conflict with its long-term consequences, people may perceive the short-term outcomes as a threat to their long-term well-being and exercise self-control involving a variety of cognitive, affective, and motivational processes. Consequently, a substantial body of literature in this tradition has focused on how people attempt to control their short-term consumption impulses to secure their long-term interests. For example, a primary self-control strategy is to make an irrevocable decision in advance by eliminating the vice alternative from the choice-set (e.g., Ainslie 1975; Thaler and Shefrin 1981). In the first empirical demonstration of such consumer preferences for precommitment, Wertenbroch (1998) showed that consumers strategically ration their purchase quantities of vice goods to avoid a potential self-control problem arising from temptations to overconsume the vice they have in stock at home. For example, many regular smokers buy their cigarettes by the pack, forgoing sizable per-unit savings that they could realize if they buy 10-pack cartons. Such purchase quantity rationing discourages excessive vice consumption by making marginal consumption more difficult and costly. Wertenbroch (1998) showed that, as a result of such self-control, vice consumers' demand increases less in response to price reductions than virtue consumers' demand, although the preferences for vices are not generally weaker than the preferences for virtues. Analyses of quantity discounts for fast-moving consumer goods (Wertenbroch 1998) and of two-part pricing schemes for services such as health clubs, mobile phone communication, and gambling (DellaVigna and Malmendier 2004) suggest that marketers' actual pricing policies are designed to make marginal vice consumption costlier than marginal virtue consumption, in line with consumer preferences for precommitment.

Research on counteractive self-control also suggests how people self-impose constraints on their otherwise preferred freedom of choice. People may steer away from short-term temptations by formulating strategies that make benefits and rewards contingent upon acting in accordance with their long-term interests. Fishbach and Trope (2000) reported that when health was subjectively important, participants in a study made receipt of a bonus contingent on completing a physically unpleasant test, although they could have earned the bonus without taking the test. Though participants risked losing the bonus by imposing this contingency on themselves, they increased their motivation to complete the test. Ariely and Wertenbroch (2002) showed that students and executives who self-imposed costly, evenly spaced deadlines (with penalties for missing them) were not only more likely to complete assignments on time but they also performed better than participants who did not self-impose such deadlines.

Relatedly, Rook and Hoch (1985) found that consumers employ a variety of distancing strategies to avoid situations in which they are likely to yield to their time-inconsistent preferences (e.g., "I immediately leave the area", and "I steer clear of record stores when I can't afford it"). Other studies have noted effectiveness of postponement (e.g., "never buy without checking other stores") and distraction as strategies against transient desires (Rook 1987). People may also proactively counteract the influence of outcomes with immediate appeal and long-term costs by devising detailed implementation of intentions (e.g., "Whenever situation Y arises, I will do X"; Gollwitzer and Brandstatter 1997).

Although there are several similarities in the conceptualizations and findings within the hedonic/utilitarian and the vice/virtue frameworks, it is important to note that the research addressing the two originates from distinct theoretical backgrounds and orientations. To date, no conceptual integration of the frameworks exists. To illustrate this lack, we next explicitly highlight points of departure between the two conceptualizations. Despite these differences, though, we then move on to showing what the two conceptualizations have in common and how they can be integrated. Specifically, we propose a model that explains consumer choice among these goods in terms of self-attribution.

Differences between conceptualizations

For simplicity, we will refer to the literature that examines trade-offs between experiential preferences and functional goals (referred to on pp. 146–150) as research in the hedonic-utilitarian paradigm and to the literature that examines experiential preferences in the context of time-inconsistent preferences (referred to on pp. 150–153) as research in the vice-virtue paradigm. These two streams of research are characterized by a number of surface differences that seem to emanate more from the theoretical perspectives, from which the research originated, than from substantive differences in conceptualizations. Nonetheless, it is worth pointing out those differences before turning to a deeper analysis of commonalities.

The hedonic-utilitarian paradigm has tended to focus on barriers to choosing the hedonic option whereas the vice-virtue paradigm has focused on the impulsivity of vice choices. For example, since choosing hedonic over utilitarian items often induces guilt consumers are seen as viewing hedonic goods with hesitation. In contrast, the vice-virtue literature generally assumes that a vice will be *automatically* chosen for immediate consumption by appealing to consumers' impulsive preferences. While seemingly in contrast with each other, we will show that these two propositions are not necessarily inconsistent.

Guilt and justification

Hedonic goods can be more difficult to justify than utilitarian goods (Dhar and Wertenbroch 2000; Thaler 1980). Compared to utilitarian goods, purchases of hedonic luxuries may therefore be associated with guilt and feelings of responsibility (Lascu 1991). Consequently, the hedonic-utilitarian literature has tried to account for the factors that facilitate the choice of the hedonic option. Findings such as the greater popularity of hedonic items as rewards than as prizes (O'Curry and Strahilevitz 2001), and stronger preferences for hedonic rewards in the face of greater effort (Kivetz and Simonson 2002a) or charitable behaviors (Khan and Dhar 2005; Strahilevitz and Myers 1998), all support the idea of greater difficulty in choosing hedonic products. Specifically, this research builds on the idea that consumers, for various reasons such as anticipated regret (e.g., Bell 1982), cognitive dissonance (e.g., Festinger 1957), or rational self-perception (e.g., Bem 1972), are often looking to justify their choices (Simonson 1989; Slovic 1975). In summary, researchers in the hedonic-utilitarian paradigm have focused on how choice of a hedonic alternative can be enhanced by providing internal or external justifications for its consumption.

Coping with temptation

A focus on temporal streams of costs and benefits, as exemplified by behavior that results in immediate gratification but delayed harm (e.g., engaging in risky sex, drinking, and smoking) is an important distinction between the hedonic-utilitarian and the vice-virtue paradigms. The vice-virtue and the want-should distinctions are defined explicitly in terms of such temporal trade-offs, while the temporal aspect is not critical to the hedonic-utilitarian distinction. Typically, work in the vice-virtue paradigm has focused primarily on contexts that give rise to time-inconsistent preferences, that is, preferences leading to choices that would not be made from a dispassionate, temporally removed perspective. Among others, time-inconsistent behavior has been studied in the context of economic policy (Kydland and Prescott 1977), saving behavior (Thaler and Shefrin 1981) and self-control (Hoch and Loewenstein 1991; Loewenstein 1996; Wertenbroch 2003). A common suggestion from these streams of research is that the affective reactions occur because of crude and rapid automatic processing while the rational reactions are generated by refined, cognitive, and deliberated reactions (Shiv and Fedorikhin 1999). The fast affective reactions can undermine the long-term goals that guide dispassionate preferences and lead to self-regulation problems (debt, addictions, and health risks). An underlying assumption is that, faced with a choice between a *virtue* and a *vice* option, people are likely to act against their better judgment and engage in impulsive behavior inconsistent with their global preferences.

Because of the view that people are impulsively attracted to vices, the literature in the vice-virtue paradigm has naturally focused on the strategies and tactics people use (consciously or unconsciously) to limit their choice of vices. Using the idea of multiple selves, Ainslie (1975) and Schelling (1984) proposed that the farsighted and conservative self attempts to restrict, in advance, the set of options that the myopic self can choose from in the future. Akin to this is Thaler and Shefrin's (1981) planner-doer model, in which the planner self limits the set of options from which the doer can later choose. Wertenbroch's (1998) demonstration that consumers are willing to pay a premium for smaller packs of vices (e.g., regular coffee, beer, potato chips, Oreo chocolate chip cookies, etc.) shows that consumers counteract a future self-control problems by self-imposing strategic constraints. Dieters may restrict the amount of groceries they purchase knowing that they would not be able to avoid the temptation when the food is in close proximity. Similarly, people may be willing to incur a penalty for missing a medical exam (due to its short-term aversiveness) to ensure better health in the future (Fishbach and Trope 2000).

Toward a common framework: a self-attribution model of hedonic choice

As the above discussion shows, the two conceptualizations have arisen within two different research paradigms. The hedonic-utilitarian distinction has come out of research on context effects in decision-making that shows systematic effects of the affective versus functional content of choice option attributes on how consumers make trade-offs between these attributes. The vice-virtue distinction has been used in research on consumer self-control to demonstrate that consumers pre-commit to consumption choices that preclude or minimize impulsive consumption. While these research traditions are not closely related, we propose that the two conceptualizations can be linked from two perspectives, in terms of the temporal streams of consequences of consumption and in terms of the goals that consumers pursue in their decision-making processes.

Commonalities

Intertemporal distribution of consumption consequences

First, note that the definition of hedonic goods as being consumed for experiential pleasure implies that the sought-after consumption benefits occur more or less simultaneously with the act of consumption. For example, drinking a bottle of fancy French wine is pleasant in and by itself, and the benefits typically stop accruing once you have finished the last glass. In contrast, the definition of utilitarian goods as being consumed for instrumental purposes implies that the sought-after consumption benefits occur after the act of consumption. For example, obtaining a college degree is instrumental to getting a good job, which occurs after you've taken classes and have graduated. Therefore, it is also possible to characterize hedonic and utilitarian goods in terms of the stream of consequences accruing from their consumption over time. Typically, hedonic goods provide immediate benefits without explicit negative delayed consequences. For example, there are no obvious delayed costs of choosing a fancy dinner instead of free groceries as a reward. Similarly, utilitarian goods typically provide their benefits post-consumption, without particular negative consequences during consumption. Nonetheless, this front- or backloading of benefits suggests that, by Wertenbroch's (1998) formal definition, hedonic goods could be characterized as vices and utilitarian goods as virtues in a direct comparison with each other. So the intertemporal framework used in the vice-virtue paradigm can be super-imposed on the hedonic-utilitarian distinction; this follows from how consumers' goals (i.e., immediate pleasure or delayed instrumentality) that are linked to the consumption item itself are distributed over time. A possible reason for why the vice-virtue paradigm has resulted in a focus on precommitment strategies is that vices are typically viewed as having immediate positive *and* delayed negative consequences, requiring an impulsive consumer to engage in self-control. The lack of an explicit attribution of delayed negative consequences to hedonic goods may have made impulse control strategies less relevant to researchers in the hedonic-utilitarian paradigm.

Choice and consumption goals

The second perspective, from which the hedonic-utilitarian and vice-virtue conceptualizations can be linked, is in terms of the goals which consumers pursue when making a consumption choice. These consumption goals can be organized at two levels, a more direct, lower-level goal linked to the consumption item itself, and a more indirect, higher-level goal linked to the process by which the item is chosen. Following Huffman *et al.*'s (2000) hierarchy of consumer goals, lower-level goals include feature preferences and benefits sought, while higher-level goals include consumption intentions, current concerns, and life values. The pursuit of higher-level goals is implicit in research on self-control through precommitment in the vice-virtue paradigm. That is because precommitment as a strategic self-control device presupposes that consumers are aware of their self-control problems (e.g., Ariely and Wertenbroch 2002; O'Donoghue and Rabin 1999). Hence, they know their character type ("I am impulsive") and make choices based on their awareness of that type. These choices can therefore be characterized as cognitively driven, top-down decisions and result from a current concern ("I am on a diet") or even a life value ("I'd like to have a virtuous character;" Huffman *et al.* 2000) to act less impulsively. In contrast, the pursuit of lower-level goals is implicit in research on context effects in choices of hedonic and utilitarian items, where consumers pursue lower-level goals such as benefits sought (e.g., pleasure versus instrumentality). Hence, research in the hedonic-utilitarian paradigm can be more easily characterized as looking at affectively driven, bottom-up choices. This research is agnostic as to whether consumers are pursuing higher-level goals such as life values (e.g., driven by an awareness of their real or ideal character type). However, research on consumer guilt (Dahl *et al.* 2003; Lascu 1991) does suggest that consumers may make inferences about their character type from their choices of hedonic and utilitarian items. For example, hedonically choosing the rich, creamy Häagen Dazs ice cream over the less tasty bowl of fresh fruit for dessert may make consumers feel guilty of indulgence and lead them to infer that they are of the indulgent type.

Preferring features or seeking benefits in line with higher-level goals, or inferring higher-level goals from feature preferences or benefits sought, requires consumers to align the different types of goals they are pursuing. Huffman *et al.* (2000) suggest that this process of alignment of higher- and lower-level goals occurs both top-down and bottom-up. Specifically, higher-level goals often shape and give meaning to lower-level goals, a process they refer to as incorporation. For example, wanting to be a virtuous person (a high-level goal) would prompt a consumer to seek benefits (a lower-level goal) that have more positive, or less negative, long-term consequences. The consumer might attribute virtuousness to him- or herself *ex ante* and choose a utilitarian item, or virtue, accordingly. At the same time, lower-level goals such as revealed feature-preferences can also shape and constrain higher-level goals, a process called abstraction (Huffman *et al.* 2000). Thus, consumers who have chosen a hedonic item, or a vice, with certain tempting features or benefits (a lower-level goal) may infer from their choice *ex post* that they are not a particularly virtuous person (thus violating or negating a high-level goal).

This discussion has shown that, despite the lack of definitional integration, the two research paradigms on hedonic and utilitarian goods and on vices and virtues share a number of commonalities. Below, we build on the above discussion to propose a self-attribution model of hedonic choice, which provides a framework to explain when and why a hedonic alternative, or vice, may be preferred over a utilitarian one, or virtue. It is important to note that, given the commonalities that we have proposed, this self-attribution model applies interchangeably to both the hedonic-utilitarian and the vice-virtue paradigms.

A self-attribution model of hedonic choice

In line with extant research, we suggest that what consumers choose may generate conscious or unconscious self-attributions. Self-perception theory first proposed the idea that people make inferences about themselves from their own behavior (Bem 1972). More recently, research on self-signaling in consumer choice has suggested that consumers' own choices provide them with valuable information about their own character (Bodner and Prelec 2001; Prelec and Bodner 2003). For example, a person who buys an expensive Prada handbag may feel stylish, frivolous, and/or indulgent at the same time. Similarly, if consumers observe themselves eating fatty food they may think that they lack self-control. On the other hand, if they observe themselves donating to a charity they may start to view themselves as more compassionate persons.

In exploring the concept of self-signaling, Bodner and Prelec (2001) argued that choices yield not just outcome utility (the utility of the anticipated consequences of choice) but also diagnostic utility (the value of what consumers learn about their disposition as signaled by their choices). Consumers incorporate both types of value into their utility function. Hence, consumer choice may be motivated purely by the *ex ante* desire to obtain a self-signal so that consumers actively seek out choices with a positive signal value. This is consistent with the results of a well-known study by Quattrone and Tversky (1984) who led their subjects to believe that their ability to submerge an arm in a container of cold water until the pain became unbearable was diagnostic of a serious but hard-to-observe heart condition. As predicted, subjects' cold water tolerance varied with whether they believed that tolerance was diagnostic of the heart condition – even though they knew that enduring the pain would not alter their susceptibility to the condition.

Although we may all seek experiential and hedonic pleasures, the purchase of such goods may often produce negative self-attributions (possibly moderated by cultural values) since such consumption is more difficult to justify, induces greater guilt, and by definition, is not essential. These negative self-attributions (e.g., "I am careless," "I am a spendthrift," "I indulge," "I lack self-control," etc.) associated with hedonic alternatives could restrict people from choosing hedonically appealing experiential alternatives. Similar negative attributions may also be associated with choosing an immediately gratifying vice over a virtuous option that lacks instant appeal but offers greater long terms benefits. For example, Dhar and Wertenbroch (2004) show that consumer preferences for choice sets depend on the signal value of a given choice from these sets. Choosing a vice from a set that also contains a virtue highlights the fact that the consumer has just chosen a vice more than choosing that vice from a set that only contains vices. Similarly, choosing a virtue from a set that also contains a vice makes the virtue choice more salient to the consumer than choosing that virtue from a set that only contains virtues. Consequently, vice-consumers derive more negative, and virtue-consumers more positive, signal values from choosing from sets that contain both vices and virtues. In other words, variability in situational factors such as the presence or absence of other choice options and the feasibility of choosing these options can highlight, or de-emphasize, alternative causes of one's choice such as the strength or weakness of one's will (cf. Bénabou and Tirole 2004).

In line with this reasoning, our self-attribution model (see Figure 8.2) proposes that hedonic choice generates certain conscious or unconscious self-attributions, which, if anticipated, in turn influence the choice outcome. Choosing a hedonic (vice) item over a more utilitarian (virtuous) alternative can generate more negative self-attributions. The negativity associated with hedonic (vice) options can then undermine their attraction and the decision-maker may end up choosing a more utilitarian (virtuous) option.

Specifically, our model in Figure 8.2 shows that lower-level goals, such as feature preferences, may lead consumers to prefer a hedonic (utilitarian) item. That preference may lead to negative (positive) self-attributions, which may induce consumers to think of themselves as indulgent (virtuous) types. This, in turn, may yield new or revised higher-level goals of pursuing indulgence (virtue) further or prudishly (indulgently) pursuing virtue (vice) instead. Therefore, self-attribution processes are the mechanism by which lower-level goals can affect higher-level goals in the model (abstraction, see Huffman *et al.* 2000).

Consistent with past research that suggests that most of consumer behavior is goal-directed (Bagozzi and Dholakia 1999), our model proposes that it is also possible for higher-level goals to affect the nature of the self-attributions prompted by a given choice. Based on the notion that different goals and goal-attainment strategies can influence trade-offs, we suggest that the negative self-attributions associated with a choice set may depend on the chooser's goals and goal-driven self-regulation strategies. For example, a person who aims to eat healthy (a benefit sought, a lower-level goal) in order to lose weight (a current concern, a higher-level goal) may associate greater negative self-attributions with choosing a tasty but unhealthy chocolate cake over a healthy but less tasty fruit salad as compared to someone who aims to exercise everyday in order to lose the same amount of

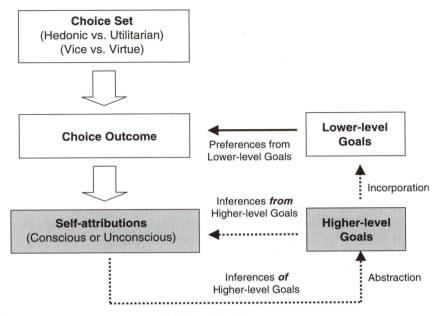

Figure 8.2 A self-attribution model of hedonic choice.

weight. Similarly, a person on a diet (a current concern, a higher-level goal) is likely to draw more negative self-attributions from the choice of the chocolate cake (a feature preference, a lower-level goal) as compared to a person who is not on a diet. Hence, our proposed self-attribution model of hedonic choice also suggests that if higher-level goals lead a consumer to anticipate negative self-attributions from choosing the hedonic or vice item, she will prefer, or at least precommit to, the utilitarian or virtuous option, which is likely to generate positive or less negative self-attributions. So the self-attributions consumers anticipate from their overt choices can in turn be determined by the goals they bring to the choice situation. Thus, our model also allows higher-level goals (pursuing virtue) to determine lower-level goals via the anticipation of self-attributions (incorporation, see Huffman *et al.* 2000).

Consistent with attribution theory (e.g., Schwarz and Clore 1983), we also propose that the preference for a hedonic or vice alternative will increase if the negative self-attributions associated with it are diminished or disconfirmed. In other words, when the choice context allows the consumer to disconfirm or neutralize any negative self-attributions attached with the choice of the hedonic or vice items she will prefer such options. Simply put, the choice of a hedonic or a vice item vis-à-vis a utilitarian or a virtuous item will be more likely when the restrictive negative self-attributions associated with it are removed. The act or item that disconfirms the negative self-attributions need not be tightly coupled with an act or item that induces negative self-attributions. For example, Khan and

Dhar (2004) illustrate that more subjects chose a pair of designer jeans over a vacuum cleaner after a seemingly unrelated charitable decision than in a control condition. Moreover, when asked to give reasons for their choices, participants in their study did not draw a connection between their initial charitable decision and the subsequent indulgent choice. This is consistent with the notion that the processes that reduce negative self-attributions may occur outside of the individual's consciousness, and without requiring intention, effort, or monitoring.

Theoretical propositions

We now present a number of theoretical propositions that follow from our self-attribution model of hedonic choice.

The role of goals. As discussed above, goals that an individual holds can affect the self-attributions she anticipates to draws from her choices, which then influence the choice outcome. Hence, a useful direction for future research would be to examine the role of different types of goals in the determination of self-attributions and choice. For example, whether people have a promotion or a prevention focus (Pham and Higgins, this volume) may influence the self-attributions they draw from their specific choices. In a promotion focus people are more likely to pursue goals that are related to advancement and accomplishment, while in a prevention focus the goals pursued are more likely to be those related to security and protection (Higgins 1998). Therefore, it is likely that a promotion-focused individual associates fewer negative self-attributions with the choice of hedonic (vice) products than an individual with a prevention focus. Future research can investigate the role of regulatory focus in a choice between hedonic (vice) and utilitarian (virtue) products.

The role of positive self-attributions. The negative self-attribution arising from a choice of hedonic or vice alternatives may be disconfirmed by countering them with positive self-attributions, which can arise through several different mechanisms. For example, higher effort may enhance the preference for a hedonic or vice item by serving to disconfirm the negative self-attributions (such as "I am being wasteful" etc.) associated with choosing such items through the generation of positive self-attributions (such as "I deserve it"). Similarly, longer waiting times may also increase preference for hedonic items by creating positive self-attributions (such as "I am patient," or "I deserve it"). Negative self-attributions may also be reduced by adding seemingly functional or practical attributes to the hedonic or vice products. For example, Patek Philippe advertises that "some people feel that you never actually own a Patek Philippe. You merely take care of it for the next generation." The positive attribution that one is buying a valuable heirloom to pass on to future generations can reduce the negative self-attributions that may be associated with buying an expensive watch for one's own use.

Moreover, negative self-attributions from hedonic or vice products may also be diminished by bundling such products with unrelated virtues. The idea here is that the act or item that generates positive self-attributions or disconfirms the negative self-attributions need not be tightly coupled with an act or item that induces negative self-attributions. In other words, seemingly unrelated decisions can induce positive self-attributions that can increase preference for relatively hedonic or vice alternatives by overriding the negative self-attributions associated with them. For example, charitable decisions (e.g., monetary or time donations) can induce positive self-attributions (e.g., "I am kindhearted," "I am conscientious," etc.) that can increase preference for unrelated hedonic or vice alternatives by overriding the negative self-attributions associated with them (e.g., "I am indulgent," "I am careless," etc.). What types of mechanisms generate positive self-attributions, and when are they effective or ineffective in reducing negative self-attributions, are useful questions for further inquiry.

The role of misattribution. Previous research has shown that the diagnosticity of the subjective experience can be modified by attribution manipulations (Schwarz and Clore 1983). We therefore propose that the impact of negative self-attributions may be diminished if they can be attributed to some external source. Similarly, the disconfirming impact of positive self-attributions may also be reduced if they attributed to some external motivation. For example, higher effort may not increase preference for hedonic or vice options if it can be attributed to an external reason (e.g., if the increased effort is seen as a result of some penalty). Future research should examine how misattribution influences consumer decision-making in the context of choosing between hedonic (vice) and utilitarian (virtuous) alternatives.

The role of non-conscious processes. Importantly, we suggest that processes that help disconfirm the self-attributions associated with consumption may lie outside of consciousness and operate independently of, and in addition, to the conscious processes discussed in earlier research (e.g., on self-control, willpower, etc.). In other words, the disconfirmation process may not require awareness, intention, effort, or monitoring on part of the consumer. For example, it is possible that promotional guilt reduction tools, such as bundling charitable donations with hedonic purchases or providing functional alibi, are effective due to a non-conscious "moral retribution" process. Therefore, such tools could easily lose their effectiveness when opportunities for misattribution are provided in the purchasing context. We believe that both the view that many of our purchase and consumption choices are driven by the attributions they allow us to make about ourselves and the view that these attributions are often non-conscious (and hence subject to equally non-conscious disconfirmation and misattribution processes) provide a fruitful perspective from which to examine and contrast hedonic and utilitarian consumption in future research.

Conclusion

In this chapter, after reviewing different loosely connected theoretical frameworks, we provided an integrative perspective regarding the distinctions between the purchase and consumption of goods for pleasure (e.g., rich creamy desserts, perfumes, and sports cars) and goods for more utilitarian and functional purposes (e.g., healthy but less tasty desserts, deodorants, and minivans). We took an inventory of these various theoretical perspectives, reviewed the empirical findings originating from them, and discussed the distinctions and commonalities in these lines of research. Building on our review and organization of the past literature, we proposed a self-attribution model of hedonic choice, which ties together the diverse theoretical views on experiential and instrumental consumption. Our model explains consumers' hedonic decisions in the light of the self-attributions that they may draw from their choices. Based on the model we put forward several propositions that provide fruitful directions for future research.

References

Ainslie, G. (1975) "Specious reward: A behavioral theory of impulsiveness and impulse control," *Psychological Bulletin* 82 (July): 463–469.

Ariely, D. and Wertenbroch, K. (2002) "Procrastination, deadlines, and performance: Self-control by precommitment," *Psychological Science* 13 (May): 219–224.

Bagozzi, R. P. and Dholakia, U. (1999) "Goal-setting and goal-striving in consumer behavior," *Journal of Marketing* 63 (October): 19–32.

Batra, R. and Ahtola, O. T. (1990) "Measuring the hedonic and utilitarian sources of consumer attitudes," *Marketing Letters* 2 (April): 159–170.

Bazerman, M. H., Tenbrunsel, A. E., and Wade-Benzoni, K. (1998) "Negotiating with yourself and losing: Understanding and managing competing internal preferences," *Academy of Management Review* 23 (April): 225–241.

Bell, D. E. (1982) "Regret in decision-making under uncertainty," *Operations Research* 30 (September/October): 961–981.

Bem, D. J. (1972) "Self-perception theory," in L. Berkowitz (ed.) *Advances in Experimental Social Psychology*, Vol. 6, New York: Academic Press: 1–62.

Bénabou, R. and Tirole, J. (2004) "Willpower and Personal Rules," *Journal of Political Economy* 112(4): 848–886.

Berry, C. J. (1994) *The Idea of Luxury: A Conceptual and Historical Investigation*, New York: Cambridge University Press.

Bodner, R. and Prelec, D. (2001) "Self-signaling and diagnostic utility in everyday decision-making," in I. Brocas and J. Carrillo (eds) *Collected Essays in Psychology and Economics*, Oxford: Oxford University Press: 1–22.

Dahl, D. W., Honea, H., and Manchanda, R. V. (2003) "The nature of self-reported guilt in consumption contexts," *Marketing Letters* 14 (October): 159–171.

Deaton, A. and Muellbauer, J. (1980) *Economics and Consumer Choice*, New York: Cambridge University Press.

DellaVigna, S. and Malmendier, U. (2004) "Contract design and self-control: Theory and evidence," *Quarterly Journal of Economics* 119 (May).

Dhar, R. and Wertenbroch, K. (2000) "Consumer choice between hedonic and utilitarian goods," *Journal of Marketing Research* 37 (February): 60–71.

Dhar, R. and Wertenbroch, K. (2004) "The costs and benefits of temptation: Choice set effects on consumption utility," Working Paper, Yale University and INSEAD.

Dubois, B., Laurent, G., and Czellar, S. (2004) "Segmentation based on ambivalent attitudes: The case of consumer attitudes toward luxury," Working Paper, HEC, France.

Festinger, L. (1957) *A Theory of Cognitive Dissonance*, Evanston, IL: Row, Peterson.

Fishbach, A. and Trope, Y. (2000) "Counteractive self-control in overcoming temptation," *Journal of Personality and Social Psychology* 79 (October): 493–506.

Frederick, S. and Fischhoff, B. (1998) "Scope (in)sensitivity in elicited valuations," *Risk, Decision, and Policy* 3 (August): 109–123.

Gollwitzer, P. M. and Brandstatter, V. (1997) "Implementation intentions and effective goal pursuit," *Journal of Personality and Social Psychology* 73 (July): 186–199.

Higgins, E. T. (1998) "Promotion and prevention: Regulatory focus as a motivational principle," in *Advances in Experimental Social Psychology*, Vol. 30, New York: Academic Press: 1–46.

Hirschman, E. C. and Holbrook, M. B. (1982) "Hedonic consumption: Emerging concepts, methods, and propositions," *Journal of Marketing* 46 (Summer): 92–101.

Hoch, S. J. and Loewenstein, G. F. (1991) "Time-inconsistent preferences and consumer self-control," *Journal of Consumer Research* 17 (March): 492–507.

Hsee, K. C. and Rottenstreich, Y. (2004) "Music, pandas, and muggers: On the affective psychology of value," *Journal of Experimental Psychology: General* 133 (March): 23–30.

Huffman, C., Ratneshwar, S., and Mick, D. G. (2000) "Consumer goal structures and goal determination processes: An integrative framework," in *The Why of Consumption: Contemporary Perspectives on Consumer Motives, Goals and Desires*, London and New York: Routledge.

Kahneman, D. (1991) "Judgment and decision-making a personal view," *Psychological Science* 2 (May): 142–145.

Kahneman, D. and Frederick, S. (2002) "Representativeness revisited: Attribute substitution in intuitive judgment," in T. Gilovich, D. Griffin, and D. Kahneman (eds) *Heuristics and Biases: The Psychology of Intuitive Judgment*, New York: Cambridge University Press: 49–81.

Kahneman, D., Ritov, I., and Schkade, D. (2000) "Economic preferences or attitude expressions? An analysis of dollar responses to public issues," in D. Kahneman and A. Tversky (eds) *Choices, Values, and Frames*, New York: Cambridge University Press: 642–672.

Khan, U. and Dhar, R. (2005) "Licensing effect in consumer choice," Working Paper, Yale University.

Kivetz, R. and Simonson, I. (2002a) "Earning the right to indulge: Effort as a determinant of customer preferences towards frequency program rewards," *Journal of Marketing Research* 39 (May): 155–170.

Kivetz, R. and Simonson, I. (2002b) "Self-control for the righteous: Toward a theory of precommitment to indulge," *Journal of Consumer Research* 29 (September): 199–217.

Kydland, F. and Prescott, E. (1977) "Rules rather than discretion: The inconsistency of optimal plans," *Journal of Political Economy* 85 (June): 473–492.

Lascu, D. N. (1991) "Consumer guilt: Examining the potential of a new marketing construct," in R. Holman and M. Solomon (eds) *Advances in Consumer Research*, Vol. 18, Provo, UT: Association for Consumer Research: 290–293.

Loewenstein, G. (1996) "Out of control: Visceral influences on behavior," *Organizational Behavior and Human Decision Process* 65 (March): 272–292.

Loewenstein, G., Read, D., and Baumeister, R. (2003) *Time and Decision: Economic and Psychological Perspectives on Intertemporal Choice*, New York: Russell Sage Foundation.

Maslow, A. H. (1968) *Toward a Psychology of Being*, 2nd edn, Princeton, NJ: Van Nostrand.

Millar, M. G. and Tesser, A. (1986) "Effects of affective and cognitive focus on the attitude-behavior relation," *Journal of Personality and Social Psychology* 51 (February): 270–276.

O'Curry, S. and Strahilevitz, M. (2001) "Probability and mode of acquisition effects on choices between hedonic and utilitarian options," *Marketing Letters* 12 (February): 37–49.

O'Donoghue, T. D. and Rabin, M. (1999) "Doing now or later," *American Economic Review* 89 (March): 103–124.

Okada, E. M. (2005) "Justification effects on consumer choice of hedonic and utilitarian goods," *Journal of Marketing Research* 42(1): 43–53.

Payne, J. W., Bettman, J. R., and Johnson, E. J. (1988) "Adaptive strategy selection in decision-making," *Journal of Experimental Psychology: Learning, Memory and Cognition* 14 (July): 534–552.

Pham, M. T. (1998) "Representativeness, relevance, and the use of feelings in decision-making," *Journal of Consumer Research* 25 (September): 144–159.

Prelec, D. and Bodner, R. (2003) "Self-signaling and self-control," in G. Loewenstein, D. Read, and R. Baumeister (eds) *Time and Decision: Economic and Psychological Perspectives on Intertemporal Choice*, New York: Russell Sage Foundation: 277–298.

Quattrone, G. A., and Tversky, A. (1984) "Causal versus diagnostic contingencies: On self-deception and on the voter's illusion," *Journal of Personality and Social Psychology* 46(2): 237–248.

Read, D., Loewenstein, G., and Kalyanaraman, S. (1999) "Mixing virtue and vice: Combining the immediacy effect and the diversification heuristic," *Journal of Behavioral Decision-Making* 12 (December): 257–273.

Read, D. and Van Leeuwen, B. (1998) "Predicting hunger: The effects of appetite and delay on choice," *Organizational Behavior and Human Decision Processes* 76 (November): 189–205.

Rook, D. W. (1987) "The buying impulse," *Journal of Consumer Research* 14 (September): 189–199.

Rook, D. W. and Hoch, S. J. (1985) "Consuming impulses," in E. C. Hirschman and M. B. Holbrook (eds) *Advances in Consumer Research*, Vol. 12, Provo, UT: Association for Consumer Research : 23–27.

Rottenstreich, Y. and Hsee, K. C. (2001) "Money, kisses and electric shocks: On the affective psychology of risk," *Psychological Science* 12 (May): 185–190.

Schelling, T. C. (1984) "Self-command in practice, in policy, and in a theory of rational choice," *American Economic Review* 74 (May): 1–11.

Schwarz, N. and Clore, G. L. (1983) "How do I feel about it? Informative functions of affective states," in K. Fiedler, and J. P. Forgas (eds) *Affect, Cognition, and Social Behavior*, Toronto: Hogrefe International: 44–62.

Shiv, B. and Fedorikhin, A. (1999) "Heart and mind in conflict: The interplay of affect and cognition in consumer decision-making," *Journal of Consumer Research* 26 (December): 278–292.

Simonson, I. (1989) "Choice based on reasons: The case of attraction and compromise effect," *Journal of Consumer Research* 16 (September): 158–174.

Slovic, P. (1975) "Choice between equally valued alternatives," *Journal of Experimental Psychology: Human Perception and Performance* 1 (August): 280–287.

Strahilevitz, M. (1999) "The effects of product type and donation magnitude on willingness to pay more for a charity-linked brand," *Journal of Consumer Psychology* 8 (Issue 3): 215–241.

Strahilevitz, M. and Myers, J. G. (1998) "Donations to charity as purchase incentives: How well they work may depend on what you are trying to sell," *Journal of Consumer Research* 24 (March): 434–446.

Thaler, R. H. (1980) "Toward a positive theory of consumer choice," *Journal of Economic Behavior and Organization* 1 (March): 39–60.

Thaler, R. H. and Shefrin, H. M. (1981) "An economic theory of self-control," *Journal of Political Economy* 89 (April): 392–406.

Wakefield, K. L. and Inman, J. (2003) "Situational price sensitivity: The role of consumption occasion, social context and income," *Journal of Retailing* 79 (Issue 4): 199–212.

Wertenbroch, K. (1998) "Consumption self-control by rationing purchase quantities of virtue and vice," *Marketing Science* 17 (Fall): 317–337.

Wertenbroch, K. (2003) "Self-rationing: Self-control in consumer choice," in G. Loewenstein, D. Read, and R. Baumeister (eds) *Time and Decision: Economic and Psychological Perspectives on Intertemporal Choice*, New York: Russell Sage Foundation: 491–516.

9 Interplay of the heart and the mind in decision-making

Baba Shiv, Alexander Fedorikhin, and Stephen M. Nowlis

A broad goal of this chapter is to take the reader on a journey, a journey involving the heart and the mind. A journey filled with cakes, pizzas, chocolates, and ice creams. A journey that will shed light on consumer motives that underlie various phenomena such as succumbing to temptation, making irrational decisions, and why tasting the same food product (e.g., Godiva chocolates) is more pleasurable under some instances than others. A journey that will reveal how many of the positive as well as negative emotions we experience in our everyday lives are rooted in brain structures such as the amygdala and the ventromedial (VM) prefrontal cortex.

The journey that the reader is about to take is organized as follows. In the next section, we present an integrative affective-cognitive framework for the interplay of emotions and cognitions in consumer decision-making, a framework rooted in both neurological and psychological theories of affect that have been proposed in the literature. In line with extensive evidence amassed by various neuroscientists (e.g., Bechara *et al.* 2002; LeDoux 1987, 1995, 1996) and psychologists (e.g., Berkowitz 1993; Buck 1985; Epstein 1993; Leventhal 1984; and Zajonc 1980) we make a distinction between "lower-order emotions" (emotions that occur spontaneously through automatic processes) and "higher-order emotions" (emotions that occur through more deliberative processes). We also discuss how these two types of emotions are likely to interact with cognitions in terms of their impact on motives and subsequently on action tendencies. In the subsequent section, we discuss the implications of, and provide empirical support for our affective-cognitive framework for various consumption-related situations. We then extend the affective-cognitive framework to somatosensory stimuli (e.g., tasting chocolate). Finally, we highlight several issues arising from the affective-cognitive framework, issues that provide promising areas for future research.

Interaction between affect and cognition – neurological and psychological theories

Let us begin our journey with a non-consumption related context, one that has often been used by neuroscientists to shed light on brain substrates that are involved in the interplay of the heart and the mind. Imagine that you are at home

and it is late in the evening. You are walking in your backyard and notice something on the grass that resembles a snake (if the reader has a phobia toward
snakes, let us assure her/him that the object is only a garden hose). According to
theories proposed by Buck (1985) and LeDoux (LeDoux 1996; see also Bechara *et
al.* 2002; Davidson *et al.* 2000; Lang 1993; Wyer *et al.* 1999), three processes are
likely to be set into motion on exposure to any affect-laden stimulus object (see
Figure 9.1). First, information related to the stimulus reaches the amygdala (an
area in the limbic structure of the brain) through direct pathways from the thal-
amus. This process gives rise to spontaneous "lower-order" emotions based on a
rapid assessment of the affective significance of the stimulus (which, according to
LeDoux's work, is determined by prior learning[1]) "without the involvement of
higher-order systems of the brain, systems believed to be involved in thinking,
reasoning, and consciousness" (LeDoux 1996: 161). These lower-order emotions
spontaneously activate action tendencies (approach or avoidance) through the
activation of basic appetitive or aversive motives. (Pham and Higgins, this volume,
make a similar distinction in their definition of prevention versus promotion
motives.) For the scenario just described, the emotions are likely to be negative,
and, therefore, the basic motives are likely to be aversive in nature, resulting in
action tendencies that might be in the form of a startle response, a response aimed
at avoiding the stimulus object.

Second, the information related to the stimulus may be subject to more deliberative, higher-order cognitive processing in the cortical structures of the brain.[2]
The outcome of these higher-order processes can serve to either overcome or
reinforce the basic motives and, thus, the action tendencies arising from lower-
order emotions. For example, a more careful examination of the stimulus object
might lead you to realize that the object is not a snake, just a garden hose. These
cognitions, arising from higher-order processes might, in turn, serve to overcome
the aversive motives and action tendencies that were triggered by the lower-order
emotions (i.e., the startle response), and cause you to continue walking in your
backyard.

Third, the cognitions associated with higher-order processing might give rise
to higher-order emotions that serve to reinforce the basic motives and action
tendencies arising from lower-order emotions. For example, even though you

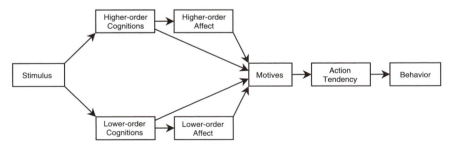

Figure 9.1 Affective-cognitive framework.

realize that the object is just a garden hose, your mind may soon get filled with thoughts about being bitten by a snake, having to be rushed to the hospital, etc., thoughts that are likely to trigger higher-order emotions through the activation of the ventromedial prefrontal (VM) cortex. In other words, you are likely to re-experience fear, albeit this time through deliberative cognitive processes, leading to a decision to head back indoors.

The processes arising from the activation of brain structures like the amygdala and the VM prefrontal cortex, and the outcomes described above can occur for pleasurable stimulus objects as well (see Bechara *et al.* 2002).[3] The key differences are likely to be in terms of the valence of the emotions that are likely to be experienced, and the motives and action tendencies that are likely to be triggered, as a consequence. Consider, for example, a situation where you decide to have a snack and you encounter two option: a piece of chocolate cake and a serving of fruit salad. Note that the chocolate cake is more affect-laden compared to the fruit salad, but also less favorable in terms of the long-term health consequences. (This situation is akin to a choice between hedonic versus utilitarian options that Khan *et al.* discuss in their chapter in this volume.) According to the affective-cognitive framework, the lower-order emotions that are likely to be triggered upon noticing the chocolate cake can result in an appetitive action tendency (i.e., a tendency to grab the cake). However, with more deliberation, you might focus on the adverse consequences of consuming the cake. Thus, these higher-order cognitions might serve to overcome the action tendency triggered by the lower-order emotions. Alternatively, you might continue to have thoughts about the cake, which, in turn, are likely to trigger higher-order emotions and, consequently, an appetitive action tendency toward the cake.

Although the affective-cognitive framework presented above is based on neuro-psychological evidence, it is also consistent with various theories that have been proposed by experimental psychologists. For example, Berkowitz (1993) has proposed a cognitive-neoassociationistic model of anger, where he distinguishes between basic or rudimentary anger, that arises from "lower-order, primitive pro-cessing," and differentiated affective reactions that arise from "higher-order, deeper processing." Much as in the affective-cognitive framework presented above, Berkowitz (1993) argues that rudimentary anger occurs very quickly before the onset of cognitive processes such as "appraisals, interpretations, schemas, attributions, and strategies" (Berkowitz 1993: 12), which form part of other theor-ies proposed by researchers such as Lazarus (1991), Ortony *et al.* (1988), and Schachter and Singer (1962). These cognitive processes could then either over-come "lower-order" affective reactions or reinforce them to give rise to more highly developed and differentiated affective experiences. The models proposed by Epstein (1993), Hoch and Loewenstein (1991), Leventhal (1984), Metcalfe and Mischel (1999), and Zajonc (1980) are also consistent with the framework pro-posed above. In line with our framework, Epstein's Cognitive-Experiential Self-Theory (CEST) proposes that two conceptual systems tend to operate in parallel in any given task: an experiential system, which is affective in nature, and is associated with crude and rapid processing, and a rational system, which is cognitive in nature, and is associated with a more refined and deliberative process-ing. Similarly, Leventhal (1984) proposes that affective reactions can arise from two routes: an "innate route" accompanied by sensory-motor processes that gen-erates primitive or partially formed affective reactions, and a memory route which involves schematic and conceptual processing. Also, Metcalfe and Mischel's (1999) "Hot/Cool System Framework" proposes that there are two types of processes involving distinct interacting systems, a hot system that is specialized for quick emotional processing, and a cool system that is specialized for slow higher-order thinking. Finally, the propositions made by Hoch and Loewenstein (1991) and Zajonc (1980) are consistent with the argument that affective reactions can occur relatively automatically without an active role of the cortical areas of the brain (the higher-order, "thinking" parts of the brain). Zajonc has argued that affect is precognitive in nature, occurring without any extensive perceptual and cognitive processes, and temporally preceding these higher-order processes. Hoch and Loewenstein propose that feelings of desire that consumers often experience in shopping situations may "occur with the minimum conscious deliberation charac-teristic of automatic or mindless behavior" and "with little or no cognition" (Hoch and Loewenstein 1991: 498). However, the difference between the proposi-tions made by Zajonc and Hoch and Loewenstein and by neuroscientists like LeDoux is that, rather than stating that affect always precedes cognition, a view taken particularly by Zajonc, LeDoux (1996) proposes that affective reactions could also arise in a relatively controlled, post-cognitive manner from deeper "high-road processing" of incoming information by the cortical structures of the brain.

In the next section, we present some of the conceptual implications of the proposed affective-cognitive framework. We also present empirical evidence in support of various aspects of the model and discuss the managerial implications of these findings. In the subsequent section, we highlight several issues related to the affective-cognitive framework that remain unexamined and provide potential directions for future research.

The affective-cognitive framework in consumption-related contexts

Let us get back to the cake-salad scenario described above and try to provide answers to several questions.[4] For instance, under what conditions would we expect lower-order processes to hold sway over higher-order processes in terms of influencing action tendencies and, thus, behaviors? What are the factors that moderate the intensity of lower-order affect and, thus, the strength of the sub-sequent action tendencies? If deliberative processes ensue, under what situations are higher-order emotions likely to be engendered?

Moderating role of cognitive load

The discussion in the previous section suggests that lower-order processes occur spontaneously and, therefore, impose few demands on processing resources. In contrast, higher-order cortical processes are deliberative in nature, and, therefore, impose demands on processing resources. As a result, any factor that constrains processing resources is likely to prevent the onset of higher-order processes, resulting in choices that are influenced by lower-order processes, i.e., by lower-order emotions. In other words, for the cake-salad scenario, since chocolate cake is more affect-laden than fruit salad, but also less favorable in terms of the long-term consequences, any factor that constrains processing resources is likely engender appetitive motives and, thus, action tendencies in favor of the cake over the salad. Shiv and Fedorikhin (1999, 2002) tested this prediction arising from the affective-cognitive framework by having some individuals memorize a seven-digit number and other individuals memorize a two-digit number prior to choosing between chocolate cake and fruit salad. Memorizing a seven-digit number was expected to impose more demands on processing resources and, thus, lead to higher choices for the chocolate cake, than memorizing a two-digit number. Consistent with this prediction, individuals were more likely to choose cake under higher than lower levels of cognitive load.

Intensity of lower-order affect: potential moderators

Although the core finding in Shiv and Fedorikhin (1999, 2002) is consistent with predictions arising from the affective-cognitive framework, it can also be accounted for by other, more cognitive, explanations. For instance, it is quite possible that the cognitive load manipulation in their experiments caused individuals to focus more on the short-term benefits than on long-term costs. In other words, cognitively busy individuals became more myopic and chose the cake, whereas less cognitively busy individuals were less myopic and considered the long-term consequences of choosing the cake over the salad (note that this "cost-benefit" account does not invoke the role of emotions). To rule out this alternative account, Shiv and Fedorikhin (1999) manipulated the affective significance of the stimulus by exposing one group of individuals to real chocolate cake and salad (real presentation-mode) and another group to photographs of the cake and salad (symbolic presentation-mode). A pretest revealed that this manipulation affects the affective significance of the chocolate cake, but not higher-order cognitions about the cake. If the cost-benefit account is valid, then choice of the cake ought to be unaffected by the presentation-mode manipulation when processing resources are constrained (i.e., when the level of cognitive load is high). After all, cognitive load ought to make individuals myopic and focus more on the cognitive benefits of choosing cake versus salad, irrespective of the presentation-mode. In contrast, if the affective-cognitive framework is valid, then under high levels of cognitive load (when lower-order affect is predicted to influences choices), choice of the cake ought to be higher with a real presentation-mode (greater affective significance and, therefore, more intense lower-order affect) rather than with a symbolic presentation-mode (lower affective significance and, therefore, less intense lower-order affect). The findings reported in Shiv and Fedorikhin (1999, experiment 1) are consistent with the latter, affect-based account, and, thus, reduce the viability of the alternative, cognitive-based account. From a broader perspective, this specific finding suggests that one factor that can affect the intensity of lower-order emotions, and their subsequent impact on action tendencies, is the nature of the presentation mode, with more vivid presentation modes engendering more intense lower-order emotions and action tendencies.

The role of higher-order emotions

Shiv and Fedorikhin's (1999) study focused on the interplay of lower-order emotions and higher-order cognitions, and the role of higher-order emotions was not examined. Specifically, their findings suggest that when processing resources are available, higher-order cognitions related to the consequences of consuming cake versus salad are likely to get activated, resulting in action tendencies (choosing the salad) that overcome the tendencies arising from spontaneously evoked lower-order emotions (choosing the cake). But, what about the role of higher-order emotions in determining action tendencies? In other words, under what conditions will higher-order processes give rise to higher-order emotions (and, therefore, action tendencies that favor the cake) rather than higher-order cognitions that focus on the consequences of consuming the cake (and, therefore, action tendencies that favor the salad)?

According to Bechara *et al.* (2002), higher-order emotions are likely to be triggered if cues related to the primary inducers (i.e., stimuli that triggered lower-order emotions) are present in the stimulus environment. For example, imagine a situation where you enter a dark room and a bat flits past you. The incident is very likely to trigger lower-order emotions (i.e., fear) in you, emotions that are centered in the amygdala. Now, imagine that a week later you again happen to enter the dark room. Even if you don't encounter the bat on this occasion, the cues in the environment (the dark room) are likely to trigger thoughts about what happened to you a week ago, triggering higher-order emotions, which are now centered in the VM pre-frontal cortex. In other words, you are again likely to experience fear even though the primary inducer (i.e., the bat) is no longer present on the second occasion. These higher-order emotions can be triggered with pleasurable stimuli as well. For example, in Shiv and Fedorikhin (2002), participants listened to sounds of neutral valence after initial exposure to cake and salad. Some participants were exposed to cues related to the primary inducer (i.e., the cake) while listening to the sounds; others were not. Participants who were exposed to the cues were more likely to focus on the affective properties of the options while making their decisions, resulting in a greater choice of the cake than those who were not exposed to such cues.

Evidence in support of the interplay of higher-order anticipatory emotions (which are centered in the VM pre-frontal cortex) and higher-order cognitions has been documented in other domains as well. For example, Shiv *et al.* (forthcoming) had normal individuals, patients with stable focal lesions in brain areas related to higher-order emotions (target-patients), and patients with focal lesions in brain regions unrelated to emotions (lesion-controls) engage in an investment task.

Participants who were endowed with $20 at the beginning of the task were told that they would be making several rounds of investment decisions, and that, in each round, they had to make a decision between two options: invest $1 or not invest. If the decision was not to invest, they would keep the dollar, and the task would advance to the next round. If the decision was to invest, they would hand over a dollar bill to the experimenter. The experimenter would then toss a coin in plain view of the subject. If the outcome of the toss were to be heads (50 percent chance), then they would lose the $1 that was invested; if the outcome of the toss were to be tails (50 percent chance), then $2.50 would be added to the participant's account. The task would then advance to the next round. The task consisted of 20 rounds of investment decisions. Note that the design of the task is such that it would behoove participants to invest in all the 20 rounds because the expected value on each round is higher if one invests ($1.25) than if one does not ($1).

An examination of the proportion of rounds (in four blocks of five rounds each) in which participants decided to invest yielded some interesting results. In the early rounds of investment decisions (the first block of five rounds), all participants seemed to make their decisions rationally, suggesting that higher-order cognitions related to notions of expected values were at play in the early rounds. However, as the rounds of investment decisions progressed, normal participants and lesion-controls became more reluctant to invest on subsequent rounds, suggesting that higher-order anticipatory emotions (fear of losing money) began to play a bigger role than higher-order cognitions in terms of their impact on the decisions. In contrast, target-patients (i.e., patients with impairments in the brain areas related to higher-order emotions) continued to invest as the rounds of investment decisions progressed. Incidentally, target-patients ended up making more money than did normal individuals and patient-controls over the 20 rounds of investment decisions.

Role of motives in the affective-cognitive framework

According to the affective-cognitive framework highlighted in Figure 9.1, the effects of exposure to affect-laden stimuli on action tendencies are mediated by consumer motives. Further, according to the framework, these motives can be activated directly by both higher-order and lower-order cognitions arising from the stimulus exposure. To test the mediating role of consumer motives, Shiv and Fedorikhin (2002, experiment 3) primed either appetitive or utilitarian motives by adapting a procedure used by Ramanathan and Menon (2004). Participants engaged in a purportedly unrelated task which involved evaluating products in three categories – cars, apartments, and mattresses. For one group of participants, the products were described on attributes such as "luxurious leather trim," "new car smell," and "sunlight streaming down the sunroof" for the car. For another group of participants, the products were described on attributes such as "high reliability," "good workmanship," and "one that will last a long time" for the car. The various attributes were selected based on separate pretests which showed that appetitive motives are activated for the former group of respondents and not for the latter. Participants then engaged in a filler task, following which they made choices between two options, a "party vacation" in Bora Bora and a "body-toning" vacation in the foothills of the Rockies. (Note that the former is more affect-laden compared to the latter but also less favorable in terms of the long-term consequences.) The results were consistent with the hypothesized mediating role of motives in the affective-cognitive framework. When utilitarian motives were primed, choice of the affect-laden option (party vacation) was higher when higher-order emotions were at play than when higher-order cognitions were at play. However, when appetitive motives were primed, choice of the affect-laden option was as high when higher-order cognitions were at play as when higher-order emotions were at play.

The findings reported in Shiv and Fedorikhin (2002) also provide support to the notion that motives can be directly activated by lower/higher-order cognitions. Further support for this notion derives from Fishbach *et al.* (2003). Their findings suggest that when individuals with chronic aversive motives in a specific domain (e.g., dieters in the domain of food) are exposed to affect-laden options in the domain (e.g., chocolate Twix bar), the aversive motives are spontaneously activated to override the temptations (i.e., appetitive motives) arising from the affective quality of the stimulus object.

Summary of evidence in support of the affective-cognitive framework and its managerial implications

The evidence presented in the previous sections seems to be largely supportive of the affective-cognitive framework. First, when higher-order processes are restricted from occurring upon exposure to a positively valenced affect-laden option (e.g., chocolate cake), the ensuing motives and action tendencies are likely to be in favor of the affect-laden option. Further, the greater the affective significance of the affect-laden option, the stronger these motives and action tendencies are likely to be. Finally, if higher-order processes occur, cognitions related to the consequences of choosing the affect-laden option are likely to overcome the motives and action tendencies triggered by lower-order emotions. However, if cues related to the primary inducers of lower-order emotions are present in the environment, then the focus of the higher-order processes are likely to be on the hedonic qualities of the affect-laden option, resulting in higher-order emotions, appetitive motives, and action tendencies that favor choosing (rejecting) this option if the emotions are positive (negative). Put together, these findings suggest that in real-world marketing contexts, the more cognitively busy or mindless the shopper is at the time of making decisions involving affect-laden options, the more likely is the shopper to choose such options. Further, more vivid presentations of affect-laden stimuli or availability of cues related to affect-laden options in the shopping environment are likely to increase the likelihood of choosing these options. For example, the findings would suggest that pleasant surprises that occur in store environments (e.g., in-store "surprise" coupons) may actually be more effective if (1) the shopper is cognitively busy at the point of purchase, (2) the surprise coupons are presented in a more vivid fashion in the store environment, and (3) more cues related to these surprise coupons are available in the store environment (see Heilman *et al.* 2002 for research on in-store surprise coupons).

Despite evidence in the literature providing support for the affective-cognitive framework, several issues related to the framework remain unexamined. We highlight some of these issues and provide potential directions for future research later in this chapter.

The affective-cognitive framework as applied to somatosensory stimuli: emerging findings

Although the discussion in the previous sections has focused on emotions arising from affect-laden *visual* stimuli (e.g., cake, party-vacation, etc.) and the interplay of these emotions with higher-order cognitions, recent studies carried out by Nowlis and Shiv (2004) suggest that the affective-cognitive framework can be applied to pleasurable somatosensory stimuli as well. But before we delve into a discussion of these findings, let us provide a context for this discussion with the following scenario. Imagine that you are at a grocery store and notice a sampling station serving a new brand of milk chocolate from Switzerland, namely Lindt. You decide to taste the chocolate so that you can decide whether to buy Lindt or another chocolate that you are familiar with, say Godiva. The question is, are you likely to derive more pleasure from the tasting experience, and thereby form stronger subsequent preferences for the tasted option if you are cognitively busy or if you are paying attention to the experience? The answer to this question might appear, at first blush, to be quite straightforward. Intuition would suggest that you would experience more pleasure during the tasting experience if you are paying attention than if you are distracted. This intuition was consistent with a survey that we conducted on individuals with expertise in food sampling programs (22 marketing executives at Pillsbury and P&G, and four professional tasters at two grocery stores in Iowa City participated in the survey). An overwhelming majority of these experts stated that food sampling campaigns would be more effective if consumers paid attention while tasting a food sample than if they were distracted.

Research on somatosensory experiences of pain, however, suggests otherwise. A series of studies by Leventhal and his colleagues (see Leventhal *et al.* 1979; also Read and Loewenstein 1999) suggests that the intensity of somatosensory experiences of pain is higher when individuals are distracted than when they pay attention during the experience. These findings suggest that, for the food-sampling scenario described above, distraction (compared to paying attention) will *increase* the intensity of somatosensory experiences of pleasure and, therefore, increase subsequent preferences for the tasted option (Lindt chocolate). Thus, what we have are two contradictory predictions, one arising from our intuition (and from the survey of experts) and the other arising from research on pain. In an attempt to resolve these contradictory predictions, Nowlis and Shiv (2005) had participants taste Lindt either under high levels of distraction (e.g., memorizing an eight-digit number) or low levels of distraction (e.g., memorizing a two-digit number). Participants then chose between the tasted option, Lindt, and Godiva (note that participants did not taste Godiva, but were familiar with this option). The findings were consistent with predictions arising from research on pain. Specifically, the choice of Lindt was significantly higher under conditions of high distraction than under conditions of low distraction.

To account for the findings reported above, Nowlis and Shiv (forthcoming) propose a Two-Component Model of Somatosensory Experiences (TCM), which has several parallels to the affective-cognitive framework discussed earlier in this chapter (see also Shiv and Nowlis 2004). According to the TCM, the somatosensory experience of tasting a food item such as chocolate (generally a pleasurable experience) is composed of two components. One component is emotional in nature (i.e., involves emotional reactions arising from the sensory experience) and is associated with automatic processes. The second component is informational in nature (for instance, its health consequences, the quality of the chocolate, its sweetness and texture, the spatio-temporal characteristics of the tasting experience, etc.). This informational component is associated with controlled processes and can be assumed to be less positively valenced than the affective component. If individuals are distracted while tasting chocolate, the affective component is likely to serve as the predominant input to the intensity of pleasure that is ultimately experienced, and, therefore, to the subsequent choice of the sampled chocolate. On the other hand, if individuals are not distracted while tasting the chocolate, both the less positively valenced informational component and the more positively valenced affective component are likely to serve as inputs. These inputs, in combination, are likely to be less positive than the affective component that is likely to predominate when the level of distraction is high. Therefore, in opposition to the predictions from the survey of experts, higher levels of distraction ought to lead to more favorable preferences for the sampled chocolate than lower levels of distraction.

Nowlis and Shiv (forthcoming) conducted several studies to test the validity of the TCM. For example, note that if the TCM is valid, then altering the affective-significance of the emotional component by having individuals consume something sweet (salty) before tasting the sampled item ought to decrease (increase) the intensity of the affective component. This should then influence subsequent preferences for the tasted option, particularly when processing resources are restricted (i.e., when the automatic emotional component is likely to predominate). The findings reported by Nowlis and Shiv (forthcoming) are consistent with this prediction. They also measured participants' emotional reactions to the taste experience (some participants responded to this measure prior to making their subsequent choices while others did so after they had made their choices; the order of measurement had no effect on the dependent variables). Tests of mediation suggest that these emotional reactions did mediate the effects of the independent variables on choice.

In sum, the findings reported in Nowlis and Shiv (2005, and Shiv and Nowlis

2004) provide further evidence that the interplay of emotions and cognitions is likely to influence not only visual stimuli but somatosensory stimuli as well. More research is needed to examine both the managerial as well as the conceptual ramifications of these findings.

Future research on issues related to the affective-cognitive framework

In this section, we highlight several issues arising from the affective-cognitive framework, issues that provide promising avenues for future research. First, we examine factors that are likely to moderate the relative impact on action tendencies of emotions and higher-order cognitions when both of these components are at play. We then examine potential factors that can moderate the intensity of lower-order emotions and the action tendencies arising from these emotions. Finally, we discuss some methodological issues related to the study of emotions in decision-making.

Interplay of emotions and higher-order cognitions: potential moderators

The affective-cognitive framework and the empirical evidence gathered thus far in support of the framework are relatively silent about what is likely to be the relative impact on action tendencies of lower-order emotions (and higher-order emotions) and higher-order cognitions if both of them are at play. In other words, under what conditions are higher-order cognitions likely to overcome lower-order emotions and vice versa? Work by Baumeister and his colleagues (e.g., Muraven and Baumeister 2000) suggests that overcoming lower-order emotions using higher-order "restraining" cognitions requires mental energy (termed in Baumeister's work as ego), and any factor that depletes this mental energy is likely to increase (decrease) the impact of lower-order emotions (higher-order cognitions). One factor that has been found to deplete mental energy required for self-control is the level of mental fatigue that the individual is experiencing. What these findings would suggest is that, in the cake-salad scenario, when both lower-order emotions and higher-order cognitions are likely to be at play (i.e., when processing resources are available), the higher is the state of mental fatigue, the greater is the likelihood that lower-order emotions would overcome higher-order "restraining" cognitions and cause the individual to give in to temptation, i.e., choose a pleasurable affect-laden option. This is a prediction that needs to be tested in future research.

Further, an assumption that Shiv and Fedorikhin (1999) make is that the higher-order cognitions are *always* restraining in nature, i.e., focus on the negative consequences of choosing the cake versus the fruit salad. We all know that higher-order cognitions can also be in the form of excuses to indulge. For example, there is nothing to prevent an individual in the cake-salad scenario from saying something like, "I have been good at watching my diet this entire week, so it is okay if I chose the cake on this occasion." In fact, in the first author's experience of running experiments involving the cake-salad paradigm, the effects of the cognitive load factor (memorizing a seven-digit number versus a two-digit number) tend to wash away if the study is conducted on Fridays (the author calls this phenomenon "the Friday Effect"). Specifically, on Fridays, even participants who are under low levels of cognitive load tend to pick the cake, much like those who are under high levels of load. An examination of participants' thought protocols suggests that participants who are under low levels of load tend to focus, in general, on the adverse consequences of choosing the cake. But on Fridays, the focus of their thoughts tends to be centered on giving excuses to indulge. Similar findings related to the role of excuses in decision-making have also been documented by Kivetz and Simonson (2002a, 2002b) and Kivetz and Zheng (2004). For example, Kivetz and Simonson (2002a) examined the impact of the level of effort participants had to invest to obtain a reward in a frequency program. The reward was either in the form of necessities or in the form of luxuries. Although, in general, individuals prefer choosing necessities over luxuries because the latter is associated with more guilt than the former, investing more effort in a frequency program causes individuals to prefer the luxury rewards presumably because the greater effort gives individuals an excuse to become indulgent ("I have invested so much in the frequency program that it is okay for me to become indulgent"). Future research needs to examine the role of excuses in moderating the relative impact on choices of lower-order (and also higher-order) emotions and higher-order cognitions, and the role of various factors that trigger excuses favoring indulgent choices (e.g., "it is a Friday"; "I have put in a lot of effort").

Future research also needs to examine the role of ambient affect (i.e., moods) in determining the relative impact of emotions and cognitions. Ample evidence has indicated that individuals under emotional distress tend to become more indulgent across various domains involving affect-laden options. For example, Slochower and Kaplan (cited in Tice *et al.* 2001) showed that inducing anxiety among individuals increased their consumption of food. Likewise, emotional distress has been shown to cause increases in smoking (Schachter *et al.* 1977), drinking (Hull *et al.* 1986), and compulsive shopping (O'Guinn and Faber 1989). In an attempt to shed light on the underlying causes of this well-documented phenomenon, Tice *et al.* (2001) found that emotional distress shifts individuals toward favoring the immediate pleasure (as a means of strategically alleviating the distress) over higher-order "restraining" cognitions. Put together, these findings suggest that when negative emotions, either lower-order or higher-order, and "restraining" cognitions are simultaneously at play, the emotions tend to win out in terms of their effects on action tendencies when the level of distress is high.

A promising area for future research is to examine whether opposite effects occur under positive mood states, i.e., the restraining higher-order cognitions have a bigger impact than emotions under these states. This would be consistent with the notion that positive mood makes people more attentive, more thorough and more efficient in their decision-making (Isen 2001). This would also be consistent with some findings in research on delay of gratification that shows that compared to neutral mood states, children in a positive mood state were more likely to choose a bigger delayed reward over a smaller immediate one (Moore *et al.* 1976; Seeman and Schwarz 1974). However, preliminary evidence does not seem to be in support of this assertion. First, work by Rook and Gardner (1993) suggests that positive mood is associated with more impulsive behaviors. Second, in a survey carried out by the first author at the University of Iowa, college football fans were asked about the activities they would engage in if the Hawkeyes won and if the Hawkeyes lost in a game against an arch rival. Most of the survey respondents stated that they would engage in indulgent behaviors following a win but not do so following a loss. It is quite possible, therefore, that both positive and negative mood states increase the impact of emotions (both lower- and higher-order) compared to that of restraining higher-order cognitions. Alternatively, it is possible that people in positive mood states are more capable of delaying gratification, but will do so only if the context is relevant (i.e., the context provides a compelling reason for exercising self-control). Work by Raghunathan and Trope (2002) points to this possibility. This research tested the effects of positive (versus, negative and neutral) moods on willingness to seek and process emotionally disturbing, but potentially useful information (e.g., the negative effects of caffeine consumption on the body). The findings suggest that people in positive moods are more receptive to such information but only if the information is relevant for them (e.g., if the individual consumes a lot of caffeine). More research is needed to examine these possibilities.

Factors that potentially affect the intensity of lower-order emotions

Although Shiv and Fedorikhin (1999) have documented the role of presentation-mode in determining the intensity of lower-order emotions, more research is needed in identifying a broader array of factors. One promising finding related to lower-order emotions is that amygdala responses to affectively significant stimuli differ in older compared to younger adults. Specifically, Mather *et al.* (2004) used event-related functional magnetic resonance imaging (fMRI) to assess whether amygdala activation in response to positive and negative emotional pictures changes with age. Both older and younger adults showed the same level of activation of the amygdala for positive emotional pictures. But for negative emotional pictures older adults showed decreased amygdala activation compared to younger adults. These findings suggest that older and younger adults may not differ when it comes to choices involving positive affect-laden stimuli (e.g., choosing between cake and salad), but older adults might be less affected by lower-order affect in situations that involve negative affect-laden stimuli. For example, one could envisage a situation where an individual is planning to buy irradiated meat, which is slightly discolored and, consequently, may elicit lower-order emotions related to disgust, but is also healthier than regular meat. A prediction arising from Mather *et al.* (2004) is that the lower-order disgust-related emotions are likely to be less intense for older adults than for younger adults, resulting in greater choices of the irradiated meat among the former than among the latter group of adults.

Another factor that can potentially affect the intensity of lower-order emotions is hunger. The work by Berridge (e.g., Berridge 2001) suggests that the affective-significance of a positively valenced food item is higher when one is hungry than when one is satiated. This, in turn suggests that the intensity of lower-order emotions is likely to be higher when one is hungry than when one is not. This is an exciting avenue for future research particularly because it points to the potential moderating role of a visceral factor, namely hunger, the effects of which have been vastly under-researched in consumption-related domains (for an exception, see Nowlis *et al.* 2004; Read and van Leeuwen 1998; see also, Loewenstein 1996 for the role of visceral factors in decision-making). For example, Gilbert *et al.* (2002) show that consumers buy more food products when they are hungry than when they are not. Future research can examine whether these findings are mediated by the intensity of emotions arising from the exposure to food items. Another issue for future research is whether hunger can moderate the intensity of affect arising from exposure to non-food-related product categories and, thereby, influence choices in these categories.

Individual differences may also play a role in the intensity of lower-order emotions that are triggered upon exposure to affect-laden stimuli. For example, Larsen and Diener (1987; see also Moore *et al.* 1995) have shown that upon exposure to affect-laden stimuli individuals who score high on the Affect Intensity Measurement (AIM) scale experience emotions with greater intensity than those who scored low on this scale. It is, therefore, quite possible that in the cake-salad scenario, individuals high on the AIM scale will experience more intense lower-order emotions and stronger action tendencies toward the cake than those low on the AIM scale. More research is needed to shed light on the role of individual differences in moderating the effects predicted by the affective-cognitive framework.

Although the thrust of this section has been on lower-order emotions, future research needs to examine if the factors highlighted above moderate the intensity of higher-order emotions as well. For example, ongoing research by Bechara and his colleagues suggests that normal ageing can affect the functioning of the VM cortex by reducing the sensitivity of this brain structure to affect-laden higher-order cognitions. It is, therefore, quite possible that age might moderate the effects of higher-order emotions in the same fashion as it does with lower-order emotions.

Finally, future research needs to examine the effects of emotions and cognitions on variables other than choice. An interesting avenue for future research is to examine whether the affective-cognitive framework applies to variety-seeking behaviors as well. As documented in the chapter by Kahn and Ratner, the amount of emotional arousal in a choice set can influence the desire for variety across items in the set. Future research needs to examine whether this phenomenon occurs with both lower-order and higher-order emotions and whether consumer motives mediate the effects.

Methodological issues

Although the affective-cognitive framework invokes the role of emotions in decision-making, the empirical evidence for emotions being involved is largely circumstantial or based on self-report measures. For example, Shiv and Fedorikhin (1999, experiment 1) manipulate the affective significance of the choice options and predict that if an emotion-based account is valid, then this manipulation ought to affect subsequent choices when the level of cognitive load is high (that is, when lower-order emotions are likely to predominate). Their data are in line with this prediction but one should keep in mind that this evidence is still circumstantial. Shiv and Fedorikhin (1999, 2002) also use self-report measures as a means of examining whether the decisions were based on emotions or cognitions. However, such self-report measures are fraught with problems. Specifically, it is quite possible that participants in Shiv and Fedorikhin's studies were inferring whether their decisions were driven by emotions or by cognitions based on the choices they had just made (the self-report measures were administered immediately after participants had made their choices). For example, if the reader had been a participant in one of these studies and had chosen the cake, the chances are high that the reader would have indicated that the choice was based on emotions ("I just chose the cake, so the decision must have been based on emotions").

The problem of using self-reported measures to get at emotions is compounded by several factors. First, many of the emotions that we experience occur without any conscious awareness (e.g., Kihlstrom *et al.* 2000). A powerful demonstration of this fact was provided by a French physician named Claparède. Each time he called on an amnesic, he would introduce himself anew (the woman had no recollection of ever having met him before). On one occasion, Claparède greeted the woman as usual by shaking her hand, but this time with a pin concealed in his hand. The woman immediately withdrew her hand in response to the lower-order emotion (pain) that she experienced. The next time Claparède called on the woman, she showed no signs of recognizing him but this time she involuntarily withdrew her hand just before she shook his. Her involuntary action tendency presumably arising from higher-order emotions had occurred completely outside conscious awareness. If she had been asked about why she withdrew her hand (through a self-report measure), she would have had no conscious recollection of why she did so, yet emotions had a role to play in her behavior.

The second problem of using self-report measures arises when the emotions are extended over a period of time. When participants are asked to make global inferences about the emotions that they have just experienced, they do not veridically integrate the momentary emotional reactions that unfolded over the period in question. Specifically, in a series of studies, Daniel Kahneman (see, Kahneman 1999 for a review) has demonstrated that individuals, when asked to respond to self-report measures of the emotions they just experienced, tend to focus more on the peak and the end of the experience.

The problems associated with the use of self-report measures to get at emotions suggest that better methods need to be used in future research. For example, one could get at emotions by measuring the physiological correlates of these emotions. These include changes in the heart rate, skin conductance, scalp-recorded brain electrical activity, etc. which have been shown to be sensitive to measuring both positive as well as negative emotions (e.g., Cacioppo *et al.* 2000). Another emerging trend is to use functional neuroimaging, but the costs involved in using this modern technology and the complexity involved in interpreting data are formidable challenges that need to be met before the use of this technique can become more widespread.

Some final words

The broad objective of this chapter was to take the reader on a journey involving the heart and the mind – a journey that was aimed at unraveling some of the psychological and neurological underpinnings of "hot" (i.e., emotional) and "cold" (i.e., cognitive) decisions. In the process of accomplishing this objective, we presented a framework that ties together emotions and cognitions, and considered factors that lead some decisions to be based on emotions and some on cognitions. We also presented empirical evidence in support of the framework, and highlighted some promising avenues for future research, including our speculation of the promise that neurological research has to offer in examining these issues. Most importantly, we hope that this journey has left the reader with a desire to learn more about the interplay of the heart and the mind in decision-making.

Notes

1   LeDoux proposes that the affective significance of a stimulus could also be hard-wired. However, in his research, LeDoux has used the classical conditioning learning paradigm to alter the affective significance of stimuli before examining the regions of the brain responsible for the generation of affective reactions.
2   For ease of exposition, the affective-cognitive framework treats the spontaneous and deliberative processes as being dichotomous. In actuality, one may view the processes as falling on a continuum from "fully automatic" to "fully deliberate." Readers may refer to Bargh (1994), which describes dimensions that help determine how automatic or deliberate a particular behavior is.
3   Although similar brain structures are involved in the generation of positive and negative emotions, evidence shows that positive and negative emotions induce distinct physiological patterns that can be detected in laboratory settings as changes in heart rate, skin conductance, respiration, and so on (Cacioppo *et al.* 2000).
4   Although our discussion in this section will center on the cake-salad scenario, the affective-cognitive framework has been examined with other stimuli as well. For example, Shiv and Fedorikhin (2002) examine the affective-cognitive framework in the context of choosing between other food items (e.g., pizza versus soup) and non-food items (e.g., an indulgent vacation in Bora-Bora versus a body-toning vacation in the foothills of the Rockies).

References

Bargh, J. A. (1994) "The four horsemen of automaticity: Awareness, efficiency, intention, and control in social cognition," in R. S. Wyer and T. K. Srull (eds) *Handbook of Social Cognition*, Hillsdale, NJ: Erlbaum, 2nd edn: 1–40.

Bechara, A., Tranel, D., and Damasio, A. S. (2002) "The somatic marker hypothesis and decision-making," in F. Boller and J. Grafman (eds) *Handbook of Neuropsychology: Frontal Lobes*, Amsterdam: Elsevier: 117–143.

Berkowitz, L. (1993) "Towards a general theory of anger and emotional aggression: Implications of the cognitive-neoassociationistic perspective for the analysis of anger and other emotions," in R. S. Wyer and T. K. Srull (eds) *Advances in Social Cognition*, Vol. 6, Hillsdale, NJ: Lawrence Erlbaum Associates: 1–46.

Berridge, K. C. (2001) "Reward learning: Reinforcement, incentives, and expectations," in D. L. Medin (ed.) *The Psychology of Learning and Motivation: Advances in Research and Theory*, Vol. 40, San Diego, CA: Academic Press: 223–278.

Buck, R. (1985) "Prime theory: An integrated view of motivation and emotion," *Psychological Review* 92 (July): 389–413.

Cacioppo, J. T., Klein, D. J., Berntson, G. G., and Hatfield, E. (2000) "The psychophysiology of emotion," in M. Lewis and J. M. Haviland (eds) *The Handbook of Emotion*, New York: Guilford Press: 173–191.

Davidson, R. J., Jackson, D. C., and Kalin, N. H. (2000) "Emotion, plasticity, context, and regulation: Perspectives from affective neuroscience," *Psychological Bulletin* 126(6) (November): 890–909.

Epstein, S. (1993) "Emotion and self-theory," in Lewis and J. M. Haviland (eds) *Handbook of Emotions*, New York: Guilford Press: 313–326.

Fishbach, A., Friedman, R. S., and Kruglanski, A. W. (2003) "Leading us not into temptation: Momentary allurements elicit overriding goal activation," *Journal of Personality and Social Psychology* 84 (February): 296–309.

Gilbert, D. T., Gill, M. J., and Wilson, T. D. (2002) "The future is now: Temporal correction in affective forecasting," *Organizational Behavior and Human Decision Processes* 88 (May): 430–444.

Heilman, C. M., Nakamoto K., and Rao, A. G. (2002) "Pleasant surprises: Consumer response to unexpected in-store coupons," *Journal of Marketing Research* 39(2) (May): 243–252.

Hoch, S. J. and Loewenstein, G. F. (1991) "Time-inconsistent preferences and consumer self-control," *Journal of Consumer Research* 17 (March): 492–507.

Hull, J. G., Young, R. D., and Jouriles, E. (1986) "Applications of the self-awareness model of alcohol consumption: Predicting patterns of use and abuse," *Journal of Personality and Social Psychology* 51(4) (October): 790–796.

Kahneman, D. (1999) "Objective happiness," in D. Kahneman, E. Diener, and N. Schwarz (eds) *Well-being: The Foundations of Hedonic Psychology*, New York: Russell Sage Foundation: 3–25.

Kihlstrom, J. F., Mulvaney, S., Tobias, B. A., and Tobis, I. P. (2000) "The emotional unconscious," in E. Eich *et al.* (eds) *Counterpoints: Cognition and Emotion*, New York: Oxford University Press: 30–86.

Kivetz, R. and Simonson, I. (2002a) "Earning the right to indulge: Effort as a determinant of customer preferences toward frequency program rewards," *Journal of Marketing Research* 39(2) (May): 155–170.

Kivetz, R. and Simonson, I. (2002b) "Self-control for the righteous: Toward a theory of precommitment to indulgence," *Journal of Consumer Research* 29(2) (September): 199–217.

Kivetz, R. and Zheng, Y. (2004) "The justification heuristic: The impact of effort versus monetary costs on the decision to indulge," Working Paper, Graduate School of Business, Columbia University, New York.

Isen, A. (2001) "An influence of positive affect on decision-making in complex situation: Theoretical issues with practical implications," *Journal of Consumer Psychology* 11(2): 75–86.

Lang, P. J. (1993) "The network model of emotion: Motivational connections," in R. S. Wyer and T. K. Srull (eds) *Advances in Social Cognition*, Vol. 6, Hillsdale, NJ: Lawrence Erlbaum Associates: 109–133.

Larsen, R. J. and Diener, E. (1987) "Affect intensity as an individual difference characteristic: A review," *Journal of Research in Personality* 21 (March): 1–39.

Lazarus, R. S. (1991) "Progress on a cognitive-motivational-relational theory of emotion," *American Psychologist* 46 (August): 819–834.

LeDoux, J. E. (1987) "Emotion," in F. Plum (ed.) *Handbook of Physiology: Section 1: The Nervous System, Higher Functions of the Brain*, Vol. 5, Bethesda, MD: American Physiological Society: 419–460.

LeDoux, J. E. (1995) "Emotion: Clues from the brain," *Annual Review of Psychology* 46: 209–305.

LeDoux, J. E. (1996) *The Emotional Brain*, New York: Simon & Schuster.

Leventhal, H. (1984) "A perceptual-motor theory of emotion," in L. Berkowitz (ed.) *Advances in Experimental Social Psychology*, Vol. 17, Orlando, FL: Academic Press: 118–182.

Leventhal, H., Donald, B., Shacham, S., and Engquist, G. (1979) "Effects of preparatory information about sensations, threat of pain, and attention on cold pressor distress," *Journal of Personality and Social Psychology* 37 (May): 688–714.

Loewenstein, G. F. (1996) "Out of control: Visceral influences on behavior," *Organizational Behavior and Human Decision Processes* 65(3) (March): 272–292.

Mather, M., Canli, T., English, T., Whitfield, S., Wais, P., Ochsner, W., Gabrieli, J. D. E., and Carstensen, L. L. (2004) "Amygdala responses to emotionally valenced stimuli in older and younger adults," *Psychological Science* 15(4) (April): 259–263.

Metcalfe, J. and Mischel, W. (1999) "A hot/cool-system analysis of delay of gratification: Dynamics of willpower," *Psychological Review* 106 (January): 3–19.

Moore, B., Clyburn, A., and Underwood, B. (1976) "The role of affect in delay of gratification," *Child Development* 8(1): 99–104.

Moore, D. J., Harris, W. D., and Chen, H. C. (1995) "Affect intensity: An individual difference response to advertising appeals," *Journal of Consumer Research* 22 (September): 154–164.

Muraven, M. and Baumeister, R. F. (2000) "Self-regulation and depletion of limited resources: Does self-control resemble a muscle?" *Psychological Bulletin* 126(2) (March): 247–259.

Nowlis, S. M., Mandel, N., and McCabe, D. B. (2004) "The effect of a delay between choice and consumption on consumption enjoyment," *Journal of Consumer Research* 31 (December): 502–510.

Nowlis, S. and Shiv, B. (2005) "The influence of consumer distractions on the effectiveness of food sampling programs," *Journal of Marketing Research* 42(2): 157–168.

O'Guinn, T. C. and Faber, R. J. (1989) "Compulsive buying: A phenomenological exploration," *Journal of Consumer Research* 16(2) (September): 147–157.

Ortony, A., Clore, G. L., and Collins, A. (1988) *The Cognitive Structure of Emotions*. New York: Cambridge University Press.

Raghunathan, R. and Trope, Y. (2002) "Walking the tightrope between feeling good and being accurate: Mood as a resource in processing persuasive messages," *Journal of Personality and Social Psychology* 83(3) (September): 510–525.

Ramanathan, Suresh and Geeta Menon (2004) "The dynamics of impulsive behavior: Construct versus goal activation effects on memory, evaluations, and choice," Working Paper, Graduate School of Business, University of Chicago.

Read, D. and van Leeuwen, B. (1998) "Predicting hunger: The effects of appetite and delay on choice," *Organizational Behavior and Human Decision Processes* 76(2) (November): 189–205.

Read, D. and Loewenstein, G. (1999) "Enduring pain for money: Decisions based on the perception and memory of pain," *Journal of Behavioral Decision-Making* 12 (March): 1–17.

Rook, D. W. and Gardner, M. P. (1993) "In the mood: Impulse buying's affective antecedents," *Research in Consumer Behavior* 6: 1–28.

Schachter S. and Singer, J. E. (1962) "Cognitive, social, and physiological determinants of emotional state," *Psychological Review* 69: 379–99.

Schachter, S., Silverstein, B., and Perlick, D. (1977) "Studies of the interaction of psychological and pharmacological determinants of smoking," *Journal of Experimental Psychology: Genera,* 106(1) (March): 31–40.

Seeman, G. and Schwarz, C. J. (1974) "Affective state and preference for immediate versus delayed reward," *Journal of Research in Personality* 7: 384–394.

Shiv, B. and Fedorikhin, A. (1999) "Heart and mind in conflict: Interplay of affect and cognition in consumer decision-making," *Journal of Consumer Research* 26 (December): 278–282.

Shiv, B. and Fedorikhin, A. (2002) "Spontaneous versus controlled influences of stimulus-based affect on choice behavior," *Organizational Behavior and Human Decision Processes* 87 (March): 342–370.

Shiv, B. and Nowlis, S. (2004) "The effect of distractions whilst tasting a food sample: The interplay of informational and effective components in subsequent choice," *Journal of Consumer Research* 31 (December): 599–608.

Shiv, B., Loewenstein, G., Bechara, A., Damasio, H., and Damasio, A. R. (forthcoming), "Investment behavior and the dark side of emotion," *Psychological Science.*

Tice, D. M., Bratslavsky, E., and Baumeister, R. F. (2001) "Emotional distress regulation takes precedence over impulse control: If you feel bad, do It!" *Journal of Personality and Social Psychology* 80(1) (January): 53–67.

Wyer, R. S. Jr., Clore, G. L., and Isbell, L. M. (1999) "Affect and information processing," in L. Berkowitz (ed.) *Advances in Experimental Social Psychology*, Vol. 31, Orlando, FL: Academic Press: 1–77.

Zajonc, R. B. (1980) "Feeling and thinking: Preferences need no inferences," *American Psychologist* 35 (February): 151–175.

10 Social marketing messages that may motivate irresponsible consumption behavior

Cornelia Pechmann and Michael D. Slater

Social marketing messages are designed to persuade people to avoid problematic or detrimental behaviors, or engage in positive behaviors, to enhance the well-being of self and/or society (Andreasen 1994). Social marketing messages are included in school programs, in educational brochures, and increasingly in the mass media ads that we see every day (Hornik 2002). Government and nonprofit entities are paying to have ads placed in the mass media, assuming that the costs are more than offset by the savings from preventing problems. Recent examples include the US Office of National Drug Control Policy's "My Anti-drug" campaign (Kelder *et al.* 2000), American Legacy Foundation's "Truth" anti-smoking campaign (Farrelly *et al.* 2003), and the US Centers for Disease Control and Prevention's "Verb" exercise campaign (Vranica 2003).

There is a potential "dark side" to social marketing campaigns, though, that is not widely discussed. There is the possibility that campaigns will have no effects. However, the "dark side" that we are going to address is that campaigns may boomerang or have adverse effects (Fishbein *et al.* 2002). In other words, running the campaigns may be worse than doing nothing at all. Commercial campaigns could also boomerang, but social marketers often try to alter major lifestyle decisions, which may increase the potential for adverse effects (Clee and Wicklund 1980).

Significant concerns about social marketing campaigns boomeranging have recently surfaced. A large-scale study concluded that anti-drinking ad campaigns on college campuses could lead at least some students to drink more (Wechsler *et al.* 2003). An evaluation of the Office of National Drug Control Policy's anti-drug ad campaign concluded that it could be adversely affecting youth (Hornik *et al.* 2002). Concerns about boomerangs, however, are not new. In 1973, the National Commission on Marijuana and Drug Abuse recommended that President Nixon freeze the dissemination of anti-drug literature (Feingold and Knapp 1977), concluding it may "merely stimulate youthful interest in drugs" (27). Reviews of studies on anti-drinking and anti-drug school programs in the 1970s found that about one in seven was counterproductive (Foxcroft *et al.* 1997; Goodstadt 1980). Feingold and Knapp (1977) found that exposing youths to anti-drug health messages over several weeks weakened negative attitudes toward drugs.

In this chapter, we will identify the eight types of adverse effects that have been talked about (see Table 10.1). Then we will address the controversial issue of whether adverse effects actually occur by examining the empirical evidence (see Table 10.2). We also examine whether adverse effects are preventable and, if so, how (see Table 10.1). One view is that boomerang effects are the fault of the advertiser, caused by poor message design and inadequate research or measures; hence they are avoidable. Another perspective is that boomerang effects are inherent to many social marketing campaigns, and occur even with well-designed messages, but only certain people may be adversely affected and so one hopes to do more good than harm. Fortunately, the evidence favors the former view.

To begin, we note that there is relatively limited empirical evidence of adverse effects, based on controlled studies. We conducted a keyword search of electronic databases and scrutinized the reference lists of retrieved articles. We identified about fifty articles mentioning the topic, of which fifteen described controlled studies in which significant adverse effects were documented relative to an unexposed control group. These fifteen articles are listed in Table 10.2 and we will focus primarily on them, because they provide the strongest evidence of adverse effects (Cook and Campbell 1979). Most of these studies were true experiments in that individual participants were randomly assigned to condition, but some were quasi-experiments in that this type of random assignment did not occur. Most were lab studies but some were conducted in the field. Virtually all of these studies examined messages to deter problem behaviors. Thus, we will not have much to say about adverse effects from campaigns that promote healthful or pro-social behaviors, although we will return to that topic in the final discussion.

It should also be noted that literally thousands of studies have been published on social marketing interventions, generally reporting favorable effects (Floyd *et al.* 2000). For instance, a recent meta-analysis (Snyder 2001) identified 48 field studies of mass media health communication campaigns in the USA and none of the studies found adverse effects. In fact, on average, "7 percent to 10 percent more of the people in the campaign (intervention) communities changed their behavior [in the positive direction] than did those in the control communities" (182). In published studies, positive effects clearly outnumber adverse effects by a wide margin. One possible conclusion that can be drawn is that adverse effects are rare and avoidable. Also, interest in studying adverse effects may be limited, with researchers preferring to demonstrate the benefits of social marketing rather than its shortcomings. Or, editors may be less willing to publish adverse effects studies, as they are with studies showing null effects, causing a "file drawer" problem. It is also conceivable that the standard research designs are not sensitive enough to document adverse effects and that nonstandard designs are required, such as longitudinal field studies of susceptible subpopulations. In any event, several studies documenting adverse effects have been published and will be discussed below.

Table 10.1 Types of adverse effects that may be caused by messages

Problem	Adverse effect	How to avoid
A. Messages that are counterinformative		
1. **Counterrisk** information is conveyed: Risk < expectation	Weakens protective risk-related beliefs	Ensure depicted risk > prior belief
2. **Counterbenefit** information is conveyed: Benefit > expectation	Strengthens belief that problem behavior is beneficial	Ensure depicted benefit < prior belief
3. **Counternorm** information is conveyed: Prevalence > expectation	Weakens protective norm-related beliefs	Ensure depicted prevalence < prior belief
4. Claim is **noninformative**; it states the obvious, a truism	Weakens belief in truism due to "pragmatic inference" that messages don't state the obvious	Avoid stating truism
B. Messages that elicit backlash		
5. Warns or forbids using an authoritarian, noncredible spokesperson	Elicits **"reactance,"** i.e., person performs behavior to assert freedom and/or savor **forbidden fruit**	Use credible spokesperson; don't be authoritarian; don't convey behavior is forbidden fruit
6. States risk but no info about how to enact advocated behavior or its efficacy	Elicits **"fear control,"** e.g., message or source derogation, denial, avoidance	Provide information to bolster efficacy perceptions
C. Inherent problems with social marketing messages		
7. **"Descriptive norm meta-message"** may be conveyed in otherwise strong message	Message that behavior is problem implies behavior is prevalent	Depict behavior as low in prevalence
8. **"Offsetting behavior"** may occur even with strong message	Lowering risk of behavior is offset by increases in behavioral intensity	Warn about risks of offsetting behavior

Note: Table focuses on messages to discourage problem behaviors.

Counterinformative messages

Counterrisk messages

A message may cause adverse effects because it is "counterinformative." That is, it may present arguments that are actually weaker than what people had previously believed. Four distinct types of counterinformative messages have been identified (see Figure 10.1). One type is a "counterrisk" message, which conveys risk estimates

Table 10.2 Studies documenting that social marketing messages caused adverse effects relative to a nonexposed control group

Article, method	Message, target, tone	Effect versus control	Possible cause
1. Feingold & Knapp 1977; *quasi-experimental lab study*	Anti-illicit drug messages, adolescents	*Attitudinal:* Less negative attitudes toward drugs	**Unclear;** too little information provided about messages
2. Foxcroft *et al.* 1977; *review of experiments*	Anti-alcohol school programs, adolescents	*Behavioral:* In 33 experiments, 16 percent of results were adverse	**Unclear;** too little information provided about messages
3. Goodstadt 1980; *review of experiments*	Anti-drug school programs, adolescents	*Behavioral, Attitudinal:* Of 125 studies, 12 percent enhanced drug use or attitudes	**Unclear;** too little information provided about messages
4. Keller *et al.* 2002; *lab experiment*	Mammogram messages on cancer risk by age, women, *negative*	*Attitudinal:* Lower estimates of getting cancer among depressed women	**Counterrisk information**
5. Cox & Cox 2001; *lab experiment*	Mammogram message on benefits, women, *positive*	*Attitudinal:* Lower perceived susceptibility to cancer, poorer mammogram attitude	**Counterrisk information**
6. Wagner & Sundar 1999; *quasi-experimental lab study*	Anti-illicit drug messages, adolescents, *negative*	*Attitudinal:* More curiosity about drug use, lower perceived risk, higher perceived peer use	**Counterrisk information**
7. Fishbein *et al.* 2002; *lab experiment*	Anti-illicit drug messages, adolescents, *positive*	*Attitudinal:* 6 of 30 PSAs rated less effective than control video	**Counterrisk information**
8. Wechsler *et al.* 2003; *quasi-experimental field study*	Norm messages, college students, *positive*	*Behavioral:* Increased drinking, especially at high-exposure schools	**Counternorm information**
9. Werch *et al.* 2000; *field experiment*	Norm messages, college students, *positive*	*Behavioral, Attitudinal:* Higher perceived acceptance of binging; increased drinking among bingers	**Counternorm information**

Article, method	Message, target, tone	Effect versus control	Possible cause
10. DeTurck & Goldhaber 1991; *quasi-experimental field study*	"No diving" sign warning of risks, adolescents, *negative*	*Behavioral:* Increased intent to dive among students who previously dove	**Reactance**
11. Hyland & Birrell 1979; *lab experiment*	Warning on risks of smoking, adults, *negative*	*Behavioral:* Increased desire to smoke among smokers	**Reactance**
12. Snyder & Blood 1992; *lab experiment*	Warning on risks of alcohol, college students, *negative*	*Behavioral, Attitudinal:* Higher perceived drinking benefits among drinkers; increased intent to drink among male drinkers	**Reactance**
13. Blood & Snyder 1993; *lab experiment*	Warning on risks of alcohol, college students, *negative*	*Behavioral:* Increased intent to drink among students with pro-drinking norms	**Reactance**
14. Bushman & Stack 1996; *lab experiment*	Warning stating violent films harmful, college students, *negative*	*Behavioral:* Increased desire to see violent films among high reactance people	**Reactance (Forbidden Fruit)**
15. Donaldson *et al.* 1994, 1995; *field experiment*	Anti-drinking refusal skills program, adolescents, *positive*	*Attitudinal:* Higher perceived drug offers among public school students	**Descriptive norm meta-message**

that are lower than what people had expected. In other words, it discusses an underwhelming threat (Atkin 2002). For instance, if people think that nearly half of smokers get lung cancer, stating the true rate of 15 percent would be a counterrisk message (Slovic 2001; Viscusi 1992). Social marketers may think it is easy to avoid counterrisk messages, but research suggests otherwise (Fishbein *et al.* 2002; Wagner and Sundar 1999). In particular, people may have exaggerated risk perceptions, and so telling them the simple truth could be counterproductive (Keller *et al.* 2002).

Researchers have found that messages that stress risk severity and/or vulnerability generally reduce the problem behavior (Floyd *et al.* 2000; Rogers 1983). However, people overestimate many types of risks, particularly those that are highly accessible in memory such as those reflecting naïve theories of disease (e.g.,

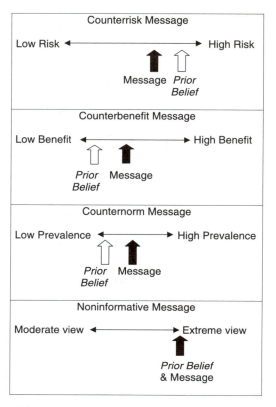

Figure 10.1 Counterinformative messages: adverse effects that are easiest to avoid. The figure focuses on messages to discourage problem behaviors.

smoking hurts lungs) and those receiving extensive news coverage (e.g., breast cancer, earthquakes) (Tversky and Kahneman 1974). Researchers have also documented individual differences in risk perceptions, for instance, adults are generally more likely to overestimate risks than adolescents (Cohn *et al.* 1995). Interestingly, though, youth rate the likelihood of certain risks that are salient in their lives higher than do adults, such as accidental pregnancies and drunk driving accidents (Millstein and Halpern-Felsher 2002).

Social marketers may therefore disseminate accurate information and yet cause adverse effects. In one study (Keller *et al.* 2002), women were given a mammogram brochure showing the actual risk of getting breast cancer by age group (e.g., at age 50, the risk is 2 percent). All women overestimated their risk of getting breast cancer. After reading the brochure, nondepressed women maintained their inflated risk estimates, while depressed woman lowered their risk estimates and became more accurate. It is conceivable that the brochure also inadvertently weakened depressed women's intent to get a mammogram by lowering their perceived cancer risk, but the study did not examine behavioral intent. In a related study (Cox and Cox 2001), exposure (versus nonexposure) to a positively framed testimonial about mammogram benefits elicited positive affect among women, lowering both perceived susceptibility to breast cancer and attitude toward mammography. The authors speculate that the positive frame weakened the risk message.

An additional study (Wagner and Sundar 1999) tested four anti-drug TV PSAs from the Partnership for a Drug-Free America among youth. Exposure to the PSAs (versus control messages) reduced the perceived risk of drug use and increased curiosity to use marijuana. Youth may have misinterpreted some of the information as counterrisk. In one PSA, young males were depicted smoking marijuana and laughing about the claim that it is dangerous. One said "I'm exactly the same as when I smoked my first joint." His mother asked: "Eddie did you even look for a job today?" and he replied "No, ma." The tagline was: "Marijuana can make nothing happen to you, too." Youth may have literally believed the tagline. In another PSA, marijuana use was compared to getting a tattoo or body-piercing and perhaps implied the risks were similarly low.

Thirty TV PSAs from the Partnership for a Drug-Free America were tested by Fishbein *et al.* (2002). Youth rated six of the PSAs as less effective than the control condition, a video with vague anti-drug references. Perceived effectiveness was measured with questions such as: "Was the message convincing?" (Fishbein *et al.* 2002: 241). The researchers did not study actual ad effectiveness; instead, they "assume that judgments of effectiveness may be a necessary (although not a sufficient) condition for producing actual change. . ." (ibid.: 239), which may not be a valid assumption.

In any event, the PSAs that were rated as ineffective used humor, argued "just say no," or tried to increase self-esteem or positive behaviors. Some of this information could have undermined prior risk perceptions, although the PSAs are not described in enough detail to draw any definitive conclusions. The PSAs that were rated as effective described serious, but realistic, negative consequences that adolescents did not already know about. Virtually all of the PSAs that were rated as effective addressed hard drugs such as heroin which pose more extreme health risks, indicating that it might possibly be more difficult to create effective anti-marijuana ads.

Yet another study (Yzer *et al.* 2003) tested Partnership TV PSAs, some of which seemed inadvertently to minimize the risks of drug use. For instance, in one PSA, a surgeon is shown smoking marijuana and giggling, trying to see if he can make a straight line with a scalpel. The intended message was that marijuana is harmful if smoked by surgeons. Some adolescents may have concluded that the risks were trivial or irrelevant to them because they are not surgeons. In this study, exposure to the anti-drug PSAs (versus control messages) did not significantly affect drug-related beliefs, attitudes or behavioral intent. However, among participants who saw the PSAs, the variability in negative beliefs was greater, indicating that the PSAs weakened some participants' risk beliefs while strengthening others' beliefs. In sum, it appears that some social marketing messages may inadvertently convey counterrisk information. However, additional research is needed to better understand the prevalence of the problem, and how best to avoid it.

Counterbenefit messages

"Counterbenefit" messages portray the benefits of detrimental behaviors in order to refute those benefits and/or attract attention but, in doing so, inadvertently increase belief in the benefits and/or belief salience (Yzer *et al.* 2003). In general, the more people view a problem behavior as beneficial or rewarding, the more likely they are to engage in it (Floyd *et al.* 2000; Rogers 1983). Nonetheless, social marketers may decide to discuss benefits to argue that the costs outweigh the benefits (Yzer *et al.* 2003). Benefits may also be depicted as a creative strategy, to attract attention, or to be clever or sarcastic. Benefits may be implied inadvertently as well. For instance, a message that is targeted at people who engage in a problem behavior may depict such people as attractive to avoid disparaging them and turning them off. The message may, however, inadvertently associate the behavior with the benefit of attractiveness.

The US Centers for Disease Control and Prevention pretested print anti-smoking ads about tobacco industry manipulation in youth focus groups, and concluded that the ads conveyed counterbenefit information (McKenna and Williams 1993). One ad, for instance, featured an attractive young model smoking a cigarette and was headlined "You get an image. They get an addict" (4). Thirty-eight percent of youths thought the ads promoted the benefits of smoking.

There is also some anecdotal evidence about counterbenefit messages. A *New York Times* columnist (Rich 1998) criticized an anti-drug TV ad for glamorizing drug users, saying: "The woman looks like Winona Ryder, she's wearing a tight tank top; there are no visible track marks" (19). Another columnist (Tuffs 2003) reported that the leading German cancer society asked the German government to stop its anti-smoking ad campaign because the ads "show attractive young people smoking, accompanied by big slogans such as 'Smoking soothes' and 'Smokers have contacts' and with statements in smaller type such as 'Right, but with carcinogenic substances such as arsenic, radon, or tar' " (360). Since substantial concerns have been raised about messages that appear to convey counterbenefit information, researchers should begin to study this issue.

Counternorm messages

A "counternorm" message states the prevalence of a problem behavior in order to show the prevalence is low, but the stated prevalence is actually higher than what people believed or is made more salient (Hovland *et al.* 1953). The prevalence of a behavior is called a "descriptive norm" and such norms have been shown to affect behavior strongly (Cialdini *et al.* 1990; Guo *et al.* 2002). People often do what they think others do, even if the behavior is harmful such as littering (Cialdini *et al.* 1990).

Explicit messages about the prevalence of binge drinking on college campuses are now widely used in campus alcohol prevention programs, and several papers claim that such efforts are successful (Haines and Spear 1996). The approach is based on research indicating that many college students drink heavily because they believe most of their peers do so and that it is expected of them too. The campaigns are intended to correct this misperception and imply that students can actually fit in better if they do not drink heavily. Recent studies have questioned the effectiveness of these anti-drinking normative campaigns, however, pointing out evidence of adverse effects.

A recent study (Wechsler *et al.* 2003) compared trends in self-reported alcohol use at 37 colleges that adopted social norm anti-drinking campaigns and 61 that did not. A typical message was "Most students have five or fewer drinks when they party" (485) and it is possible that such messages were counternormative for some students. Normative beliefs were not measured, though; only behavior was assessed. Students were surveyed in 1997 prior to when the campaigns commenced, and again in 2001. All campaigns were in place at least one year. Colleges that ran (versus did not run) the campaigns tended to be large and public and have higher drinking rates. To control for such differences, student-level data were adjusted based on age, gender, race, and survey response rate. Such adjustments cannot, however, ensure comparability (Cook and Campbell 1979).

It was found that heavy episodic drinking increased from 46 percent to 49 percent in schools that ran the anti-drinking campaigns, but stayed at about 41 percent in schools without the campaigns. The researchers concluded that the social norm campaigns likely caused the increases in drinking. However, the schools using the campaigns had more serious drinking problems to begin with, and so it is possible that the campaigns were simply ineffective at "stemming the tide" and did not actually make things worse than they otherwise would have been.

In a field study (Werch *et al.* 2000), college students were randomly assigned either to receive or not receive post cards and a phone call that were designed to convey anti-drinking norms. A sample message was: "In a recent study of our students living in the dorms, 64 percent reported that they have *not* engaged in heavy drinking recently" (86). Exposure (versus nonexposure) to social norm messages caused students who were in the preparation stage of heavy drinking, in that they had drunk heavily on occasion, to consume alcohol more frequently and perceive their peers as more accepting of heavy drinking. The messages worked among other students. The messages may have boomeranged among those who already planned to engage in heavy drinking by making the heavy drinking rate (36 percent) more salient.

In sum, it appears that to avoid adverse effects from social norm messages, (1) the stated prevalence of the problem behavior must clearly be lower than what was previously believed by the vast majority of the target audience, and (2) the stated prevalence must be low enough to suggest that the behavior is truly deviant or marginal. Normative beliefs, however, likely vary by audience segment. It would be useful to conduct research on how to create effective norm-based campaigns when there is considerable heterogeneity in normative beliefs.

Noninformative messages

A "noninformative" message states a truism, something that virtually everyone believes. It inadvertently weakens beliefs in the truism because it causes people to question its veracity (Gruenfeld and Wyer 1992). One might assume that social marketers would avoid restating the obvious, but several experts have voiced concerns about this issue (Cappella *et al.* 2001). One paper (Fishbein *et al.* 2002) opined: "it is unfortunately true that messages often target beliefs that are already strongly held by the population in question (e.g., 'smoking is harmful to health')" (238). Others have pointed out that if a celebrity who is presumed to be drug-free claims not to use drugs, youths may suddenly question whether the celebrity is drug-free after all (Feingold and Knapp 1977).

Researchers who have examined this issue (Gruenfeld and Wyer 1992) argue that messages not only convey literal meanings, but also pragmatic implications about why the messages were generated. A key pragmatic implication is that the messenger seeks to convey information that the recipient does not already have. This is called the "informativeness principle." If a message appears to restate the obvious, recipients assume the statement must not be so obvious; otherwise the informativeness principle would be violated. The researchers (ibid.: 45) found, for example, that exposure (versus nonexposure) to a newspaper headline stating "Republican congressmen belong to elitist country clubs" actually reduced people's belief in this statement, due to pragmatic implications. Future research should examine if the phenomenon extends to social marketing messages and, if so, under what circumstances.

How to avoid counterinformative messages

Counterinformative messages seem to be caused by poor message design, and presumably can be avoided by consulting experts and conducting research with potential audience members. Research should be conducted to understand audience members' prior beliefs and messages should be constructed that strengthen rather than weaken protective beliefs (Cappella *et al.* 2001; Fishbein *et al.* 2002). Messages should also be quantitatively copy-tested prior to airing (Atkin 2002; Fishbein *et al.* 2002; for guidance see Foley and Pechmann 2004). The copy-testing should involve not only the primary target audience, but also other groups that will be exposed to the campaign and are nontrivial in size. One should pay particular attention to individuals who are not predisposed to engage in the problem behavior. These individuals may have strong prior beliefs that are protective; hence, they may find the arguments to be weaker than prior beliefs. Messages should also be copy-tested among individuals who have engaged or intend to engage in the problem behavior. They may selectively attend to and/or overweigh any information that is conveyed about the benefits or prevalence of the behavior, even if that information is later countered (Petty and Cacioppo 1986).

Messages that elicit backlash

Messages that elicit reactance

Another reason why social marketing messages may boomerang is because they may elicit backlash. One type of backlash is called "psychological reactance" (Bensley and Wu 1991; Brehm 1972; Bushman 1998). When people feel pressured by others to make a change or even just comply with a recommendation, they may sometimes feel reactance or a drive to move in the opposite direction (Brehm 1972). Reactance actually increases people's attraction to the target belief, attitude, or behavior. One review paper (Clee and Wicklund 1980: 401) explains "It is the subject's knowledge that someone else wants to exert control or influence his/her behavior that generates the motivation to resist, and to behave in contrary ways."

Research suggests that several factors increase the likelihood of reactance (Brehm 1972; Clee and Wicklund 1980; Ringold 2002; Stewart and Martin 1994). First, reactance tends to be stimulated by highly overt influence attempts, including dogmatism and authoritarianism (Bensley and Wu 1991). Second, a low credibility spokesperson has been shown to trigger reactance (Brehm 1972; Clee and Wicklund 1980). Third, reactance appears to be more likely if the threatened freedom is highly important to the individual. Hence, social marketing messages are especially prone to elicit reactance if targeted at individuals who already engage in the problem behavior and thus presumably value the freedom to do so (Clee and Wicklund 1980). A reactance personality, defined as a strong desire to make one's own choices, can augment reactance effects (Hong and Page 1989). Finally, adolescents and young adults appear to be more prone to reactance than older adults (Hong *et al.* 1994). Note that reactance can be elicited even if the recommended course of action is viable and efficacious. People are not necessarily reacting against the merits of the recommendation; they are mainly reacting against the recommendation being made and/or the manner in which it was made.

In one study of reactance (Bensley and Wu 1991), college students read either a high or low dogmatic alcohol abstinence message and then participated in an ostensibly unrelated beer taste test. The highly dogmatic message used wording such as "any reasonable person must acknowledge these conclusions" whereas the less dogmatic message was worded "we believe that these conclusions are reasonable" (ibid.: 1114). Male heavy drinkers who read the high (versus low) dogmatic message drank significantly more. However, it is unclear whether there was a net negative effect of the dogmatic message relative to a no message control, because no control group was included.

In a more naturalistic field study (deTurck and Goldhaber 1991: 69), researchers posted signs by shallow ends of two school pools stating "No Diving. Danger. Shallow Water. You Can Be Paralyzed." Two other schools' pools were not provided with signs and served as controls. Posting (versus not posting) the signs increased intent to dive in the shallow end of the pool among adolescents who had previously done so.

A UK study exposed adults to cigarette ads with (versus without) the government health warning. Seeing the warning increased smokers' desire to smoke but had no effect on nonsmokers (Hyland and Birrell 1979). A similar study (Snyder and Blood 1992) examined US college students' reactions to the Surgeon General's warning not to drink alcohol when pregnant or driving due to the health risks. Seeing (versus not seeing) the warning increased drinkers' ratings of the benefits of drinking, and caused male drinkers to increase their intent to drink, but had no effect on nondrinkers. In a follow-up study (Blood and Snyder 1993), the warning increased intent to drink and drive, but only among those with pro-drinking normative beliefs. However, other researchers (MacKinnon and Lapin 1998) have been unable to replicate the Snyder results.

Some evidence suggests that messages evoke contrary behavior not only through motivational processes and reactance, but through related informational processes (Stewart and Martin 1994). Warnings may inform people that a behavior is "forbidden fruit" which in and of itself may increase its allure (Bushman 1998; Bushman and Stack 1996). For instance, by labeling a movie R-rated, one may inform people that it contains sex and violence and some people may be looking for these attributes. As one paper explains (Stewart and Martin 1994: 13), "warnings that . . . serve as signals for risk-taking opportunities or make a product more attractive may produce behavior that is exactly the opposite of that intended . . ."

One study (Bushman and Stack 1996) manipulated the warning label on violent films. The Surgeon General warning stated "This film contains some violent content. The US Surgeon General has concluded that television violence has harmful effects on viewers of all ages" (ibid.: 212). The "no-source" warning provided the same information without attributing it to the Surgeon General. The warning labels increased college students' desire to see violent films, relative to a no-label control. Also, the Surgeon General (versus no-source) warning increased choice of a violent film in a behavioral task. A follow-up study indicated that the warning labels enhanced the appeal of violent films among participants who had a reactance personality.

In sum, several studies have shown that authoritarian warnings can elicit reactance and be counterproductive. Restrictive laws can elicit reactance too (Mazis *et al.* 1973). Reactance seems particularly likely among people who engage in the problem behavior and/or have reactance personalities. However, few reactance studies have examined PSAs which tend to be more image-oriented and subtle than warnings, and perhaps less likely to elicit reactance. More research focusing on PSAs should be conducted.

Messages that elicit fear control

Threatening messages that evoke extreme fear may boomerang because they elicit a type of backlash called "fear control" (Witte 1991; Witte and Allen 2000). People may try to protect themselves from feelings of fear by minimizing the perceived risks. Fear control may involve message or source derogation ("you can't believe those studies"), defensive denial or wishful thinking ("that won't happen to me"), and/or defensive avoidance ("I am just not going to think about it"). Once fear is lessened, people may be less likely to engage in corrective actions to avoid the dangers that still face them (Witte 1991; Witte and Allen 2000). In a classic study (Janis and Feshbach 1953), a highly threatening message about dental hygiene had no effect on willingness to engage in the advocated behaviors (e.g., flossing), whereas a low-fear appeal increased willingness to engage in those behaviors.

Subsequent research based on Protection Motivation Theory (Rogers 1983) and the related Extended Parallel Processing Model (Witte 1991) indicates that whether a fear appeal is effective or counterproductive depends on both the degree of the threat and the ability to respond which itself is a function of both response efficacy and self-efficacy. Response efficacy refers to how effective a recommended behavior is believed to be in addressing the threat. (Older readers may remember "duck and cover" in case of a nuclear attack as an example of low response efficacy.) Self-efficacy refers to a person's perception that he or she can successfully execute the recommended behavior. If threat is high and efficacy is high, a person can be expected to modify his or her actions to reduce the danger. If threat is high but efficacy is low, a person can be expected to engage in counterproductive fear control rather than danger control (ibid.).

A meta-analysis of thirteen relevant studies (Witte and Allen 2000) found that problematic fear control responses do tend to increase with the extent of fear aroused, and decrease as efficacy elements in the message become stronger. However, comparisons with nonexposed control groups generally have not been reported or have been nonsignificant. Thus, there is sparse empirical evidence that, given low efficacy, strong fear appeals are counterproductive relative to seeing no fear appeals. What the evidence does suggest is that, given low efficacy, weaker fear appeals may be preferable to stronger ones.

One experiment crossed low, moderate or high threat AIDS messages with low or high condom efficacy information (Witte 1991). Threat was manipulated through the vividness of the photos showing AIDS health effects, and the similarity of the AIDS patient to the college student participants. Participants were screened to be sexually active. The high threat-high efficacy message led to positive behavior change at six week follow-up. The high threat-low efficacy message produced no behavior change relative to the no-message control, and led to fear control in the form of defensive avoidance.

Another study (Sturges and Rogers 1996) tested anti-smoking appeals. The pattern of results indicates that in the low efficacy condition, the high (versus low) threat message weakened intent to not smoke among adolescents and young adults. Among young adults, the mean intent to smoke was somewhat higher in the high threat-low efficacy condition than in the control condition, indicating a possible net adverse effect. However, the researchers did not statistically compare the means.

Other researchers (Nye *et al.* 1999) showed college students who were heavy drinkers "self-focusing" information about their typical drinking frequency based on a screening, and/or "normative" information about normal drinking. Students' problem recognition increased with either self-focusing or normative information. The combined information evoked the most negative affect but caused problem recognition to revert back to baseline (mirroring the control), among those who scored high on self-deception. These students tended to deny the accuracy of the information about their typical drinking. The problem may have been that none of the messages addressed efficacy, and students' baseline efficacy at cutting back on drinking may have been low. Interestingly, an earlier study (Agostinelli *et al.* 1995) found that the combined information (versus a control) reduced self-reported drinking at six-week follow-up, indicating no long-term adverse effect and, in fact, a positive effect. Hence, the findings are inconclusive.

In sum, low threat messages seem to work better than high threat messages given low efficacy. However, there is surprisingly little evidence that given low efficacy, high threat messages yield worse behavioral or attitudinal outcomes than no message. It is troubling, though, that low efficacy-high threat messages have been shown to evoke negative cognitions such as defensive avoidance. More research is needed to determine if, and when, such negative cognitions might produce adverse behavioral effects.

How to avoid messages that elicit backlash

To minimize the likelihood that social marketing messages will elicit backlash in the form of reactance, authoritarian spokespeople and wording should be avoided. Useful new information should be provided: not mandates. When young people are asked to react to PSAs, they often make comments such as "give us the facts and let us draw our own conclusions" (Teenage Research Unlimited 2003) and this approach should indeed reduce reactance. Also, credible spokespeople should be used. US broadcast laws require that sponsors be identified but, if the sponsor is the government or other authority figure, this information should probably be deemphasized. Also, it may help to brand the campaign with a credible name and logo. It has been argued that the national anti-smoking ad campaign called "Truth" is a good example of effective branding (Farrelly *et al.* 2003).

Witte and Allen (2000) discuss how to construct fear appeals that bolster feelings of efficacy and avoid backlash. They advise: "To increase perceptions of self-efficacy, practitioners should identify barriers that inhibit one's perceived ability to perform a recommended action and directly address these in the message" and that "To increase perceptions of response efficacy, practitioners should clearly outline how, why, and when a recommended response eliminates or decreases the chances of experiencing the health threat" (Witte and Allen 2000: 606). They also recommend that "fear control responses such as denial, defensive avoidance, and reactance should be assessed in evaluations" (ibid.: 606). Further, it may be necessary to try to avoid reaching entrenched users who may feel incapable of performing the protective behavior.

Inherent problems with social marketing campaigns

Descriptive norm meta-messages

Social marketing messages that are well constructed and avoid the afore-mentioned pitfalls could still conceivably boomerang by implying that the problem behavior is widespread or prevalent. According to Norm Theory (Kahneman and Miller 1986), judgments of normativeness are based on the salience of exemplars. Social marketing messages could inadvertently make salient problem behaviors and therefore suggest that those behaviors are the norm and common. We will refer to this type of adverse effect as a descriptive norm meta-message (Hornik *et al.* 2003). A descriptive norm refers to the perceived prevalence of a behavior and, in general, the higher the perceived prevalence, the more likely that others will engage in the behavior (Cialdini *et al.* 1990). For instance, a major factor that increases adolescents' risk of drug use is the degree to which they believe it is prevalent among peers (Guo *et al.* 2002). Some research even indicates that descriptive norms about what people do have more influence on behavior than injunctive norms about what people should do (Buunk and Bakker 1995; Cialdini *et al.* 1990).

Two empirical studies suggest that anti-drug messages may boomerang among adolescents by implying that drug use is widespread (Donaldson *et al.* 1995; Hornik *et al.* 2002). The best documented example comes from a field experiment of four types of in-school alcohol prevention programs. The programs addressed resistance skills, norm education, negative health consequences, or a combination of the three (Donaldson *et al.* 1994; Donaldson *et al.* 1995). The resistance skills curricula inadvertently increased the perceived prevalence of alcohol and drug offers among public (but not Catholic) school students (Donaldson *et al.* 1995). The researchers posited that the resistance skills training may have inadvertently implied that drug offers were commonplace. By contrast, the combined program which included both resistance skills and norm education reduced the perceived prevalence of alcohol and drug offers (ibid.) which, in turn, lowered substance use (Donaldson *et al.* 1994). These findings suggest that it may be possible to counter an implied meta-message that drug use is prevalent by explicitly stating that prevalence is low.

Additional evidence of a possible descriptive norm meta-message effect, although more tentative, comes from an evaluation of the US Office of National Drug Control Policy's National Youth Anti-drug Media Campaign (Hornik *et al.* 2002). Independent evaluators conducted both cross-sectional and longitudinal (panel) household surveys of parents and their children. Among youth (12–18 years old) who had not tried marijuana at baseline, self-reports indicating greater initial exposure to the anti-drug ad campaign were correlated with higher perceptions that marijuana use was prevalent and acceptable and increased intent to use marijuana at 12–18 month follow-up, even after controlling for several confounds. There were no significant behavioral effects.

These longitudinal results are somewhat inconclusive, however, because they were not replicated in the cross-sectional results either at baseline or follow-up. In other words, there was no concurrent adverse effect, only a lagged adverse effect, which is difficult to explain based on standard theories of communication effects. Another concern is that the research relies on self-reported measures of ad exposure which may be subject to reverse causation. That is, youth who were contemplating marijuana use, and a year or so later actually used, may have been more attentive to the anti-drug ads initially than those who had no intent to use. The analyses included propensity scores (similar to covariates) to correct for such confounds but these methods are imperfect (Cook and Campbell 1979). Further, a well-respected school-based survey, Monitoring the Future, has documented a downward trend in adolescent drug use since the campaign commenced (Johnston *et al.* 2003), and no adverse effects. Finally, if adverse effects did indeed occur, it is uncertain whether they were caused by descriptive norm meta-messages or other problems. Many of the early campaign ads were not quantitatively copy-tested before airing and some may have contained weak messages (Foley and Pechmann 2004).

Offsetting behavior

Another inherent problem that might conceivably plague social marketing campaigns is what economists refer to as "offsetting behavior" (Calkins and Zlatoper 2001; Peltzman 1975) The notion is that some people may decide to engage in a risky behavior such as speeding for benefits such as shorter travel time. Each person has an acceptable level of risk and seeks to adjust his/her behavioral intensity to avoid exceeding the acceptable level. If a law is enacted that requires drivers to wear seat belts, the risk of speeding to drivers decreases due to the added protection the seat belt affords. As a result, drivers may increase their speeding up to their acceptable risk levels. The offsetting behavior of increased speeding is itself an adverse effect and it, in turn, could cause other adverse effects such as more accidents. In analyzing secondary data, some economists have found evidence of offsetting behavior and related adverse effects.

In particular, some economists have empirically demonstrated that seat belt laws may increase speeding, leading to more car accidents (Asch *et al.* 1991; Chirinko and Harper 1993), more injuries and deaths to nonoccupants including pedestrians (Calkins and Zlatoper 2001; Chirinko and Harper 1993; Peltzman 1975), and more property damage (Peltzman 1975). One study even suggests that seat belt laws may increase total fatalities (Calkins and Zlatoper 2001), although other studies have concluded that fatalities decrease (Asch *et al.* 1991), particularly among occupants (Peltzman 1975).

Social marketing messages could conceivably cause offsetting behavior, as shown in Figure 10.2. To our knowledge, consumer and health promotion researchers have not yet studied the phenomenon. Concerns about offsetting behavior, however, are often voiced. For instance, it is argued that promoting birth control could increase sexual promiscuity and sexually transmitted diseases. Consumer research on this topic is sorely needed.

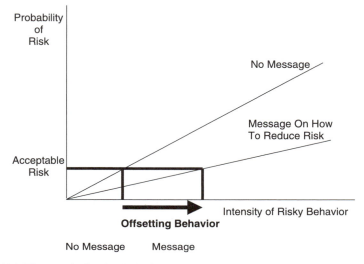

Figure 10.2 Theory of offsetting behavior.

How to minimize inherent problems with messages

Donaldson *et al.*'s (1994) study indicates that, to prevent meta-messages implying that a problem behavior is prevalent, one should include explicit messages regarding the behavior's low prevalence and unacceptability. Certain contexts may be especially conducive to descriptive norm meta-message effects and, if so, extra precaution may be needed to test for and prevent such effects. In particular, meta-message problems may arise when (1) actual levels of the behavior are not reliably known, as with illegal behaviors such as marijuana use, also known as pluralistic ignorance (Katz 1983); (2) discussion of the topic had previously been virtually absent in the media channels used by the population of interest; and (3) exposure to the topic is suddenly and dramatically increased in those channels. Descriptive norm meta-message effects may be unlikely for topics such as alcohol and tobacco that are already very visible in mainstream media.

Turning to the problem of offsetting behavior, if it does occur, one solution may be to promote behaviors that cannot readily be offset. For instance, findings indicate that laws reducing speed limits evoke less offsetting behavior than seat belt laws (Chirinko and Harper 1993). Another solution may be to warn people about the risks of the offsetting behavior. For instance, if people think they can speed more safely when wearing seatbelts, perhaps they should be warned of the risks of killing pedestrians.

Substantive conclusions

Based on our review of the literature, we conclude that a great deal could conceivably go wrong with social marketing campaigns. Without proper audience research, campaigns could do worse than fail; they could have adverse effects. Most importantly, messages that are created without an adequate understanding of audience members' prior beliefs could be counterinformative. They may weaken people's beliefs about the risks of a problem behavior and/or strengthen beliefs about its benefits or prevalence. Poorly constructed messages could also cause a backlash. People may decide to behave contrary to the social marketer's recommendation in order to assert their independence. Or, if a message arouses fear without offering viable solutions, people may discount it to reduce their fear. Most of these problems have been documented.

Fortunately, it appears likely that many of these problems can be avoided by educating advertising professions about potential adverse effects and how to avoid them, conducting high-quality audience research, and quantitatively pretesting all messages prior to airing to ensure they produce the desired changes in beliefs and intent and have no adverse effects (Atkin 2002; Fishbein *et al.* 2002). Foley and Pechmann (2004) provide detailed guidance on how to quantitatively pretest messages.

Some of the literature suggests that social marketing campaigns could at times be plagued by inherent problems that cannot readily be avoided. Even well-constructed messages could inadvertently imply that the problem behavior is commonplace and thus promote copycat behavior. Or, messages on how to lower the risks of a behavior could inadvertently increase the frequency of that behavior because it is now perceived as being safer; this is called offsetting behavior. However, there is very little empirical evidence that these types of inherent problems actually occur. While the effects are theoretically possible, they are not well documented. More research is needed before drawing any firm conclusions.

In sum, social marketers should not assume that any message is better than no message. At minimum, messages should be quantitatively pretested prior to airing using methods that are sensitive to adverse effects (Foley and Pechmann 2004). On the other hand, social marketers should not be dissuaded from running campaigns because of the potential for adverse effects. Most, if not all, adverse effects seem to be preventable.

Research issues and future directions

In our review of the literature, we considered whether any higher-order factors pertaining to message or research approach might help to explain the adverse effects that have been documented. We asked: Are adverse effects more prevalent for behavioral versus non-behavioral dependent variables, or for lab versus field designs? Referring back to Table 10.2, it can be seen that adverse effects occurred in all cases and neither factor seemed to matter much, based on the studies listed. Also, about half of the messages were positive in tone in that they discussed benefits or positive descriptive norms, while half were negative in that they addressed risks (see Table 10.2). Based on this 50–50 split, message valence does not appear to be associated with adverse effects, but more research is clearly needed. Also, adverse effects have been shown with both print and TV messages, and with health programs, but delivery mechanism may nonetheless matter and should be studied. For example, a complex message might be understood in print but misunderstood in a brief TV ad.

In this review, it was not possible to examine the roles of consumer motivation, ability or opportunity to process messages. These variables were neither manipulated or measured in most past studies. Future research should examine if adverse effects are more likely when motivation, ability and/or opportunity are low. Also, considerably more research is needed on social marketing campaigns that promote pro-social behavior to see if they might inadvertently encourage social loafing or free-riding. We could not find a single paper on this topic and it deserves attention. If people believe that a pro-social campaign (e.g., promoting recycling) will cause others to contribute to the common good, some might feel the problem is resolved and they no longer need to do anything. A recent study on the "reverse third person effect" suggests that people infer that social marketing campaigns will have less of an effect on others than on themselves, which might mitigate this type of problem, but the findings are by no means conclusive (Henriksen and Flora 1999).

Finally, it is possible that social marketing campaigns may inadvertently motivate political opposition to the advocated causes. For instance, in Belgium, it is often claimed that government campaigns to promote cultural tolerance are used by extreme right-wing groups to stimulate anti-immigrant and anti-government feelings. In effect, a social marketing campaign could polarize a society with respect to the focal issue, which could hurt the cause. We were unable to find research on this topic but encourage that it be done. Ironically enough, research on adverse effects could itself boomerang in that, if there is evidence that social marketing campaigns may boomerang, there may be fewer such campaigns in the future. Nonetheless, more research on adverse effects should be conducted. Many critical issues remain unresolved, or even unexplored.

Acknowledgments

The authors thank Craig Andrews, Rick Netemeyer, Luk Warlop and the editors for their insightful reviews of our earlier draft. We especially thank the reviewers for their substantial input into the last section of this chapter. We also thank Max Seraj for his assistance.

References

Agostinelli, G., Brown, J. M., and. Miller, W. R. (1995) "Effects of normative feedback on consumption among heavy drinking college students," *Journal of Drug Education* 25(1): 31–40.

Andreasen, A. (1994) "Social marketing: Definition and domain," *Journal of Public Policy and Marketing* 13(1): 109–114.

Asch, P., Levy, D. T., Shea, D., and Bodenhorn, H. (1991) "Risk compensation and the effectiveness of safety belt use laws: A case study of New Jersey," *Policy Sciences* 24: 181–197.

Atkin, C. K. (2002) "Promising strategies for media health campaigns," in W. D. Crano and M. Burgoon (eds) *Mass Media and Drug Prevention: Classic and Contemporary Theories and Research*, Mahwah, NY: Lawrence Erlbaum Associates: 35–64.

Bensley, L. S. and Wu, R. (1991) "The role of psychological reactance in drinking following alcohol prevention messages," *Journal of Applied Social Psychology* 21(13): 1111–1124.

Blood, D. J. and Snyder, L. B. (1993) "Why warnings boomerang: The failure of the Surgeon General's alcohol warning to affect young adults," presented at International Communication Association Conference, Health Communication Division, Washington, DC.

Brehm, J. (1972) *Responses to Loss of Freedom: A Theory of Psychological Reactance*, Morristown, NJ: General Learning Press.

Bushman, B. J. (1998) "Effects of warning and information labels on consumption of full-fat, reduced-fat, and no-fat products," *Journal of Applied Psychology* 83(1): 97–101.

Bushman, B. J. and Stack, A. D. (1996) "Forbidden fruit versus tainted fruit: Effects of warning labels on attraction to television violence," *Journal of Experimental Psychology: Applied* 2(3): 207–226.

Buunk, B. P. and Bakker, A. B. (1995) "Extradyadic sex: The role of descriptive and injunctive norms," *Journal of Sex Research* 32(4): 313–318.

Calkins, L. N. and Zlatoper, T. J. (2001) "The effects of mandatory seat belt laws on motor vehicle fatalities in the United States," *Social Science Quarterly* 82(4): 716–732.

Cappella, J. N., Fishbein, M., Hornik, R., Ahern, R. K., and Sayeed, S. (2001) "Using theory to select messages in anti-drug media campaigns: Reasoned action and media priming," in R. E. Rice and C. K. Atkin (eds) *Public Communication Campaigns*, Thousand Oaks, CA: Sage Publications: 214–230.

Chirinko, R. S. and Harper, E. P. Jr. (1993) "Buckle up or slow down? New estimates of offsetting behavior and their implications for automobile safety regulation," *Journal of Policy Analysis and Management* 12(2): 270–296.

Cialdini, R. B., Reno, R. R., and Kallgren, C. A. (1990) "A focus theory of normative conduct: Recycling the concept of norms to reduce littering in public places," *Journal of Personality and Social Psychology* 58(6): 1015–1026.

Clee, M. A. and Wicklund, R. A. (1980) "Consumer behavior and psychological reactance," *Journal of Consumer Research* 6(4): 389–405.

Cohn, L. D., Macfarlane, S., Yanez, C., and Imai, W. K. (1995) "Risk-perception: Differences between adolescents and adults," *Health Psychology* 14(3): 217–222.

Cook, T. D. and Campbell, D. T. (1979) *Quasi-Experimentation: Design and Analysis Issues for Field Settings*, Boston, MA: Houghton Mifflin.

Cox, D. and Cox, A. D. (2001) "Communicating the consequences of early detection: The role of evidence and framing," *Journal of Marketing* 65(3): 91–103.

deTurck, M. A. and Goldhaber, G. M. (1991) "A developmental analysis of warning signs: The case of familiarity and gender," *Journal of Products Liability* 13(1): 65–78.

Donaldson, S. I., Graham, J. W., and W. B. Hansen (1994) "Testing the generalizability of intervening mechanism theories: Understanding the effects of adolescent drug use prevention interventions," *Journal of Behavioral Medicine* 17(2): 195–216.

Donaldson, S. I., Graham, J. W., Piccinin, A. M., and Hansen, W. B. (1995) "Resistance-skills training and onset of alcohol use: Evidence for beneficial and potentially harmful effects in public schools and in private catholic schools," *Health Psychology* 14(4): 291–300.

Farrelly, M. C., Niederdeppe, J., and Yarsevich, J. (2003) "Youth tobacco prevention mass media campaigns: Past, present, and future directions," *Tobacco Control* 12 (Suppl I): ii35–i47.

Feingold, P. C. and Knapp M. L. (1977) "Anti-drug abuse commercials," *Journal of Communication* 27(1): 20–28.

Fishbein, M., Hall-Jamieson, K., Zimmer, E., von Haeften, I., and Nabi, R. (2002) "Avoiding the boomerang: Testing the relative effectiveness of anti-drug public service announcements before a national campaign," *American Journal of Public Health* 92(2): 238–245.

Floyd, D. L., Prentice-Dunn, S., and Rogers, R. W. (2000) "A meta-analysis of research on protection motivation theory," *Journal of Applied Social Psychology* 30(2): 407–429.

Foley, D. and Pechmann, C. (2004) "The national youth anti-drug media campaign copy test system," *Social Marketing Quarterly* 10(2): 34–42.

Foxcroft, D. R., Lister-Sharp, D., and Lowe, G. (1997) "Alcohol misuse prevention for young people: A systematic review reveals methodological concerns and lack of reliable evidence of effectiveness," *Addiction* 92(5): 531–537.

Goodstadt, M. S. (1980) "Drug education – A turn on or a turn off?" *Journal of Drug Education* 10(2): 89–99.

Gruenfeld, D. H. and Wyer, R. S. (1992) "Semantics and pragmatics of social influence: How affirmations and denials affect beliefs in referent propositions," *Journal of Personality and Social Psychology* 62(1): 38–49.

Guo, J., Hill, K. G., Hawkins, J. D., Catalano, R. E., and Abbott, R. D. (2002), "A developmental analysis of sociodemographic, family, and peer effects on adolescent illicit drug initiation," *Journal of American Academy of Child Adolescent Psychiatry* 41(7): 838–845.

Haines, M. and Spear, S. F. (1996) "Changing the perception of the norm: A strategy to decrease binge drinking among college students," *Journal of American College Health* 45(3): 134–140.

Henriksen, L. and Flora, J. A. (1999) "Third-person perception and children: Perceived impact of pro- and anti-smoking ads," *Communication Research* 26(6): 643–665.

Hong, S.-M., Giannakopoulos, E., Laing, D., and Williams, N. A. (1994) "Psychological reactance: Effects of age and gender," *Journal of Social Psychology*, 134(2): 223–228.

Hong, S.-M. and Page, S. (1989) "A psychological reactance scale: Development, factor structure and reliability," *Psychological Reports* 64 (3, Part 2): 1323–1326.

Hornik, R. (2002) *Public Health Communication: Evidence for Behavior Change*, Mahwah, NJ: Lawrence Erlbaum Associates.

Hornik, R., Barmada, C. H., Romantan, A., Henderson, V. R., Jacobsohn, L. S., and Cappella, J. N. (2003) "Evaluation of the national youth anti-drug media campaign: Results after three years of research," presented at Annual Conference of the International Communication Association, San Diego, CA.

Hornik, R., Maklan, D., Cadell, D., Barmada, C. H., Jacobsohn, L., Prado, A., Romantan, A., Orwin, R., Sridharan, S., Zanutto, E., Baskin, R., Chu, A., Morin, C., Taylor, K., and Steele, D. (2002) *Evaluation of the National Youth Anti-Drug Media Campaign: Fifth Semi-Annual Report of Findings*, Rockville, MD: National Institute on Drug Abuse, National Institutes of Health.

Hovland, C. I., Janis, I. L., and Kelley, H. H. (1953) *Communication and Persuasion*, New Haven, CT: Yale University Press.

Hyland, M. and Birrell, J. (1979) "Government health warnings and the 'boomerang' effect," *Psychological Reports* 44(2): 643–647.

Janis, I. L. and Feshbach, S. (1953) "Effect of fear-arousing communications," *Journal of Abnormal and Social Psychology* 48(1): 78–92.

Johnston, L. D., O'Malley, P. M., and Bachman, J. G. (2003) *Monitoring the Future National Results on Adolescent Drug Use: Overview of Key Findings, 2002* (NIH Publication No. 03–5374 ed.), Bethesda, MD: National Institute on Drug Abuse.

Kahneman, D. and Miller, D. T. (1986) "Norm theory: Comparing reality to its alternatives," *Psychological Review* 93(2): 136–153.

Katz, E. (1983) "Publicity and pluralistic ignorance: Notes on the spiral of silence," in H. Baier, H. M. Kepplinger, and K. Reumann (eds) *Mass Communication Review Yearbook*, Beverly Hills, CA: Sage Publications: 89–99.

Kelder, S. H., Maibach, E., Worden, J. K., Biglan, A. and Levitt, A. (2000) "Planning and initiation of the ONDCP national youth anti-drug media campaign," *Journal of Public Health Management Practice* 6(3): 14–26.

Keller, P. A., Lipkus, I. M., and Rimer, B. K. (2002) "Depressive realism and health risk accuracy: The negative consequences of positive mood," *Journal of Consumer Research* 29(1): 57–69.

McKenna, J. W. and Williams, K. N. (1993) "Crafting effective tobacco counter advertisements: Lessons from a failed campaign directed at teenagers," *Public Health Reports* 108 (Suppl. 1): 85–89.

MacKinnon, D. P. and Lapin, A. (1998) "Effects of alcohol warnings and advertisements: A test of the boomerang hypothesis," *Psychology and Marketing* Special Issue 15(7): 707–726.

Mazis, M. B., Settle, R. B., and Leslie, D. C. (1973) "Elimination of phosphate detergents and psychological reactance," *Journal of Marketing Research* 10(4): 390–395.

Millstein, S. G. and Halpern-Felsher, B. L. (2002) "Perceptions of risk and vulnerability," *Journal of Adolescent Health* 31 (Suppl. 1): 10–27.

Nye, E. C., Agostinelli, G., and Smith, J. E. (1999) "Enhancing alcohol problem recognition: A self-regulation model for the effects of self-focusing and normative information," *Journal of Studies on Alcohol* 60(5): 685–693.

Peltzman, S. (1975) "The effects of automobile safety regulations," *Journal of Political Economy* 84(4): 677–726.

Petty, R. E. and Cacioppo, J. T. (1986) *Communication and Persuasion: Central and Peripheral Routes to Attitude Change*, New York: Springer.

Rich, F.(1998) "Just Say $1 Billion," *New York Times*, July 15, A19.

Ringold, D. J. (2002) "Boomerang effects in response to public health inventions: Some unintended consequences in the alcoholic beverage market," *Journal of Consumer Policy* 25(1): 27–63.

Rogers, R. W. (1983) "Cognitive and physiological process in fear appeals and attitude change: A revised theory of protection motivation," in J. Cacioppo and R. Petty (eds) *Social Psychophysiology: A Source Book*, New York: Guilford Press: 153–176.

Slovic, P. (2001) "Cigarette smokers: Rational actors or rational fools?," in P. Slovic (ed.) *Smoking: Risk, Perception, and Policy*, Thousand Oaks, CA: Sage Publications: 97–124.

Snyder, L. B. (2001) "How effective are mediated health campaigns," in R. E. Rice and C. K. Atkin (eds) *Public Communication Campaigns*, Thousand Oaks, CA: Sage Publications: 181–190.

Snyder, L. B. and Blood, D. J. (1992) "Caution: The Surgeon General's alcohol warnings and alcohol advertising may have adverse effects on young adults," *Journal of Applied Communication Research* 20(1): 37–53.

Stewart, D. W. and Martin, I. M. (1994) "Intended and unintended consequences of warning messages: A review and synthesis of empirical research," *Journal of Public Policy and Marketing* 13(1): 1–19.

Sturges, J. W. and Rogers, R. W. (1996) "Preventive health psychology from a developmental perspective: An extension of protection motivation theory," *Health Psychology* 15(3): 158–166.

Teenage Research Unlimited (2003) "Focus groups of youth rank tobacco company's ads last among several anti-smoking campaigns," at http://www.tobaccofreekids.org/reports/smokescreen/study.shtml/.

Tuffs, A. (2003) "German government under attack for anti-smoking advertisements," *BMJ* 327 (7411): 360.

Tversky, A. and Kahneman, D. (1974) "Judgment under uncertainty: Heuristics and biases," *Science* 185 (4157): 1124–1131.

Viscusi, W. K. (1992) *Smoking: Making the Risky Decision*, Oxford: Oxford University Press.

Vranica, S. (2003) "Critics fault antiobesity ads as not reaching far enough," *Wall Street Journal*, April 11, B6.

Wagner, C. B. and Sundar, S. S. (1999) "The curiosity-arousing function of anti-drug PSAs," presented at 49th Annual Conference of the International Communication Association, San Francisco, CA.

Wechsler, H., Nelson, T. E., Lee, J. E., Seibring, M., Lewis, C., and Keeling, R. P. (2003) "Perception and reality: A national evaluation of social norms marketing interventions to reduce college students' heavy alcohol use," *Journal of Studies on Alcohol* 64(4): 484–494.

Werch, C. E., Pappas, D. M., Carlson, J. M., DiClemente, C. C., Chally, P. S., and Sinder, J. A. (2000) "Results of a social norm intervention to prevent binge drinking among first-year residential college students," *Journal of American College Health* 49(2): 85–92.

Witte, K. (1991) "The role of threat and efficacy in AIDS prevention," *International Quarterly of Community Health Education* 12(3): 225–249.

Witte, K. and Allen, M. (2000) "A meta-analysis of fear appeals: Implications for effective public health," *Health Education and Behavior* 27(5): 591–615.

Yzer, M. C., Cappella, J. N., Fishbein, M., Hornik, R., and Ahern, R. K. (2003) "The effectiveness of gateway communications in anti-marijuana campaigns," *Journal Health Communication* 8(2): 129–143.

11 We are who we were

Intergenerational influences in consumer behavior

Elizabeth S. Moore and William L. Wilkie

Does childhood continue to exert powerful influence on our consumer behavior as adults? This interesting question involves the topic of intergenerational influence (IG), which is defined as the transmission of information, resources, and beliefs from one generation to the next within families. Intergenerational influences constitute an interesting and often-overlooked set of forces that help to guide our consumption behaviors in our daily lives as adults. Given that childhood learning is prolonged and powerful, the fact that some beliefs and attitudes formed within the household will persist well into adulthood comes as no surprise. It is the *nature* of these influences that is of interest, a topic that has been studied in the fields of sociology, psychology, political science, and more recently, consumer behavior.

The nature of intergenerational influences

Socialization theory provides a backdrop

Viewed broadly, socialization is the process through which individuals develop specific patterns of socially relevant behavior through interactions with others (Ziegler and Child 1969). Socialization helps a society to function by reinforcing particular beliefs, traditions, and values (Brim 1968). In this manner socialization also helps individuals in developing their personal identities, and in assuming new roles as they move through their life cycle. Socialization is both pervasive and powerful. As an area of inquiry, socialization has a long tradition in sociology and cultural anthropology, as well as in social learning, developmental, and personality theories in psychology (e.g., Levine 1969; Peterson and Rollins 1987).

A range of "socializing institutions" stands ready for this work. The family (parents and relatives), the educational system, the mass media, religious institutions, and peers each can contribute in important and different ways to the process of childhood socialization. The family is the setting in which most children spend the greatest amount of their time, and is the first and typically most powerful agent of socialization. As time unfolds, each family develops its own distinct lifestyle, its own patterns of decision-making, and its own body of shared experience, preferences, and views of the world (Sillars 1995). During this time, the children are learning, continuously, day by day and week by week, over a period of many years until leaving the household nest as young adults. They not only observe parental beliefs, values, and behaviors, but also come to internalize some of these for themselves. No other agent of socialization enjoys such a cumulative edge in exposure, communication, and receptivity. Parents and other family members serve as important channels of information, and as sources of social pressure as well as support for one another.

Although socialization is a life-long process, childhood and adolescence are particularly crucial times. During childhood, socialization involves not only learning for the present, but also the learning of roles and behaviors that will be needed in the future (McNeal 1987, 1992). Selective exposure to a particular family lifestyle, moreover, usually means that it comes to be accepted as the child's personal norm (Sears 1983).

This brief foundation in socialization theory provides several useful perspectives on the nature of IG influences. For example, socialization theory highlights the long time span for IG development and that, fundamentally, IG transfer is a process of social influence. IG internalization then occurs when a child adopts a parent's opinion and integrates it into his or her own belief system (Kelman 1960). Further, some of these beliefs will be sustained long after the source of the information has been forgotten. Thus, these IG influences began as social phenomena, but have been transmuted to now reside deep within a person's heart and mind, embedded within that person's self-identity. As we shall shortly discuss, in our own research we have seen that many IG effects are based on considerable cognitive and emotional investment, and are not at all fragile (e.g., Moore *et al.* 2002). Also, while socialization implies an internal acceptance of what the child learns, the full manifestation of such learning in later adult behaviors brings an additional set of research issues to be considered. Given that much of IG has been long internalized as a child enters adulthood, it can be quite challenging to identify and isolate the unique effects of family interactions on the now adult consumer.

Though traditional theories of socialization have focused primarily on the transfer from parent to child, it is also the case that there are domains in which this flow may be reversed (e.g., Ekstrom *et al.* 1987; Moschis 1988). Socialization occurs for everyone throughout life: adulthood brings both new demands as well as greater freedoms to choose the roles one would most like to pursue. Children can be an important source that adults can learn from, particularly as they reach the teen years and early adulthood. To this point there has been surprisingly little systematic study of "reverse socialization."

Another key element of socialization theory recognizes that households are not static entities: both children and parents continue to progress through the life cycle, and household structures can change as well, sometimes sharply (Moore *et al.* 2001). Also, parents experience changes in their work status, health, or lifestyle that can alter family interactions significantly. Simultaneously, children and siblings are maturing, taking on new responsibilities, and seeking more independence: in adolescence, parent–child relations often need to be redefined (e.g., Aquilino 1997).

In general the IG research area is challenging to study precisely because of its intrinsic set of properties. To start, because IG impacts are embedded within an individual's sense of self, they can be largely hidden from view, and possibly not consciously available for reporting. Further, the fact that IG develops over long time frames and across life cycle stages seems to suggest longitudinal research designs, yet these are not often feasible. Families are also private social groups, and therefore not easy to observe in anything approximating a rigorous fashion (Wilkie 1994). Most IG researchers have therefore tended to search for evidence of IG in obtainable objective measurements, searching for attitudinal and behavioral similarities between parents and their now-grown adult children.

IG influences have been discovered in many spheres

Intergenerational research in the social sciences has a long tradition. Evidence shows that many forms of influence are transmitted along generational lines, including political party affiliation, candidate preferences, achievement orientation, religious values, as well as gender and racial attitudes (e.g., Bao *et al.* 1999; Beck and Jennings 1991; Cashmore and Goodnow 1985; Moen *et al.* 1997; Whitbeck and Gecas 1988). Although effect sizes are modest in some cases, the essential finding of intergenerational similarity is quite robust. Several of these studies have employed longitudinal designs in which the attitudes of parents and children were compared over a time frame spanning 20 to 30 years (e.g., Moen *et al.* 1997; Niemi and Jennings 1991; Miller and Glass 1989). At least within the political arena, these effects are not limited to the United States, but have been observed in other Western nations as well (Jennings 1984; Nieuwbeerta and Wittebrood 1995).

The extent of intergenerational consensus does vary considerably by topic. For example, parent–child similarity is highest within religious and political arenas, least apparent on lifestyle dimensions (Troll and Bengston 1979), and appears to be related to underlying properties such as topics that are concrete, visible, and salient (Acock 1984; Jennings and Niemi 1974). Further, defining the *precise focus of analysis* can influence results. In the political sphere, for example, high levels of correspondence have been observed in the "partisanship" of family members (e.g., political party affiliation, candidate preferences), while more moderate levels surface for specific political issues (e.g., school prayer), and lower levels of agreement obtain for especially abstract and diffuse topics such as "cosmopolitanism." These differences have been attributed, in part, to the relative ease of learning when there is a concrete referent, consistent reinforcement, and long-term visibility within the household (Beck and Jennings 1991).

Intergenerational influences in consumer behavior

The core research base of IG influences in consumer behavior remains small to the present time, even though the study of IG was formally introduced into consumer research in the early 1970s (e.g., Arndt 1971, 1972; Miller 1975). Fortunately, however, a considerable body of additional consumer research on children, adolescents and family decision-making is available to supplement theory and findings (see, e.g., the excellent review by John 1999). For example, *consumer socialization* represents one aspect of this broader process. It has been defined as "the processes by which young people acquire skills, knowledge and attitudes relevant to their functioning in the marketplace" (Ward 1974: 2). Research on the consumer socialization of young children and teens has provided a basis for understanding parent–child interaction in household purchase decisions, impacts of parenting style and scope of parental influence (e.g., Beatty and Talpade 1994; Carlson and Grossbart 1988; Foxman *et al.* 1989; Moschis 1987; Palan and Wilkes 1997). Further, early work on both family decision-making and the "Family Life Cycle" also recognized the existence and role of IG influences (see Davis 1976; Wells and Gubar 1966).

IG transfer of brand and product preferences

A significant portion of IG consumer research has focused on measures that hold direct implications for marketing strategy. Chief among these is the IG transmission of product and brand preferences. An early study established that these effects can be large and enduring when conditions are right: Woodson *et al.*'s (1976) analysis of auto insurance purchases revealed that 32 percent of men reported that the insurance company with which they dealt also supplied coverage to their fathers. The greatest degree of overlap (62 percent) was reported among men in their twenties, then this proportion fell as men matured. Even at age 50 however, almost 20 percent of men reported similar patronage as their fathers. Of course, some unique characteristics of this product category likely promote IG transfer in several ways. First, parents often purchase auto insurance for their teenage children initially, as a rider to their own policies. Also, they are likely to use an insurance agent, resulting in a channel structure that may be somewhat less accessible to young adults. Further, insurance is an infrequent purchase decision and one that is hard to evaluate, so may not be especially susceptible to change.

Multiple levels of IG findings: an illustration

IG research can actually involve a great deal more than the single numerical index of parent/child similarity just reported for auto insurance. Recently, for example, Moore *et al.* (2002) were interested in learning how robust IG effects might be under more difficult marketplace conditions, so they undertook a study for 24 consumer packaged goods. Note that for frequently purchased packaged goods, family purchase decisions are made in a highly competitive marketplace characterized by frequent new product introductions and substantial promotional activity designed to induce switching behavior (Kahn and McAlister 1997). At the same time, however, many packaged goods meet the basic criteria researchers have suggested are important for intergenerational effects to occur: that a brand should have a relatively long life cycle, be used by households with children, and provide satisfaction over time (Shah and Mittal 1997; Woodson *et al.* 1976).

Our study developed a "parallel" survey in which young adult daughters living off campus and away from their family home were paired with their mothers to form family dyads. Each person filled out the survey, but without contact or discussion concerning its contents. Our interest was in examining the similarity of their responses, then statistically testing whether the levels observed represented signs of intergenerational influences at work (i.e., mother/daughter agreements at greater levels than general marketplace forces for that product category would suggest). Three "IG Hierarchy" measures were assessed across the 24 product classes:

- *"Daughter Aware of Mother's Favorite Brand":* First, across all products daughters were aware of their mother's preferred brand 69 percent of the time, or an average of 17 correct predictions of the 24 brands possible. This score ranged from 95 percent correct for soup to only 49 percent for paper towels.
- *"A Shared Choice Set for Daughter and Mother":* Does the brand the mother most prefers also appear in the daughter's consideration set? Across all products this occurred 60 percent of the time, or for 14.5 of the 24 categories. Comparing this result to that above, it is clear that some daughters, though knowing of their mother's favorite, have chosen not to consider it for themselves. The extent of this decline differed across products, with personal care (soap) and foods (coffee, tea) especially susceptible.
- *"A Shared Brand Preference for Daughter and Mother":* In how many families do the mother and daughter report an identical brand preference (this included products for which one member does not use, so is conservative). This measure showed an average brand preference agreement over all families and products to be 36 percent – far above chance for this marketplace, and strongly supportive of IG impacts. The crucial statistical test here was significant for 23 of the 24 categories.[1]

Turning to the individual brands themselves, powerful impacts of IG continued to emerge:

- *"High IG Brands":* These are brands we identified as having high IG brand equity (i.e., statistically higher than expected if no IG effect were operating in their category). The highest score overall was registered by Newman's Own Spaghetti Sauce, with 86 percent of its support coming from mothers and daughters in the same families.[2] Some product categories had a single dominant IG brand, others had two, and some had three. We termed this the *"IG Silo Effect":* there are Crest households and Colgate households, Tylenol households and Advil households, and Peter Pan, Jif, and Skippy households as well, all living near each other, but with different brand dynamics operating within each home – an interesting perspective on the landscape of the consumer marketplace!
- *"Brands With IG Potential":* This category is worth mentioning here, because it reflects research challenges in the IG area. Within our study, these were

brands with indications of possible IG influence, but for which either the sample size was too small, or the score was not sufficiently distinct from the category average (i.e., an artifact may be operating). In a managerial context, these would be candidates for further diagnostic evaluation.

- *"Brands With No or Low IG Impact"*: This category is very important, since it suggests that the IG influence phenomenon does not extend to every brand in the market, but is instead selectively applied. Some of the well-known and successful brands in this category were Hunts Catsup, Chicken of the Sea Tuna, and Scott Paper Towels. Here the sample size was large enough for us to be confident that their lack of IG impact is real (at least for this sample).

Overall, this brief research description shows the nature of data and findings illustrative of IG research on brand preference. It illustrates that intergenerational influence can be manifested in an array of measures, and also that statistical and analytical issues are important in attempting to isolate IG impacts from other influences also operating in the dynamic consumer marketplace. Also, of course, it is useful in illustrating the power and potential of IG as a source of continuing influence on consumer behavior.

While our illustration was confined to packaged consumer goods, consumer researchers have examined IG preference influences across different types of product categories as well. For example, Heckler *et al.* (1989) assessed perceived purchase similarities among parents and adult children and, as hypothesized, found stronger IG impacts for convenience goods than for shopping goods. Further, interesting cross-cultural research has also supported the notion that cultural effects are embedded in the IG phenomenon (Childers and Rao 1992). Here, among US families, adult children reported having been influenced by their parents on brand choices for "privately consumed necessities" (e.g., shopping goods – lamps, refrigerators, mattresses whose brand names are not readily perceived by anyone other than the family), but having not been particularly influenced in purchases of "publicly consumed luxury" goods (where the brand name would be easily perceived by friends and neighbors). In contrast, among Thai families, the IG effects were observed across both product types, consistent with a stronger cultural norm favoring collectivism and extended family living arrangements.

Consumer orientations and buying style

Beyond brand preferences, IG also manifests itself in consumers' buying styles, decision strategies, and generalized beliefs about the marketplace, and thereby acts to guide a wide range of consumer activities. If, for example, a child adopts a parent's habits of saving and spending, many decisions will be affected, both those that direct resource allocation and those involving specific purchases. From the field's beginnings, consumer researchers have searched to discover which particular broader manifestations of consumer behavior seem to spring from IG influences (e.g., Arndt 1971, 1972; Hill 1970). For example, Hill's (1970) famous longitudinal study found that financial planning skills and deficits were transmitted across three generations. This was particularly true among families who were poor financial managers, and who tended to spend impulsively. Other aspects of consumer buying styles have been investigated as well, sometimes with mixed results. For example, Arndt (1971) reported significant agreement between college students and their parents on opinion leadership behavior (e.g., giving advice), innovative behavior (e.g., receptiveness to new products), and store preferences, yet not on product importance ratings. Moore and Lutz (1988) revealed shared marketplace and choice rules (also noted by Carlson *et al.* 1994), and Obermiller and Spangenburg (2000) reported IG transfers between family members on their skepticism toward advertising. Most recently, Cotte and Wood (2004) have extended IG research to include siblings and have shown that both parents and siblings can influence innovativeness.

Consumer researchers have also started to examine factors that might influence the level of IG consensus. For example, an exploratory study by Moore and Berchmans (1996) found that children who believe that their parents have strong financial management skills tend to develop similar approaches, and become more confident in their ability to control their economic future. However, the tenor of parent-child communication did moderate the level of IG consensus observed (e.g., when children had experienced significant conflict with parents about money matters, they tended to explicitly reject their parents' views). These findings are intriguing yet only preliminary; additional research is clearly needed to understand how household dynamics actually operate to strengthen, or in some cases, weaken IG ties.

Exploring IG's motivational dimensions

While the empirical emphasis in consumer IG research has been on detecting the presence of IG impacts in consumer behavior, less studied have been the motivational characteristics of these intergenerational influences. What is the nature of these IG bonds? Why do these IG bonds persist? Why are some sustained over many years, while others are easily broken?

Figure 11.1 summarizes a portion of an illustrative conceptual framework we developed to reflect some ways in which IG influences are manifested in young adults. It should be noted that our source work here dealt only with consumer packaged goods, so our observations are clearly limited to this domain (see Moore *et al.* 2002, for research details and the complete framework). A surprising number of motivationally related insights emerged in this work, which employed three depth interviews conducted over the course of several days (at home, then in-store, and then in-pantry) with 25 young adult women.[3] Our informants were female college students who lived in off-campus housing and shopped regularly for groceries. Some had been independent shoppers for as little as a few months, and others for as long as two and a half years.

IG influences as simplifying forces	IG influences as emotional bonds
– Functional performance – Familiarity – Inertia – Low involvement – Trust in mom's expertise – Risk protection	– Nostalgia – Trust – Overcoming loneliness & trepidation – Resentments and brand avoidance – Brand as a symbol of allegiance – Love – Gratitude – Happiness – Anger – Guilt – Frustration
Other IG insights regarding products and brands	**Other IG dimensions: "Beyond the brand..."**
– IG as a brand portfolio – IG as competitive barrier/opportunity – IG as desired brand tier – IG as new product propensity – IG as preference for product forms – IG as a limiting brand force – IG as a reverse influence flow	– Shopping style and preference – "Good consumership" – Following the rules: norms for behavior – Packaging entire assortment – Adoption of lifestyle dimensions – Ties to personal identity (remembered rituals, ethnic heritage)

Note: Adapted from Moore *et al.* (2002).
Figure 11.1 Marketplace manifestations of intergenerational (IG) influences.

IG as a simplifying force

As indicated in Figure 11.1, one contribution of IG influences is to offer a range of simple decision heuristics for young consumers to employ as they encounter the complexities of the modern marketplace (Heckler *et al.* 1989). Within our depth interviews the informants frequently mentioned IG brands as the ones they now purchase as young adults. In probing the motivations underlying these purchases, a number of functional considerations began to surface. For some, purchase of an IG brand represents a normal decision rule that offers *efficiency in obtaining a satisfactory level of functional benefits*. To the extent that particular brand preferences have been internalized now as personal favorites, these brands represent a natural choice. Brands may also be chosen out of *familiarity and inertia* – and with no reason to change, the status quo is maintained. *Low involvement*, whereby little thought or effort is given to the decision, may account for some of these decisions.

In other cases, choices are based more on the *trust placed in a parent's extensive experience and expertise*. In this regard, IG influences *protect against purchase risks* in newly encountered sectors of the marketplace. Willing to presume that their mothers had researched available alternatives and determined which were best, often the daughters were quite willing to confidently rely on her judgments. Thus, here we see more deliberative effort involved in the formation of a decision rule, one that may be used to advantage across a number of product categories. So, functional considerations seem to underlie some of the IG-related decisions that we observed.

IG as an emotional bond

Continuing in Figure 11.1, we note that, in contrast to serving as a basis for a simplifying decision heuristic, IG influences also often reflect emotional bonds with roots deep in parent–child family relationships. This is a striking element of IG research, reflecting both embeddedness and staying power over the adult years. Because our work focused on brands, a range of object-centered emotions emerged, reflecting special emotional ties between a daughter and a particular brand, interwoven with family-related thoughts and feelings. At times, this was manifested in *nostalgia*, with the brand serving as a warm reminder of home and family. Nostalgic ties to past consumption experiences can create a special fondness for brands (Holbrook 1993), thus leading to preferences that are likely to be strong and enduring. It was also evident that these IG brands were imbued with great *trust* based on longstanding household use. Sometimes, IG brands were relied on for *reassurance*, particularly as daughters, out on their own, experienced feelings of loneliness.

> I like Jell-O and pudding but . . . I didn't do that much this year. My mom even said something about it. When we came here she said "Oh Beth, you didn't make Jell-O this summer." (R8)

> It's like what I was saying about the Bisquik. This is going to sound stupid, but it's kind of comforting to have it sitting in my cupboard. It makes the kitchen homey. (R23)

> They're sitting in my cabinet for that one day – that you buy Oreos for no reason. My mom did that. She comes home with this thing of Oreos and I was like "What's the point?" She said "We haven't had them in a long time and I just needed them." I really think that there's something in women that forces them – they have to have Oreos at some point in their life. It just makes sense. (R9)

We also found that brands can serve as symbolic markers of significant personal relationships, both positive and negative. Occasionally a brand has come to represent long-standing *resentments or other negative feelings* related to family life. In this case, the brand is explicitly avoided, perhaps as a symbolic statement about family relationships. However, when a brand becomes a *symbol of allegiance* to a loved family member, preference for it can become virtually unshakeable. These dimensions are consistent with Olsen's (1993) findings, which suggested that brand loyalties sometimes emerge as a reflection of affection and respect, thus functioning as a "bridge" or reinforcer of familial bonds.

> I like Brownberry bread . . . because it has sentimental value for me. Which sounds really dumb but it is true. Before my dad remarried, we would always eat healthy food, well relatively healthy. And, I would eat my vegetables and we would have Brownberry wheat bread. (R1)

> I buy things that my Dad buys. I like my Dad . . . You could also say that I don't buy the things my stepmother buys because I don't like her. (R1)

Overall, we were intrigued by the range of emotions that surfaced in connection with what are often considered as low-involvement packaged goods. *A priori*, we might not have expected such strong feelings to be linked to IG brands in these categories. However, it does suggest a fruitful area for future research. To what extent do emotions underpin IG influences, and what roles do emotional considerations play in sustaining IG impacts?

As we noted at the start, IG influences develop naturally in the midst of every-day home life for children. Their families are acquiring and spending money day after day, year after year. All of this consumption-related activity is embedded within close, personal relationships. Emotions manifest themselves in the process of making household decisions, and in the consumption these decisions produce. In a research project currently in progress we are attempting to examine the forces within the family that either support or work against the transmission of beliefs and practices across generations (see Moore *et al.* 2005 for more information). Here we collected written life histories from 110 young adults.[4] In these personal narratives, informants describe how childhood experiences within their families have influenced their current consumption.

One of the striking results to emerge in these data so far has been the powerful emotions that are reported in connection with specific consumption episodes: emotions ranging from expressions of *love, gratitude, and happiness* to the opposing extremes of *anger, guilt, and frustration*. To illustrate, some informants described their parents' personal sacrifices to provide for them, and the immense gratitude they feel as a result. They then note how this has translated into their own careful saving and spending behavior. Others relate how shopping with one of their parents became a highly valued family ritual because these were times when they felt particularly close and cared for.

> My mom is always careful in buying things. She keeps to a strict budget. If and only if she has extra money, will she buy anything for herself. She always puts my needs ahead of her own. My view on spending is very similar to my mom's. I think that it is similar because I grew up with her ideas and guidance. I always budget my money and am very careful about what I spend it on. I have often considered buying something and then talked myself out of it because I felt guilty about spending the money on myself. (I108)

> I have always had a love for shopping and I think this is because I spent a lot of time with my mom in shopping situations. We have always considered going to the mall as a bonding moment. (I112)

At the other end of the spectrum, other informants described how angry and hurt they feel at times, particularly when parents fight about money.

> . . . they don't like the phone bills to skyrocket. I remember my freshman year, I was having a lot of trouble adjusting to being away from home and would call fairly often, and my mom would sometimes rush me off of the phone. I was always hurt and felt that she cared more about the bill than talking to me. (I105)

> There were occasionally big conflicts over money and over the way my mother was being left to raise the children on a small amount of money while my father was able to go abroad on business and stay in luxury hotels. As the children got older, my mother's anger turned to the fact that she wasn't able to go with my father because we couldn't afford it. She began to resent the fact that now even though she was working very hard she was unable to go on holidays abroad like all her friends were doing . . . During my childhood I didn't really pay attention to or fully comprehend all the arguments around me about these matters, but in later years I began to remember them and feel a bit guilty about all the demands I made for toys and things which could be partly the reason why I myself am so reluctant to spend these days. (I130)

Obviously these memories have endured and are exerting influence today, but what about the issue of IG endurance more generally?

Issues of the endurance of IG influences into adulthood

The long-term impacts of IG influences are felt in adulthood. Yet, the potential of IG to guide consumer behavior is constrained by how long these influences endure. Both parents and children may change over time, in response to life cycle transitions, cultural changes, and the influence of others. Determining the extent to which IG influences endure ("persist"), and the factors that work to sustain or disrupt them is a key research topic. Researchers have explored this issue conceptually, and contrasting points of view have emerged.

On the one hand, socialization theorists suggest that parents and children may retain some shared beliefs and attitudes over the life course, but that these commonalities likely diminish over time. As children leave home, the frequency of interaction with parents typically declines, resulting in less reinforcement of childhood attitudes. At the same time, the young adult is being socialized into other social groups through work, community activities, and perhaps through marriage. These may espouse different norms and values than those learned as a child. In contrast, proponents of developmental aging or status inheritance models suggest that parents and children may actually converge over time as children assume adult status, role demands and responsibilities (e.g., Glass *et al.* 1986; Miller and Glass 1989). The idea here is that as youth age, they are likely to attain a social status or position akin to their parents'. As a result, they may come to hold similar views that surface as they begin to have children, buy property, and work on a full-time basis.

Few studies have addressed this question empirically, yet results are interesting. In studies of political and social ideologies, as well as religious beliefs, parents and their adult children reveal little or no convergence over time. That is, parents and their adult children do not seem to become more alike on these issues over the life course, though they may share similar roles and responsibilities. Instead, as predicted by socialization theory, parent–child attitude similarity is likely to decline over time. However, even though convergence may not occur, vestiges of parental influence do remain for individuals, even well into middle-age. For example, Moen *et al.* (1997) showed that daughters' gender role ideology in the late 1980s was positively related to their mothers' gender role ideology observed almost 25 years before. The greatest erosion seems to occur during the first few years after a young adult leaves home, but there are indications of a leveling off (by the late 20s or early 30s), and then stabilization over time (see Beck and Jennings 1991; Glass *et al.* 1986; Niemi and Jennings 1991; Whitbeck and Gecas 1988). In a sense this is what might be expected, as socialization does occur throughout life. Thus, while IG effects are commonly thought to be about stability alone, in the larger context our concern is about change over time, how adaptation within adulthood is managed, and the extent to which this rests on the foundations built as a child.

Disruptive forces in adulthood

As shown in Figure 11.2, one of the most powerful agents of change as a young adult leaves the family home is the rise of *new influencers*. New people, whether peers, roommates or spouses help to shape the patterns of daily life. As new living arrangements are encountered, each new party brings his or her own set of existing consumer preferences and decision styles to bear in the negotiation of joint purchases. Discussions, joint shopping trips, and shared consumption experiences can all initiate the introduction of new brands, products and purchase criteria. *Informational social influence* is clearly brought to bear in this manner, and over numerous occasions, as in our first quote below. *Normative social influence* is also likely to be present, and can also serve to disrupt the enactment of some existing IG influences. For example, our informants reported that social disdain from peers can be a surprising experience for a young person who discovers that the IG preferences he or she holds are not the norm, as in our second quote:

> I would never buy this on my own because my Mom has never done the boxed spaghetti thing. She always makes it from scratch. I didn't even really know it was available or if I did, I probably wouldn't think it was very good.

New influencers: spouse, roommates, and peers	New lives bring shifting lifestyle demands
– Joint purchase decisions – Introduction of new options and categories – Influences on choice criteria – New roles: purchasing agent for others – Informational & normative social influence – Social disdain: peers and media – Conformity pressures	– Income constraints – Mobility – Time at a premium – Plenty of personal meal occasions – Period of experimentation
Altered marketplace experiences	**Other insights on IG disruption**
– Lack of brand availability – results in frustration – Sales promotions, sampling, premiums – New products, information, and metrics – Mismatched package sizes – Product line deletion	– Incomplete IG knowledge – Parents change as life cycle continues – Behavior is not the only measure of IG – Time and distance

Note: Adapted from Moore *et al.* (2002).
Figure 11.2 Sources with potential to disrupt intergenerational (IG) influences.

But one of my roommates left it and so I ate it one night when there was nothing left to eat and it was wonderful. So now, I buy it. (R6)

Everyone always makes fun of me because my Mom always put Miracle Whip on my sandwiches, instead of mayonnaise. And Kevin always yells at me about stuff like that. (R11)

Beyond social interactions, the move away from home can also bring significant changes in *lifestyle demands*. Financial constraints may narrow the range of purchase options. Independent living may also alter some basic product needs: for example, grocery purchases may be geared more toward personal meal occasions, and convenience products. Many of our informants perceived time to be a premium, and thus opted for easy preparations. Others viewed their new living arrangements as an opportunity to explore new options. In some cases, the *structure of the marketplace* may threaten IG preferences. Lack of IG brand availability in the new marketplace, or disruptions caused by competitive promotional programs can each attenuate IG ties. Also, in major ways, the *dynamic nature of the marketplace is at work* to undo IG influences – competing brands are promoted and offered on specials, new options are introduced and intrusively promoted for their enhanced benefits, and support is sometimes withdrawn for older items dropped from product lines.

If I could afford to stick with certain brands I would, but due to my budget I more often than not, switch. But, I don't really want to, I don't think. (R1)

It was weird going grocery shopping for myself . . . I actually had to make my own meals . . . I don't know how to do it. So . . . I buy a lot of . . . just stuff that's easy . . . (R8)

. . . And another thing . . . they don't carry my brand of cottage cheese in this huge grocery store . . . Do they have it? No they don't . . . you can get it in a huge jumbo size . . . but I don't need that, so let's go! (R6)

. . . Buffalo Don's drinking water . . . they don't have here, and that makes me really mad. (R10)

Other factors at work to disrupt IG preferences include *larger geographic distances, longer time frames away from home,* and *socialization into new institutional living* circumstances such as military service. Thus, those segments of the population who never move far from home and family might be expected to hold more tightly to certain IG characteristics. Also, the parents will be modifying some of their own preferences and behaviors as they progress through their life cycles, and this will provide less support for some IG preferences. Finally, our own interviews also brought forth an interesting conceptual issue: that an excessive reliance on behavioral indicators might overstate "IG disruption." Reflecting the theorists' predictions of convergence during later adulthood, some of our informants indicated that they had stopped using particular products temporarily due to present circumstances, but that they fully planned to return to them once their income and lifestyle needs allowed. With respect to future IG research, this indicates that both attitudinal and behavioral measures may be needed to capture some IG effects.

Sustaining forces in adulthood

Despite the many forces at work to disrupt IG influences, some IG brand and product preferences do persist in the marketplace. This is partially due to the presence of a supporting structure of sustaining forces that can be called upon by the young adult (as shown in Figure 11.3). At a basic level, one category of sustainers includes *forces that support repetitive purchase.* Many of these relate to those mentioned earlier in the context of motivational underpinnings – IG brands that offer strong functional performance, low involvement in a product category or simple inertia. We also found that risk aversion may help to sustain IG preferences when young adults view themselves as novices, and therefore subject to making mistakes.

When I first started, I probably purchased them a lot because I didn't really know what else to buy, and I knew that those would be healthy for me 'cause

---

Forces that support repetitive purchase

- Performance, familiarity, inertia, low involvement
- Risk aversion
- Regularity as a reinforcer
- Seasonal rituals as IG support

Parents as IG sustainers

- IG purchases as continued loyalty to parent
- Proximity is a key issue
- Family shopping outings as reinforcers
- Parents as product suppliers
- Inputs from afar: coupons from home
- IG influence attempts continue to occur in adulthood

Maintenance of self-identity

- Ethnic identity as IG sustainers
- Select lifestyles shape choice options
- IG brand as "safe harbor"
- IG as basis for influence attempts on others
- Loosened constraints allow IG enactment
- Reverse IG: bringing parents back

Note: Adapted from Moore *et al.* (2002).

Figure 11.3 Sustaining forces for intergenerational (IG) influences.

she always chose things that were healthy for us. I knew that I liked them and I didn't want to go wrong 'cause it was my own money. (R7)

Parents can also sustain IG preferences. Parental visits and interactions, as well as joint shopping trips (albeit less frequently), gift supplies, and coupons can all serve as continuing reinforcements of preferences and shopping orientations learned previously. In some cases, more emotional ties were evident in our interviews, with the IG brand having come to symbolize family loyalty and affiliation.

My parents stock me up. Last time I went home I came back with so much food, I filled up my cabinet and had to start a new one. Because she [mother] said "I know you won't go down there." So, I don't have to go grocery shopping. (R18)

At a more intrinsic level, perhaps the most powerful sustainers of IG influences are those that *tie to personal identity*. For some consumers, IG brands are bound to central aspects of their sense of self. A number of these factors surfaced in our data. For example, some young women expressed a strong desire to retain their personal ethnic identity through consumption enactments. Pursuit of a particular lifestyle learned at home (e.g., healthy lifestyle, vegetarianism) also had strong impacts, but now extending beyond specific brands to broad choice criteria (these also reduce the potential for disruptive effects brought by either peers or marketing activities involving violations of the chosen lifestyle). Finally, this drive for expression of self-identity could also stimulate attempts to influence peers and parents.

> When we were in high school all three of us were in sports so we had on the go meals. And now that I'm in college and I don't want to make a huge meal for a family, I have on the go meals too. And so, a lot of them have continued, like the pastas and rice dishes and stuff. (R7)

> And bagels are important. Big and Crusty bagels because they remind me of, you have to have – I'm going to bring back real, real bagels – just because I think that everybody needs to experience a real bagel. Yeah, you guys need to experience the real New York deli bagel. I'll do that over Thanksgiving. (R9)

> After I went to college I started eating wheat bread, and then one time I came home from college and I said "Dad, why don't you buy Brownberry wheat bread anymore?" And then he just started buying it, and now he buys it again. (R1)

Research challenges and opportunities for the future

The intergenerational influence topic offers many fruitful avenues for future discovery. Here are eight of the most interesting and important research opportunities we see on the horizon for IG research:

Building on theories of human development

The genesis of IG is much more complex than the traditional research matching studies are able to reflect. In some sense, this complexity is what makes IG such a fascinating topic, yet at the same time it poses serious research challenges. Consider, for example, that IG influences are deeply embedded within a person's sense of self, and that they co-exist along with a myriad of other influences acting on that individual, all within a dynamic context. The effects of IG can indeed be captured in measures of generational similarities, but in reality these are only small indicators of a much richer latent construct. IG may be assessed in our research in terms of effects, but in reality it is part of a broader process by which an individual develops. To this point the boundaries of IG have not been delineated well, nor has there been adequate specification of the set of causal agents and processes at work in the family household.

For example, there has been a strong tendency for us to conceive of the fundamental nature of IG primarily through the lens of socialization theory. However, other theories of human development are likely quite capable of complementing and enriching our field's understanding. To illustrate, Lewin's Field Theory provides an overarching perspective from which to consider IG. It suggests that human behavior is a function of both person and the environment, which together comprise an individual's "life space" or psychological field. Life space is represented as the totality of forces, internal and external, acting on a person at a particular point in time (in Wilkie 1994). In this regard, age-old debates about "nature versus nurture" (or rather the interaction of the two) are relevant here, as families not only share the same environment, but are also linked genetically. Thus there may be genetic influences on consumer behavior that have not yet been addressed in our literature.[5] Research on twins does show that attitudes, preferences, and behavior can have a genetic basis (e.g., McCall *et al.* 1997), and it is reasonable to assume that some IG effects might be grounded in heredity, and not just in learning processes (e.g., certainly genetic transfer appears to be relevant to certain problem consumption behaviors such as alcoholism and obesity). While developing an understanding of the role of heredity in IG may be quite challenging, we do see it as a fertile direction for future work. More generally, our point here is that it will be worthwhile for researchers in this area to recognize both the value and the limits of the traditional *socialization* basis for their IG work, and for scholars to consider ways to develop a richer theoretical base for this area.

Explicating the domain for consumer IG

Within consumer research, perhaps the most fundamental research need is to more fully specify the IG domain. To be sure, much progress has been made in identifying IG impacts as empirical findings have cumulated over time. However, the full scope and depth of IG influences at work in consumer behavior has not been documented. For example, even some basic consumption activities such as information search and shopping preferences, savings behavior, and consumer expertise have yet to be explored as possible IG effects. The potentials for IG impacts of a more aesthetic nature such as stylistic preferences for interior design and colors, literary genres or music might also be considered. Also, gift-giving and family inheritance are worthy topics to learn of IG communication and adult sustenance (e.g., Price *et al.* 2000). For business practitioners, it would be extremely useful to examine the scope of product-related IG influences. For example, which product and service categories – such as cars, kitchen appliances, tools, sewing machines, and financial services – are most subject to IG influences, and which are not? There is little need to pursue further options here, as readers may enjoy the process of considering further topics in consumer behavior that may be beneficiaries of IG influences.

Delving more deeply into the emotional components of IG

Our research has convinced us of the power and centrality of emotion in IG, yet this interesting avenue for study has not been investigated in detail in consumer research (this may be because the field to this point has focused on finding IG impacts in the first place, and has thereby tended to view the IG phenomenon as more cognitive than emotional in nature).

As noted earlier, our own research has found that the character of emotions can run a wide gamut, from love and gratitude to anger and guilt, and can reach high levels of intensity, even when expressed years after the original triggering episodes. We have come to a view that it is helpful to search for the extent to which IG emotion is being enacted or expressed through such consumption-related vehicles as a joint shopping trip with a parent or a special gift-giving occasion. We have also seen indications that underlying emotions can be at work in the creation of specific aspirations the child may come to have for himself/herself. For example, in our life-history data evidence appeared that a parent's earlier history of per-ceived selflessness and generosity had motivated the overt desire in the now young adult to strive to be similarly charitable in her interactions with others.

Beyond the substantive domain for IG, there are also emotion-related options to consider within existing research paradigms. For example, let us briefly take up the matter of perspective. From the consumer's point of view, the emotional component of some IG is clearly characterized by intensity and richness. From the researcher's perspective, therefore, it is worthwhile to ask whether our existing measures of consumption behavior are tapping into that intensity in a sufficient manner. For example, measurement of parent-child shared brand preference (which we've reported on earlier in this chapter) is necessarily limited when treated as a single indicant, and could miss salient IG impacts of emotions. One such case would involve negative emotions, if these have resulted in a strong rejection of a particular brand or particular product category. In these instances the lack of parent–child correspondence would have been seen as evidence of no IG impact, when in fact there is an IG impact, but in the opposite direction from that expected.

In sum, we believe that emotional and motivational drivers are likely, at times, to be powerful forces in creating and sustaining IG. We believe that they warrant considerably more conceptualization, perhaps best based upon the burgeoning attention to the topic of emotional components of consumer behavior in general. We also believe that empirical studies are needed, first to ascertain which parti-cular emotions are most likely operative in the IG arena, and then to assess the extent to which these appear and operate differentially within the consumer population. However approached, emotion within IG warrants further study.

Assessing IG dynamics during adulthood

There are a number of potential research issues related to the workings of IG through adulthood. One issue in particular, the question of IG's persistence over time, has predominated thus far. This remains an important topic for future research, and brings with it some significant measurement challenges. Although longitudinal research designs would be optimal, these may often not be feasible. Perhaps a reasonable alternative would involve cross-sectional surveys of con-sumers within different age groups or life stages, with sufficiently large samples to make valid comparisons across them. Beyond this, further work needs to be focused on the underpinnings of endurance, the forces that work to either sustain or disrupt IG in its many manifestations. As part of this analysis, it would be useful to gain additional insight as to whether and under what conditions consumer IG influences might converge, as the former children now enter structured stages of their own family life cycles, including parenthood.

A second topic that has not yet received much empirical attention centers on the dynamic aspect of parents' behavior. As we observed in our depth interviews, parents' preferences may also change over time, and they may continue to provide advice to their now adult children. Thus, socialization may still occur, yet clearly this is no longer a process of "childhood learning." When both participants in the socialization process are adults, we might ask whether this is a conceptually different form of IG, or not. Given that adults have many more options in terms of information acquisition, it is interesting to consider under what circumstances parents might be consulted, and why.

Exploring the "reverse flow" of IG influences in today's world

Given the dynamic nature of the consumer marketplace, "reverse IG" is a particularly relevant topic for study in our field. Here interest is in those domains in which the flow of influence is reversed, moving from the child to the parent (e.g., Ekstrom *et al.* 1987; Moschis 1988), particularly among families with teenagers and young adults. Though published research to date has produced little systematic study of "reverse IG," it is likely that this is a substantial influence in particular categories. For example, young adults may impact the family's decision to invest in an innovative technology, consume in a new product category, or choose a particular brand and special features. They may also educate the parents about how new products work, thus enhancing the actual consumption experience (reverse IG is also likely in the fashion world: in our life history narratives a number of informants reported efforts to update the style of clothing their parents would wear). Further investigation of reverse IG should be a fruitful research topic for marketing-related research as well. More broadly, extending this sphere to include sibling influences is a natural possibility as well (e.g., Cotte and Wood 2004).

Broader consideration of the concept of reverse IG is also needed. We would suggest that it is more than a simple reversal of the direction of influence. Reverse IG cannot be captured within the childhood learning model that socialization theory provides. The basic phenomenon of adults learning from their offspring (at various stages in their development) is likely subject to different causal factors and processes than existing models of IG include. So, while we would consider child-to-parent influence a form of IG influence, it has some unique properties that need to be studied and understood.

Attending to the distinction between "Q" and "R" analyses of IG influences

Employing a factor analysis analogy, one of the primary issues to recognize in this area is that empirical studies can be undertaken with either people (Q) or objects (R) as the primary focus. The primary emphasis in consumer research to this point has been on documenting IG effects and the forms it may take (perhaps arising in part from the early focus on managerial concerns in this area). This corresponds to the "object" focus. There is, however, the alternative perspective of focusing on families rather than the IG effects themselves, which would provide us with the opportunity to look at the determinants of IG (NB, some consumer research has done this, but much opportunity exists in this direction). For example, families likely vary considerably in the strength of IG influences, particularly in terms of shared preferences and behavior. What are these differences, and what leads to their development? If a portion of future IG research would focus on the consumers and/or the families themselves, a different and potentially richer view of the IG phenomenon is possible.

A number of theoretical frameworks that focus on family dynamics exist (e.g., family systems theory). These should be helpful in conceptualizing "Q" analyses of IG influences. For example, within consumer research the "parental style" paradigm (see Carlson and Grossbart 1988) provides insights into how parents interact with their children about consumption-related issues. This particular model differentiates parents on the basis of their approach to socialization, how they communicate with their children, and their permissiveness (or lack thereof). This can be a useful starting point for understanding how families differ with regard to IG and why (see also Moore and Berchmans 1996). More broadly, attention to issues of family dynamics is an important research direction for the future, if we are to fully understand the true nature of IG influences.

Advancing consumer IG measurement methodologies

Beyond questions of the larger conceptual domain for IG, it is also the case that there presently is no ideal measure of IG, nor clear agreement as to the underlying information that needs to be gathered, and then analyzed. There is a significant need for directed attention to these issues in future research undertakings. For example, although interpretivist methods have recently been employed, consumer researchers have traditionally relied on survey methods for IG data generation. Some key studies have relied upon the "key informant" approach using measures collected from the younger family member (e.g., Childers and Rao 1992; Heckler *et al.* 1989). Note that this approach assumes that the young person is sufficiently knowledgeable to answer on behalf of the parent or family. In contrast, other key IG studies have measured both sides of the parent–child dyad, then compared responses to assess similarity (e.g., Arndt 1971; Obermiller and Spangenburg 2000; Viswanathan *et al.* 2000). Most recently this approach has been expanded to assess family triads, including a sibling (Cotte and Wood 2004). Note here that these approaches necessitate dyadic or triadic data analyses, which can become considerably more complex in their statistical assumptions. Is either survey approach sufficient? Is one approach superior? Further, what exactly *should* be measured? Intergenerational influences are a mere fraction of the many influences that guide consumer behavior, and, as mentioned previously, some aspects of IG are deeply embedded within a person's self-identity. A primary research challenge is to identify and then disentangle IG from these other influences (e.g., how can/should ethnic identification be separated from parent to child influence transmission?). This challenge is then complicated by the recognition that IG is not a single effect, but rather a range of effects that can operate at multiple levels (e.g., product non-use, store patronage, decision heuristics, brand preference, etc.). Given these complexities, how do we know that our inferences are valid? The topic of IG measurement and analysis remains an area for fruitful investigation.

Increasing sensitivity to the impacts of IG's darker sides

Though the emphasis in the IG literature to this point has focused on its positive dimensions, it would be worthwhile for future IG research to recognize that intergenerational influences are at times associated with personal anxieties, poor consumer decision-making, and dysfunctional behaviors. For example, some of the earliest work on IG by Hill (1970) suggested that financial planning skills were shared across generations, and that this was particularly true among families who tended to spend impulsively. Poor financial management may be an IG influence that is continuing to create havoc on saving and spending decisions in future families. Other consumption-related behaviors that are essentially negative may well also be readily transmitted from one family generation to the next, such as consumer fraud (e.g, abuse of credit, shoplifting), compulsive buying, and uninformed or impulsive decision-making styles learned within the family home. Further, long-term deleterious health effects can result from smoking behaviors, alcohol abuse, or overeating, all of which may well be subject to IG influences. From a research perspective, it would seem that there is a need to identify potentially negative forms of IG, and to determine what effects they may be exerting within families. Also, of course, intervention researchers concerned with ameliorating these problems should also be encouraged to examine IG as a potentially significant causal agent.

A final note

In this tour of the intergenerational influence research area we have covered a range of conceptual, empirical, and applied issues. Hopefully it is now clear that IG constitutes an interesting and often-overlooked set of forces that guide our everyday consumption behaviors. These effects can be powerful, but are also subtle and complex. This leads to the many intriguing research challenges that lie ahead, where much remains to be discovered.

Acknowledgments

The authors would like to thank our reviewers Les Carlson, June Cotte, and Terry Childers, and the editors for their thoughtful comments and suggestions. This chapter was significantly enriched by their insights.

Notes

1 Only canned vegetables did not demonstrate an IG brand preference effect. However, in a parallel analysis (not discussed here) of IG effects on product usage versus product nonusage, significant IG impacts had appeared for canned vegetables (i.e., if a mother does not use canned vegetables, her daughter is likely to also avoid canned vegetables). Actually, then, all 24 of our product categories in the study showed statistically significant impacts of intergenerational influences.
2 It should be noted that all brands listed here are larger share of market entries: our statistical tests required threshold sample sizes, so smaller or specialty brands could not be tested, though they may well exhibit IG brand equity as well.
3 This was a different sample of young women from the survey results noted earlier. All interviews were audio-taped and transcribed verbatim. Based on the aims and pro-cedures of grounded theory (Glaser and Strauss 1967; Strauss and Corbin 1990), an extensive and highly structured analytic process was used to identify and preserve essential conceptual categories and relationships in the data. The authors read and independently coded each interview. Emergent categories were compared in detail for the first six interviews. These initial categories were used as the structural basis for coding the remaining interviews, with added enrichments as necessitated by the data. All interviews were independently coded and compared on a line-by-line basis. Few discrepancies arose, and these were resolved through discussion.
4 The life history method belongs to a broader domain of biographical research methods that tap into personal experience through the use of narrative such as profiles, memoirs, life stories, autobiographies, and diaries.
5 We would like to thank Terry Childers for this valuable insight.

References

Acock, A. C. (1984) "Parents and their children: The study of inter-generational influence," *Sociology and Social Research* 68(2): 151–171.

Aquilino, W. S. (1997) "From adolescent to young adult: A prospective study of parent–child relations during the transition to adulthood," *Journal of Marriage and the Family* 59 (August): 670–686.

Arndt, J. (1971) "A research note on intergenerational overlap of selected consumer vari-ables," *Markeds Kommunikasjon* 3: 1–8.

Arndt, J. (1972) "Intra familial homogeneity for perceived risk and opinion leadership," *Journal of Advertising* 1(1): 40–47.

Bao, W., Whitbeck, L. B., Hoyt, D. R., and Conger, R. D. (1999) "Perceived parental acceptance as a moderator of religious transmission among adolescent boys and girls," *Journal of Marriage and the Family* 61 (May): 362–374.

Beatty, S. E. and Talpade, S. (1994) "Adolescent influence in family decision-making: A replication with extension," *Journal of Consumer Research* 21 (September): 332–341.

Beck, P. A. and Jennings, M. K. (1991) "Family traditions, political periods, and the devel-opment of partisan orientations," *Journal of Politics* 53 (August): 742–763.

Brim, O. G., Jr. (1968) "Adult socialization," in J. Clausen (ed.) *Socialization and Society*, Boston, MA: Little Brown: 183–226.

Carlson, L. and Grossbart, S. (1988) "Parental style and consumer socialization of children," *Journal of Consumer Research* 15 (June): 77–94.

Carlson, L., Walsh, A., Laczniak, R. N., and Grossbart, S. (1994) "Family communication patterns and marketplace motivations, attitudes, and behaviors of children and mothers," *Journal of Consumer Affairs* 28(1): 25–53.

Cashmore, J. E. and Goodnow, J. J. (1985) "Agreement between generations: A two-process approach," *Child Development* 56: 493–501.

Childers, T. L. and Rao, A. R. (1992) "The influence of familial and peer-based reference groups on consumer decisions," *Journal of Consumer Research* 19 (September): 198–211.

Cotte, J. and Wood, S. L. (2004) "Families and innovative consumer behavior: A triadic analysis of sibling and parental influence," *Journal of Consumer Research* 31 (June): 78–86.

Davis, H. L. (1976) "Decision-making within the household," *Journal of Consumer Research* 2 (March): 241–260.

Ekstrom, K. M., Tansuhaj, P. S., and Foxman, E. R. (1987) "Children's influence in family decisions and consumer socialization," in M. Wallendorf and P. Anderson (eds) *Advances in Consumer Research*, Vol. 14, Provo, UT: Association for Consumer Research: 283–287.

Foxman, E. R., Tansuhaj, P. S., and Ekstrom, K. M. (1989) "Family members' perceptions of adolescents' influence in family decision-making," *Journal of Consumer Research* 15 (March): 482–491.

Glaser, B. G. and Strauss, A. L. (1967) *The Discovery of Grounded Theory: Strategies for Qualitative Research*, Chicago, IL: Aldine.

Glass, J., Bengston, V. L., and Dunham, C. C. (1986) "Attitude similarity in three-generation families: Socialization, status inheritance, or reciprocal influence?" *American Sociological Review* 51 (October): 685–698.

Heckler, S. E., Childers, T. L., and Arunchalam, R. (1989) "Intergenerational influences in adult buying behaviors: An examination of moderating factors," in T. K. Srull (ed.) *Advances in Consumer Research*, Vol. 16, Provo, UT: Association for Consumer Research: 276–284.

Hill, R. (1970) *Family Development in Three Generations*, Cambridge, MA: Schenkman.

Holbrook, M. B. (1993) "Nostalgia and consumption preferences: Some emerging patterns of consumer tastes," *Journal of Consumer Research* 20 (September): 245–256.

Jennings, M. K. (1984) "The intergenerational transfer of political ideologies in eight western nations," *European Journal of Political Research* 12: 261–276.

Jennings, M. K. and Niemi, R. G. (1974) *The Political Character of Adolescence*, Princeton, NJ: Princeton University Press.

John, D. R. (1999) "Consumer socialization of children: A retrospective look at twenty-five years of research," *Journal of Consumer Research* 26 (December): 183–213.

Kahn, B. E. and McAlister, L. (1997) *Grocery Revolution – The New Focus on the Consumer*, New York: Addison-Wesley.

Kelman, H. C. (1960) "Compliance, identification and internalization: Three processes of attitude change," *Journal of Conflict Resolution* 2: 51–60.

Levine, R. A. (1969) "Culture, personality and behavior: An evolutionary view," in D. Goslin (ed.) *Handbook of Socialization Theory and Research*, Chicago, IL: Rand McNally.

McCall, B. P., Cavanaugh, M. A., and Arvey, R. D. (1997) "Genetic influences on job and occupational switching," *Journal of Vocational Behavior* 50: 60–77.

McNeal, J. U. (1987) *Children as Consumers*, Lexington, MA: D. C. Heath.

McNeal, J. U. (1992) *Kids as Customers*, New York: Lexington.

Miller, B. C. (1975) "Intergenerational patterns of consumer behavior," in M. J. Schlinger (ed.) *Advances in Consumer Research*, Vol. 2, Ann Arbor, MI: Association for Consumer Research: 93–101.

Miller, R. B. and Glass, J. (1989) "Parent–child attitude similarity across the life course," *Journal of Marriage and the Family* 51 (November): 991–997.

Moen, P., Erickson, M. A., and Dempster-McClain, D. (1997) "Their mother's daughters? The intergenerational transmission of gender attitudes in a world of changing roles," *Journal of Marriage and the Family* 59 (May): 281–294.

Moore, E. S. and Berchmans, B. M. (1996) "The role of the family environment in the development of shared consumption values: An intergenerational approach," in K. Corfman and J. Lynch (eds) *Advances in Consumer Research*, Vol. 23, Provo, UT: Association for Consumer Research: 484–490.

Moore, E. S. and Lutz, R. J. (1988) "Intergenerational influences in the formation of consumer attitudes and beliefs about the marketplace: Mothers and daughters," in M. J. Houston (ed.) *Advances in Consumer Research*, Vol. 15, Provo, UT: Association for Consumer Research: 461–467.

Moore, E. S., Wilkie, W. A., and Alder, J. A. (2001) "Lighting the torch: How do intergenerational influences develop?" in M. C. Gilly and J. Meyers-Levy (eds) *Advances in Consumer Research*, Vol. 28, Valdosta, GA: Association for Consumer Research: 287–293.

Moore, E. S., Wilkie, W. A., and Berchmans, B. M. (2005) "Intergenerational relations and the continuity of consumption styles," Working Paper, University of Notre Dame.

Moore, E. S., Wilkie, W. L., and Lutz, R. J. (2002) "Passing the torch: Intergenerational influences as a source of brand equity," *Journal of Marketing* 66 (April): 17–37.

Moschis, G. P. (1987) *Consumer Socialization*, Lexington, MA: Lexington Books.

Moschis, G. P. (1988) "Methodological issues in studying intergenerational influences on consumer behavior," in M. Houston (ed.) *Advances in Consumer Research*, Vol. 15, Provo, UT: Association for Consumer Research: 569–573.

Niemi, R. G. and Jennings, M. K. (1991) "Issues and inheritance in the formation of party identification," *American Journal of Political Science* 35 (November): 969–988.

Nieuwbeerta, P. and Wittebrood, K. (1995) "Intergenerational transmission of political party preference in the Netherlands," *Social Science Research* 24: 243–261.

Obermiller, C. and Spangenburg, E. R. (2000) "On the origin and distinctness of skepticism toward advertising," *Marketing Letters* 11(4): 311–322.

Olsen, B. (1993) "Brand loyalty and lineage: Exploring new dimensions for research," in L. McAlister and M. L. Rothschild (eds) *Advances in Consumer Research*, Vol. 20, Provo, UT: Association for Consumer Research: 276–284.

Palan, K. M. and Wilkes, R. E. (1997) "Adolescent–parent interaction in family decision-making," *Journal of Consumer Research* 24 (September): 159–169.

Peterson, G. W. and Rollins, B. C. (1987) "Parent–child socialization," in M. B. Sussman and S. K. Steinmetz (eds) *Handbook of Marriage and the Family*, New York: Plenum: 471–507.

Price, L. L., Arnould E. J., and Curasi, C. F. (2000) "Older consumers' disposition of special possessions," *Journal of Consumer Research* 27 (September): 179–201.

Sears, D. O. (1983) "The persistence of early political predispositions," in L. Wheeler and P. Shaver (eds) *Review of Personality and Social Psychology*: 79–116.

Shah, R. H. and Mittal, B. (1997) "Toward a theory of intergenerational influence in consumer behavior: An exploratory essay," in M. Brucks and D. J. MacInnis (eds) *Advances in Consumer Research*, Vol. 24, Provo, UT: Association for Consumer Research: 55–60.

Sillars, A. L. (1995) "Communication and family culture," in M. A. Fitzpatrick and A. L. Vangelisti (eds) *Explaining Family Interactions*, Thousand Oaks, CA: Sage: 375–399.

Strauss, A. L. and Corbin, J. (1990) *Basics of Qualitative Research: Grounded Theory Procedures and Techniques*, Newbury Park, CA: Sage.

Troll, L. and Bengston, V. (1979) "Generations in the family," in W. R. Burr (ed.) *Contemporary Theories about the Family*, Vol. 1, Reuben Hill, F. I. Nye, and I. L. Reiss, New York: Free Press: 127–161.

Viswanathan, M., Childers, T. L., and Moore, E. S. (2000) "The measurement of intergenerational communication and influence on consumption: Development, validation and cross-cultural comparison of the IGEN scale," *Journal of the Academy of Marketing Science* 28 (Summer): 406–424.

Ward, S. (1974) "Consumer socialization," *Journal of Consumer Research* 1 (September): 1–14.

Wells, W. D. and Gubar, G. (1966) "Life cycle concept in marketing research," *Journal of Marketing Research* 3 (November): 355–363.

Whitbeck, L. B. and Gecas, V. (1988) "Value attributions and value transmission between parents and children," *Journal of Marriage and the Family* 50 (August): 829–840.

Wilkie, W. L. (1994) *Consumer Behavior*, 3rd edn, New York: Wiley.

Wilkie, W. L. and Moore, E. S. (2004) "Challenges facing intergenerational research in marketing," Working Paper, University of Notre Dame.

Woodson, L. G., Childers, T. L., and Winn, P. R. (1976) "Intergenerational influences in the purchase of auto insurance," in W. B. Locander (ed.) *Marketing Looking Outward: 1976 Business Proceedings*, Chicago, IL: American Marketing Association: 43–49.

Ziegler, E. and Child, I. L. (1969) *Socialization and Personality Development*, Reading, MA: Addison-Wesley.

12 Consumer identity motives in the information age

John Deighton

In a typical marketplace transaction, for example buying milk in a store, the seller is identified and the buyer is anonymous. Sellers use identifiers like trademarks and brand names to build reputations for their offerings, but mass-market buyers lack countervailing reputational power. To the extent that buyers have reputations, they are those that sellers ascribe to them when they assign them to stylized market segments. The information age, and in particular the progress in storage, transmission, and retrieval of personally individuating information over the past thirty years, is beginning to undermine this historical fact by putting the resources of identity and reputation into buyers' hands. First came credit cards, which detached buyers' reputations for creditworthiness from particular retail stores ("store charge cards") and made them elements of personal, portable identities. Later came loyalty cards to mark buyers' worth to airlines, hotels, supermarkets, car rental companies, bookstores, movie theaters, photo-finishing chains, ski resorts, and fast-food chains to name just a few. Soon biometrics may liberate buyers from the need to carry cards and make possession of marketplace identities more pervasive and less conspicuous. Digital identity is increasingly a factor to be reckoned with in consumer behavior.

The theme of this chapter is what it is beginning to mean for the "why" of consumption that buyers increasingly can be offered and can accept or reject the power and burden of identity in markets. Only seller-initiated identity offerings will be considered, because that is where advances in technology give us something new to investigate. The information technologies needed to mobilize buyer identities have large fixed costs that must be sponsored, and while buyers can in principle form cooperatives to share these costs, that possibility is not explored here.

The chapter begins by locating anonymity and identity in historical context. Next I define identification as it will be used in the chapter. The term "customer brand" will be used to refer to the identity that a seller offers to a buyer within a specific buyer – seller relationship – a means by which buyers can be individually known, and know that they are known, in a manner somewhat symmetrical with what branding offers to products. Four degrees of intensity of customer brandedness are distinguished: transitory tag branding, persistent tag branding, role branding and self-expressive branding. For each level of intensity, the chapter explores a set of implications for the operation of markets and the experience of consumption. Finally the chapter examines consumer privacy as a particular motive governing self-presentation with the power to unsettle the transition from product branding to customer branding.

Anonymity's short history

The essence of anonymity is to be unrecognized in a second encounter. To live anonymously in the social world is not to be unnoticed in the first encounter, which would be to be invisible, but to be seen and dealt with in the knowledge that once you are gone there will be no getting back to you. It is a stance that was hard to perform as recently as two centuries ago. Strangers were a social category both rare and dangerous for most of human history, until large cities began to form in the early 1800s and mass transportation began to make travel more than a rarity. In 1700 only 48 European towns were larger than 40,000 people, and 85 percent of Europe's population lived in nucleated settlements, farms, and hamlets. Most people lived with so little mobility, embedded in such persisting social networks, that identity was all but inescapable (Tuan 1982). To appear in a social setting without an identity was to be conspicuous and arouse suspicion. The cultural legacy persists in the form of prejudice against vagrants and nomads, and the social prestige that attaches to rootedness.

This absence of anonymity took two forms. First, people possessed social identities in the eyes of the people they lived with. They lived in circumstances of physical intimacy that we would find intolerable today. Tuan's (1982) sweeping review of personal living arrangements from the Middle Ages to the recent past, in Europe, China, Brazil, and the Kalahari, concludes that life before the modern age, "lived in the open, visible to all members of the group" (Tuan 1982: 28) faced challenges to cohesiveness that did not exist after systems of mass communication became prevalent.

> In premodern times, literacy, if it existed, was limited to a few elite members of society. Touch and speech in face-to-face contact were the only effective means of communication. Social cohesion required that people move almost constantly in each other's presence. Gregariousness was a necessity whether the group was egalitarian or hierarchial.
>
> (Tuan 1982: 26)

Huizinga (1954: 9–10) summed up the Middle Ages thus, "All things in life were a proud and cruel publicity."

Second, people possessed formal identities recorded in documents that they carried whenever they strayed from those who could vouch for them. As recently as two hundred years ago it was imprudent to appear in a community without some claim, usually written but sometimes in the form of distinctive garb or ornamentation, to an identity (Groebner 2001). Throughout Europe from the Middle Ages until the rise of nation states, it fell to communal institutions to supply the means to vouch for identity. Guilds issued documentation to journeymen traveling to pursue training in trades, soldiers carried passes and wore insignia, pilgrims pinned papers to their clothing, and diplomats carried letters of testimony. Later the nation state took over the function of imposing an identity on people. Caplan (2001: 49) cites the German philosopher Fichte, writing in 1796: "The chief principle of a well-regulated police state is this: That each citizen shall be at all times and places . . . recognized as this or that particular person." As late as the early twentieth century intra-national travel required papers and registration with a local police station in several European countries.

At just the historical moment that local recognition of a person's identity could no longer be relied on to regulate the social order, nations throughout Europe began to take a bureaucratic interest in the identities of their populations. Arguably the first step was to fix the names that people carried (Caplan 2001). Relatively fluid naming regimes gave way to the registration of names at birth. France required certification of births in 1792, and in 1794 forbade citizens from bearing names other than those registered at birth. Prussia forbade the use of a name other than one's own in 1822. England took registration of births out of the hands of its established church and made it a civil obligation in 1837. Jeremy Bentham proposed the universal adoption of a naming regime that included tattooing first and last names on the wrist, pointing out in defense of the idea that it was "a common custom among English sailors" and would be "a new spring for morality, a new source of power for the laws, an almost infallible precaution against a multitude of offences" (Caplan 2001: 65). Bentham's proposal for a Panopticon (1787/1995), a "penitentiary inspection house" in which prisoners would live backlit and in silhouette perpetually visible to an inspector, forms a central metaphor in Foucault's (1995) analysis of how a state of conscious and permanent visibility assures the automatic functioning of power. Anonymity, it seems, is a state of affairs not much loved by the institutions that regulate the social order.

Anonymity flourished in the chaos of Victorian urbanization, but its heyday was brief. With the weakening of informal scrutiny by local communities, the State rushed to fill the void with formal protocols. Today all modern nation states impose compulsory identity and surveillance at a multitude of points of contact: for taxation, for military registration, for voting, for motor vehicle operation, for home ownership, and for international travel. And to the extent that there is privacy, it is a prerogative of the more affluent, whose stake in the status quo can be more taken for granted. Those of lowest social status, such as welfare recipients, the indigent elderly, and offenders against the law, are as scrupulously labeled and monitored today as any medieval serf was.

The market, however, has been far slower than the State to fill the identity void. Over the last two centuries it has been easy to stylize the buying side of markets as anonymous and to treat identified buyers as a quaint exception. Buyers came to think of privacy as a right, and sellers to think of buyer anonymity as an unfortunate fact. Now the information age is bringing marketplace anonymity's brief reign to an end, filling the identity void with new market structures. The motive to be identified and to identify, to evade identification and to police it, is occupying an increasingly prominent place in consumer behavior and marketing strategy if we look for it.

What is it to be identified? Shaping and being shaped

By an identity I mean some of the characteristics of a self that are exhibited in a social setting, and which in sum specify to others and to oneself who one is. By digital identity I mean simply the subset of these characteristics that can be coded so that they can be electronically manipulated. In a cybernetic sense, an identity is some of the meanings that serve as a standard or reference for who one is or intends to be (Burke 1991; Burke and Tully 1977), and to which the self-concept attempts to return when disturbed by reflected appraisals from the social environment. Its importance to consumption has been recognized: it has been described as the organizing construct through which ordinary consumption activities can be understood (Kleine *et al.* 1993).

To be identified is to recognize that one is observed or at least observable. It enables the deployment of "face," as when T. S. Eliot has Alfred J. Prufrock speak of preparing the "face to meet the faces that you meet," or when Madonna credits Rita Hayworth with "giving good face." There are false faces and poker faces, straight faces and faces that face up, faces that fail to conceal ("written all over your face") and faces that bear the brunt of failure ("egg on your face"). In this view of things the face is where the world and we collide, where the self shines through or dissembles. Because the face is understood to be a rhetorical plane, questions of trust or authenticity arise. Does the face deserve the reputation it asserts?

But the causality runs in both directions, so that the face is an interface, not only giving expression but also modeling what is impressed on it. It is not just that the face projects or refracts or distorts out from some notional self into the world, but that the world shapes the face and the face creates the self. When Goffman (1959) writes of "face-work," he describes a back-and-forth process in which the two parties in a face-to-face encounter each try to converge on a single "definition of the situation." People will often go out of their way to avoid being "difficult," or disagreeing about what is actually going on, and in the process of being polite or agreeable or getting along they will find themselves doing things that they had not quite expected themselves to be doing. Identities are not only the sum of the face work we pursue selfishly, but also include the face-saving we engage in to maintain our place in a network of social affiliations. This two-way trade requires that theorizing about identity must pay attention to the way it shapes action and also to the way it is shaped by action. Identity is an expression of preferences and also an influence upon preferences. It enacts motive and it constructs motive.

In this chapter I am concerned with the face resources offered to us in the marketplace by identity devices designed by buyers for sellers, such as for example airline and hotel frequent-flyer programs, or Amazon's well-known collaborative filtering engine that tells us about products that people like us have liked. I shall view them not simply as faces but as interfaces. To what extent do they serve us, and to what extent do they make us? Is an identity program a vehicle for the expression of who I want to be, carefully designed to take into account who I am and what I need? Or is it a seductive mask that transforms me into the role that the mask enables me to perform, a maker of tastes more than it is a marker? I shall claim that it is both, in proportions determined by just how central is the self-presentation task that it enables.

The more an identity program engages the central life themes of the buyer, the more it shapes the buyer's tastes. Supermarket frequent-shopper programs are, it seems, weak face resources. They confer membership whose rewards are mainly economic – members pay lower prices – and while there are people for whom paying lower prices is a self-actualizing experience, termed by Schindler (1998) "smart shoppers," for others the more expressive domains of life are fields like recreation and entertainment, and it is here that memberships are correspondingly more self-expressive. A casino chain, Harrah's, offers resources for the frequent visitor to its casinos that are fulfilling on dimensions besides the economic. By enabling loyal patrons to perform according to a stylized notion of the high roller, Harrah's rewards program makes casino visits more fun and more status-enhancing, while shaping and modeling the behaviors that serve the casino's interests. They show gamers how to be big shots. Harley Davidson invites its riders to play the role that the bike enables through its Hog (Harley Owners Group) program. More intensely, the passion of a member of the fan base of a baseball team feeds on the passion of other members, in the stadium and in the out-of-stadium events of the fan club. Individuals perform their roles more vigorously because the actions of other individuals draw them into the performance (Deighton 1992).

Degrees of identity

The identity mobilized by an identity program is conceived here as continuous: a buyer who abandons anonymity faces options of increasing complexity, both with respect to the number of dimensions available for face work and the grading on each dimension. Creditworthiness, of the kind established by a credit card, is one such dimension, and its gradations are played out with the help of color codes, from plain cards to silver to gold and so on. But creditworthiness, in the form of check-cashing privileges, is just one dimension of the resource offered by a hotel frequent-guest program. A rich face resource is better for a buyer bent on self-expression than a simple resource, although richness is costly to use and live up to, so there is, at least notionally, an optimal level and dimensionality of resource for a given level of buyer involvement with the seller's offering. Anonymity and the four degrees of intensity with which customers can be branded are summarized in Figure 12.1 and developed in the sections that follow.

Transitory identity

A precondition for a buyer to have any sense that they are identified (and equivalently that they are not anonymous and can be gotten back to) is that they possess

Anonymity	The buyer acts with confidence that the seller can take no subsequent action that is contingent on the first action.
Transitory Identity	In the eyes of the seller the buyer is described by a unique means of address that permits seller response to be conditioned on the buyer's action.
Persistent Identity	The seller knows the buyer by a persistent address by which the seller can reach the buyer in the future, so that seller responses can be conditioned on a pattern of buyer actions over time.
Role-specific Identity	When the pattern of buyer actions conforms to a role, the seller rewards the buyer with resources that are valued within the role.
Self-expressive Identity	The pattern of buyer actions is an integral element of the buyer's self-concept, and supported by seller resources that are valued resources for self-definition.

Figure 12.1 Degrees of buyer identity.

an address (Blattberg and Deighton 1991). An addressable buyer is located in time and space so that the seller can reach out with a context-specific offering and match the response (or lack of a response) to the address. Obvious examples include a mailing address, a telephone number, or an email address. For a less obvious example consider what happens when a customer appears in front of the cash register at a supermarket where, based on the contents of the customer's shopping basket, she or he is given a set of context-relevant coupons. At that moment the buyer is addressable, and although that individual's response to the coupon cannot be measured by the marketer because the address does not persist, the aggregate effectiveness of matching a particular purchase to a particular coupon can be. A web-enabled desktop computer with an internet protocol (IP) address is another example. The user is addressable by pop-up advertising in response to typing a search term into an Internet search engine or a website address into an Internet browser, and again the marketer can measure the aggregate effectiveness of the match between cue (the search term "refinance" for example) and the response (a pop-up ad for a specific mortgage loan originator for example).

Addresses in the examples above are of two kinds – transitory and persistent. By a transitory address I mean one that exists for just a single encounter, after which the seller has no way to identify that buyer again. The presence of the shopper at a supermarket checkout or the possession of a temporary IP address are both transitory. The weakest face resource, then, is that conferred by possession of a transitory address, when a buyer recognizes that he or she in an interaction where the seller's response is conditioned on the buyer's action or identity, but the system lacks memory. Even such a weak face can induce impression management. To illustrate, a supermarket shopper (personal communication) noticed that the Catalina system for disseminating discount coupons to shoppers was programmed to give a coupon entitling the buyer to a large discount on Brand A whenever Brand B was bought, and a smaller face-value coupon whenever Brand B was bought by redeeming the large discount coupon. The buyer, being relatively indifferent between Brands A and B, took to managing the impression they were giving off to the machine by buying in the sequence B, A, A, B, A, A. Thus even weak customer branding influenced the buyer's self-presentation.

Persistent identity

A persistent address allows for interaction beyond the single encounter. An address is a mailbox, a phone number, an IP address, or a computer hard drive containing a cookie. At its minimum, the address is no more than a tag, preserving much of the buyer's anonymity but allowing the seller to leave signed messages and the buyer to reply if they choose, as for example when someone registers on a website with an email address that they reserve for use with websites they suspect will send spam. This capacity for two-way communication marks the end of mass marketing; for example, it opens up the possibility of direct marketing. More generally, it makes possible what I shall call customer branding.

When a persistent identity is available, a seller may "brand" the buyer in the sense of conferring individuality on the buyer. By letting the buyer know that they are recognized and remembered, distinctive and distinguishable among all other buyers whenever they exchange with that seller, the identifying tag allows the buyer to lay claim to some points of differentiation relative to other buyers, perhaps to demonstrate loyalty, perhaps to be less expensive to serve, or perhaps to possess idiosyncratic tastes. In sum, when a buyer has a persistent address or tag, it is possible to have a reputation.

Reputation, whether of product or customer, is the core of what it means to be branded. A persistent address makes reputation effects possible. Marketing campaigns can judge their audiences not merely by reading the generalized effects of broadcast marketing, and not just with the reaction-sensitive tools of direct marketing, but by forming impressions of individual identities. They can reach out to a particular customer, observe the response, and reach out again in a manner that takes account of that response. Their marketing can begin to take on the form of conversation. Using only the fact of a persistent address, interactive marketing begins to engage with identity, reacting to it and shaping it. Demeanor starts to matter. The etiquette of soliciting an identity tag, for example, influences the quality of the subsequent relationship. Without the cooperation of the buyer, uninvited communication over time is interpreted as pestering or spamming. Tag branding is commonly done with the buyer's cooperation, by such gestures as inviting registration or extending membership.

Examples of this weak form of customer branding that is made possible by a persistent address, which I am calling tag branding, include membership of supermarket frequent-shopper programs, subscriptions to Netflix's digital video disk subscription service, subscription to Tivo's digital video recorder service, bank customers, phone subscribers, and shoppers who register with Amazon. In the case of Tivo, Netflix, and Amazon, the consumer grants the marketer the right to address them because it is impossible to get the service without an address to which it can be delivered. Addressable marketing communications, such as Tivo's pitches on behalf of new television pay-per-view programming or Amazon's book recommendations, are part of the offering. That is not the case with supermarket frequent-shopper programs. To induce the shopper to register, there needs to be a bribe in the form of discounted prices for members.

Reputation is a property with very large consequences for the operation of markets. When positive reputation exists in an exchange, we can afford to be less vigilant about squaring what we give against what we get. We can be indulgent, and others can be indulgent to us. Exchanges that might not have happened, or at best would have gone forward as pinched and crabbed little trades between mutually suspicious parties, can flourish. This social generosity occurs because a reputation in another's eyes can be thought of as a claim on unrealized value from the exchange, or a store of value accrued but not yet captured. Without an identity, each exchange must net out within the life of the transaction if it is to be a success. Identity's consequence, reputation, is the assurance that allows us to leave something on the table and come back for it later. In summary, what happens to the operation of markets when customers have identities in the eyes of those who are selling to them is the possibility of humane dealing – trust, reciprocity, and kindness. So too, of course, is the possibility of betrayal, discrimination, and cruelty, against which only reputation can protect.

Thus, identity and reputation turn matters of transaction into matters of relationship. The distinction between transactions and relationships, it should be emphasized, is not necessarily marked by the time it takes for the exchange to unfold. There are short transactions and long transactions. As easily as a buyer can, quite anonymously, buy a bus ticket, he or she can, still anonymously, buy a season ticket on a bus for a week or a month, with the ticket serving as a transitory identity marker. Indeed, in principle, the buyer can buy a ticket for five or even ten years if there is a bus company willing to set a price that far ahead and the buyer can trust them to stay in business that long. These are all transactions, and the terms are set before the deal is struck. The buyer can do all these things anonymously or with a transitory identity. What the buyer cannot do without a persistent identity is enter into an open-ended process of progressive reputation development. For that, he or she must have an identity the seller can count on. In the bus example, there is a relationship when the terms the bus company offers are subject to change to reflect its growing (or evaporating) confidence that it can count on the buyer to do whatever they want of a good customer.

The distinction between a transaction and a relationship, as used here, is this. The terms of transactions are set before we enter the exchange, while the terms of relationships are always in play. The duration of a transaction is one of the fixed terms, while the duration of a relationship is indeterminate. A transaction is over when its term expires, but a relationship is over when the value of reputation is exhausted and identity has become irrelevant. Markets are more efficient when both sides have the power to build reputations because, as noted, the expected give and the get do not have to net out in the term of the transaction. Ackerlof (1970) made famous the problem that, in a market where some products are "lemons" and others are perfectly good, if sellers have no reputation then even the good products will sell at the value of a lemon. Less attention has been paid to the reciprocal problem – what if some buyers are "lemons"? If some customers are more valuable over time than others, but anonymity prevents sellers from knowing who they are, then sellers run the risk of spending money to acquire a customer who turns out to be a "lemon." In such situations, sellers will likely underspend on customer acquisition. Some buyers who would have derived great utility from becoming the customers of the seller will never come to know of the seller's existence. The market will, to some degree, have failed.

Role-specific identity

Mere addressability confers a sketchy identity. Some forms of customer branding confer richer identities and place more face resources at the disposal of members. I shall call them role-specific identities, because there are role obligations to be borne for the benefits to be enjoyed, and because the benefits are experienced in the context of the role. A role, in this sense, is a blueprint for being. It is seductive in the sense of enticing the buyer into a private social consensus (Deighton and Grayson 1995). It puts at the consumer's disposal a script for asking for things that are valued in the role and also a system to respond to the scripted requests. A familiar example of this next level of identity is that conferred by a credit card. Marketers will not offer the identity unless they expect that the recipient will live up to the obligation expected of a good credit risk. Similarly a "road warrior" role is required if all the advantages of frequent-flyer programs are to be enjoyed: the lounge as a refuge during recurrent layovers, and the small kindnesses from flight attendants that restore a salesperson's dignity. While infrequent travelers can belong to the programs, an accelerated schedule of benefits ensures that the advantages of membership are greatest for those whose travel schedules are most grueling.

An example is American Airlines' AAdvantage program. The tagging elements, which comprise the frequent-flyer card and the schedule of free flights to be earned in exchange for paid flights, are to be seen as no more than the enticement to sign up. They give the airline permission to build a profile of the customer and the ability to know what value lies therein. Initially they give the traveler an incentive, and not a particularly strong one, to tilt his or her patronage toward American Airlines occasionally when the burden of doing so is not too onerous. As the traveler's potential value becomes clearer, the airline elevates her or his brand from plain member to Gold member to Platinum member and still higher. As the member's status inflates, so do the demands of the role and the willingness of the airline to meet those demands. For example one of the marks of a frequent traveler is wariness of airport baggage-handling systems, but, confident of being invited to board first, these customers know they can carry their hand luggage onto the plane and find overhead space. It is shared space, as the flight attendant announcements declare, but not equally shared. High-status passengers get upgraded to first or business class when there is unsold capacity in those ranks, and in the coach class cabin they are much more likely to have an empty seat next to them than low-status passengers.

As important as the contractual entitlements of the role are the non-contractual elements. A buyer with a unique identity and transaction history, confident of being remembered for that uniqueness between transaction occasions, is endowed with negotiating resources that are not available to the anonymous buyer. When an anonymous buyer has to ask, "Do you know who I am?" in an effort to recover from a bad service encounter, the answer that hangs in the air is "No" and the battle is half lost before it begins. Frequent flyers pass on stories to each another of being recognized in service encounters and receiving preferential service, and the stories themselves become quasi-contractual terms of role entitlement.

Self-expressive identity

The fourth level of analysis marks a shift from membership as an instrumental role to membership as an expressive element of selfhood. The membership is no longer a mantle to be donned or doffed as circumstances dictate, but an integral, persistent element of the actor's sense of who they are. Sarbin (1986), writing in the tradition of role theorists, describes gradations in the gap between role and self: they run from, at one extreme, the role enacted quite cynically, to the role enacted unselfconsciously, to, at the extreme, the merging of role and self. At this last extreme, a proffered identity is so fully accepted that it becomes a component of who the buyer believes himself or herself to be.

One marker of the transition from a role to a self-expressive identity is a shift in the buyer's audience from the seller alone to the seller and the buyer's broader social network. A role-specific brand identity program starts to become a self-expressive program when membership starts to acquire expressive value to the member in relations with parties other than the seller. The seller's value offering is not just an end in itself to the buyer, but a means to social ends.

What are some examples of identity programs that attain this fourth, self-expressive level? University education can be construed as such a program. Most of the students in full-time, full-immersion business schools are not merely applying to buy MBA degrees – they are seeking to acquire lifelong identities, lifelong networks of friendship and collegiality, lifelong patterns of ambition, and lifelong styles of interaction with others. Alumni databases store the identities of members, and lifetime email addresses enable easy access among members and between the seller and the community of buyers. Multi-tier identity offerings range from a line in a donor list, to a name on the university library and a seat on the Board of Trustees. So intense is the sense of identity that some graduates return to the college chapel to marry and later to be buried. Admission to membership of elite universities is more sought-after than offered, suggesting that an identity program that operates at the more self-expressive end of the spectrum must be careful to admit to membership only those who can be relied on to live up to the character of the customer brand.

Other self-expressive identity offerings and tiered membership structures can be found in political parties, religious organizations, and philanthropic causes. Among commercial examples, the Harley-Davidson Owners' Group and the Winnebago-Itaska Travelers Club elicit the kind of deep and persistent inter-penetration of life projects and membership that characterize this level of analysis. The Harrah's Total Rewards program spans the boundary between the customer brand as role and as self-expression. For many members it is just a tool to help perform the role of the weekend gamer. The company however characterizes the benefit that customers derive from gambling as the sensation of being "exuber-antly alive" (Lal and Carrolo 2002), and for some members that state becomes the purpose of life itself.

The core of the argument in this chapter is that a single motive accounts for engagement in a progression of social behaviors, from acting anonymously to seeking identification for narrowly instrumental motives, to taking on an identity adopted to make it easier to play a role dictated by broader instrumental motives, and finally to assuming an identity that is self-expressive in the sense of being indis-tinguishable from at least part of the individual's sense of self (see Figure 12.2). The force restraining the operation of this motive is risk, the fear of aversive consequences to the progressive surrender of control over self-related informa-tion. With each stage in the progression the individual is induced to draw a wider boundary between what is private and what is public. The private sphere expands to include more of the rest of society. When we join a frequent-shopper program we accept that our food-buying habits will no longer be private information. When we join a frequent-flyer program we accept that others will know where

Transitory Identity	Persistent Identity	Role-specific Identity	Self-expressive Identity
e.g. Catalina coupons	e.g. frequent-shopper program	e.g. airline frequent-flyer program	e.g. MBA degree
Anonymity	*Progressive sharing of self-related information*		*Identity*
Motive to conceal information	**Narrowly instrumental motive to share information**	**Broader instrumental motive to share information**	**Expressive motive to share information**

Figure 12.2 How identity programs engage the motive to share self-related information.

we travel. When we join a church we accept that others will know something of our beliefs.

With each increment in shared information comes an increase in vulnerability. Anonymity protects against retribution, while identity leaves one vulnerable in perpetuity. Why do buyers volunteer to become vulnerable? Of necessity, it is a condition for exchanging in some markets. Some degrees of relationality cannot happen without reciprocal vulnerability. When the operation of markets depends on the self-expressive degree of identity and the intimacy it makes possible, there is often some discomfort in describing them as markets. Marriage, the parent–child bond, and friendship are all exchange relationships of this ilk. Market-style analyses of such matters, such as Becker's (1991) economic analysis of marriage failures, often strike clinicians as impoverished views of the phenomena. At a minimum they serve the purpose of indicating the *reductio ad absurdum* of this argument.

Vulnerability is a precarious state, open to betrayal and necessitating sensitive management. Aaker *et al.* (2004) offer the word "transgression" as a collective noun for all of the ways that a seller can act to hurt the process of relationship development; to wind back the skein of reputation, tolerated vulnerability, and identity that together builds intensity in a relationship. As relationships become more intimate, the resources available to accommodate transgression grow. Yet, paradoxically, the cost of using the resources grows too. The result is that customer branding at the self-expressive end of the spectrum can be long-enduring, but it can also be prone to brittleness.

Identity and loyalty

The programs I have discussed here, by which buyers are granted identity by the initiatives of sellers, are sometimes called loyalty programs. I have avoided that term in this chapter for two reasons. First, these programs are viewed here for what they can do for (or to) buyers. When they are called loyalty programs, it is often because the perspective taken is what they can do for sellers. The second reason is that while it is obvious that these programs confer identity, it is not at all inevitable that they induce loyalty.

Table 12.1 attempts to draw generalizations about the effect of level of identity on the intensity of the exchange relationship. If loyalty means buyer behavior that exhibits more regularity than can be explained by the terms of the seller's offer on each choice occasion, then the present conjecture is that there is no loyalty in a loyalty program unless it induces the buyer to play a role or offers self-expressive possibilities.

Privacy

Privacy invasion is to the information economy what pollution is to the industrial economy – a social cost borne not by those who benefit from the pollution, but by the rest of society. Because those who produce it do not feel its costs, too much

Table 12.1 Buyer identity and implications for exchange relations

	Buyer interest	*Response to seller*	*Loyalty?*
Transitory identity	Exploitation of seller	Responsive to isolated promotional inducements	Self-interested behavior on discrete choice occasions
Persistent identity	Compliance with seller's inducements	Adaptive to pattern of specific inducements over time	Self-interested gaming behavior
Role-specific identity	Conformity to seller-defined role	Conforming to a script whose scope is more general than the inducements	Role-consistent stable behavior
Self-expressive identity	Fealty to seller values	Sincere adherence to a role	Allegiance

privacy invasion tends to get produced in a free market. To the extent that buyers do not care to have their privacy invaded, they push back at the users of information and demand regulation. But laws, rules, and guidelines are blunt tools. They hurt as well as help, so that the desire for privacy poses a large threat to the flowering of the information economy in general and interactive, relational marketing in particular.

Fortunately, when we empower customers by giving them a negotiable marketplace identity, we give them a way to deal with the problem of privacy. Customer brands can become safe harbors against unwelcome intrusion, or at least they can become safe enough so that their reputations are not punished.

The semantics of privacy

Words like "privacy" are politically contested terms. Their meanings arise from a process by which people negotiate back and forth, sometimes reaching a consensus but often not. The process is one in which a variety of interest groups, civil rights activists and business interests for example, contend for control of "the" significance of a range of information technology practices. Sometimes victory is declared and manifested in legislation or in a social norm, but often the skirmishes go on for decades with no resolution. It took twenty years or so beyond the widespread adoption of telemarketing to introduce even rudimentary control of telephone intrusions into private homes in the form of "do not call" lists. (After more than a hundred years there is still no similar consensus on mail in the USA.) Substantial interests, both economic and social, depend on these various outcomes, and it is useful to be able to anticipate how quickly and in which directions consensus is likely to form.

In this section, which draws on arguments in Deighton (2003), I shall hazard some speculations about the path to consensus. To do so I shall use four terms, anonymity, identity, marketable assets, and moral rights, and show how they function as framing tools in the hands of interest groups advocating on questions raised by individual identity in the information age. The four terms allow us to distinguish four framings. Questions of privacy can be framed as issues of either anonymity or identity, and both questions can be framed either as matters of moral right or as making a market in an asset. These four contending interpretations are available for any question related to personal information. The "right to privacy" frame is rather popular in public policy discussions, yet there are strong interests on the side of making a market in information. It is the strength of constituencies arguing for privacy on the one hand, and for making consumer information available to marketers on the other hand, which makes the idea of privacy so fundamentally a politically contested matter. This interplay of anonymity as both an entitlement of consumers and a cost to the efficient operation of markets, and of identity as both an invasion on rights and a source of consumer power, is developed in the next two sections of the chapter.

Anonymity and identity

Three terms need to be used to build this argument: anonymity, identity, and privacy. Anonymity and identity mark two ends of a single dimension. Anonymity is the state of being unidentified by observers. Identity is the opposite: the state in which the observers recognize us, using a set of characteristics that specifies who or what we are taken to be. Anonymity lets an individual escape intrusion or accountability by being unreachable, undetectable, or out of the presence or view of others. We shift from being anonymous to being identified by so simple an act as signing in or lifting a veil. So anonymity is transitory or temporary, while identity is persistent. Granted, identities may change, but the change occurs slowly because identities reside as much in the minds of observers as in the wishes of the actors. The third term in this argument, privacy, is a different kind of idea. My use of the word is close to the way that privacy advocates use it, as a motivational state. Privacy is the motivation to be in control of information about oneself (Marx 1999). We use the privacy motive to turn the tap by which we regulate where we are, or want to be, on the spectrum between anonymity and identity. People set the privacy tap differently for different social contexts – they decide when to assert privacy, or when to ignore privacy, depending on the costs and benefits of doing so.

In the realm of legal and policy usage, where the emphasis is on management issues, privacy has just this motivational flavor. The legal scholar Katsh (1995) describes privacy as the power to control what others can come to know about you. The emphasis is on our ability to regulate the flow of information about ourselves. When we are in control of the regulation, and shut off the flow, we have exercised privacy and there is anonymity. When information flows more freely, either because we deliberately increase the flow or because we lose control of the flow, there is identity. They are end-points on a continuum, so that a gain in one comes at the price of a loss of the other. Lessig (1999) amplifies the notion of regulation or control, pointing out that it covers two activities. First there is an individual's power to control monitoring of his or her conduct and activities, and second there is the individual's power to limit search of possessions and property. Thus anonymity is the consequence of privacy management in which the emphasis is on defending against inferences from information revealed in conduct, activities, possessions, and property. And identity is the consequence of not managing privacy, and inviting inferences from information projected in conduct, activities, possessions, and property.

Privacy is relinquished in order to assert particular entitlements, while it is sought in order to evade particular impositions. Because what we seek to evade often occurs in the same context as what we seek to claim, setting the privacy tap often presents a dilemma. The same mail, email, and telephone addresses bring us welcome and unwelcome communications. The same medical history is a useful element of our identity in dealings with a physician but not with a medical insurer. An item of personal data can be a burden or a resource depending on social context.

Managing privacy in a market setting

The principle of customer branding may be able to reconcile the motive for privacy, or personal control of personal information, with the motive for identity and the desire to deploy the market power it represents. In agreeing to wear a customer brand, the buyer in effect concedes a limited surrender of the power to control privacy, allowing his or her transaction history and demographic profile to be put together by a seller in exchange for discounts and superior service, plus a branded assurance against the worst abuses of identity exploitation. The plethora of consensual databases that have come into being on the Internet and as a result of offline identity programs can be viewed as a patchwork of "walled-garden" sanctuaries from the hurly-burly unregulated market in identities that characterizes the world outside the walls.

Consider a supermarket frequent-shopper program as an example of a local solution to privacy anxiety. The identity of an individual household is valuable not primarily to the grocery store but to manufacturers to whom the store can sell access. The program becomes a medium through which a manufacturer can communicate directly to its customers, or, more important, to those who are not its customers. By making a market in this information, the grocer magnifies its value. Under a market regime, that value is available to manufacturers, improving the efficiency of their marketing methods. In return, shoppers capture some of the value. In a market of competing frequent-shopper programs, grocers bid for the right to gather a shopper's data by offering discounts and in some cases nonprice benefits such as superior service to program members.

How does an institutional solution of this kind protect the consumer against unwelcome intrusion? The grocer, by virtue of having linked the program to its reputation, finds itself responsible for mistreatment of its customers. It therefore has an incentive to police the actions of the parties to whom it sells the data, and to conduct its own interactions with civility, because its interests are aligned with those of its customers. In the credit-card industry, one US card issuer (Capital One) makes protecting customers from intrusions a point of differentiation by making the advertising claim, "No telemarketing." This vendor thus makes a market on the promise of privacy. To the extent that consumers value privacy over a low interest rate or other features, Capital One prospers. To the extent that they regard the price of privacy as too high, the card issuer suffers.

Even in the acutely sensitive realm of health care, there exist programs in which patients surrender the anonymity to which most health-service regimes entitle them in exchange for participation in disease-specific intervention programs. Corporations like Landacorp, American Healthways, ProChange, and Matria Healthcare exist to provide communication and support to sufferers from chronic medical conditions. Patients with active disease conditions (like congestive heart failure), usually view the identification necessary for such interventions in a positive light. When the disease or condition in question is covert or absent (as in the case of a negative colon-cancer screening), practitioners report that identification is experienced as a privacy violation.

Because a customer's transaction information is more valuable to an industry when pooled with information from the consumer's transactions with competitors, showing shifts in market share, enterprises are emerging that pool the transaction databases of ostensible competitors. Thus the Star Alliance combines the frequent-flyer programs of United Airlines, Air Canada, Singapore Airlines, and eleven other airlines to create a single managed identity for a member. A firm called Abacus pools the transaction records of over one thousand direct mail catalog retailers. Conceivably, then, today's patchwork of walled gardens will evolve into a near-universal regime of market-based customer identification under the protective umbrella of sponsor brand reputations.

Conclusion

"You have no privacy, get over it." So said the chairman of Sun Microsystems, in sketching a future where technology upsets today's notions of personal identity, in which lost children can be traced because they have radio-frequency identification devices embedded on their bodies and adults carry Java identification cards. He argues,

> If there were no audit trails and no fingerprints, there would be a lot more crime in this world. Audit trails deter lots of criminal activity. So all I'm suggesting, given that we all have ID cards anyhow, is to use the biometric and other forms of authentication that are way more powerful and way more accurate than the garbage we use today . . . It's called a Java card. It's already done – the technology's all there . . . Identifying yourself is way different from creating a database on you. And I have no problem with it being illegal for

the government to create a database on anybody. But you can get wiretap authority; you could also get the same authority to agree to build a database on [an individual]. And because we have an audit trail of you at your bank, at your airline, and your Internet service provider and all the rest of it, if we think you are a potential terrorist and we've gone to the courts and shown enough evidence, the government should be able to quickly build a national database on you for just that instance, for that particular issue . . . I get all this random hate mail from these lunatics – you can't believe the anger these folks have. But just because you have an ID card doesn't mean the police have the right to walk over and say, "Produce it."

(Tennant 2001: 27)

McNealy stands on the fault line of a social earthquake. The rules of decorum and protocol that have governed the presentation of self in markets and in society at large have changed little in millennia. Now suddenly new rules are being developed on the fly as we find ourselves confronted by technologies that make it possible to have portable identities and perform or be the victims of unobtrusive surveillance. The age of the anonymous consumer is drawing to a close, and the shape of what will follow it is not completely clear yet.

But an outline of the future of personal identification in the information age can be conjectured. This chapter starts with the assumption that buyers will not find it easy to deploy these technologies unaided for reasons of cost. To economize on scale and scope it seems more likely that sellers will take charge of the process of identifying buyers in marketplace settings. This chapter offers the idea of customer brands to stand for the process by which sellers offer these identity resources to buyers. Four degrees of branding are described, corresponding to four degrees of personal identification and four levels of surrender of control over personally identifying information in exchange for relational benefits.

Loyalty programs, which I prefer to call identity programs, are not usually viewed as very consequential – not by customers, and not even by the firms that create them. To many, they are just cents-off discounting devices, little better than plastic green stamps. But as we try to anticipate the threats and opportunities, commercial and societal, of pervasive portable digital identities, this chapter argues that we have more to learn from the workings of these programs than from any other current manifestation of the coming age. They represent a glimpse of life when some version of our reputations travels with us wherever we go, whether we like it or not. On one hand, such programs put identity's power at our disposal. When customers have a rich and multidimensional identity in their dealings with sellers, such customers are stronger negotiators, and those with prime track records can command better terms of trade and access. On the other hand, such programs also impose identity's liabilities on us. Those buyers whose identities are worth less, or are less well-defined, find that they are disadvantaged in the market. Research into digitally enabled identity, its motivating force and its management for and on behalf of consumers, is likely to be of increasing importance to the agenda of consumer research as the information age unfolds.

Acknowledgments

The support of the Teradata Center for Customer Relationship Management at Duke University's Fuqua School of Business during the writing of this manuscript is gratefully acknowledged. I thank Fuqua's marketing faculty, and in particular Christine Moorman, Joel Huber, and Richard Staelin, for comments on a seminar presentation. I thank Eric Arnold, Suraj Commuri, Susan Spiggle, Susan Kleine, and Charlotte Mason for reading an early draft of the paper and supplying many stimulating comments, which either influenced this chapter or should have.

References

Aaker, J., Fournier, S., and Brasel, A. (2004) "When good brands do bad: Personalities, acts of transgression and the evolution of relationship strength," *Journal of Consumer Research* 31 (June): 1–18.

Ackerlof, George A. (1970) "The market for 'lemons': Quality uncertainty and the market mechanism," *Quarterly Journal of Economics* 84(3) (August): 488–500.

Becker, Gary S. (1991) *A Treatise on the Family*, Cambridge, MA: Harvard University Press.

Bentham, J. (1787/1995) *The Panopticon Writings*, M. Bozovic (ed.), London: Verso.

Blattberg, R. C. and Deighton, J. (1991) "Interactive marketing: Exploiting the age of addressability," *Sloan Management Review* 33 (Fall): 5–14.

Burke, P. J. (1991) "Identity processes and social stress," *American Sociological Review* 56 (December): 836–849.

Burke, P. J. and Tully, J. (1977) "The measurement of role/identity," *Social Forces* 55: 881–897.

Caplan, J. (2001) " 'This or that particular person': Protocols of identification in nineteenth-century Europe," in J. Caplan and J. Torpey (eds) *Documenting Individual Identity*, Princeton, NJ: Princeton University Press.

Deighton, J. (1992) "The consumption of performance," *Journal of Consumer Research* 19 (December): 362–372.

Deighton, J. (2003) "Market solutions to privacy problems?" in C. Nicoll, J. E. J. Prins, and M. J. M. van Dellen (eds) *Digital Anonymity and the Law – Tensions and Dimensions*, Information Technology and Law Series Vol. 2, The Hague: T. M. C. Asser Press.

Deighton, J. and Grayson, K. (1995) "Marketing and seduction: Building exchange relationships by managing social consensus," *Journal of Consumer Research* 21 (March): 660–676.

Foucault, M. (1995) *Discipline and Punish: The Birth of the Prison*, New York: Vintage Books.

Goffman, E. (1959) *The Presentation of Self in Everyday Life*, Garden City, NY: Doubleday.

Groebner, V. (2001) "Describing the person, reading the signs in late medieval and renaissance Europe: Identity papers, vested figures, and the limits of identification, 1400–1600," in J. Caplan and J. Torpey (eds) *Documenting Individual Identity*, Princeton, NJ: Princeton University Press.

Huizinga, J. (1954) *The Waning of the Middle Ages*, Garden City, NY: Doubleday.

Katsh, M. E. (1995) *Law in a Digital World*, New York: Oxford University Press.

Kleine, R. E. III, Kleine S. S., and Kernan, J. (1993) "Mundane consumption and the self: A social identity perspective," *Journal of Consumer Psychology* 2(3): 209–235.

Lal, R. and Carrolo, P. M. (2001) *Harrah's Entertainment, Inc.*, Boston, MA: HBS Publishing.

Lessig, L. (1999) *Code and Other Laws of Cyberspace*, New York: Basic Books.

Marx, G. T. (1999) "What's in a name? Some reflections on the sociology of anonymity," *The Information Society* 15(2): 99–112.

Sarbin, T. (1986) "Emotion and act: Roles and rhetoric," in R. Harre (ed.) *The Social Construction of Emotion*, Oxford: Blackwell.

Schindler, R. M. (1998) "Consequences of perceiving oneself as responsible for obtaining a discount: Evidence for smart-shopper feelings," *Journal of Consumer Psychology* 7(4): 371–392.

Tennant, D. (2001) "Q&A: McNealy defends Sun reliability, personal privacy views," *Computerworld* (November): 27.

Tuan, Y. (1982) *Segmented Worlds and Self: Group Life and Individual Consciousness*, Minneapolis: University of Minnesota Press.

13 Communal consumption and the brand

Thomas C. O'Guinn and
Albert M. Muñiz, Jr

The vast majority of the marketing and consumer behavior literature emanating from American business schools is about one quasi-dyadic relationship: marketer and individual consumer. In this literature, the why of consumption is typically explained in terms of attitudes, attribute bundles, affect, judgment biases and decision heuristics – all at the individual level. While these factors are no doubt important, the truly social aspects of consumption have been relatively overlooked and undervalued. To be sure, social psychologists attempt (more or less) to account for the influence of others on individual consumers' thoughts and judgments. But this is hardly the same as studying social behavior as social behavior in its social context: consumer behavior formed and enacted within and by aggregations, themselves shaped, sanctioned, and grounded in relationships, institutions and other collectives.

In "the field" of consumer research (the field as defined by researchers in US business schools), the social is most often constructed as a moderating variable to the cognitive processes of individuals, a weak modifier of all things psychological. It is the relatively rare occurrence when the social is studied beyond this narrow and limited construction. In the wider academic world the social is better represented. In this chapter, we will bridge this gap and make a case for why, and how, the social should be better represented in the field of consumer research. We cast the why of consumption differently: not a single heuristic is mentioned. Instead, we observe active and meaningful negotiation of the brand between consumer collectives and market institutions. Holt (this volume), argues for the need to understand brands in their societal context. We feel that it is equally important to understand brands at the group/community level as such an understanding reveals much that is important about the why of consumption.

We start by reviewing the two constructs that are central to this endeavor, community and brands. We will examine the historical legacy of community in modern social thought, arguing for its centrality to the study of consumption by illustrating its relationship to brands in contemporary market economies. We then explore the quintessential example of this relationship, the brand community. After connecting the particulars of brand communities to the why of consumption, we will explore another, closely related, group brand phenomnon, the polit-brand. These two closely related phenomena reveal important aspects of the socially situated and constructed nature of brands. Many of the aspects, enactments, and other behaviors surrounding brands are significant for consumers, and thus should be to consumer researchers and practitioners as well.

Community

The idea of community has been used in the pursuit of understanding human beings for over two hundred years. Community was important to Immanuel Kant in 1781, and to Fredrich Nietzsche a century later (1886). It was given its modern sociological nomenclature in 1887 by Ferdinand Tönnies: Gemeinschaft und Gesellschaft (roughly Community and Society). From that point forward community was canonical to sociology. Simmel in the early twentieth century (1904), then Max Weber (1922) and Royce (1969), viewed it as essential social theory, vital to understanding modern social existence. Today, community remains a staple of political, religious, and scholarly discourse (Bauman 2001; Boorstin 1973; Fischer 1975; Maffesoli 1996; Wellman 1979; Putnam 2000). Not inconsequential is that community is present in everyday utterance, and matters to publics well beyond the academy.

Yet it has taken the nascent field of consumer research well into its third decade to more than mention community, even in passing. The reasons for this are, as always, essentially political in nature, and are rooted in the vagaries of academic history, including the wholesale adoption of psychology as the sanctioned science of US business schools (the field). It is Pollyanna-ish to think that this absence of social thought was unrelated to the hegemony of the field's psychological atomism, which holds that while there is a social, it is relatively inconsequential compared to cognitive process. The field as defined above has produced scant literature involving social and institutional production, politics, and history. Yet, to discuss consumption outside these social forces is a mistake.

Several years ago, we became interested in applying the notion of community to consumption (Muñiz and O'Guinn 1995). Like a handful of others (Fischer *et al.* 1996; Fournier 1998; Maffesoli 1996; Schouten and McAlexander 1995), we believed we were observing a form of community playing out in the marketplace. After thinking about this for a bit, we came to believe that as broadly as the notion of community applies, marketplace behavior has a particularly important place in community research. After all, the very idea of community is historically and fundamentally connected to the marketplace. Community scholarship begins with a concern for community's condition in the wake of modernity, market capitalism, and then ubiquitous consumer culture. The branded society in which we now live has been traditionally implicated in the purported demise of community, or at least its cooptation. So at a theoretical and fundamental level, community and consumption are no strangers. Community is (or should be) a fundamental consumer behavior term. We believe the interplay of community and contemporary consumption is important to a fuller understanding of how we live and why we consume as we do.

Brands

To most scholars, it is absolutely axiomatic that there is no such thing as just a thing. To sociologists, anthropologists, and many more, all material objects carry with them meaning – even the ones mislabeled as "utilitarian." This point has been made too many times by too many celebrated scholars (e.g., Goody 1993; Sahlins 1972; Schudson 1984) to belabor it here. The entire human record consists of no place where materiality, social construction, and meaning are strangers. Goods have always had social meaning. The same holds true for *branded* goods.

Brands are particularly marked things, their power being derived from being marked. Brands have a special relationship to modern market economies, those economies defined by marketing, advertising, and consumption. In the late nineteenth century, brands replaced many "unmarked" commodities. While it is true that there were some branded products prior to this period, it is during the last two decades of the nineteenth century that the ubiquitous branding we know today began. Between 1875 and 1900, thousands of branded products replaced unbranded commodities. The phenomenal growth first took place in package goods. Soap, previously sold by weight from a generally unbranded cake, becomes Ivory (1882) and Sapolio (circa 1875). Beer, previously drawn from an unnamed keg, becomes Budweiser (1891) and Pabst (1873). All across the spectrum of goods and services, existing commodities became brands, as did the flood of new things designed for the modern marketplace of 1900.

It was a necessity of modern market capitalism to discover and promulgate brands. Consider the economics. Commodities (beer, soap) have elastic demand functions. If there is no distinction between soaps, all soaps are completely interchangeable. The set of acceptable substitutes is large and the demand is price elastic; price increases are met with decreases in demand. But when soap became Ivory in 1882, all that changed. Procter and Gamble began to impart different, additional and particular meanings to the previously unmarked commodity. Due to the new marketplace meanings of Ivory brand soap, there were far fewer acceptable substitutes at any given price. Value (and profit) was added. Ivory's demand function became inelastic. Brands made good economic sense, and modern market capitalism became reliant on branding. It is no coincidence that this period is also known as the birth of the modern advertising industry (Fox 1984). Major advertising agencies such as J. Walter Thompson and N. W. Ayer were founded during this period. The growth is obvious in a tenfold increase (ibid.) in advertising spending between 1864 ($50 million) and 1900 ($500 million.) Brands were created and projected into national consciousness by ad men.

Ivory would claim purity during a period when purity was of vital concern to Americans. The average life expectancy in the USA in 1900 was 49.2 years (Sullivan 1926). Infant mortality was twice what it would be just twenty-five years later (ibid.). A concerned public pushed Congress to pass the Pure Food and Drug Act in 1904. Purity was more than a word; it was, at that time, one of the few things the public believed might prevent them, or their children, from dying young. So, Ivory floats. Its purity was demonstrated by a market logic. No one really had to understand the physical mechanism that related purity to floating; it became a marketplace myth. Social context gave meaning to Ivory's branding, its advertising claim, its marketplace logic, and the meaning of a bar of soap that floated. Ivory *meant* something. It was pure, 99 44/100 pure. Ivory was no longer a commodity; its set of acceptable substitutes shriveled. The same was true of countless other branded goods and services.

During the last years of the nineteenth and the first two decades of the twentieth century, the practice of branding exploded. Advertising and branding pushed marketplace modernity along; they were its engines, its mode. Over the next eight or so decades, the branding tide rose to cover just about everything. By the end of the twentieth century, religions rushed to brand, as did universities, cities, and national parks. Even dirt and water were branded. Few things were left behind. Brands came to be important in the lives of citizens. Citizens became consumers, consumers of brands. We became a branded society, and brands had meaning, social meaning, meaning that cannot be isolated from its historical, political, cultural, and social grounding.

The modern concern with community's demise

The parallel storyline of this play is about what was supposedly happening to community. Remember, it was mass-marketed, branded society that was the prime suspect in the slaying of "true" community. This meta-narrative is the leitmotif of modern social thought: commercial urban life destroyed true community. How ironic is it to now be writing of their admixture: brand community? Yet, since the postmodern is marked by irony, then perhaps brand community is perfectly of its time (Maffesoli 1996). Or, maybe, the two constructs (brand and community) have always shared more, and were less antithetical, than modernist doctrine allowed. The latter is our belief.

Now, after two centuries or so, we arrive at this moment where three things are true: (1) brands are a ubiquitous aspect of daily life; (2) brands are at some level meaningful to ordinary contemporary citizens; and (3) community was not so easily done away with – the communal urge of humans and the benefits that accrue to collectives and institutions ensured community's adaptive longevity. Community endures in all sorts of forms, in all sorts of places, including the marketplace. Community, of a particular sort, is found in the form of brand community. Brand communities possess the hallmarks of traditional communities, but have their own unique market logics and expression. In the following, we explore brand communities and the why of consumption, drawing on ten years of research conducted by both authors into a variety of brands (Muñiz and Hamer 2001; Muñiz and O'Guinn 2001; Muñiz and O'Guinn 1995; Muñiz *et al.* 2005; Muñiz and Schau 2005; O'Guinn and Muñiz 2004; O'Guinn and Muñiz 2000; Schau and Muñiz 2002). These data include observation, participant observation, and interview data from a variety of settings including face-to-face and online environments.

The characteristics of brand communities

Brand communities, just like other forms of community, possess three defining characteristics: consciousness of kind, evidence of rituals and traditions, and a sense of obligation to the community and its members. The ways in which these characteristics manifest, and the fact that they manifest in communities centered on brands, reveal much about the why of consumption.

Consciousness of kind

The most important attribute of community is consciousness of kind. To be a community, a group of people have to feel a collective similarity to one another and the group, and a collective difference both individually and collectively from other groups. Our research has shown considerable evidence of consciousness of kind in a variety of brand communities in several different product categories. Consider the following exemplar from an online Mazda Miata community post:

> Truth be told, I just "found" this group and I'm a happy little person now that I've found there are other people out there like me that love their Miatas!

This verbatim reveals language of someone being happy because they realized that there are others just like them . . . out there . . . who get it . . . who see what they see as enthusiastically as they do. The promise of community is here: not to be alone, to share appreciation, no matter how odd, inappropriate, misplaced, trivial, or wrong others might feel it to be. The informant's language looks much like that of someone saying that they discovered others with the same sexual orientation, the same health problems, or the same religion. No matter how others might judge this shared affection, it is clearly consciousness of kind. It is often the case that communities form precisely because others find the focal object unusual and/or objectionable. Communities have historically served (among others) the otherwise isolated and outside. Consciousness of kind transcends geographic boundaries. Because so much occurs online, and is, after all, about far-flung brands and mass-mediated creations, face-to-face interaction is unnecessary.

Many brand communities have a stated populism. In brand communities, stratification characteristics that might determine an individual's standing in another community, such as income, age or gender, are *said* to be unimportant. Rather, status in brand communities is more often influenced by such factors as how long consumers have been using the brand, the historical value of the model they own, the number of models that they own, and their knowledge and experiences with the brand. In this way, brand communities are officially egalitarian, at least in a traditional socioeconomic sense. As a result, and as a testimony to its strength, consciousness of kind is often experienced and expressed by members with diverse backgrounds.

One informant tells of holding up traffic at a McDonald's one morning because the employee working the drive-through window was a fellow Saab owner. The two members "ignored" their stratification inequities to carry out an expected ritual of Saab community members, even if it meant holding up everyone else in the busy service line. The informant was a successful professional. The employee was assumed to be of a lower SES category, but owned a much older Saab, one with historical value and enhanced community social cachet. Many of our informants tell similar tales of lengthy encounters with others with whom they share little beyond a shared appreciation of the brand. In this manner, benefits accrue to the individuals in several ways, not least of which is a sense of their own egalitarianism, fairness, and goodness. The belief in a "democracy of goods," (Marchand 1985) also serves to ameliorate and justify the realities of even severe social stratification inequities in market economies. It protects and reifies marketplace ideology. If a community of things can make us equal, then other inequalities may be more easily accepted or ignored.

Communal feelings of consciousness of kind underscore the significance of brands and brand meaning to contemporary consumer culture. Brands are easy to see and carry a host of strong and pervasively cultivated meanings. They facilitate the community-forming process by making the identification of like-minded others visible and vivid. It is easy to gather around brands. The why of consumption here lies in recognizing that brands say much about the groups that use them. Brands demonstrate shared beliefs, beliefs consumers like to recognize.

Rituals and traditions

Communities typically develop rituals and traditions that serve to reify the community and its culture. This is one way in which communities stay vital. Brand community examples of this are plentiful. Methods and modes include celebrating the history of brand; sharing brand stories and myths; ritualistic communication and utterances; special lexicon; and communal appropriation of advertising, market icons, and commercial text. One obvious example is the way Saab, VW Beetle, Miata, and Jeep drivers wave, beep their horn, or flash their lights to other drivers of the same brand. One informant told us: "If you own a Saab, you just do this, it's expected." When asked who expected it, he said, "the Saab folks" – in other words, the brand community, the others in the know. The collective has behavioral expectations.

Communities educate their members (particularly the young) in community history. Communities, whether traditional or brand, rely on a known-in-common history to keep the community alive, vital, and centered. Thus, user-created webpages devoted to these brands are replete with historical narratives. The textual nature of the Web provides an excellent forum in which members share their knowledge of the brand's origins, often replete with illustrations and photographs. Consider the following, from an ambitious user-created Volkswagen website:

> The idea for the Beetle came from a German engineer, Ferdinand Porsche, in the early 1930's. The final design for the Beetle was completed in 1938 and the first bug prototype saw the light of day in 1939. Unfortunately, WW2

ceased production shortly thereafter. Fortunately, in the summer of 1945, production restarted and Beetles couldn't be produced fast enough. In 1958, Volkswagen of America was established and Beetles soon made their way onto American soil. By the mid 1960's the VW Beetle was out selling all American made vehicles in the US. The Beetle was mass-produced for a record 30 years, undergoing over 50,000 design modifications along the way. Loved for its unique road handling and its adorable style, the Beetle stands proudly today as the top selling imported car in US automotive history.

Similar texts and retellings are common within most brand communities. The VW Bug has special significance for the VW brand community because it was the car that started it all. In much the same way, the date of January 24, 1984 (when the Macintosh was launched) has significance for many Apple brand community members. Hence, it is frequently chronicled. Communities need marked dates or celebrated events. Through this the community bestows significance upon the event and gives it meaning, meaning which is transmitted and affirmed though the socially enacted celebration.

One of the most frequently encountered forms of communal affirmation is ritualized story-telling. Communities (re)create their history, their values, and other aspects through communal stories. Religious narratives, stories of national heroes and battles, and even school anthems are examples of this. The same is true in brand communities. In the Saab brand community a common critical communal myth is the "saved my life story." Saab positions itself as a safe car, and its brand community embraces this positioning as well, building on it and incorporating it into their experience with the brand. Here is one example of its telling:

I love my Saab. It is my second one, the first one got totaled when a stupid [driver] pulled right out in front of me. I was going about 50mph and slammed on my brakes as hard as I could (there was a truck coming in the other lane). Everything went into slow motion and I braced myself for the crash. My car held straight, didn't waver or slip on the wet pavement and it also saved my life. I walked away . . . she wasn't so lucky. The cop told me Saabs . . . are the safest in crashes that he has seen.

Think about this story: The Saab is totaled (it gives its life for its driver). The Saab driver "walked away" while the other driver didn't. A policeman is present (miracles often need an objective authority figure as confirmation) and proclaims Saabs to be safe. This story is full of critical distillations of the brand's constellation of meaning. It is economical in its conveyance. Most members have such a story in their repertoire, referring to firsthand experience or someone they know. These stories are not generated by Saab, but are organic, created by consumers for consumers.

These stories are ritualistically told, re-told, and re-told again. Reactions are always the same, amazement and affirmation. When one thinks about communication from a psychological point of view, communication is typically explained as the transmission of information bundle x́ between parties a and b. Here, in a communal setting, we see something completely different, a different sort of communication. Here, the purpose is not to get consumer b to learn something new; both consumers already possess this knowledge. They know "that Saab also builds jets," that "Apple created the first windows-based desktop operating system" or that "Newton created the PDA market." Why do they do this, if all the parties already possess information bundle x́? The why here is communal affirmation. Here the speech act is to publicly affirm and reify a key community belief: Saabs are like jets, Apple is a computer pioneer. It is affirmative and ritualistic communication, an authoritative performance (Arnould and Price 2000). It is communication that serves a larger social purpose, to maintain the collective and its boundaries, and keep its rules. It is communal communication serving the individual and the collective.

(Moral) obligation

The third, and probably most controversial aspect of brand community is the degree to which moral obligation is/is not present. To nineteenth-century social theorists, publicly enacted morality was a vital aspect of face-to-face community. In contemporary times, what constitutes group morality is a much more open question. Here, it is more narrowly construed, limited, and fungible. We hold that a certain type of soft moral obligation does exist in brand communities. Here, the sense of responsibility sometimes involves brand advice, repair, and service help. Such sentiments are regarded as commonsense by members, as the following quote from a Volkswagen community forum makes clear:

> So if you are driving through Cincinnati and see a white 67 Beetle at the side of the highway, hopefully it will not be me this time. If you do see a bug stranded by the side of the road, remember that it is good VW etiquette to stop and see what is wrong.

Similar etiquette shows up in Saab drivers who help other Saab drivers when their cars break down on the side of the road, among Macintosh users who will help an acquaintance rescue a defective Mac hard drive, and Pocket PC users who will donate their troubleshooting efforts to the collective. A particularly powerful sense of responsibility exists in the brand community centered on the Apple Newton, a product that Apple discontinued in 1998. The Apple Newton brand community innovates the product and software, provides parts sources, technical support, and advertises the brand to others. Here, the sense of responsibility is quite strong as the community is the *only* source for support.

Responsibility also manifests via an apostolic function. Members of brand communities, generally think that new members (but only appropriate new members) should be recruited to keep the community alive. This is seen as a group moral duty. Most brand community members have engaged in this behavior at some level or another, ranging from showing off what the brand can do to more openly explicit persuasive attempts. Most love to share stories of successful conversion efforts. Brand communities, like traditional communities, are often most morally offended when defections occur. In brand communities, this means buying or using the competing brand. Defectors are labeled "turncoats," or are accused of "betrayal." Reasons for staying in the community are publicly rehearsed and restated, as in Mac pages that list "the reasons Macs are superior to Windows pcs." While serving to elevate the brand, such statements also serve as a publicly performed reminder to stay loyal to the brand, and to rehearse counter-arguments against "leaving the fold."

Brand communities are similar to communities of limited liability (Jannowitz 1952). These communities are intentional, voluntary, and partial in the level of involvement they engender (ibid.; Hunter and Suttles 1972), but still vital to contemporary life, meaningful, and maybe modal. We argue that the morality that manifests in brand communities is a small case "m", morality, even a marketplace morality. Still it exists, and the marketplace is the central stage of contemporary society. Brand community members do feel a type of obligation to other members, and the collective, that has at its core a morality: a loosely codified sense of right and wrong, duty and obligation. The why here is to perpetuate the brand and what is stands for, and to help others who share this appreciation.

Of particular marketplace relevance

There are some aspects of brand communities that have the particular flavor of the marketplace, and yet are very similar to the same basic dynamic observed in traditional communities.

Oppositional brand loyalty

Just as in any other form of community, members of brand communities also note a critical demarcation between users of their brand and users of other brands: "We are different from them." This phenomenon is observed in brand communities in which the very defining nature of the community is its opposition to another brand and its community. One example of this can be found in the Apple Macintosh brand community, and its nemesis, Windows-Intel (or Wintel). Consider the following from a typical user-created Apple website:

> These are some pictures, sounds and links that express my hate for Microsoft and Windows PC's, I do not hate pc's, just pc's running Windows. Please wait half a minute while it loads (kinda like opening the "Windows" directory in Winblows 95), but unlike Windows – its worth the wait . . .

The purpose of the Apple community is as much anti-Wintel as it is pro-Apple. In fact, a good part of what the Apple brand means is that it is *not* Wintel. In a similar fashion, Saab is not Volvo and Volkswagen is not Honda.

Another great illustration of oppositional brand loyalty and the resulting tensions comes from the PDA market. It is a market with two fiercely competing operating systems: PocketPC and Palm. Users of these two operating systems seek market dominance, recognizing the benefits afforded via network effects. In the following, one can even see the oppositional community as intertwined with geographical metaphor, the wrong part of town:

> I gave a sales rep a demo of my iPaq a few weeks ago at Franklin Covey. That place is scary, it's like wall to wall Palm. I felt like I had wandered into the wrong part of town.

Much like in traditional communities, members of brand communities use familiar spatial metaphors to highlight the shared consumption topography.

This phenomenon shows up in other brands as well (Muñiz and Hamer 2001). Users of a variety of brands appear to define their preference by the brand that it is not. These rivalries occasionally surface in the context of online conversations, leading to brand preference debates that can range from simple name-calling to sophisticated and passionate discussions of why each brand is better. Such conversations underscore the social and communal nature of brands, even among those who feel little to no affiliation with their fellow brand-users. When a user of the competing brand insults their brand of choice, even those who feel no connection to their fellow brand-users will pull together in a temporary communal affiliation of sorts. The why here is the desire of the group to define themselves, particularly by who and what they are not. Obviously, history is replete with examples of communities and other social collectives that have done the same. Still, it's the completely unremarkable everydayness about the marketplace language of opposition that marks it as so completely consumer culture.

Marketplace legitimacy

Another brand community facet is revealed in issues of legitimacy. These occur on two fronts: is the brand "real," and is the brand community member legitimate? Again, issues of pretenders and true believers have long been part of community discourse. Communal status hierarchies are often premised on degrees of passion and shades of authenticity. Yet, marketplace legitimacy has a particular dimension to it in that it reveals the shifting power relations between those traditionally in control of the brand (the marketer) and consumer collectives. Members make distinctions between those who are appropriate for the brand and those who aren't, the impostors being those attracted to the brand for the wrong reasons.

Consider the following exchange, from a Saab brand community forum. The Saab brand community has long struggled with issues of legitimacy. These issues started when yuppies began to embrace the brand in the 1980s and continued as General Motors took complete control of the Saab brand, redesigning the models and repositioning the brand to make them more mainstream and marketable to a more affluent market segment. Members were discussing who proper Saab drivers were versus who they were perceived to be, when one member voiced a common belief among long-time devotees:

> I tend to avert my gaze in disgust when passing a NG900 (New Gen, No Good – take yer pick) So-called-Saabs, so I never noticed what drives them (always assumed yuppie scum).

Here, the assumption was made that those driving newer Saabs, those produced since GM had taken over (hence, new generation), were Yuppies, while those who favored the classic, pre-GM models were the true aficionados. Demonstrating the tensions surrounding these issues, another member takes issue with this characterization and replies with the following:

> Wow, I've been reading this newsgroup for over a year and never knew how much some of you were disgusted with NG900/9–3's. I'm sorry to have bought a product that sullies YOUR image. Here's yuppie scum for you . . . I'm a 25 y/o married guy that works as a warehouse manager and is enlisted in the Navy Reserve (after 4 years of Active service). I drive a 2K 9–3. My 28 y/o wife is an administrative assistant for the CEO of an e-bank. She's a veteran as well. She drives a 1998 900S. Working people (that probably make less than some of you yuppie scum) own the cars that you snub your noses at. We drive our Saabs, not for status, but because they are extremely fun to drive. Neither car is an automatic, and both are run hard on a daily basis. Besides a sunroof motor on my 9–3, neither car has ever had a problem. My Mother and Father in law both own early 900 turbo's. My Mother in law because of safety issues, my Father in law because he's an absolute speed demon and loves to perform most of the work on the car himself. They are professional people, probably like you. There's only one difference, they would never "pigeon-hole" someone (especially us) as yuppie scum for wanting a nice, fun car.

Of course, from the marketer's point of view, having its core or "lead" users actively policing community membership (and purchase), is a problem. Many drivers of newer Saabs, like the driver above, are likely to be offended by such characterizations. Some may even be dissuaded from repurchasing the brand.

In a very similar way, members of the Volkswagen brand community differentiate between the original Beetle, produced between 1945 and 1981, and the new VW Beetle introduced in 1997. The original Beetle is a large part of the meaning of the VW brand community. Its unusual appearance and underdog origins are a source of pride among VW enthusiasts. To most long-term VW aficionados, the New Beetle is nothing but a pale, marketing-inspired imitation of the original Bug designed to move VW upstream, and further away from its economy-minded roots. The VW brand community is a factious collective, having segments favoring air-cooled over water-cooled models, each with differing claims to legitimacy.

Through actions to define and enforce these standards of legitimacy, the active brand community can represent a marketplace power inversion.

Desired marginality

A closely related phenomenon is desired marginality. Here, brand community members actively try to keep the community small and marginal. A brand like Apple, with an approximate 3 percent share of the US computer market, has marginality as part of its brand meaning. The original VW Bug had it too, its underdog status cleverly and famously used by Doyle Dane Bernbach to market the brand. Sometimes brand community members actively work against share growth. They must walk a tricky path between rejecting willing new members and sustaining a large enough market share to keep the brand viable. Here, the why is in maintaining cultural cachet. If the brand gains too much market share or if it becomes too mainstream, cultural cachet is lost and the brand is no longer deemed "hip." This dynamic maps on to the alternative ethos in which a band or a filmmaker or some other artist is deemed to be "cool" until they are signed by a major label or too widely discovered. (For a similar example of how this happened to the Mexican beer brand Corona, see Holt, this volume.) Here, the boundaries of community and brand are upheld by the collective. By enforcing community standards of legitimacy, they ensure marginality.

Rumor

Much content in brand communities takes the form of rumor. The history of the brand and personal stories centered on the brand are often transmitted via communal rumor. Rumors play an important role in the consumer construction of the brand as rumors allows the community to express properties of the brand that may not be true, but reflect what the community *wants* to be true.

Cultural capital and issues of credibility loom large in brand communities. These communities are structured, with complex hierarchies. The contribution of a new and valuable piece of communal brand talk carries status. The search for new information, such as modifications the manufacturer intends to make to the product or new line entries, can be intensely competitive. As a result, consumers sometimes share brand-related information from non-reputable sources. Such utterances are particularly relevant in the Internet age as they may be afforded the same credibility as official information and become part of the brand's communally accepted legacy. The multi-media nature of the Web provides an excellent forum in which members can share their knowledge of the brand's origins, often replete with illustrations, photographs, and video.

Rumors surrounded the reintroduction of the New Beetle in 1997 as community members looked for reasons to be optimistic that the New Beetle would honor its roots. As a result, rumors about the new model, including the use of the original plans and the re-hiring of retired designers were rife in the months leading up to the launch of the New Beetle. Long-time community members wanted to believe that the New Beetle would be true to the ethos of the original, despite fearing otherwise. In a similar way, members of the Saab brand community spend considerable time discussing the future of Saab, including rumors on future Saab models. These rumors have arisen largely in response to Saab's acquisition by GM and the fears that GM would change the essence of the brand.

Rumors of the creator's return constitute a recurring narrative phenomenon in the abandoned Apple Newton brand community: Is Apple coming back to the market that it created? Such beliefs, despite the low likelihood of their occurrence, are common. Co-mingled with these beliefs are rumors and tales of secret labs and hidden signs that a new Newton is being developed and tested. Consider the following example from an online Newton forum:

> I dunno. I saw *something* at Disneyland out here in California. It wasn't a newton, and they usually used newtons for taking surveys and things. It was a color device with an apple logo. This was months ago. I know I should have kicked his ass and ran out of the park with the device, but going to jail is not one of my "cool" things to do on my weekends :). All I know is that there is something going on. What with all the spare newtons on ebay, (could be a sign that apple is about to drop some cool sh**) it will make sense.

The possibility of reintroduction is an important source of optimism in the Newton brand community. Here, as in most brand community rumors, the why is often the communal desire to ensure the survival of the brand and what the community wants it to represent. Via rumors and community narratives, the community attempts to exercise control.

Communities of a fashion

Given that we see these and other traditional markers of community, we hold that brand communities are communities of a sort. This does not, by any means, assert that they are the same as pre-industrial villages, or any such thing. Obviously, they are not situated in the same late nineteenth-century dynamic of nascent urban modernity, labor and capital politics, or dominant academic critique. Instead, brand communities, as well as other consumption communities, are their contemporary milieu: existing in late modernity, with a fully embedded and normalized (hyper)-consumer ethic, the product of a mass-mediated connectivity that is quickly becoming the mode of community connection and communication. Why these previously antagonistic forces (if they really ever were so unambiguously antagonistic) are now less antagonistic is an important why question for researchers working in the domain of Consumer Culture Theory (Arnould and Thompson 2005). Is there something so appealing about the communal form, that consumers now living in a branded world, appropriate it and build on it, apparently quite comfortably? It appears so.

An important and related question centers on where brand communities can be found: what leads to the formation of a brand community? After ten years of research in this area, we can offer some conditions under which brand communities are likely to flourish. While we cannot assert that a combination of any or all of these properties will definitely exist in or produce a brand community, we can state with some confidence that these properties have been common in the brand communities that we have witnessed. Brand communities fare best when the brand in question has a unique and distinctive set of meanings. Such meanings allow the brand, and the resulting community, to stand out from others. Grassroots communities appear to fare better than inorganic or created communities. The attempts to build a community around the Saturn brand of automobile have created a far weaker form of brand community than those that exist around Saab, Volkswagen, or Jeep. This is not to say that a marketer cannot create a successful brand community or cannot encourage an existing brand community. Rather, we believe that the strongest brand communities form out of a necessity. A challenge gives the community a reason to exist and persevere. This challenge can take many forms: low market share (Saab, Macintosh), difficulty of use (Jaguar), derision and ridicule (Volkswagen Beetle), marketplace abandonment (Apple Newton), or a strong rivalry (Coke versus Pepsi, Apple versus Wintel, Pocket PC versus Palm). Tension is crucial to maintaining cohesiveness. Finally, many brand communities appear to have the capacity for powerful and transformative consumption experiences. We have encountered clear examples of brand communities in a variety of brands: Bronco, Jeep, Macintosh, Miata, Newton, Palm, Pocket PC, Saab, and Volkswagen. Many of these communities have been demonstrated to be capable of consumption experiences that have a profound impact on their users, moving their users beyond the mundane, remaking them. Many of these transformative experiences have been dependent on the communal setting for reification and reaffirmation.

Further, we are not just talking about fanatical consumers. More and more consumers of every stripe are getting their information about brands through non-marketer controlled channels in a way that is unprecedented. True, some of the data reported here and elsewhere come from active brand community members. But for many consumers, brands provide an admittedly small, but not altogether trivial communal bond. For every person who actually posts on a brand community website, there are certainly more who feel some communal connection, but do not act, and others who act only rarely. It would clearly be an unusual social network or community that did not have such a distribution of activism/passivism. Further, it would be entirely odd for a mass-market material object existing in the consumer (brand) society milieu *not* to possess some aspect of we-ness in its global brand meaning. Even for the relatively passive, the communal ethos of a brand becomes part of what the brand means, an important part.

So the point that typically gets only the passing nod in "the field" becomes vital: humans are social creatures, and this holds true if the human is a sixteenth-century villager or a twenty-first-century consumer. Humans desire to congregate, affiliate, and associate with like-minded/spirited others. It is a powerful, basic human expression. Community endures and finds at its center the things most cherished by its members – institutions, political causes, religious affiliations, even brands. Community emerges where it will, *despite* the rationalizing effects of markets (see Ritzer *et al.*, this volume). Do benefits accrue to other interested institutions, political actors, ideologies, and systemic engines around which communities form? Yes, clearly they do. There are philosophical, economic, and political benefits to those collectives, just as there are for brand communities, making branded consumption not only a social marker, but a social goal as well.

The polit-brand

Brands are sometimes explicitly political. One example is the particularly politicized brand, which we have dubbed the polit-brand (O'Guinn and Muñiz 2004). The post-1972 (US/Western European) political left fights market capitalism's hegemony through purchases, as opposed to boycotts of brands from major corporations; the new revolutionary leftist strikes blows against the capitalist empire by buying things. But, these things have to have been granted community approval. Here, the brand community is at once centered on a brand *and* a political goal. While the use of brands in revolution has been discussed elsewhere, most notably in Frank's (1997) *Conquest of Cool*, we offer a significantly different take on the dynamics and meaning of the phenomenon.

Circa 1972 the old "new left," to all intents and purposes, perished (Schulman 2001). It was replaced by a more consumption-ambivalent "revolution." In this new socio-political order, revolutionary politics are enacted not through choices of consuming or not consuming, but in identification, group sanctioning, and community championing of brands that are deemed by the collective to be the best vessels of the group's "alternative" politics. Such social processes can be seen in such brands as Apple, Ben and Jerry's, Blackspot, Carhart, Diesel, MAC, REI, SweatX, and Tom's of Maine. We believe that notions of branding and their place in social thought have something to gain from the broadening border-crossing of brand and politics. These are communal brands, inherently tied to communal politics, and it is impossible to deny the inherent social nature of this consumption. Here, the why of consumption is about advancing a social movement's politics.

One of the earliest politicized brands was Coca-Cola, a brand whose political legacy is still the topic of communal discourse. Consider the following comment:

> My mother's family swears by Coca-Cola. It used to be, in fact, that in order to receive permission to marry into her family, three basic qualifications had to be met. The prospective in-law had to: (1) Be a Democrat, (2) Drive a Ford, and (3) Drink Coca-Cola.

Such sentiments, divulged as long-standing and "understood," reveal the depth of the co-mingling of politics and brands by different groups of consumers. In a similar fashion, during 2004, members of less affluent Chicago neighborhoods made their "right" to have Starbuck's a matter of front-page city politics (Mihalopoulos and Olivo 2004). To have one's neighborhood served and marked by this brand became a matter of rights, disenfranchisement, and social equity. Aldermen/women were asked to get the neighborhoods Starbuck's. This is very interesting in contrast to the traditional critique: here there is a reported lack of concern of displacing local "mom and pop" coffee outlets. These are brand politics, and obviously, have a powerful and literal communal component.

Intentionally or not, Apple Computer has become a politicized brand. This is the result of several factors, most the subject of story, speculation, and rumor, oftentimes reflecting what various factions *desire* to be true. The Apple brand community has strong feelings about this. This is from a discussion entitled "Apple=Democrats?"

> 1. It's well-known that Jobs is a liberal and has contributed liberally (pun intended) to liberal causes and liberal political campaigns. I've heard this discussed for years.
> 2. A Democratic administration has brought Microsoft to the brink of destruction as the entity we all know. This is of benefit to Jobs and to Apple Computer . . .

Such characterizations are consistent with those encountered previously, such as the Apple community member who characterized "IBM people" as wearing suits and voting for Reagan and "Apple people" as wearing jeans and not voting for Reagan. Such descriptions may reflect Apple's position as a David fighting the Goliath of then IBM, now Microsoft. Still, this is not the entire story. Others note figures from the right side of the political spectrum who use Macs and challenge the liberal characterization. In this way, the community-accepted political ideology for the brand is continually negotiated, regardless of marketer intent, much like the quasi-political characterization of the typical Saab driver (yuppie or not) is continually negotiated in the Saab brand community.

Recently, more actively marketer-politicized brands have emerged on the scene. Two examples of this are SweatX clothes and Blackspot sneakers. SweatX is an anti-sweat shop brand. It is strongly supported by an online brand community. In fact, without the associated collective, it would have far less market meaning and potency. However, the most controversial polit-brand is the so-called "anti-brand brand," Blackspot, by AdBusters, an ostensibly anti-advertising and anti-consumer culture magazine. AdBusters is marketing the Blackspot to its members (themselves a form of brand community) to challenge a particularly chaotically politicized brand, Nike.

> We're selling real, authentic empowerment. If you wear the Blackspot sneaker, you're helping to demolish a big, bad corporation [Nike] that has done dirty deeds in the Third World.
>
> (Adbuster Publisher, Kalle Lasn)

By targeting Nike, Blackspot further complicates the politics of Nike, polarizing both supporter and detractor communities. Very clearly, brands, politics, and national ideology intersect. Holt (this volume) offers evidence on this marketplace reality. To deny the inherently social form of human politics would fly in the face of reason, not to mention the evidence of everyday experience.

Who owns the brand?

This is an obvious question posed by the issues explored in this chapter. Brand communities assert considerable claims on ownership, claims that are only complicated by the politicization of brands. These impassioned and empowered consumer collectives assert more channel power and make claims on core competencies formerly reserved for the marketer. Brand community members increasingly regard marketers not as owners of the brands, but as temporary stewards, stewards who can be held immediately and directly accountable for transgressions, such as undesired modifications or violations of privacy (see Deighton, this volume). Community members recognize that their interests in the brand may surpass those of the marketer and that they may be better aware of the realities in which the product is used.

In the following, a Body Shop customer and brand community member goes online to tell the community about her dissatisfaction with a recent change in Body Shop management policy.

> I hate this sort of waste. I went to the Body Shop recently to get a refill for my foundation and they didn't have my color. The sales being informed me that they "were phasing out the refills because they 'recycle'." Like that's an environmental step forward. Sheesh. I refused to buy an entire new case, that's absurd and wasteful. I switched brands because of it. I think Body Shop is selling out to profits over the environment.

Marketers must be more accountable because consumers are acting as social collectives, not individual marketplace atoms. The PocketPC (a Microsoft product) user group organized online enough to be a lobbying force to Microsoft . . . not as individual customers, but as an organized, politicized, and powerful social collective. Representing the extreme case is the brand community centered on the Apple Newton. There, the brand is no longer produced by the manufacturer, but by the community. Moving beyond the co-creation of the brand, the collective becomes the marketer and keeps the brand and its meaning alive. While certainly not typical, the actions of the Newton brand community demonstrate what brand communities are capable of.

In brand communities marketplace power relations are destabilized. It is via the continued creative and interpretive actions of the community that the brand is continually co-created with the marketer. If the meanings suggested by the marketer resonate with the members of the community, these meanings will be amplified in the stories they tell and the images they create. If the marketer-suggested meanings do not map onto the brand as created by the community, then the community will attempt to drown out those marketer-suggested meanings. The community will reject those marketer-created images and endeavor to create their own. Potential buyers of a new car may "Google Saab" and be put into immediate contact with Saab community members who present an image of the appropriate buyer that is not what Saab management would like for them to see.

These effects extend to *all* brands. While not all brands have thriving brand communities, all brands have communal aspects. All brands are situated socially. User-created brand talk is common. Regardless of whether they are consumed publicly or not, all brands convey complex meanings to others, meanings that are continually negotiated between the marketer and consumers.

Discussion

It is time to see brands as more than summed attitudes floating in preference factor space. We need to see them as complex bundles of meaning, where negotiation between marketer and groups of consumers is instrumental and meaningful to both parties, the marketplace, and society at large. Brands are co-mingling with, or substantially emulating, the form and function of traditional social institutions. This obviously impacts the why of consumption. In this chapter we argue that we must significantly rethink our views of brands, brand communication, and the obsession with the individual consumer and his or her thoughts. Contemporary society floats on a true sea-change in mediated human communication that makes it easier for consumers to exchange information and organize. Brands are social creations, and this reality has never been more important.

This research provides an important perspective via its boundary-spanning nature, occupying the intersection of blind spots for two different fields. Consumer behavior research, for the first three decades of its existence, has had a blind spot concerning things truly social. The field has developed little knowledge on consumption in its social context, as it is affected by the various groups, institutions, and collectives centered on it. Sociology, on the other hand, has extensively explicated the social, but has a significant blind spot with regards to the marketplace beyond its essentialist critique. Sociology has failed to recognize consumption as providing important and emically legitimate social bonds for contemporary society. We are advocating a position where the substantive area of consumer inquiry can contribute to both fields and beyond, thus enriching at least two genres via truly interdisciplinary thought. Community should be added to the study of consumption, and consumption to the study of community.

The thing so long called "brand loyalty" is more and more thought to be informed by social relationships and communal sensibilities and forces – and not just by consumer sociologists but by brand managers as well. Brands were always socially constructed, but recently the power ratio of their builders has changed significantly. Brand managers have recently begun to publicly fret over the "newly empowered consumer." Hardly brands with small shares, Pepsi and Coca-Cola have brand communities. P&G and HP, just to mention a couple, actively acknowledge, court, and seek to "manage" brand community. It is not industry that has been slow to see brand community's power.

Conclusion

Brands are not trivial to human existence, no matter how hard one tries to wish this reality away. As branded things grew more important in people's lives and consumption became more central to everyday life, community did not subside, but began to coalesce around icons of society's new center – consumption. Ultimately, brand communities matter because they look and behave like other forms of community, and community is an essential human phenomenon. These are socially embedded and entrenched entities, and thus extremely durable. The increasing legitimacy of consumer society has changed the world. In short, consumption and brands matter. Brand communities and other social aggregations of empowered consumers are not going away. In fact, society's need for trust (Cook 2001) and security (Bauman 2001) have rarely been more profound. This provides us with heretofore unknown research opportunities. But, this requires new thinking and conceptualizations.

Brands and the talk of brands are everywhere. Yet, this ubiquity does not counter their importance, just the opposite. Brands are constellations of meaning, meaning that cannot be cleanly detached from culture and history. Brands are not just names of marketed things, but increasingly part of the social fabric and centers of social organization. Our models, our thinking, and our practice need to catch up with this reality.

Acknowledgments

The authors wish to thank Gary Fine, David Mick, Hope Schau, and Jim Twitchell for their comments on an earlier draft of this manuscript.

References

Arnould, E. J. and Price, L. L. (2000) "Authenticating acts and authoritative performances: Questing for self and community," in S. Ratneshwar, D. G. Mick, and C. Huffman (eds) *The Why of Consumption: Contemporary Perspectives on Consumer Motives, Goals, and Desires*, London: Routledge: 140–163.

Arnould, E. J. and Thompson, C. J. (2005) "Consumer culture theory (CCT): Twenty years of research," *Journal of Consumer Research*, March (forthcoming).

Bauman, Z. (2001) *Community: Seeking Safety in an Insecure World*, Oxford: Polity Press.

Boorstin, D. (1973) *The Americans: The Democratic Experience*, New York: Random House.

Cook, K. S. (2001) *Trust in Society*, New York: Russell Sage.

Fischer, C. S. (1975) "Toward a subcultural theory of urbanism," *American Journal of Sociology* 80 (May): 1319–1341.

Fischer, E., Bristor, J., and Gainer, B. (1996) "Creating or escaping community? An exploratory study of internet consumers' behaviors," in K. Corfman and J. Lynch (eds) *Advances in Consumer Research*, Vol. 23, Provo, UT: Association for Consumer Research: 178–182.

Fournier, S. (1998) "Customers and their brands: Developing relationship theory in consumer research," *Journal of Consumer Research* 24 (March): 343–373.

Fox, S. (1984) *The Mirror Makers: A History of American Advertising and Its Creators*, New York: Vintage.

Frank, Thomas (1997) *The Conquest of Cool: Business Culture, Counterculture, and the Rise of Hip Consumerism*, Chicago, IL: University of Chicago Press.

Goody, J. (1993) *The Culture of Flowers*, Cambridge: Cambridge University Press.

Hunter, A. and Suttles, G. D. (1972) "The Expanding Community of Limited Liability," in G. D. Suttles (ed.) *The Social Construction of Communities*, Chicago, IL: University of Chicago Press: 44–80.

Jannowitz, M. (1952) *The Community Press in an Urban Setting*, Glencoe, IL: The Free Press.

Kant, I. (1980 [1790]) *The Critique of Judgement*, trans. James Creed Meredith, Oxford: Clarendon Press.

Maffesoli, M. (1996) *The Time of the Tribes: The Decline of Individualism in Mass Society*, Thousand Oaks, CA: Sage.

Marchand, R. (1985) *Advertising: The American Dream*, Berkeley, CA: University of California Press.

Mihalopoulos, D. and Olivo, A. (2004) "For Some It's Coffee; For Others It's Class," *Chicago Tribune*, July 16: 1.

Muñiz, A. M. Jr. and Hamer, L. O. (2001) "Us versus them: Oppositional brand loyalty and the cola wars," *Advances in Consumer Research*, Provo, Utah: Association for Consumer Research, Vol. 28: 355–361.

Muñiz, A. M. Jr. and O'Guinn, T. C. (2001) "Brand community," *Journal of Consumer Research* 27(4): 412–431.

Muñiz, A. M. Jr. and O'Guinn, T. C. (1995) "Brand community and the sociology of brands," Paper presented at Association for Consumer Research Annual Conference, Minneapolis, MN.

Muñiz, A. M. Jr. and Schau, H. J. (2005) "Religiosity in the abandoned Apple Newton brand community," *Journal of Consumer Research* (forthcoming).

Muñiz, A. M. Jr., O'Guinn, T. C., and Fine, G. A. (2005) "Rumor in brand community," in *Advances in Theory and Methodology in Social and Organizational Psychology: A Tribute to Ralph Rosnow*, Mahwah, NJ: Erlbaum (forthcoming).

Nietzsche, F. (1990 [1886]) *Beyond Good and Evil: Prelude to a Philosophy of the Future*, trans. R. J. Hollingdale, New York: Penguin Books.

O'Guinn, T. C. and Muñiz, A. M. Jr (2000) "Correlates of brand communal affiliation strength in high technology products," Paper presented at the Association for Consumer Research Annual Conference, Salt Lake City, UT.

O'Guinn, T. C. and Muñiz, A. M. Jr. (2004) "The polit-brand and blows against the empire," Paper presented to Association for Consumer Research Annual Conference, Toronto, ON.

Putnam, R. D. (2000) *Bowling Alone: The Collapse and Revival of American Community*, New York: Simon and Schuster.

Royce, J. (1969) *The Basic Writings of Josiah Royce*, J. J. McDermott (ed.), Chicago, IL: University of Chicago Press.

Sahlins, M. (1972) "The first affluent society," in M. Sahlins (ed.) *Stone Age Economics*, Chicago, IL: Aldine.

Schau, H. J. and Muñiz, A. M. Jr (2002) "Brand communities and personal identities: Negotiations in cyberspace," in S. M. Broniarczyk and K. Nakamoto (eds) *Advances in Consumer Research*, Provo, UT: Association for Consumer Research, Vol. 29: 344–349.

Schouten, J. W. and McAlexander, J. (1995) "Subcultures of consumption: An ethnography of the new bikers," *Journal of Consumer Research* 22 (June): 43–61.

Schudson, M. (1984) *Advertising, The Uneasy Persuasion*, New York: Basic Books: 129–146.

Schulman, B. J. (2001) *The Seventies: The Great Shift in American Culture, Society, and Politics*, Cambridge, MA: Da Capo.

Simmel, G. (1981/1904] "Fashion," in G. B. Proles (ed.) *Perspective on Fashion*, Minneapolis, MN: Burgress: 130–155.

Sullivan, M. (1926) " 'Immense decrease in the death rate', " in R. Rhodes (ed.) *Visions of Technology: A Century of Debate About Machines, Systems and the Human World*, New York: Touchstone: 88–89.

Tönnies, F. (1957 [1887]) *Gemeinschaft und Gesellschaft*, trans. C. P. Loomis, East Lansing, MI: Michigan State University Press.

Weber, M. (1978 [1922]) *Economy and Society*, Berkeley, CA: University of California Press.

Wellman, B. (1979) "The community question: The intimate networks of east yorkers," *American Journal of Sociology* 84(5): 1201–1231.

14 How societies desire brands

Using cultural theory to explain brand symbolism

Douglas B. Holt

Conventional psychological theories of branding have an Achilles heel that we should no longer ignore. Outside of certain technology- and service-driven categories, where brands are built largely through reputation effects, branding's big stakes are decided increasingly by cultural symbolism. Brand symbolism delivers customer value by providing culturally resonant stories and images that customers use to buttress their identities.

Brand symbolism was introduced into consumer research by motivation researchers (Ernst Dichter, Sidney Levy, Joe Newman, Pierre Martineau, and their colleagues) nearly a half-century ago. Yet, despite its central and growing importance, brand symbolism has been all but ignored for decades by the top journals in marketing. Instead, marketing's brand theories have yoked brand symbolism to the dominant psychological models without considering its distinctive qualities. To address this gap, I have developed a cultural theory of branding conceived specifically to explain how brands create identity value through their symbolism. To do so requires an entirely different theory of consumer motivations and desires: moving from the essentialist, static, individual-level constructs of existing theories to social and cultural constructs that are grounded in historical contexts.

To motivate the discussion, consider a few examples of iconic brands. Iconic brands are brands that have become cultural symbols and, hence, are the most successful in delivering identity value to consumers. Iconic brands are some of the most powerful brands in the world: by my calculation they account for nearly half of the 100 most valuable brands in the world (as ranked by Interbrand's Global Brand Scorecard printed annually in *Business Week*). In many cases, the brand's identity value is the central driver of brand value: witness Coke and Pepsi, Budweiser and Guinness, Levi's and Diesel, Absolut and Jack Daniels. In other cases, identity value commingles with the brand's reputation for quality, reliability, and innovation, such as with brands like BMW, McDonald's, IBM, and Apple.[1] Any theory that claims to explain brand symbolism should be able to explain how these iconic brands have become so. Consider a few examples:

> *Marlboro*: Marlboro was restaged in 1955 as a filtered cigarette targeted to
> men. The new advertising portrayed tough men from a variety of occupations

sporting a military tattoo on the top of one hand. The ads told stories of these men enjoying themselves alone in conventionally masculine endeavors: working on their car, fishing, racing cars. The launch was a great success and the brand quickly climbed to a 5 percent share. The tattoo campaign was pulled in 1959. For the next four years, Leo Burnett and Phillip Morris experimented with a variety of creative ideas intended to communicate masculinity – some ads used famous football players, some ads featured male encounters with sexy women – to no avail as the brand's share faltered. Since the beginning, the team had experimented with a variety of ads featuring cowboys, none of which broke through. Finally in 1965 the brand finally took off again with a campaign depicting the autonomous life of industrious cowboys laboring on the range, with music from *The Magnificent Seven* playing in the background, and named this new imaginary place Marlboro Country. These vignettes about ranch life sent the identity value of Marlboro skyrocketing, doubling the brand's share from 1965 to 1970. In 1971, cigarette companies agreed to a voluntary ban on television advertising, effectively freezing symbolic competition in the category.

Budweiser. Budweiser was a competitive but not dominating brand in the 1970s, strongly challenged by Miller, Schlitz, and Lite Beer from Miller. Anheuser-Busch struggled to find advertising to respond to Miller's successful "Miller Time" campaign. Finally, in 1983, Anheuser-Busch launched "This Bud's for You," a campaign that showcased men working cheerfully and industriously in artisanal trades, men whom Bud saluted with a baritone-voiced announcer proclaiming "this Bud's for you!" The results were startling. American men, particularly working class men, flocked to the beer. By the middle of the decade, Budweiser was unchallenged as the most desirable beer in the country, dominating the premium segment. Anheuser-Busch successfully extended the campaign for seven years, but around 1990 the advertising stopped working, sending Bud's brand equity into a tailspin. For the next seven years, management tried a variety of very different campaigns to revive the brand, all of which failed. Finally, two new campaigns – "Lizards" and "Whassup?!" – which developed entirely different symbolism combined to rekindle Bud.

Mountain Dew: PepsiCo's Mountain Dew was a regional soft drink that took off in the 1980s with a BBDO ad campaign depicting young guys in scenic rurale locales performing vigorous improvised stunts to the applause of appreciative young women, always ending in a Freudian plunge into a swimming hole. The team abandoned the campaign in 1991, and, after three years of experimentation, hit upon an ad featuring four "Dew Dudes" who mocked the challenge of death-defying extreme sports stunts. This ad sent the soft drink's identity value skyrocketing. The ad was quickly expanded into the "Do the Dew" campaign with a number of similar ads produced. Within a year, though, the new campaign's symbolism began to fade. PepsiCo and

BBDO successfully changed the campaign by launching a series of pop culture parodies featuring the Dew Dudes mixing it up with the likes of Mel Torme and Jackie Chan, once again playfully mocking crazy stunts. Mountain Dew became the fastest growing carbonated soft drink in the United States during the 1990s as a result.

Academic theories of brands, if they are going to contribute insight to real world branding, should be able to explain why these brands become iconic, and also why they lose their iconic power as often as not.

This essay consists of three parts. In the first section I will critique the way in which brand symbolism is treated in the dominant theory of branding in American marketing – what Kevin Keller calls the consumer-based brand equity (CBBE) model. Second, I offer a brief genealogy of Corona beer to ground the exposition of the new model. Finally, I introduce a new cultural branding model to address this class of branding phenomena and point out its primary points-of-difference versus the CBBE model.

A critique of the CBBE model's treatment of brand symbolism

Kevin Keller's exposition of the CBBE model (Keller 1993, 1998, 2002, 2003a, 2003b) offers the most widely accepted and comprehensive treatment of branding in American marketing. Keller's essay on customer-based brand equity (Keller 1993) received the Maynard Award. Later the Marketing Science Institute commissioned Keller to write the discipline's definitive treatment of brands (Keller 2002), and the *Journal of Consumer Research* also invited him to write an essay on branding (Keller 2003b). The CBBE model is a more academically oriented version of a related model developed earlier by David Aaker (1991, 1996; Aaker and Joachimsthaler 2000). Aaker's and Keller's publications are unique in American marketing in that they have developed synthetic branding frameworks that are intended to apply to all aspects of branding, including brand symbolism.

While Keller and Aaker never trace the lineage of the CBBE model, its roots are evident to anyone who has worked in the marketing profession over the past 30 years.[2] It is an academic treatment of a branding model that has long dominated brand management and advertising, what I term the "mind share model" of branding (Holt 2003, 2004). This model has its roots in the early attempts to make branding into a science by Stan Resor and David Ogilvy in the 1950s, and is especially influenced by Ries and Trout's famous book *Positioning: The Battle for Your Mind* (Ries and Trout 1981). The mind share model is based upon the assumption that the goal of branding is to claim virgin cognitive associations in a product category, and consistently communicate these associations in everything the brand does over time to sustain the brand's hold on this cognitive territory. In the 1990s, these mind share assumptions were incorporated into a variety of brand metrics sold by market research companies and ad agencies (e.g., the Young and Rubicam Brandvaluator, which Keller draws upon extensively in his writings).

Theoretical issues

The CBBE model does not treat brand symbolism as a qualitatively distinctive feature of the brand. Rather symbolism is rolled into the general model as one type of brand association. So the axiomatic assumptions of CBBE are assumed to apply to brand symbolism:

Axiom #1: Brand symbolism consists of abstract associations. The core of the brand – what Keller calls the *core brand values* and, in short form, the *brand mantra*, and what in industry is more commonly referred to as the *brand DNA* or *brand essence* – is defined as the set of abstract associations (attributes and benefits) that characterize the most important dimensions of the brand (Keller 2003a: 151). Like Aaker, Keller typologizes these associations to include categories such as product benefits, personality, symbolism, organization, quality perceptions, and user imagery. For example Keller (ibid.: 66) specifies the Apple brand in terms of its product associations (Powerbook, Macintosh, graphics, Desktop Publishing) and its "intangibles" (cool, creative, fun, educational, innovative, friendly). In the CBBE model, brand symbolism is treated as a subset of these associations, part of the brand's intangible associations.

Cultural research challenges this assumption. Research exploring how consumers understand, use, and value brand symbolism has consistently demonstrated that people understand brand symbolism in terms of concrete stories and images, not abstract associations (e.g., Mick and Buhl 1992; Thompson 1997; Fournier 1998). The CBBE model, like all of the psychological models that have preceded it, assumes that people find intrinsic value in abstract concepts like "fun." This is a methodological artifact. People find great value in the particular details of the stories and images that they associate with particular brands, not with generic concepts. The fact that they are able to simplify these experiences to abstract concepts like "fun" in an experiment or survey when they are asked to do so is hardly proof that it is the abstraction that consumers value. Marketing has reduced the complexities of brand symbolism to generic concepts simply because they are tractable via preferred methods.

Axiom #2: Brand associations exist as "knowledge structures" in the minds of individual consumers. According to Keller, a brand exists as a knowledge structure in the mind of the consumer: "the power of a brand lies in what resides in the minds of customers" (Keller 2002: 59). And, so, according to the conventional information-processing intuition that underlies the model, "thinking" about these associations leads to a stronger brand. The CBBE model views brand symbolism as a particularly abstract ("deep" "higher level") type of knowledge structure: Keller offers examples such as Coke (Americana), Marlboro (Western), Disney (fun and magic).

While treating the brand as knowledge makes sense for functional aspects of a brand, knowledge is of negligible importance for brand symbolism. For example, Keller claims that the Nike brand is based upon the "mantra of authentic athletic performance," which exists as a knowledge structure in customers' minds. Yet, consumers' knowledge of Nike's athletic performance is inconsequential: they hold similar knowledge structures for Adidas, Puma, and other athletic brands.

This knowledge does not differentiate success from failure, and has nothing to do with why consumers value Nike's brand symbolism.

Rather, interpretive studies such as those referenced above have demonstrated time and again that consumers use brand symbolism in their identity projects as a material resource with which they construct life narratives. Consumers value Nike primarily because they find value in the stories that have been embedded in Nike, its symbolism, and draw upon these stories in their everyday lives to buttress their identities.

Further, cultural theory challenges the CBBE's claim that brand symbolism is, in the first instance, a property of the mind. Brands, as symbols, gain their power from two characteristics ignored by the CBBE model. First, symbols are valued because they are established as cultural conventions: their meanings are intersubjectively shared (Holt 2002, 2004). It is the fact that the brand exists in public culture as a conventional sign that gives the brand's symbolism its social value. Second, when brand symbolism is successful, it gets woven into the fabric of social life as consumers use these symbols to interact: to forge affiliations, to claim status, and to socialize (see Holt 1995). Although the vast majority of brands do not have formal brand communities of any size, all brands with strong symbolism act as symbolic resources that consumers use to negotiate their lives in society (Holt 2002). While it is surely true that consumers have cognitive representations of brand symbolism, these representations are the consequence of their stature in public culture and social life. Cognitive representations exist well down the causal pecking order from these socio-cultural dimensions of brand symbolism.

Axiom #3: Brand symbolism is successful when it is strong, favorable, and unique. Keller insists that brands become successful when their associations are "strong, favorable, and unique," a phrase he uses repeatedly. So the CBBE model seeks to explain the success of particular brand symbolism by assessing the symbolism in terms of these three criteria.

The most obvious problem with this approach is that these three properties are metrics, not components of an explanatory model. To demonstrate that a brand has "strong, favorable, and unique" associations is to provide a present-tense description. A satisfactory theory must specify the processes through which particular brands build these associations, showing how these processes differ from brands that do not have such glowing report cards. The CBBE model does not offer such an explanation.

There is a logical reason for this missing explanation. An individual-level model cannot possibly explain the collective resonance of a brand's symbolism. The CBBE model views the brand in relationship to individual consumers. Yet, brand symbolism becomes powerful only when it is accepted and used by a large population. It is logically impossible for an individual-level model to explain these social patterns; socio-cultural theories are required (Holt 1997). Further, the CBBE model is premised upon generic universal constructs (e.g., fun, quality, adventurous, and so on), which cannot explain why a particular society finds so much value in particular brand symbolism. So the CBBE model's theoretical assumptions lead to garbled arguments when its advocates attempt to explain the successes and failures of brands that rely on symbolism.

Axiom #4: Strong brands result from expressing the brand's symbolism consistently over time. Both Keller and Aaker assume that consumers value brands because they provide a distinctive and stable heuristic. So both insist that brands can be successful over time only if they maintain consistency in the brand's associations – brand symbolism included.

But this is an essentialized model that cannot account for the historical specificity of a brand's resonance. The CBBE model argues that the brand exists as a trans-historical timeless entity abstracted from the ebb and flow of social and cultural changes. The CBBE model yanks the brand and consumer out of history to posit a brand–consumer connection that is not dependent upon historical context. Such a theory cannot explain how iconic brands work, because their cultural resonance is always historically specific: Budweiser's symbolism resonated powerfully for about seven years, lost its value, and then regained resonance only with entirely different symbolism; Mountain Dew's symbolism had to be significantly altered several times to maintain its resonance.

Empirical issues

Keller regularly uses the CBBE model to discuss iconic brands and offers numerous examples. Aaker takes a similar approach in his books as well. Keller garners authority for these views by positioning the CBBE model as a synthesis and application of academic research: he states that the model is "well grounded in the academic literature," uses headers like "the science of branding," and fills his expositions with academic references (e.g., Keller 1998, 2003). Yet the empirical basis for these applications to brand symbolism is questionable.

Aaker and Keller both developed their academic reputations by conducting well-regarded experimental studies on branding. But this research focused mostly on cognitive issues concerning the extendability of a brand, a question well-suited to experimental research using psychological theories. Neither scholar has conducted research on brand symbolism. In fact, to the best of my knowledge, there is not a single experimental study in the major American marketing journals that examines how brand symbolism works. This is not surprising since the methodological constraints of experiments limit the ability to study how brand symbolism resonates throughout a society (which requires exiting the closed conditions of the lab) in particular historical moments (which requires historical analysis).

Rather than drawing inferences from published experimental studies, Keller and Aaker induct their assertions about brand symbolism by studying actual brands – a valid approach to theory-building when done well and informed by appropriate theories. However, when viewed as case studies, their analyses do not meet the standard criteria for case research in the social sciences.

For example, Keller (2003a: 648) analyzes Pepsi branding by tracking changes in the brand's tagline. This approach implies that the branding impact of Pepsi advertising can be understood without examining the ads in which these taglines were embedded (and given meaning). He claims that the changes in Pepsi taglines reveals whether or not the brand was well positioned as a "youthful" beverage, suggesting that the taglines that explicitly invoked youth were somehow more effective – an overly literal view of how advertising works to develop brand symbolism. Further, Keller claims that Pepsi's performance ebbed and flowed with these tagline changes: youth taglines produced better results than non-youth taglines. In fact, Pepsi's share of the CSD category fell by nearly 40 percent during this period, regardless of tagline. Rather than buttressing the CBBE model, Pepsi is a key counter-example: a veritable branding disaster that is tied to a brand strategy premised upon the CBBE model's insistence on consistency in abstract associations.[3]

To take another example, Keller states that

> an even cursory examination of the brands that have maintained market leadership for the last 50 or 100 years or so is a testament to the advantages of staying consistent. Brands such as Budweiser, Coca-Cola, Hershey, and others have been remarkably consistent in their strategies once they achieved a preeminent market leadership position.
>
> (Keller 2002: 635)

Yet even a cursory examination of the historical records of Budweiser and Coca-Cola demonstrates that they have undergone dramatic revisions in their strategies over time (see Holt 2004). In interviews with Anheuser-Busch management for instance, a senior manager told me that Anheuser-Busch was forced to give up Budweiser's "work-reward" strategy in the early nineties because American men no longer believed in it.

Similarly, Keller (2002: 635) claims that Marlboro has been "single-mindedly focused in its marketing communications" since the 1950s. He relies on a *Wall Street Journal* story to recount the oft-told story that Marlboro was repositioned from a woman's cigarette to a brand whose image relied on the Western cowboy. Lacking primary data, Keller fails to note that Marlboro was launched with a tattoo campaign, that a wide variety of replacement campaigns were tried in the period 1959–1964, that early cowboy ads were not particularly successful, and that US television advertising ceased in 1971 due to the voluntary television ban.

When Keller does examine primary data, his interpretations gloss over the distinctive qualities of the branding effort compared to the brand's rivals. For example, Keller (1998) describes the rise of Nike in the late eighties as due to a surge of interest in sports and the fame of Nike's endorser, Michael Jordan. Of course a "surge of interest in sports" cannot explain why one particular brand took off. Jordan was a key element for Nike, but "endorsement fame" is not credible given that Nike is largely credited (even by Jordan himself) in creating that fame. Further, Nike didn't take off until several years after they hired Jordan when they began to portray him differently in their advertising, alongside other breakthrough ads ("Revolution," "Bo Knows," and so on). Specifically, Michael Jordan became one of the most powerful cultural icons in the USA only after Nike launched Spike Lee's seminal "Spike and Mike" ads. Keller does not consider the impact of Nike's intensive use of African-American vernacular and imagery, even though Nike's advertising was renowned for the way in which it drew upon the culture of the African-American ghetto. Instead, the campaign is interpreted as "subtly urging Americans to participate more actively in sports." This analysis misses the point that the campaign's "Just Do It" declarations were metaphorical rather than literally about sport (few people used their Nike gear to play competitive athletics). An explanation of Nike's success needs to pay attention to the distinctive qualities of Nike's branding: the particular characteristics of the advertising that Nike produced with its sponsored athletes, different from competitors like Adidas, Reebok, and Converse, which caused the brand to resonate so powerfully with American desires beginning in the late 1980s. By ignoring the crucial details of Nike's branding efforts, Keller's explanation for successful brand symbolism describes generic aspects of branding that are common to all brands in the category.

In one final example, Keller (2001) analyzes the decline of the Levi's brand in the 1990s. Yet, as with Nike, the analysis does not consider any details of Levi's branding efforts, nor any social changes to explain Levi's fall from grace. Instead, the MSI report offers up an explanation that verges on tautology: Levi's lost resonance, lost favorability, and lost distinctiveness. In other words, the Levi's brand became less desirable, so its brand metrics (all of which correlate heavily with desirability) must have fallen. Keller adds as an aside: "competitive actions, consumer shifts, environmental changes, and other such forces can change the nature of brand associations, often fairly quickly." Of course this is true. Therefore, any viable theory of branding must specify these forces and link them to specific changes in brand equity.

More generally, the CBBE model cannot explain how iconic brands work because it does not seriously examine the phenomena to be explained: What are the collective desires that iconic brands tap into? And what are the particular qualities of brand symbolism that sate these desires? Iconic brands are built through branding activities (usually sponsored films such as television ads) that resonate with a substantial fraction of a country's population at a particular historical moment. So a plausible theory must pay close attention to the fit between the brand's particular actions and what is going on in society and culture that shapes people's identity desires. In other words, we need a theory that explains the social construction of desire across a nation, and, then, we need to specify what precisely it is that successful brands do to attend to these desires.

In my recent writings (Holt 2002a, 2002b, 2003a, 2003b, 2004), I have conducted socio-cultural research, informed by contemporary cultural theory, to attend to this gap. In this research, I use a variant of the cultural-historical method, which I call a brand genealogy (this methodology is detailed in Holt 2004). To outline some of the differences of the cultural branding model versus CBBE, consider a much-abbreviated genealogy of a brand familiar to many readers – Corona beer.[4]

A short genealogy of Corona beer

The Mexican beer Corona was one of the most successful American identity brands of the 1990s. Corona sales quickly climbed to become the leading imported beer in the United States, far outpacing the once dominant Heineken.[5] According to the CBBE model, building a strong brand requires first staking out a distinctive and important category association and then consistently reinforcing this association over time. Yet Corona executed neither of these steps.

Corona's first brief climb to iconic status came in the mid-1980s and peaked around 1988. At the time, Corona was one of the cheapest beers in Mexico, the price brand of the large Mexican brewery Cervecería Modelo. American distribution was mostly limited to the Southwest, where Mexican-Americans tended to live and where Mexican culture influenced the Anglo population.

In the 1980s, the idea of a hedonistic "Spring Break" vacation had caught on spectacularly across American colleges and was widely celebrated in the media. Coeds from across the country stormed Daytona Beach, Florida, South Padre Island, Texas, and – most popular of all – the beach resorts of Mexico. These vacations were carnivals of excess: 24/7 drinking, wet T-shirt contests, dirty dancing, and sexual escapades, real and imagined.

Corona cost about $4.00 per case, so the price was certainly appealing. In addition, Corona had a leg up on other Mexican beers for two reasons. First, Corona had a distinctive package design with all of the right connotations. A clear returnable bottle with the logo roughly painted straight on the glass, this package was understood as an authentic Mexican beer (read: offbeat noncommercial product of a less industrialized country) compared with the foil labels and brightly colored cans used by the more expensive Mexican beers. Also, somewhere along the way, American students started putting lime in their Coronas. This was a beer analogue to another of their favorite party rituals, licking some salt, drinking a shot of tequila, and sucking on a lime wedge.

As college students returned to campus with debauched stories of fun in the sun, Corona was frequently a prop. Distribution followed the students as they entered professional lives in major metropolitan areas, particularly in places like Texas, California, and Arizona where a disproportionate number of college kids traveled to Mexico for Spring Break. As Corona-laced myths of sun-and-debauchery spread, the beer soon became the drink of choice among young professionals throughout the nation, the quintessential beer for an evening out of partying at bars and clubs. In a quintessentially socio-cultural process, Corona's first rise in identity value was the product of its Mexican branding reframed by American consumers so that the beer embodied a myth that was particularly potent for the so-called "yuppies" of the 1980s.

The CBBE model would claim that Corona owned strong and favorable "partying" associations and related user imagery, which are particularly valued in the beer category. However, this observation does not work as an explanation. Recall that, at the same time, Bud Light was beginning an extraordinary sales climb with its Spuds McKenzie, "the official party animal," campaign. Bud Light apparently owned "partying" too. Nor were these two brands alone, as other beer brands tried to convey a partying attitude, albeit with less good fortune. Further, beer brands had worked hard to capture this partying association before, but never with such success as Corona and Bud Light. A persuasive explanation must detail what Corona did differently than other brands that accounts for its success.

Beer-drinkers didn't value "partying" as a generic concept associated with the brand. Rather, beer brands were more valued when they told the partying story that best resonated in American culture. In the 1980s, Corona and Bud Light had the most compelling partying myths. Other brands did not. Partying was one of several category benefits available to brewers to use as a platform on which to build culturally specific myths. Corona's success came from its authentic role as a key prop in the Mexican Spring Break myth. Corona won out because it embodied one of most resonant party-centered myths circulating in American culture at the time.

What happened next is a good example of what often happens when customers act as the primary authors of the brand's myth. As Corona became popular, the trend-leading consumers who had initially propagated Corona's myth watched the insider coolness of their Corona-drinking evaporate. The Corona story lost its cachet, and so they moved on to other beers.

Because Corona's US distributor was not airing ads that advanced Corona's myth, when these insider customers moved on to less popular beers, the brand effectively lost its myth. Corona became a short-lived fad. By 1990, sales had collapsed, returning to pre-1987 levels. For five years the brand struggled to return to growth without success. Other beers had replaced Corona as more desirable party drinks for young people. Corona became the Mexican beer that used to be cool. The CBBE model, because it is a psychological model, cannot account for these social processes.

Corona's next move directly violated CBBE principles. The brand team ditched the brand's supposed partying brand essence and concocted the "Change Your Lattitude" campaign. The ads depicted an idyllic beach scene – what Americans understood as a Mexican beach – viewed through the eyes of a couple lounging beachside. The ads had little in the way of action and no music moved the ad along. Time stood still. Instead the audience was gradually introduced to a simple setting: a beach, a couple relaxing, and Coronas.

The campaign's breakthrough spot, *Pager*, opens with a long shot of the blue ocean, a gentle surf washing onto white sand with the familiar sounds of the sea – seagulls, wind, and waves. Then a rock skips across the water. The camera pulls back and we can see that a woman is lounging on the beach next to a table. On the table rests a Corona, a man's watch, a half-dozen small saucer-shaped rocks, and a pager. The arm of the woman's male companion reaches into the frame and grabs a rock and skips another across the surf. The man begins to repeat the motion when the pager goes off, the vibrating beep causing the pager to bounce around the table. His arm hesitates, changes direction, grabs the pager and skips it across the surf, like he skipped the rocks. The woman, unperturbed, sweeps her hair back and stares mindlessly out at the ocean. The tagline tells us "Miles Away from the Ordinary." As the campaign developed, the tagline was switched to "Change Your Lattitude."

Corona immediately took off, soon hitting sales numbers far beyond the 1980s peak and, unlike its first fifteen minutes of fame, sustained extraordinary sales growth for a decade, becoming far-and-away the leading imported beer in the USA. How do we explain Corona's success?

The CBBE model would argue that Corona succeeded because the brand now owned the "relaxation" association. But simply noting that the Corona was now associated with relaxation does not work as an explanation. Relaxation had been a central benefit in the beer category for many decades, long before Corona had significant distribution in the United States. Budweiser had emphasized a relaxation theme as far back as the 1950s and other beer brands had followed Bud's lead. The fact that Corona was generically associated with relaxation cannot explain its success. Rather, we have to look at Corona's particular expression of relaxation and explain why, in the United States of the 1990s, this particular expression was far more resonant than those offered by other beer brands.

What Corona's American consumers bought when they slapped down $7.00 for a six-pack of the former bargain basement beer was a chance to experience, through the ritual gulp of the yellow liquid, a glimmer of the American ideal of a tranquil beach vacation. What the new advertising campaign had done was to grab hold of Corona's valuable but dormant cultural real estate – the Mexican beach – to develop a different and more meaningful myth. It was still true that Corona, with its roots as a working class Mexican beer and its Spring Break reputation, was indelibly etched in the collective American imagination as a key prop in a winter beach vacation. This asset, however, lay dormant, underutilized.

Mexican beaches had another meaning that Corona's managers adapted. Sitting on a beach relaxing with a beer or margarita had come to be one of the most salient American dreams for "getting away from it all" – of taking a time out from the rat race of work to relax and de-stress. This ideal, equating relaxation with escaping to a beach in a less-developed country, a place far removed from the highly competitive company life, a place where time slowed down, was tremendously appealing to overworked Americans. To tap into this cultural opportunity, Corona authored an evocative myth that used the Mexican beach stories to imbue their beer with the idea of escaping from everyday routines.

Corona's new campaign registered so powerfully because the United States had just undergone a profound shift in its labor market. A new flexible network organizational model had emerged out of the early 1990s recession that relied upon a flexible white-collar workforce to respond to changing marketplace conditions. For the first time in the century, middle-class salaried jobs were now routinely subject to lay-offs and firings. Work became intensely competitive, and work-related stresses dominated everyday life. In this environment, "relaxation" took on a new historically specific meaning. No longer was relaxation simply kicking back at the end of the day to chill out with a cold beer – a common relaxation story told by Budweiser and Schlitz and Pabst from the 1950s through 1970s. Job demands now followed workers into their homes, so this made no sense. Now relaxation required more radical escapes. Professional men and women now dreamed of getting away to places far removed from the rat race.

Corona used its authority to represent the Mexican beach so as to encapsulate these desires for a sanctuary from day-to-day work pressures in 30 seconds of film. Corona gave beer-drinkers access to the perfect antidote that they could now gulp down, even while sitting at home on a Wednesday night after a bruising day at the office.

To do so, Corona branding violated the CBBE model by shifting its supposed brand associations from wild partying to tranquil relaxation. But consumers didn't seem to be miffed because they never understood the brand in terms of stable abstracted knowledge structures. Instead, the story connected and Corona came to embody one of the most potent expressions of relaxation in American culture. In so doing, the brand didn't represent relaxation in a generic way, as an abstract concept stripped bare of connotations, reduced to its dictionary definition. Rather Corona owned a particularly evocative representation of relaxation in American culture: doing absolutely nothing on a faraway Mexican beach.

Corona's success has resulted, not from generic ownership of the abstract concepts of partying and then relaxation, but from performing particular identity myths about partying and relaxation that offered American beer-drinkers symbolic sustenance. Corona's iconic value resided in the particulars of these distinctive myths, not in the abstractions that the CBBE model emphasizes.

Further, Corona succeeded only when it radically shifted its myth, from a story about lascivious partying in Mexico to a story about relaxing in isolation on a quiet beach. Rather than stewarding the brand's knowledge structures to maintain consistency at all costs, Corona succeeded when managers paid close attention to historical changes and made the appropriate adjustments to better align the particular stories the brand performed with important tensions in American society.

Like Corona, all of the iconic brands that I've studied exhibit the lauded metrics that, according to the CBBE model, correlate with strong brands: they have strong, distinctive, and favorable associations and they have core consumers with deep emotional attachments. But these observed characteristics are the *consequences* of successful mythmaking, not the cause. When a brand performs an identity myth that addresses an acute anxiety in society, consumers develop favorable associations, emote, and gather together around the brand. Hence, while the CBBE model provides a useful metric for appraising the brand's identity value, the inferences that Aaker and Keller make about why identity brands become strong are inadequate, if not faulty. To understand why particular brands become widely favored as symbols to address people's identities requires a theory of desires that is constructed at the level of society and culture.

The cultural branding model

To build an explanatory theory of identity brands, I have used the brand genealogy method to study in much more detail other iconic brands including Budweiser,

Marlboro, Volkswagen, Mountain Dew, Nike, ESPN, and Patagonia. My analysis iterated between inducting patterns from these cases and deducing conceptual direction from the extensive academic literature on (non-brand) cultural icons.

Let me sketch the theory, which I develop at length in a recent book *How Brands Become Icons: The Principles of Cultural Branding* (Holt 2004), as well as in several management articles (Holt 2003a, 2003b). First we need to theorize how societies come to desire brand symbolism, and then we need to explain what iconic brands do that results in addressing these desires so successfully.

National ideology

Nations require a moral consensus to function. Citizens must identify with the nation, accept its institutions, and work toward its betterment. Nations are organized around a set of values that define what is good and just. These moral imperatives propel people to pursue national goals as they strive to meet society's definition of success and respect. This is ideology, a system of ideas that forges links between everyday life – the aspirations of individuals, families, and communities – and those of the nation. To be effective, a nation's ideology can't be coerced or learned as though from a textbook. Rather, it must be deeply felt, taken for granted as the natural truth. National ideology is usually the most powerful root of consumer demand for myth (though national ideology often intersects and competes with other bases of group identity, especially ethnic-religious identities).

Ideology is never expressed directly, as a declarative statement. Instead, ideologies are conveyed through myths. A variety of important American myths are critical for the nation to function, such as the self-made man (which addresses the path to the country's idea of rugged individualism leading to economic success), the frontier (which addresses the quest for ever-expanding opportunities, and the country's global mission to convert the rest of the world to its ideals), and the melting pot (which expresses ideals about how immigrants become a cohesive people). These myths link the meaning of individual lives to the country's collective nation-building project: how Americans see themselves as part of the team to build the nation's economic and political power. These myths are usually constructed around ideals of individual success and of manhood – what it takes to be a man. Tracing the evolution of such myths as they are updated to address contemporary social issues is central to charting myth markets.

Cultural contradictions

Americans don't naturally inhabit the nation's ideology simply because they are citizens of the United States. Rather, it takes work to forge these identifications. While ideology sets the collective vision to which the nation aspires, people in different walks of life understand and use ideology differently and their life circumstances make it easier or harder to realize these values. These cultural contradictions – tensions between ideology and individual experience – produce intense desires and anxieties, fueling demand for symbolic resolutions that smooth over the tensions. National ideologies create models for living. The distance between that model and everyday life acts as a cultural engine, creating demand for myths that manage these differences. These tensions are particularly acute when the nation's ideology shifts. Periods of cultural ferment produce myriad contradictions, which in turn create veins of intense anxieties and desires that ripple throughout society.

Myth markets

Contradictions in the national ideology create myth markets. A wide variety of cultural products compete to provide the most compelling myths: stories that will provide symbolic sustenance to shore up the contradiction. At any given time in American society, there are a number of important cultural contradictions. And each contradiction spawns a distinctive myth market.

Think of myth markets as implicit national conversations in which the center of the conversation is the national ideology. American ideology is taken up by a variety of contenders advocating different viewpoints. These contenders are popular culture in all of its forms: films, music, television, books, politicians, talk radio, video games, and, of particular interest here, brands. We usually think of popular culture as light entertainment and a record of current events, important in terms of economics but trivial in terms of culture. Most of the time this is true. But myths are much more than merely entertaining or newsworthy. Popular culture is also a national conversation in which myths circulate. Myths come packaged in all types of popular culture products: in films, television programs, music, books, magazines, newspapers, sports, politics, even in the news. Brands perform myths through the stories with which they become associated, primarily through advertisements. These stories are relived by customers as they ritually consume the product.

Iconic brands rarely develop their myths from wholly original cloth. Rather, these brands typically borrow and add to existing myths circulated by other cultural products. Generally parasitic, an iconic brand seldom competes head-on with other cultural products – films, television, and the like. In terms of myth performances, brands rarely compete with films, politicians, or musicians. Even the best 60-second ad (say, Nike's "Revolution" or Apple's "1984"), can't compete with John Wayne's films, Ronald Reagan's speeches, or Kurt Cobain's songs and concerts.

But brands have an advantage over these more ephemeral performances because they provide a material connection to the myth. Brands load the myth into products used every day, so brands allow for ritual action (the ability to viscerally experience the myth through one's actions) in a way that a poster in a bedroom or an occasional gathering for a rally or concert cannot.

With only a handful of exceptions (Nike and Volkswagen stand out), brands do not so much originate new expressive culture as they recycle materials placed into circulation by other media (e.g., film, television, music, journalism, books). Take Mountain Dew for example. In the 1960s Mountain Dew invented a hillbilly story that borrowed liberally from the *Li'l Abner* cartoon (e.g., stereotypes about drinking moonshine and running barefoot) and was informed by other contemporaneous myths, like *The Beverly Hillbillies*. Later, in the 1980s, Mountain Dew's myth was substantially influenced by, and played off, the television program *The Dukes of Hazzard*. And finally, in the 1990s, the brand presented the slacker "Dew Dudes" who were taken by extreme sports, a myth that was tremendously influenced both by *Wayne's World* and by MTV's portrayal of extreme sports. Iconic brands leap into emerging myth markets usually led by other mass-cultural products. The most successful identity brands develop a distinctive point of view and aesthetic as they recycle these cultural materials.

Identity myths and iconic brands

Brands become iconic when they perform powerful identity myths: simple fictions that address cultural anxieties from afar, from imaginary worlds rather than from worlds that the consumer lives in. Identity myths are useful fictions that stitch back together otherwise damaging tears in the cultural fabric of the nation. These tears are experienced by people in their everyday life as personal anxieties. People use myths to smooth over these tensions, helping them to create purpose in their lives, to cement their desired identity in place when it is under stress. Academic research has demonstrated that the extraordinary appeal of the most successful cultural products has been due to their mythic qualities – from Horatio Alger's rags-to-riches dime novels of the nineteenth century, to John Wayne Westerns, to Harlequin romance novels, to the action-adventure films of Willis, Schwarzenegger, and Stallone. Iconic brands work the same way.

Brands become iconic when they address societal desires, not individual ones. Iconic brands perform myths (usually via advertising) that symbolically resolve the identity desires and anxieties stemming from an important cultural contradiction. Iconic brands earn extraordinary value because they address the collective anxieties and desires of the nation. We experience our identities – our self-understandings and aspirations – as intensely personal quests. But when scholars examine consumer identities in the aggregate, they find that identity desires and anxieties are widely shared across a broad swath of a nation's citizens. These similarities result because, even though they may come from different walks of life, people construct their identities in response to the same historical changes that impact the entire nation.

To take up of the examples from the beginning of the chapter, Budweiser became the most desirable beer in the 1980s because the brand addressed one of the most acute contradictions of the day. Working men were powerfully moved by Ronald Reagan's battle cry, invoking America's frontier myth to restore the country's economic might. The country's economic and political meltdown in the 1970s, along with the increasing independence of women, had left them feeling emasculated. So Reagan's call-to-arms gave them hope that they would soon regain their lost manhood. However, these same men were beginning to realize that their vocations as skilled manual laborers, their primary source of masculine identity, was becoming obsolete as these jobs were outsourced overseas, replaced with service jobs. Budweiser targeted this acute tension between America's revived ideals of manhood and economic realities that made realizing these ideals nearly impossible for many men.

Over time, as the brand performs its myth, the audience comes to perceive that the myth resides in the product. The brand becomes a symbol, a material embodiment of the myth. So as customers drink or drive or wear the product, they experience a bit of the myth. This is a modern secular example of the *rituals* that anthropologists have documented in every human society. But rather than religious myth, in modern societies the most powerful myths have to do with identities. Customers use iconic brands as symbolic salves. Through the products in which they are embedded, customers grab hold of the myth and use it in their lives to make their identity burdens a bit less burdensome. Great myths provide for their consumers little epiphanies – moments of recognition that put images and sounds and feelings on barely perceptible desires. Customers who make use of the brand's myth for their identities forge powerful emotional connections to the brand.

Rethinking how brands work

The CBBE model ignores the cultural properties of brands because it has been crafted within a paradigm that assumes that all explanations of marketing phenomena must emanate from cognitive structures in individual minds. The model is no different from the rest of mainstream consumer research, where the assumption that marketing can be treated as a natural science has led to search for durable universals using research methods that fail to grapple with the social and cultural properties of real brands. The result is a "debate" that moves back and forth between microscopic (now neurological) to universal (now evolutionary psychology) levels of analysis, bypassing along the way the unit of analysis where we most desperately need theory – society and culture. To traverse from the psychological assumptions of the CBBE model to socio-cultural axioms, such as those outlined here, requires conceptual reorientation along the following lines:

From building associations to performing myths

The CBBE model assumes that brand symbolism consist of abstract associations in the consumer's mind. Thus, the purpose of advertising is to influence these associations. The communication content is treated as instrumental rhetoric. Consumers are assumed to discard this rhetorical material and only absorb (or not, depending on the success of the ad) associations to the brand.

The cultural branding model turns this view of brand communications on its head. For iconic brands like Coke, Nike, and Budweiser, the brand's communications are the center of customer value. Customers buy the product primarily to experience the stories that the brand performs. The product is simply a conduit through which customers get to experience the stories that the brand tells. When consumers sip a Coke, or a Corona, or a Snapple, they are imbibing in more than a beverage. Rather they are drinking in identity myths that have become imbued in these drinks. The brand is a *storied product*: a product that has distinctive brand-markers (trademark, design, etc.) through which customers experience identity myths. Because the CBBE model ignores the particular contents of the brand's communications, the model is unable to decipher how brand symbolism works.

From abstractions to cultural expressions

The CBBE model proposes that the brand consists of a set of abstractions. Descriptions of brands are full of abstract adjectives and nouns like security and performance and quality and ruggedness. In cultural branding, in contrast, the brand's value is located in the particulars of the brand's cultural expression: the particular cultural contents of the brand's myth and the particular expression of these contents in the communication. For Corona, the brand exists in the Mexican beach, and the evocative expression of the beach in its "nothing's happening" style of advertising. For Coke, in "Teach the World to Sing," the brand existed in the idea that in the hippie counterculture could be found the seeds of peace and racial harmony. For Snapple's breakthrough "100 percent Natural" campaign, the brand was centered in loud-mouthed Wendy telling silly stories of Snapple drinkers, and in the barbed political soliloquies of Howard Stern and Rush Limbaugh. Abstracting these cultural expressions to "relaxation" and "friendship" and "quirky," respectively, strips these brands of their most valuable assets.

The CBBE model abstracts away the messiness of society and history in search of the brand's purified essence. This distilled model denies the brand a role as an historical actor in society. In its insistence that brands forge a transcendental identity lodged in consumers' minds, the CBBE model ignores that identity value is created and transformed in particular historical contexts. A model of identity-branding must detail the brand's stakes in the transformation of culture and society and the particular cultural expressions the brand uses to push for these transformations.

From transcendental consistency to historical fit

In the CBBE model, the brand's associations transcend time and space. Therefore explanations of the evolution of brands boil down to whether or not the brand maintains consistency in the face of organizational and competitive pressures that push for zigging and zagging. Brand management is about stewardship: finding the brand's true "identity" and maintaining this compass point come hell or high water.

Yet Corona succeeded by moving away from their initial branding – their supposed DNA at the time – to address shifting currents in American society. In fact, all of the iconic brands that I've studied, with histories extending more than a decade, have had to make significant shifts in order to remain iconic. Brands that haven't adjusted properly – like Pepsi, Levi's, and Miller – have lost much of the brand equity. These reinterpretations of the brand are necessary because, for a myth to generate identity value, it must directly engage the most acute cultural tensions of the day. Coke celebrated America's triumphs against Nazi Germany in World War II, but then suddenly shifted to dramatize ways to heal internal strife around war in the early 1970s and then racial divisions in the early 1980s. Corona, originally a brand that represented collegiate hedonism, later was retooled to provide a soothing antidote to the compression and anxieties of the networked free agent work that came to a head in the 1990s.

Iconic brands are built using a philosophy the opposite of that espoused by the CBBE model. That is, the brand is an historical entity whose desirability comes from performing myths that address the most important social tensions that pulse through the nation. For identity brands, success depends upon how well the brand's myth is modified to fit historical exigencies, not by its consistency in the face of historical change.

The cultural branding model outlined here is a preliminary effort. Much work remains to be done. But, to develop this area, the discipline of marketing must embrace theories and methods that it has for decades pushed to the margins, and it must not continue to insist, against all evidence, that its favored psychological assumptions are universally applicable for resolving all important branding questions.

Notes

1   I develop this multidimensional view of brand value in more detail in Holt 2002b.
2   I worked as a brand manager at Clorox (a Procter & Gamble spin-off) and Dole in the mid-1980s and was indoctrinated into a branding model very similar to the CBBE model. Keller reports spending considerable time with managers at companies like Clorox and Nike, and so it is likely that his exposition of the CBBE model has been influenced by these interactions.
3   Similarly, Keller reports that Mountain Dew's urban Busta Rhymes campaign and an urban beeper promotion were key elements of the brand's success. Yet both of these efforts were failures according to interviews I've conducted with PepsiCo executives, and also according to market data: Mountain Dew continues to index extremely low with urban minorities.
4   This case is adapted from Holt 2004. It is sufficient to draw out my main points of argument, but readers should note that the other genealogies reported in the book are considerably more detailed.
5   See Rohit Deshpande, Kirsten J. O'Neil-Massaro, and Gustavo A. Herrero, "Corona Beer (A)" (Harvard Business School Case #9–502–023, 2001). Anheuser-Busch now owns 50 percent of Cervecería Modelo, the brewer of Corona.

References

Aaker, D. A. (1991) *Managing Brand Equity*, New York: The Free Press.
Aaker, D. A. (1996) *Building Strong Brands*, New York: The Free Press.
Aaker, D. A. and Joachimsthaler, E. (2000) *Brand Leadership*, New York: The Free Press.

Fournier, S. (1998) "Consumers and their brands: Developing relationship theory in consumer research," *Journal of Consumer Research* 24 (March): 343–373.

Holt, D. B. (1995) "How consumers consume: A typology of consumption practices," *Journal of Consumer Research* 22 (June): 1–16.

Holt, D. B. (1997) "Poststructuralist lifestyle analysis: Conceptualizing the social patterning of consumption," *Journal of Consumer Research* 23 (March): 326–350.

Holt, D. B. (2002a) "Why do brands cause trouble? A dialectical theory of consumer culture and branding," *Journal of Consumer Research* 29 (June): 70–90.

Holt, D. B. (2002b) Brands and Branding, HBS Note #503045, Boston, MA: HBS Publishing.

Holt, D. B. (2003a) "What becomes an icon most?" *Harvard Business Review*, March.

Holt, D. B. (2003b) "How to build an iconic brand," *Market Leader*, Summer: 35–42.

Holt, D. B. (2004) *How Brands Become Icons: The Principles of Cultural Branding*, Cambridge, MA: Harvard Business School Press.

Keller, K. L. (1993) "Conceptualizing, measuring, and managing customer-based brand equity," *Journal of Marketing* 57 (January): 1–29.

Keller, K. L. (1998) *Strategic Brand Management*, Upper Saddle River, NJ: Prentice-Hall.

Keller, K. L. (2001) "Building customer-based brand equity: A blueprint for creating strong brands," MSI Report Number 01–107, Boston, MA: Marketing Science Institute.

Keller, K. L. (2002a) *Branding and Brand Equity*, Cambridge, MA: Marketing Science Institute Relevant Knowledge Series, 02–601.

Keller, K. L. (2003a) *Strategic Brand Management*, 2nd edn, Upper Saddle River, NJ: Prentice Hall.

Keller, K. L. (2003b) "Brand synthesis: The multidimensionality of brand knowledge," *Journal of Consumer Research* 29 (March): 595–600.

Mick, D. G. and Buhl, C. (1992) "A meaning-based model of advertising experiences," *Journal of Consumer Research* 19 (December): 317–338.

Ries, A. and Trout, J. (1981) *Positioning: The Battle for Your Mind*, New York: McGraw-Hill.

Thompson, C. (1997) "Interpreting consumers: A hermeneutical framework for deriving marketing insights from the texts of consumers' consumption stories," *Journal of Marketing Research* 34 (November): 438–455.

15 Transformations in consumer settings

Landscapes and beyond

George Ritzer, Michael Ryan, and Jeffrey Stepnisky

Consumer settings have dotted the geography of our existence for centuries. The advent of a capitalist mode of production, however, has intensified the quantity (though arguably not the quality) of these settings. The last half-century has seemed particularly explosive in terms of the creation of new methods of attracting consumers and their dollars. In particular, the 1980s and the 1990s saw the emergence of "cathedrals of consumptions" (Ritzer 2005) – spectacular, themed, shopping and entertainment environments that drew crowds and consumers *en masse*. More recently, we have seen the emergence of what we will call (borrowing a term from sociologist Sharon Zukin) "landscapes of consumption" – *locales that encompass two or more cathedrals of consumption that allow, encourage, and even compel people to consume.* If the cathedral of consumption is best captured by the image of the suburban mall, the cruise line, or the themed restaurant, then the landscape of consumption is best captured by the image of the Las Vegas Strip, a collection of consumer settings that work synergistically to generate an energy of place that cannot be reduced to any single setting.

To pursue the question of the "why" of consumption we will develop this concept of landscape of consumption through a case study – Easton Town Center, in Columbus, Ohio. Easton has been described as a "streetscape," "lifestyle center," "leisure-time center," and "urban village." What is unique about Easton is that it captures a more general trend in urban design – to fuse aspects of the hyperconsumption propagated through the cathedrals of consumption, with a more easy-going, relaxed street life built around ideals of community. Easton is particularly evocative because it aims to simulate a community of 1950s America,[1] even as it becomes home to flagship stores for such big-name companies as Express for Men, Lazarus, and even McDonald's. In effect, Easton is a shopping mall designed on the model of small-town America. Herein lies a contradiction, and the basis of our critical analysis. Despite Easton's attempts to become a place of substance and meaning for contemporary consumers, it remains an example of the many rationalized structures that, in fact, threaten, on a global scale, the substantial and meaningful social forms they attempt to reproduce. Therefore, part of the problem in unpacking the why of consumption is to understand how entrepreneurs and urban designers tap into consumer desire for spectacle, as well as the nostalgia for shopping and living environments of the past, but at the same time to understand the contradictions within these designs, and therefore their likelihood of success.

We develop this set of problems across three sections. In the first, we place our study in the context of theoretical writing in the sociology of space, and consumer research on cathedrals of consumption, servicescapes and retroscapes. In the second section, we describe Easton with a focus on the techniques that the owners, planners, and designers of Easton have used to position it as a unique consumption environment. In the third section, we describe the contradictions that run through Easton with a special interest in the characteristics that make it a "non-place." Indeed, despite its efforts to become a place of substance and meaning, "something," Easton still shares many of the features of what Ritzer (2004) has recently called "nothing."

The sociology of space and the landscapes of consumption

Our interest in consumer settings is related to a more general sociological interest in the study of space. In the context of social theory, Edward Soja (1989) argues that attention to space corrects a previous neglect of modern social theories that exclusively focused on social change, history, and time. For example, Marx grounded his theory of social change in a historical materialist perspective, which emphasized the dialectical transformation of societies across time. The increasing interconnectedness of the world has placed communities and societies into regular contact so that now it is possible to say that "we are in the epoch of simultaneity; we are in the epoch of juxtaposition, the epoch of the near and far, of the side-by-side" (Foucault 1986: 22). Neo-Marxist theorists, such as the aforementioned Edward Soja (1989, 1996), but also the influential French theorist, Henri Lefebvre (1991), argue that in the present era, capitalism increasingly turns its attention to the manipulation and control of space. In Lefebvre's words we have moved from a concern with "the mode of production of things in space" to the "mode of production of space" (Lefebvre 1991: 410). In this way, space is not only a means of production, but it is also a form of social control. Indeed, as a theorist of "everyday life," Lefebvre shows us that the organization of space controls activities so that in their very "habitus" persons reproduce the kinds of spaces central to the operation of capitalism.

More specifically, scholars have studied the way that entrepreneurs create shopping and entertainment spaces that attract, and in some instances, control consumers. Though department stores and other "dreams worlds" were first developed in the nineteenth century (Benjamin 1999; Miller 1981; Williams 1982), the last half of the twentieth century saw an explosion in the development of spaces that could offer consumers unique, new, and especially stimulating experiences. Gottdiener (1998) points to an important shift from shopping malls designed for efficiency and functionality to shopping malls designed to attract consumers through the use of culturally charged symbols. In this view, the shopping mall is not merely the end point of consumption (a place in which people buy items that they have seen advertised and promoted elsewhere), but rather is a vital link in constituting a consumer culture more generally. Numerous scholars, including Ritzer (2005), have argued that these new locations use postmodern, aesthetic techniques to attract consumers. Spectacle is created through the implosion of a diversity of previously discrete social and cultural forms, the creation of themed environments, the manipulation of time and space, and the simulation of fantastical and imaginary realities. In effect, these "new means of consumption" offer a total, "phantasmagoric" (Benjamin 1999) experience clearly distinguished from the mundane realities of everyday life. Insofar as the consumption setting is unified under a common theme, diverse elements are granted a continuity that becomes a focal point for the articulation of experience and the elaboration of meaning. The new means of consumption attract consumers not only because they are centralized locations where commodities can be purchased, but because they embody, give concrete form to, and even help to create the ideals and images that circulate within consumer culture.

In this context, consumer researchers have also introduced suggestive terms such as "servicescape," "brandscape," and "retroscape" (see Sherry 1998a). Brown and Sherry (2003) use the concept "retroscape" to describe consumer environments (including cathedrals of consumption such as themed Irish pubs, Historyland in Hayward Wisconsin and, what we would call, landscapes of consumption such as Huntington Beach) that are unified under nostalgic themes. These spaces submit time to the logic of space, and to spectacular effect. Retroscapes attract people through the nostalgic appeal for the past (reminding consumers of a better time and better place) and, in some cases, give consumers the total experience of stepping out of their everyday lives and into the past.

Alternately, in his analysis of the brand outlet "Nike Town Chicago," Sherry (1998b) argues that the brandscape (one example of the more encompassing concept, servicescape) is not merely a product of designer intention and spatial layout, but that its meaning and form also rely upon the activity of consumers who imaginatively and viscerally experience the brand as it is laid out in geographical space.

Sherry's work gets us into the controversial debate over the relative agency of consumers in these constructed settings. Indeed, contemporary research in consumer culture regularly shows that consumers are not mere "dupes" of capitalist entrepreneurs (see Mick *et al.* 2004). Rather, consumers are able to make personal meaning out of mass-produced, branded commodities and the environments in which they are sold (see O'Guinn and Muñiz, this volume, as well as Holt, this volume). Nevertheless, the position taken in this chapter is that even as consumers are able to find meaning and generate community in consumer spaces, these activities are regularly underpinned by a logic of rationalization which is tied to the larger project of global capitalism. The meaning brought to consumption by individual consumers does not detract from the larger social forces that guide the development and design of landscapes of consumption, and the contradictions that reside therein. Indeed, part of explaining the why of consumption comes in understanding the larger social forces that generate opportunities for and patterns of consumption, as well as the way that the settings of consumption attract consumers, but are also continually updated and transformed (thus taking on new surface features) so as to not become boring to consumers (a point taken up at the end of this chapter).

We most closely follow the sociologist Sharon Zukin (1991) in our use of the term "landscape of consumption." Taking a macrosciological approach, Zukin argues that in the United States, the shift from industrial society to post-industrial society has led to the destruction of old social geographies. This has pushed the problem of space to the center of social theory. In formulating her concept of landscape, Zukin introduces a number of ideas that are of interest to us. For one, landscape and power are deeply and intricately connected. Large-scale, bureaucratic, economic structures attempt to impose a new order upon an existing geographic location. Though these attempts to create a landscape are oftentimes met with resistance, Zukin concludes that ultimately old forms of organization give way as a result of the demands of capital. Second, Zukin argues that landscapes of power are characterized by a "structural coherence." Against the postmodern view that contemporary landscapes are ephemeral, everchanging aesthetic displays, she claims that at base, there is a tendency to homogenization – "repetition and singularity" – largely a result of the profit motive.

Both of these points are instructive. We also hold that landscapes of consumption are generated by large-scale, economic interests that reflect powerful social forces and these forces are often homogenizing. However, despite its influence, Zukin's discussion of landscapes of power in general, and landscapes of consumption in particular, retains a *productivist* bias. It is difficult in Zukin's work to distinguish clearly landscapes of consumption from the related concepts of "landscapes," "landscapes of power," and "landscapes of production." In some cases, the settings that Zukin includes under the heading of landscapes of consumption also involve production settings (for example, cities [e.g. Miami, Los Angeles] and suburbs [e.g. Westchester]). To Zukin, consumption is often secondary to production. It has been over a decade since Zukin's book was published and since then there have been numerous studies and arguments made that treat consumption as an entity that can be analytically distinguished from production (Slater 1997; Ritzer *et al.* 2001; Goodman and Cohen 2004). For this reason, we reorient this concept by placing it squarely in the realm of consumption, and argue that unlike the spaces described in Zukin's book we are now witnessing the emergence of landscapes of consumption that are primarily dedicated to the goals of consumption. These are *first* places where people consume – commodities, brands, lifestyles, identities – and only *second* are they places where people work, and live as residents. These landscapes, though inevitably tied to the work that is necessary to the production of consumption, attract people not as places to work (or "produce") but rather as places to consume.

In this essay, we focus on a new type of landscape of consumption – Easton Town Center in Columbus, Ohio.[2] We have chosen Easton, not only because it exemplifies more general principles of landscapes of consumption, but because it is a kind of landscape of consumption that we expect to become more prevalent in coming years. The management team that designed and runs Easton plans to create similar structures with Greene Town Center in Dayton, Ohio and Bayshore Mall in Milwaukee, Wisconsin. A total of at least 14 developers were set to have opened similar "lifestyle centers" by 2004 (Shopping Center World 2003).

In our discussion of Easton, we are especially interested in the way that it creates a kind of *spectacle* by *simulating* a small town. Simulation is one of the principal techniques used by entrepreneurs to attract consumers to cathedrals of consumption (Ritzer 2005). A reality unavailable to everyday experience is created by designing an environment that appears more real than reality itself. Indeed, many of the spaces in which people now live and shop increasingly obscure the boundary between reality and unreality. Easton is a simulation that taps into an American collective memory (Halbwachs 1992; Middleton and Edwards 1990; Zerubavel 1996) of small-town life. In this regard, Easton is also a kind of simulation that reverses the grand spectacle often observed in mega-malls and other cathedrals of consumption (e.g. cruise ships, Las Vegas casino-hotels). Though Easton encompasses some spectacular elements, it largely operates through what Sandikci and Holt (1998) have called the "commodification of the social" (334); a technique that they argue has become central to the design of malls and, by extension, to landscapes of consumptions. Easton is not only a place where commodities can be purchased, and it does not primarily rely upon grand displays and overwhelming spectacles to attract consumers (though there are some elements of this in Easton). Instead it is a place that promotes a certain kind of (or collection of) social experiences. In particular, Easton "remembers" a time when consumption was fused with everyday life, even as it promotes the newest and most spectacular brand commodities and the chain store settings in which they are on offer.

Easton: beyond the cathedrals of consumption

Easton Town Center started as the far-off dream of fashion mogul, Leslie Wexner, CEO of The Limited, Inc. During the 1980s and early 1990s, The Limited began acquiring pieces of former farmland on Columbus's northeast side to build a new distribution center and warehouses. These developments never came to be, however, as local infrastructure improvements, including a federally funded project to widen the Columbus Beltway (I-270), made Wexner realize he was sitting on a gold mine. He knew the land was too valuable for just warehouses and "so they decided on a planned community" (Palmieri 2003). Easton was constructed at a cost of over $300 million to date and is owned and operated by Steiner + Associates, The Georgetown Company, The Limited Brands (formerly known as The Limited, Inc.), and California governor Arnold Schwarzennegger. Two of these investors, Steiner + Associates and Limited Brands are also based in Columbus.

Easton is currently a 7 million square-foot endeavor, although the developed area of Easton will eventually have over 12 million square feet of office, hotel, residential, and retail space. The main focus of the town, the "downtown" so to speak, is a 1.5 million square foot retail area composed of an indoor shopping area known as Easton Station and six city blocks of outdoor "small town" shopping. There are currently over 160 tenants (over 30 of which are brand new to the Columbus market – for example, Virgin Records, Nordstrom, Anthropologie, The Container Store, The Cheesecake Factory, and set to open in March 2005, Crate and Barrel) drawing in an excess of 30 million visitors in 2003 (up from 18 million in 2002). The Center has already been the recipient of a number of honors and awards including the International Council of Shopping Center's award for Innovative Design and Construction of a New Project in 2000 and the Business First Corporate Caring Award for small businesses in the Health and Human Services category in 2003.

The presence of Easton has unquestionably had a large impact on the city of Columbus at large. Over 25,000 jobs have already been created by this undertaking and it is projected that over 40,000 will be linked with the Center by 2010 (Easton Website). The projected tax revenue over 30 years is estimated at $1.5 billion (Blackford 1995). It has also brought many new retailers to the area and in this way helped to diversify the Columbus market. In fact, some shoppers even cite their inability to find certain stores anywhere else in the Columbus market as their primary draw to Easton.

Shoppers from all over Ohio, the Midwest, and beyond are now moving Easton higher up on their list of travel destinations. One Indianapolis resident and visitor to Easton said, "Easton just reminds me of the way shopping used to be – more about seeing people and less about buying things."[3] Another group of five women who were former roommates at Ohio State University take an annual shopping trip somewhere. Even though they now live all over the country they chose Easton as this year's destination. That puts Easton in such company as San Francisco which was their choice last year and Disney World which is their choice for next year (Gebolys 2001).

Easton exists in relationship to extant cathedrals of consumption, and its design can be read as a response to the failure of many of them to maintain the illusion of spectacle. Easton ups the ante on spectacle, as it were, at once overcoming the limitations of single cathedrals of consumption but at the same introducing new kinds of spectacle. We examine three elements of this spectacle. First, like many mega-malls and even landscapes of consumption that have preceded it, Easton collects numerous cathedrals of consumption in a single location thereby creating an atmosphere highly conducive to *hyperconsumption*. The collection of cathedrals of consumption is one of the appeals of Easton. As Sherry (1998b) has suggested in his analysis of the larger retail environment in which Nike Town Chicago (NTC) is located, the combined effect of such a collection of brand name outlets creates a synergy that cannot be created by any single cathedral of consumption. He calls Michigan Avenue (the "Boule Miche") a "canyon of consumption" and argues that the prestige and energy of this street "contribute to the immediacy of NTC's external presence" (119). Though Easton cannot be described as a canyon of consumption (indeed, as will be argued later, one of the appeals of Easton is that it underwhelms rather than overwhelms consumers), it is nevertheless the case that the combined presence of these single cathedrals of consumption fosters a heightened level of consumption. Though we borrow from Sherry the idea that a collection of cathedrals of consumption can create an effect larger than any of the single cathedrals, we are also aware that much of Sherry's analysis focuses on Nike Town, rather than the larger landscape of consumption of Michigan Avenue of which it is a part.

A second aspect is that Easton combines indoor and outdoor spectacle. Many cathedrals of consumption have utilized both naturalistic and urban themes to create spectacle. Designers bring the outdoors inside, unite it under a common theme, and thereby generate great energy and attachment to the space. Kozinets *et al.* (2002), though using the term differently than we are here, identify "landscape" themes as one of the four common techniques used by brand stores to attract consumers. These cathedrals of consumption mimic an outdoor environment through associations with "nature, Earth, animals and the physical body" (2002: 19). Examples of these kinds of places include Bass Pro Shops, which feature indoor stocked fishing pools, and REI (Recreational Equipment Incorporated) outlets, which feature artificial rock-climbing walls, and, in France, the outdoor store Nature & Découvertes (Hetzel 1996). Similarly, large malls such as the Mall of America simulate urban settings using park benches, stylized handrailings, and urban facades. In these instances, the spectacle resides in the hyperreal quality of the interior landscapes (Baudrillard 1983).

But there are also limits to this simulation. As with all spectacles, the continuing appeal of phantasmagoria depends upon maintaining a quality of newness, as well as the spectacle's perceived distance from the mundane realities of everyday life. So that spectacle does not become an instance of "more of the same," and thereby indistinguishable from everyday life, cathedrals of consumption routinely change and update the "spectacle" (this is one explanation for the continual transformation of mega-malls, strip malls, and suburban big box stores). In this regard, Easton is understood as yet another move in the effort to extend the spectacle once contained within single cathedrals of consumption. This is a consumption space that allows people to move from the phantasmagoria produced inside particular shopping and entertainment complexes to the natural phantasmagoria of the outdoors. In this respect, the limits to the size of indoor spectacle are overcome as cathedrals of consumption intermingle with the natural expanse of the surrounding land and overhead sky, and shopping is returned to its "natural" environs. At the same time, anticipating our third aspect of the simulation, this appeal to the outdoors dovetails with images of shopping from previous eras. If single cathedrals of consumption brought the outdoors inside, then Easton also brings the indoors outside, and into the past.

Easton also seeks to underwhelm rather than simply to overwhelm the visitor with size. The idea is to make the space seem manageable. The streets are small and easy to walk (indeed the space is constructed with an emphasis on pedestrian as opposed to vehicular mobility), the building heights are limited to two stories (with the exception of the central Easton Station) and the store ceiling heights are restricted to about 13 feet. The designers of Easton write that: "Cobblestone brick streets, stylized lighting and telephone booths combine with many other carefully planned architectural elements to create a 'sense of place' – the feeling that this is a distinct, memorable environment." The big box stores (e.g. Target, Wal-Mart, Best Buy), restaurants with drive-thrus, and parking lots are located on the periphery in order not to interfere with the small town feel.

In some ways, this aspect of Easton resembles a time in America before the widespread development of suburban malls and big box stores, when shops lined the streets of, for example, downtown areas (for more on this, see Cohen 2003). Even recently, through processes of gentrification and urban restoration, outdoor shopping districts are experiencing a revival, replacing (or at least existing alongside) the mall and the big box store as central means of consumption (see for example Zukin's [1991] discussion of downtown New York). Nevertheless, Easton is different from these urban spaces. For one, Easton is not actually a neighborhood or a town, but instead was designed to *simulate* a town. Furthermore, unlike previous outdoor shopping environments, Easton's shops are not indigenous, local establishments, but rather they are brand name stores with national and international reputations. Although many of the stores in Easton are not as large and spectacular as stores found in mega-malls (but certainly some are), at least some of them strive to simulate alternative realities. For example, "the McDonald's built its restaurant in the style of its 1950s hamburger joints, and there is also an old-time ice cream shop" (Mander 2001). Not only do each of the individual shops, eating establishments, and entertainment areas offer a kind of simulation and spectacle, but they are all united under a common set of themes: nostalgia for the American small town of the 1950s.

This is the third sense in which Easton provides spectacle. Easton operates as a kind of retroscape by simulating the atmosphere of 1950s small-town America. The president of the design and development company that took the lead in creating Easton said "I look at it as this Norman Rockwell middle American hometown vernacular" (ibid.). This kind of manipulation of time in space is, of course, a technique that has been practiced by marketers for many years, though not in the unique combination that is found in Easton Town Center. Many large malls such as the Mall of America feature shopping areas dedicated to the theme of Main Street USA, which evoke "the ideology of pedestrian, city life" (Gottdiener 1998: 40). Arnold *et al.* (2001) have shown that Wal-Mart attempted to overcome its image as a community-destroying monolith by presenting itself as an all-American, mainstreet America, organization. Nevertheless, in these examples, the nostalgia for past forms of life and the ideals of small-town America remain distant and distinct from everyday life. In the Mall of America, Main Street USA is indoors, a shopping destination at a clear distance from everyday life. And in the case of Wal-Mart, the Main Street USA image is a semiotic achievement, not embodied in a geographic main street. In this regard, Easton is unique because it not only offers shoppers and vacationers a short-term encounter with the past, but it also offers potential residents the possibility of revivifying the American dream of small-town community life.

Perhaps the most valuable attempt undertaken by Easton to make itself more of a town is its attempt at recreating social events nostalgic of typical

American cities 50 years ago. For example, in the summer there are outdoor music concerts, art shows, and even a farmers' market. During the Christmas season there is a parade and a ceremony to light the town Christmas tree, horse-drawn carriages are available to take you all around the town (for a small fee of course), and carolers in period clothing roam the premises which are lit by over half a million white lights. These simulations of the past are furthered through institutions designed to promote an ethic of community. For example, Easton's management has set aside a community meeting room that is available free of charge for use by local groups. There is also a mobile "community booth" that can be used to give groups public exposure. Easton management supports a scholarship program for local high school students and a Change for Charities program that has, to date, donated over $160,000, a portion of the revenues generated by the parking meters and tickets, to area non-profits. Steiner + Associates said of the program, "The innovative concept of helping the local community via parking meters and parking tickets, truly reflects the vision of Easton Town Center . . . Even when a customer is dropping a quarter into a meter, that customer becomes part of the experience and makes a difference in the community" (Easton Website 2). We might say that these and other activities "brand" Easton as a small town that enables a certain kind of lifestyle – a desire for the past, a desire for community. Clearly, as O'Guinn and Muñiz point out in their chapter in this volume, the desire for community is alive and well in contemporary consumer society. Further, they demonstrate that consumers can be quite creative in realizing community through branded commodities. What we want to emphasize is that even as certain commodities, brands, and spectacular environments can become a source of meaning in contemporary life, these activities remain caught up in the web of rational techniques used to design places like Easton.

It is important to remember that, at least in its original design, despite its appearance as a small town, Easton is not a town designed around living. Rather, it is a town designed around consumption. The ambience of small-town America is therefore a marketing achievement rather than a product of residents and indigenous businesspersons. Nevertheless, as the interest in Easton has become apparent, apartments are beginning to appear with the probability of many more being built in the future. Thus, it not only looks like a town, but with the addition of these apartments, it is becoming a town! Developers are currently building 800 apartments in addition to the approximately 700 already constructed and have considered breaking ground on luxury condominiums. In fact, the developer now regrets not putting apartments among the shops (rather than making them a separate development) and his current project – Kansas City's Zona Rosa – will do just that with apartments placed in the center of the retail area (Ritter 2004). These apartments are not merely housing for the staff and salespersons in Easton, but are meant to appeal to those who would like to live in a place like Easton. One local resident said, "I would love to live out at Easton! It has just about everything you can think of and you don't have to go very far to get it." Though, in some respects Easton is becoming a place to live, it is also different from planned developments, such as Celebration, Florida and Kentlands, Maryland, that have been designed to resemble small towns, because the priority in Easton is on consumption and it is designed to reflect a town from a specific time period – the 1950s. Thus, the throwback to small-town America is co-mingled with the spectacle of hyperconsumption. Easton *both* simulates the small town life of an era gone by and is a site of hyperconsumption.

We suggest, then, that one of the central appeals of Easton is that it brings together activities of everyday life and community with opportunities promised in a consumer culture. Easton exemplifies a particular type of landscape that seeks to reproduce a kind of community that seems to have been lost in the midst of an increasingly ubiquitous consumer culture (Sklair 2002). Ironically, even as the rise of consumer culture has been vilified as one of the primary causes of the demise of idealized forms of community, Easton aims to reconcile community with the forces of hyperconsumption that are often blamed for its demise. This adds a new dynamic to the understanding of consumption settings, and as we argue in the following section, it introduces a set of contradictions that inform our speculations about their future.

Contradictions in the landscape of consumption

There are contradictions in cathedrals of consumption, and by extension in landscapes of consumption. On the one hand, they offer simulation and spectacle that enables people to live in realities that they are unlikely to encounter in everyday life. On the other hand, they are built on principles of rationality and control. The commodities that are sold in these places are mass-produced and the success of a product depends upon its extensive distribution and sale. In service of these aims, despite their spectacular and phantasmagoric appeal, cathedrals and landscapes of consumption are, at base, carefully designed environments that manipulate and control consumers in order to increase profitability. Furthermore, cathedrals of consumption continually change in order to keep up spectacle and to hide the rational structures that determine their form. In the previous section, we described some of the techniques that Easton – a landscape of consumption that encompasses a number of cathedrals of consumption – uses in order to overcome previous limitations. Most important is the fact that Easton simulates small-town America, and in a sense offers an alternative to the grand spectacles associated with the mega-malls and Las Vegas-style consumer settings. Nevertheless, Easton remains a rationally designed space, and as such it embodies contradictions and is vulnerable to the same weaknesses as characterized extant cathedrals of consumption. In this section we explore several contradictions within Easton that threaten both the continued appeal of its spectacle as well as the potential for community it attempts to recreate.

Unlike most towns that emerge in organic relationship with their environment and community, Easton Town Center was created as a landscape of consumption. In contrast to smaller neighborhoods in which shops and entertainment facilities emerged in response to residents' needs (see, for example, Oldenburg's *The Great*

Good Place in which he describes local taverns and cafes that were closely related to the needs of everyday life), in Easton the lay-out and design of the landscape is conceived as a totality with the ultimate aim of increasing profitability. That is, it was not, at least originally, a town in which people lived and that developed consumption sites in order to satisfy the needs of residents and/or those who came to town from the hinterlands to purchase needed goods and services. Indeed, there were no residents, at least at first. Rather, Easton Town Center was, and is, a landscape of consumption designed to be a "destination" for consumers. It is not a reorganization of an existing social space that struggles to integrate aspects of an existing geography with aspects of an emerging geography. Rather like malls, amusement parks, or even gated communities, Easton was constructed from the top-down, as it were, and in its very design was able to control for "resistance."

Precisely because Easton is a totally designed space, it is unable to reproduce the organic relationship that, at least in its idealized form, characterized those earlier times and places. Even as it appears to be a community that enables the warmth and freedom of earlier eras, it is grounded in what Hetzl has elsewhere called a near "totalitarian" logic of control (Hetzel 1996: 183). In this regard, even as Easton strives to distinguish itself as a unique locale, it still participates in more general processes of rationalization. James Scott (1998), in *Seeing Like a State*, though writing from another perspective, provides extensive historical evidence which shows that top-down community and urban design is always devastating to the people who live in these areas. He argues that communities are only able to thrive when there is a close relationship between the design of place and the practical knowledge acquired in everyday life. Thus, even as Easton strives to simulate the community atmosphere of small-town America, its very rationality threatens to destroy the kind of community-building efforts that it strives to simulate.

Recently, Ritzer (2004) has theorized the rationalization of society through the distinction between something and nothing. *Nothing* refers to "generally centrally conceived and controlled social forms that are comparatively devoid of distinctive substantive content" (xi). In contrast, *something* is a social form "that is generally indigenously conceived, controlled and, and comparatively rich in distinctive substantive content" (7). For example, the McDonald's Big Mac is an instance of nothing. Furthermore, the particular commodity – the Big Mac – is closely linked to other forms of nothing. The people who serve the Big Macs (non-persons), the way in which the Big Macs are served (non-services), and the restaurant in which they are served (a non-place), are all centrally conceived, controlled, and devoid of distinctive content. Indeed, social forms characterized by nothing are insidious because they link together a whole range of social activities, demanding that they conform to the principles of rational design and control. It is not only particular commodities that are emptied of distinctive content but also places, relationships, and all forms of human contact that are emptied of content. One of the reasons why the world of consumption is increasingly characterized by nothing is because nothing can be relatively easily reproduced and exported. In this respect, the spread of nothing is closely linked to cultural homogenization, and it becomes increasingly difficult for social forms characterized by something to maintain a foothold. As forms of nothing spread across the globe, cultures and communities previously distinct from one another come to resemble one another more and more closely. Most important for our discussion of Easton, and the landscapes of consumption more generally: To what extent is Easton an instance of nothing rather than an instance of something?

Of particular interest is the concept of non-place, because Easton is promoted as a unique setting that restores something to a world increasingly dominated by nothing. Indeed, as a landscape of consumption, the simulation of place is the fulcrum around which all other aspects of Easton revolve. The anthropologist Marc Augé (1995) argues that the contemporary world is increasingly character-ized by "non-places." Augé's concept of non-place is developed in opposition to the kinds of places that were central to previous eras. These places were stable settings that symbolically embodied a continuous relationship to the past (monu-ments and architecture reminded community members of their position within a shared time), and allowed the formation of deep and meaningful relationships. More to the point, place emerged in an organic relationship with the surrounding environment, as groups of people regularly (through, for example, Durkheimian acts of collective effervescence) endowed their places with myths, stories, and the everyday practices that they held in common. In contrast, non-places are emptied out of historical content and meaning. They dis-embed persons from particular locales, cast them into an ever-changing symbolic universe and lead to the forma-tion of ego-centered individualism. Furthermore, Augé argues that in response to the proliferation of non-places, our culture collectively struggles to fill these places up with memories, so that the present meaninglessness and emptiness of non-places is hidden from view.

Clearly, the designers of Easton have attempted to create a *place* that has the qualities of *something*, particularly that which is unique. In this regard, the appeal of Easton for consumers is not only that it offers consumer goods, but that, at least on the surface, it provides an experience of *something* in a world increasingly characterized by spectacular forms of *nothing*. It is not necessary to travel through other non-places (like airports, highways, and subway systems) to get there, espe-cially if one already lives in Easton. Furthermore, brand name retailers such as Lazarus, Express, and McDonald's have used Easton as a testing ground for innovations in their retail strategies, content, and layouts. Centrally, the appeal of Easton resides in its simulation of small-town America from the 1950s – one that evokes rich imagery of a particular place and substance. Through its resemblance to small-town America Easton acquires, if only on the surface, the ability to conjure up the fantasy of *something*. Of course, this should not be understood as a "real" return to small-town America. Rather, as Augé leads us to believe, Easton's simulation of the American past is symptomatic of the kind of emptiness that pervades all non-places. The non-places, by virtue of their emptiness, call out for people to fill their spaces with memories and symbols of substance. Here nostalgia for the past combats postmodern dislocation, by offering a space that seems continuous with times in which place actually was central to everyday life. As such, even as Easton aims to distinguish itself from other consumption settings and other types of non-places that proliferate in the present world, it is still, at base, a rationalized space. It is not endowed with meanings and histories shared by members of a community. Rather, the meanings contained in this space are generated by the designers of Easton and the many brand name retailers it encompasses.

The non-place of Easton is connected to, and indeed constitutive of, other forms of nothing. Non-things are sold everywhere in Easton. The products offered in most Easton stores are not indigenous creations, but rather they come from the same template as products and commodities sold in innumerable other locations across America and around the world. Non-services exist throughout Easton in its ATMs, restaurants, and fast-food establishments. Finally, there are many non-people in Easton. A non-person is someone "who does not interact with others as a person, and perhaps more importantly is not treated by others as a person" (Ritzer 2004: 59–60). Non-personhood often emerges in the context of non-places, non-services, and non-things. These "nullities" promote behavior that is scripted and inattentive to the particularities of others. Certainly, there are plenty of scripted encounters and engagements with non-persons in the shops and entertainment centers of Easton – despite the claim that Easton is like small-town America in which it is implied, at least, that everyone knows everyone else. In this, Easton is not necessarily different from the other cathedrals and landscapes of consumption in which non-services and non-people reign. But more intriguing is the possibility that the *residents* of Easton increasingly become non-persons, especially when they are out and about in the town. If Easton is primarily a non-place, essentially lacking in the kind of spaces that promote substantial relationships between persons, then it seems likely that the people who live in these places will by necessity come to develop the characteristics of non-personhood that pervade non-places. Constantly surrounded by cathedrals of consumption, it is possible that residents of Easton would take on many of the qualities of Disney "cast members."

Why, then, do consumers come to visit, and, in some cases, live in these emptied-out non-places? One reason is the ubiquity of nothing in the contemporary world. In a society increasingly dominated by principles of McDonaldization, Americanization, and other forms of capitalist expansion, forms of nothing dominate the landscape. Although some groups have sought to create communities of meaning that exist at a distance from the consumer culture (Kozinets 2002), it becomes increasingly difficult for consumers to find alternatives to nothing. Consumers have little to choose from, and when pressed, are likely to seek out places that at least appear to be something. There is another reason why people are attracted to non-places. As Ritzer (2004) has argued elsewhere, despite their lack of distinct and meaningful content, non-places (and instances of nothing more generally) can often come to have great meaning for people. Indeed, because they are empty, the various forms of nothing make it easier to take "various actions to change them so that they can be more laden with content, and therefore meaningful" (154). For example, despite its basic form, a pair of blue jeans can be decorated and designed to reflect the interest and desires of any single person. Similarly, non-places are popular because they are empty and readily filled with diverse fantasies and meanings. They can, as in the case of Easton, become repositories of memory, or in other instances new kinds of meaning can be laid over the same framework. In this respect, a non-place like Easton offers a rich set of opportunities for people to restore a kind of meaning to their lives, once supplied by stable, organic communities. This doesn't change the fact, however, that non-places are still rationalized settings rife with contradictions. It only helps us to understand the general attraction of these non-places.

There is one last contradiction that interests us. As a general rule, cathedrals of consumption are able to maintain their spectacular appeal – keep up the simulation, as it were – precisely because they remain at a distance from everyday life. Cathedrals of consumption are successful because they provide an escape from everyday reality by offering the opportunity to imagine worlds and participate in fantasies that cannot be had outside of these spectacular settings. Indeed, when cathedrals of consumption get too close to everyday life, become too familiar and mundane, they quickly lose their appeal and are forced to update and change or go extinct. In this, the cathedrals of consumption embody a more general logic of consumer culture that is based on novelty and the constant reinvention of desire. Indeed, the greatest spectacles of our time are the vacation spots, such as Disney World and Las Vegas, that most people can only afford to visit once, or a few times, in their lives. Furthermore, because these cathedrals of consumption remain at a distance from everyday life, the underlying rationality and sheer manipulativeness of these places are more likely to remain hidden from consumers. People who work as "cast members" and employees in these fantastic settings, however, quickly become disenchanted with them (Ritzer 2005). They come to see that despite the magic on the surface, these kinds of spectacle and simulation depend upon rational systems that are largely devoid of meaningful content. The regular visitor to a cathedral or landscape of consumption, let alone one who lives there, is prone to a similar type of disenchantment.

Easton, as another attempt to create spectacle and attract consumers, is vulnerable to these weaknesses. The contradictions embedded in previous cathedrals of consumption are exacerbated by the fact that even though it was initially designed as a consumption setting, Easton has also become a place in which people live. Granted, at present, Easton relies much more on "out-of-town" visitors than it does local residences for profits. However, the developers have noted that they aim to experiment further with these kind of residential-entertainment communities, thereby implying the importance of attracting people to live within such town centers. In another sense, it is important for Easton to maintain residences if it is to retain its image as a small-town community. While Easton, no doubt, heavily relies upon its landscape to simulate small-town America, the presence of residences as physical structures, regardless of the people who actually inhabit them, contributes to the general atmosphere and feeling that this is a "real" town. This will become especially important in future projects that aim to more fully integrate apartments into the consumption setting. However, precisely because people live in Easton and regularly participate in its simulated reality, they are more likely to see through it (particularly its rationality) and to become bored with it. This places even greater pressure on this kind of landscape of consumption to change and continually introduce new kinds of spectacle. Since Easton is relatively new, this has not yet led to a major revamping of the landscape. However, there is evidence that the management team is oriented to introducing constantly new kinds of spectacle into Easton. At its website, it offers a regular update of the new brand name stores that will move into the Center. If our argument is correct, this will be a never-ending process. In order to keeps itself "fresh," Easton will be forced to introduce continually new elements of spectacle. The question is whether Easton, like other cathedrals of consumption, will reach a limit in its ability to up the ante on spectacle, and still hide the contradiction that resides in this process. By continually providing new forms of spectacle, the simulation of small-town America, premised on stability and comfort, is potentially undermined, and the rationalizing impulse at the base of Easton revealed. In this context, Easton will be seen as just another spectacle – just another simulation – and rather than shopping, dining, and seeking entertainment in Easton Town Center, residents and visitors will seek out new settings and new kinds spectacle that offer what they perceive to be a greater promise of happiness and the "good" life.

Acknowledgments

The authors would like to thank the editors of this volume for their careful reading of and feedback on an earlier version of this chapter. Also, thanks to reviewers Ray Oldenburg, Robert Kozinets, and Patrick Hetzl for helpful commentary on the piece.

Notes

1   The specific time period of the attempted re-creation is of important emphasis. It is not a contemporary small town that Easton wishes to simulate. In fact, the lived reality of many of the visitors to Easton is that of one of the many neighboring small towns. Instead, Easton strives to re-create a town from a particular time period – the 1950s – and fill it with the most contemporary alternatives for hyperconsumption.
2   There are numerous kinds of landscapes of consumption, which while sharing general definitional similarities, also embody different characteristics. The most striking distinction is that these other landscapes were not originally designed with the sole purpose of being landscapes of consumption. Pigeon Forge, Tennessee, the landscape around the Duomo in Milan, Italy, and Branson, Missouri, for example, were all initially residential landscapes.
3   Interviews conducted by Michael Ryan on site at Easton Town Center.

References

Arnold, S., Kozinets, R., and Handelman, J. (2001) "Hometown ideology and retailer legitimation: The institutional semiotics of Wal-Mart flyers," *Journal of Retailing* 77(2): 243–271.

Augé, M. (1995) *Non-places: An Introduction to an Anthropology of Supermodernity* (trans. J. Howe), New York: Verso.

Baudrillard, J. (1983) *Simulations* (trans. P. Foss, P. Patton and P. Beitchman), New York: Semiotext(e).

Benjamin, W. (1999) *The Arcades Project*, Cambridge, MA: Harvard University Press.

Blackford, D. (1995) "Wexner has vision for Northeast," *The Columbus Dispatch*, March 5.

Brown, S. and Sherry, J. Jr (2003) *Time, Space, and the Market: Retroscapes Rising*, London: M. E. Sharpe.

Cohen, L. (2003) *A Consumers' Republic: The Politics of Mass Consumption in Postwar America*, New York: Alfred A. Knopf.

Easton Website (2004) Easton Town Center, <http://www.eastontowncenter.com>, accessed July 13.

Easton Website 2 (2004) "Easton town center announces 2003 beneficiaries of change for charity program," <http://www.eastontowncenter.com/news/change2003.cfm>, accessed July 13.

Foucault, M. (1986) "Of other spaces," *Diacritics* 16(1): 22–27.

Gebolys, D. (2001) "Packing 'em in," *The Columbus Dispatch*, December 9: 01E.

Goodman, D. and Cohen, M. (2004) *Consumer Culture*, Santa Barbara, CA: ABC-CLIO.

Gottdiener, M. (1998) "The semiotics of consumer spaces: The growing importance of themed environments," in J. Sherry Jr (ed.) *Servicescapes: The Concept of Place in Contemporary Markets*, Chicago, IL: NTC Business Books: 29–54.

Halbwachs, M. (1992) *On Collective Memory* (trans. L. Coser), Chicago, IL: University of Chicago Press.

Hetzel, P. (1996) "The fall and rise of marketing fundamentalism: The case of the 'Nature & Découvertes' distribution concept," in S. Brown, J. Bell and D. Carson (eds) *Marketing Apocalypse: Eschatology, Escapology and the Illusion of the End*, London: Routledge: 171–188.

Kozinets, R. (2002) "Can consumers escape the market? Emancipatory illuminations from burning man," *Journal of Consumer Research* 29: 20–38.

Kozinets, R., Sherry, J. Jr., DeBerry-Spencel, B., Duhachek, A., Nuttavuthisit, K., and Storm, D. (2002) "Themed flagship brand stores in the new millennium: Theory, practice, prospects," *Journal of Retailing* 78(1): 17–29.

Lefebvre, H. (1991) *The Production of Space* (trans. D. Nicholson-Smith), Oxford: Blackwell.

Mander, E. (2001) "Columbus discovers streetscape concept," *Shopping Centers Today*, October, <http://www.icsc.org/srch/sct/current/sct1001/page1c.html>, accessed July 13.

Mick, D., Burroughs, J., Hetzl, P., and Brannen, M. (2004) "Pursuing the meaning of meaning in the commercial world: An international review of marketing and customer research founded on semiotics," *Semiotica* 152(1/4): 1–74.

Middleton, D. and Edwards, D. (1990) *Collective Remembering*, London: Sage.

Miller, M. (1981) *The Bon Marché: Bourgeois Culture and the Department Store, 1869–1920*. Princeton, NJ: Princeton University Press.

Oldenburg, R. (1987) *The Great Good Place*, New York: Paragon.

Palmieri, J. (2003) "Is this the future of retail?" *Retail Strategies*, May 12.

Ritter, I. (2004) "Newer urbanism: Yaromir Steiner's Zona Rosa opens in Kansas City next month," *Shopping Centers Today* April, <http://www.icsc.org/srch/sct/sct0404/page15.html>, accessed July 13.

Ritzer, G. (2004) *The Globalization of Nothing*, Thousand Oaks, CA: Pine Forge Press.

Ritzer, G. (2005) *Enchanting a Disenchanted World: Revolutionizing the Means of Consumption*, 2nd edn, Thousand Oaks, CA: Pine Forge Press.

Ritzer, G., Goodman, D., and Wiedenhoft, W. (2001) "Theories of consumption," in G. Ritzer and B. Smart (eds) *Handbook of Social Theory*, Thousand Oaks, CA: Sage: 410–427.

Sandikci, O. and Holt, D. (1998) "Malling society: Mall consumption practices and the future of public space," in J. F. Sherry Jr (ed.) *Servicescapes: The Concept of Place in Contemporary Markets*, Chicago, IL: NTC Business Books: 305–336.

Scott, J. (1998) *Seeing Like a State: How Certain Schemes to Improve the Human Condition Have Failed*. New Haven, CT: Yale University Press.

Sherry, J. F., Jr (1998a) *Servicescapes: The Concept of Place in Contemporary Markets*, Chicago, IL: NTC Business Books.

Sherry, J. F., Jr (1998b) "The soul of the company store: Nike town Chicago and the emplaced brandscape," in J. F. Sherry Jr (ed.) *Servicescapes: The Concept of Place in Contemporary Markets*. Chicago, IL: NTC Business Books: 109–146.

Shopping Center World (2003) "Developers' expansion plans," *Shopping Center World*, April 1: 4.

Sklair, L. (2002) *Globalization: Capitalism and Its Alternatives*, Oxford: Oxford University Press.

Slater, D. (1997) *Consumer Culture and Modernity*, Cambridge: Polity Press.

Soja, E. (1989) *Postmodern Geographies: The Reassertion of Space in Social Theory*, New York: Verso.

Soja, E. (1996) *Thirdspace: Journeys to Los Angeles and Other Real-and-Imagined Places*, Cambridge, MA: Blackwell.

Steiner + Associates Website (2004) <http://www.steiner.com/portfolio/eastontowncenter%5Cphototour/phototour.cfm>, accessed July 13.

Williams, R. (1982) *Dream Worlds: Mass Consumption in Late Nineteenth-Century France*, Berkeley, CA: University of California Press.

Zerubavel, E. (1996) "Social memories: Steps to a sociology of the past," *Qualitative Sociology* 19(3): 283–299.

Zukin, S. (1991) *Landscapes of Power: From Detroit to Disney World*, Berkeley, CA: University of California Press.

16 Star gazing

The mythology and commodification of Vincent van Gogh

Gary J. Bamossy

> People say that what we're all seeking is a meaning for life. I don't think that's what we're really seeking. I think that what we're seeking is an experience of being alive, so that our life experiences on the purely physical plane will have resonances within our own innermost being and reality, so that we actually feel the rapture of being alive.
>
> (Joseph Campbell, *The Power of Myth*, 1988)

Vincent van Gogh exemplifies personalization of artistic greatness. His work was made into an enigma; his life into a legend; his relative poverty, misery, self-mutilation, and suicide into a scandal. The places he went and the objects he touched have become relics; his paintings have sold at record prices in auction and are exhibited in the global spotlight (Heinich 1996). During the twentieth century he has been cast as a misunderstood genius, *peintre maudit*, paradigm of the modern artist, saint, martyr, hero, an enduring and evolving icon of popular culture, an artist who sold only one painting during his lifetime, and the painter whose work by the end of the twentieth century fetched the highest prices ever paid for art. Admirers travel the world to see authentic works of van Gogh; pilgrims pay homage at his gravesite, and visitors go to the van Gogh Museum to say they've "been there," signaling their arrival and passage in the form of mailed postcards. Some come to the museum for 30 minutes, while others stay the entire day.

While there is nothing incongruous about calling van Gogh a genius, calling him a saint, a hero, or a powerful icon of popular culture entails myth-making. Campbell describes myths[1] as "the stories of our search through the ages for truth, for meaning, for significance. We all need to tell our story and to understand our story ... we need for life to signify, to touch the eternal, to understand the mysterious, to find out who we are" (Campbell 1988: 5). Similar to the processes described by Holt (this volume) as to how societies come to produce and consume the mythical qualities related to highly desirable brands, the life and work of van Gogh has undergone a process of recounting, reinterpretation, and blending of fact and lore by a diverse group of story-tellers. This chapter explores these heterogeneous systems of myth-building, contextualizing the many acts of consumption that we create, sustain, experience, buy, and buy into, and in doing so, perpetuate and celebrate the myths of Vincent's life.

Why does Vincent van Gogh serve as such a powerful conduit, satisfying our needs for both believing and consuming myths? There are clear examples of contemporary artists, such as Andy Warhol and Pablo Picasso, who have made very effective use of public relations and mass media in order to shape and frame their image and fame as artists and celebrities. Public recognition for an artist in van Gogh's time was much more likely to come from third parties: art critics publishing in influential magazines and newspapers, or from the sale of an artist's work in commercial auction often organized by an art dealer. As an artist, Warhol consciously chose celebrity subjects – from Campbell's soup and Coca-Cola to Marilyn Monroe – to represent his pop-culture "comments on America." As a person and celebrity, Warhol was a masterful *producer* of cultural discourse (see Schroeder 1997). In stark contrast, van Gogh's paintings *became* the objects of pop cultural discourses, and his life *became* the subject matter of both scholarly and (pop) cultural discourses. Vincent van Gogh is a myth of substance, and it will be argued in this chapter that the myth is just as important to consumers as are his paintings.

The systems of producing Vincent's myths

Vincent's suicide in France on July 29, 1890, was followed six months later by the death of his brother, agent, and life-long supporter, Theo, in a mental asylum in Holland. Theo's death left the task of introducing van Gogh's oeuvre to Theo's widow, Johanna. But others – painters, critics, song-writers, novelists, film directors, actors, forgers, art historians, psychiatrists, collectors, patrons, pilgrims, curators, and art dealers – have been instrumental in creating the myths surrounding van Gogh. These various discourses not only *create* knowledge about Vincent's life and works, they also become the *reality* they appear to describe. Even when scholars correct "errors" in Vincent's biography, they are often just challenging an outmoded myth, only to create a new one in its place. This chapter shows how the mythical images of Vincent van Gogh have developed over time. Developing a critical assessment of the various discourses of his life helps to highlight the ongoing myth-making process, and the ways in which these discourses convey meaning to the consumer and to the consumed (Costa 1998; Hulsker 1985).

Heinich (1996) traces the chronological developments and intellectual discourses of van Gogh as a hero and mythical figure, highlighting what they are made of in contrast to "average men," and describing the nature and content of the average man's admiration for the hero. Herein lies the starting point for tracing and understanding the development of van Gogh's reputation as an artist, as well as his eventual multiple personae of genius, saint, madman, pop icon, and co-opted endorser for products, services, and kitsch.

Art reviews of van Gogh's style, and the establishment of new critical criteria

Critical reviews regarding van Gogh's work primarily began after his suicide, although "Vincent" received his public patronym in the first favorable article published during his lifetime – a review of select paintings shown in an exhibition during the final year of his life (Aurier 1890). In letters subsequent to the exhibit and review, Vincent wrote to his brother Theo, and to the author Aurier, describing his great unease with the review, and his desire not to be spoken of or written about (*Letters of Vincent van Gogh to His Brother Theo*, 629, 20 April, 1890 III). Seizing on this, later art critics, scholars, and biographers interpreted Vincent's response as a personal objection to the perceived false values associated with fame and renown. With this, the making of the myth of the man and painter was well underway by the late 1890s.

Ironically, Aurier's favorable review of van Gogh was of more immediate benefit to Aurier's own career as an art critic than to van Gogh's as a painter. First, Aurier chose an artist characterized by the unique and innovative qualities of his work, rather than by respect for the common values of the academy that were most accessible to non-specialists. Second, Aurier focused less on the subject or referent of the paintings, and more on the signifier, illustrated by comments such as "investigations of a most curious order, sometimes, but not always great style." Aurier's review thereby broke from the standard criteria of criticism and established him as Paris' leading writer of aesthetic avant-gardism (Heinich 1996: 13). Others followed suit throughout the 1890s, describing Vincent as an "instinctive, rare genius, tormented spirit, gifted with a power of expression that is extraordinary, one who 'glimpses objects within nature but only really sees them within himself' . . . a harmonious strangeness in which line and color unite" (Leclerq 1890); having "magnificent sincerity, colorist's temperament to render the excesses of nature" (Retté 1894). Importantly, publication of a work of aesthetics in which van Gogh's name appears for the first time next to those of established artists, such as Moreau, Redon, Gauguin, and Cézanne also occurs (Mellerio 1896).

Throughout the last decade of the nineteenth century, reviews by art critics, as well as memoirs by other artists (notably Émile Bernard 1893; Paul Gauguin 1894), began to establish the theme of van Gogh as a genius. During this period, his brilliance as a painter is closely linked to his presumed madness as a person. This is important, in that during this period in Europe, madness allowed for an affirmation of deviance; instead of branding van Gogh with the stigma of incoherence, his deviance, in his paintings and his life, caused him to be celebrated as an exceptional figure. Art critics began using new criteria and adjectives to assess van Gogh – excess, personality, subjectivity, originality, madness, mystery, and marginality – and to distinguish him from generally accepted criteria of what it was to be an artist and painter at that time. Interestingly, several of these images/dimensions of madness, excessiveness, and marginality regarding van Gogh reappear as pop cultural objects (postcards, posters) in the postmodern market place of the late twentieth century.[2] The construction and subsequent glorification of van Gogh as an artist and as a unique man of great frailty *and* strength establishes his singularity, and crowns this decade of commentaries among French critics (Heinich 1996; Zemel 1980). This discourse among art critics and fellow artists opens a hermeneutic space, a universe of systems of interpretation within which van Gogh's name has been taken up in such diverse disciplines as psychology, psychiatry, aesthetics, history, and medicine. With such a broad array of contributing scholars, the myths grew exponentially, and eventually spread from a small circle of experts to the larger public.

Scholars: between truth and myth

The sheer amount of academic literature written about van Gogh the painter, and Vincent the man, confirms his uniqueness.[3] Trails of theoretical and empirical work from a wide range of disciplines have represented, misrepresented, and mythologized Vincent since the early part of the twentieth century. For example, psychiatrists, psychologists, and anthropologists have been concerned with both Vincent's deviance and his singularity; scholars of religious history have used metaphors to describe his sacrifices and rise to greatness; and sociologists of religion have developed accounts regarding the creation of van Gogh relics, and have drawn parallels between pilgrimages to van Gogh sites and journeys that trace the paths of Jesus' life. Art historians and theorists have examined the dynamics of auctions and the continuously rising prices of van Gogh's paintings, debating and occasionally lamenting the value of his work, relative to the value attributed *to* the work. Critical theorists in economics and sociology have also examined the prices paid and argued that the ceilings are imposed by the buyer's financial resources rather than the presumed value of the art. Thus, successfully outbidding rival bidders on a live, televised auction demonstrates both an interest in van Gogh's work and the financial superiority of the winner while competing on a global stage amongst the super-rich. Van Gogh's poignant *Irises*, which sold in auction for $53.9 million in 1987, serves not only as a representation of the lonely artist, but as an icon of how much people are willing to pay for his paintings.

Invariably, with so much written about van Gogh, inaccuracies will occur. Subjective accounts, rumors, speculation, and simple misunderstandings have acquired the authority of fact in the academic literature on the painter. Once in the public domain, even incorrect information provides a basis for myth. In these cases, myths are woven not from established facts, but from information that seems reasonably probable, or at least not improbable. By the same token, newly discovered facts may be rejected if they prove to be incompatible with the prevailing images, or if they do not appeal to the public at a given time. In this way, the body of "knowledge" about van Gogh may be likened to Foucault's (1970) "discourse" or perhaps Kuhn's (1962) "paradigm."

As one example, van Gogh's sister-in-law, Elisabeth du Quesne van-Gogh, published her (German language) *Personal Recollections of van Gogh* in 1910. In this book, she argued that the beginning of Vincent's road to insanity began in his late teens, when Ursula Loyer, daughter of van Gogh's landlady during his brief employment in London, rejected Vincent's expression of love. Numerous French scholars picked up this anecdotal story some years later; the debate centered on the nuances of various French words and expressions attributed to Vincent in letters to his family describing the rebuff. Throughout 40 years of scholarly debate regarding Vincent's adolescent love crisis as the starting point of his psychosis, no one seems to have acknowledged the likelihood of translation errors. French scholars debated meanings based on fourth-generation translations from Dutch to German to English and finally to French. Notably, van Gogh did not speak or write French during his early life (Hulsker 1993).

In a different instance also stemming from du Quesne's biography, myths about van Gogh arose among the Japanese, depicting him as a virtuous man who disdained commerce and business. Du Quesne indicated that Vincent was dismissed from his position as an apprentice to an art dealer in The Hague for declaring in public that commerce was the pursuit of gain and thus ultimately tantamount to theft. This anecdote was repeated in a series of subsequent academic publications. Eventually, the story was embellished, and Vincent was quoted as saying "organized theft," then "business is greed, and greed is incessant theft" (Shūji 1993: 156). Shūji goes on to say that as a result, he was dismissed from his position. These misquoted elaborations struck a deep chord with the Shirakaba group, Japan's intelligentsia of the early 1900s. In spite of the fact that van Gogh was desperate to sell his paintings during his own life time, the myth of van Gogh as a suffering artist who had contempt for commerce and business was well established in Japan. Japanese were among the first pilgrims to make the long journey to van Gogh's burial place in France, and Japanese art collectors later propelled van Gogh into the international spotlight as a result of record auction prices paid for his paintings.

While both of these scholarly examples are relatively minor misrepresentations, they point to ways in which enduring myths of Vincent – aspects of his madness, his suffering artist persona, and a disdain for commercial enterprise – are generated. The scholarly work of authoritative "experts" continues to influence both the number and content of myths that arise from the popular press, and from film and other mass media. When conjecture, fallacy, and fabrication are perpetuated often enough by successive authors, they eventually acquire a ring of truth.

As a hero of biography and fiction

In September 1891, the painter Émile Bernard offered the first genuine biographical account of van Gogh's career and life (Bernard 1891). In this brief article, and in a longer subsequent article (1893), Bernard brings his friend van Gogh back to life with physical ("red-headed . . . an eagle look and an incisive mouth"), as well as spiritual ("excessive in everything, vehement") descriptions. These two biographies served to introduce van Gogh's personal history to a general audience. Including a copy of one of Vincent's self-portraits, Bernard's 1883 publication served to ensure that Vincent's face, his works, and his personality were no longer recognized by just a small circle of art connoisseurs, but became known to a broader public. A memoir by the artist Paul Gauguin (1894), who was at the center of the incident in which Vincent severed his ear, also provided a first-person biographical accounting of Vincent's life. While some notable and critically regarded biographers of van Gogh did not know Vincent personally (see the collective works of Jan Hulsker), it is nevertheless easily argued that legends and myths about van Gogh have spread in part through numerous and conjectural biographies. Pabst and Nagahiro (1993) compiled a bibliography of literature inspired by van Gogh, and developed categories of poetry, biographical novels, short stories, drama, fiction, literary reviews, and essays. More than 440 entries include literature in every major language in the world, as well as dozens of minor languages. Irving Stone's (1934) *Lust for Life*, a highly fictionalized novel on van Gogh's life and work, has sold millions of copies, in 39 different languages.[4] However, many other authors have tried to correct the modern misconceptions and myths about van Gogh. For example, as director of the van Gogh Museum, John Leighton fielded many questions pertaining to which painting van Gogh was working on at the time he committed suicide. Eventually, Leighton (1999) wrote a book to correct the popular misconception that it was *Wheatfield with Crows, 1890*.

Illness and madness

Although some authors have been influenced by and have accurately represented material in van Gogh's letters, many more have produced fictionalized biographies, using poetic license in their interpretation of information, for the purpose of filling in gaps. One influential study, and the origin of many of the views perpetuated by later biographers regarding van Gogh's character came from Doiteau and Leroy's (1928) book, *La Folie de van Gogh* (*Van Gogh's Insanity*). Both authors were medical doctors (Leroy was the director of the asylum in St Rémy, but long after the time when van Gogh voluntarily had himself committed there), and their book was based on articles which each had published earlier in medical journals. The book seems unfortunately titled, given that their conclusion is that van Gogh was actually sane. Their final diagnosis, most commonly accepted in medical circles today, was that van Gogh suffered from a latent epileptic form of psychosis. While the authors proclaimed that van Gogh was not insane, and was in fact witty and lucid, they also went on to indicate:

> The most conspicuous aspect of Vincent van Gogh's personality, a trait obvious even to a layman, is his irascibility, which in unquestionably pathological; he is never content with himself or his work, nor with anyone else . . . Vincent is also irritable, unsociable, and unstable. He has never been able to accept criticism, to agree with an opinion different from his own, or to take advice. Nor has he ever remained in one place for any length of time . . . Vincent is distrustful and suspicious.
>
> (Doiteau and Leroy 1928: 103, 111, 125)

No direct evidence is offered for this assessment, and the authors' tone and writing style suggests they had known van Gogh personally, although neither had ever met him.

While temporal lobe epilepsy is the most accepted diagnosis (Lubin 1996), physicians, psychiatrists, historians, and others have strongly fueled myths about Vincent by speculating on other possible illnesses, primarily based not on examining van Gogh himself, but on his letters and paintings, and medical records from the asylum in St Rémy. Van Dooren (1982) provides a thorough review of the various posthumous diagnoses: schizophrenia, manic depression, a wide variety of other psychogenic illnesses, neurosis, character aberrations, epilepsy, tumors, alcohol poisoning/addiction (absinthe), digitalis, turpentine, or paint (lead) poisoning, eye diseases, and Ménière's disease (a rare affliction of the ear).[5]

The diagnosis of Ménière's disease is a particularly striking example of modern myth-building. In 1990, the centenary year of van Gogh's death, a team of American specialists announced they had discovered the actual cause of van Gogh's physical and mental problems, and possibly his suicide. Claiming to have examined 796 letters written between 1884 and Vincent's suicide in 1890, the authors titled the article, published in the prestigious *Journal of the American Medical Association*, "van Gogh had Ménière's disease, and not epilepsy" (Kaufman *et al.* 1990). This diagnosis is all the more amazing, given that there are only 300 known letters by or about van Gogh during the period 1884–1890, while the total of all his known letters at the time of the *JAMA* publication was 652.[6] It was the *JAMA* authors' addition of the word *nausea* to the original letter written by Dr Peyron, van Gogh's asylum physician in 1889, which allowed them to make their diagnosis (Hulsker 1993; Peyron, 604F in de Leeuw 1996).

From scholars to biographers to doctors, the myths of van Gogh originated, multiplied, and metamorphosed into new versions of familiar themes. Based on Vincent's work and letters, his personality, his marginalized life as a painter, the severing of his ear, and his time in an asylum, Vincent's posthumous biography slowly transformed to hagiography, the system of learning that examines saints and their worship.

Pilgrimages and saintliness

Among the first group of pilgrims to pay homage to van Gogh the painter and Vincent the man was the Shirakaba group of Japan, starting around 1910. These Japanese intellectuals' enthusiasm for van Gogh was fired by their strong pro-European feeling and their cult of "self." The Shirakaba understanding of van Gogh was more about the man, and considerably less about his paintings. Based primarily on their reading of the first German biography of van Gogh, these Japanese saw Vincent as "a new type in the artistic poverty of our time: the artist who not only does not sell, but convinced of the futility of the effort, gives up any attempt and gains from this insight not bitterness, but on the contrary, pure joy" (J. Meier-Graefe, quoted in Zemel 1980: 116). This is an interesting conclusion, given the abundant evidence in Vincent's letters to his brother Theo that

Vincent was genuinely desperate to sell his paintings and to become less dependent on Theo's financial support.

Early on, these Japanese intellectuals were able to pay personal visits to Dr Gachet, van Gogh's somewhat eccentric physician in Auvers, and to JoAnna Bongers, Theo's widow and Vincent's sister-in-law. Dr Gachet tended to "hold court" for his visitors and acquired 26 of van Gogh's paintings in the 70 days that Vincent was in his care. Later, Gachet's son, Paul Gachet Jr, styled himself as an expert on the final months of van Gogh's life despite limited and sketchy contact with van Gogh – the artist committed suicide when Gachet Jr was only eight years old – and hosted many Japanese and European guests. Gachet Jr made his living primarily from exhibiting, selling, and ultimately donating many of the paintings his father had acquired. Clearly, Gachet Jr enjoyed a life as a professional van Gogh myth-maker.

Nagahiro (1993: 398) describes the motivations of early Japanese pilgrims to van Gogh's grave, focusing on the Japanese desire to see the "authentic":

> Japanese artists earnestly aspired to absorb and internalize the human qual-
> ities of van Gogh. Yet they felt slightly inadequate, knowing that they had
> only seen van Gogh's works in reproduction. This clash between pride and
> self doubt stemming from the knowledge that their convictions were based
> solely on reproductions, fostered a longing for "the real thing," which pervades
> the pilgrimages that the Japanese made through the world of van Gogh. . . .
> In short, it was the quest of the "real Vincent van Gogh" that the Japanese
> pilgrims made their journeys. The climax was invariably a visit to van Gogh's
> grave. . . . The act of visiting a grave in order to commune with the spirit
> buried there is essentially analogous to trying to understand an artist's inner
> being by studying reproductions of his work. The mind that has gained
> intimacy through reproductions tries to consolidate that mental act by paying
> respects at the grave . . . To this day, it is not so much a desire to understand
> his paintings as the hope of penetrating his very essence as a human being
> that defines the way the Japanese regard Vincent van Gogh.

While Nagahiro's descriptions of Japanese pilgrims capture the motivations of early Japanese visitors and provide a more general cultural sense of what it means to visit Auvers-sur-Oise, Nagahiro does not focus on the more recent role of the Japanese in van Gogh's auction prices, nor on the influences of pop culture on van Gogh's modern image in Japan. In the summer of 2001, I interviewed a number of Japanese and Asian visitors to Vincent's gravesite, generating a more current mix of the meaning of van Gogh to young Japanese consumers:

I: What brings you to Auvers-sur-Oise?

R_{jf}:   We are here for a few days, away from our tour group in Paris. We wanted to come and see the place of Mr van Gogh.

I: Why is that?

R_{jf}:   We have learned about Mr van Gogh in school, and admire his painting, especially his studies of Japanese prints. Uh, we know about him because of the high prices that have been paid for his paintings in our country. He is very well known to Japanese people for his expensive prices.

I: I'm sure you have noticed that there are no paintings of van Gogh here in Auvers. There are many of his paintings in the museums in Paris.

R$_{jf}$: Yes. We have seen those the other day. We are here to visit his grave, and to see this places [*sic*] where he walked and lived. Also, my boy friend [gestures to partner] has the same birthday.

R$_{jm}$: Yes. Eric Clapton.

I: Eric Clapton?

R$_{jf}$: Yes. Eric Clapton, Vincent van Gogh, and he [*gestures again to partner*] are all born on the same day, March 30.

The cemetery in Auvers is simple, unpretentious, well-kept, wears well the patina of time, and is small enough that no signage is necessary for tourists to find Vincent's and Theo's joint grave. During the tourist season, tourists and pilgrims form a small but steady flow. The tourists themselves provide the "signage" to point the way to the gravesite; their cameras and dress serve to distinguish them from the locals who also visit and care for graves. The Town Council of Auvers has made a conscious effort to erect signs within the small town center to guide the visitor along a pleasant route, up village stairs made famous by a van Gogh painting.[7] From there, tourists pass to the Auvers church, where another sign makes it clear that this is precisely the spot from which Vincent painted his masterpiece of the building. Down a dirt road another 100 meters, through well-manicured wheat fields, lies the cemetery. The beautiful wheat fields are no coincidence; they provide a planned "atmosphere-accessory" managed by the Town Council, offering reference and context to van Gogh's most famous paintings from his time in Auvers. Of all the offerings left on Vincent's grave by visitors, a shaft of wheat from the nearby field is by far the most common. These wheat sheaves contribute to the lore of the painting, and sustain the legend and myth of van Gogh. However, there are also more substantial offerings that pay homage to van Gogh and his life:

One evening at the restaurant I joined a Japanese gentleman who was finishing his meal. He spoke good English. And he seemed very tired. He just arrived in France in the same afternoon, from Japan. We spoke about the many tourists who come to Auvers, including Japanese tourists. He was pleased to hear that many Japanese come to my restaurant, and visit Vincent's room [which is upstairs from the dining area]. I noticed that he had a large urn on the floor, next to the chair where he was eating. I asked what is was, and he said it is the ashes of his friend; that his friend was cremated this past winter [2001], and that he had left this man money in his will to pay for his trip to Auvers. To carry out the wishes in the will, the man's task was to scatter his friend's ashes on van Gogh's grave, and in the wheat fields. I've seen many offerings of locks of hair, jewelry, tea sets, and pottery from the Japanese who come here, but these offerings are taken by the locals rather quickly. This is the first time I've seen ashes. I remember thinking that I hoped the Town Council did not see him doing this!

(Personal interview, D. C. Janssens, owner of Auberge Ravoux, June 2001)

Auvers' Mémoire des Lieux society is dedicated to identifying the motifs in Auvers painted by van Gogh, and to placing reproductions of his paintings in those places. Not only the objects that van Gogh touched and used (his pallets, letters, paint boxes, pencils, and possessions), but also the objects represented in his painting have become "relics." Both the Yellow House in Arles, as well as the Auberge Ravoux in Auvers, have been rebuilt or remodeled as replicas of the original buildings, thereby providing the visitor with the feeling of walking in a painting, or in history itself. These physical replicas and advisory signs indicating where he stood, and offering his exact perspective of the objects that he painted, are part of creating the cult of an idol, not unlike Christianity's Stations of the Cross. The town councils of Arles and Auvers, and entrepreneurs like Mr Janssens (a Proctor & Gamble marketing vice-president prior to his passionate "van Gogh career") serve to create and organize van Gogh shrines, providing consumers with opportunities to eat where Vincent ate, stand where Vincent stood, see the objects that Vincent saw, pay respects to the artist by visiting the very room in which he died in the arms of his brother Theo, and walk the funeral route to Vincent's and Theo's grave.

Thus, Auvers provides a locale where one can celebrate the actual life and the constructed myths of van Gogh. However, perhaps the most powerful impact on the modern myth-making of van Gogh comes from the films that portray his life. In Kurosawa's (1990) film *Dreams*, a man walks through an Arles landscape composed of oversized images of van Gogh's paintings. "What better expression of a painter's power than the creation of a fictional world that can later serve as a model for reality?" (Heinich 1996: 125). I turn now to a discussion of this powerful myth-maker, the film.

Film as myth-maker

While the previous sections have set out van Gogh as the ultimate signifier of discourses on artistic temperament and suffering, creativity, alienation, and post-mortem glorification, perhaps the greatest impact on myth-making of van Gogh comes from popular films. In the period from 1948 to 1990, 85 films and documentaries about van Gogh were produced, coinciding with the substantial and direct visual impact that stemmed from the growing popularity of cinema and television. The prominent list of cast members and directors, particularly from the Hollywood genre of van Gogh films, is impressive: directors Robert Altman (*Vincent and Theo* 1990), Akira Kurosawa (*Dreams* 1990), and Vincent Minnelli (*Lust for Life* 1956); actors Kirk Douglas as Vincent, and Anthony Quinn's supporting actor academy award winning role as Gauguin, and Martin Scorsese as Vincent in Kurosawa's fifth *Dream* sequence. *Lust for Life* is perhaps the most influential Hollywood film on van Gogh, and presents the major components of the legend and myths of Vincent as a suffering genius and mad artist, using powerful visual images and dramatic characters.

Vincent van Gogh shot himself with a small pistol on Sunday, July 27, 1890. He apparently aimed for his heart and missed, and died two days later from blood loss and untreated infection. (The manner of his death raised doubts about Dr Gachet's medical skills, and led to further myth-making regarding van Gogh's suffering.) Many films, Minnelli's *Lust for Life* in particular, represent the artist as shooting himself while painting *Wheatfield with Crows*. The painting portrays an ominous black sky, with two paths that diverge, ending pointlessly in the fields of wheat. Crows seem to harass the scene, and the artist. Psychiatrists have aggressively analyzed the symbolism of this setting, and have speculated that it represents the choice of life or death, van Gogh's delusions, or even schizophrenia.

While youth tend to garner their supply of van Gogh images and myths from many different sources, the impact of films is particularly important in understanding the ways in which van Gogh is appreciated and consumed, particularly among tourists and patrons who are middle-aged. This interview in 1997 with an American woman who was visiting the van Gogh Museum is illustrative:

I:	What is it that makes you interested in van Gogh, and brings you to the museum?
R_{af}:	Well, I remember seeing this wonderful film, "Lust for Life" starring Kirk Douglas. What a fascinating man! My husband is here [Amsterdam] for some work, so I've come to see the paintings of van Gogh. Did you see the movie?
I:	Yes. Kirk Douglas, and directed by Vincent Minnelli.
R_{af}:	Didn't you just love all the colors? And at the end of the film, I remember seeing the credits, where a lot of well-known Hollywood actors had donated their original van Gogh's for use in the movie.

This short transcript is indicative of the larger role of Hollywood films and televised images that motivate consumers to visit places, view objects, and connect to their visually mediated experiences. In several interviews at the van Gogh Museum, (primarily American) respondents discussed their impressions of the museum while simultaneously describing visits to the Eiffel Tower in Paris, Big Ben in London, or the leaning tower of Pisa. Bamossy *et al.* (1999) found that these visual destinations in Europe have their American counterparts, including, for example, the sign spelling out "Hollywood" resting in the hills overlooking the famous community, or the dramatic rock formations of Monument Valley, famous from Western films, particularly those directed by John Ford, and often depicted as the ideal backdrop to persuade Europeans to buy a 4×4 SUV. Films create emotional connections with places and objects, and many visitors to the van Gogh

Museum come there to connect with the places and objects they've seen in movies concerning van Gogh's life and work.

The commercial, the kitsch, and the postmodern: van Gogh, unincorporated

In the summer of 1990, the circus came to Amsterdam – not the two-week visit by *Circus Rens*, Europe's version of Ringling Bros/Barnum and Bailey Circus, but the van Gogh Centenary Exhibition, commemorating the 100th year of Vincent van Gogh's death on July 28, 1890. At Center Ring was the venerable van Gogh Museum, which houses the largest permanent collection of van Gogh's works and had, for this celebration, assembled many of the masterpieces that had been scattered around the world since his death. The centenary exhibit not only marked the passing of van Gogh, it also provided a perfect marketing opportunity for the museum, and for the city of Amsterdam. Museums may be viewed as societies' institutions for preserving and glorifying high art, but they are also organizations that stage blockbuster shows in an effort to develop and sustain financial resources (see Joy and Sherry 2003a for a provocative essay on the relationship between the art market and the art world).

The centennial drew over 1.3 million visitors, more attendance during the four months of summer than during an entire "normal" year. The exhibition was so successful that the museum's management required visitors to buy a ticket for a specific time slot as a method of crowd control. While the exhibit itself was clearly a celebration of Vincent's life and works, the festivities were not limited to art and objects produced by the museums and exhibited inside their walls displaying van Gogh's oeuvre. The exhibit's carnivalesque atmosphere spilled into the large and beautiful museum square (and its highly commercial "van Gogh Village"), into the city, and east across the country to the sleepy town of Otterlo, which houses the world's second largest collection of van Gogh's works.

A sacred institution such as a museum may represent "high culture," continuity, and the housing of cultural treasures, yet the van Gogh exhibit produced a cultural scene that could also be described in more postmodern terms as "one giant hyperreal amalgam which continually effaces modernist distinctions between fiction, fact, image, simulations, and the 'real' " (Thompson 2000: 123). The museum exhibit became a clear example of "a cultural (dis)order of fragmented, superficial signs and images whose only coherent linkage lies in their hyperstimu-lating ephemerality" (ibid.). Consider the following sideshows, which emerged and evolved over the course of the 1990 celebration:

- An explosion of van Gogh images on literally hundreds of (sometimes improbable) product and service offerings touted during the time frame of the exhibit. These images ranged from accurate representations of van Gogh's works linked to a product or retail outlet, to a variety of postmodern representations relating the persona of van Gogh as an object to his paintings or his life, also sometimes linked to a product or service.

- The intriguing atmosphere of black market and street auctioneering of (sometimes forged) tickets for a time slot to enter the museum, particularly during the busy summer months. This market often took place in the same Museum Square (*het museumplein*) where street performers (jugglers, fire-eaters, musicians, magicians, unicyclists/acrobats) plied their trade for the entertainment of tourists.

- The non-commercial celebrations surrounding the centenary exhibit: youth primarily from Europe and North America who designate the Museum Square as the "hip" place to meet; spontaneous musical performances (not for spare change), in particular the singing of Don McLean's "Vincent" ("Starry, Starry Night"); smoking of hash and marijuana in preparation for using one's "time-slot" ticket or as part of sharing personal experiences following (or instead of) the museum visit; showing/trading van Gogh postcards.

- A daily stream of frantic and ticketless tourists, pleading with the ticket-takers at the museum entrance to allow them access to the museum gift shop so they could purchase gifts and postcards. When told by the ticket-takers that one could purchase postcards and van Gogh souvenirs from literally hundreds of kiosks and shops near the museum and throughout the city, a typical response was "But I want to say that I purchased them (cards) from the van Gogh museum."

The centenary exhibit provided a highly focused venue and a set of time constraints for the celebration of van Gogh, yet the creation and sustaining of the many images and myths concerning Vincent is hardly ephemeral. In the following section, consumer data will be presented which describes and explores consumer stories and lore about Vincent and his works. In doing so, the data illuminate the ways in which the myths circulate, how consumers use myths to anchor their experiences, and how art influences our processes of desire, and inspires our imagination and behaviors.

Data collection reported in this study began in 1989, becoming more systematic and focused in 1990, and continuing through the present; it involved extensive participant observation, personal interviews, and the gathering and observation of writings, words, images, and behaviors relating to van Gogh. Interviewees since 1990 include museum patrons and visitors, art scholars, research librarians at the van Gogh library, museum managers, curators, commercial retail managers/ owners (including the owner of the *auberge* in Auvers-sur-Oise, France, where van Gogh died), members of the van Gogh Foundation Board of Directors (including a great niece of van Gogh, Costa and Bamossy 1995), and pilgrims from countries around the world who have paid their respects at Vincent's grave. In general, the interviews have been ongoing, and were conducted at various times throughout the year, each year since 1990.

In addition to the personal interviews and observations, I have had my own scholarly and personal journey of discovery of Vincent, and of van Gogh. This includes visits to most of the places he lived, as well as a pilgrimage to his final resting place in Auvers-sur-Oise in 2001. With the exception of a few masterpieces privately housed in Japan, I have been to most major repositories of van Gogh's works numerous times since 1990, including Dutch museums (Amsterdam, Otterlo), American museums (New York, Malibu, Chicago), and French museums (Paris). I own a small library of books on van Gogh (written in Dutch or English) and several oil or print reproductions of his masterpieces, which hang in my home or office. I have specialized literature on van Gogh's writings, have viewed several documentaries and films on his life, and have reviewed original documents in the archive section of the van Gogh Foundation Library.

My own personal and scholarly investment in van Gogh has raised my level of sensitivity to doing research on this man and his works. I am keenly aware that by inducing subjects (admirers, museum visitors, pilgrims by the graveside) to provide an account of their experience, I am forcing them temporarily out of their participatory stance, often putting them into a position of justification. In interviewing subjects (as opposed to "experts" or "professionals"), I am displacing both the position of the object observed, and the position of the observer. I have learned throughout the research experience that often one cannot avoid an emotional engagement. So it goes with admiration. The mere fact of distancing oneself by taking an interest in the characteristics of admiration, rather than in the admired object, implies withdrawal, detachment, or disengagement. From the point of view of the interviewed subject, such an attitude tends to be perceived as a refusal to admire and, directly or indirectly, as a critique of admiration itself. There is no "neutral position," as every neutralization *per se* means taking a stand. The notion of "axiological neutrality" assigned to the scholar runs the risk of disappointing the expectations of the artist's admirers, and this cannot be avoided (see Heinich 1996).

For the industries of advertising, branding, mass producers of countless souvenirs, fashion accessories and interior design services, van Gogh is "gold." The van Gogh family copyright on his works expired 50 years after his death, and the van Gogh Foundation has never registered the artist's name as a trademark. As a result, common forms of artist commercialism such as printed reproductions in books, calendars, posters, and postcards have expanded into other product arenas. Vincent's image, his paintings, and the subjects and objects of his art can be found on products and services as diverse as Italian sugar packages, Dutch gin and vodka, branded potatoes, pre-paid French telephone cards, American house paint, refrigerator magnets, and computer mouse pads. The Amsterdam entrepreneur and multi-millionaire Jaap Dekker has registered the name of "Vincent van Gogh," and of his company, van Gogh International, and collects royalties from manufacturers of perfumes, cosmetics, clothing and textiles, watches, fashion accessories, pens, T-shirts, scarves, and neckties in 60 countries. Over 30 years ago, Hammacher (1970: 32) observed that the popular interest in van Gogh had developed into "a kind of van Gogh semiology, a socio-aesthetic van Gogh language, people beginning to live according to van Gogh symbols. These trends manifest themselves in the lucrative industry producing books, booklets, calendars, illustrations of all shapes and sizes, films, and plays."

Postmodernists would argue that parodies and (mis)appropriations of images result naturally and necessarily through the breaking away from the canons of normal representation. Van Gogh represents the *sine qua non* of this break for artists and their works, and for historical figures generally. The thousands of "low art" and "kitsch" reproductions of Vincent[8] and of his paintings provide many consumers with crude and transient images of who he was, and what he created. It may be that these postmodern representations of van Gogh and his work, provided by the advertising industry and delivered via mass media, help lead the way to a shift in some consumers' contemporary needs for myth, and ultimately, to their understanding of the man and his works. One of the recurring themes in the interview data, among both American and European youth, is that there is something intimate occurring – that visiting the museum for the purpose of seeing van Gogh's paintings, or visiting for the purpose of "being there" in the social scene provided by the museum, is a way to come closer to greatness, to approach and observe the line between insanity and genius, and to visit the unknowable nature of a great artist. Interviews conducted over several years at the van Gogh Museum suggest that youth find it gratifying to see genius and productivity coming from an individual who was marginalized and who suffered. This gratification seems related to, and amplified by, a perceived "connection" between Vincent and other popular icons and with manifestations of "rebellious" behavior in their own experiences:

I: It's a beautiful day today. What brings you to the museum?

R_{am1}:   Well, we've just got a whole day sort of planned . . . spent some time at the Bulldog [A touristy Amsterdam coffee shop, where you can sit and smoke marijuana and/or hash] now we're here. Later we're going for Indonesian food, and then back to another coffee shop. We're only here for two days.

I: Have you been hitting lots of museums on your trip around Europe?

R_{am1}:   [*Laughing*] No . . . not really. This is the first one.

I: How come this one?

R_{am1}:   Well, he's a trip. The whole ear thing; not well received during his life; poor. And we've got some girls back home who told us to go. We're getting them some stuff at the gift shop.

I: So what do you know about van Gogh? Did you do any special preparation before coming here?

R_{am1}:   Yeah. We went to the Bulldog! [*more laughing*].

I: Yeah, I noticed. How come?

R_{am1}:   Well, he's a trip. Lots of colors, and we've been seeing some great postcards of him around town. Just thought it would be a good way to come.

I: Postcards around town?

R_{am2}:   Yeah. You know. Sunflowers and weed, or van Gogh wearing a walkman and doing a joint, with a bandage on his ear. Pretty funny shit.

I: Does van Gogh remind you of anyone in particular from your life?

R$_{am1}$:   What'd you mean?

I: Whatever . . . another artist? Or someone who is a public figure?

R$_{am1}$:   [*Pause* . . .] Maybe Kurt Cobain. Or Jimi Hendrix. You know, on the edge and suicide.

R$_{am2}$:   Or Che Guevara.

I: Che Guevara?

R$_{am2}$:   You know. Sort of a revolutionary type. Also has an image like van Gogh's.

I: How's that?

R$_{am2}$:   They both have that same thing in their photographs. You know that shot of Che? [We establish that he is referring to the 1960 photo of Che taken by Alberto Korda, although the respondent did not recognize the name of the photographer]. van Gogh has that same sort of image.

Like Vincent, Che's image is ubiquitous – his figure staring out at us from coffee mugs, posters, key rings, T-shirts, and various props at rock concerts. This apotheosis of Che's image has been accompanied by a parallel disappearance of the real man, who, like Vincent, has been swallowed by the myth. Remarkably, when pressed to discuss the similarities of Vincent with Che, Cobain, or Hendrix, the connections are most often superficially elaborated – premature death (suicide for van Gogh and Cobain, execution for Che, accidental drug overdose for Hendrix), a rebel/romantic image – but little is offered in the way of substance. This erasure of complexity seems to be the normal fate of many icons. In a (youth) culture that consumes imagery incessantly, modifying those images becomes inevitable. What familiarity breeds is not contempt, but recycling. Over a period of time, these commercial, postmodern images of Vincent and his works sustain the myths, contextualize the myths by linking them with others, and provide consumers with a simplified handle on which to hang their perceptions.

Some final observations on the "Why" of consuming van Gogh

This chapter provides an overview and analysis of the scholarly discourses, biographies, and hagiographies that frame the early and current myths of van Gogh. Early myths generated a discussion of

(1) the nature and motivations of van Gogh pilgrimages,
(2) the influences of film,
(3) pop culture, and
(4) the kitsch and the commercial that create, sustain, and produce more recent myths that are a large part of the cult of Vincent van Gogh.

However, any promise to provide insights into the "why" of consuming van Gogh must first acknowledge van Gogh's oeuvre. The primary and secondary data presented in this chapter offer insights into the celebrity and cult of Vincent, as well as the multidisciplinary interpretations of his paintings as they relate to myth-making. Many of the interviews I conducted over the past 14 years provided personal insights into van Gogh's art, and artistic style.[9] I believe, however, that what simply stands alone, with no need for explanation as to why people spend their time and money to view van Gogh's paintings, is the magnificent uniqueness of the work itself. Distinct from the work of virtually any other artist prior to or since his time, van Gogh's art is instantly recognizable and presents an aesthetic window on a reality all its own (see Holbrook and Hirschman 1982 for a discussion on hedonic and aesthetic consumption; see also Joy and Sherry 2003b).

The experience is emotional. My personal encounters with van Gogh have led to moments of epiphany, revelation, and radiance. Our use of words always involves qualifications and limitations, and when I speak of the emotion that van Gogh can evoke, it is not just of the beautiful, but of the sublime. Some visitors are moved to tears, leaving the museum feeling as if their life has been changed and enriched. Others come on a lark, or as part of a day of cultural grazing which includes getting stoned, buying souvenirs, and eating Indonesian food. Herein lies an additional insight regarding the "why" of consuming van Gogh – he is accessible at so many different levels, and offers a variety of meanings, embodied in his person, his myths, and his works.

Consumers often have complex motives for visiting the van Gogh Museum, searching for or constructing an experience that meets a wide variety of their emotional needs. In the Fall of 1996 I interviewed an Italian male in his late 20s, whom I had noticed throughout the course of the afternoon in the museum was spending all of his time in front of van Gogh's *Wheatfield with Crows*:

I: [*after briefly establishing some rapport*] . . . I notice that you have been spending much of your time here, in front of *Wheatfield with Crows*. Is there something special about this painting for you?

R_{It1}:   Yes, I do like it very much. But I am also staying here because I believe that should someone else find this painting particularly attractive, then there is a good chance that we will be very emotionally compatible.

I: How so? Can you help me understand?

R_{It1}:   Well, this painting is not only beautiful, but it is dark [I establish that he means "emotionally dark," and not in terms of the colors, which are very bright] and powerful. It speaks of death and separation, and passion.

I: So, what do you believe the connection might be with someone who also enjoys this painting?

R_{It1}:   [*Laughing*] . . . well, honestly, I am hoping to find a young woman who sees the beauty and passion of this painting, and that I will be able to talk with her, and perhaps spend some more time with her after the museum.

I: Oh! Has this approach been successful for you?

R$_{It1}$:   Not as yet, today [I establish that he has been here twice before, and always in front of this painting]. But the other day was quite good.

I: Good?

R$_{It1}$:   Yes. An American girl from Boston.

I: And what happens if you are not successful in arranging some time with someone? Do you feel disappointed that you have spent all your time in front of this one specific painting?

R$_{It1}$:   No. Even if there is no promise of further engagement after, I find it very interesting to talk with anyone, women or not, about the feelings of this painting.

I: OK, so apart from the particular painting, is there any particular reason you choose the van Gogh Museum? There are many museums in Amsterdam, and many masterpieces.

R$_{It1}$:   The other museum [Rijksmuseum] is too impersonal, and too serious. I like the sort of woman who comes to this museum.

When the entrepreneur Jaap Dekker was considering potential "returns" on the investment necessary to register "Vincent van Gogh" as a trademark, he carried out a number of studies. While to the European mind van Gogh's name was associated with Impressionism, rich colors, and flowers, Dekker's research indicated that Americans associate the artist's name with exclusive, luxury items such as yachts, caviar, and champagne (Kasumi 1993). The Americans' associations are perplexing; van Gogh never painted any of those objects, and his lifestyle was a far cry from luxury. Perhaps the high prices of his auctioned paintings or the celebrity status van Gogh acquired as the focus of films directed by and starring Hollywood's best provide the most likely explanation.

Just as many associations about van Gogh seem superficial, van Gogh's art itself is accessible at the novice level. Elementary school children introduced to "high art" are often presented with van Gogh's paintings; experience has taught art teachers that young children can relate easily to his work (Dubelaar and Bruijn 1990). At a young age, having a positive affective response sets the stage for deeper levels of learning and appreciation (Bamossy 1982). Similarly, many adults who know very little about van Gogh exhibit positive attitudes about the man and his art; the adage "I don't know art, but I know what I like" has rarely been more true. For consumers who feel that "high art" is neither their preference nor priority, as in the case of some tourist youth in this study, using drugs and consuming the postmodern parodies of van Gogh are also ways to connect to the man, the pop icon, and his art. For the young Italian male visitor who had multiple agendas for spending his time at the van Gogh Museum, the connection was clearly to a specific painting, while the painting itself potentially (hopefully?) served as an emotional connection that was beyond the art itself.

For more serious admirers, pilgrims, and patrons, van Gogh offers richness well beyond the price of a museum admission ticket, or the travel expenses necessary to trace his footsteps. Regardless of whether one's understanding of van Gogh is based on fact, myth, or some personal and unique combination of both, contemplating his works while musing over who he was, and what may have led him to create as he did, provides a deeply meaningful experience. Campbell (1988) describes the value of myths in many ways. Myths bring us to a level of consciousness that is spiritual. Myths show us how to deal with great human problems and achievements, and how to respond to crises of disappointment or delight, failure or success. For all of these reasons, myths of Vincent the man, and van Gogh the artist, surround and support multiple consumption forms, meanings, and experiences. Both Vincent and van Gogh's art will continue to be contemporary myths of substance.

Acknowledgments

The development of this study has benefited from presentations made to the marketing departments at the University of Utah, California State University Northridge, and the Vrije Universiteit, Amsterdam. My thanks to Guliz Ger, Annamma Joy, and Jonathan Schroeder for their friendly and insightful reviews, and to Russ Belk, Jaap Boter, Kymberly Meyer, and David Mick for their thoughtful comments on an earlier draft of this chapter. I am grateful to Janeen Costa, who has helped me throughout my exploration and thinking about Vincent, his work, and the nature of art, beauty, and love.

Notes

1   Myths are generally meant to explain the origins of the world, and the experiences of the supernatural. Legends focus on heroes, both historical and non-historical, while lore has to do with the anecdotal information or stories of a more restricted nature.
2   For several levels of analysis offered in the chapter, the visual data would be useful to the reader. Go to: http://c3.business.utah.edu/Vincent for access to these images. Additionally, this site offers a Power Point file on *The Mythology and Commodification of Vincent van Gogh* which the reader may find useful for a lecture/class discussion.
3   Reading about van Gogh, and then writing about him, involves making distinctions between the artist and the cult of the man. The biographical treatments of Vincent (the man) borrow several motifs from the heroic tradition, and the use of the name "Vincent" (his signature on both letters and painting) designates the man. References to van Gogh tend to allude to his individual works and oeuvre. The use of "Vincent" in this manuscript follows the tradition of speaking about the particularized person, while the use of "van Gogh" signifies reference to his works.
4   A search during Spring 2004 for "van Gogh" on Google's Search Engine returned over 1.7 million links to his name.
5   Published academic/medical literature on van Gogh's illness shows an interesting pattern both chronologically and geographically, starting with the Germans, who took the lead in psychiatric analyses. In addition, many art historians and physicians offer examples of van Gogh's innovative representations of the sun, and starts as evidence of hallucinations induced by poisoning from alcohol, lead paint, or other eye diseases. Further details of the literature streams, and examples of van Gogh's painting which are offered as speculative evidence of his ailments can be found in the Power Point presentation at: http://c3.business.utah.edu/Vincent.
6   As of Spring 2004, there are 874 known letters. See http://www.vangoghgallery.com/

for an inventory of all letters. This is the most complete, authoritative website on Vincent van Gogh.

7   The village stairs were destroyed following van Gogh's death, but the Town Council reconstructed them, faithfully following the "look and feel" of the stairs as represented in his painting. Local admirers have placed a reproduction of the painting near the stairs, so that visitors can admire the replica's faithful representation of the painting. Life occasionally does imitate art.

8   A diverse set of examples of these postmodern images of Vincent, and the use of his image, or the subjects and objects represented in his paintings as parody, advertising, or branding can be found in the Power Point presentation at: http://c3.business. utah.edu/Vincent

9   As a general trend over the 14 years of interview data, I would conclude that European visitors and patrons to the museum are more likely to relate van Gogh to other artists, and particularly artists from the respondent's home country. American interview data is more likely to link van Gogh to film, popular culture, or myths about the man. These are defendable characterizations to make on the data as a whole, but of course, Europeans also place van Gogh in the context of pop culture, just as some American respondents had thoughtful comments on van Gogh as an artist.

References

Altman, R. (1990) *Vincent and Theo* (film), Hilversum: VARA TV.

Aurier, G. (1890) "Les isolés: Vincent van Gogh," *Le Mercure de France*, January.

Bamossy, G. J. (1982) "Socializing experiences as predictors of performing arts patronage behavior," *Journal of Cultural Economics* 6(2): 119–124.

Bamossy, G. J., Hogg, M., and Askegaard, S. (1999) "Europeans' imagination of the American west," in L. J. Shurm *et al.* (eds) *Proceedings of the Association for Consumer Research*, Paris.

Bernard, É. (1891) "Vincent van Gogh," *La Plume*, September.

Bernard, É. (1893) "Vincent van Gogh," *Le Mercure de France*, April.

Campbell, J. (1988) *The Power of Myth*, New York: Doubleday.

Costa, J. A. (1998) "Paradisal discourse: A critical analysis of marketing and consuming Hawaii," *Consumption, Markets and Culture* 1: 303–346.

Costa, J. A., and G. J. Bamossy (1995) "Culture and the 'marketing of culture': The museum-retail context," in J. A. Costa and G. J. Bamossy (eds) *Marketing in a Multicultural World: Ethnicity, Nationalism, and Cultural Identity*, Newbury Park, CA: Sage Publications: 299–328.

De Leeuw, R. (1996) *The Letters of Vincent van Gogh*, London: Penguin.

Doiteau, V. and Leroy, E. (1928) *La Folie de van Gogh*, Paris.

Dubelaar, T. and Bruijn, R. (1990) *Op zoek naar Vincent* (*In Search of Vincent*), Amsterdam: Uitgeverij Ploegsma.

Foucault, M. (1970) *The Order of Things: An Archaeology of the Human Sciences*, New York: Vintage Books.

Gauguin, P. (1894) "Natures mortes," *Essais d'art libre* IV, January.

Hammacher, A. M. (1970) "van Gogh and the words," in J.-B. de la Faille (ed.) *The Works of Vincent van Gogh*, Amsterdam.

Heinich, N. (1996) *The Glory of van Gogh: An Anthropology of Admiration*, Princeton, NJ: Princeton University Press.

Holbrook, M. B. and Hirschman, E. C. (1982) "The experiential aspects of consumption: Consumer fantasies, feelings, and fun," *Journal of Consumer Research* 9: 132–140.

Hulsker, J. (1985) *Lotgenoten, het leven van Vincent en Theo van Gogh*, Weesp, The Netherlands: Agathon/Unieboek bv.

Hulsker, J. (1993) "The Borinage episode, the misrepresentation of van Gogh, and the creation of a new myth," in T. Kōdera (ed.) *The Mythology of Vincent van Gogh*, Tokyo and Amsterdam: Asahi National Broadcasting Ltd and John Benjamins BV: 309–323.

Joy, A. and Sherry, J. F. Jr (2003a) "Disentangling the paradoxical alliances between art market and art world," *Consumption Markets and Culture* 6 (September): 155–182.

Joy, A. and Sherry, J. F. Jr (2003b) "Speaking of art as embodied imagination: A multisensory approach to understanding aesthetic experience," *Journal of Consumer Research* 30 (Sept): 259–282.

Kasumi, F. (1993) "The van Gogh industry" in T. Kōdera (ed.) *The Mythology of Vincent van Gogh*, Tokyo and Amsterdam: Asahi National Broadcasting Ltd and John Benjamins BV:409–418.

Kaufman, A. *et al.* (1990) "Van Gogh had Ménière's disease and not epilepsy," *Journal of the American Medical Association* 264: 491–493.

Kuhn, T. (1962) *The Structure of Scientific Revolutions*, Chicago, IL: University of Chicago Press.

Kurosawa, A. (1990) *Dreams* (film), Kurosawa Production, Warner Bros.

Leclercq, J. (1890) "Beaux-Arts. Aux Indépendants," *Le Mecure de France*, May.

Leighton, J. L. (1999) *Vincent van Gogh: Wheatfield with Crows*, Zwolle, The Netherlands: Uitgeverij Waanders, bv.

Lubin, A. J. (1996) *Stranger on the Earth: A Psychological Biography of Vincent van Gogh*, New York: Da Capo Press.

Mellerio, A. (1896) *Le mouvement idéaliste en peinture*, Paris: Floury.

Minnelli, V. (1956) *Lust for Life* (film), MGM.

Nagahiro, K. (1993) "The Japanese pilgrims and their journeys through the world of van Gogh" in T. Kōdera (ed.) *The Mythology of Vincent van Gogh*, Tokyo and Amsterdam: Asahi National Broadcasting Ltd and John Benjamins BV: 397–408.

Pabst, F. and Nagahiro, K. (1993) "Literature inspired by Vincent van Gogh," in T. Kōdera (ed.) *The Mythology of Vincent van Gogh*, Tokyo and Amsterdam: Asahi National Broadcasting Ltd and John Benjamins BV: 431–439.

Pollock, G. (1980) "Artists, media, mythologies: Genius, madness and art history," *Screen* 21: 57–96.

Powers, K. P. (1998) *At Eternity's Gate: A Spiritual Vision of Vincent van Gogh*, Grand Rapids, MI: Eerdmans Press.

Retté, A. (1894) "Notes de voyage," *La Plume*, September.

Schroeder, J. E. (1997) "Andy Warhol: Consumer researcher" in M. Brucks and D. MacInnis (eds) *Advances in Consumer Research*, Vol. 24: 476–482.

Shūji, T. (1993) "The formation of the 'van Gogh mythology' in Japan," in T. Kōdera (ed.) *The Mythology of Vincent van Gogh*, Tokyo and Amsterdam: Asahi National Broadcasting Ltd and John Benjamins BV: 151–173.

Stone, I. (1934) *Lust for Life: The Novel of Vincent van Gogh*, Garden City, NY: Doubleday.

Thompson, C. (2000) "Postmodern consumer goals made easy!!!!" in S. Ratneshwar, D. G. Mick, and C. Huffman (eds) *The Why of Consumption: Contemporary Perspectives on Consumer Motives, Goals and Desires*, London: Routledge: 120–139.

Van Dooren, E. (1982) "Vincent van Gogh: Ziekte en Creatie," scriptie, Universiteit van Amsterdam ("Vincent van Gogh: Sickness and Creation," Masters thesis, University of Amsterdam). Available in the van Gogh Foundation research library, Amsterdam.

Zemel, C. M. (1980) *The Formation of a Legend: van Gogh Criticism, 1890–1920*, Ann Arbor, MI: UMI Research Press.

17 Conscious and unconscious processing in consumer motives, goals, and desires

W. Fred van Raaij and Gewei Ye

Do consumers know all of their motives, goals, and desires? Consumer researchers often assume so and ask consumers in interviews and questionnaires about their buying plans, intentions, objectives, and goals. In the same way, researchers ask consumers about their motives and desires. At times, researchers are skeptical about the validity of these answers, but nevertheless they continue to assume that consumers are fully aware of their motives and desires, and that consumers consciously go on to realize their plans and desires.

For instance, making a decision that a specific purchase contributes to reaching a goal is a rational and conscious process or, at least, consumers often try to be rational in collecting and processing information to make the "best" decision. But is this the complete story? Are we consciously aware of all factors that play a role in our decisions? Are we fully aware of our motives, preferences, desires, and emotions in our decision-making? Wilson (2002) argues that we are strangers to ourselves, lacking sufficient self-knowledge. Goal-setting, for instance, seems to be a conscious activity. But events in the environment can trigger goals and direct our behavior outside conscious awareness. Do we "calculate" what will be the "best" alternative, or do we sometimes intuitively "feel" what is the best option? Or do we disagree with the "best" alternative we calculated according to a rational, and thus conscious, approach?

Several approaches should be distinguished in decision-making and choice:

(1) normative approaches of how we should make a decision;
(2) prescriptive approaches of what is or should be the "best" decision;
(3) predictive approaches of what will be the most likely outcome of a decision process;
(4) and, finally, the descriptive approach of how consumers proceed to make actual decisions in "real life."

Especially for the predictive and descriptive approaches, it is worthwhile to include in research all relevant factors that play a role in actual consumer decision-making and choice. Decision rules sometime are like legal rules, to be followed consistently. Whereas legal rules are normative or prescriptive, consumers follow decision rules to facilitate their decisions and to justify such decisions to themselves and others (Amir *et al.*, this volume).

In this commentary chapter, we develop a model of levels of decision-making, and discuss the chapters of this volume from this perspective. The approach in most of the chapters can be categorized as systematic information-processing. Some of the approaches contain elements of lower (unconscious) levels of processing.

Levels of decision-making

Western consumers live in a world with an overload of advertising and store merchandise, and they are unable to process all the ensuing information carefully. It is even not functional to process all this information because it may distract consumers from the tasks they are performing. Consumer involvement with advertising messages and even choice between brands may be low. Only in a limited number of cases are consumers sufficiently personally or situationally involved to collect a lot of information and process this information carefully. In cases of high involvement, consumers will pay much attention to relevant messages and explicitly learn from them. See Figure 17.1 for a model, adapted and developed from a low-involvement model by Heath (2003). Depending on involvement and attention to stimuli, this model contains three stages: (1) levels of

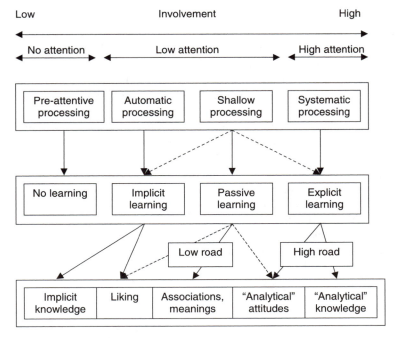

Figure 17.1 Levels of processing model.

information-processing, (2) types of learning, and (3) effects of learning. The distinction between low- versus high-road emotions comes from Shiv *et al.* (this volume). We will use this model (Figure 17.1) in our commentary on the chapters in this volume.

The difference between systematic and shallow processing is similar to the systematic-heuristic distinction (Chaiken 1980) and the distinction between the central and the peripheral route in the elaboration likelihood model (Petty and Cacioppo 1986). Systematic and deliberate processing occurs if consumers have the motivation, ability, and opportunity to process the information. In the case of systematic processing, consumers actively seek information, attend to the content of the message, and try to process the information in a rational way, e.g., they try to understand technical product benefits. Shallow processing occurs if consumers lack the motivation, ability, or opportunity to process the information. In the case of shallow processing, consumers pay attention to cues in the message or message source, and form associations and change their attitudes based on these peripheral cues.

Systematic processing leads to conscious, active, and explicit learning and to "analytical" (reasoned) knowledge and attitude change (persuasion). "Analytical" means that the attitude is based on a number of evaluated beliefs. Shiv *et al.* (this volume) classify "higher-order cognitions" and "high-road emotions" in this category.

Shallow processing leads to less conscious and passive learning, to associations and meanings, a liking of and preference for objects, and to a gradual (small-step) attitude change. Krugman (1965) introduced the concept of low-involvement learning, for instance, learning when being exposed to television commercials. Shiv *et al.* (this volume) call the effects of this type of learning "lower-order cognitions" and "low-road emotions."

Automatic processing leads to implicit learning. In this case, consumers are not aware that they are learning when exposed to messages. They do not recall or recognize the information presented, but the implicit-learning effect shows up in their liking, preferences, and behaviors. In this sense, advertising may have more effects than can be measured with common recall and recognition tests that measure only the effects of explicit and passive learning (Van Raaij 1989).

"Explicit" means here that people are fully aware of what they are doing, or, at least, the research model takes only the factors and information into account that people are aware of, and neglects factors and information that people are not aware of. Shiv *et al.* (this volume) report that when processing resources are limited, spontaneously evoked affective reactions rather than cognitions tend to have a greater impact on choice. To extend this, we may argue that implicit learning, either cognitive or affective, has a great impact in many choice situations, because consumers often experience effort or time constraints when collecting information for a decision.

When people act on their implicit preferences they are often tempted by and attracted to "relative vices," products with a short-term hedonic value (Khan *et al.*, this volume). The explicit choice between hedonic and utilitarian products will be normatively in favor of the utilitarian alternative. Implicitly, consumers may reject this choice and prefer instead the hedonic alternative. This means that the real preference for the hedonic alternative may be overruled by the normative view that the utilitarian product is better in the long term and is easier to justify both to oneself and to others. Consumers may employ self-control devices to control their implicit wishes and desires, short-term orientation, and selfishness (Khan *et al.*, this volume).

Explicit and implicit factors

As shown in the model of Figure 17.1, we have to distinguish explicit and implicit factors in cognition and attitude. In the social cognition approach (Greenwald and Banaji 1995), implicit attitude is taken into account. Explicit attitude is based on components that people are aware of and that people can systematically manipulate, i.e., can use to make a good decision and a good impression on others (social desirability; political correctness). But people may be influenced by their implicit attitude, i.e., the component of attitude that people are not aware of and that plays a role in their "real" preferences. Implicit attitudes cannot be measured with paper-and-pencil tests but with other means such as reaction times and behavioral changes.

The problem with pure explicit choice (i.e., choice that does not incorporate implicit components) is that it may be an incomplete description of consumer behavior. Explicit choice is only the tip of the iceberg, while implicit information-processing remains hidden under water (Wilson 2002; Zaltman 2003). To arrive at a more complete understanding and comprehensive description of the judgment, goal formation, and choice processes of consumers, it is advantageous to include implicit factors in consumer research (Loewenstein 2001; Bargh 2002). In the discussion of the chapters of this volume, we distinguish (1) approaches that can be extended to automatic processing and implicit learning, (2) approaches in which the basic motivation may be implicit, and (3) the interaction of systematic and automatic processing and, consequently, explicit and implicit learning.

Extension to automatic processing possible?

Some chapters in this book are almost completely in the domain of systematic information-processing and explicit learning. Amir *et al.* (this volume) describe consumer decisions by following rules. Following rules may facilitate decisions, but may be dysfunctional when they lead to choices that are inconsistent with one's preferences. Rule following seems to be an example of systematic information-processing, although it would be interesting to investigate whether these rules have become almost automatic ways to process information and to make choices.

Intergenerational influences in consumer behavior (Moore and Wilkie, this volume) take place mainly during childhood, not so much by explicit learning but by observational, participative, passive, and implicit learning, and thus accepting norms and values, preferences, and habits from the older generation. These norms, values, preferences, and habits become internalized as associations, meanings, preferences, and implicit knowledge. Intergenerational influences may thus exist at the conscious (brand preference and loyalty) and less conscious (decision heuristics) levels.

O'Guinn and Muñiz (this volume) discuss brand communities (Apple, Saab). Members of brand communities develop brand associations, stories, and brand loyalty. These brand associations and stories are not only the result of systematic information-processing, but to a large degree the result of biased, less conscious, self-serving information-processing.

Pechmann and Slater (this volume) discuss the possible adverse effects of social-marketing campaigns. These campaigns may provide information about undesirable behaviors that are less negative than the prior beliefs of segments of the target groups. Consumers may then conclude that the risks, costs, or prevalence of the undesirable behaviors are lower than expected. They may then engage in these undesirable behaviors more rather than less frequently, and thus cause the social-marketing campaign to have adverse effects. Learning that 15 percent of smokers will get lung cancer, while the prior belief was that nearly half of smokers will get lung cancer, may be a relief for smokers and induce them to continue smoking or even smoke more, rather than less, after the campaign. The prior belief was not based on the true rate but was probably an intuitive inference from earlier campaigns on smoking and health.

Framing this message as "the chance to get lung cancer is three time higher for smokers than for non-smokers" would probably not cause such an adverse effect. Pechmann and Slater do not discuss the effects of message-framing, although message-framing may reduce or eliminate some of the adverse effects of public service campaigns.

Pechmann and Slater also discuss consumer reactance (in order to keep one's freedom) as a response to "dogmatic" campaigns designed to stop undesirable behaviors. They also discuss offsetting behaviors to remain at an acceptable level of risk. Both effects are considered to be the effect of explicit information-processing. But remarkably little empirical research has been done on offsetting behaviors. In the studies on reactance and offsetting, behaviors before and after the campaign are compared. The reasons for the behavioral changes are then either assessed directly from the participants or inferred from the actual behaviors. We expect that many consumers may intuitively adapt to the new situation with shallow or no awareness of their motives and changed behavior. However, this expectation waits for an empirical test.

Automatic processing and implicit learning as a basic motivation

For many approaches in this volume, the basic consumer motivation may be in the domain of automatic processing and implicit learning. Wilson (2002) argues that people are often not aware of their own feelings or the information-processing that is going on while they focus on another subject. Theories can just be repositioned to include, and sometimes even to start from, implicit factors.

Pham and Higgins (this volume) discuss *regulatory focus theory*, a motivational theory distinguishing *promotion* (approach) and *prevention* (avoidance) as conscious modes of self-regulation. They employ a model of stages of consumer decision-making, starting with problem recognition. If problem recognition includes conscious approach or avoidance orientations, regulatory focus is considered to be a conscious process. However, consumers may not always be aware of their promotion or prevention focus. Such focus could unconsciously determine their search for information and their decisions, for instance to focus on a desirable end state or to focus on the solution of a problem. The situation and the choice alternatives may "prime" promotion or prevention focus in consumers, and then unconsciously evoke eagerness or vigilance that affects their information search, decisions, and choices.

Regulatory focus theory could add an individual differences factor to signal detection theory (Tashchian *et al.* 1988) in the sense that individuals in a state of eagerness from a promotion focus are motivated to score "hits," while individuals in a state of vigilance from a prevention focus are motivated to ensure "correct rejections." Saying "yes" to a signal or "no" to noise in an ambiguous situation may largely depend on vague memory or even liking of the stimulus (see Zajonc 1968 on "mere exposure" effects). This means that it is not too difficult to extend regulatory focus theory to unconscious processes and implicit learning. It is an interesting research issue for the near future to consider promotion and prevention focus not only as a conscious but also as an unconscious orientation.

Hope as a source of motivation (de Mello and MacInnis, this volume) has a similar distinction between desired end states and problems to be solved. The hope of a better future is either promotion or prevention focused. "Being hopeful" is the expectation level to the possibility of a goal-congruent outcome (MacInnis *et al.* 2004), but may also be a basic and less conscious orientation of consumers towards setting goals and making decisions. "Being hopeful" is then a generalized, less conscious, non-quantified, even counterfactual, dreamful, pleasant, and optimistic orientation of consumers that a desired outcome or a solution of a problem may be possible. Perhaps, we should give a new name to this new meaning of the concept "being hopeful." Based on this less conscious orientation, preferences may develop for particular products, services, and behaviors.

De Mello and MacInnis state that "the marketplace is rife with products and services that the dispassionate consumer would term, at best, as of dubious effectiveness." Nevertheless these products are sold, not because consumers rationally expect that these products will have the desired effects, but because of a vague, almost unconscious hope that this will be so. This results in motivated reasoning, biased processing, and even self-deception that "the hoped-for outcome will occur." Buying these dubious products often will induce a good mood, i.e., a generalized, less conscious, pleasant orientation. A less conscious and even unconscious orientation (being hopeful, mood) may thus affect preference and buying behavior, and may be affected by buying behavior as well.

Kahn and Ratner (this volume) discuss consumer diversification and variety-seeking. They cite the study by Kahneman and Snell (1992) that people are poor forecasters of their own preferences. Consumers generally assume that their preferences for repeated items will decline more than they actually do. Consumers are ineffective at predicting satiation effects over time. "People have inaccurate beliefs about how to space things over time to maximize utility" (Kahn and Ratner, this volume). In a similar way, for products with varied appeals, there is a difference between preference in memory and preference in real time. This points to a divergence between cognitive and affective evaluations, and probably between systematic processing (explicit learning) and automatic processing (tasting; implicit learning). Varied experiences are easier to retrieve from memory and are associated with an increased affect and, hence, preference. Ease of processing and retrieving stimuli is an explanation for implicit learning, and thus for liking and preference (Janiszewski and Meyvis 2001).

Holt (this volume) discusses "identity myths" of brands such as Budweiser, Corona, Marlboro, and Nike. An advertising theme may connect a brand to a deep, almost subconscious social anxiety, tension or desire of people and thus become successful. Corona connects to relaxation, doing nothing on a faraway Mexican beach. Marlboro connects to an authentic, adventurous, and independent lifestyle: Marlboro Country. Consumers may forget the advertising, but the identity myth for which the iconic brand stands lingers as a deep-rooted meaning and liking. Kaiser and Ketchum (this volume), in their chapter on fashion, employ a similar concept: "mood as a collective emotion that renders a sense of cultural resonance."

Awareness of mortality is a hallmark of humanity, concludes Turley in his explanation of the work of Zigmunt Bauman. It fuels the drive to escape and to secure immortality. We are not always thinking of our death, but it is always a less conscious background motivation to consume now ("You live only once") and to leave "markers" behind to secure immortality.

Interactions of systematic and automatic processing

Shiv *et al.* (this volume) discuss the interactions of "high-road" and "low-road" cognitions and emotions. Low-road emotions and cognitions are often related to "vices," alternatives that are attractive in the short run (demerit goods). If enough resources are available, higher-order cognitions are activated, restraining low-road emotions to determine behavior and to give way to "vices." However, higher-order cognitions may also be used to find excuses to indulge in the behavior "suggested" by the low-road emotion. High-road emotions may also determine behavior, if people remember earlier experiences that gave rise to an emotional reaction. In the latter case, there is an interplay of high-road emotions and higher-order cognitions.

The intensity of the experience of pain is higher when individuals are distracted than when they pay attention (Leventhal *et al.* 1979). In a similar way, it may be more effective to have consumers sample food when they are distracted than when they are paying attention to the tasting (Shiv *et al.*, this volume). This is contrary to expert knowledge that consumers should pay attention to the food they taste. This means that low-road emotions arising from sensory experience, associated with automatic processing, may be more intense when higher-order cognitions are blocked. The higher-order cognitions are associated with systematic, controlled, and deliberate processing. In a similar way, advertising messages may become more persuasive, when consumers do not consciously think about them. If not enough resources are available, higher-order cognitions cannot exert cognitive defense or cognitive control, and thus cannot restrain low-road emotions to determine behavior.

Khan *et al.* (this volume) distinguish utilitarian and hedonic consumption and, correspondingly, systematic and shallow/automatic processing. Utilitarian (affect-poor) alternatives evoke an evaluation based on systematic processing, whereas hedonic (affect-rich) alternatives evoke a feeling evaluation that is largely based on shallow and automatic processing (Hsee and Rottenstreich 2004). It is found that loss aversion is higher for hedonic goods than for utilitarian goods. Consumers are less willing to give up hedonic features of alternatives than utilitarian features (Dhar and Wertenbroch 2000).

Consumers often experience the conflict between heart and mind, vice and virtue, want and should, doing versus planning, the enjoyment of a party tonight versus the approaching deadline of work to be finished. Impulses of immediately gratifying activities or purchases have to be controlled in order to reach a long-term goal. When processing resources (time, effort) are limited, automatically evoked affective reactions, rather than systematically processed cognitions, tend to have a greater impact on decisions. Affective reaction as an effect of automatic processing can undermine people's long-term goals and may lead to self-regulation problems (debt, addiction, health risk). Systematic processing of information, explicit learning, "high-road cognitions," and well-planned behavior are then needed for self-control of automatic processing of information, implicit learning, "low-road emotions," and impulsive behavior. However, consumers may anticipate regret and negative self-perception, and thus avoid the temptation of "vices" by "installing" pre-commitments and constraints. Following personal rules may be another possible constraint (Amir *et al.*, this volume).

Although hedonic products are generally more attractive in the short term than utilitarian products, consumers need more justification to select a hedonic product. Consciously or unconsciously they anticipate negative self-attributions, e.g., feel guilty or feel regret, when they select the hedonic alternative. Justifications like "I deserve it" or "I have earned it" make the hedonic alternative more acceptable. Conscious processes include willpower and self-control, whereas unconscious processes include guilt reduction and "moral retribution." Khan *et al.* (this volume) conclude that these non-conscious attributions are a fruitful perspective to examine utilitarian and hedonic consumption in future research.

Conclusions

It is worthwhile to read the chapters of this volume from a specific perspective. We read the chapters with a level-of-information-processing perspective in mind. Most conceptual and measurement approaches could be extended to less conscious processes and implicit learning. We expect that this will provide richer and more insightful explanations and conclusions. We need to employ new research methodology to collect data on automatic processing and implicit learning. Measurement of mental constructs such as cognitions and attitudes will then be extended to behavioral measures such as response latencies and behavioral changes.

One step further is the theoretical extension from systematic to automatic processing and implicit learning. It is the idea that we are not consciously aware of all motives and desires that affect our behavior. Research on motives may not always be the most informative way to understand what is going on in the mind of consumers. Priming, for instance due to exposure to advertising and store environments, may activate specific cognitive networks and, thus, behavioral intentions and behavior (Bargh 2002). Theories may be repositioned to include or even to start with implicit factors rather than to consider explicit factors only.

The third step is the interaction of systematic and automatic processing and, consequently, explicit and implicit learning. The availability of resources determines whether systematic or automatic processes dominate. If enough resources such as time and effort are available, systematic processing determines behavior, whereas if resources are lacking, automatic processing determines behavior. But this is not the whole story. Long-term systematic processing and explicit learning may control short-term automatic processing and implicit learning: virtues may dominate vices. On the other hand, systematic processing and explicit learning may also provide justification for vices. We expect that the interaction of systematic and automatic processing will become a major approach for future research on consumer motives, goals, and desires.

References

Bargh, J. A. (2002) "Losing consciousness: Automatic influences on consumer judgment, behavior, and motivation," *Journal of Consumer Research* 29: 280–285.

Chaiken, S. (1980) "Heuristic versus systematic information processing and the use of source versus message cues in persuasion," *Journal of Personality and Social Psychology* 39: 752–766.

Dhar, R. and Wertenbroch, K. (2000) "Consumer choice between utilitarian and hedonic goods," *Journal of Marketing Research* 37: 60–71.

Greenwald, A. G. and Banaji, M. (1995) "Implicit social cognition: Attitude, self-esteem, and stereotype," *Psychological Review* 102: 4–27.

Heath, R. (2003) *The Hidden Power of Advertising*, Admap Monograph No. 7, Henley-on-Thames, UK: Admap Publications.

Hsee, K. C. and Rottenstreich, Y. (2004) "Music, pandas and muggers: On the affective psychology of value," *Journal of Experimental Psychology: General* 133: 23–30.

Janiszewski, C. and Meyvis, T. (2001) "Effects of brand logo complexity, repetition, and spacing on processing fluency and judgment," *Journal of Consumer Research* 28: 18–32.

Kahneman, D. and Snell, J. S. (1992) "Predicting a changing taste: Do people know what they will like?" *Journal of Behavioral Decision-Making* 5(3): 187–200.

Krugman, H. E. (1965) "The impact of television advertising: Learning without involvement," *Public Opinion Quarterly* 29: 349–356.

Leventhal, H. B. D., Shacham, S., and Engquist, G. (1979) "Effects of preparatory information about sensations, threat of pain, and attention to cold pressor distress," *Journal of Personality and Social Psychology* 37: 688–714.

Loewenstein, G. (2001) "The creative destruction of decision research," *Journal of Consumer Research* 28(3): 499–505.

MacInnis, D. J., de Mello, G., and Patrick, V. M. (2004) "Consumer hopefulness: Construct, relevance to internet marketing, antecedents and consequences," *International Journal of Internet Marketing and Advertising* 1: 174–195.

Petty, R. E. and Cacioppo, J. T. (1986) "The elaboration likelihood model of persuasion," in L. Berkowitz (ed.) *Advances in Experimental Social Psychology*, Vol. 18, New York: Academic Press.

Tashchian, A., White, D., and Pak, S. (1988) "Signal detection analysis and advertising recognition: An introduction to measurement and interpretation issues," *Journal of Marketing Research* 25: 397–404.

Van Raaij, W. F. (1989) "How consumers react to advertising," *International Journal of Advertising* 8: 261–273.

Wilson, T. D. (2002) *Strangers to Ourselves: Discovering the Adaptive Unconscious*, Cambridge, MA: The Belknap Press.

Zajonc, R. B. (1968) "Attitudinal effects of mere exposure," *Journal of Personality and Social Psychology, Monographs* 9 (2, Pt 2): 1–27.

Zaltman, G. (2003) *How Customers Think: Essential Insights into the Mind of the Market*, Boston, MA: Harvard Business School Press.

18 What consumers desire

Goals and motives in the consumption environment

Marsha L. Richins

Motivations are messy, disorganized affairs of the heart and mind. Despite our attempts to appear "rational" and to make everyday decisions in a logical fashion, most of us consistently fall short of that ideal. Conflicting goals, unconscious motivations, and imperfect information about ourselves and the decision environment often lead to choices that are difficult to explain or justify and that ultimately fail to provide us with optimal outcomes.

Several chapters in this volume describe complexities in consumers' evaluation and choice processes that sometimes result in suboptimal or inconsistent choices. For instance, de Mello and MacInnis describe how the state of "having hope" can bias the way consumers evaluate information and make decisions. Shiv *et al.*, in their exploration of how affective processes proceed in different areas of the brain, note how environmental, personal, or stimulus characteristics can truncate processing, leading to inconsistent or suboptimal choices. Amir *et al.* explore how rule-following by consumers can undermine preference maximization, and Kahn and Ratner show how the desire for variety can lead to over-diversification and a resulting decline in utility.

These chapters, and similar investigations into motivational processes in other venues (e.g., Bagozzi and Dholakia 1999; Hoch and Loewenstein 1991; Ratneshwar *et al.* 2000), are gradually bringing consumer scholars to an understanding of how consumers navigate the messy complexities of their lives and environments so that they can make a multitude of decisions every day while keeping their sanity and, in most cases, being reasonably satisfied. In fact, large portions of the motivation literature focus on the "how" of motivation, that is, the way in which motivations influence information-processing and other facets of decision-making. Less attention, however, has been paid to the "what" of consumer motivation. What, really, is it that consumers desire?

An underlying theme in writings about consumers' motivations is that people seek to achieve gains and avoid losses when they make consumption and other choices in their lives. In this volume, this idea is most clearly evident in the chapter by Pham and Higgins as they discuss promotion and prevention focus in the pursuit of goals, and it resonates through other chapters as well. But to understand the "why" of consumption, we need also to know exactly *what* gains consumers hope to achieve and *what* losses they wish to avoid.

Because of the messiness and diversity of consumer desires, scholars have been reluctant to conceptualize them in a comprehensive way. Early attempts by Maslow, Dichter, and others to enumerate or categorize consumer desires have been viewed as incomplete, internally inconsistent, or flawed in other ways (see Austin and Vancouver 1996 for a review). Yet without an understanding of what it is that people desire, we are limited in our ability to understand their behavior in pursuit of these desires.

Some consumer goals

In keeping with the tradition of prior research on motivation in consumer behavior, the authors of most of the chapters in this book don't address the specifics of what it is that consumers desire or the specific goals they pursue. However, it is possible to catch glimpses of consumer desires and goals in their writings, and this section synthesizes information about the specific gains and losses alluded to in the chapters of this volume.

Staying alive

Despite the recognition by needs theorists of the fundamental importance of physical security and safety, these concerns were not discussed very much in the chapters of this volume. This may well be due to the fact that, until quite recently, security and safety have been taken a bit for granted in contemporary American society, the location from which most of the authors of this volume are writing. A notable and timely exception, however, is provided in the chapter by Darach Turley, which places this issue front and center in our consciousness, making even sophisticated readers pause as he describes us all as "consumers on death row," struggling to postpone our physical decay and to repress our mortality. According to Turley and other authors (e.g., Becker 1973), attempts to manage our fear of these inevitabilities drive many aspects of consumer behavior (see also Rindfleisch and Burroughs 2004).

Fitting in

Social needs and the desire to belong to a group received more attention in this book. Group membership can be important and satisfying, whether one belongs to a real group or a virtual group, and fitting in with the group can be a strong motivating force. Pechmann and Slater, for instance, describe how the desire to fit in with peer groups influence consumers' (particularly young consumers') reception of social-marketing messages designed to promote socially or medically approved behaviors. More abstract groups can also be important, as O'Guinn and Muñiz report in their discussion of brand communities in which like-minded consumers form mutually reinforcing (often virtual) groups centered on a brand. The desire for group affiliation can also be satisfied to some extent by an illusory group. Ritzer *et al.*'s discussion of consumption landscapes reveals how even the illusion of community can be satisfying to consumers, at least for a brief period of time.

Being me

The need to fit in and be part of a crowd is complemented by the need to be separate, in the sense of having one's own identity, and considerable consumer effort in modern societies is devoted to walking the thin line that divides conformity and individuation. The chapter by Kaiser and Ketchum explains the appeal of fashion to many consumers because of its flexibility in presenting the self, enabling consumers to find just the right ensemble that will allow them to fit in, whatever the occasion or group may be, while simultaneously expressing some facet of the self that distinguishes the individual from others. Perhaps because our identities are so malleable in Western societies (McCracken 1986), they may at times be a bit fragile. As a result, identity confirmation can be a powerful marketing tool to generate brand loyalty, particularly through advertising (as aptly described by Holt) and through adept product placement in movies and television programming.

Feeling good and (being) spiritual

Despite the central role that pleasure seeking has in the lives of consumers in affluent societies, hedonic desires have received little attention in the consumer behavior literature (with some notable exceptions such as Hirschman and Holbrook 1982, Arnold and Reynolds 2003, and a number of studies that address control of pleasure-seeking drives). So the chapters in this volume that focused on hedonic impulses are particularly welcome. Khan *et al.* review the literatures on hedonic and ultilitarian goods and suggest some processes that guide affective consumption. More directly, Bamossy describes the appreciation of beauty as being hedonically fulfilling, enabling consumers to experience, in Joseph Campbell's words, "the rapture of being alive." His description of the consumption of the art of Vincent van Gogh illustrates the difficulty in some cases of drawing a distinction between the hedonic and the spiritual. The blurring of the hedonic and the spiritual is evident in many religious practices and groups throughout the centuries (among thirteenth-century mystics, Tantric Buddhists, Shakers, and Pentecostals to name a few).

Hoping and dreaming

Hope, in the various incarnations described by de Mello and MacInnis, may be the ultimate motivational force. Without hope, there is little motivation to continue with life's tasks or to even worry about staying alive; depression and sometimes suicide are the consequences of loss of hope (Beck *et al.* 1993). There are hints of the importance of hope in several of the other chapters in this volume. The iconic brands described by Holt owe some of their success to the hope their advertisements instill through the consumption myths they express.

The landscapes of consumption described by Ritzer *et al.* are designed to elicit fantasies and foster dreaming, an activity that both savors and nourishes hope.

Controlling

Control is both a process variable and a goal in the motivational world. As such, it crops up frequently in the chapters in this volume. We can see control at work as a process variable when consumers attempt to control their decision processes in a way that allows them to achieve goals, avoid losses, and manage risk. This process of achieving and maintaining control is the subject of regulatory focus theory (e.g., Higgins 1998; Pham and Higgins, this volume). The use of personal rules (described by Amir *et al.*) is another way to maintain control in decision processes because it simplifies complex decision situations while allowing the consumer to achieve consistency and maintain fidelity to important principles of the self or understandings of the world.

But control is also a desired goal state, and thus the desire for control has strong motivational properties. The ultimate control goals, of course, concern death and personal decay, as so aptly described by Darach Turley. But concerns for control pervade other aspects of our lives as well. Pechmann and Slater, in discussing reactance, highlight the importance that individuals place on maintaining control over their own behavior. We also wish to have control over how others see us. Deighton describes consumers' desires for privacy in the increasingly unprivate world of Internet commerce. This desire for privacy is essentially a desire to control what people know about us and extends beyond the Internet to numerous other domains of our lives to include information about ourselves in medical, sexual, financial, and other contexts. In a sense, the desire for privacy complements the concept of identity expression, as described in the chapter by Kaiser and Ketchum and in other writings about identity expression (e.g., Richins 1999; Wicklund and Gollwitzer 1982). Essentially, attempts to manipulate the way we appear to others are actually attempts to maintain privacy – to disguise the real self (sometimes in a literal sense) by presenting an "appearance."

It is clear that in addition to striving to control decision processes, consumers also desire the end state of being "in control," the sense that we are effectively managing our personal, social, financial, and other resources without undue interference. In a messy world full of competing obligations and limited resources, being "in control" for many assumes a dreamlike quality – something we long for but can never quite achieve. The elusiveness of this highly desired quality leads us to the last goal on our list – spiritual sustenance.

Spiritual sustenance

In a difficult world, the spirit needs comfort, reassurance, and sustenance. By spirit, I mean the essential energizing force of a person – that which gives us vigor, hope, and power. The wear and tear of daily life erodes one's spirit, and invigorating and sustaining activities are needed to begin each day, each season, and each year anew. Interpersonal relationships and hedonic activities (described above) can be a source of sustenance, as can retreat to an idealized or sustaining environment such as a vacation locale, a visit to a landscape of consumption (Ritzer *et al.*), or an hour in a house of worship. Holt notes how iconic advertising can provide symbolic sustenance of the self, but this function is not limited to advertising alone. Media in its many forms do more than offer simple entertainment. Books, television programming, and movies can sustain our spirit by giving us hope, showing others who have overcome difficulties similar to our own, and affirming who we are. All of these things can refresh the spirit and provide a renewed vigor for living.

And the rest of the goals . . .

Each of the goals described above has been addressed, directly or tangentially, by the authors in this volume. This list of consumer motives, however, is far from complete, as enumerating consumers' desires and goals was not the objective of any of the chapters in this volume. Even a casual glance at these categories reveals that all of them could be more nuanced. Social goals, for instance, come in a variety of guises, including desires for the respect of others, for sexual intimacy, and for a sense of community. Some goals (mastery, status, and creative expression, for instance) are not mentioned at all. Furthermore, potential overlaps among goal categories (among hope, hedonism, and sustenance, for example) suggest the difficulty of developing taxonomies or lists of goals. Nonetheless, a number of scholars in other fields have attempted to identify more comprehensive lists of human motivations and goals, and these can serve as useful resources for consumer behavior scholars interested in understanding the what and why of consumer motivation. Most notable are the works of Austin and Vancouver (1996), Ford and Nichols (1987), and Chulef *et al.* (2001). While these taxonomies are not in complete agreement with each other (see Chulef *et al.* 2001 for a review), they offer useful starting points as well as valuable illustrations of the complexities of understanding consumer goals.

As helpful as these goal enumerations may be, however, they are still works in progress. One deficiency that astute readers may notice when examining these enumerations and other studies of motivation reported in the literature is the absence of the consumer's voice in the analysis of motivations. For the most part, the goals described in these taxonomies are derived theoretically or by statistical analysis of the perceptions of expert or lay judges. As a supplement to (and a validation check upon) these frameworks, it would be fruitful to ask consumers themselves what they desire and to examine their narratives and the descriptions of their hopes and worries as they proceed through their daily lives of acquisition and consumption. Although we have seen some of this in the consumer behavior literature (for instance, interpretive work such as that done by Mick and Fournier 1998 and means-end analyses such as the one by Pieters *et al.* 2001), we have heard far too little from consumers themselves about the goals that shape their consumption desires, consumption activities, and satisfactions.

Why we need to know

Clearly, the definitive work to develop a taxonomy of human goals remains to be done. More specifically of interest to consumer behavior scholars, we have little knowledge of how the various human goals operate in the consumption sphere. A better understanding of *consumer* goals would enable us to study nuances in consumption motivation processes that are currently unavailable to researchers, as well as allowing scholars to extend the study of motivation beyond process itself. Some potential expansions of knowledge that would be enabled by a better understanding and enumeration of consumer goals are described below.

Goal conflicts

A particularly difficult problem for consumers to manage and consumer scholars to penetrate is goal conflict. By their very nature as desired states in a milieu of limited resources, goals invite conflict. There is not enough time and not enough money for consumers to reach all their goals, resulting in *goal-priority conflict.* Further conflict arises when two desirable states are inherently incompatible, such as simultaneously held goals of achieving mastery by learning to play the piano and of fostering sustenance by reducing demands on one's time – an example of *goal-incompatibility conflict.* Understanding exactly what consumers' goals are and how they are invoked would make it easier to understand the conditions under which goal conflicts occur, the consequences of goal conflict, and goal-conflict resolution strategies. Study of these phenomena may reveal marketing opportunities for new products that help consumers resolve goal conflicts. It may also suggest effective advertising strategies that assist consumers in conflict resolution or that provide the appearance of conflict resolution. thereby creating positive brand attitude.

Goal complexity

Some forms of consumption may be undertaken for the sake of achieving one specific goal (health insurance, for instance). The motives for other product acquisitions are more complex. Products that are purchased for many reasons or to fulfill many needs are imbued with multiplex goals of varying importance, some of which may be less salient than others or even unknown at a conscious level by the consumer. Knowledge about the range and intensity of consumption goals a particular product or product-related activity is able to satisfy may be indicative of its "involvement potential" and may help explain the strong appeal of such product classes as cars, guns, and fashionable clothing to significant groups of people, while products such as refrigerators generate little enduring involvement in anyone. Goal complexity may also be related to a number of decision variables such as extensiveness of search, decision latency, and extent of information-processing errors.

Goal satisfaction and product satisfaction

Although it is generally understood that product satisfaction is related to the extent to which a product fulfills the goals or expectations a consumer holds for that product, scholars have done little to understand exactly what those goals are (see, however, Gardial *et al.* 1994). We also don't know under which conditions achievement of all goals is necessary to produce satisfaction, or when the consumer will be satisfied when just some of the goals have been achieved. Perhaps for each purchase the consumer has a core goal or set of goals that must be reached to result in satisfaction, while other goals are less central to the specific purchase or usage situation and thus less crucial for product satisfaction. Having a taxonomy of consumption goals will help researchers investigate the relationship between satisfaction and goals in a more complex way than has been done so far, as well as allow a deeper understanding of brand loyalty and other post-purchase phenomena.

Goals and consumer–product relationships

Consumption goals may also be a useful mechanism with which to explore the nature of consumer–product relationships. Consumers, in a sense, have relationships with their possessions. Some possessions are loved and some disliked, some are friends, and some (a recalcitrant lawn mower, a poorly functioning printer) may be viewed as enemies. Although Fournier (1998) has examined the relationships people have with brands, less attention has been paid to possession relationships. By studying product-related behaviors, consumption goals, and consumption-related affect, it may be possible to identify a set of product-relationship types that can help elucidate a variety of consumer constructs and behaviors, including satisfaction, word-of-mouth, brand loyalty, and product disposition.

Despite a lengthy history of research in motivation, consumer behavior scholars have much to learn about how consumers navigate the complexities of the consumption environment. Although this volume and other scholarly work is moving us toward a better understanding of motivational processes, we have much to learn about the specific goals that consumers pursue, how these goals relate to one another, how priority is assigned among competing goals, and how goal conflicts form and get resolved. The consumer's own voice is an important but underutilized instrument in the task of developing this understanding.

References

Arnold, M. J. and Reynolds, K. E. (2003) "Hedonic shopping motivations," *Journal of Retailing* 79 (Summer): 77–95.

Austin, J. T. and Vancouver, J. B. (1996) "Goal constructs in psychology: Structure, process, and content," *Psychological Bulletin* 120(3): 338–375.

Bagozzi, R. P. and Dholakia, U. (1999) "Goal setting and goal striving in consumer behavior," *Journal of Marketing* 63 (Special Issue): 19–32.

Beck, A. T., Steer, R. A., Beck, J. S., and Newman, C. F. (1993) "Hopelessness, depression, suicidal ideation, and clinical diagnosis of depression," *Suicide and Life-Threatening Behavior* 23 (Summer): 139–145.

Becker, E. (1973) *The Denial of Death*, New York: Free Press.

Chulef, A. S., Read, S. J., and Walsh, D. A. (2001) "A hierarchical taxonomy of human goals," *Motivation and Emotion* 25 (September): 191–232.

Ford, M. E. and Nichols, C. W. (1987) "A taxonomy of human goals and some possible applications," in M. E. Ford and D. H. Ford (eds) *Humans as Self-Constructing Living Systems: Putting the Framework to Work*, Hillsdale, NJ: Lawrence Erlbaum Associates: 289–311.

Fournier, S. (1998) "Consumers and their brands: Developing relationship theory in consumer research," *Journal of Consumer Research* 24 (March): 343–373.

Gardial, S. F., Clemons, D. S., Woodruff, R. B., Schumann, D. W., and Burns, M. J. (1994) "Comparing consumers' recall of prepurchase and postpurchase product evaluation experiences," *Journal of Consumer Research* 20 (March): 548–560.

Higgins, E. T. (1998) "Promotion and prevention: Regulatory focus as a motivational principle," *Advances in Experimental Social Psychology* 30: 1–46.

Hirschman, E. C. and Holbrook, M. B. (1982) "Hedonic consumption: Emerging concepts, methods, and propositions," *Journal of Marketing* 46 (Summer): 92–101.

Hoch, S. J. and Loewenstein, G. F. (1991) "Time-inconsistent preferences and consumer self-control," *Journal of Consumer Research* 17 (March): 492–507.

McCracken, G. (1986) "Culture and consumption: A theoretical account of the structure and movement of the cultural meaning of consumer goods," *Journal of Consumer Research* 13 (June): 71–84.

Mick, D. G. and Fournier, S. (1998) "Paradoxes of technology: Consumer cognizance, emotions, and coping strategies," *Journal of Consumer Research* 25 (September): 123–143.

Pieters, R., Allen, D., and Baumgartner, H. (2001) "A means-end conceptualization of goal-directed consumer behavior," in T. J. Reynolds and J. C. Olson (eds) *Understanding Consumer Decision-Making: The Means-End Approach to Marketing and Advertising Strategy*, Mahwah, NJ: Lawrence Erlbaum: 413–433.

Ratneshwar, S., Mick, D.G., and Huffman, C. (2000) *The Why of Consumption: Contemporary Perspectives on Consumer Motives, Goals, and Desires*, New York: Routledge.

Richins, M. L. (1999) "Possessions, materialism, and other-directedness in the expression of self," in M. B. Holbrook (ed.) *Consumer Value: A Framework for Analysis and Research*, New York: Routledge: 85–104.

Rindfleisch, A. and Burroughs, J. E. (2004) "Terrifying thoughts, terrible materialism? Contemplations on a terror management account of materialism and consumer behavior," *Journal of Consumer Psychology* 14(3): 219–224.

Wicklund, R. A. and Gollwitzer, P. M. (1982) *Symbolic Self-Completion*, Hillsdale, NJ: Lawrence Erlbaum.

Author index

Aaker, D. A. 275
Aaker, J. L. 24–5, 250, 275, 278
Abelson, R. P. 106
Ackerlof, G. A. 241
Ainslie, G. 87, 90–3, 98, 151–2, 154
Aldag, R. J. 115
Alloy, L. B. 52
Amir, O. 93, 95–6, 99
Ariely, D. 113, 152, 156
Arndt, J. 67
Arnold, M. J. 342
Arnold, R. 134
Arnold, S. 299
Arnould, E. J. 259, 264
Asch, S. E. 59
Augé, M. 303
Austin, J. T. 341, 344
Avnet, T. 18

Bagozzi, R. P. 56–7, 158, 340
Bamossy, G. J. 326
Bargh, J. A. 338
Baron, J. 87, 90, 98
Barthes, R. 131
Bass, F. M. 107
Batra, R. 147
Baudrillard, J. 298
Bauman, Z. 67, 70–3, 77–8, 82
Baumeister, R. F. 176
Bazerman, M. H. 149–151
Beatty, S. E. 18, 211
Bechara, A. 166–7, 171
Beck, P. A. 210
Becker, E. 67
Belk, R. W. 45, 52, 72, 77, 81
Bell, D. E. 154
Bem, D. J. 154, 157
Benabou, R. 158
Benjamin, W. 293–4

Bensley, L. S. 195
Berkowitz, L. 166, 168
Berlyne, D. E. 103
Bernard, É 313
Berridge, K. C. 179
Berry, C. J. 146
Bettman, J. R. 17, 19, 22, 28, 38
Birch, L. L. 105
Blattberg, R. C. 238
Bless, H. 18
Bodner, R. 157
Bonsu, S. K. 69
Bourdieu, P. 73
Brehm, J. 195
Brendl, C. M. 35
Breward, C. 138
Brickman, P. 106
Briley, D. A. 27, 33–4
Brockner, J. 22
Broniarczyk, S. M. 115
Brown, C. L. 59
Brown, S. 294
Brucks, M. 18
Brunner, G. C. 14
Buck, R. 166–7
Burke, P. J. 236
Bushman, B. J. 196

Cacioppo, J. T. 181
Camacho, C. J. 36
Campbell, C. 77
Campbell, J. 309, 327
Caplan, J. 235
Carlson, L. 211, 227
Carver, C. S. 10
Celsi, R. L. 78
Cesario, J. 25, 36
Chaiken, S. 332
Chernev, A. 116

Childers, T. L. 213
Chow, Y. S. 106
Chowdhury, T. G. 21, 34
Chulef, A. S. 344
Cialdini, R. B. 93, 192, 199
Clee, M. A. 195
Cohen, J. 44
Coombs, C. 103, 104
Costa, J. A. 310
Cotte, J. 214, 227
Crane, D. 122
Crowe, E. 10, 11, 18, 19, 31, 36

Dahl, D. W. 156
Davidson, R. J. 167
Davis, F. 122, 126, 132–3, 136
Deaton, A. 146
Deighton, J. 241, 246
DellaVigna, S. 152
Dellu, F. 103
Dhar, R. 30, 145–6, 149, 153, 158
Doiteau, V. 314
Donaldson, S. I. 199, 201
Drolet, A. 108

Ellsworth, P. C. 45, 49
Epstein, S. 166, 168

Faison, E. W. J. 103
Feingold, P. C. 185, 194
Festinger, L. 115, 154
Fischoff, B. 90
Fishbach, A. 152, 155, 173
Fishbein, M. 189, 191, 194
Fiske, A. P. 91, 93, 98
Fiske, S. T. 54
Foley, D. 202
Ford, M. E. 344
Förster, J. 11, 18, 20, 26, 31
Foucault, M. 235, 293
Fournier, S. 253, 276, 346
Fox, C. R. 107, 117
Foxall, G. R. 102
Frank, T. 125
Frederick, S. 88, 90, 94, 148
Freitas, A. J. 129, 137
Freud, S. 9, 70, 74
Friedman, R. S. 12, 18, 21
Frijda, N. H. 45

Gardial, S. F. 346
Garrison, M. 135
Gelwick, R. 47
Gentry, J. W. 69

Giddens, A. 69, 79
Gilbert, D. T. 90, 179
Gilovich, T. 57
Glass, J. 219
Goffman, E. 236
Gollwitzer, P. M. 46, 153
Gottdiener, M. 293
Gray, P. N. 89
Groopman, J. 49
Grunfeld, D. H. 194
Guy, A. 122

Haase, J. E. 47
Habermas, J. 90
Hammacher, A. M. 322
Harvey, D. 125
Hauser, J. R. 20
Hauser, K. 139
Heath, R. 231
Hegel, G. W. F. 140
Heidegger, M. 67
Heilman, C. M. 174
Heinich, N. 309–10
Herman, C. P. 105
Herrnstein, R. J. 110
Hetherington, M. M. 105
Hetzel, P. 302
Higgins, E. T. 8–13, 16, 19, 24–5, 31,
  36–7, 46, 61, 160
Hill, R. 213
Hirschman, E. C. 72, 145–6, 342
Hoch, S. J. 145, 150, 154, 168–9,
  340
Holbrook, M. B. 83, 216, 325
Holt, D. B. 277, 285
Hornik, R. 185, 199
Hovland, C. I. 192
Hoyer, W. D. 17
Hsee, C. K. 88, 94, 98, 148–9
Huber, J. 33
Huffman, C. 56, 115, 156–9
Hull, C. L. 10

Idson, L. C. 12, 35–6
Isen, A. 49, 177
Iyenger, S. S. 115

Jain, S. P. 51
Jakobson, R. 130
Janiszewski, C. 336
John, D. R. 211
Johnson, A. R. 44
Johnson, E. J. 30
Joy, A. 325

Kahn, B. E. 34, 38, 104–6, 109–10, 115
Kahneman, D. 30, 88, 91, 106, 110–11, 144, 147–8, 180, 199
Kardes, F. R. 10, 61
Kasser, T. 67
Kastrinakis, S. 134
Katsh, M. E. 246
Keller, K. L. 275–80
Keller, P. A. 189–90
Khan, U. 148, 153, 159–60
Kierkegaard, S. 134
Kihlstrom, J. F. 180
Kim, H. 108, 113
Kimle, P. A. 125, 127
Kivetz, R. 34, 146, 148, 153, 177
Kleine, R. E. 236
Klinger, E. 1
Kozinets, R. 298, 304
Kruglanski, A. W. 50
Krugman, H. E. 332
Kunda, Z. 53, 59
Kydland, F. 154

Lancaster, K. 104
Lang, P. J. 10, 167
Langer, E. J. 92, 98
Larsen, R. J. 179
Lascu, D. N. 153, 156
Lazarus, R. S. 44, 46, 59–60, 168
LeDoux, J. E. 166, 167
Lee, A. Y. 13, 24, 26, 27, 33
Lefebvre, H. 293
Lehmann, U. 134
Lessig, L. 247
Leventhal, H. 166, 168–9, 174
Levine, R. A. 208
Lewin, K. 2, 9, 11
Liberman, N. 12, 13, 18, 30
Loewenstein, G. F. 95, 109–10, 145, 154, 179
Lord, C. G. 51

McAlister, L. 104, 106
McCracken, G. 128
MacInnis, D. J. 45
McNeal, J. U. 209
Madrian, B. C. 30
Maine, H. S. 89
March, J. G. 87, 90, 93–4, 98
Markus, H. 55
Maslow, A. H. 144, 146
Mather, M. 178
Matlin, M. 55
Meloy, M. G. 51

Menon, G. 65
Menon, S. 104, 108
Metcalfe, J. 168–9
Mick, D. G. 276, 294, 344
Middleton, D. 296
Miller, G. A. 10
Mitchell, D. J. 104
Moen, P. 210
Molden, D. C. 12
Moller, D. W. 73
Moore, B. 178, 179
Moore, E. S. 209, 214, 227
Morales, A. 116
Moschis, G. P. 211
Mowrer, O. H. 9
Muggleton, D. 124
Muñiz, A. 253, 255
Muraven, M. 176

Nisbett, R. E. 90
Novemsky, N. 111
Nowlis, S. 174–5, 179

O'Curry, S. 145, 148–9, 153
O'Donoghue, T. D. 156
O'Guinn, T. C. 177, 255
Okada, E. M. 147, 149, 151
Ortony, A. 168

Pavia, T. 68–9
Payne, J. W. 19, 88, 144
Pessemier, E. 106
Peterson, G. W. 208
Petty, R. E. 50, 194, 332
Pham, M. T. 8, 13, 16, 18–19, 25–6, 36, 38, 147
Pieper, J. 47
Pieters, R. 344
Polhemus, T. 124
Prelec, D. 87, 90, 92, 98, 157
Price, L. L. 69
Pyszczynski, T. 67

Quattrone, G. A. 157

Raghunathan, R. 31, 178
Raju, P. S. 103
Ramanathan, S. 172
Ratner, R. K. 93, 109–10, 112–13, 115
Ratneshwar, S. 1–2, 33, 340
Raz, J. 87, 88, 90, 91, 92, 96
Read, D. 102, 106–9, 111, 151, 174, 179
Reagan, D. T. 92
Richins, M. L. 343

Ries, A. 291
Ritzer, G. 292–3, 296, 302, 304
Roese, N. J. 36
Rogers, R. W. 189
Rolls, B. J. 105
Rolls, E. T. 105
Rook, D. W. 152, 178
Roseman, I. J. 45
Ross, W. 110
Roth, A. E. 94
Rottenstreich, Y. 145, 147, 149
Russo, J. E. 51
Rycroft, C. 47

Safer, D. A. 19, 24
Sanbonmatsu, D. M. 53
Sandikci, O. 296
Schachter, S. 168, 177
Schelling, T. C. 154
Schouten, J. W. 253
Schwartz, S. H. 90
Schwarz, N. 26, 36, 147, 159, 161
Seeman, G. 178
Shafir, E. 87
Shah, J. Y. 27, 12–13, 22, 24
Shaver, P. 45
Sherry, J. F. 294, 297
Shimanoff, S. B. 44
Shin, J. 116
Shiv, B. 117, 150–1, 154, 170–3, 176, 178, 180
Shocker, A. D. 20
Silberberg, E. 104
Simonson, I. 33, 38, 87, 106, 108, 154
Slack, J. D. 128
Slater, D. 126
Slovic, P. 154
Snyder, C. R. 61
Snyder, L. B. 186
Soja, E. 293

Solomon, M. R. 127
Spiegel, S. 25
Staats, S. 47
Steenkamp, J. B. 103
Stewart, D. W. 195–6
Stone, G. P. 126–27
Stotland, E. 47, 49, 60
Strahilevitz, M. 146, 148–9, 153

Thaler, R. H. 152–4
Thibaut, J. W. 115
Thompson, C. 276, 320
Trope, Y. 53, 59
Tuan, Y. 234
Tversky, A. 28, 88, 90, 111

Venkatesan, M. 103
Viswanathan, M. 227

Wang, J. 24, 25
Ward, S. 211
Wechsler, H. 193
Werch, C. E. 193
Wertenbroch, K. 145, 150–2, 154–5
Westbrook, R. A. 36
Wicklund, R. A. 343
Williams, R. 137
Wilson, E. 123, 135
Wilson, T. D. 55, 330, 333
Witte, K. 196–8
Wyer, R. S. 167

Yzer, M. C. 191–2

Zajonc, R. B. 166, 168–9, 335
Zaltman, G. 333
Zhou, R. 13, 17, 23–4, 27, 31–2, 38
Ziegler, E. 208
Zukin, S. 295, 299

Subject index

action: planning 57; tendencies 167, 170–3
advertising 81–2, 125, 140, 274, 279–80, 282, 289, 322; celebrity endorsers 279–80; *see also* social marketing campaigns
aesthetics 311, 325
affect 26, 117, 147, 150, 154–5, 342; individual differences 179; intensity measurement scale 179; *see also* affective-cognitive framework; *see also* emotions
affective-cognitive framework 166–7; applied to somatosensory stimuli 174–6; methodological issues 180–1; moderators 169–72, 176–8; neurological and psychological theories 167–9; relationship to brain structures 166–8, 171, 178–9
ambiguity 123, 126–28
anonymity 234–5, 246–47; *see also* privacy
anti-drinking/anti-drug/anti-smoking ads: *see* social marketing campaigns
anxiety 74, 134–5, 287
appraisal theory 45–6
approach/avoidance behaviors 2–3, 9–11, 61, 167
arousal 103
attention 15, 331,
attitudes 69, 188–9, 331–2
authenticity 261–2, 267, 302–4, 316
authoritative performances 259, 267
aversive motives 167
awareness 330, 332

behavioral decision theory 144–5; *see also* decision-making
bias 102, 109; *see also* motivated reasoning
brand communities 252, 255, 264–6; communal communications 259; consciousness of kind 256–7; desired marginality 263, 282; marketplace legitimacy 261–3; moral obligation 259–60; oppositional brand loyalty 260–1; polit-brands 266–7; rituals and traditions 257–9, 281–2; rumor 263–4
brands 6, 198, 233, 254–5; abstract associations 276–7, 281, 283, 326; beliefs 257, 259, 276; brandscapes 294; critique of brand equity model 275–80; cultural symbolism 273, 277, 283; cultural theory and branding 273, 280, 283–5, 288–90; genealogy 281–4; iconic brands 273–5, 280, 287–8, 309, 312, 323; identity and meanings 257–8, 265, 267, 270, 277, 281; intergenerational influences 212–13, 215–18; loyalty 260; myth making 281–4, 286–8, 336; packaging 281; personification 258; positioning 275; relationship to national ideology 285; social purpose 259, 265; story-telling 257–8, 264, 276–7, 286; who owns the brand 267–9; *see also* brand communities; *see also* customer brands
bricolage 136–7
buyer–seller exchange relationships 233, 240, 244–5
buying styles 213–14

capitalism 125–6, 131, 138, 141, 264, 292–4
celebrity endorsers 279–80
choice 3–4, 82, 104; consumption goals 156–9; context effects 33–4, 104, 108, 145; hedonic/utilitarian 144–5, 153; impulsive 145, 155–6; intertemporal

95, 151, 154; post-choice processes
34–5; reason-based 97; status quo 28,
30; variety-seeking 102, 107–9; *see also*
decision-making
choice sets 103, 107–8, 115–16, 158;
see also consideration sets
cognitions 8, 88, 150, 154, 331, 336–7;
cognitive load 169–70, 173–4;
higher/lower order 167, 176–8; *see also*
affective-cognitive framework
commodification 309, 322, 324
communication effects: *see* advertising;
see social marketing campaigns
community and consumption 131, 252–3,
255, 257, 292, 300, 303; desired
marginality 263
compromise effect 33–4
conflict 150, 152
consciousness of motives 330, 338
consideration sets: composition 21;
construction process 22; size 20–1
consumption 48, 50, 74, 76–7; adverse
effects 186–9, 201–3; beliefs 187, 257;
cathedrals 292, 305; communities
252–3, 255, 292, 300, 303; decisions
4–5, 86, 168–70; fashion 122–3,
128–30, 141; food sampling 174–5;
goals 156–9; hedonic/utilitarian 144–5,
150–3; hyperconsumption 292;
landscapes 292–5, 297, 301–3; myths
309–10, 326–7; politics 266–7; settings
292, 301, 317–18, 320; socio-cultural
processes 281–2; to reduce anxiety
287–8; transformative experiences 265
context effects in choice 33–4, 104, 108,
145
control 343
counterfactual thinking 36
creativity 125, 128, 136
cultural mood 122–3; ambiguity 132, 134;
ambivalence 132, 135–7; anxiety
134–5; bricolage 136; fashion 122–3;
intersubjectivity 134–5; metaphor
132–3; mood boards 136–7; motivation
133; shopping 135
culture: collectivist/individualist 13, 33–4,
113; consumer culture 257, 294; cultural
capital 263; cultural symbolism 273,
277, 283, 293; cultural theory and
branding 273, 280, 283–5, 288–90;
meaning of death 71–3, 82; *see also*
cultural mood
customer brands 233, 247, 249; identity
tags 233; persistent identity 233,

239–41; reputation 239–40; role-specific
identity 233, 241–2; self-expressive
identity 233, 242–4; transitory identity
233, 237–9

death: as my death 70; as unreasonable
70; denial/acceptance 69; relationship
to culture 71–3, 82; survival strategy 73,
75; thanatology 69; *see also* mortality
decision-making: approaches 330–1;
consideration set formation 20–1;
evaluation of alternatives 22–3;
evaluation strategy 26–7; heart vs. mind
150, 166–7, 170, 173, 177, 179;
heuristics 87–8, 106, 215–16;
information-processing modes 331–3;
information search 17; levels 331;
problem recognition 13–15; rules 22,
28–9, 86–8, 90–2; uncertainty 106, 149;
see also choice
de-marketing: *see* social marketing
campaigns
dependence 80
desire 77, 81, 130, 150, 280, 284–5;
communal 261, 264, 267; desired
end-state 9–10, 14–15; freedom and
expertise 79–81; innovation and
immortality 76–8; overcome satiation
104–5; peak experiences and fitness
78–9; societal 287; spectacle 292
dissonance 35–6, 154
diversification bias 102, 109
do's and don'ts 88
dream worlds 293, 343
drinking 192–3
drives 103

Easton Town Center 292, 296–7, 301–4
elaboration likelihood model 332
emotions 35–6, 133, 135, 325;
anticipatory 171; emotional bonds
215–18, 224–5; higher/lower order
167–9, 173–4, 336; related to hope
45–7; *see also* affect
evaluation of alternatives 22–3; evaluation
strategy 26–7; sensitivity to evaluative
content 23–4; having hope 57
experiential 145–6, 153, 157
expertise 79–81
exploratory behavior 103

fashion: aesthetic 124; ambiguity 123,
126–8; consumption 122–3, 128–30,
141; counterculture 125; cultural mood

122–3, 132–4; flexibility 123–6, 140;
identity 137, 139; materiality 123,
137–40; metaphor 122–3, 128–30
fear control 196–8
films 318–19
fitting in 341
flexibility 123–6
forbidden fruit 187, 189, 196
framing of gains/losses 13, 24, 27, 31, 35
freedom 79–81

goals 1, 10, 20, 28, 34–5, 88, 155–60,
340–1, 344, 346; abstraction 157–9;
achievement 47–9, 60–1; alignment
156; complexity 345; conflicts 345;
congruence 45–6; controlling 343;
determination 56, 330; enactment 51,
56; functional 145–7;
hedonic/utilitarian 146–7;
higher/lower level 156–9; hope 51,
56–7; incorporation 56, 159;
taxonomies 344; *see also* regulatory focus
theory
guilt 89, 153, 156

heart vs. mind in decision-making 150,
166; role of hunger 179
hedonic consumption 9, 24, 117, 144–5,
333; self-attribution 157–60
heuristics 87–8, 94, 106, 215–16
hope 9, 44–5, 69, 81, 128, 135, 335, 342;
appraisal theory perspective 45–6;
consequences 59–60; coping and well-
being 60; emotion 45, 47, 56; goal
achievement 47–9, 58, 60; goal
congruence 45–6; goal enactment 51,
56–7; having/sustaining 51;
marketplace as a source 49–50;
motivated reasoning 50–2, 59; product
evaluation 57; risky behaviors 61;
self-deception 61–2; three facets 46–7
human body 137, 139–40
hyperconsumption 297, 301

identity 5–6, 117, 128, 132, 137, 139, 209,
222, 238, 245, 267, 277, 287, 332, 343;
community 256–7, 261, 267; digital
236; face 236–7; identity programs
236–7, 249–50; national 285–6;
persistent 233, 239–41; role-specific
233, 241–2; self-expressive 233, 242–4;
social 234–5, 341; tagged as a customer
brand 233; transitory 233, 237–9
ideology 257, 285–6, 299

images 124, 129, 137, 343
immortality: deconstructed 75–6; desire
for innovation 76–8; postmodern
survival strategy 75–6; secular 72–3;
see also mortality
impulsive choice 145, 155–6
information age 233, 238, 243, 248–9,
257, 265
information processing 88; automatic
processing 333–6; conscious processing
330, 338; interactions of systematic and
automatic processing 336–7; modes of
processing for making decisions 331–3;
shallow processing 331–2; systematic
processing 331–2
information search 17;
alternative/attribute-based 19;
extensiveness 18; global/local 20;
internal/external 18/19
information sharing 243; *see also* privacy
interactive marketing 239,
intergenerational influences:
brand/product preference 211–13;
buying style 213–14; disruptive forces
219–20; emotional bonds 215–18, 224–5;
enduring 218–23; learning 333–4;
measurement 227; motivational
dimensions 214–15; negative forms 228;
reverse flow 226; simplifying force
215–16; socialization theory 208–10
intertemporal choice 95, 151, 154
intertextuality 124
involvement 117–18, 215, 217, 221–2,
331–2, 345

justification of behavior 153–4

kitsch 322–3

learning 331; explicit 332–4, 338; implicit
332–4, 338
loyalty programs 236–7, 241, 244, 247,
249–50
luxuries 146, 177

Marxist analysis 137, 293
materialism 67
memory for experiences 111–12
metaphors 122–3, 128–30; meaning
construction 129–31
misattribution 161
mix and match 126, 136–7
mood 177–8; *see also* cultural mood
moral obligation 259–60

mortality 67, 341; awareness of mortality as hallmark of humanity 81; deconstructed 73–5; motivation 67, 77; salience 67; *see also* death; *see also* immortality

motivated reasoning 50, 335; biased processing 52–4; biased thoughts and images 54–5; confirmation and disconfirmation biases 53–4; having hope 51–2; perception of objectivity 59; perceptual defense 53

motivational dimensions of intergenerational influences 214–15

motives 9–12, 16, 18, 60, 67, 77, 102–3, 133, 166–7, 172–3, 325, 340; consciousness 330, 338; consumer's voice 344; expressive 243; identity 233; instrumental 243; social 112–13

museums 320–1

myth making 281–4, 286–8, 309–10, 318–19

necessities 146, 177

need for uniqueness 113

negotiation behavior 94

Neo-Marxist theorists 292

nonconscious processes 161

non-places 302–4

norms of behavior 86, 90–1, 93, 97, 192–3, 197, 199

nostalgia 294, 296, 299–300

nothingness 302–4

novelty 103–5

offsetting behaviors 200–1

packaging 281

parental style 227

peak experiences 78

personal responsibility 74, 259

pilgrimages 315–17

positioning 275, 279

possessions: consumer relationships 346; disposition 69

postmodernism 311, 320, 323; survival strategy 75–6

preferences 88–9, 92, 108; construction 8; experiential 145–6, 153; inconsistencies 94–6, 145, 150–2; misprediction 110–11; time-inconsistent 145, 150–2

price sensitivity 86, 88, 90, 93, 95

priming manipulations 16, 27, 32, 96–7, 172–3

privacy 343: anonymity and identity 234–5, 246–7; invasion 244–5; managing privacy in a market setting 247–8; semantics 245–6

processing: *see* information processing

product obsolescence 77

production 123, 125–6, 137–40, 293, 295

professionalization of medical care 73

promotion/prevention 10, 46, 61, 113, 160, 340; activation 16–17, 27; risk-taking 31–3; *see also* decision-making; *see also* regulatory focus theory

PSA's: *see* social marketing campaigns

purposeful behavior 1

range effects 148–9

rationalization of society 302

reactance 185, 195–6

regret 36–7

regulatory focus theory 8, 335; approach/avoidance 9–11; ideals/oughts 12; matching principle 23–4; motivation 9–12; pain/pleasure 9; regulatory anticipation 9–11; regulatory reference 9–10; risk 31; self-regulation 10; signal detection 10–12, 19–21; sources 12–13; support 11–12; vigilance 10; *see also* promotion/prevention; *see also* decision-making

repeat purchase 221–2

response mode effects 147–8, 151

retroscapes 294, 299–300

risk 31–3, 106, 190–1, 243; risky behaviors 61, 187, 200–1

rituals 257–9, 281–2

rules: activation 93–4; compared to heuristics 88; decision-making 86, 88, 90–2, 333; downside 90; higher-order principles 87; individual differences 95–6; legal system 89; override 96–7; use 94–5; value-seeking 88, 94

rumor 263–4

satiation 104–5

satisfaction 34–5, 104, 346; processed-based 37–8

self: independent/interdependent 24, 27; *see also* identity

self-attribution theory 157–60

self-control 91–2, 152, 155

self-discrepancy theory 12–13
semiotics 76, 124, 128–31, 134, 140, 299, 311
sense/sensibility in consumption 4–5
shopping 78, 82, 135, 173–4, 238, 292–3, 297
signal detection theory 10–12, 35
simulation 296, 298–9, 301, 305–6
social influences 219–20
social marketing campaigns 185–6, 334; adverse effects on consumption 186–9, 201–3; counterbenefit messages 192; counterinformative messages 187, 190; counternorm messages 192–3; counterrisk messages 189–91; descriptive norm 199–200; fear control 196–8; message backlash 187, 195, 198; noninformative messages 194; offsetting behavior 200–1; problems 199; reactance 189
social obligation 259–60
socialization theory 208–10, 218–20
sociology of space 293–6
somatosensory experiences: two-component model 175
somatosensory stimuli 174–6
spectacle 292, 294, 296–9, 305–6, 320
spiritual sustenance 333–4
stimulation 103–4, 293
style: *see* fashion

temptation 145, 154, 173, 177

terror management theory 67
thanatology 69
time-inconsistent preferences 145, 150–2
trade-offs 88, 91–4, 97, 144, 146, 153, 155, 158
traditions 257–9

uncertainty 88, 106, 149
unconscious processes 330, 335, 338
utilitarian consumption 24, 117, 144–5
utility 88, 92, 97, 102, 117, 157; global/local 109–10

van Gogh 309; commodification 322; myths 312–14, 318–19, 326–7; pilgrims 315–17
variety-seeking behavior 33, 336; arbitrary dimensions of variety 107–8; diversification bias 102, 109; drive for stimulation 103–4; evaluated favorably 114–15; high-involvement 117–18; normative value 102; reducing 116–17; satiation 104–5; social motivations 112–13
vices 150–1, 155, 159, 332–3
virtues 150–1, 155, 159

wants 150
willpower 150
wish lists 78